ARAFAT

ALSO BY JANET WALLACH AND JOHN WALLACH

Still Small Voices

The New Palestinians

BY JANET WALLACH

Desert Queen: The Extraordinary Life of Gertrude Bell

ARAFAT

In the Eyes of the Beholder

Revised and Updated

Janet Wallach and John Wallach

A Birch Lane Press Book
Published by Carol Publishing Group

To the memory of

YITZHAK RABIN

a soldier statesman

who made Israel more secure

by making peace

A Birch Lane Press Book
Published by Carol Publishing Group
Birch Lane Press is a registered trademark of Carol Communications, Inc.

Editorial, sales and distribution, rights and permissions inquiries should be
addressed to Carol Publishing Group, 120 Enterprise Avenue, Secaucus,
N.J. 07094

In Canada: Canadian Manda Group, One Atlantic Avenue, Suite 105,
Toronto, Ontario, M6K 3E7

Carol Publishing Group books may be purchased in bulk at special
discounts for sales promotion, fund-raising, or educational purposes.
Special editions can be created to specifications. For details, contact
Special Sales Department, 120 Enterprise Avenue, Secaucus, N.J. 07094.

Manufactured in the United States of America
10 9 8 7 6 5 4 3 2 1

Library of Congress Cataloging-in-Publication Data

Wallach, Janet.
    Arafat : in the eyes of the beholder / Janet Wallach and John
Wallach.—Rev. and updated.
        p.   cm.
    "A Birch Lane Press Book".
    Includes bibliographical references and index.
    ISBN 1–55972–403–X (hc)
    1. Arafat, Yasir, 1929–   . 2. Palestinian Arabs—Biography.
3. Israel-Arab conflicts.   4. Jewish-Arab relations—1949–
5. Middle East–Politics and government—1945–   I. Title.
DS119.7.A6785W35   1997
322.4'2'092—dc21
[B]   97–5565
                                                              CIP

Contents

Foreword by Shimon Peres

From a Foe to a Partner

The first meeting that took place between Yitzhak Rabin and myself with Yasser Arafat at the White House in Washington on September 13, 1993, was close to being traumatic. Rabin was very hesitant about coming to Washington, but he finally did participate. After shaking Arafat's hand, he turned to me and whispered in my ear: "Now it's your turn!"

Indeed, we both stood on the brink of an abysmally difficult step. In order to fully understand the implications of these events, it has to be kept in mind that Israel and Israel's leaders were about to cross one of the most momentous bridges that people have to cross in the course of their lifetime. To do this we had to surmount a barrier of a magnitude much greater than any geographical or political one—a psychological barrier.

It has to be taken into account that Yasser Arafat was possibly the most abhorred figure in Israel for three decades. He generated fear and anger and distrust. All efforts on the part of the common acquaintances to placate the massive resistance encountered and to present Arafat in a more palatable light met with complete failure.

I heard his voice as it came over the telephone in the course of a number of conversations held by the late Norwegian Foreign Minister Holst in his mediation attempts, when I was in Sweden on that crucial night of August 17, 1993—a fateful night, when the negotiations could either collapse or end in an accord. The discourses lasted well into the night. While Holst held the receiver, Arafat's voice was clearly distinguishable as it echoed across the room. I could sense the emotion that gripped the speaker on the other end of the line, the intensity of which could be felt in spite of the considerable distance between Tunis (from where he was speaking) and Stockholm (from where we were calling).

The meeting with the Palestinian leader was one of the most significant milestones of the twentieth century—the importance of which could be measured not so much by the number of people directly affected by the event but by the complexity of the problem and the depth of the conflict which characterized the relationship between the two peoples during most of the twentieth century. The source of the dispute was twofold; the first, historical—two peoples whose destinies led them to the same place at the same time, but having no form of agreement regarding the place or the time; the second, geographical—two peoples sorely in need of a peaceful solution, occupying a stretch of land so small that, by the nature of things, any acceptable partition of the territory would be a feat hard to achieve. The schism deepened even more with the blood that was shed as a result of our failure to reach an agreement. Not only soldiers, but women and children too, lost their lives to terrorism.

Overcoming the complexities of the situation was a difficult task; however, on our part, the accord with the Palestinians was motivated by a moral issue—we no longer wanted to have control over another people. From the Palestinian standpoint, this presented a dramatic political shift: substituting dialogue for terrorism.

And that is how it came about that Yasser Arafat became the first Palestinian leader in this century to meet us face to face, knowing full well, just as we did, that the meeting would result in compromise, not victory.

In the course of one of our discussions, Arafat said to me: "Just see what you did to me: from a popular figure in the eyes of my people, you have turned me into a controversial personality in the eyes of the Palestinians and the whole of the Arab world."

My reply to that was "Historically, it is at times preferable to be controversial than popular," adding that the Palestinian people had been led for forty-three years by the Great Mufti of Jerusalem, Haj Amin El-Husseini. El-Husseini mounted terrorist units with the object of attacking Jews. It was he who ordered the Arabs to get out of Israeli during the War of Independence in 1948, assuring them they would return as victors. Thus, he created the refugee problem. He had even gone so far as to collaborate with Hitler. What was *his* legacy to the Palestinian people? Only calamity, tragedy and loss of life.

"El-Husseini never ceased to be popular, nor did his people ever cease to be miserable.

"Then you came along, Yasser Arafat, and for more than twenty years you continued to advocate terrorism, boycott and hostility. True, you too were very popular. But what did this popularity bring you? Or more specifically, what did it bring your people? Once again, only destitution, loss of life, hatred and despair.

"You have now decided to make a historical change. It is true that many criticize you. Some of your people are even out to get you. But consider this: you are the very first Palestinian in history who has already given his people a territorial address, administrative authority, the taste of freedom and hope for the future. In a single year, you have achieved what others have failed to do in a century."

This is indeed a leader's true test, making difficult historical decisions that might arouse the ire of certain segments of the population but on the other hand could bring about positive changes in the long run.

When we got to know one another, deep in our hearts we might have felt sorry for all the years of animosity that characterized our relationship. Looking at the person who was standing before me now, not subjectively but objectively, what I saw was a wise man, with a sense of humor, fully able to make decisions. Like all of us, he, too, had his weaknesses, which I will refrain from elaborating upon. Indeed, it sometimes seems to me that nothing makes us more human than our foibles, in the same manner that nothing exemplifies a responsible leader better than his ability to withstand controversy.

We used to be foes. Today we are partners. Not an easy partnership, it is true, but one which makes it possible, for the first time in the history of our relationship, to realize our ambition to safeguard human lives in the region rather than inflict pain, to act with mutual respect rather than sink into eternal enmity.

In the present edition of Janet and John Wallach's book, a chapter has been added. This new chapter deals with the Oslo Accord. I do not know whether this is indeed the last chapter in this rich biography, but it is no doubt the most important one: peace is the peak that every leader aspires to reach.

Tel-Aviv, December 23, 1996

Preface to the Revised Edition

Few regions of conflict have seemed so resistant to peace as the Middle East. When we embarked on this project in 1990, nearly fifty years had gone by with little change. If someone had told us then that five years later Yasser Arafat would return to his ancestral home in Gaza as head of a democratically elected Palestinian government recognized by Israel; that the Jewish nation would withdraw its troops from Gaza and a third of the West Bank, and that the PNC would vote to abrogate its covenant to destroy Israel, we would have found it difficult to believe.

Yet there has been more progress in resolving the Arab-Israeli conflict, and the Israeli-Palestinian dispute at its heart, in the last decade than in the entire half century since the creation of Israel. Historians will point to two events as the primary cause: the *intifada*, the Palestinian uprising in the occupied territories, which weakened Israel politically and ideologically, and the Gulf War, which weakened the Palestinians who sided with Iraqi despot Saddam Hussein. Peace finally came to this region, historians will conclude, because the Soviet Union collapsed, because other radical forces were in retreat and because the Israelis and Palestinians simply exhausted each other and themselves.

But such a shorthand version of history fails to credit the personalities who took the risks required to end decades of hostility and war. When we completed our biography of the PLO leader in 1990, we concluded that despite the widespread abhorrence of him,

Yasser Arafat was both capable of and personally committed to finding what he called "a just peace" with Israel. Few took him at his word when, in Geneva in 1988, he publicly recognized Israel's right to exist and renounced the use of terrorism. Yet in the last seven years he has fulfilled both pledges. He has used the new Palestinian police force to crack down on Hamas and other terrorist groups. He has proved his desire for peace by dropping demands for a Palestinian state as a precondition for negotiating agreements with Israel. He has demonstrated statesmanship by his willingness to postpone resolution of the controversies over Jerusalem, the settlements, refugees and statehood. Above all, he has shown understanding, even wisdom, in agreeing to the security guarantees that Israel requires in order to withdraw its forces from Gaza and parts of the West Bank.

Perhaps this is the most noticeable change in the Yasser Arafat we knew in the late 1980s and the leader who has emerged today. Throughout most of his career as a revolutionary, he sought recognition from the United States, believing that America would somehow force Israel to yield to Palestinian demands. Thus, he could avoid dealing directly with the Jewish state. We concluded in our earlier edition that peace would emerge only when Arafat understood that he "must speak openly and directly" to the legitimate fears and concerns of the Israeli people: that it was only Israel which could deliver the United States and not vice versa. In the last four years, Yasser Arafat has emerged as a leader because he understood this prerequisite and the need for compassion and patience. No doubt, as Uri Savir has noted, he has also mellowed and matured because he has had to deal with real issues and his place in history. But he also was fortunate in finding the man, or men, he was searching for.

When we spent long hours interviewing him in Tunis, Yasser Arafat constantly reminded us that he needed an Israeli De Gaulle. He found him not in a single individual but in the two elder statesmen of Israel, Yitzhak Rabin and Shimon Peres. Without the strategic vision of the war hero Rabin, there would have been no September 1993 agreement on the White House lawn. Rabin recognized that Israel was strong enough to give the Palestinians what they wanted—a roadmap to eventual statehood—and that Israel would actually be more secure by doing so. Rabin understood from virtually his first act in office—freezing the expansion of settlement activity—that territory, *and* autonomy, was the key to a solution. But it was Peres's boldness in recognizing that only the PLO, and only

Yasser Arafat, could deliver the Palestinians that created the opportunity for the secret channels in Oslo to succeed. Peres's skill as a negotiator and his gentleness and humanity were indispensable in earning the trust required in the final two weeks of the marathon Oslo negotiations.

In updating and revising this work, we left the basic biography intact because we felt it was important for the reader to understand the history of the Palestinian struggle and Arafat's central role in shaping it. Without his cunning, treachery and talent for turning defeat into victory, and without his ability to survive not only his Israeli foes, but to navigate between Syrian, Jordanian and radical Palestinian rivals, all of whom wanted to destroy him, the Palestinians would have been overpowered or swallowed up by pan-Arab nationalism, Islamic fundamentalism or Palestinian extremism.

In the final chapter we hope we have shown how Yasser Arafat has redeemed his lifelong dream of putting the Palestinian people on the road to statehood *and* of making peace with Israel. At this writing, Benjamin Netanyahu, the new Israeli leader, has fulfilled the earlier Rabin-Peres pledge to withdraw Israeli troops from the biblical city of Hebron. There is hope again that momentum will be restored to the peace process. Time has been the perennial enemy in the Middle East. When a friend informed him recently that a new edition of our biography was being published, Arafat exclaimed: "It is not finished. It was not finished. I need more time. It is the time which lacks." Since we wrote the first edition, Arafat has married, his wife has given birth to a baby girl, a Palestinian legislature has been freely elected, a police force has been established and a Palestinian president has been sworn into office. But Yasser Arafat is still racing against the clock. He remains enigmatic, authoritarian and unpredictable. It may be too soon to hail him as the George Washington of his people, but in our view Yasser Arafat has already secured an important place in history.

JANET AND JOHN WALLACH
January 1997
Washington, Connecticut

Preface to the First Edition

Mention the name Yasser Arafat and many Westerners still say he should shave off his scruffy beard and change into civilian clothes. In their eyes his smug air of self-confidence and guerrilla uniform fit the tailor-made image of a terrorist. His embrace of Saddam Hussein following Iraq's invasion of Kuwait has reinforced the revulsion to him. Yet to many of his own people, he is a saint: the same scruffiness is a mark of Arafat's refusal to fit the mold of more conventional Middle East rulers; the *kafeeyah* headdress and pistol symbolize the defiant Palestinian struggle to gain a homeland.

To understand Arafat, we sought to find out how he sees himself, seeking clues from him, his family, his friends and his foes. To understand how the beholders see Arafat, we had to know how they view themselves—how other Palestinians, Jordanians, Syrians and Israelis see their own interests, their own ambitions, their own role in the Arab-Israeli conflict and how the history of the last fifty years has shaped that role.

In dealing with Arabs and Israelis, history is everything, a prism in which all of these people are trapped by their own historical environment and what that environment has done to them. Some desperately want to get out of this prison but cannot. For a man like Arafat, it is even more difficult, because he has lived in a world of half-truths where ambiguity is a prerequisite for survival. We have tried to depict the environment in which he has lived, not as an effort to justify or excuse his behavior, but as part of an effort to understand it.

We asked leaders in the region who have dealt with Arafat to give us the benefit of their first-hand experience. Whether Israeli, Syrian or Jordanian, they believe as deeply as Arafat in the righteousness of their cause. Their views are shaped by their own rich cultures and traditions as well as by narrower self-interests which are often opposed to those of Palestinians. Therefore, we have provided much of the historical background that colors their perception of this charismatic and menacing figure.

To many Israelis, Arafat is a constant reminder that the extermination of six million Jews did not end the threat of another Holocaust. Some would still agree with Israeli official Avi Pazner, who said the real aim of the PLO was to create a state "in the very heart of our country, a Palestinian state which would serve as a base for aggression against Israel until Israel is weakened enough to be dealt the final blow." While opinions have changed about Arafat's real intent, there still are many Israelis who believe the PLO wants to destroy Israel.

To many Syrians, Arafat seems an equal threat, an upstart and an impostor who came out of nowhere to challenge age-old claims to leadership of the Arab world. Until recently, historic Palestine was regarded as merely a small corner of what was once Greater Syria; Arafat's efforts to unify the Arab world behind the Palestinian cause imperiled the dreams of Syrian leaders to restore Damascus as the capital of that world. In addition, intense personal suspicion and hatred have fueled the conflict between Syrian President Hafez al-Assad and Yasser Arafat.

To many Jordanians also, Arafat has been a danger, a symbol of the divided loyalties among Jordan's Palestinian majority. His popularity in the West Bank is a reminder that the historic Hashemite Kingdom may have to accommodate the West Bank and Gaza Palestinians, creating a federation with them in order to survive. For Hussein, there is also the bitter memory of Black September in 1970–71 when hostile PLO rhetoric spilled over into a violent campaign to topple him, leaving more than two thousand people dead.

Finally, to Moslem fundamentalists and more radical Palestinians, Arafat seems corrupt and deceitful, a once-proud revolutionary who has renounced the armed struggle for the duplicity of diplomacy and connived with the West to accept the permanence of a colonial implant. For them, Israel itself is the daily reminder that a Jewish state, even a secular one, has no place in the Middle East; unlike Arafat, these Arabs have not given up the struggle to liberate all the land which was once part of historic Palestine.

How has Arafat managed to chart a course between the Scylla of the Arab world and the Charybdis of Israel? What has enabled him to survive in a region where violent death and destruction are almost as common as birth and belief? "I have always speculated about the degree to which he is an empty vessel that shapes itself in response to the wishes or needs of the receiver," observes Washington psychologist Jerrold Post. "It is a peculiar thing: as if there are twenty different Arafats."

To unravel the mystery of which is the "real" Arafat, and why he has not only survived but flourished in a region often inimical to him, we talked to those who know him best: his family, close relatives and childhood friends; the leaders who have dealt with him as an ally and as an adversary; Palestinians who worship him and others who regard him as a traitor; and, of course, Arafat himself. Through the eyes of all, we hoped to gain a better understanding of the qualities that have enabled this seemingly unkempt, brash and bearded revolutionary to bring the Palestinians back from what author and *New York Times* correspondent Thomas Friedman described as the "desert of obscurity to a land of prime time." We wanted to find out if Arafat was capable of leading his people, as Friedman put it, "from prime time to Palestine."

In the course of this endeavor, which we began in 1988, we traveled from Tunis to Cairo to Amman to Damascus to Jerusalem and back again, taping countless hours of interviews with more than a hundred people, all the while trying to keep the central question before us: Is this a leader whose chameleonlike ability to shape himself to situations and people and survive the treachery of endless foes enables him to make peace in this troubled part of the world? This book is by no means authorized by Yasser Arafat, yet he and his advisers were generous in the time they gave us. All of Arafat's own words as well as those of all the other people quoted, unless otherwise noted, are from the interviews we conducted. It was difficult to persuade Arafat to talk of his childhood and his early years. Where possible, we have tried to shed some new light on this aspect of his life.

Over the years, there has been much misinformation purveyed about Yasser Arafat, some of which he encourages to maintain the aura of mystery about his roots and some of which is deliberately engendered by those who want to destroy his credibility. We tried, as much as possible, to ignore the hearsay, the disinformation and the malicious gossip, most of it bred in ignorance or sheer hatred. Wherever we went, of course, we heard conflicting and often contradictory stories about Yasser Arafat.

His origins, for example, are emblematic of the ambiguity that is Arafat. He passionately contends he was born in Jerusalem and therefore is a Palestinian by birth; others claim with equal assurance he was born in Cairo or Gaza. An Egyptian birth certificate exists, and it seems to support such claims. However, we found virtually no one in his family who believed he was born in Egypt. We suggest an answer to the riddle of Arafat's birth: that he was, as he claims, born in Jerusalem, but in circumstances that still deeply embarrass him, circumstances of which he has never spoken openly because they involve the marital problems of his parents. A close relative even suggested the birth certificate was a forgery, manufactured to help win Arafat the free university admission to which all Egyptians were entitled.

We approached conflicts like this one as journalists, investigating the facts, attempting to discover the truth, but basing our conclusions on empirical evidence that we gathered ourselves. Where we could not establish the truth conclusively, we present all the evidence and allow readers to draw their own conclusion.

Our principal aim was to get closer to the real human being than has yet been possible. Until now, Arafat has been prejudged by many. We haven't covered up his past or brushed it under the rug. But we also wanted Arafat to be seen for what he is, not a reflection of someone's imagination or a cardboard cutout or caricature. Israeli author Uri Avneri noted a few years ago that "when a journalist lends a hand to the dehumanization of an entire people, then the blood of those people can be spilt freely. We, the Jews, know this better than anyone else. Once a Jew is described as subhuman, he can be killed with impunity. Once a Palestinian refugee is described as a 'terrorist,' he can be bombed, shelled, expelled and denied human rights and dignity."

We hope this book will contribute to less spilt blood and greater understanding.

Acknowledgments

T he two-year journey that we have taken from Washington to the West Bank and Gaza and on to Tunis, Damascus, Cairo, Amman and Jerusalem has given us an opportunity to look at the Arab-Israeli conflict from all perspectives. We have been privileged to spend time with heads of state and foreign ministers who shared their views and ideas unsparingly. We have had the great fortune to hear the thoughts of numerous scholars, writers and political leaders, intelligent and informed people on all sides of the issue.

We are grateful to Yasser Arafat for the amount of time he spent with us and his willingness to indulge our persistent questioning over the course of a month in Tunis and in earlier interviews. He sat patiently with us for hours and hours and spoke about his childhood and student years, shedding light on subjects he has refused to discuss in the past. He facilitated meetings for us with members of his family, including his brother Fathi in Cairo, and with his cousins Sheihk Musa Abu Saud and Hisham Abu Saud and with Muheideen al-Husseini, the son-in-law of Haj Amin al-Husseini.

None of this would have been possible without the help we received from Munib al-Masri, a Palestinian businessman who has devoted much of his life to bridging gaps of misunderstanding. Not only is he gracious and hospitable, he has the compassion to understand the other side and the keen ability to present his people's position sympathetically and intelligently.

Bassam Abu Sharif, who deserves credit for persuading the Palestine Liberation Organization to moderate its position, paved the way to make this book possible. He gave us his time and energy and offered us solace, sustenance and insight in the anxious waits between interviews. He was always available when we needed him, even if we were not always ready when he called in the wee hours of the morning and ordered us to be downstairs "in five minutes."

Yasser Abed Rabbo also was unsparing of his time. His observations were among the most perceptive of anyone we met. A big share of thanks goes to Rita Hauser, who had the courage to take brave steps on a perilous path. We are confident she will one day be recognized as an important pioneer in the Jewish community. She graciously shared invaluable information and insights.

Swedish Foreign Minister Sten Andersson went out of his way to see us during the United Nations General Assembly session in New York and on several other occasions. From the first day that we met him, we felt we were in the company of an extraordinary diplomat who was deeply and personally committed to making peace between Arabs and Israelis. It was Andersson's idea to involve the American Jewish community directly in the peace effort; his devotion to this cause is a tribute to the non-traditional diplomacy that distinguishes Andersson and that makes him such a natural successor to the late Swedish Prime Minister Olaf Palme and Swedish envoy Gunnar Jarring, who devoted their lives to similar causes.

We could not have written this book without Danny Rubinstein, who edited the initial draft of our manuscript as well as our first book *Still Small Voices*. He always shared his extraordinary knowledge with us in ways that illuminated complex issues and enabled us to grasp their significance. Few Israeli journalists have his grasp of the humanity that is at the root of this crisis or carry the daily pain and suffering of the Palestinians as sensitively as Danny. If all Israelis were as proud of their heritage while also conscious of the rights of others, the conflict would have been settled long ago.

From the very beginning, when we first raised the possibility of writing a book about such a controversial subject, Chuck Lewis, former bureau chief of the Associated Press, was a pillar of support. He encouraged us to persevere when the going got rough, reminding us that the "creative tension" we were experiencing in our marriage ultimately would produce a better book. He was exceptionally generous in allowing one partner to use his allotted vacation and "comp time" to work on this project. We will always be grateful for his kindness and wise counsel, qualities that distinguish him as the bureau chief of The Hearst Newspapers, and as a valued friend.

Among the Palestinians we met in Tunis are many whose moderate voices need to be heard in the United States and in Israel. They include Hassan Khadar, Akram Hanieh, Ahmed Abdul Rahman, Mahjoub Omar, Nizzar Amar, Jamil Hilel, Hani al-Hassan and his brother Ambassador-at-large Khaled al-Hassan. We also had interviews in Tunis with Hakim Belawi, Abu Iyad, Um Jihad, George Habash, Mohammed Milhem, Faisal Oweida and Mohammed Bilal.

We are appreciative of the help we received in Tunis from Ambassador Robert Pelletreau, Jr., whose gentle way and gracious hospitality have given the PLO a kinder, gentler image of the United States. He has performed one of the most difficult of diplomatic tasks with grace, humor and quiet intelligence. There are so many others to whom we are indebted in Tunis: Hamid Zaouche made his country feel like home for us. Egyptian Ambassador Ali Maher gave us the benefit of his years of experience in the Arab world.

In Cairo we wish especially to thank Foreign Minister Ismet Abdul Meguid, who worked tirelessly at Geneva to persuade the PLO to follow through with its historic compromise; also Minister of State for Foreign Affairs Bhutros Ghali, whose wry observations were the perfect backdrop for our reporting; Nabil Sha'ath, whose insights have provided the intellectual foundation for the new PLO course; Mohammed Heikal, who shared with us his rich experiences as a close aide to former President Gamal Abdel Nassar.

Ambassador Frank Wisner smoothed the way for us, taking time out of his busy schedule to provide wise counsel, wonderful books and a good meal. He is an unpretentious man whose thoughtful ways have endeared him to the Egyptian government. Few people are as knowledgeable about the extensive history of the Jews in Egypt as Israeli Ambassador Shimon Shamir. A scholarly diplomat and kind human being, he shared much of his work with us and encouraged us to be painstaking in our own research. The Egyptian government is fortunate to have Mohammed Agami serve the needs of visiting journalists; he was always there when we needed him with a smile and a hug even when we were depressed because a hoped-for interview did not materialize. He made us feel as if the success of our task was just as important to him, and for that alone we will remember him. Our thanks also to Information Minister Safwat al-Sharif; to Ahmed al-Ebrashy, director of the State Information Service, and to Mohammed Wahby of the Egyptian Press Office in Washington; and to so many others in Cairo, including classmates who shared their recollections of Yasser Arafat as a student leader, among them, Khaled Mohiedeen, Zakaria Neel, Kamal Naguib, Sami Suleiman, Said Kamal and Said Yassin. Egyptian Ambassador Abdel Raouf al-Reedy provided his usually expert guidance.

We are extremely grateful to His Majesty King Hussein, who was generous with his time and who graciously shared his wisdom and memories with us; Her Majesty Queen Noor was not only hospitable but helpful and patient. Among the Jordanian leaders, past and current, who shared their insights were: Adnan Abu Odeh, His Majesty's principal adviser on Palestinian affairs; Foreign Minister Tahir al-Masri; former Prime Minister Zeid Rifai; former Foreign Minister Marwan Kassem; His Majesty's press counselor Fouad Ayoub; Ahmed Qatanni, who is in charge of Palestinian affairs for the Jordanian government; Abdul Majeed Shoman, former treasurer of the Palestine National Fund and Akram Zuaiter, who gave us a compelling account of his role in the 1936 Arab riots in Jerusalem.

In Amman we are also indebted to Professor Abu Jaber, a noted historian; to Ruhi al-Khatib, the mayor of Jerusalem from 1950 to 1967; and Omar al-Khatib, the Fatah representative in Jordan who was the second-in-command to Abu Jihad in Lebanon. Our special thanks to Hamid Abu Sitta, who crossed the Suez Canal with Arafat in a rowboat; lawyer Ali Zubi for his recollections of Jerusalem in the 1930s; and Abdul Jawad Saleh, the former mayor of El Bireh who heads the Jerusalem Center for Development Studies in the Jordanian capital and was in charge of constructing hospitals and bomb shelters for the refugees in Lebanon. Our thanks also to American Ambassador Roscoe Suddarth III and to distinguished diplomat Richard Viets, the former U.S. ambassador to Jordan who has constantly sought a dialogue between Arabs and Israelis.

In Syria, among the many people who also helped us were Damascus University Professor Hussan al-Khatib; Mohammed Nashashibi, former Palestine National Council speaker Khaled al-Fahoum, the Democratic Front for the Liberation of Palestine's Nayaf Hawatmeh and Abu Laila and the leaders of PLO splinter groups who took the time to explain patiently the reasons for their disaffection with Fatah, among them: Omar Sha'abi, head of the Foreign Relations Department of the Popular Front for the Liberation of Palestine-General Command, Sami Kandil, an official of Saiqa, Abdul Jawad and Abdul Hadi al-Mashash of "Fatah Uprising."

We consider ourselves very fortunate to have as friends Ambassador and Mrs. Edward Djerejian who spent hours briefing us on the intricacies of Syrian politics, and helped us obtain access to always hard-to-see Syrian officials, including Defense Minister Moustafa Tlass; Information Minister Salman and others. Our thanks to Alexandre Zotov, the Soviet ambassador in Damascus, who shared his insights with us while we were there, and to Rolff Gauffin, the Swedish ambassador in the Syrian capital whose knowledge of Lebanon is as impressive as his contacts with Palestinians.

In Jerusalem we are grateful to Prime Minister Yitzhak Shamir and former Defense Minister Yitzhak Rabin, who both made time to see us despite their heavy schedules; to spokesman Avi Pazner, whose friendship is dear and who has always helped us despite our philosophical differences. David Cassuto, Israel Harel and Miriam Levinger also enabled us to understand the righteous beliefs of many Jewish settlers. Although we do not share their aims, we believe their views should be heard.

Among the many wise and courageous Palestinians in the West Bank who taught us much of their perseverance and commitment to peace, we wish particularly to thank Radwan Abu Ayash, whose leadership qualities are a great asset to his people; Professor Sari Nusseibeh, for his scholarly insights; Faisal Husseini, whose moderate voice has made him a natural inheritor of his family's prestigious status among Palestinians, and Ziad Abu Zayyad, who has always reached out to bridge the gap between Palestinians and Israelis.

There were so many friends in Washington who helped us, but in particular we want to thank those who took the time to read all or parts of our manuscript and give us their criticisms and advice: veteran newspapermen James Dorsey and Steve Hagey, former State Department officials Nicholas Veliotes, Charles Hill and Peter Rodman. The PLO's capable representative in Washington, Hassan Abdul Rahman, was always ready to help as was the articulate spokesman for the League of Arab States, Ambassador Clovis

Maksoud. The Brookings Institution's William Quandt provided us valuable assistance. Few Americans are as knowledgeable on this issue as noted scholar Helena Cobban. We are grateful for her support.

Swedish Ambassador Anders Thunborg, who represented the United Nations in Lebanon during the trauma of the PLO's evacuation from Beirut, gave us the benefit of his dignified counsel. Roger Edde, a Lebanese citizen who has taken many risks to help end his nation's long nightmare, was tireless in teaching us about his war-torn country. We are also grateful to all the official and unofficial envoys who told us their stories: Ambassador Philip Habib; Ambassador John Gunther Dean; John Mroz, President of the Center for East-West Studies; Merle Thorpe, the President of the Foundation for Middle East Peace, and Gail Pressberg; Landrum Bolling; Judith Kipper of Brookings and the Council on Foreign Relations and Wat Cluverius, the former U.S. counsel in Jerusalem, both of whom played key roles in the 1985–86 peace effort with Jordan.

Before we left for the Middle East, we had the opportunity to discuss U.S. policy with Secretary of State James A. Baker and with his adviser Ambassador Dennis Ross, with former national security adviser Zbigniew Brzezinski and with Columbia University professor Gary Sick; also helpful were Martin Indyk, director of The Washington Institute for Near East Policy, and Geoffrey Kemp, senior associate of The Carnegie Endowment; Jerry Bremer, the State Department's former counterterrorism adviser; U.S. officials Tony Wayne and Steve Strain; former government psychologist Jerald Post and Richard Haass, the senior Middle East adviser on the National Security Council. We thank all of them for taking time from their busy schedules to prepare us for our stay in the region.

In transcribing the hundreds of interviews we taped over two years, we were fortunate to have the assistance of Catherine Torrance, Richard Eisendorff and John Wilner in Washington. Najla Rizk in Cairo helped us get access to individuals we otherwise could not have obtained and worked diligently to help us. Karma Nabulsi helped us in London. We are thankful to Ron Goldfarb, who encouraged us in this project, and to Carole Stuart, who believed in it from the beginning. Bruce Shostak, our editor, was patient with us at difficult times and provided valuable guidance. We also want to thank Aaron Miller, senior member of the State Department's Policy

Planning Staff, for never hesitating to criticize our work and for encouraging us to revise several initial drafts. His advice was truly invaluable; his friendship is treasured even more. Finaly, we could not have completed this task without the understanding and support of our children, Michael and David, who often had their dinners served late and had to suffer through our noisy battles. Their love saw us through to the end.

ACKNOWLEDGMENTS TO THE REVISED EDITION

More momentous events took place in the relatively short time span since we completed the first edition of this book than in the half century since the Arab-Israeli conflict began. We are therefore indebted to the Israelis and Palestinians who took the time to update us on their own involvement in the Oslo process and in the subsequent events that have determined the future of the peace process. First and foremost, we would like to thank Shimon Peres, who graciously agreed to write the foreword for this edition. It is probably the first time that any high-ranking Israeli official, let alone a former prime minister, has agreed to introduce a figure who was for so long the nemesis of the Israeli people. Both Uri Savir, the former director-general of the Israeli Foreign Ministry, and Yossi Beilin, the deputy prime minister, also spent time with us. Without them, there would have been no Oslo accord. We first met Uri in the 1980s when he was the Israeli consul-general in New York. He took time then to attend our talks, come to a book signing for *Still Small Voices*, and to give us the benefit of his unique wisdom and humanity, as he did on more recent occasions.

Understandably, Yasser Arafat, shouldering the heavy responsibilities of president, could not give us the many hours that he did when we were with him in Tunis, Amman, Baghdad and other capitals between 1988 and 1991. However, we are grateful that he did respond, directly and through intermediaries, to our new queries about his indispensable role in this process. We have been privileged to spend so much time with him and hope that this work will provide both admirers and detractors a more objective lens to judge him. Other Palestinians also were helpful, particularly Hasan Abdul Rahman, the senior Palestinian envoy to the United States; Raymonda Tawil, the mother of Suha Arafat; Hanan Ashrawi, the Palestinian minister of higher education; Leila Shaheed, the senior Palestinian envoy to France; and Munib Masri, who has been a personal as well as professional friend and whose guidance has been invaluable.

There also were Americans whom we would like to thank. High on the list is the Honorable Aaron Miller, a distinguished State Department official who, as deputy to Dennis Ross, may be in the background of television footage but who will always be in the forefront of our hearts. He provided important insights for us and took the time to read, comment on and correct our manuscript. We would like to thank Bruce Bender of Carol Publishing for having the confidence in us to republish this work and Donald J. Davidson, a sensitive and intelligent editor who put up with our many last-minute changes as the situation itself evolved. Most of all, we would like to thank S. Daniel Abraham, the founder of the Center for Middle East Peace and Economic Cooperation, which has played an increasingly vital role in facilitating greater understanding in the region. Danny has spared no effort in bringing Israeli and Palestinian leaders together, most recently Yasser Arafat and Benjamin Netanyahu. The center's president, Wayne Owens, a former congressman and member of the House Foreign Affairs Committee, has also been helpful in providing access for us to important background material. He is a rare combination of public servant, scholar and private citizen who has done as much as any diplomat to make peace a reality.

Finally, we dedicated this edition to Yitzhak Rabin in gratitude for the many hours he spent with us over the course of the last decade. Beginning in the summer of 1989 when he invited us to brief him on this project in Tel Aviv, we were constantly struck by his desire to learn all he could about his adversary. He probably anticipated even then, as a great general would, the eventual need to deal with Yasser Arafat. Yitzhak Rabin's personal courage and stamina ended generations of warfare and put the Middle East on a new course towards prosperity, cooperation and hope. We hope this book will help speed that process.

I

Arafat Unveiled

1

A Mystery Inside an Enigma

THE ELDERLY *Arab vendor sat behind a small table in Hebron's souk, while the chickens he was selling squawked at the reporter from the Jerusalem Post. In fluent Hebrew, the merchant insisted that he too had rights, that the Arabs had been in Palestine for hundreds of years: "The Jews say this was their land first. It is true that the Jews were here 2,000 years ago, 3,000 years ago. Who destroyed them? Nebuchadnezzar destroyed them. The Romans destroyed them. Not the Moslems. There were no Moslems then. When the Moslems captured this land, it was from the Romans, not the Jews. So whose land is it?"*

The question is as old as the Bible itself.

It has been approximately 4,000 years since Abraham, the primordial ancestor of Arabs and Jews, bought a burial place for his wife Sarah and himself. The Book of Genesis describes this first recorded land purchase in Hebron, some 3,000 feet up in the Judean Hills, about twenty miles south of Jerusalem. It was there, in the Cave of Machpelah, that the Bible says Abraham, Sarah, their son

Isaac and his wife Rebecca and their son Jacob and his wife Leah are buried.

Jews trace their roots to Abraham through Isaac, and Arabs trace their roots through Abraham's son Ishmael, born by Hagar, the handmaiden of Sarah. Today, Palestinians assert they are a people distinct from the rest of the Arabs, a people with roots that predate even those of the ancient Hebrews. They trace their heritage back to the Canaanites, who inhabited Mesopotamia and built the cities of Megiddo, Hatzor and Jerusalem in the third millennium before Christ.

During the Late Bronze Age (1500–1200 B.C.) Canaan was a battleground between the two empires of Egypt and the Hittites of Asia Minor. It was around this time that Moses led the Hebrews out of Egypt, and during the transition from the Late Bronze to Early Iron Age (about 1250 B.C.) that the Israelites first settled in Canaan.

A hundred years later, the Philistines invaded from Crete and other Mediterranean islands and managed to establish a foothold on the southern coast of Canaan, where they formed a coalition of five city-states: Gaza, Ascalon, Ashdod, Ekron and Gerar. It is from this people, the Philistines, that the name Palestine originally derives.

Around 1000 B.C., under the leadership of David, the Israelites defeated the Canaanites and Philistines and unified Judah in the south with Samaria and Galilee in the north, establishing the ancient kingdom of Israel. David was crowned in Hebron and later traveled to Jerusalem, where the first great temple was built by his son Solomon for the national and religious capital of the Jews.

For most of the next 1,600 years, the Jews were ruled by the Assyrians, Babylonians, Persians, Greeks, Egyptians and Romans. While they dreamed of a "Return to Zion" during the Babylonian exile, this theme did not become dominant in Jewish scripture until the Romans destroyed the Second Temple in A.D. 70. The Jews were forced to flee from Jerusalem, and for nearly 2,000 years thereafter they were scattered throughout the Middle East and the rest of the world. In A.D.132, the Roman emperor, Hadrian, changed Judea (the Greek form of Judah) to Palaestina.

For the next 1,384 years, during Byzantine rule and after the advent of Mohammed in the seventh century, Palestine was repeatedly invaded by foreign armies: by the Persians in A.D. 614, by the

Baghdad-based Abbasids, by the Egyptian Fatimids, Seljuk Turks, Crusaders, Mamluks and by the Ottomans in 1516. By the time of the Ottoman Empire in the sixteenth century, the Jews had become a scant minority among the Moslems; and although some scholars assert Jerusalem had a Jewish majority in the mid-nineteenth century, the Arabs made up more than 90 percent of the population when Britain occupied Palestine in World War I.

Although the Koran, the Moslem holy book, does not mention Jerusalem by name, it tells the story of Mohammed: that he was awakened one night by the archangel Gabriel, who carried him away on a winged horse to the masjad al-Aqsa, the "furthermost place." From there they ascended together to Heaven and Mohammed met God, returning the same night with the commandments he had received for the people of Islam. Jerusalem became identified as the "furthermost place," and al-Aqsa Mosque, built on the grounds of Solomon's Temple, became known as the very spot from which Mohammed rose to Heaven. Today, more than 700 million Moslems consider Jerusalem subordinate only to the holy cities of Mecca, Mohammed's birthplace, and Medina, where the prophet fled in hejira ("flight") in A.D. 622.

The new religion spread so quickly that within ten years of Mohammed's flight from Mecca, Islam (Arabic for "submission") had triumphed throughout Arabia; and less than a century after Mohammed's death in A.D. 632, Arab armies had conquered a domain that stretched from Spain to India. However, the holy cities of Mecca, Medina and Jerusalem remain the heart of the Moslem empire.

According to Judaism, God promised the same land to his chosen people, the Israelites. The Bible says that God told Joshua, "Therefore arise, go over this Jordan [River], thou and all thy people, onto the land which I do give to them, even to the children of Israel. Every place that the sole of your foot shall tread upon, to you I have given it, as I spoke unto Moses. From the wilderness, and this Lebanon, even onto the great river, the river Euphrates, all the land of the Hittites, and onto the Great Sea [the Mediterranean], toward the going down of the sun, shall be your border."

So, four thousand years later, whose land is it? Does it belong to the descendants of Abraham and Isaac, the Jews who built Solomon's

Temple? Or does it belong to the children of Ishmael, the Moslems who follow the preachings of the prophet Mohammed?

————————————————

————————

Like a modern Bedouin trekking across the desert, Yasser Arafat trots about the globe, working the world from an airplane. His momentary home, an executive jet borrowed from Iraq, Algeria, Kuwait, Tunisia or Saudi Arabia, seats no more than eleven and flies on his command to Beijing or Baghdad or Addis Ababa. "Believe me," he says plaintively, "I am living in this airplane more than on the ground."

The PLO chairman has just returned to Tunis from a wearying trip, "fifty-two hours and a half, within five days." His stops included North Korea, Laos, Peking, Hanoi and Bangladesh. On the way, Arafat adds, he visited Afghanistan as a guest of the pro-Soviet regime and also met with the antigovernment rebels, helping win the freedom of an American photographer held captive by the commandos.

A guerrilla on the go, he plays the role of peacemaker, patching up squabbles here, helping release hostages there. Yet for all his success with others, he has not brought peace to his own people. "Peace needs courageous men," he says. But too many times it has slipped between his fingers. For all his travels, Arafat races to keep himself in place at the center of attention.

For security reasons he maintains an extra pilot on his staff and keeps his destination a secret even to his fellow passengers until the plane is well in the air. He shies away from public places like movie theaters and restaurants, and cannot even recall his last meal out. "After Beirut I had one, but I don't remember it," he says.

No matter where he travels, the sixty-one-year-old Arafat eats only food that has been prepared and inspected by a trusted aide, and even this has not stopped attempts to poison him. In the most famous incident in Lebanon in the 1970s, an associate tried to slip a deadly substance in his rice. "It was the Israelis, the Mossad," says Abu Iyad, Arafat's second in command.[2]

Arafat travels light. His wardrobe includes a security blanket—an old blue jogging suit (and newer ones in yellow and green) —a Rolex watch, Bally boots, a well-worn British army coat, long woolen underwear and a handful of fatigues. His five almost identical uniforms, bought in Tunis, consist of neatly pressed trousers and breast-pocketed, long-sleeved shirts with epaulettes—three in olive drab for summer, two in khaki for winter. He keeps one of the outfits, nearly twenty years old, for special occasions and favors its more formal jacket for ceremonial affairs. His is the uniform of the guerrilla, a meaningful symbol for his people, a convenient style for his ascetic, nomadic life.

He recalls the last time he put on a suit, in 1968, when he made an overnight stop in Paris on his way to Algiers. "I couldn't go like this," he says looking down at his pseudomilitary clothes. Since then, the five-foot-four, thick-waisted leader always wears his uniform, whether he meets with chiefs of state decked out in full military regalia, or attends summits with Arab sheiks swathed in flowing *djellabahs,* or consults with Western leaders wearing tailored suits from Saville Row.

The others may top their heads with hats or crowns or go bareheaded, but Arafat always wears his *kafeeyah,* the checkered cloth he shapes in a point to symbolize the jagged map of Palestine. "I use it as my style. Arafat's style, yes?" he asks, smiling as he touches the black and white fabric. "The others are not using this style. I have my own style," he gloats.

The PLO chairman is defensive about his rough beard, rumored to hide a skin disease. "I like it," he grins. "Every three months I have someone shave it, but not completely."

In Tunis, where he is based, there are no obvious signs of Arafat, no images of him pasted on the walls, no visible PLO flags flapping in the wind. Tunis is a quiet city, a calm Mediterranean port where sparkling white houses brushed with brilliant blue doors reflect crystal beaches and an azure sea. Unlike their Algerian neighbors who fought a long and bloody war against the French, the Tunisians won their freedom peacefully and appear oblivious to Palestinian revolutionaries in their midst. In this soft spot of North Africa, mild-mannered people gather in cafes, where they grumble over local politics and the suffering economy, and muster up a hearty laugh at the oil-rich Libyans next door who must come shopping in downtown Tunis for such amenities as refrigerators and television sets.

But the underside of Tunis reeks of revolution. The city has become a political battlefront for the leaders of the Palestine Liberation Organization, who fled here after the Israelis forced them out of Lebanon in the summer of 1982. Red and white striped guardhouses outside their villas, government-provided Tunisian soldiers, and khaki-clad Palestinian gunmen lurking in the background illustrate the dangers surrounding the PLO chiefs. Nevertheless, their large, middle-class houses, some on lavish grounds with landscaped gardens, are furnished with Oriental carpets, richly fitted bathrooms and bars stocked with Scotch.

Ask one of the PLO leaders where he lives, and he may provide you with the address for a house in Tunis that he calls home. But Yasser Arafat claims no particular villa as his own. Instead he shifts from house to house, changing his location on a whim in the middle of the night. Arafat lives, quite rightly, in constant fear of some of the world's most skillful intelligence agencies, who have tried more than once to kill him. He evades them by traveling stealthily and often, not only in Tunis but around the world.

Arafat is holding court well past midnight in a safe-house in Belvedere, a posh Tunisian neighborhood of whitewashed villas hidden behind high stone walls and thick palm trees. Ordinarily, his neighbors, foreign diplomats and prosperous businessmen, are fast asleep, and the only signs of life are a passing police car or someone driving home from a late-night rendezvous. But on nights when Yasser Arafat, or Abu Amar, as his supporters call him, is here, the area converts to a war zone.

An eerie blackness covers the road. Streetlights are extinguished and houses are darkened. A dozen or more burly bodyguards, members of Arafat's Force 17 security troop, lean against the old Mercedes and BMWs parked in front of the house, their lighted cigarettes providing the only glow. With Soviet Kalashnikov automatic rifles swinging from their shoulders and Czechoslovak Scorpion pistols protruding from their hip pockets, their job is to protect the PLO chairman from enemy attack, whether it be Israeli, Syrian, or even extremist elements from within his own organization. Troops of Force 17 have been involved in the past in terrorist attacks; now they speak in quiet tones as they monitor the stream of visitors who enter the villa to see Arafat.

Inside the large but barely furnished house the air is stagnant; cigarette ashes fill small dishes on the tables and stamped-out butts spill on the floor. Bodyguards wander through the empty rooms, relieving their boredom by twirling their guns. Thirsty from too much tobacco, they gulp bottled water, Bedouin style, pouring it into their mouths without letting it touch their lips.

From a room in the back, Bassam Abu Sharif, once an active member of the radical Popular Front for the Liberation of Palestine, led by George Habash, and now a close aide to Arafat, can be heard shouting on the telephone, switching back and forth from Arabic to English. Abu Sharif's blaring is due, in part, to deafness in one ear, a result of a letter bomb sent to him in Beirut by the Israelis, he says, in 1972. He lost one eye, and the left side of his face was also damaged by the explosion, but it is not really noticeable until you see a photograph of the Palestinian before the package arrived and you realize how handsome a man he was. The Israelis were paying him back for his role in a series of international airline hijackings the PFLP organized in 1970.

Here and everywhere, Arafat is besieged with requests for interviews and harassed with endless meetings. Clusters of people, waiting for hours, stand wearily in the dim corridor or slouch half asleep in a drably furnished room usually reserved for meetings of the fifteen-member PLO Executive Committee. The only decoration is a picture of Arafat on the wall.

A coterie of Palestinians—translators, advisers, businessmen and exiled West Bankers—wander from room to room, part of the permanent cast of characters who complain they must always be ready to be at the side of the indefatigable chairman. Arafat works a sixteen-hour day and is at his best from nine P.M. to midnight. He sleeps only when he must, in the early morning or in the late afternoon, usually catching his eight hours four at a time. He guards his health cautiously, takes quantities of vitamins and an assortment of pills that cause his hands to tremble. He has medical check-ups every three months, and exercises regularly every afternoon with a brisk half-hour walk. His brother Fathi, a physician in Cairo, regards his health as amazingly good for someone with such a peripatetic existence. "If I have a patient who tells me he travels every day, nine or ten hours, for the last ten years," says Fathi, "I ask, 'Why are you coming to me?'"[3] But white spots on Arafat's arms and hand may indicate a loss of pigment from a lack of sun. Recently, he tried to cure this condition by taking infrared treatments, but the only result was he burned his hands. Arafat watches his diet carefully. He prefers fish and yogurt for lunch, and finishes his meal with fresh fruits as often as he can. He indulges in jars of his favorite honey from Yemen or Germany and halvah late at night. He snacks on Tunisian dates and kenafas made of sugar, shredded wheat and cheese and sometimes sneaks in marron glacé or a chocolate or two. He never drinks alcohol or coffee and never takes tobacco. But as abstemious as he is, he closes his eyes to the hedonism of his colleagues, knowing that for all he does not drink or smoke or womanize or live in splendor, they make up for it in quantities.

A group of PLO ambassadors, once guerrilla fighters but now well-dressed representatives to world capitals, pace the halls. Their first-class air tickets and hotel rooms cost a small fortune, and they will probably see Arafat for no more than a minute or two, but for various reasons, the chairman has summoned them from places like London or the Hague. One young envoy has been called from Copenhagen because of news reports that the wife of a Palestinian official who lives in Denmark has been caught spying inside Israel. The ambassador understands that it is safer to discuss certain matters in person than to risk having Israeli Mossad agents intercept a phone call. Nevertheless, he suggests with a yawn, he would rather be in bed back at home.

While others grumble, a menagerie of artists from Madame Tussaud's Wax Museum flaps around the rooms, at work on a statue of Arafat soon to be displayed in the London gallery. A bright-eyed delegation of West Bank Palestinian women all rouged and coiffed despite the hour, wait for a handshake or even a hug from Abu Amar. A group of Italian Communists, rumpled and shy, hope for a moment of inspiration from their revolutionary idol.

Three or four European journalists, based in Tunis and assigned to cover the chairman, growl that, as usual, they have been roused from their sleep with the promise of an interview, but whether or not they get it remains to be seen. An interview with the chairman is now a precious commodity, highly valued and not easily attained. Currently he does not pursue the press; instead he courts them by playing the reluctant lover. It is precisely his reticence that is so seductive.

Arafat is illusive and shrouds himself in myth: He is an outcast driven by a sense of betrayal; a victim who suffers the pain of martyrdom; Ishmael, born of a servant woman, abandoned by his father Abraham, sent into the wilderness with little more than God's promise that he will make a nation. And yet he pictures himself as a conqueror, an invincible moral master. He calls himself the phoenix, the mythological Egyptian bird that consumes itself in fire, then rises from its own ashes.

The ordinary facts of Arafat's life—his place of birth, his parents, his childhood, his adolescence—lay buried in the soil of his distant homeland. Unlike the other leaders of the PLO, married men with families and private lives, he has traded his personal life for Palestine, dedicated his time, his money and his energy exclusively to the cause. No details identify him as a regular human being, no wife, no children, no house of his own.

Even his love life has been veiled in secrecy, fueling the rumors spread by his enemies in Damascus and Tel Aviv that he is homosexual. He speaks haltingly of a time in Beirut in 1973 when he and a married woman were deeply in love, and whispers sadly about her death. Some of his friends suggest that Arafat suffers from being shy and that he has been hurt by several women who rejected his offers of marriage. "The Palestinian women are not accepting me," he says. His familiar phrase "I am married to all the women of Palestine" may be as much a cover to heal his unrequited love as it is a cloak of armor in which to hide himself.

He has had his brief time of wealth, houses, fast cars and fancy suits, but he renounced those and more; he has taken the oath of self-denial in return for the singular passion that drives him, the resolution to see an independent homeland for the Palestinians.

For now the stage is set behind closed French doors in the high-ceilinged salon where television lights glare on the pallid faces of a dozen weary people. Arafat's aides huddle in the smoke-filled room, tensely watching a British Broadcasting Corporation TV crew. At the far end of the room Arafat looks out, his body nearly swallowed up behind a large desk, his face bearded with its perpetual three-day growth, his bright eyes bulging, his thick lower lip drooping in disgust. Surprisingly small, unexpectedly neat and clean, he is nevertheless an odd-looking man made instantly recognizable by the omnipresent olive-green uniform and his trademark checkered *ka-feeyah*. As he speaks his eyes dart mockingly about the room, his knee jerks like a nervous teenager's and his small fingers thump on the desk.

BBC journalist Marie Colvin asks about his peace plan. Arafat smiles, pleased at the image she helps him project. But her next question is unclear, and the chairman sneers, unsure of the reporter's intent. "You were the leader of the PLO. Were you unable to control these extremist groups?" she asks, referring to terrorist attacks by constituent factions of the PLO. Arafat gives a circuitous reply, playing to the camera like a lover. "The superpower, the United States of America, haven't the ability to stop the attempts to kill Reagan and the assassination of John Kennedy." The reporter's next question hits harder, touching a raw nerve. Is he personally responsible for terrorism? she asks. Arafat rages in response, his eyes bulge even more, his body jumps up and down, his finger points accusingly. "Is this an investigation?" he thunders. "You are speaking to the chairman of the PLO. The president of the state of Palestine. Be careful with your investigation!"[4]

He slams his hands on the desk and stands up in a fury, a Smith and Wesson pistol showing from his holster, six clean bullets lined up at his hip. With a dramatic flourish, he dismisses the group and walks quickly out into the corridor, brushing aside the reporter and the crew. Arafat is instantly transformed: his warmth freezes into icy anger, his charm turns into ugly hate. He marches past his lounging bodyguards into the narrow hallway, revealing a glimpse of the raging guerrilla leader, back arched stolidly, eyes staring straight ahead.

He is a master of theatrics, a versatile actor who hides behind his costumes, switching from politician to guerrilla as quickly as he whips off his *kafeeyah* and snaps on his army cap. A deft manipulator of his own emotions, he is a spigot of passions who one minute pours hugs and kisses, and the next spews angry tirades, and other times sobs soft tears. He is solicitous of women one moment, plying them with gifts, and surly the next, stomping off like a spoiled child. He is contemptuous of his enemies: "I am not Begin," he says. "I am not talking to God." Yet he is desperate to be accepted as their equal: "I am like Dayan. I am well educated." He is defiant: "I have many reasons not to trust any of the American promises." He is distressed: "[Undersecretary of State Lawrence] Eagleburger is insulting me. I do not know why." He depicts his people as martyrs: "We are the victims." He portrays himself as a valiant world figure: "I am a man of history."

He is small and scrappy, shrewd and street smart, cunning enough to outwit his enemies and clever enough to outlast his friends. He is not an intellectual, yet he relishes rhetoric, delights in double talk, and enjoys nothing so much as an argument. His friends joke that when Arafat is alone, he cannot resist fighting with himself in the mirror. His life is melodramatic, his moves mysterious, his existence riddled with question marks. What is he really like? Why does he have that beard? Why does he wear that *kafeeyah*? Is he married? Does he like women? Who is this man who claims to be the leader of at least five million people? Is he their leader? Is he legitimate? Can we deal with him?

His secretary Kawlah, an attractive thirtyish woman with streaked brown hair and smart-looking clothes, rushes after him, bringing a glass and a bottle of water to quench his thirst. An aide grabs the chance to whisper in his ear that Madame Toussaud's artists need him to pose again, while another pleads that an American journalist really must speak with him soon. He brushes aside their petitions and marches into the conference room, a broad smile now painted on his face, to greet the group of Communists who have come to pay him homage. He hugs their leader, plants moist kisses on both cheeks, and waits while they stand in awe, trying bashfully to speak in awkward English. Long minutes go by before the group presents him with a gift, an original poster of the *intifada* entitled *"kaffiiya."* Arafat grins with pride, but rebukes their spelling and their choice of white for the headdress. He cannot resist the opportunity to lecture his listeners: "The white is for civilians, those living in the cities. The red and white is for the desert, for the Bedouins especially in the south of our country and in Jordan and in Saudi Arabia. The black and white is for the peasants." The meeting over, he moves down the line and embraces each man with ebullience, the poses snapped by his personal photographer, leaving tremors of adoration in his wake. Then he is off, back to the salon where his attendants are reassembling, readying themselves for another in the endless round of interviews.

Returning to his desk, he shuffles through a stack of papers, some of them faxed reports of the latest news of the *intifada*, some of them letters requesting funds. With his photographic memory, he recalls papers and people filed in his brain dozens of years before. "I have a very good memory," Arafat says. Adds Bassam Abu Sharif: "He remembers every single paper that he signed fifteen, seventeen years ago."[5] Another time his aide says, "He remembers he had put twelve years ago a green file in the library of Mr. X in Damascus which had three papers: 'The middle one is important, and it carries this sentence...' He has an electronic memory for information, faces and names."[6]

Arafat's seemingly perpetual, upside-down days are filled with a steady paper flow, a constant stream of phone calls and a continuous course of meetings. Working always to stay master of his universe, he keeps in touch with his constituents, more than five million people scattered around the world, followers of multifarious ideologies, believers in numerous religions and subjects of other governments—almost half of them under Israeli control. Approximately 1.6 million Palestinians live in the West Bank and Gaza Strip, another 710,000 live inside Israel itself as Israeli citizens; 1.3 million Palestinians live in Jordan and have Jordanian passports; 750,000 refugees are in Syria and Lebanon; 700,000 live in the Arabian Gulf, in Kuwait, Saudi Arabia, Qatar and the Arab Emirates; and several hundred thousand are in Egypt, Europe, the United States and South America.

His electronic network allows him to "contact all my headquarters anywhere, anytime, by all means: fax, telephone, wireless, telex," the chairman says, adding that the PLO owns a share in Arabsat, the Arab countries' multibillion dollar, private communications satellite. "I am using the American technology: satellites. I have my own Star Wars," he says. One day soon, jokes Bassam Abu Sharif, the PLO will launch its own satellite into space. For now, Abu Sharif calls the fax "a daily life machine" and claims, "We have forty-eight faxes in Ain Hilwa refugee camp alone. In the territories, there are hundreds of faxes. If an incident happens in any small village in the West Bank or Gaza, he gets a report in fifteen minutes by fax." The messages are telephoned from East Jerusalem to Europe and then passed on to headquarters. Their prevalence is inescapable in Tunis, where almost every phone call to a PLO office is met with the familiar piercing ring of a fax machine.

Says Abu Sharif, "Of course, many of the faxes are coded and have scramblers with the other faxes. The other party has to have the same machine. It won't receive unless it is coded. You can't intercept it. If you try to, you will only get scrambled messages." The aide explains that this sophisticated system of communications started when the PLO was fighting in Jordan in 1970; they had thousands of fighters but no telephone lines to communicate. "We used the best Western and Japanese technology. It is all coded," he says. The equipment, purchased primarily from the Sharp Corporation of Japan, is so intricate that according to Abu Sharif it would take years for a computer to decode one of the PLO's private communications.

Despite this modern system, Arafat's job of maintaining a nation is complicated, if not impossible: he has no country, no territory, not even an acre to call his own; he has no official taxes to collect nor authorized services to render, no police protection or fire trucks, no postal delivery or social security; no permanent manner in which to demonstrate his leadership or demand the loyalty of his people.

Nevertheless, from his PLO base in Tunis, Arafat reigns as president of a complex and comprehensive government-in-exile, a state-in-waiting recognized by 130 countries. Though his critics, even within the PLO, accuse him of refusing to delegate responsibility, Arafat often boasts that the PLO is an organization run by consensus. Certainly he has built a parapet of government, with an inevitable bureaucracy estimated at 5,000 employees. "We have a very accurate and organized system," declares Arafat.

The PLO has a complex structure:

—an Executive Committee of fifteen people representing all factions of the Palestinians. It includes the mainstream Fatah, the Democratic Front for the Liberation of Palestine (DFLP), the militant Popular Front for the Liberation of Palestine (PFLP), the Iraqi-backed Arab Liberation Front (ALF), the extreme fringe Palestine Liberation Front (PLF), the Palestinian Communist Party (PCP) and independents. It meets monthly in Tunis, Cairo, Algiers or Bagdhad to oversee the workings of the PLO. The current PLO Executive Committee includes:

Yasser Arafat (Abu Amar): Fatah; chairman of the Executive Committee and head of the Military Department.

Farouk Kaddoumi (Abu Lutuf): Fatah; head of the Political Department.

Mahmoud Abbas (Abu Mazzen): Fatah; head of the Department of Arab and International affairs.

Yasser Abed Rabbo (Abu Bashir): DFLP; head of the Department of Information.

Mustafa al-Zabari (Abu Ali Mustafa): PFLP; head of the Department of Repatriates.

Ahmed Abdul Rahim: ALF; head of the Popular Organizations Department.

Suleiman al-Najab: PCP; head of the Department of Social Affairs.

Mohammed Abbas (Abul Abbas): PLF; head of Department for Refugees.

Jamal al-Surani: Independent; secretary-general of the Executive Committee and head of Department of Administrative Affairs.

Abdul Razak Yahya (Abu Anas): Independent; head of the Economic Department.

Bishop Ilia Khouri (Abu Mahar): Independent

Abdullah Hourani: Independent; head of Department of Cultural Affairs.

Mahmoud Darwish: Independent; chairman of the Supreme Council for Education, Propaganda and Heritage.

Jaweed al-Ghussein (Abu Tufiq): Independent; chairman of the board of directors for the Palestine National Fund.

Mohammed Milhem (Abu A'Ala): Independent; head of Department of Occupied Homeland Affairs and the Department of Higher Education.

—a Finance Board composed of twenty-seven people that supervises an annual budget of more than $300 million and oversees the tens of millions of dollars required to maintain organization inside the West Bank and Gaza;

—a Health Ministry, the Palestine Red Crescent Society, headed by Arafat's brother, Fathi Arafat, with a staff of physicians that runs fifteen major hospitals, nine in Lebanon, four in Syria, one in Egypt and one in Yemen; two major medical complexes in Syria; and forty-four clinics and infirmaries spread out through Lebanon, Syria, Sudan, Egypt, Tunisia and Qatar. The ministry also provides medical outcare to the sick and pays medical insurance to the wounded victims of the *intifada* in the Israeli-occupied territories.

—an Education Department which runs schools for the children of Palestinian martyrs, provides scholarship funds for higher education, and boasts that its people have the highest literacy rate in the Arab world. In addition to the traditional curriculum of reading, writing and arithmetic, the department ensures that students are drilled in Palestinian history, culture and politics.

—a Political Department headed by a putative foreign minister, Farouk Kaddoumi, with a diplomatic corps ensconced in eighty-five embassies worldwide and accredited in over one-hundred countries.

—the Palestine Liberation Army, a military organization that maintains a skeleton army with brigades in Iraq, Egypt, Yemen, Sudan and Algeria, each under the control of the local government. Asked if his army is composed only of guerrilla fighters, Arafat scoffs: "For your information, we are not *fedayeen* (guerrillas). We have a very good army. One of the best armies among the Arabs. And we have some high officers, some who have been trained in the United States, some of them have been trained in France." Arafat is eager to surpass his competition, the Arab states, and aches to equal his enemy, Israel. "For your information, we were the first army in the region, three months after the Israelis, to use a computer to direct artillery. It was in 1981."

Several thousand Palestinians are at hand in Tunis, but the Tunisian government is strict and does not allow gun-toting members of the PLO to ride herd on its citizens. The Tunisians remember what happened to Jordan in 1970 when the Palestinians terrorized the population and created a state within a state; they know what happened to Lebanon when the Palestinians came and the country was torn apart by civil war; they do not want the same thing to happen to them. Rarely do the worlds of Tunisians and Palestinians mix, but when members of the PLO leadership sunbathe poolside or on the beach at the luxurious Hotel Abu Nawas, their bodyguards keep their pistols hidden in paper bags or tucked into designer carryalls.

The Tunisians know that their own safety is fragile. Once in a while the brutality of the war between the Palestinians and the Israelis spills over and injures the hosts. In October 1985 the Israelis flew into a Tunis suburb and bombed the seven-acre PLO Force 17 headquarters in Hammam al-Shatt where Arafat took his breakfast almost every morning of the week; twenty-four Palestinians, including Arafat's secretary, were killed, fourteen Tunisian workers were found dead, and many others were injured. It was thanks to his daily exercise that Arafat says he escaped. "Jogging saved me during the air raid," he claims. Some say that he had been paying a condolence call on a widow living nearby, while still others imply he was warned.

The bombing was in retribution for the September 1985 murder of three Israeli tourists, killed aboard their yacht in Lanarca, Cyprus, most likely by members of Force 17. According to the PLO, one of the Israelis was Sylvia Raphael, supposedly a Mossad agent who helped plan the death of Ali Hassan Salameh, the former head of the PLO's security department. Salameh was chief of operations in Europe for Black September, a clandestine terrorist group within Fatah, and was personally responsible for plotting the death of eleven Israeli athletes participating in the 1972 summer Olympics in Munich. In the never-ending cycle of violence and revenge, members of the Palestinian Liberation Front led by Abul Abbas reacted less than a week after the October 1985 Tunis bombing with a plan to hijack an Italian cruise ship, the *Achille Lauro*, when it reached the Israeli port of Ashdod and to blow up an Israeli munitions depot. But the guerrillas panicked when they sensed Israeli agents had discovered they were on board and hijacked the ship just after it left Alexandria, Egypt. Brandishing their weapons, the terrorists held eighty passengers at gunpoint and shot Leon Klinghoffer, a crippled American Jew, in the head, then shoved his body and wheelchair overboard.

Violent actions, demonstrations and strikes in the Israeli-occupied West Bank and Gaza followed for two years, foreshadowing the uprising which exploded in December 1987. In early 1988 the Israelis retaliated. They returned to PLO headquarters in Tunis and assassinated Abu Jihad, the PLO's second in command, the official responsible for Palestinian activities in the West Bank and Gaza. This time the Israelis performed a "surgical operation." They arrived in the middle of the night and plugged Abu Jihad's body with 75 bullets, but left unharmed his wife and two-year-old son, who were both in the bedroom with him.

While dozens of PLO leaders have been killed by enemies, Arafat's ability to escape death has become legendary among Palestinians. His aides swear he can smell danger coming. He has been known to stand up suddenly in the middle of a meeting and say, "Everybody out!" Countless tales tell of swift escapes from cars and from buildings that were bombed only moments after PLO leaders had fled. In Syria the government tried twice to ambush Arafat, but succeeded only in killing his bodyguard. In 1982 in Beirut he was hunted obsessively by Ariel Sharon, the then Israeli defense minister, who sent his fighter planes on constant search-and-destroy missions over the city. Arafat changed his location as much as he could but often met with his colleagues in Beirut's high-rise office buildings. On one occasion, late on an August night in 1982, Arafat was in his office in a fourteen-story building when he was informed that the Italian ambassador wished to see him. Sensing danger, the chairman changed locations immediately, moving his cohorts across the street. At 2:05 A.M. the Fatah leaders looked out the window to see an explosion destroy the building they had been in. "It was like an atom bomb," recalls Ahmed Abdul Rahman, spokesman for Fatah, who was there at the time. "There was nothing one minute and you wondered what happened because you didn't hear the noise of the plane. You only heard the noise afterward."[7] Two hundred fifty people were killed, he says; Arafat and his colleagues escaped unharmed.

In the West Bank, where he traveled in disguise in 1967, "the closest call," Arafat remembers, "was in a small village, even smaller, a few houses. This was my headquarters. At eleven I got up. I don't know why. There were only two of us in this house and I said, 'We should leave.'" When his associate asked him why, Arafat told him, "I feel we are in danger." The friend argued and went outside to look around, insisting there was no danger. Arafat grew angry and said, "We have to leave. If not, I will leave alone." The two men walked to the village of Deir Salam and arrived there just toward dawn. "We looked back to see where we had left," says Arafat. "And there were army vehicles. When he turned around, my friend began to weep with joy."

That intuition, which Arafat calls "a dog's sense," is one reason the chairman has been able to survive for so long in the wily Arab world. Another is his Machiavellian ability to befriend the right governments at the right time, whether they be Egypt, Iraq, Syria, Lebanon, Jordan, the United States or the Soviet Union; to stay friendly with his opponents and to switch sides whenever necessary. Even within his own umbrella organization of the PLO, Arafat has managed to maintain a consensus. He has balanced himself between the extremists, using them as leverage against the world. Aware that the Palestinians have been rendered impotent by having neither land nor authority, he has gained his power by unifying his people through the institutions of the PLO, and he continually reaffirms that unity by pushing them to agreement.

He has been in the forefront of Palestinian thinking, a pragmatist trying to preserve a realistic political process, knowing full well that on one side some complain that he moves too slowly toward peace with Israel, while on the other side some accuse him of being a traitor and call him "a Zionist agent," and that all sides of the PLO scheme to impose their own brands of ideology. His staying power as chairman of the PLO is due as much to his absolute determination to remain independent of any Arab government as it is to gain a homeland for the Palestinian people. For those Palestinian refugees scattered around the world, but citizens of nowhere, their homeland is the PLO; their identity is Arafat.

Arafat crawls into bed at four or five A.M. wearing his pajamas or a jogging suit, awakes around ten in the morning and starts his day with a quick ride on his sleek, Carnielli stationary bicycle or a twenty-minute round of jogging and Swedish exercises. A practicing Moslem, he often combines the five daily prayers into one and always wears a white gold chain and pendant engraved with a verse of the Koran.

He lingers in the shower and spends more than half an hour preparing to dress but saves time by not shaving: "It would be very difficult for me to waste fifteen minutes shaving because I would lose 450 minutes a month, seven and a half hours. Too much, because I have no time as it is," he says. Besides, he adds, "In our area of the world, this is not something bad to have your beard."[8] He has no hair to comb—he began balding when he was in his twenties—and rarely lets himself be seen bareheaded, covering up his pate with his signature black and white *kafeeyah*. It was in June 1967 that Arafat began to wear the headcloth. "It was directly after the Six-Day War," he recalls. "I went there, inside the Arab territories, where I spent more than four months. I used the *kafeeyah* as our peasants do. Then I continued using it as my own style." He grins, touching the pointed tip of the headdress and repeats, "I have my own style."

He breakfasts daily on cornflakes with honey and tea, eaten while he meets with some of his advisers or military staff. A session with those on his staff who are in contact with the occupied territories comes next, then a meeting with the ambassadors from the Arab League, followed by a working lunch with his financial advisers. Later in the day he might call a meeting of the central committee of Fatah, the fat cat of the PLO, the biggest and richest of all its factions.

The PLO's financial operations are controlled by the Palestine National Fund, which once had assets of more than one billion dollars but now, because of the oil glut and the cost of the *intifada,* sets its wealth at 600 to 800 million dollars. Its worldwide holdings, run by SAMED, part of the economic bureau headed by Ahmed Kureah (Abu Ala), who worked at the Arab Bank, include farms and production plants in Yemen, Sudan, Somalia, Guinea, Mali, Guinea-Bisseau and Poland. "We have investments, farms and houses everywhere," says Khalid al-Fahoum, former speaker of the Palestine National Council and now a bitter opponent of Arafat. "In Africa, in particular, because land is cheap there, and because we want to have good relations, and it is easy to make friends with the African rulers because they don't ask for too much money."[9] In Poland the PNF owns a nail factory, in Hungary a shoe factory, in Nicaragua part of the national airline, Aeronica. There are PLO-owned radio stations in Algiers, Yemen and Baghdad, reputed partial ownership in the influential Radio Monte Carlo, and at least a dozen newspapers and periodicals that come under the PLO's umbrella.[10]

From its operating budget of $300-$400 million a year, the PLO gives 60 percent of its money to Fatah and the balance to the PFLP, the DFLP and the other factions of the PLO. In addition, it provides $90 to $100 million a year to the Palestine Liberation Army and distributes funds to the Palestine Red Crescent, its political bureau, "al-Dareh al-Siyasiya" and to the welfare of orphans and widow. The PNF's funds come from private donations, personal loans and annual contributions of $85 million from the Saudi government and $235 million from other Arab states, jeopardized now by the Gulf crisis.

Despite the agreement by all Arab countries to support the Palestine National Fund, the recent oil glut has also forced a cutback on their expenditures, and the fund currently operates at a deficit. Private donations as well as contributions from Arafat, who sometimes dips into the deep Fatah treasury, have helped to offset the losses. Nevertheless, the board of directors, whose treasurer is Jaweed al-Ghussein, chairman of the Cordoba Development Company, wrings its hands in frustration. The "Compradors," as Arafat dubs his combined billionaire backers, include Abdul Majeed Shoman, the chairman of the Arab Bank; Hassib Sabagh, the Athens-based chief of CCC, the largest construction company in the Middle East; Munib al-Masri, the London-based chairman of EDGO engineering company; and Abdul Muhsin al-Qattan, a Kuwaiti-based contractor.

Since August 1988, when King Hussein withdrew his administration from the West Bank and Gaza, the PLO has assumed much of the cost of social services in the occupied territories. In addition to the fees they had already been paying, a one-time gift of 2,000 Jordanian dinars ($3,000) to families of martyrs and 500 Jordanian dinars ($750) to families of the wounded, the PLO reportedly sends thirty to forty million dollars a month to the West Bank and Gaza; only about thirteen million of that sum comes from the special Arab Fund. One of the PLO's greatest challenges has become channeling its money into the occupied territories. Israeli authorities examine all Arabs at the borders, detaining them for hours, often making them strip naked, and subjecting them to body searches to make sure they are not smuggling guns or money for the *intifada* into the West Bank and Gaza.

The Palestinians dance around the Israelis with a number of inventive techniques. "There are many ways to get money into a certain country," observes Ahmed Qatanani, head of Jordan's Department of Palestinian Affairs. "Since you have people who travel from the territories abroad, or back and forth, with different nationalities—people who like to make money—even Israelis can be agents for transferring. This is taking place."[11]

One of the most convenient methods of transferring funds is through banks in Amman. "The PLO has been using different channels. For instance, they put money in accounts of various people and institutions in Amman, and money has been going sporadically through people. If the Israelis know of a procedure of getting money in and have no reason to believe that money now goes solely for support of *intifada*, they will even give permission to the people to get the money in," says Qatanani. Deposits made in the Cairo-Amman bank, which has branches in Jordan and in the West Bank, can be withdrawn in Nablus or Ramallah. "If you listen to the radio," explains Qatanani, "it says, 'We have sent you 400 dinars through the Cairo-Amman Bank. This comes from Kuwait to someone in Nablus.' Over the radio they tell them to go to the Cairo-Amman Bank and receive the money we have sent. This is a half-hour program that is broadcast on the radio twice a day."

In addition to the Arab-owned banks, the Palestinians take advantage of Israeli institutions. Perhaps the most clever is the use of savings accounts and bonds which, in a paradigm of Middle Eastern paradox, helps the Israeli economy while it maneuvers to destroy it. "Most of our money is invested in Germany, England and Switzerland," says Khaled al-Fahoum the former speaker of the PNC. A current financial adviser says that approximately 20 percent of the funds are kept in Abdul Majeed Shoman's Arab Bank headquartered in Amman and Cairo, 30 percent in Swiss institutions, 30 percent in American banks located in New York—in the clearinghouses of Chase Manhattan Bank and Republic National Bank—and the balance scattered around the world. A close aide to Arafat says, that in a twist of irony, some of the assets deposited in New York have been in Israeli-owned banks, easily transferable to accounts of Israeli Arabs or even Jews who can withdraw the money in Tel Aviv, Haifa or Jerusalem for the Palestinians. "There are Israeli channels to get the money in," confirms Qatanani. PLO funds have also been invested in Israeli government savings bonds which can be presented at any Israeli bank before maturity, redeemable for the face value minus a penalty charge. To Palestinians it is worth the nearly 20 percent loss to be able to cash their bonds inside Israel.

But perhaps the most exasperating scheme to the Israelis has been the PLO's system of borrowing money at high interest rates from ultra-Orthodox Jews. Some Hasidic groups who go so far as to call themselves Palestinians believe that, until the arrival of the Messiah, Israel has no right to exist as a Jewish state. Anxious to counteract Zionism, they help the PLO create a Palestinian entity in place of Israel, working eagerly, especially when they can do so at a profit.

While the directors of the Palestine National Fund contrive ways to transfer money to the territories, Arafat keeps tight control over his own organization's finances; Fatah has its own direct sources of income, siphoning off 5 percent of the salaries of every Palestinian worker in Saudi Arabia, where the government makes certain the money is paid. A similar sum has been less strictly paid out in Kuwait and the Gulf states. Fatah's secret assets are known only to three or four people, and Arafat's signature must appear on all of Fatah's checks.

Arafat controls more than just the funds of Fatah. "Anyone who does not control the money does not control power," Arafat tells his friends. His hold is so tight that his associates say if he is killed, no one will know where all the money is kept. Arafat has at least one dozen bank accounts which require his signature, and they are scattered around the world. Not long ago a member of the PFLP asked him, "Where are the funds for the *intifada?*" "Here I am," answered Arafat.

Once in a while, problems arise for people who need Arafat's endorsement. One incident reported by Herb Denton in the *Washington Post* tells of a reserve soldier in the Palestine Liberation Army who left his home in Cairo to fight in Lebanon against the Israelis in 1982. The army colonel had brought $200 with him, but the money was stolen from his hotel room. Desperate, he went to Arafat to ask for help. The chairman responded at once, writing a note generously authorizing money for the soldier and telling him to take it to the finance office.

When the colonel presented the chit to the clerk at the finance office, however, he was told that such a large amount would have to be approved by the PLO Executive Committee. The only problem was that the committee would not be meeting for another month and the site of the meeting would be Damascus. Disgusted and confused, the colonel showed Arafat's note to a friend, who told him this was Arafat's "third signature." What the colonel needed to do, said the friend, was to see Arafat again and ask him for his "first signature."

The distraught soldier returned to Arafat and proceeded to ask for his "first signature." Arafat burst out laughing and said, "You son of a bitch, how did you know?" With that he quickly signed another note. Just as quickly the colonel took the note to the finance office. And just as quickly the clerk gave him his money.[12]

Despite these legendary tricks, Arafat's authority to hand out money puts him at a special advantage, on an elevated plateau far above any other Palestinian leader. To the tens of thousands of refugees in the West Bank and Gaza, in Jordan, Lebanon and Iraq who rely on Fatah for their food, their clothing and their health care, Arafat is close to God. To the thousands of widows and children of Palestinian martyrs living in the Middle East and Europe, who rely on Fatah for their pensions and their college tuition, Arafat is an icon. He provides not only the bread and bandages to brace them for their daily lives, but most important, he gives them a dream they can cling to, the hope of a homeland.

Sitting now in the middle of the night in his temporary house in his temporary headquarters in Tunis, Yasser Arafat reads faxed reports of conversations held by West Bank Palestinians with Israeli Prime Minister Yitzhak Shamir and Defense Minister Yitzhak Rabin. As he reads, he glances toward us and nods almost imperceptibly for this interview to begin. When we ask who might represent the Palestinians at negotiations with the Israelis over elections in the West Bank and Gaza, Arafat fumes: "Nobody can ask this question, because there is one man only in the Middle East who can nominate. It's not for the American, for the Israelis, for Sharon himself, for Modai, for Levi," he shouts, reeling off a list of right-wing Israeli leaders. "They know it is only one man who can give his stamp."

We change the subject and ask about the chairman's childhood: Arafat arches his back in response. The enigmatic leader has made it his mission to keep his early years a mystery, his own murky identity a metaphor for all the Palestinians. He is the fatherless father, the motherless son, the homeless leader of a homeless nation, the selfless symbol of a people without identity, the ultimate man without a country.

He was born, he says, a child of violence and destiny, in a Moslem waqf, a compound of thirteen stone houses that abutted the Wailing Wall, the oldest, most venerated symbol of the ancient Jewish kingdom that for seventy years—3,000 years ago—gave birth to the Zionist dream of nationhood and that for one thousand two hundred years has been a holy symbol for Islam. Many others say he was born in Cairo, and a birth certificate confirms this. But the document may be a forgery: like everything else about him, even Arafat's birth is layered in mystery, as though the facts themselves might undermine his mythical existence.

The story his family and close friends reveal is that his parents were continually feuding: In an act considered shameful for an Arab woman, his mother left her husband's apartment in Sakakini, a middle-class section of Cairo well-populated with Jews, and traveled to Jerusalem to have her baby in her family's home, in the womb of the Moslem world, next to the very wall from which Mohammed ascended to heaven. Here, in August 1929, an Arab boy was born without his father, near a wall that was enshrined in the heart of two ancient cultures at the meeting place of two devout religions in the holiest city on earth.

On the day Arafat was born, there were probably disturbances only a stone's throw away from the Abu Saud "Zawia" (religious compound), when Jews dared, as they had for several weeks, to sit on benches as they prayed at the last remaining rampart of the Second Temple. The life that began that day would be filled with the seething hatreds, blood feuds and communal strife that were already spilling forth between Arabs and Jews and that would culminate in the creation of a state for the Jews and in a violent nationalist struggle by the Palestinians to give life to their own dream for a homeland. From that day more than sixty years ago, Yasser Arafat has only returned to Jerusalem as a guerrilla leader. He is still fighting to go home.

His birth certificate states that Arafat was born in Egypt on August 24, 1929. The death of his mother, he acknowledges, took place in Cairo only four years later. His Egyptian accent substantiates a childhood spent in Cairo's schools. But on this evening and in the course of numerous other interviews, Arafat stubbornly maintains that he was born on a different day in a different place, August 4, 1929, not in Egypt, but in Palestine. "I was born in Jerusalem," he repeats again and again. "I lived there until 1942."

"He was born in the house of his Uncle Selim," confirms his cousin, Sheik Musa Abu Saud, who shows an old, worn photograph of Arafat's birthplace, a stone building that once clung to the Western Wall, but was razed by the Israelis after the war in 1967.[12] Like all Arab sons, the boy carried his own given name as well as the names of his father, his father's family, his father's extended family, and his father's extended clan. But Mohammed Abder Rauf Arafat al-Kudwa al-Husseini would soon be known as Yasser (meaning "easygoing") Arafat. Much later he would adopt the name of a follower of the prophet Mohammed, the fighter Amar ibn Yasser, and take as his own nom de guerre Abu Amar.

The romantic image of being born in a house abutting the Wailing Wall, a child of the tortuous intermingling of the Jewish and Arab ancient past, is a notion that appeals to him. Yet the Egyptian document contradicts this story.

Why this cover-up? Perhaps he fears his Egyptian birthplace weakens his credentials as a Palestinian leader. Perhaps he was born in Jerusalem, and like many in Egypt, his Gazan father later registered him in Cairo so that he could receive a free Egyptian education. Most likely, his mother, Zahwa Abu Saud, who came from a prominent Jerusalem clan, gave birth in her family home and when she returned to Cairo several weeks later, she registered her baby's birth. Perhaps he doesn't know himself. Whatever the answer, Arafat relishes the mystery.

Yasser Arafat was the sixth of seven children; he had three older sisters, Inam, Khadiga and Yusra, two older brothers, Gamal and Mustafa, and a younger brother Fathi. His father, Abder Rauf Arafat, who hailed from a landowning family in Gaza, a distant branch of the eminent Husseini clan, lived for some time in Jerusalem, then moved in 1927 to Cairo. For the first few years of his life Arafat lived in Egypt with the rest of the family. But after his mother's sudden death from kidney disease, four-year-old Yasser and his younger brother Fathi were sent off to their maternal Abu Saud family in Jerusalem. "I went to live with my uncle because my mother had died when I was very young," confirms Arafat. The two boys were shuttled like unwanted orphans from the apartment in Cairo to their father's family house in Gaza to the Abu Saud home in Jerusalem.

Their father made his money as a merchant, selling cheese, wheat, rice, sugar and the popular Nabulsi soap. "I asked him once," says Arafat, "why he left Jerusalem, and he said we had a big trading company. His partners, one from the Alami family, another from the Dajanis, asked him to go to Egypt, and they stayed in Jerusalem."

There was little contact between Arafat and his father, and the times when they lived together were unhappy at best. A religious man who married twice more after the death of his first wife, Abder Rauf brought the young boys back to Cairo when he took his second and third wives. The fights between the women and the children were bitter, but if Yasser worried about each new stepmother, he will not admit it now. "It was she who had to be afraid," Arafat says with a laugh. "There were seven of us and only one of her. She had to be afraid of me."

Asked of his best memory of his father, Yasser Arafat pauses for a minute, then answers slowly, "He never treated us as his sons. He always treated us as his friends." Silent for a few moments, he thinks some more and says, "I learned a lot from my father. My father was pious. He was a good man. He was very keen that I should be sincere, honest and genuine. I was never to lie or hide secrets from him." Nevertheless, he rarely confided in the older man, even keeping secret the fact that he wanted to go to college in the United States. "Heart to heart was something different with my father," he acknowledges. Having squandered the family's money and land in a major legal battle, Abder Rauf died in Gaza in 1954. Yasser Arafat did not attend the funeral.

The man who did treat him like a son was his uncle, Salim Abu Saud. A striking man with a big mustache, Salim had no children of his own and took the two boys, Yasser and Fathi, under his wing, making room for them in his house within the family compound in Jerusalem. Sheik Hassan Abu Saud, another relative and a prominent mufti in charge of the courts of Islamic law, also took an interest in Yasser. The Sheik worked closely with the grand mufti of Jerusalem, Haj Amin al-Husseini, the most important Moslem leader in Palestine during British rule. He watched over the young Yasser, introducing him to the concept of Arab nationalism and exposing him to the anticolonial ideas which would permeate Arafat's thinking. It was Sheik Hassan Abu Saud and Haj Amin al-Husseini who played major roles in directing Arafat's life.

But the chairman does not wish to speak about his childhood; he has spent enough time on personal matters. He pushes the interview onto a political track and talks about his first major victory, the battle of Karameh, which took place in Jordan against the Israelis in 1968.

After the devastating defeat of the Arab states in the Six-Day War in June 1967, when the Israelis won the West Bank, Gaza, Jerusalem and the Golan Heights, the outwitted Arabs went home, their armies destroyed, their egos demolished. The Palestinians, disgusted with their ineffective cousins in Egypt, Jordan and Syria, ran guerrilla operations of their own, sneaking across the Jordanian border and attacking kibbutzim along the river front. The Israelis retaliated by shelling Jordanian farms in the Jordan Valley. The Palestinians continued with more incursions, firing on buildings in several collectives, provoking the Israelis to plan a major attack. As Arafat remembers, "The Israelis were massing in an arrogant way."

The Palestinian fighters, more a ragtag bunch of guerrillas than a regular army batallion, knew they could not count on the other Arabs for support, and many of them did not want to fight the Israelis alone. But Yasser Arafat, as one of their leaders, urged his Fatah guerrillas to face the enemy army deploying across the river. The small band of Palestinian soldiers, with help from the Jordanian army, stood their ground as the Israelis came across, battling the soldiers and destroying a number of their tanks and armored vehicles. After twelve hours of fighting, the enemy retreated in haste with ninety Israeli soldiers wounded and twenty-nine Israelis dead.

Of the Palestinians, ninety-seven fighters were killed, but Arafat, the spokesman for Fatah, could claim overwhelming victory, calling it the Arabs' first triumph over Israel. As Arafat understood so well, Karameh was not so much a strategic victory as it was a victory of morale. The Arab countries could now reclaim their pride; they owed their dignity to the Palestinians in general, and to the steadfast Arafat in particular. But Arafat also revealed another side that would stand him in good stead: like a precinct boss stealing an election, he never mentioned that Jordanian tanks made the crucial difference in the Israeli defeat.

As Fatah's spokesman, Arafat was superb. His flare for the dramatic, his clever use of words, his bold exaggeration and his ability to tell different constituencies what they wanted to hear made him a first-rate publicist. Those skills, combined with the real military accomplishment, made Arafat a true hero. He spread the message of Karameh around the world so successfully that Fatah was swarmed with volunteers; from a small band of fighters it swelled to an army of thousands, too big in fact for its officers to control.

Within two years the Palestinian guerrillas in Jordan had become reckless with power; they set up roadblocks and checkpoints throughout the Hashemite Kingdom, extorting money and terrorizing Jordanian citizens in an effort to take over Jordan and assassinate the king. The rebellion was finally ended by the Jordanian government in June 1971 after a series of brutal battles that the PLO calls Black September; but Fatah would rise again.

From Jordan the Palestinians moved to nearby Lebanon, where they consumed eleven years engaged in a bloody civil war. Encouraged by the PLO, factions of Lebanese Moslems—Sunni, Shiite and Druse—battled against the numerous militia groups of the Lebanese Christians in a struggle for control of the country. Syrian forces intervened on behalf of the Christians, and the killing grew worse as the Moslems and the PLO fought against the Christians and their new allies. With the country mutilated by the fighting, factions broke off and allegiances changed; the PLO switched loyalties, the Lebanese switched sides, and the massacres continued as Christians battled Christians and Moslems battled Moslems. By the summer of 1982, when the Israelis invaded the country and Beirut was under siege for eighty-eight days, Arafat and his fighters were rendered helpless. Not only had no Arab countries come to his aid to help him fight the Israelis, but worse, the Syrians had squeezed him to such a point that they were dictating his actions. Arafat was forced to withdraw. The world watched as a seemingly humiliated Arafat and his brigades of weary men evacuated Lebanon. It appeared to be a major defeat for the PLO and the end of Yasser Arafat.

Asked why he retreated, the chairman leans over to answer. Narrowing his eyes and wagging his finger he says, "Believe me, it is only the Lebanese, my allies, who pushed me to leave Beirut. Only when they told me 'Please, Arafat, this is enough.... What are you waiting for, Abu Amar? Look, we are here facing death, shelling, bombing from the sea, from the land, from the air.' I began to feel the responsibility of killing their children. By insisting on carrying on this steadfastness and the fighting, I am killing their children. I felt guilty."

The Lebanese leaders knew that the other Arab states had deserted the Palestinians. If the PLO leader withdrew, the Lebanese believed the fighting would cease. "What are you waiting for?" they begged him. "Is there any support or help coming to you from the Arabs?" He shakes his head in disgust. The Arabs had betrayed him, as they had done so many times before. He lowers his voice and whispers bitterly, "No help."

Characteristically, Arafat went back to Tripoli to defy the Syrians, and to prove that his persona was stronger than the force of Arab armies. When he retreated, after his troops were completely surrounded, it was to Egypt that he traveled, embracing his former enemy, Hosni Mubarak, president of the only Arab country to sign a peace treaty with Israel.

Others might have felt saddened by this defeat, but Arafat took it as a challenge. "They have tried many times to cancel me and to liquidate me." But, he snaps back, "The phoenix bird is still alive!"

Suddenly he turns aside. "I will give you this picture," he says and digs through his papers for a drawing of the mythical Egyptian bird. An aide finds it, and Arafat thrusts it at us. "Look how beautiful, this phoenix bird! Bird on fire! Uprising from the ashes!"

The ancient Egyptians created the phoenix as a symbol of indestructibility. Yasser Arafat sees himself as the modern embodiment of the Palestinians' unbreakable dream. He is their phoenix, their hope, their claim that will not disappear. From Lebanon he could have gone to Egypt or Iraq, but instead he made his first stop in Greece, sending word to his Arab cousins that he rejected any false offers of friendship in favor of independence. "It is a message for all the coming generations," he says. "Because I didn't receive the Arabs' help, for this reason I insisted on going to Greece. This is a message for the future, for new generations."

An agreement negotiated with the help of the Americans forced him to settle away from the area of Palestinian conflict, and Tunis eventually offered the best solution for this exile from exile. But for Arafat, who had been forced to make the journey from Palestine to Cairo, who had been expelled from Egypt, banished from Syria, ejected from Jordan and expunged from Lebanon, there was really only one place left to go. With hope and determination that has made him the consummate Palestinian leader, he spoke out, not only to his own people, but to the Arabs and to the Western world. "The next stop is Palestine," he declared.

2

The Holy Wall

"WHAT TOOK YOU SO LONG?" Yassar Arafat snaps at us. We are startled by the sight of the chairman with his bald head bared and his shirt sleeves rolled up. He is upstairs in his favorite safe house, sitting at his desk in a small, simple office; only a television in one corner and an exercise bicycle in another offer diversions from his work. He laughs when asked if he would appear on American television dressed like this. "Sure. Why not?" he says, grinning. But his PLO colleagues complain that even after years of hearing their pleas, Arafat will not appear in public without his kafeeyah.

He turns back to his work. Miffed that he has had to wait for his visitors, he hardly raises his head when he talks, showing more interest in the pile of papers on his desk. One by one he works his way through the stack, signing each sheet with a felt-tip pen, using red ink to emphasize action, approving requests for funds from various Palestinians in need. "These are concerning some aged persons in Lebanon," he points out. "And these are from Lebanon, some of them are civilians, some of them are our volunteers in our military forces. They are asking for the Red Crescent to take care of them, to send them for medical operations outside in one of the brotherly countries. I have to give the orders."

Despite the PLO's considerable staff, it is always Arafat who gives the orders, signs the checks and runs the organization in his chaotic and highly personal style. "He makes decisions and they become de facto decisions," says a colleague. "He doesn't abide by the spirit of collective decision making. He doesn't want to delegate authority. He wants all the strings in his hands, from the smallest financial detail to the administrative to the military."

It is Arafat who has written so many notes on so many pieces of paper that he sometimes suffers from pains in his number 5 and 6 vertebrae that travel to his arm and shoulder. Because of this he sleeps on a special pillow and wears a neck brace from time to time. It is Arafat who is heralded like the Pied Piper when he visits the Palestinians living in the refugee camps; Arafat who flies off to meet with Soviet President Mikhail Gorbachev, French Prime Minister François Mitterand, Egyptian President Hosni Mubarak, or dozens of other heads of state; Arafat who holds the purse strings; and Arafat who creates the consensus within the PLO.

"I am the commander," he declares, and few would disagree; he has earned his stripes by facing Israeli bullets and confronting the enmity of Arab states. Seeing himself as a soldier-statesman, he says that the American president he most admires was Dwight David Eisenhower, and the few decorations in his office give testimony to his reverence for military leaders: a sword swathed in green and white from Panama's former military ruler, General Manuel Antonio Noriega, hangs near his desk on one wall; a framed letter to the French troops signed by General Charles De Gaulle hangs on another. "I am searching for a new De Gaulle," he likes to say, referring to the general's withdrawal of French troops from Algiers in 1962. A photograph from the intifada offers evidence of the chairman's popularity with his own people: a group of young boys, muffled in kafeeyahs, march down a West Bank street holding a Palestinian flag emblazoned with Arafat's picture. How different the image in a photo that shows Arafat in Saudi Arabia, looking more like Gandhi than like a guerrilla. Kneeling, his head bare and his

body draped in a plain white sheet, he is a good Moslem making a pilgrimage to Mecca.

"I am a good Moslem," he likes to say, "and a good Jew." Islam incorporates three religions, he explains. "For your information, to be a good Moslem, you have to be a good Christian and a good Jew." Leaning back in his swivel chair, he says to his Jewish listeners, "Judaism is part of my religion." The references he often makes, to his cousins the Jews, to the Diaspora, to the biblical chapter of Exodus, to the right of return, and to David and Goliath are meant to prey on a sense of moral guilt over the displaced Palestinians. The reaction from Jews runs from mild agreement to raging fury; some concur; many feel he rubs salt in a festering wound; still many others believe he is mocking their suffering, making odious comparisons between Jews who have been brutally victimized by the Nazis and Palestinians who, they believe, have chosen to be victims by refusing in 1947 to accept a partitioned state.

Nevertheless, biblical allusions and the idea of betrayal run throughout Arafat's rhetoric. He links his people's plight to the historic vulnerability of the Jews: We are cousins, he constantly reminds his audience, the children of Isaac and Ishmael, two semitic lines descendant from the same father, Abraham. "The Jews are very intelligent. They are the elite...and we are the elite. We are like our cousins, the Jews." We have both been victims, betrayed by the world, he repeats.

If it was once the Jewish David who had to fight bare-handed with only stones to slay the monstrous enemy Goliath, now, he says, the Palestinians must fight the same way by means of the intifada. "For the first time in history the Jews have become invaders and conquerors," he whispers. "You and I know the meaning of the reality of Judaism. And for this, the symbol was David and Goliath." Narrowing his eyes and shaking his finger, he says, "But now the Palestinians are the Davids, and Israel is the Goliath. These stones of the intifada are going to do the same thing that David did against Goliath."

Arafat's aide, Bassam Abu Sharif, takes credit for the idea of recreating the Exodus, a ship that would bring Palestinians to their homeland. The trip would have mimicked an historic journey in 1947, when a ship called the Exodus, crammed with 4,500 Jewish survivors of the Holocaust, sailed from Hamburg, Germany, to

Palestine. But the British officials who met the vessel in Palestine refused to allow the 400 pregnant women and the rest of the refugees off the ship; instead they forced the captain to turn the boat around and sail it back to Germany.

Acting on Abu Sharif's brainwave, in February 1988, the PLO announced that it would hire a Greek ship, name it al-Awda, (the Return) and fill it with Palestinian refugees, 130 people who had been deported earlier from Israel. When, according to the PLO, an Israeli captain agreed to pilot the ship from Athens to Haifa, the PLO rubbed its collective hands, thinking the idea would succeed as a brilliant public relations ploy. Two hundred journalists and two hundred observers, including former American Congressman Paul Findley, British politician Lord Mayhew and Italian Senator Ranier Lavalle, had all agreed to accompany the voyagers across the sea. Arafat says he even received a letter from the captain of the 1947 Exodus, who wrote that he wanted to join the trip because "you have the right to return to your homeland."

Israeli Prime Minister Yitzhak Shamir publicly denounced the plan, claiming that when the PLO talks of "home," it still wants all of Palestine: "The return of the Arabs is a slogan, a declaration of war against the entire Israeli nation and the state of Israel," he said, and Foreign Minister Shimon Peres announced on television that the ship would not be allowed to enter Israeli waters. At night, the empty boat was blown up by Israeli Mossad agents who planted explosives in a Cyprus port.

The episode received wide publicity inside Israel. "The Israelis reacted because they know what it means in ideology and history," says Abu Sharif. "Sometimes when I read or listen to Israeli officials' reactions, I laugh, because they are exactly like us, the way they react, the way they stick to things. The 'return' is a key word in Jewish history. We were telling the Israelis that the right of return is not only theirs, but ours. Any human being should be able to return to his home."[1]

The Palestinians' more than forty-year struggle with the Israelis wearies all the PLO leaders, particularly the gray-bearded Arafat. He compares himself to the beleaguered Moses in the story of the golden calf told in the book of Exodus. When Moses returned to the desert, after a forty-day trip to Mount Sinai, he found that the monotheistic

Chosen People had become corrupt idolaters worshipping a molten calf. An angry God ordered Moses to punish the sinners. "I still remember how the people were arguing with God in Sinai about the color of the cow," says Arafat. "Even Moses was completely tired." Pleased with his point, even though he has confused the story about the golden calf, he grins and repeats, "I am a good Jew."

If Arafat's allusions to Judaism anger the Jews, their pronouncements about Zionism bring out his wrath. The Palestinians' struggle "is a resistance against Israeli occupation," he says. "Don't forget," he reprimands his listeners, who he fears might confuse the modern Palestinian-Israeli conflict with an older Moslem-Jewish connection, "we were together in Europe, in Spain, facing the same Inquisition courts. We were together. It is not Moslems who harmed Jews. It was the Europeans. Not us."

As he speaks, an aide enters the room carrying a box of Baci chocolates wrapped in gold foil, a jar of honey and a spoon. Arafat's face softens and he smiles, nodding toward us. "Try some of this honey," he urges. "This is very special, very famous." The thick yellow nectar from South Yemen has a smoky taste, less sweet than common brands. Arafat dips the spoon in, takes a dollop, and licks his lips in pleasure.

But his momentary delight hardly diverts his attention. He comes back quickly to the subject at hand: "Zionism is very modern. Does that mean that all the Jews before Zionism were not real Jews? Because Zionism is a new item. Does this mean that pre-Zionist Jews were not real Jews? Zionism is a political movement."

We argue that Zionism is a nationalist movement of a people for a homeland. "Like Fatah," adds Arafat's secretary. But Arafat is adamant. His voice rising, he bangs his black-framed eyeglasses on the desk and says that Israel is exclusionary, unlike the secular, democratic Palestinian state he dreams of: "Fatah says Jews can live with Moslems; Zionists say only Jews." We answer that for Zionists a Jewish state was necessary after the extermination of six million Jews in the Holocaust. Arafat responds: "When I was in Poland I went to those concentration camps to see the tragedy of the Jews. Auschwitz. I was against it. And I am still against what had happened." But, he protests, sloughing off the argument, "It was not from me." Although the guilt lies with the Europeans, he says, it is the Arabs who have suffered instead.

The debate is interrupted by a signal to the chairman. He rises and his secretary invites us to join him for a meal. It is three A.M. *and we are not quite sure if this will be breakfast, lunch or dinner, but the dining room table is laden with food: platters brim over with lebneh, balls of white cheese; squares of jibneh; fried goat cheese; hard-boiled eggs; fried eggs; green olives; tomatoes; cucumbers; green peppers; foul, crushed beans with olive oil; fennel; watermelon; yogurt; pita bread; honey and halvah. Arafat attacks the food, chewing heartily on his pita bread and cheese. He picks up the discussion about Zionism, wolfing down several slices of watermelon, one after another.*

It was the Zionist movement, he says, not the Jews themselves, that displaced the Arabs in 1948, turning them into homeless refugees. Even now, Arafat quarrels not with Judaism, but with those who turned it into a political movement. The very notion of Arab nationalism, he argues, is a cultural phenomenon, a unity of language, literature and history. Arab nationalism, he insists, includes Moslem, Christians and Jews who lived in the Arab world. To be an Arab does not mean to be a Christian or a Moslem, but to speak the language, share the same music, wear the same kind of clothes, and live the same way of extended family life. The Jews who came from the Islamic world, he suggests, behave like the Arabs. Judaism is not a nationality, he says; the Arab Jews are Arabs because they share the same traits.

Religion is one thing, Arafat admonishes; "Nationality is something different. If we have to speak about [Jewish] nationality only, it is religious nationality. It is something completely different. This means that all the Jews have to be concentrated in one place, all the Moslems have to be concentrated in one place, all the Christians have to be concentrated in one place.

"It was after the partition plan decision of '47 that we began to understand there is a conspiracy against our existence as Palestinians. And it is not only a matter of partition, but of annihilation for the Palestinian people. And we were right."

Ready to leave the table, he stands and, ignoring the others, moves brusquely to his office, where he goes back to work. The conversation is over, but his anger propels him to add one more thing: the house in which he grew up was destroyed by the Israelis soon after they annexed East Jerusalem in 1967. For him, the tangible memories of Palestine were obliterated by Zionism. But the roots of his anger reach back 100 years to the deteriorating Ottoman Empire.

T he streams of nationalism trickled through the sands of the Middle East at the end of the late nineteenth century. Small uprisings for autonomy, including one by a group of Arabs in Palestine, had been squelched by the Ottoman Turks, but the once powerful Ottoman Empire that had ruled the Arabs for four hundred years, dominating a stretch of land that reached from as far north as Syria to as far south as Yemen, would soon yield to the British and the French. The European victors of World War I would sweeten their presence with the promise of independence. The ancestors of Yasser Arafat could almost taste their own Arab state.

The British had already established their place in the Middle East when they assumed control of the Suez Canal in 1875. This vital waterway linking Europe with the Far East, first attempted by the Egyptian King Sesostris II in 1850 B.C., then rebuilt by Pharaoh Necho in 609 B.C. and the Persian Emperor Darius in 520 B.C., would become a reality of riches and influence for the English.[2] The passageway would allow merchant ships to carry spices, perfumes, cottons and silks from China and India to London and Edinburgh without having to travel around the Cape of Good Hope. Even more important, it would ease the way for the flow of oil, the vital fluid upon which Britain would come to depend in the twentieth century.

With the Suez Canal under its influence, Britain became the protector of Egypt, and the country became the main base of the British during World War I. From there, General Allenby led his army as he marched toward the Turks in Palestine and Syria. On December 9, 1917, the people of Jerusalem lined the streets and stood on their balconies to watch as Allenby and his men rode victoriously on horseback into the holy city.

Further to the south, in the Hejaz, British officer T. E. Lawrence organized an Arab revolt against the Turks. The strange, poetic

Lawrence of Arabia encouraged the Arabs into rebellion by reinforcing the British pledge of an Arab kingdom after the war. The future domain, he promised, would be ruled by Hussein, the Sharif of Mecca, the head of the prominent Hashemite family which claimed direct descent from the prophet Mohammed. The Sharif's son, Prince Faisal, led his Arab fighters north through the desert, battling against Turkish brigades, heading toward Syria. Among his officers was Amin al-Husseini, the twenty-year-old scion of a powerful family from Palestine.[3] Like Prince Faisal, Amin al-Husseini dreamed of an Arab kingdom. It would be Husseini, a distant relative of Yasser Arafat, who would pass on that dream to the future chairman of the PLO.

But unbeknownst to Lawrence, British and French diplomats had made a secret agreement dividing up the same lands that Lawrence had promised to the Arabs. The secret document, known as the Sykes-Picot Agreement, signed by the British Sir Mark Sykes and the Frenchman, Charles Picot, split the area into two spheres of influence: the Levant, composed of Syria and Lebanon, would be under French control; Iraq, Transjordan and the Gulf area would be under British rule; Palestine would be divided under British and international control.

Prince Faisal arrived in Damascus in October 1918. Settling in place with his battalions, he worked, with the help of the British and French who were temporarily in charge of the area, to create an Arab administration. By 1920 he announced himself the emir of Syria. His kingdom was to include the area known as Greater Syria: Syria, Lebanon, Jordan and Palestine.

In Palestine, Faisal's former soldier Amin al-Husseini celebrated with demonstrations in the streets, proclaiming Faisal's kingdom and confirming the link between Palestine and Syria. But Faisal's Emirate lasted only ten weeks, and al-Husseini's career took him in a far different direction.

The European allies, meeting at the League of Nations, declared that Syria was under the mandate of the French. Swiftly and easily, the French removed King Faisal from his throne. But the British were obliged to find him another seat of power, and installed him almost immediately as the king of Iraq. To make further amends, Faisal's brother, Prince Abdullah, was made the emir of Transjordan, a desert area that stretched from the Iraq to the Jordan River.

The British were given the mandate to rule Palestine, the narrow strip of land between the Mediterranean Sea and the eastern border of Transjordan. The 600,000 Arabs, mostly Moslems with a small minority of Christians, and a portion of the 75,000 Jews had lived together under the rule of the Ottoman Turks, and although tempers sometimes flared over the rights to holy places, the two groups usually coexisted comfortably. The mutual roots of their religions and respect for each other's cultures softened the harshness of momentary blow. Nevertheless, by the time the British arrived in Palestine, the streams of nationalism were becoming deeper and wider.

The majority of the Jews in the British mandate of Palestine had come from Europe after the turn of the century in search of Zion, the Promised Land. The new nationalist movement of Zionism had been conceived by a Viennese Jewish writer, Theodore Herzl, who preferred assimilation to the separation imposed in Europe upon his people. But the wealthy, flamboyant Herzl had witnessed the ugly anti-Semitism of the notorious Dreyfus affair in France and had watched the progression of pogroms sweeping across Russia and eastern Europe. He responded by approaching influential leaders, calling for a piece of land that the Jews could claim as their own. In his brief book, *The Jewish State*, Herzl pleaded, "We are a people, one people. We have everywhere tried to honestly integrate with the national communities surrounding us and to retain only our faith. We are not permitted to do so."[4]

In 1897 Herzl organized a congress in Basel, Switzerland, with delegates from sixteen countries. The theatrical thinker, wanting to do away with the notion of Jews as poor, wretched souls of the ghettos, insisted that those who came to his convention should dress for the opening session in black formal clothes and white tie.[5] The independent Jewish state that Herzl dreamed of would be a land run by the rich and influential. Herzl's concept of Zionism captured the imagination of some European Jews; the first to arrive in the historical homeland of Palestine were bourgeois people seeking economic and social stability. Like the Germans and other groups of European settlers who had come to Palestine, they established small agricultural colonies scattered around the country.

But the nature of the Zionists changed after 1905. The new pioneers were young idealists who, having seen their dream of a socialist revolution in Russia turn into a nightmare, wanted to re-evoke the communal concept in Palestine. The Zionist spirit grew with such speed that more than 25,000 Jews immigrated to Palestine between 1904 and 1914. The members of the World Zionist Organization had established their own development bureau in the mandate. They had created their own institutions, including the Jewish National Fund; had designed their own flag, using the blue and white colors of the prayer shawl; and had their own national anthem, the Hatikvah.

The British, who had received Jewish support for their efforts in World War I, responded favorably to Herzl's movement. In November 1917, British Foreign Secretary Lord Balfour declared in a letter to Lord Rothschild and the Zionist organization that Britain would "view with favor the establishment in Palestine of a national home for the Jewish people." Balfour went on to say that "nothing shall be done to prejudice the civil and religious rights of existing non-Jewish communities in Palestine."[6]

At the Paris Peace Conference in 1919, the president of the World Zionist Organization, Chaim Weizmann, underscored the Balfour Declaration and proclaimed that once the Jews became a majority in Palestine, which they planned to do through massive immigration, they would form an independent government. Zionism's goal, Weizmann told the conference, was that "Palestine become as Jewish as England is English." Emir Faisal, who led the Arab delegation to the conference, could identify with the Jewish desire for a homeland. "The Arabs," he said, "especially the educated among us, look with deepest sympathy on the Zionist movement."[7]

But few Arabs saw the Balfour Declaration through the same lens as the emir. Most Arabs viewed the movement for a Jewish homeland as a direct threat to their own nationalist campaign. The Balfour Declaration enraged them; it not only refuted the promises made to them for the establishment of an Arab state, but even ignored the Sykes-Picot agreement that placed Palestine under British and international control.

Haj Amin al-Husseini, who had fought briefly with Prince Faisal in World War I, set out to destroy the declaration. In 1919 he joined with a group of young Arabs in Damascus to form the Palestinian Society, which would promote the Palestinian cause, and he helped establish the Society of Palestinian Youth, which carried out military actions against the British and the Jews. In spite of such objections, when the League of Nations confirmed the British mandate over Palestine in 1920 and 1922, the Balfour Declaration, favoring a Jewish state, was included in the terms of reference.

When the British took over, they named their new country Palestina Ei (a combination of the Arab name Palestine and the Jewish Eretz Israel) and sent an English Jew, Sir Herbert Samuel, to Jerusalem as their first high commissioner. The Arabs sensed a clear message of betrayal: despite the promises of an Arab state, Palestine would become a Jewish homeland with Jerusalem as its capital. What had begun as two small streams of nationalism would flood into an ocean of hate.

The ancient city of Jerusalem sat high on a hill above the dry, undulating earth of Palestine. Below it, shepherds guided their flocks along dusty paths strewn with pale stones, and farmers coaxed olive oil from the fruit of the twisted trees. High stone walls built in the sixteenth century by the Turkish sultan, Suleiman the Magnificent, surrounded the small houses crowded together in the city. Behind the ramparts, the cobblestone streets were divided into four major ethnic and religious areas: in the west were the Christian and Armenian quarters, where pilgrims walked the Via Dolorosa and followed the Stations of the Cross; in the east, around the Temple Mount, called Haram al-Sharif, was the Moslem quarter, marked by the mosques and the wailing of muezzin calling the faithful to prayer; in the south was the Jewish quarter, overlooking the 2,000-year-old ruins of the walls on the same Temple Mount.

For both the Arabs and the Jews, Jerusalem was a holy city, a shrine of their religions. It was here, on the site of Mount Moriah, that Abraham, father of both Judaism and Islam, offered his son Isaac as a sacrifice to show his loyalty to God. And it was here, around 960 B.C., that the Jewish leader, King Solomon, built the First Temple, which was later destroyed by the Babylonians, and here, on the same site, that the Second Temple was begun under the patronage of the Persian King Cyrus in the sixth century B.C. and completed by Herod in the first century B.C. It was here, the Moslems believed, that Mohammed arrived from Mecca astride his winged horse al-Buraq and here that he stopped and tied his magical animal to the wall before he ascended to heaven. The religions were so entwined that a remnant of the wall of the Second Temple, known as the Wailing Wall, formed part of the wall of the Haram al-Sharif, site of the Dome of the Rock, the house of worship in which the Moslems prayed. And it was here that Yasser Arafat says he was born.

Jerusalem had been an important religious center under the Turkish Empire, but the area had little significance for the Ottoman administrative government. When the British created their administration, Jerusalem became, as it had been in ancient times, the capital of Palestine. The city flourished as new money poured in for building construction and civic development; the British increased the water supply, improved the sanitary conditions and installed new roads. Slowly the population spread beyond the old stone walls, creating new neighborhoods for Arabs and for Jews on the hills surrounding the Old City.

But if the establishment of the British administration brought prosperity to the Arabs, it also roused their suspicion. Weizmann's words still swirling in their heads, the Arabs watched in fear as more Jews arrived in Palestine, some buying land to settle on, others establishing businesses in competition with the Arab merchants and craftsmen. The Moslems in Jerusalem, particularly those from the large, aristocratic clans whose homes were close to the mosques on the Temple Mount, felt threatened by the growing numbers of Jews parading through the Arab quarter on their way to the Western Wall of the Temple Mount. When some religious Jews blew the ram's horn, a traditional ritual on Rosh Hashanah, or placed benches near the wall for elderly men to sit on, the Arabs protested. These acts, they said, were a small example of the creeping danger of Zionism. The Jewish nationalist movement, they claimed, was in direct opposition to nascent Arab nationalism.

Despite these concerns, the 1920s brought a booming economy and relative calm, although some Arabs organized protests and a few disturbances marred the city's life. During demonstrations in 1920 and 1921 the Arabs, who blamed the British for the influx of Jews, demanded that the mandate be ended and, more particularly, that the Balfour Declaration be canceled.

One of the organizers of these demonstrations was young activist Haj Amin al-Husseini. This slight young man, with his gaunt cheeks, thick mustache and closely cropped beard, looked intense and proudly defiant. A member of the rich Husseini clan which traced its roots in Palestine at least to the sixteenth century, the fair-haired, blue-eyed Haj Amin inherited a leading role in Palestinian affairs. The only real competition to the Husseinis came from the Nashashibis, a wealthy, landowning clan which had settled in Jerusalem in the fifteenth century and claimed equal power and influence.

The clan was the backbone of the society; loyalty to it came before loyalty to politics or religion, and membership in a clan was a status of which one could be fiercely proud. Family members married within the clan, and the family name was carried proudly, like a banner. Typically, the father of Yasser Arafat, Abder Rauf Arafat, a member of a small branch of the Husseinis, married a woman from the Abu Saud family, another branch of the same clan.

The Husseinis had been mayors, muftis and officials in the Ottoman administration. Before joining Faisal's army, Haj Amin had already been trained for political leadership: he had been sent to study at the Ottoman Turkish school of administration in Istanbul, at the Islamic College in Cairo, and at the Jewish French Alliance school in Jerusalem. It was in Cairo, at the center of Islamic and Arabic studies, that he heard ideas of Islamic reform and Arab nationalism. There he became not only a Palestinian leader but a Moslem Arab nationalist.

In March 1920, on the day that his former commander Faisal proclaimed himself king of Syria, Haj Amin al-Husseini organized demonstrations in Palestine to confirm the Arabs' link to the new Syrian kingdom. One month later, during a week of religious celebrations for Moslems, Christians and Jews, when the holidays of Nabi Musa, Easter and Passover converged, Haj Amin arranged more protests, in which five Jews and four Arabs were killed and many others were wounded. Angered by his activities, the British tried to arrest him, but Haj Amin escaped and fled with a colleague to Transjordan where they hid with a Bedouin tribe. The British military court sentenced him in absentia to ten years in prison.

Several weeks later, however, in a move to calm Arab fears, the British high commissioner declared a pardon for Haj Amin. Sir Herbert recognized the young Arab's ability to galvanize his followers and hoped to gain his loyalty to the British administration; a few months later he nominated Haj Amin as grand mufti of Jerusalem, the highest Islamic post in Palestine. The mufti, distinct in his black robe with a high white turban capped on his head, would be in control of the Moslem religious courts, the schools, the orphanages and the wealthy charitable foundations called the *waqf*.

The high commissioner was carefully balancing power between the two competing clans, the Husseinis and the Nashashibis. The head of the Nashashibi family, Rageb Nashashibi, had been named the mayor of Jerusalem, and Sir Herbert needed to defuse the growing hostility between the clans by giving the Husseinis the important office of the grand mufti. With equanimity restored in 1921, the number of disturbances decreased. Shortly afterward, Haj Amin was appointed president of the Supreme Moslem Council a position of even greater power and influence than that of mufti.

Jerusalem remained fairly tranquil for several years, but in 1924 a large group of Jews from Poland, suffering under anti-Semitism that surfaced with the newly established independent Polish regime, tried to emigrate to western Europe and the United States. However, their path to the United States was blocked because of the Johnson-Reed Immigration Act passed by Congress that year; they instead turned toward Palestine.

The Arabs witnessed this new wave of Jewish arrivals with mounting fear. That same year trouble broke out in Jaffa when the Jews of the city celebrated the festival of Purim, a remembrance of the first recorded significant act of anti-Semitism. In the traditional manner of commemorating the ancient victory of the Jews over Haman, some Jews dressed up in Arab costumes to portray the Persian villain. The Moslems in the city, taking this as a sign of mockery, became enraged. Violent fights broke out; a number of people were killed and wounded.

An anxious Arab leadership warily observed the encroaching Zionism. As the Jewish community developed into a stronger and larger body, the Jews established an economic and social infrastructure. They developed prestigious neighborhoods in Jerusalem, in Haifa and in Tel Aviv, and built new settlements (kibbutzim) everywhere in Palestine, particularly along the coastline of the Mediterranean and in the valleys of the Galilee. Jewish trade unions were organized and vocational centers and schools were established; in 1925 Lord Balfour laid the cornerstone for Jerusalem's Hebrew University at the top of Mount Scopus. The Arabs, claiming that the school was built on expropriated Arab land, responded by calling for a strike.

With an eye on easing the strained atmosphere, the British tried to establish some local autonomy around Palestine. Despite competition from the Nashashibi clan, by 1929 Haj Amin emerged as the most influential Arab political figure in Palestine, and Jerusalem emerged, both religiously and politically, as its most important city.

Haj Amin's intent was to establish an independent Arab state. His close friend and associate, the Mufti Sheik Hassan Abu Saud, was leader of a prominent religious family of Jerusalem. It was to this family that Yasser Arafat's mother belonged, and it was this man, Sheik Hassan Abu Saud, who would play a pivotal role in Arafat's upbringing. The two activists, Sheik Hassan and Haj Amin, operated in tandem: the mufti of al-Shafaria preached Arab nationalism to those who came to pray at al-Aqsa Mosque in Jerusalem; the Grand Mufti Haj Amin organized campaigns outside Palestine to stir Arab support for Jerusalem as a holy city and central place for Islam. Envoys were dispersed throughout the Moslem world, to Egypt, India, Iraq, Kuwait, Bahrain and Hejaz, not only to raise money to restore the mosques on the Temple Mount, even gilding the dome, but to create Moslem awareness of the Jewish threat.[8] The Jews had tried unsuccessfully to buy the Arab land around the Temple Mount; if they could not own the area, they at least wanted authority over the holy site. Haj Amin knew what troubles lay ahead if the British succumbed to the demands of the Jewish immigrants.

The focus of Arab and Jewish attention centered on a hundred-foot-long stone wall within the Old City, part of the ancient retaining wall that surrounded the Temple Mount. The Wailing Wall, or Western Wall, as it was known, was a holy site for the Jews who came there to pray. Built in the biblical era of King Solomon, it stood on the edge of the Maghreb neighborhood, a rundown section named for the poor North African Moslems who had settled there. The Jews would walk through the Arab alley until they reached the end of the narrow path which stopped directly in front of the Wall. There they touched the heavy stones, said their prayers, wept for their ancient Israel and wrote their wishes on tiny pieces of paper which they slipped between the stones.

Like the Jews, the Moslems attached holiness to this same site. Moslems made the pilgrimage from all parts of the world to celebrate Mohammed's Night of Ascension at the Western Wall. They believed that not only the wall, but the entire area, was holy, because beyond the wall was the Temple Mount, the sacred area of the mosques of the Haram al-Sharif (Noble Sanctuary). Some of the most religious Moslem leaders, members of the Supreme Moslem Council, built their stone homes abutting that wall, constructing them in such a manner that part of the house would be outside the wall, part inside and opening onto the Temple Mount.

The Western Wall had belonged to the Moslems since the Caliph Abdel Malik built the Mosque of Omar in A.D. 691. Later, during the Crusades, the Christian soldiers turned the mosque into a church run by the Knights Templar.[9] But by 1187 the area was back in the hands of the Moslems, soon administered by the Moslem Waqf, the Islamic charitable foundation. For hundreds of years the Jews were given permission to pray at the wall, and over the course of time arrangements were made and customs developed on how both religious groups were to behave. But in modern times, as the number of Jews who visited the area increased, the Moslems held tightly to their rights, believing that the smallest steps taken by the Jews could lead to larger strides of possession and usurpation.

During the 1920s, as more Jews arrived in Palestine and some transgressed the accepted rules at the wall, the Moslems tried to stop them and fights broke out. Members of the Supreme Moslem Council complained that the Jews abused their rights: they put benches where no seats were allowed; they placed objects on the ground, which the Moslems had proscribed; they blew the shofar on the high holidays, disturbing those who lived nearby. Those acts were looked upon by the Moslems as attempts to establish a strong presence and take control of the property.

The Jews complained that the Moslems were exaggerating the significance of their acts; that indeed they were simply carrying out the rituals of their religion. They charged that the Moslems dirtied the area intentionally; that they deliberately drove their cows and sheep through the alleyways; that they purposely made noise banging cymbals and gongs during the Jewish prayer to provoke the worshipers. During August 1928, a year when about 10,000 Jews arrived from Europe, the Jews put up a screen to separate the sexes, and a fight broke out between Jews and Moslems. The bloody riots that followed presaged the violent uprisings to come.

On their most holy Day of Atonement in August 1929, the Jews were again accused of trying to expand their area by bringing special lights, placing their books on stands and setting up a screen which they left standing overnight, none of which was allowed. Under Haj Amin's watchful eye, Sheik Hassan Abu Saud, wearing his high white hat and official black robe, waded into the crowd of Jews to protest. As the sheik's son recalls, the feeling was, "They wanted to extend the Wailing Wall area.... If the Moslems accepted this, then they would go to the next step. That's why my father went through them all, alone, and the grand mufti of Palestine was standing in his window, looking at him, afraid somebody would kill him or shoot him." The sheik "closed the book, put off the light and came back," says his son. "From that time the Moslems felt the Jews were going to go step by step to gain rights they were not allowed to gain. From that a revolution started."[10]

Following the incident at the wall, thousands of protesters marched, and more riots broke out in other parts of Palestine. Sixty-seven Jews were massacred in the town of Hebron; more killings took place in Safad, in Haifa and in other cities. In total, 135 Jews were killed and 340 wounded, and 116 Arabs were killed and 240 wounded. The riots jolted the Jewish community and rallied the Moslems not only in Palestine but around the Arab world. They marked a turning point in the Arab-Jewish relationship, a watershed after which the conflict over the future of the land became cruel and brutal.

No longer could Jews and Arabs pretend to live side by side like brothers under patriarchal British rule. To the Arabs, the Jews had become the favorite son of the British, the Isaac to their father Abraham. The Jewish nationalist movement of Zionism loomed as a menacing threat to the very existence of the Arabs in Palestine. But the Moslems would fight hard before they followed in the footsteps of Ishmael to become exiles from their home.

The future leader of the Palestinians grew up at the center of the Arab-Jewish conflict. The houses Arafat lived in, the family that surrounded him, the places where he played, his entire early life were integral parts of the violent disputes over the claims to the holy city and the rights to a homeland.

The homes in which Arafat spent most of his early years were part of the Abu Saud Zawia, a religious compound of about thirteen houses. The two- and three-story stone buildings reflected the long and rich history of Jerusalem; the foundations were dug in Herod's time, the walls constructed adjacent to the Western Wall of the Temple Mount.

From the large homes that threaded the wall, the children could look out across the Temple Mount and watch the religious Moslems, dressed in their long robes, coming for Friday noon prayers; only a short while later, just before sundown, they could stare at the pious Jews, black felt hats on their heads, twists of curls coming down their cheeks, long black coats covering their black pants, coming to pray at the Wailing Wall. Once in a while the youngsters would see scuffles in the alley between Moslems and Jews.

The home of Sheik Hassan Abu Saud was always open to religious Moslems who came to pray at the mosque, and meals were often shared among the families in the compound. Recalls his son Sheik Musa, "My mother used to step from here to there to there to see if anybody needs any help." Sometimes, he says, "she would send us to the other houses and tell them not to cook today. She made a lot of food for all, and they put it in the middle of the area of our houses, and we came together to eat." As the sheik remembers it, "The life of our family was very good. Yasser saw that very well and liked it. As a child, he liked to stay with us more than anywhere else."[11]

Dinner talk was often of Arab nationalism, British betrayal and the dangerous spread of Zionism. Over plates of stuffed grape leaves and crushed beans, the stories were frequently repeated of Haj Amin's inspiring work to organize the Arabs and of Sheik Hassan's heroic efforts to stop the Jews from expanding their place at the wall.

In the years after 1929, turbulence surrounded Jerusalem and the wall. In 1930 three Arabs were hanged, seventeen were sentenced with life imprisonments and 800 more Arabs were jailed for their activities in the riots, yet few Jews were imprisoned for their role in the fighting. The Arabs watched in futility as they saw what they felt was mounting British injustice: in 1930 the Jews were given valuable long-term mineral rights to the Dead Sea; the Jews were allowed to buy up land where Arab farmers toiled and were allowed to dismiss the Arab workers; large numbers of Jews were allowed to immigrate legally, and when even more came illegally in desperate flight from pogroms and anti-Semitism, the British averted their eyes.[12] In 1931 the Arabs demonstrated around the country, and in August of that year the Arab Executive Committee called for a general strike.

The waves of Jews immigrating to Palestine were increasing;

despite the rise of the Nazis in Germany, the welcoming doors had been shut in Europe and the United States. In 1932, 9,500 Jews came to Palestine; in 1933, as Hitler came into power, that number rose to more than 30,000 and the total number reached 230,000.[12] While the Arabs demonstrated and called for strikes, the Jews had few other places for their escape. In 1934 there were 42,000 legal Jewish immigrants, and in 1935, 61,000 more fled from Europe. By 1936 there were about 400,000 Jews and 1,000,000 Arabs. When the British first arrived in Palestine, the Jews represented less than 20 percent of the population. By 1936 they represented almost a third of the people living there.[13]

In 1936 the Arabs in Syria waged a strike against the ruling French government; the result was an agreement for Syrian independence. The Palestinian Arabs took that national movement as their cue; after several people were killed in violent skirmishes near Nablus and Tel Aviv, the Palestinians formed the Arab National Committee in Nablus and called for a strike. A leader of the group, Akram Zua'iter, recalls that the committee's motto was "Britain is the origin of the disease, the mandate is responsible for every catastrophe."

Zua'iter, now an octogenarian who still relishes his fights against the British, says, "We were directing our struggle against the British mandate, against the government rather than against the Jews, because the Jews were not as responsible as the mandate government." During a demonstration in Nablus, Zua'iter rallied the crowd with a fiery speech. "I talked about the responsibility of the mandate," he remembers. "I asked them, 'If you have one bullet and you want to use it, and you have a Jewish soldier and an English soldier, who are you going to attack?' They all answered: 'The British.'"[14]

In contrast to Zua'iter's anti-British rallies, Haj Amin, whose office of grand mufti was actually part of the British government, targeted his battles directly against the Jews. But several days after the Nablus committee was formed, Palestinian notables around the country established the Arab Higher Committee, choosing Haj Amin al-Husseini as chairman. Well aware of the popular feelings against the British, Haj Amin accepted the will of the committee, called for civil disobedience and ordered a general strike.

The goals of the strike, now clearly aimed at the British, were to halt Jewish immigration, to stop land transfers to the Jews and to establish a national government with parliamentary representation. "The strike was mostly at the British," recalls Akram Zua'iter. "But it was taken for granted that why you were fighting the British was because they were supporting the national home for Zionists. It was taken for granted that we declared the revolution against both, but especially against the British."

United under the mufti, the strike was welcomed by Arabs all over Palestine: everyone took part, including children; for Yasser Arafat and his cousins in the Abu Saud compound, the strike meant a chance for them to act too. As one of the family members, Muheideen al-Husseini recalls, "Every Palestinian knew it was revolution. Every small child thought we are fighting the Zionists and the British, and we have to hurt them in any way we can!"[15] Like the other children, Yasser put nails in the roads, slashed the tires of the British cars and threw rocks, familiar actions that would be repeated fifty years later in the *intifada*, the uprising against the Israelis.

The strike lasted six months; in retaliation, the British broke into the homes of Arab activists, beat the men and sometimes arrested them. Yasser Arafat still recalls the night when his uncle was seized from his bed and taken to jail. "They stormed the house and I found soldiers all around me. They hit me and hit my brother, Fathi. He was a small child, and I was about seven years old. They left me after hitting me, but they arrested my uncle and took him away."

Despite the determination of the Arabs in Palestine, in October 1936 the leaders of Saudi Arabia and other Arab countries, at the behest of the British, requested that Haj Amin and his organizers end their rebellion. The following summer, the British responded with a recommendation by an investigative committee headed by Lord Peel. The Peel Commission advocated partition of Palestine into three areas: a Jewish state, an Arab state that would be united with Transjordan, and a separate British zone that would include Jerusalem.

The Jews accepted the plan in principle, but the Arabs rejected the concept of a divided land; they responded with increased violence and brutality. The Arab revolt had begun. Shortly afterward, the British disbanded the Arab councils and arrested and tried to imprison a number of strike leaders. During the first week of September, recalls Ali Zubi, a supporter of the Husseini clan who now lives in Amman, "a friend of mine and I were having dinner down at the Dead Sea. On the way back, about one o'clock in the morning, we were ambushed six or seven times by the British. We learned later that the mufti had disappeared that very night we were searched. The British were prepared to arrest him."[16] But Haj Amin had escaped and gone into exile. Sheik Musa Abu Saud was captured by the British. His son remembers that the religious men of the family gathered in the house to try and stop the arrest. At their pleading, the high commissioner ordered the release of Sheik Hassan, and he, along with other nationalist activists, fled the country. With the family protectors gone, Yasser Arafat and his brother Fathi left by rail for Cairo, only to return to Palestine shortly thereafter.

Although the leaders of the strike were either deported or imprisoned, the nationalist revolution gained strength. Arabs attacked Jewish settlements, cut telephone wires, blew up bridges, derailed trains and attacked police stations. An effective boycott of Jewish products considerably cut the income of Jewish merchants. Weapons were stolen from police stations while more attacks were carried out by nationalist guerrillas against towns and government buildings. The revolution became widespread and well organized, and even received financial and moral support from Syria, Lebanon, Transjordan, Saudi Arabia, Egypt, Iraq and Yemen. To show their allegiance to the revolution's leaders, who wore the traditional Arab headdress, all Palestinian Arabs took to wearing the *kafeeyah*, now the trademark of Yasser Arafat.

The revolution continued until 1939, but military victory seemed illusive and internal tensions led to brutality among the Palestinians, Arabs killing Arabs. In an effort to stop the fighting, the British canceled the Peel partition plan and met in London with Jewish leaders, exiled Palestinian Arabs and with representatives of other Arab states. Under the terms of the resulting White Paper the British would agree to support a future independent Palestine controlled by the Arabs; Jewish immigration would be slowed, then halted; Jews would only be allowed to buy land in areas where they were already the majority. Although the White Paper was never actually authorized, the exhausted Palestinian Arabs called a halt to the fighting. With the outbreak of World War II the revolt came to an end. "It stopped as if there were an electric light, and you switched it off," says Ali Zubi.

But the spirit of Arab nationalism remained unabated. For Yasser Arafat and the other Moslem children who played together in the alleys of the holy site, no greater heroes existed than his relatives Haj Amin al-Husseini and Sheik Hassan Abu Saud. The uprising they experienced had many of the markings of the *intifada* which was to come fifty years later, in 1987: the formation of popular committees; the concept of general strikes; the violence of throwing rocks and burning tires; the brutality against their own people; the economic boycotts against the Jews; and the stimulation of Palestinian awareness through clothing, folklore and other local customs were all instruments learned in the earlier Arab revolt. The rebellion would remain a burning imprint in the collective memory of Palestinians. But the future would bring another lesson as well: Haj Amin's efforts would end in defeat; Arafat was determined to win.

3

Cairo Youth

IN THE EARLY HOURS *of another morning, as the North African night melts into the soft pink day, Yasser Arafat meets with his inner circle. The handful of men, with him from the beginning, serve as his antennas to the world. Some of his closest colleagues, of course, have been killed: men like the intelligent and respected Khalil Wazir, code named Abu Jihad, riddled with Israeli bullets in his Tunis bedroom in the middle of the night in 1988; or Ali Hassan Salameh, chief of security and head of Fatah's famed Force 17, killed by Israelis in Beirut in 1978.*

But still there are those who have survived. The stocky, cunning Salah Khalaf, code-named Abu Iyad, mastermind of the 1972 Munich kidnapping and assassination of Israeli Olympic athletes and now the second most powerful man in the PLO, has been a supporter of Yasser Arafat from his student organizing days at Cairo University. The gruff and muscular Farouk Kaddoumi, code-named Abu Lutuf, was another early member of Fatah; his tough revolutionary bent has made him the voice for the PLO's hard-line, left-wing constituency.

54

Hani al-Hassan and Khaled al-Hassan, two activist brothers who met Arafat in Kuwait in the 1960s, have both been involved in peacemaking efforts around the world. The burly Hani, the more impulsive of the two, led the "mad" faction inside Fatah that lobbied for military actions against the Israelis almost from its beginning stages. The black-haired Khaled, physically towering, prides himself on intellectually towering above the others as well and calls himself Fatah's resident philosopher. Bassam Abu Sharif, the PFLP guerrilla-turned-diplomat, once known for his role in airline hijackings in the late 1960s and early 1970s, is recognized now for his moderate voice toward the West and his flexibility in negotiations with the United States and Europe. Mahmoud Abbas, code-named Abu Mazzen, is a loyal follower of Arafat and a member of the PLO Executive Committee. Now the successor to Abu Jihad, Abu Mazzen keeps a low profile, is in charge of Israeli affairs and calls for coexistence with Israel. Yasser Abed Rabbo, a sophisticated thinker who has long been a member of the radical DFLP, reads books like Getting to Yes, the American best-seller on negotiation strategies, while he leads the PLO team in its official talks with the United States. Hail Abdul Hamid, code-named Abu al-Houl, is responsible for the Western Section, including the West Bank and Gaza. A member of Fatah, he succeeded Ali Hassan Salameh and was chief of Arafat's personal security force.

"The Old Man," as these colleagues sometimes affectionately call Arafat, has summoned them for a working session at an hour when most normal men are fast asleep. The leaders of the PLO consider themselves to be normal men; not so their chief, who often functions better past midnight than most people do during the day. In the room, the mood is relaxed and informal: they swap jokes, tease friends and catch up on gossip. They wish those who just returned from the latest trip with the chairman a speedy recovery and ridicule them for not having avoided the nightmarish flights that mark Arafat's existence.

The chairman's closest aides have learned to find excuses— demanding wives, sick children—that will relieve them from taking the dreaded trips. Talking about Arafat's most recent journey, fifty-two hours of flying time that took him from Tunis to Peking, Pyongyang, Laos, Hanoi, Bangladesh, Kabul and back to Tunis, Abu Sharif shakes his head firmly and says, "I ran away from that." But then he adds, "Before that trip I was in Japan. Before that I was in Peking. Before that I was with him at the Africa Summit, and we visited five countries in four days. We went to Mauritania, Senegal and Mali in three days. It is something nobody else can do."[1]

Travel with Abu Amar means an average of ten trips a month, seemingly endless, often turbulent flights on a small airplane cramped with people, paper and crates of ammunition, round-the-clock work and no time set aside for sleep. The chairman thrives on these journeys, seeking solace in the Koran when the bumps are rough, catnapping in his jogging suit, his eyes shaded by a black sleeping mask, his neck resting on his special small pillow. But his aides return home looking pale and wan, exhausted from the nerve-wracking schedule.

The group laughs when someone makes the standard offer to find a wife for Arafat; only then, it is suggested, would he sleep in his own bed and allow them to sleep in theirs. The Old Man laughs, but they all know it is too late in his life for marriage.

Arafat's attitude toward women is the subject of much discussion by friends and foes. His enemies suggest he is homosexual or revolting to women. Says Syrian Defense Minister Moustafa Tlass, who is known for his womanizing, *"Women like the pocket of Arafat because Arafat is considered one of the richest men in the world."* The beguilingly handsome general sneers at his foe: *"One with ugly features does not hope to have women. He doesn't bathe. One would be afraid of shaking hands with him."*[2]

Jamil Hilel, a longtime colleague, says: *"He is a religious man and a fairly ethical man. I don't think he would have any homosexual tendencies. He isn't married for reasons of practicality; he doesn't have the time. He also is very affectionate toward women, in the way he speaks to them and holds them. He puts his arm around them and even kisses them. He is very sensitive. Women like him because he is a leader. He isn't handsome, but he has become an international figure."*[3]

Some of Arafat's colleagues insist he is simply uninterested while others swear he has had his share of love and women. *"I believe there is a relationship between sex and power,"* says an aide who first met Arafat in 1967. *"I believe that he had this sexual desire more than any of his colleagues. He used to be surprised how Abu Iyad could leave his wife for six months and be totally engaged in his work."* But this *aide feels that power became Arafat's aphrodisiac. "I believe that Arafat got to a stage of being so powerful that it sort of replaces his sexual desire. Sometimes the selfishness of acquiring power is that one doesn't want to share anything with anyone. We are talking about the leadership of a resistance movement. He is really extracting his power with blood, rather than by elections."*

Friends and family frequently deny that Arafat has had any romantic relationships, claiming that he is too religious or too driven in his work to have room in his life for women.

Says Hamid Abu Sitta, who has known him since adolescence, "Abu Amar never had time for women. He has had a special life."[4]

Says Khalid Mohiedeen, who trained him as an officer at Cairo University, "He was strict. He was a good Moslem and I know he didn't touch women. This I am sure of."[5]

Says Abdul Jawad Saleh, a former member of the PLO Executive Committee, "I saw him in Beirut. He used to look at one of the women journalists in Beirut. You could see his eyes glittering with love."[6]

Majoub Omar, an Egyptian intellectual who has been close to Arafat for more than twenty years, says, "I doubt that he ever loved a woman." But Omar insists that Arafat's personal life should not even be discussed. "In the West," he explains, "it is normal to present a symbol with his personal life. But in the East, no. Arafat is a symbol of the whole movement, so we gain nothing from presenting him [in public]. Everyone is weak sometimes and strong sometimes, but for a leader, they will not forgive him for the weak times."[7]

Adds his younger brother Fathi Arafat, "As a brother with a weakness for these things, I say I hope that he has a family. But as one responsible in the revolution, I don't want him to have a family. I feel that he must be for all. I want him to be free for the Palestinian revolution."[8]

Arafat prides himself on his relationship with youngsters. "All children are my children," he likes to say, and they in turn show him much affection, believing him to be larger than life. Youngsters in the occupied territories, who know him through television or the written press, think of him as a superhero. Typically, when the six-year-old son of Ziad Abu Zayyad, a PLO supporter in the West Bank, rode past an Israeli prison where Palestinians were being held in detention, the boy announced defiantly: "I will go to Yasser Arafat, bring him with his men, and we will bring guns and blow up these walls. We will free all the prisoners who are inside." Says the boy's mother, "He was quite serious about it."[9]

The chairman dotes on the sons and daughters of the revolution, particularly on "al-Shuhada," the children of Palestinians who have been killed, seeing to it that orphan boys are given his code name "Amar" and sending the children extra stipends for their education. "They are my weakness and my strength," he says. Jamil Hilel observes, "I think he would have liked to have been a father. He compensates for this by spending his spare time with children." Adds Hilel, "We have a school for the children of martyrs. One way of trying to help them is to find husbands [for the daughters] so they can live a normal family life."

One PLO representative who would like to see Arafat become a father tried recently to play marriage broker. He mentioned to the chairman that he knew an eligible woman worthy of him. "I asked him whether he was interested," says the man. Arafat answered, "Where is she?" The matchmaker had an attractive Egyptian woman in mind: "very elegant, wealthy, well-educated and able to speak seven languages." The PLO official arranged a meeting on the pretense that the woman might work for the chairman, but after twenty minutes Arafat indicated he was not interested. "I think because she was too strong," says the friend with obvious disappointment. Another friend tells of a recently ended tryst between Arafat and a well-educated, middle-aged Egyptian woman who made several visits to Tunis.

There have been some women, Arafat acknowledges under continuous questioning, with whom he has been romantically linked, though who and where and when are left vague at best. "He was always in conflict whether to get married and fearing to get married," says Abu Iyad, whose own wife and children live far away. "He is afraid marriage will impose limitations on him. Regardless of how busy you are, you need some time for a wife and children. Abu Amar cannot afford to do this."[10]

During their university days in Cairo, says Bassam Abu Sharif, Arafat met a young Egyptian woman he cared for and proposed to her in the proper style. "He had asked her parents to allow them to be married," says Abu Sharif. The answer came back, "No." Only later, it seems, when Arafat had the courage to ask why she rejected *him, she told him she had not realized it was he who wanted to marry her. "This particular incident really affected him and made Abu Amar not think of marriage. From 1955 to 1967 he did not think of marriage," says Abu Iyad. Adds Abu Sharif: "I think he had a very rich personal life before '65. He was rich and young. Of the girls I know that he liked, they are beautiful and mature."*

In 1967, says Abu Iyad, Arafat met a Jordanian, a dark-haired, dark-eyed young woman who spoke in a sultry voice and had the kind of confidence and intelligence that intrigued Arafat. But in those years in Jordan when he was mounting guerrilla operations against the Israelis, he would allow nothing to interfere. Says Abu Iyad, "Abu Amar is a normal man. Things did not work out because of him, not because of the girl. At that time, he felt that if anything was about to stop his work, he would stop [the relationship]." She married another man and now lives in London. If Arafat is sorry he did not marry her, he does not say so. He can, if he wishes, still hear her throaty voice as she broadcasts the news in Arabic for the BBC. After all, as Abu Iyad says, "He is very romantic."

"He is so romantic," Majoub Omar says of his friend, "he may be fragile emotionally."

Another Palestinian who has known Arafat since 1967 says flatly, "The kind of women Arafat likes are aggressive, active and out-going." This aide recalls a somewhat embarrassing time when he introduced Arafat to his own girlfriend, an attractive reporter. The twenty-six-year-old American woman, eager to write a feature story, begged for an interview with Arafat. The chairman was unusually generous, giving the journalist large chunks of his time, taking her with him wherever he went, from army bases to schools, even giving her gifts of jewelry and antiquities. The man who introduced them at first looked innocently upon their friendship. "I was wondering if he was trying to win her as a journalist to his side." Still, the aide was in a quandary. "I was worried that my leader would fall in love with my girlfriend." But he does not believe the relationship ever moved beyond the platonic stage. "It wasn't consummated; rather, it was suppressed." Nevertheless, he confesses with a laugh, "I put a stop to it."

Of all of Arafat's relationships, certainly the one with Nada Yashruti has had the most enduring impact on him; but even this love affair was so burdened with politics that it was fated to be destroyed.

Nada was highly intelligent, first in her class at the American University of Beirut, and later a PLO activist whom Arafat says he had known "for a long time." She had lived with her husband, a Fatah leader, in Lebanon and had become friends with influential Lebanese, including the Christian politician Suleiman Franjieh. Arafat met Nada when, after being ousted from Jordan in 1971, he and his PLO colleagues moved to Beirut. A small, energetic woman with dark brown hair and pale white skin, she was in her mid-thirties when Arafat professed his love for her. Nada's husband Khaled had been an engineer in charge of constructing a large apartment complex in Beirut and was killed when a bag of cement fell on him at the site. Though no one was ever charged in connection with his death, the accident has caused some skeptics to wonder if it had been planned.

In Lebanon, an Arab country divided between Christians and Moslems, the Palestinians aligned themselves with the Moslems and gained control of the south, creating a frontline base from which they could carry out military operations across the border into northern Israel. The Israelis retaliated against the Lebanese, punishing the Christian-led government for allowing the PLO raids to take place. Tensions increased in the country as the Christians attacked the Palestinians in their refugee camps in the south. By 1973 the fighting between the two sides had gone well beyond the boundaries of the Palestinian camps; for two days the sound of gunshots could be heard around Beirut, a preface to the civil war that broke out in 1975.

Because of her friendship with Lebanese President Franjieh, Nada Yashruti was a perfect liaison between the PLO and its enemy, the Christians, and was asked to talk to Franjieh, the commander of the Christians' Lebanese army, to persuade him to lift the siege. The woman paid a call on Franjieh at the presidential palace in Beirut. After a long meeting, she returned home late that night in 1973 and found someone waiting at her door. Within moments, she was assassinated.

Some Palestinians say she was sent to see Franjieh for a more devious purpose, to eavesdrop on his conversations. They claim that when she was discovered by a Franjieh loyalist, she was thought to be a spy for the PLO. "She had many friends in the republican palace," says Khaled al-Fahoum. "The story I heard was that she had meetings at the palace. One day when she was leaving, she heard talk in one of the rooms. She stopped and listened. It happened that this talk was confidential. She was discovered by the Lebanese intelligence service, the deuxième bureau. They noticed her, and they went to her room, and waited for her at night. When she opened the door, they shot her."[11]

Some Palestinian leaders, like Yasser Abed Rabbo, who was with Arafat at the time of the murder, believe her death was politically motivated. "It was an action, I believe, against Arafat. At that moment," he explains, "there were some people who were interested in not solving the problem with the Lebanese army. They wanted to make a confrontation....She was trying to resolve the situation and she was close to Arafat."[12] PLO spokesman Jamil Hilel explains why he believes the murderer was a Christian Lebanese: "The Phalangists were preparing the scene for the outbreak of civil war. Maybe they killed her just to build up the psychological atmosphere of hatred. They knew she was in love with Arafat and killing her was a way of punishing Arafat."

News of Nada Yashruti's death was brought to the chairman while he was in a meeting with the chief of staff of the Lebanese army. Arafat became pale and distraught. "He cried like a baby," remembers Said Kamal, who watched in dismay as the PLO leader banged his head on the wall.[13]

"It is true," says a soft-spoken Arafat when asked if he was in love with Nada Yashruti. "She was very beautiful," he remembers. "I was going to marry her. She had accepted, and then she was killed."

I t was Zahwa Abu Saud, Arafat's mother, who was his first source of grief. Her death, when he was four, caused his father to send him from Cairo to Jerusalem. Arafat lived as an outcast among the Abu Saud family: his relatives in Jerusalem may have been generous and welcoming, but the young Yasser who came to stay with them was a stranger, not an intimate member of the prestigious clan. His connection to the family was through his mother, and in the patriarchal circle of Arab culture, where men were at the center, he was a pariah, a child unwanted by his own father. In this world where family life revolved around the husband, children belonged in their father's house; the dispatching of Arafat to his mother's family was nearly total rejection. In this world where even the houses of the men extended upward, layer upon layer, male generation on top of male generation, Arafat was an outsider. If Yasser occasionally traveled with his father to Gaza or Egypt during the summer, he was still more a foundling than a full-fledged family member.

It was not until 1942, in Cairo, that the thirteen-year-old Arafat could begin to feel at home. World War II was raging across Europe and North Africa, and in Egypt the Allies and the Axis powers were battling; but Abder Rauf Arafat, still living in Egypt and married for the third time, wanted his family back together. "I left Jerusalem in '42," Yasser Arafat recalls. "It was during the war. But in that period, I still remember, it was dangerous in Cairo because the battles were [close by], near Alexandria."

But back in Egypt, Yasser had to suffer with Inam, his oldest sister, who was now in charge of the family. Strict, strong-minded and dour, Inam would constantly challenge his wily ways. The multiple marriages of their father did not bring any happiness to the children either, and caused more tension in the household. Abu Iyad, a friend of Arafat's from their college years, says that Abder Rauf's marriages were "bitter and painful for Arafat. That is one of the reasons he didn't want to get married. All the brothers got married late." Arafat's father's many wives, says Abu Iyad, "were emotionally disturbing."

When his father was at home, Arafat could not help but be aware of the older man's erratic behavior. With the same kind of nervous energy as his son Yasser, Abder Rauf was a merchant who ran the Egyptian end of the trading business he had formed with two other Palestinian Arabs. A good Moslem, Abder Rauf came from the Kudwa clan in Gaza, a small, distant branch of the Husseinis. Arafat claims the family still owns considerable property. "You know what we have in Palestine?" he asks proudly. "From my mother, we have a big area of land. And my father's land, you can go ask the meaning of al-Radwan Waqf. We have the biggest area of land in Gaza for my family." An Israeli authority suggests that the al-Radwan clan is one of some 100 aristocratic Arab families in Israel that belong to the waqf. A custodian, appointed by the families, administers the property and donates the income from the land to charity. Although the revenues cannot be taxed, neither can the descendants' share in the wealth.

A religious man, Abder Rauf was active with the Islamic Council. But perhaps what consumed most of his time was a lawsuit he started against the Egyptian government. He believed that he was the rightful owner of much of Abassiya, a principal section of Cairo. The strong-willed merchant had convinced himself that he belonged to the prominent Egyptian family, named Demerdash, which had once owned the valuable acreage. The son-in-law of Haj Amin, Muheideen Husseini, says, "His father, for a period of time, claimed that he owned one of the most important pieces of land in Cairo, and he raised hell about it.... There was something wrong with his father, a little bit mad...he had something wrong with his mind."[14] The land, it seemed, had once belonged to the Demerdash family, but had been taken over by the Egyptian government, the Emiri, under the rule of the Turks. Says Muheideen al-Husseini, "He claimed it belonged to his forefathers. He claimed it was sold by marriage or by one of his grandmothers."

The case caused such a furor that it was reported in the press. A friend of the family, Hamid Abu Sitta, was startled when he saw the story. "I remember I read in the newspaper, *Mussawar,* that a man claimed the territory of Abassiya." When he questioned his friend Yasser, "Abu Amar laughed about it. He said, 'My father is searching for his old holdings.'" But the family could hardly laugh. Friends and relatives reveal that Abder Rauf squandered much of the family's property in Gaza, selling off land to pay for his long, drawn-out case.

After years of legal battles, the Moslem religious court declared Abder Rauf the rightful owner. But the Egyptian government, under King Farouk, refused to accept the decision in the civil court. In 1948 Abder Rauf was sent into exile and spent the rest of his life in Gaza.

Like almost all Gazan clans, the Arafats felt closer to Egypt than most other Palestinians did. Abder Rauf's Kudwa branch of the family traced their roots to Khan Yunis and Gaza, geographically and historically an extension of Egypt. Gaza's proximity had a profound effect upon its people: they had religious ties to the Moslem Brotherhood, an Egyptian Islamic group with a fundamentalist and militaristic ideology; they sought their higher education from Egyptian universities; they had similar cultural interests and even spoke with the same accent as the Egyptians.

Of first meeting Arafat in 1967, Nizar Amar, a PLO official, says, "I found a young small man. His voice was very soft. I was surprised by Arafat's Egyptian accent. He spoke as if he was an Egyptian."[15] While most Palestinians use the Arabic dialect common to Damascus, Arafat often surprises acquaintances with his lyrical Egyptian style, pronouncing "g" hard, as in Gamal rather than Jamal, using expressions like *"Zayak?* instead of *"Keefak?"* to ask "How are you?', saying *"Zayy?"* "How do you know?" or *Yanni aih?"* "What do you mean?" or *"aluz aaoul"* "I want to say."

But in Egypt, Arafat has no accent; in Cairo he sounds like everyone else. Even today, he fits comfortably into the culture of the Cairenes, a man with sisters and brothers and a house he still remembers from his school days. Only in Cairo does Arafat feel secure enough to send away most of his bodyguards while he sleeps soundly in the city's womb. Here, where his family has lived for more than fifty years, he sometimes visits his talkative sister Khadiga, still residing in the family house at number five Damascus Street in Heliopolis, or stays on the broad, main thoroughfare of Baron Street with his sister Inam, nicknamed long ago "Mother of the Faithful." Even his younger brother Fathi, head of the worldwide Palestine Red Crescent Society, whose looks—same small build, same nervous energy, same darting eyes, large nose and thick lips—let him pass for Yasser's identical twin, lives with his wife and children in Cairo.

Since his boyhood days, Egypt has provided sanctuary, a giant safe house in which Arafat could take refuge. Cairo's frenetic energy matches his nervous pace. Its crowded streets and masses of people suit his politician's character. Egypt's role as a leading Arab state mirrors his personal ambition; its place at the center of the Arab world reflects his own egocentric needs. Its ancestry in Arab culture reinforces the roots of his own upbringing; its heritage of Islam feeds his own religious faith. Its military leaders are role models for his own career.

Life in Jerusalem had meant scarred memories of living as a misplaced person in other people's homes, fears of middle-of-the-night intrusions by the British, and angry scenes of riots in the streets against colonial rule. But in Cairo Arafat lived with his own family. If he fought with his sisters and brothers and his own stubbornness clashed with his father's strong will, that would serve to strengthen him. If he battled miserably with his father's latest wife, or with Inam, his protective sister and surrogate mother, they were his battles fought within the context of his own family. From the age of thirteen, Egypt became Arafat's real home, Cairo the city where he still feels most at ease.

Back and forth on his childhood train trips from Jerusalem to Cairo, Arafat could sense the differences between the cities. Jerusalem may have grown under the British, but Cairo bustled with its multitudes, a melting pot of Arabs, Africans and Europeans, of Moslems, Christians and Jews. It was a city of superlatives: the largest city in Africa in the most populous country in the Arab world; it was the spiritual center of Islamic learning, the home of al-Azhar, the oldest continuously active university in the world. Cairo was a city of contrasts: a land of pagans that had embraced Christianity in its infancy, now it was home to millions of Christian Copts, descendants of the ancient Egyptians; Cairo, with its pyramids, recalled the biblical land where the Jews once served as slaves, yet with its strategic position as a center for trade, it had become home to prosperous Jewish merchants from Europe and the East.

The city sprawled into neighborhoods: lower-class slums crammed with endless families spilling out from swollen tenements into the garbage-filled streets; upper-class areas along the Nile shaded by palm trees and dotted with palatial estates, their colorful residences recalling eras of Turkish pashas and British nobles; middle-class sections lined with balconied apartment buildings and interspersed with mosques and churches, shops and schools.

In the center of Cairo was Abassiya, a large area that included the middle-class neighborhoods of Dahir and Sakakini. The grand, imposing, gray stone palace of the pasha Sakakinin sat in a circle of grounds covered by palm trees and surrounded by bushes and walls. A core of wealth and influence in the center of the area, it dominated the neighborhood, and still stands as a monument to colonialism and power. Like spokes on a wheel, the narrow streets spun out from the center, each street filled with houses and shops. Successful merchants and businessmen of different origins—Greeks, Armenians, Italians, Arabs from Palestine and Lebanon, Sephardic Jews from Spain and Morocco—settled their families into spacious flats in Sakakini.

Abder Rauf rented a seven-room apartment in an old building on

Kubessi Street. The large flat provided ample room for the Arafat children to live and play; the dining room table often doubled for Ping Pong, and the big balcony served as a perfect location for the younger boys to roller-skate. On Fridays, the dining room turned into a discussion center; as part of his work for the Islamic Council and as a good religious deed, Abder Rauf invited young Palestinians studying in Cairo to join the family for lunch or dinner. The conversations centered on religion, politics and the latest news of the war.

The Palestinians, living in Egypt under British rule, once again saw the English as an oppressive colonial power and the corrupt, pro-British monarchy as a travesty upon the Arabs. Like Arab nationalists everywhere in the Middle East, during World War II they sympathized with the British enemy, the Nazis. The Palestinians' nationalist leader, Haj Amin al-Husseini, exiled from Jerusalem, had escaped to Iraq, where he tried to help in the Iraqi Arab revolt against the British. But forced by the ruling power to flee again, he moved to Italy, where he formed a friendship with Benito Mussolini.

The Nazis showed great contempt for the dark-skinned Arabs, even calling them a lower form of life; Adolph Hitler had gone so far as to describe the Arabs as "half apes."[16] But the fair-haired, blue-eyed Haj Amin was able to convince both Mussolini and Hitler that the Arabs could be of service to the Axis powers in their fight against the British. The mufti promised the Nazis that he would supply them with fighters; his recruits, mostly Moslems living in Yugoslavia, would not only fight in battle, but could perform vital military sabotage, disrupting British communications and cutting off the British supply of oil. In exchange for these activities during the war, Haj Amin wanted Axis help to fight the Jews in Palestine after the war. Mussolini embraced the mufti and, in 1941, responded to his pleas by declaring, "If the Jews want [a state] they should establish Tel Aviv in America."[17]

By April 1942, the mufti convinced both Hitler and Mussolini to support him and persuaded the fascist leaders to agree to a secret document. In a letter addressed to Haj Amin and signed by German Foreign Minister Joachim von Ribbentrop and Italian Foreign Minister Count Galeazzo Ciano, the Axis powers promised to help the Arab countries with "every possible aid in their fight for liberation...as well as to the abolition of the Jewish National Homeland in Palestine."[18] In admiration, says Ali Zubi, the Arabs dubbed Hitler "Abu Ali," the "good fighter."[19]

In May 1942, only a few weeks after he received the confidential document, the mufti and his associates settled in Germany and went to work helping the Nazis. On a radio program broadcast in Berlin and transmitted to the Arab world, Haj Amin called for his Moslem brothers' help: "Oh, Arabs, use and avenge your martyrs. Avenge your honor. Fight for your independence. I, mufti of Palestine, declare this war a holy war against the British yoke of injustice, indecency and tyranny."[20]

Haj Amin was also determined to stop the transport of German Jews to Palestine. The Nazis, concerned about the safety of German citizens living in Palestine, had struck a deal to exchange German and East European Jews for their own natives. But in a letter to the German foreign minister the religious leader of the Moslems begged the Germans not to send 4,000 Jewish children and 500 Jewish adults to Palestine; similar letters were sent to Romania, where 1,800 Jewish children and 200 Jewish adults were about to be transported, and to Hungary, where 900 Jewish children and 100 Jewish adults were to be transferred. Instead, the mufti recommended that these Jews all be sent to concentration camps in Poland.[21]

By 1945, when the war ended with the Nazis' defeat, Haj Amin's efforts had come to little fruition. But he escaped formal charges by the Soviets and the Yugoslavs as well as attempts of Jewish groups to bring him to trial at Nuremburg and, after a search for safety, fled in disguise to Egypt, where he asked King Farouk for asylum for himself and his colleagues. Ensconced so close to Palestine, he set to work once again to establish an independent Arab state. With him in Egypt were dozens of close associates, among them Arafat's relative, Sheik Hassan Abu Saud, and another family member, the military leader Abdel Kadar al-Husseini.

The young Arafat sat at the Friday dinner table in Cairo absorbing the students' talk about the hated colonialists, about the courageous efforts of his relative Haj Amin and about the Arabs' alliance with the Nazis. Recalls Fathi Arafat, "I remember my father saying, 'What is going on is colonialism. It is not the Jews. This is a game of high stakes.'" Throughout the Middle East, Arabs were active in anti-British affairs. In Egypt, secret anticolonial, pro-Axis cells were formed by young officers like Anwar Sadat and others; in Iraq, there had been an attempted revolt against the British; around the area, in Lebanon, Syria, Iraq, Palestine and Egypt, many Arabs were working as German agents fighting against the local British enemy.

Like most boys, Arafat enjoyed the high tales of warfare. He, however, had the added pleasure not only of knowing the valiant mufti, but of being related to him. Although he was physically small, his own leadership skills became evident early on. He played out his militaristic fantasies with his friends, organizing battalions of Arab boys in the neighborhood. "He liked making camps in the garden of our house," his sister Inam recalled. "He formed them into groups and made them march and drill."[22] Arafat, the commander, took his position seriously, beating the boys and bullying them into action. His brother Fathi says he put metal dishes on the heads of local children and marched them up and down the street, striking them with a stick if they disobeyed.[23]

On other occasions, the hyperenergetic young Yasser, ignoring the intense Egyptian heat and sporting a favorite knitted cap on his head, might have skipped along the streets of Sakakini past rows of six-story apartment buildings, shops—grocers, bakeries or dry goods—belonging to Jews, a mosque, a church or a synagogue. Fifteen thousand Jews lived in Sakakini, and unlike their brothers in Jerusalem who clashed continually with the Arabs, those in Egypt belonged to a thriving community, accepted within local Arab society. Arafat delights in talking about the Egyptian Jews, boasting of their influence, exaggerating their role and their riches. "Sakakinin was a Jew who worked in the palace of the king. And the whole section of Abassiya is named by him as a Jew," he says, although, in truth, the pasha Sakakinin was actually a wealthy Moslem, married, like many Egyptians, to a Jewish woman.

Certainly, the Jews prospered and lived comfortably in Cairo, and Arafat could not help but feel the Jewish presence in the area. Conspicuously different from the Moslems who stopped their work on Fridays, the Jews closed their shops for the Sabbath on Saturday. When they were open the rest of the week, their conversations in Yiddish or Ladino could be heard everywhere. Friday nights and Saturday mornings, on holidays like Rosh Hashanah and Yom Kippur, Sukkoth, Purim or Pesach, and for all their weddings and bar mitzvahs, the Jews streamed into three grand synagogues in the area, their Hebrew chants floating through the air outside. Jewish schools supplied education, Jewish centers offered sports; at the best-known of these clubs, the Maccabees, Yasser Arafat often played basketball or skated in the yard. "In that period," he says now, "we didn't differentiate among Jews, Christians, Moslems and Copts. All of them went to the same schools, lived on the same streets in the same area."

Arafat may have generous memories of his relationship with the Jews, but he had other intentions when he befriended the Maccabees. As an adolescent, he joined in the games of his Jewish friends, but he also taunted them, going into the streets after early morning prayers to wake up the sleeping Jews with his shouts of *"Allah Akhbar!"* ("God is Great!") Recalls his sister Inam, "He had been back in Cairo only a short time when he started to go to the places and the clubs where the Jews gathered. . . . He told us that he wanted to study their mentality."[24]

Arafat acknowledges that in his years as a high school and university student, he was aware of Jewish thinkers and writers. "Don't forget," he says now in his office in Tunis, "before this confrontation with Palestine, those Jewish writers, Jewish artists, Jewish poets were a part of our lives."

From the eighth century to the fifteenth century, much Jewish literature was written almost entirely in Arabic. Major Jewish thinkers like Maimonides, author of *A Guide for the Perplexed*, and several Jewish poets like Ibn Ezra, Ibn Gabirol and Al-Harizi wrote their works in Arabic. For the 700 years of the "golden age in Spain" Arab and Jewish life were intertwined. "In Arab history, if you are speaking about generosity, you will hear the Arabs speak of Samuel," says Arafat; the biblical Jewish judge "is part of our history."

Hungry for any information that would give him insight into the Zionist movement, the politically active student made it a point to read Zionist books like the writings of Theodor Herzl and Vladimir Jabotinsky. "Even now I read them," he says. "I have to understand my enemy." He points to a book on his desk and says, "This is by a famous Jewish writer. He is speaking about the relationship between the Arabs and the Jews." Arafat is asked if he speaks any Hebrew. "Ani ohev otah," he answers. "I love you."

Arafat's passion for politics, even as a youth, far outweighed his boredom in the classroom. On school mornings, Inam complained, she made sure to take her brother to school herself, but he was often not there when she went back to meet him in the afternoon. In the evenings, when he did seem to be interested in his homework, his studiousness was a cover for something else. He would frequently invite friends over, telling his sister that they were at the house to study. But when she brought tea or snacks to the boys, she would hear Yasser announce, "Here comes the General!" The students would snap to attention and pretend to be hard at work. It was only later that she discovered they were deeply involved in political talk.[25]

Arafat's cousin, Musa Abu Saud, a son of Sheik Hassan Abu Saud, recalls that he and Yasser learned about a special group of Jewish girls in the neighborhood who were making clandestine broadcasts. "They were Zionists with a secret radio. The Zionists were doing secret things," he explains "sending many people to Egypt from outside."[26] The Jewish Zionist Youth Movement had been actively bringing young people from Palestine to Egypt, trying to encourage Egyptian Jews to join their movement. When the boys discovered what was happening, they reported it to the Egyptian police, but the authorities almost arrested them. "The police were not well educated at that time," says the cousin. "We were subject to be captured instead of these people who were running the radio." But the Arab boys felt vindicated when a young woman named Yolanda Harmar, a spy for the Haganah and a leader of the group, was forced to flee the country.

On days when the rebellious Yasser ran off, he often visited old friends and acquaintances from Jerusalem. "He always joined in Egyptian demonstrations. Many times I ran after him to bring him back home...to try to keep him out of trouble," said his sister.[27] She took her role as surrogate mother seriously, demanding strict behavior, cutting off his allowance when he didn't obey. But the mischievous teenager continued to disappear, a habit that is still part of his behavior. "In secondary school," Arafat explains, "I was involved in all the Egyptian national movements. And during that period they were boiling against the British occupation."

By 1946 prominent Palestinian nationalists like Haj Amin al-Husseini, Sheik Hassan Abu Saud and the military leader, Abdel Kader al-Husseini, had settled in Cairo, where they established the Arab Higher Committee. Like most Palestinian students, seventeen-year-old Arafat spent time at the home of Sheik Hassan or the mufti's house in Heliopolis engaged in discussions about Arab nationalism, Islamic movements and secret military plans, the very themes that still dominate his life. Arafat's intensity did not escape the notice of the mufti, who encouraged his future leadership.

From their Egyptian base, the members of the Higher Committee began a new drive to oust the British from the mandate and to create their own Arab state. Their immediate aim was to build a military force to counter the Jewish underground groups which had been able to acquire arms. Zionists like David Ben-Gurion had organized the widespread Haganah, which doubled as an illegal nationalist movement under the cover of being the official Jewish brigade within the British army in Palestine; other Zionists, like Menachem Begin, helped form the more radical Irgun, or, like Yitzhak Shamir, started the similarly extremist Lehi.

In the years right after the war, when tens of thousands of Jewish emigrants had come into Palestine illegally, the mufti and his colleagues appealed to Islamic interests to repel the Zionists. They not only recruited young Palestinians living in Cairo, but roused the support of Egyptian religious fundamentalists who belonged to the underground Moslem Brotherhood. But with the British still in control of Egypt, the young fighters had to be trained covertly. Although Abdel Kader spent most of his time in Palestine, where he led his forces in military operations against the Jews, he traveled back and forth to Cairo, where he trained the young volunteers. "He was my leader. I was seventeen and he was older. I was one of the youngest officers," Arafat recalls. Faisal Husseini, the son of Abdel Kader and then a small child, remembers that Arafat would sometimes visit them at home. There, in Abdel Kader's kitchen, young Palestinians learned to make bombs and defuse them; on different occasions Arafat and other students were secretly trained to be commandos by a German officer who had traveled with Haj Amin to Egypt.

But the guerrillas needed guns as much as they needed volunteers. Although both the Allied and the Axis troops had left behind a vast supply of weapons, procuring the arms was even more difficult than training the men. Yasser Arafat was sent on secret missions. He was assigned to take agents arriving from Palestine, their pockets stuffed with cash, to underground dealers in Cairo and Alexandria. There, they could buy weapons which had been left behind after World War

II. But buying arms was illegal and the price often exorbitant; with his Egyptian accent, Arafat could pass for a local boy and strike a better bargain than the Palestinian strangers who spoke in a different dialect. Faisal Husseini, now a Palestinian leader in the West Bank, recalls how he and his brothers would play with the old British rifles that his father brought home. Their favorite game was to carefully clean the old guns and then pretend to shoot them. From Cairo, the weapons were smuggled out on airplanes owned by the imam of Yemen to an old British airstrip in Jericho, recalls Muheideen Husseini.

When the supply of armaments diminished in the cities, Arafat led the gunrunners on more dangerous excursions through the desert; if they survived the knives and rifles of ruthless bandits hiding in the sandy wilderness, they could buy secret caches of arms from the Bedouins. But there was competition from their enemy, the Zionists, who were building up their own munitions supply. Arafat recalls one of his more daring missions: "I had heard that the Zionists had sent some of their men to buy weapons left in the Western Desert, in the el-Alamein area, and I decided to go. I found some of them buying weapons and transporting them to a ship off the coast." The shrewd Arafat contacted the Arab League, which notified the Egyptian government about the illegal sale to the Jews. "I managed to stop it," he says with a smile.

To win the struggle for their own state, the Palestinians had to have the moral and financial help of the other Arab countries and needed better weapons for their own soldiers. In Cairo, they had to capture the attention of the Egyptians and the Arab League, a group of independent Arab states organized in 1945 for the purpose of Arab unity. The teenage Arafat thought of a plan to persuade the Egyptians to legalize arms sales. On one of his gun-buying expeditions he had found an old German Tiger tank that British soldiers had taken and sold to a scrap-metal dealer. He bought the junk heap from the dealer, he says, "for twenty-five Egyptian pounds." With the help of a few dozen friends he pushed the tank to the Foreign Ministry where they draped it with banners and held a demonstration. In the end, their efforts proved fruitless, but Arafat succeeded in winning the attention of the officials.

By the end of 1947 the fighting between the Arabs and the Jews in Palestine had become so deep and widespread that it soon became clear to the British that they would have to give up control of Palestine. In November 1947 the British announced they were withdrawing their administration from the mandate. They asked that, in their place, the United Nations declare two states: one Arab, one Jewish. With help from Swedish judiciary expert, Emil Sandstrum, on November 29, 1947, the United Nations announced its resolution for a partitioned state. After much heated debate, the Jews accepted the plan, but the Arabs, infuriated that they should give up any of their land, rejected it flatly. Both sides prepared for war.

Under the direction of Abdel Kader in Jerusalem and Hassan Salama in Ramle, the Arabs fortified their positions and solidified their battalions. In addition to the weapons they bought in Egypt, they purchased arms from Transjordan, Iraq, Syria and other Middle East countries. As the fighting intensified, they gained important strategic territory. Nevertheless, the Jews won a series of important battles, gaining control of Tiberias, Haifa, Safad and some Arab areas of Jerusalem.

By the beginning of April 1948 Abdel Kader and his men were in control of the main highway linking Tel Aviv with Jerusalem. If they could gain the capital, they could win the war. The Arabs took hold of Kastel, a tiny village hidden in the hills only a few kilometers from the holy city. On an early April day, the Jewish fighters from the Haganah entered Kastel, and after several hours of fighting, took possession of an important site. That night the Jewish soldiers fired shots at some Arab soldiers strolling through the village; not until the next day did the Zionists learn that they had killed the Arabs' leader, Abdel Kader. Thousands of Arabs streamed into Jerusalem for the funeral of their martyr. The soldiers who had fought with him at Kastel came to pay their respects; in their absence the Jews took control of the area and soon succeeded in winning Jerusalem.

During this same period members of the extremist Jewish group, the Irgun, entered the Arab village of Deir Yassin and attacked the residents: 254 men, women and children were killed. The massacre became a symbol of brutality; the fear that it could be repeated prompted 250,000 Arabs to take flight from their homes. They became the first Palestinian refugees.

Word of Deir Yassin and of Abdel Kader's death spread like wildfire around the Arab world. In Egypt, as everywhere, the Palestinian students were shattered by the news. At Cairo University they held demonstrations and rallies to recruit more fighters for the war. One of those who marshaled the students was Hamid Abu Sitta, a third-year engineering student and member of the Moslem Brothers. Abu Sitta, who had been trained for a year by Abdel Kader in Syria, had already fought in Palestine and come back to the university. He attracted a group of about fifty students in front of the headquarters of the Moslem Brotherhood and gave a rousing speech. "What is the use of education when you are losing your homeland?" he cried. Abu Sitta called for the young men to show their anger and burn their books. "This is no time to study," he shouted, as the students tossed texts and papers into the fire. "Our country needs us now. Our women and our children are being killed by the Jews. We have to go to defend our people. Let us go!"

Students who had received military training were encouraged by Abu Sitta to leave at once for Palestine. Those who hadn't been trained, he insisted, should stay in Cairo and learn how to fight. Yasser Arafat, whose father was a longtime friend of Abu Sitta's father, approached him immediately. "He came up to me and said, 'I want to go with you.'" But Abu Sitta answered, "You are not trained. You are very small." Arafat was stubborn: "I want to fight, really fight. I'm trained and you can depend on me." Toward the end of April, Arafat, Abu Sitta and a group of almost fifty students left for Palestine.

Accompanied by a major of the Egyptian army, Mahmoud Labib, Arafat and Abu Sitta traveled by train from Cairo to Qantara, a town at the Suez Canal. But the young men had no passports or official papers and waited impatiently until nighttime to make the illegal crossing. Under the cover of darkness, they slipped into a small boat and rowed for ten minutes across the canal. Believing they were armed with little more than enthusiasm, Arafat said, "Here we are, three men going to fight Jews. Three men with only one weapon. We must be crazy."[28] But unbeknownst to him, the Egyptian soldier had hidden weapons in the bottom of the boat. By prearrangement, several cars awaited their arrival; when they reached shore, the three men transferred the rifles and pistols to the automobiles and drove to Gaza.

From Gaza the men went their separate ways. As Arafat recalls, "I didn't participate with Hamid Abu Sitta, because he stayed in Gaza. I didn't participate in any military activities in Gaza. I continued to

Jerusalem." Arafat joined a group of soldiers from the Moslem Brotherhood who had been fighting under Abdel Kader, but he found the situation in Jerusalem terribly frustrating. "It wasn't easy," he says with disgust, "because we were very poor with equipment." The Jews, he states, "had everything. There was an attempt to overtake our positions many times." Arafat was stationed in the Old City, in the areas of Bab al-Halil—the Jaffa Gate—and Sheik Jarrah and in the village of Silwan. At one point, he says, pointing to a lightly swollen black scar near his ankle, a bullet ricocheted and penetrated his leg. He shrugs when asked who did it; some people suggest he accidentally shot himself.

The Palestinians in Jerusalem could hardly fight back against the Jews. Asked if he engaged in battle, Arafat derides the question. "You are completely ignorant, I am sorry to say. You have no idea. The British army was still there with all its armaments. The main British forces were in Jerusalem."

On May 15, 1948, when the British withdrew and the Jews declared their state of Israel, the Arab forces from Egypt, Iraq, Syria, Lebanon and Transjordan attacked. But secret talks between King Abdullah of Transjordan, who was supported by the Nashashibi clan, and Golda Meir, a minister in the new Israeli government, promised the Hashemite leader a part of Palestine, including East Jerusalem, in exchange for a cease-fire inside Jewish territory. Abdullah agreed to back the formation of a Jewish state if the Jews would support his move to take over more Arab territory. Although a formal agreement was never reached, the talks played a significant role in easing hostility between the Hashemites and Israel, but only at the expense of the nationalist Arabs—the Husseinis and Haj Amin who were supported by the Egyptians. Three years later, a group of Palestinians, under the guidance of Haj Amin, assassinated King Abdullah.

When Arab support troops finally arrived in Palestine, the local Arabs sighed with relief. The official, organized Arab armies, however, worried about the local guerrillas who could not be kept under control, refused to allow the Palestinians to engage in battle, and immediately disarmed them. Says Arafat, "I still remember when the Arabs took the decision, and they began to prevent the Palestinians from participating. The Egyptian army took my armaments. They guarded us and took our weapons." When Arafat and his

Palestinian colleagues protested, the Egyptians answered, "These weapons will be kept for you for another round."

Says Arafat, "I was furious. They took our weapons and we began to feel that there was something wrong. There was a betrayal." He sneers at the Arab leaders: "Actually, they were not running a real war [but only] paying lip service to the idea." Now he observes that this was "one of the fatal mistakes of the Arabs. They said no [to partition] but they did nothing."

Arafat is certain in his belief that the Arabs should have accepted partition. If they were not prepared to fight, he says, then they should have accepted the United Nations proposal. "Why didn't they accept the partition? Why didn't they have the desire and the will to continue the war?" he asks contemptuously. "This was the cause of all the military coups all over the Arab world...Nasser...the Syrians, and the Iraqi revolution. All the Arab world became upside down after this treason."

After the invasion of the Arab forces, 700,000 Palestinians fled their homes, some going north to Lebanon and Syria, others south to Gaza and yet others across the river into Transjordan. The flood of refugees had begun. Like so many others, Yasser Arafat left Jerusalem, but he was fortunate to be able to return to his family's home in Cairo. For thousands of other Palestinian Arabs, the flight became a lifetime of bitter experiences: some were able to relocate in countries where they could find work; many others were forced to live in refugee camps or in areas where they were denied full citizenship.

Less than a year later, in February 1949, the United Nations concluded an armistice agreement between Israel and its four bordering Arab neighbors—Egypt, Lebanon, Jordan and Syria. The Palestinians had already dispersed throughout the area. They could remember their villages, their homes, even the fruit trees in their backyards, yet they had lost their identity in the eyes of the rest of the world. They had no passports to travel, sometimes no right to work in the countries where they lived, no say in the governments that ruled them. They were homeless, stateless people wanting only to return to their Palestine. They would never allow their Arab brothers to forget their plight; they would never allow their enemy, Israel, to live in peace.

4

Commitment to Fight

DARKNESS CLOAKS *the armored gray Mercedes waiting in the driveway of the safe house. In the same blackness of the night, Yasser Arafat steals out of the villa and sneaks into the car. The driver shifts gears, the engine rumbles, and the heavy car speeds across the roads of Tunis, heading directly for the runway at the airport.*

Arafat is off again, this time to Cairo for a meeting with Hosni Mubarak, the president of Egypt. Few events delight Arafat as much as the opportunity to meet tête-à-tête with heads of state. The chance to act as an equal to legitimate world leaders sends him rushing around the globe, from Kabul to Teheran, Cambodia to Moscow, playing peacemaker, winning points that he hopes he can cash in for friendship. When an American photographer accompanying the Mujahadeen rebels was arrested in the spring of 1989 by the government of Afghanistan, it was Yasser Arafat who showed up in Kabul and helped convince the authorities to release him. When militant Iranian students took more than sixty American diplomats hostage in November 1979, it was Yasser Arafat who argued with the

77

Ayatollah Khomeini to release the captives. When radical Lebanese Shiites took two Soviet citizens hostage in Beirut in 1985, it was Yasser Arafat who helped save them. With the Cambodian government discredited as a Vietnamese puppet and fighting would-be rulers from the cold-blooded Khmer Rouge, it was Arafat who appeared in Phnom Penh in June 1989 to try and mediate the feud.

The meeting he will have with Mubarak is to discuss the proposals to bridge gaps between Israel's plan for elections in the West Bank and Palestinian efforts to link elections to a process of Palestinian nation building. There will be numerous sessions between Arafat and the Egyptian leader, and dozens more flights, shuttles between Tunis and Cairo, Tunis and Amman, Tunis and Baghdad. Arafat is in a constant swirl of motion, moving towards what he hopes will be the best political solution for his people.

Back in Tunis, there will be more meetings, not just with members of his own organization or with other Arabs, but with Americans acting as secret channels. Self-appointed confidential envoys quietly encouraged by the State Department, American Jews eager for an end to hostilities, delegates from Quakers, international lawyers, journalists and former diplomats, they all seek an audience with Arafat. Through his aides, he urges them to come, then listens to their pleas and argues with them for hours, speaking to each interest group in the language they want to hear, playing on their sympathies and their angst.

When Americans discuss Israeli leaders, he tells them that he knew Moshe Dayan. "Did you ever talk to him? they ask. "No, no, no. One of my cousins was an officer with him during the British occupation," he says. "In the same regiment where Dayan served." Oddly enough, there were both Arabs and Jews together in a British brigade fighting the French Vichy government in Syria. It was during one of these battles that Moshe Dayan lost an eye. Arafat tells the Jews that his Moslem religion makes him one of them and speaks with personal interest about the fights in Israel between the two major factions. "I cannot accept what is going on between the Sephardim and the Ashkenazim," he declares. "This is against my religion." As for the government of Prime Minister Yitzhak Shamir, he says, it "is spoiling not only the Palestinian life, they are spoiling Judaism."

To the Quakers, Arafat speaks in a gentle voice, still mourning the 1982 massacres of Palestinians in Sabra and Shatila by Lebanese

Phalangists, crying about the conditions in the refugee camps, denouncing Israeli abuses of Palestinians' civil rights. To the lawyers he argues angrily about United Nations declarations and the legitimate right of the Palestinian people to have a homeland. To the journalists he lashes out at their questions about progress in the peace talks and excuses the intransigence of the PLO by claiming that the PLO is the most entity egalitarian in the Arab world. "We are one of the most important democratic oases in the area," he says. "Maybe it's one of our tragedies."

But no matter what rhetoric he recites to each group, he relishes the role of the underdog. He cleverly exploits the image of constantly being betrayed, while using the relationship with the superpowers to depict himself as a revolutionary who can hobnob with the leaders of the world. Whatever words he uses, his message is always the same: his is a history of broken promises and shattered dreams. "I have bitterness," he says. "I have paid a very high price."

He has been betrayed, he says, by a long list of people, beginning in Palestine with the British. But the British fraud against the Arabs marked only the beginning of what he sees as a long, continuing deceit. His Arab cousins who came to fight and took away his weapons were early proof that the Palestinians had no friends they could count on. The secret promises made by Abdullah, emir of Transjordan, to support the Israelis in exchange for more Arab land for himself proved how shameful Arafat's brothers could be. Later the Syrians would show themselves to be odious enemies. No matter that Arafat operated as a freewheeling fighter, not only would they arrest and imprison him, and twice try to assassinate him, but they would squeeze him during the war in Lebanon until he could no longer breathe. Then there would be the Lebanese who, though he believed he fought for their freedom, begged him to leave their country. Of course, he would not even have been in Beirut if not for the Jordanians, who threw him out in 1971 after the deaths of thousands of people. Then there was Sadat. "He was my friend," says Arafat. "I knew him before the Egyptian revolution. I knew him before he married Jehan." But after Sadat announced his trip to Jerusalem, Arafat never spoke to him again.

And lately, there were the Americans. The Americans urged him to evacuate Lebanon and promised him protection for the families of the fighters who stayed behind; afterwards came the horror of the massacres at Sabra and Shatila. The Americans told him that if he left

Lebanon, they would deliver "a political bonus," which he thought meant self-determination for the Palestinian people. "I have many reasons not to trust the Americans," says Arafat. "My file is full of promises. Not only verbal promises, but written promises, written documents." It will take a great deal of trust, he suggests, to travel down the road to peace with Israel. "We are fed up with being cheated and deceived. We are fed up."

He had felt betrayed in Jerusalem, first by the British, and then in 1948 by his Arab brothers, who stripped away his weapons and forced him to give up the fight against the Zionists. Once more he left the holy city, thrust into the world as the outcast Ishmael. He returned to Cairo depressed and in despair. If he had learned anything from his experience, it was that the Palestinians could not rely on anyone else to help them. In fact, if they were to reconquer their land, they would have to remain independent of any other Arab regime. After all, the Arab rulers had all been installed by colonial powers; the corrupt regimes were betraying the Arab people who lived under their rule. It was a lesson he would take with him through life.

For the moment, Arafat saw little hope for his own people to return home. What was worse, he saw the prejudice against them as refugees, the contempt from the rest of the Arab world that would sear the souls of the Palestinians.

A people without homes or land who suddenly poured into the neighboring countries in search of food, housing and jobs, the Palestinians became a threat to the local populations, who had their own difficulties just to sustain themselves. In Gaza, where Arafat's father still owned considerable land, 250,000 refugees from what was now Israel were resettled in shanty towns with no electricity or running water or sewerage, sheltered at best under canvas tents and, only with the help of the United Nations Relief and Works Agency, given flour and rice to eat and milk and water to drink. Throughout the Arab world, the Palestinian refugees were treated as second-class citizens, if they were given citizenship at all.

The Palestinians were kept apart from the local population, not allowed to assimilate even if they wanted to. Travel restrictions were tight, passports rarely given, and the only documents issued by most states were temporary. Even today, Palestinians in Tunis must apply for a laissez-passer, and in Syria, Libya and Iraq, no passports are granted to Palestinians.

In Egypt refugees were required to have an Egyptian document to leave and a visa to return. In Cairo, where the Egyptians generously opened their colleges, Palestinians were not allowed to participate fully in university life, barring them from Egyptian student organizations and forbidding them to join the Egyptian army.

For Arafat, as for many Palestinians, the answer to his future lay in earning a university degree. Like the Jews, the Palestinian Arabs sought education as a means of upgrading their status in the world. Without land to claim as their wealth, at least they would have transportable knowledge; the Palestinians would become the intellectuals and professionals of the Arab world, the doctors, lawyers and engineers who would serve the less-educated but oil-rich countries of the Middle East.

Abder Rauf insisted that his sons pursue their education. "My father was anxious for his sons to be doctors. He tried with the chairman, but he said 'no,'" recalls Fathi, now the head physician of the PLO.[1] Even as a child, Yasser's deftness for design was apparent in the paper cameras and ham radios he constructed for his younger brother. Always clever at mathematics and chess, Yasser had decided to study engineering. But after his bitter experience in Palestine he wanted a different setting; relatives in Gaza had suggested he join them at the oil engineering school at the University of Texas.

Afraid to tell his father he wanted to leave Egypt, he applied secretly to the school. "I wanted to go to the U.S.," he recalls. "And when my father found out later that I wanted to go, he asked me 'Why are you keeping this a secret? If you want to study in the U.S., we will work for it. If you want to go, we can arrange it.'" But after several months without receiving an answer, he says, "I changed my mind." The approval came too late; Mohammed Abder Rauf Arafat known to his friends as Yasser Arafat, enrolled once again at the modern, westernized University of King Fuad the First, later renamed Cairo University.

The family had moved from Sakakini to the more prosperous neighborhood of Heliopolis, and once again Inam was in charge of the household. That same year, 1948, Abder Rauf was forced to leave the country. His long court battle against the Egyptian government was ended, his claim to much of the area of Abassiya dismissed, and he was exiled from Egypt. He lived out his life in Gaza.

In their apartment Yasser shared a room with his brother Fathi, who recalls that "he was a delicate person." As a medical student at the same university, Fathi would bring home skeletons or skulls to study. "We were in the same room," says Fathi smiling. "He could not stay in the room one hour before he would say, 'What's this?' I would answer, 'You know I have to study it.'" But the future guerrilla leader was too upset by the sight. "I can't," he would shout, and leave. "He could not stay in the same room with the skull," says Fathi.

Every morning Arafat jumped the gate in front of the house and walked down the street where he met his Egyptian classmates, Sami Suleiman and Kamal Naguib. Together they would ride in a car or take the forty-five-minute bus ride across town to the engineering school. They would walk past the main gates of Cairo University's campus, not far from the road to the ancient pyramids, and head towards the engineering college, one of the huge university's best-known schools. Large stone buildings filled the city campus, and thousands of Arab students from all over the Middle East milled about the grounds. At the entrance to the buildings, old men wearing fezzes and long white caftans greeted the students and bowed to the professors who entered the venerable halls.

Arafat's decision to stay in Cairo meant not only that he would study in Egypt, but that he would continue to be involved in the conflict against the British. Haj Amin and his entourage were still installed in Cairo, but the Egyptian government was not encouraging any more military activities against the Israelis. Arafat sensed, however, that if Egypt freed itself from the yoke of the British, it would be more likely to support an independent home for the Palestinians.

As a Palestinian, Arafat was not supposed to participate in Egyptian student affairs, but as an Arab nationalist it was difficult to resist submerging himself in the political and military struggle against British imperialism. His student days were filled with military training, meetings of the students' association and, when he had time, engineering classes.

Occasionally his friends invited Arafat to join them for relaxing weekends at their classmate Kamal Naguib's country house, but when Yasser went along, he rarely took part in the chess matches or card games the others enjoyed. It wasn't cards but the colonialists who dominated his thinking. If he brooded over bridge, it was not how to play the game but how to blow one up. While his friends indulged in movies, soccer games and dating, Arafat was obsessed with politics and warfare. Kamal Naguib, who still lives in Cairo, recalls: "He was always immersed in his political motivations, and you couldn't even discuss otherwise with him. It was the dream and hope of his life. He ate, drank, slept the issue."[2] His only other interest seemed to be religion. "Arafat has always been a devout Moslem." says Naguib. "He has never smoked a cigarette nor even had a glass of beer and he prayed regularly." As for flirtations with the opposite sex, notes his former classmate, "He never had a girlfriend nor did we ever know him to have a fling."

Khalid Mohiedeen, the brother-in-law of Arafat's friend Sami Suleiman, taught military classes at the university. Now leader of the left-wing National Progressive-Unionist Rally Party in Egypt, Mohiedeen remembers first meeting Arafat at Sami Suleiman's house in 1949. "At that time we were talking politics and he was telling me that this idea was an opinion of the Marxists and that idea was an opinion of the Moslem Brothers. I was astonished that a young student knew the literature of all the political trends."[3] To the surprise of Mohiedeen, Arafat's love of politics went beyond Palestinian affairs. "He was enthusiastic about the problems of Egypt. He was talking about the Egyptian people that were fighting, even though he was a Palestinian. He was so interested in the struggle of Egypt for independence that it struck me at the time."

Mohiedeen, who was several years older than the others, was in charge of military training at the university's school for volunteer reserve officers, the equivalent of the American ROTC. Each morning before classes, six days a week from seven A.M. to nine A.M., he would drill the Egyptian students in shooting rifles, using machine guns and setting mines. Arafat made sure he was at every class. "He wanted to be a good soldier, a good officer," recalls Mohiedeen. After ninety sessions in the morning plus two months of training at military camp during the summer, the students were given a reserve officers' certificate.

Many of the young men took the instruction to avoid active military duty, but Arafat proved to be an exception. Says his former teacher: "Some people came just to get the certificate. He came to do it for the training. He wanted to be trained for the fight." Ordinarily, students born outside of Egypt were allowed to take the training but were not eligible for the diploma; but Arafat, who had an Egyptian birth record, managed to obtain a certificate. A few years later that card would help him gain access to government officials.

If Arafat felt compulsive about attending military training sessions, he was not very concerned about showing up for engineering classes. The typical first-year schedule included three courses a day in mathematics, chemistry and physics. Arafat was often absent and graduated long after his classmates. "He was not a good student because he didn't concentrate on studies," says Sami Suleiman, who remembers that Arafat switched from civil to architectural engineering. "It is easier," explains Suleiman.[4] One course that Arafat did enjoy was called National Studies and Morality. Kamal Naguib recalls: "We studied that a nation must have its land and its people. The people must have patriotism to keep them together." Notes Naguib, "That was Yasser's view at the time."

Arafat would often disappear from the university, going off as a secret volunteer with the Moslem Brothers, who were fighting the British near the Suez Canal. "He used to vanish at will," says Sami Suleiman.

After years of contention over their presence in Egypt, the British had finally begun to withdraw their forces, gradually moving them back to their bases near the Suez Canal in the triangular area of Port Said, Abu Kabib and Suez City. But anti-imperialist Egyptians, especially extremist groups like the Moslem Brotherhood, wanted the British to evacuate completely. The Moslem fundamentalists sought an independent state in which Islamic law, called Sha'ria, would prevail, and they did not hesitate to use violent and brutal means to their end. The Brotherhood tried to convince King Farouk and his prime minister, Mustapha Nahas, to allow them to engage in a guerrilla offensive against the British.

In 1950 the Islamic activists had been given implicit permission by the Egyptian government to carry out sabotage activities. Yasser Arafat, whose nationalist and religious sympathies lay with the Islamic fundamentalists, left school to help the Moslem Brothers in Abu Kabib where they were carrying out hit-and-run operations against the British troops. The volunteers would strike at the barracks, steal their weapons and flee. "I was one of the leaders of the resistance against British occupation," Arafat boasts.

During these raids the young Arafat met some of the Egyptian military leaders who were forming the Free Officers Movement. "We began to make contacts with the Egyptian officers and they used to give us weapons and ammunition," Arafat says. The movement, an underground group formed in anger over Egypt's embarrassing loss in Palestine, blamed the army's failure on the corruption of the monarchy. The Free Officers, who included Arafat's former military instructor, Khalid Mohiedeen, as well as the future leaders Gamal Abdel Nasser and Anwar Sadat, planned to overthrow the profligate King Farouk and replace him with their own Revolutionary Command Council.

Like almost everyone else, Arafat knew that the Egyptian army had been destroyed during the war in Palestine in 1948, but he shrewdly recognized that the government was anxious for recruits to fight against the British; the problem lay in Egypt's lack of facilities to train the volunteers. Arafat realized that such facilities could also serve as a training ground for young Palestinians eager to renew the battle for their homeland.

The fighting in Suez gave Arafat credentials as a soldier and helped him make important contacts with the military. When he returned to Cairo, he requested permission from Egyptian authorities to set up a training camp at his school. He was given the right to establish an instruction center at the university for any students willing to go on missions against the British, which he sometimes accompanied. The program was so successful that Arafat soon received approval to expand it to other schools. "For a certain period of time," he says, "I was responsible for the training of all these universities—one called Ibrahim Pasha University, one called Fuad al-Awal University in Alexandria."

As senior military instructor for the students and captain in the Egyptian army reserves, Arafat became well known on campus. "We had this open, legitimate training facility," he says. "This is why I became famous." Naturally Arafat, active politically as well as militarily, belonged to the Palestinian students' association; but unlike his brothers, he was allowed to join the Egyptian students' union, an organization ordinarily closed to non-Egyptians. "I was the only Palestinian who had been elected in the Egyptian Union of Students in Cairo University."

With the encouragement of Haj Amin, he also set his sights on the presidency of the Palestinian students' association. The union was not supposed to engage in political activities, but working under the cover of cultural affairs, it served as an instrument for unifying Palestinians. Explains Arafat, "Because the infrastructure of the Palestinians had been destroyed, we had nothing. So the students' organization actually was not a union of students: it was one of the establishments for unity, identity, and support. Because we had to depend on ourselves for everything, we had to work hard, to struggle, to achieve, to get help."

During this period, in 1951, Arafat met Salah Khalaf, a literature student from Gaza who was attending al-Azhar, an important center of Islamic studies. A member of the Moslem Brotherhood, which was supported by the mufti, Salah Khalaf had heard about Arafat and his plan to lead the Palestinians' association. With their widespread influence and strong-arm methods, the Moslem Brothers could help a presidential candidate to win or make sure he was defeated. Khalaf was suspicious of the younger Arafat, who had adamantly refused to join the fundamentalists' group. Khalaf's doubts were reinforced as soon as he heard Arafat speak: "From a purely Palestinian point of view, I did not like his Egyptian accent. I did not like it at all."[5] Nevertheless, he could not ignore Arafat's self-assurance. "I was very impressed by his obvious leadership qualities as I watched him training the students. He was very dynamic. Very tough. Very passionate. And I like the way he used to talk to the students. I remember him saying: 'If you walk like this and do like this you will make the ground tremble under your feet, and you will cause an explosion like a volcano.'"[6]

Salah Khalaf agreed to give Arafat the backing he needed. Arafat gladly accepted the Moslem Brothers' help and, in return, included Khalaf on the list of people who would be in his "Cabinet." Nevertheless, Arafat insisted on maintaining his independence. He began a personal campaign of going out to meet every Palestinian student he could, literally knocking on every door, greeting every Palestinian who arrived on an Egyptian campus, and offering any help he could give to the students. Abu Adeeb, one of the young men who had recently arrived from Gaza, recalls his first meeting with Arafat: "I was one of about fifty students who went from Gaza to Cairo to have their higher education. Every five or six students used to rent and share one apartment. I remember how surprised we were when Arafat called on us. He introduced himself and then said, 'I am here to serve you. What can I do to help?'" Adds the former classmate, "He did the same with each group that came to Cairo."[7]

Most important, Arafat knew how to portray himself favorably to each potential voter, how to be all things to all men. Omar Khatib, a member of the student association at the time, recalls how Arafat appealed to different constituencies. "We were a group in the student union who considered ourselves independent; Arafat used to present himself to us as an independent. There were some Communists in the union; he used to present himself to them as a Communist. To the Moslem Brotherhood he presented himself as a Moslem brother."[8] The lessons of dividing the students and persuading each of them of his loyalty has proved invaluable in Arafat's dealings with the rival leaders in the Arab world. Observes Sami Kandil, "Today he survives on the contradictions among the Arab regimes."[9]

His ability to speak simultaneously in so many tongues has allowed him to survive. Even today it marks the chairman's style, and if he cannot do it all himself, he uses his inner cabinet to address his various constituencies. While Bassam Abu Sharif writes engaging op-ed pieces for the *New York Times* or the *Washington Post*, Farouk Kaddoumi reassures the Iraqis and the Gulf states that the PLO will maintain a hard line. While Abu al-Houl ("the Sphinx") encourages activists in the *intifada*, Abu Iyad sends a videotape to a peace group meeting in Jerusalem. Each knows what his role is, each plays to his particular audience at a given time. And if anyone finds this intolerable, Arafat can argue that his is a democratic institution.

Arafat, however, will not yield to any other country's demands to represent him or control him. His stubborn insistence on remaining independent of the other Arab states, learned from his bitter experience in Palestine, has cost him the support of the Syrians and tested his friendship with Saudi Arabia, Jordan and Egypt. "The moment I let anybody else decide for me, as the president of the state of Palestine and the chairman of the PLO, this means the next time they will deal with those who I gave the authority to."

Arafat's leadership style of personal contact, also developed in his student days, remains another of his trademarks. While some politicians distance themselves from their constituents, Arafat enjoys immersing himself in crowds or seeking out individuals for an affectionate greeting. In most of his travels, Arafat is careful to keep a low public profile, hidden and protected from any possible physical attack. He knows that he is a constant target of the Israeli Mossad, th Syrian secret intelligence and extremist elements within his own PLO. But Arafat is, after all, a politician, and from time to time he indulges his desire for adulation.

On a visit to the late President Nicolae Ceausescu's totalitarian Romania, officials proudly took the PLO leader on their subway and ordered the train to stop only at a station that had been cleared of people. But Arafat was annoyed, disappointed that no one was there to greet him. The chairman insisted they continue to the next station where the platform was jammed with ordinary rush-hour travelers. Knowing that no one in Ceaucescu's dictatorship would dare to do him harm, Arafat plunged into the thick crowd, beaming with pride when the Romanians all recognized him.

Much of his popularity among the Palestinians living in the refugee camps of Lebanon, Jordan or Iraq comes from his personal visits to their schools and hospitals. He pays house calls on widows and families of martyrs and makes sure they feel his personal interest in their lives. He remembers their names and their children's names and the names of those who died; his intimate questions about their health, their studies and other personal matters make him the object of their undivided affection. No other Palestinian leader gives or receives such personal devotion.

Once in a while his efforts to express sympathy for mourners have turned out to be slightly awkward. On a visit to Cairo in the autumn of 1967, Arafat arrived at the airport and was told that the head of the Coptic church had just died. Arafat went directly to the house of his friend, Clovis Maksoud, an official with the Arab League, and told him that the pope was dead. Surprised, Maksoud asked, "Which pope?" "The Coptic pope," answered Arafat. "You must come with me." Maksoud agreed, and the two men went together to pay their respects to the Copts. When they arrived at the place of mourning, they found a group of religious leaders sitting in a circle in the dark. Arafat walked around the room, kissing every bishop and arch-bishop in turn. As he moved to kiss the next man, however, he suddenly pulled away. "Clovis," he whispered, "what is this?" Maksoud could not suppress a smile. Looking at the very stiff figure, he whispered back, "This is a cadaver."[10]

On a different occasion, Arafat paid a condolence call to the brother of the former president of Lebanon, Fouad Chehab. The body of the late president was on view in a private room laid out in full regalia, dressed in military uniform, his medals pinned to his chest. Although Arafat had once been imprisoned by Chehab and felt little remorse, he thought it his duty to pay his respects and arrived at the house with a group of people including, once again, Clovis Maksoud. Somewhat hesitantly, he walked into the room, leaned over the body, and bent his *kafeeyah*-covered head over the corpse as if to give it a kiss. But when he started to get up, he was stuck. The medals had caught on his *kafeeyah*. The bereaved brother, thinking Arafat was very fond of the president, walked around the room saying, "See how much he likes him," while the nervous Arafat, his head bobbing up and down, fumbled to release himself from the cadaver.

But even mourning calls and door-to-door campaigning are not enough to sustain Arafat now, nor were they enough to win the election in his student days. Arafat needed time to organize his voters, but the date of the annual election was fast approaching; the only way to postpone it was with the approval of the Egyptian Bureau of Central Services. He knew he could not secure permission from the intelligence department for a postponement, but the quick-witted candidate could *appear* to have the okay.

Recalls Sami Kandil, another leader in the Palestinian students' movement: "He claimed that the Egyptian leaders, for security reasons, wanted to postpone the elections. The students didn't believe him. So he brought a piece of paper with the name of one of the security authorities at the top. On that paper he wrote: 'All pre-election meetings are prevented. Elections are to be postponed until further notice.'" Another friend remembers that Arafat took a sheet of paper and wrote out what looked like an official letter of permission to delay the elections. "Then he took a ten-piaster coin, dipped it in ink, and stamped the imprint on the top of the paper: what appeared was an official-looking seal. The scheme worked. When Arafat held up the sheet of paper and showed it to people standing at a distance, they believed him. He was able to get the elections postponed." Adds Kandil, "Some of the students believed that the Egyptian authorities were backing Arafat and they felt scared of him."

Once Arafat gained the delay, he and Salah Khalaf schemed of other ways to ensure victory. On the day of the election the several hundred Palestinian students poured in from all over Cairo to cast their votes. Salah Khalaf had talked to a group of independent students—sightless Palestinians from his Islamic college, al-Azhar—and convinced them that Arafat was an independent candidate worthy of their votes. But the students had no means of transportation to the voting place. Salah Khalaf hired enough cabs to bring all the blind students to the building where the elections were taking place. Says former fellow student Omar Khatib, "What a sight it was to see so many taxis." To make sure the students voted correctly, Arafat and Khalaf had formed a committee of helpers. Recalls Khatib, "One person from that committee stood next to the blind person voting and wrote the vote down for him."

If some of the students resented this tricky maneuver, others respected Arafat's cunning. Says Khatib, "It was very apparent that he was playing around." But he adds admiringly, "He was able to manipulate all these people into getting him into office. This is what a real politician does!" Arafat won the election in 1952 and went on to turn the association into a powerful organization with several thousand students.

By the summer of 1952 the Free Officers' Movement had already gained enough backing to carry out their coup; on July 23 they succeeded in overthrowing King Farouk. The officers' Revolutionary Council installed General Mohammed Naguib as the puppet head, but it soon became apparent that Gamal Abdel Nasser held the reins of power. Arafat immediately used his friendship with the Free Officers to help his own organization. Together with a handful of other students, he wrote a letter to the new Egyptian government begging them not to forget the Palestinian refugees. Then, with great drama, they all pricked their fingers and signed the petition in blood.

Arafat tried to arrange a meeting with General Naguib to present the paper. "It was Nasser who made the appointment for me with Mohammed Naguib," he recalls. "I still remember that I contacted him and he gave the order to the military secretary of Mohammed Naguib to open the gate for us." The meeting was photographed and appeared on page three of *al-Ahram*, the Egyptian newspaper that backed the Free Officers' revolution. Arafat's message read, "Don't Forget Palestine." Arafat sought a change in the status of the Palestinian students' association, wanting it to be not merely a cultural club but a political group called the General Union of Palestinian Students. He also requested that the students be allowed to publish their own magazine. Recalling his friendship with the Free Officers, he says, "I had very strong relations with them from the Suez period. So the moment they came to power they gave me the license. It was the first license for the GUPS. From that moment GUPS became one of the most important structures for the Palestinians."

The students distributed their magazine around the Arab world. Its message of unity with underground Palestinian groups throughout the Middle East gave Arafat and his organization enormous influence. The student leader also used the Palestinians' refugee status to appeal to other Arab states for financial aid. While the Egyptians had always provided the Palestinians with free tuition, until Arafat took over the students were required to pay two pounds per month for their own sports and health care. "This was my achievement," he says proudly. "Even these two pounds were paid by the Arab League." In some cases, the Arab League even paid more. "It depended on the faculty, because part of it was for health treatments, and part of it for sport and social. I succeeded in getting the Arab League to pay six pounds per month for hardship cases among the students."

Winning financial support for the students put Arafat in a strong position at the university, while having the backing of the student body also gave him influence with the government.

"I had such good relations with Nasser and his men that I could get any facilities from them," he explains. "You don't know what facilities I had offered to me. After the Egyptian revolution, the first facility, as an example, was an office in the Egyptian military college for the Palestinians. It was me who opened it." In addition, every new student who wanted to receive financial aid had to obtain it through the organization. "Even the pilgrims coming from Gaza had to go through GUPS because they knew we could offer the facilities." This aid, he emphasizes, "was not only for the students. The facilities became a response to the plight of the Palestinian people."

Although several thousand Palestinians were studying in Egypt, GUPS was the only Palestinian organization, and Arafat was able to receive aid for it from the Egyptian government, the Arab League and from private sources such as the Palestinian-owned Arab Bank. Abdul Majeed Shoman, now chairman of the worldwide bank started by his father and a board member of the Palestinian National Fund, recalls that Arafat would visit their main office in Cairo. "I always knew him as Yasser," he says. "He would come to the bank and ask for donations. He was always polite and a gentleman. My father gave him small amounts, not more than a hundred dollars."[11]

Nabil Sha'ath, whose father was manager of the Alexandria branch of the Arab Bank, also remembers Arafat coming to ask for student scholarships. Sha'ath was struck by Arafat's air of confidence, an attitude unmatched by most Palestinians. "He was not cowed by the intelligence community. The way he talked to Egyptian policemen and so on was very confident. He was never an Uncle Tom in that sense. You have to understand about Palestinians—they had a tough time in the Arab countries from the different intelligence and police organizations, but he talked with confidence to them, almost like he was their equal. He didn't have to say those key words of obsequience. In Egypt, in particular, the police officers who were in charge of the Palestinian students had a lot of authority to deport or to jail."[12]

Like all young Palestinians at the time, Sha'ath belonged to the student association at his school, the University of Alexandria. On Friday afternoons they would gather to go on picnics at one of Egypt's vast parks. The students would bring their own lunches, the association would provide chartered buses, and they would ride to the rally, singing and chanting Palestinian songs. As much as the afternoons were social occasions, Sha'ath recalls, "the Friday picnic would always turn into a political meeting of some sort."

Sha'ath, an eloquent proponent of the PLO who still lives in Egypt, recalls: "In his demeanor, his talk about he future, his authority, Arafat acted as if he were the president of the Palestinians, not the president of the association. He had the authority of a leader very clearly. He was also a politician in the sense that he was one of the very few who could get both the Moslem Brothers and the Communists to vote for him. He was always a rallying point. Arafat was close to the Brothers, the Communists and the Baathists. That's why he personally was always elected to be at the helm.''

Although his classmates graduated in 1953, Arafat remained in school another two years, catching up with the many classes he missed while fighting in Suez or campaigning on campus in Cairo. As head of GUPS Arafat first spoke publicly about independent Palestinians fighting for their homeland. "It was in one of the meetings for the election of the committee of the students," the chairman recalls. "It was, if I still remember, in '54, in the American University [of Cairo] Hall. There were two thousand students and I said, 'We have to continue in our march from here to liberate Jerusalem.'" The Palestinian students were hearing the idea of Fatah. They cheered him on. "It was the first hope for them as a group."

But that same year had its disappointments. In an attempt to replace Mohammed Neguib, who was close to the Moslem Brotherhood, the Revolutionary Council named Gamal Abdel Nasser as prime minister. Nasser was eager to calm Egypt's relationship with the British so that he could convince them to withdraw completely from the Suez Canal. Nasser ordered a halt to the guerrilla raids against British troops in Gaza. As a result, Arafat's training centers, where the young commandos were receiving instruction, were also closed.

Unhappy with Nasser, the Moslem Brotherhood, which had backed Neguib, plotted to overthrow the new leader. Their assassination attempt was aborted, but Yasser Arafat, known to be close to the Islamic fundamentalists, was arrested. "They knew that I knew where the weapons were," recalls the chairman, "because I was the leader of the resistance." But Arafat refused to divulge the information to the police. "When they came to investigate and they asked me, I said: 'Ask Nasser, ask Khalid Muhiedeen. They are my partners. Don't ask me.'" For two months Arafat was forced to stay in prison but, he says with a hint of irritation, his friends Kamal Hussein and Khalid Muhiedeen came to get him released, "Eventually."

The following year, 1955, held better things in store. For the first time, the General Union of Palestinian Students was invited to an international conference of Communist youth organizations. Arafat knew that this invitation meant world acknowledgment of the Palestinians as a separate entity. Poor but exhilarated, he, Salah Khalaf and three other students set off for Warsaw, where the conference would be held. "Among the five of us we had only two dollars," he remembers.

They stole their way on board a ferryboat and found an unlocked car to hide in. All was fine, until Arafat accidentally hit the steering wheel and set off the horn. Khalaf remembers that "the guards woke up, arrested Abu Amar and the other fellow and took them to prison." It seemed that Arafat had chosen the car of someone "important" on the ship and was detained until they reached port.[13]

Khalaf recalls that they made their way to Genoa, where they met some pretty girls traveling with their mother. Arafat and another fellow wanted to go out with the girls, but the mother was a problem. Thinking they could count on Khalaf to help them, they asked him to look after the elderly woman for a while. But Khalaf did not want to stay with her either, and disappeared, leaving the woman alone. When Arafat and the girls returned late at night and asked about their mother, Khalaf just shrugged and said, 'She's not with me." The girls left quickly, and Arafat never saw them again.

From Genoa they went to Venice, but by now, with no money, they were miserable. "We had to live for one week as a dog," Arafat says. Instead of enjoying the city, sightseeing at the cathedrals, gliding along the canals or sipping cappucino in the cafes, they scrounged around for two days, eating only apples and sleeping in public gardens. But Arafat was undaunted. Even today, he smiles broadly as he wags his finger and says triumphantly, "We were traveling to be the first representatives of Palestinians in these festivals."

While Arafat was taking the diplomatic route through Europe, his Palestinian colleagues in Gaza, commanded in part by Khalil Wazir (code-named Abu Jihad), were instigating guerrilla raids against the Israelis, hoping that the Israelis would retaliate and embarrass Nasser into a war against Israel. A spate of military actions by these *fedayeen* from Gaza into Israel naturally provoked Israeli reprisals.

Abu Jihad led the Palestinians in protests and demonstrations, marching and waving handkerchiefs that had been dipped in the blood of the dead soldiers, publicly humiliating the Egyptian president. In addition, Abu Jihad organized envoys who visited other Arab countries and in meetings with the press described the Israeli attack and the Egyptian defeat. Newspaper stories in the Middle East and elsewhere vividly recounted the embarrassing tale. Egypt, whose army had been virtually destroyed in Palestine in 1948, was forced once again to prepare for war against Israel. Ironically, Nasser bought arms and ammunition from Czechoslovakia, the same country that helped supply the Zionists in 1948.

In reaction to Egypt's arms buildup the United States and England withdrew their financial support for a major Egyptian construction project, the Aswan Dam. On July 26, 1956, Gamal Abdel Nasser retaliated against the West and nationalized the Suez Canal. The British, dependent on the canal for all of their oil imports, were livid. In an agreement with France and Israel, on October 29, 1956, Britain and France attacked Egyptian airfields and military installations while the Israelis invaded Gaza and the Canal Zone.

The Egyptian army went into action. Yasser Arafat, now a graduate of the engineering school, immediately joined as a volunteer and was put in charge of the bomb-disposal squad in Port Said. But his career was short-circuited when the war came to an abrupt halt only a few days later. The United States refused to support its allies and demanded that Britain, France and Israel withdraw their forces. American President Dwight Eisenhower quickly became Yasser Arafat's hero. "We have to remember Eisenhower," he says. "He didn't alert them. He said 'You must withdraw,' and he didn't even answer the phone. He didn't answer their calls. He refused. And what happened? They withdrew." Angrily, Arafat compares current Israeli defiance of American pressure for peace talks with the PLO to the reaction of the British and French during the Suez crisis. Baffled by what he sees as Israel's insolence, he shakes his head and says, "No one in Europe can say no to the Americans." Stubbornly mistaken, he seems sure that the United States can "deliver" Israel the way Eisenhower delivered the canal back to Egypt.

Israel's forces remained in Gaza for several months while its allies called an immediate halt to their attacks. The Israeli occupation of Gaza brought forth a rash of protests and clashes from the Palestinians living there. Not only were the citizens of Gaza suffering at home, but their sons who were students in Egypt were no longer receiving financial aid from the Arab League. Led by Yasser Arafat, who was still active with GUPS, the students marched to the headquarters of the Arab League to demand their money. The Egyptian police refused to let them enter the building. One of the protesters was Omar Khatib, who recalls, "Arafat went up the stairs and talked to the officer who was standing at the door. He agreed on a small group of them going in and talking to the representatives of the League of Arab States. When we went in as a small group, I asked Arafat, 'What did you tell the officer?' Arafat replied, 'I told them nothing more than I'm an officer in the Egyptian army and I want to go in.'" Arafat, then in the reserves, had flashed his military I.D. and said he was an officer. But as Khatib explains, once again Arafat used his cunning: "With his finger he just hid the reserves part of it and showed it to the officer." As a result of the meeting, the students received their financial aid.

Nevertheless, the Palestinians were not placated; Israel's occupation was intolerable, and the students protested to President Nasser. Once again they marched, this time to the presidential palace, and once again, to make their point, they dramatized the event by signing a petition. With Arafat at the helm they pushed their way towards the palace entrance and after much arguing convinced the authorities to allow a group of forty to see the president. Arafat presented the petition to Nasser, saying that the Palestinians were ready to liberate Gaza themselves if they had the support of the Egyptian government. Nasser promised them he would not abandon Gaza. "But give me some time," he begged the students.

By March 1957 Egypt and Israel had negotiated an agreement: Israel was forced to withdraw from Gaza; Egypt was precluded from any Palestinian incursions into Israel. Nasser came through on his promise to save Gaza, but he would no longer tolerate any attacks across the border by the *fedayeen* nor would he allow any nationalist political movements by the Palestinians in Egypt.

The rebellion by the Gazans against the Israelis inspired Arafat and his colleagues, Abu Jihad and Salah Khalaf, to think in terms of a broader and more unified Palestinian revolt. Meeting in Cairo under the cover of GUPS or secretly in each other's houses, the group devised the concept of a revolutionary Palestinian organization which would act independently of other political parties and other Arab states.

But Nasser's pact meant that Arafat was no longer welcome in Egypt. The Palestinian would have to find work as an engineer in some other country. Waiting in an airport, en route to an interview in Saudi Arabia, he met his old friend Hamid Abu Sitta. "What are you doing here?" Abu Sitta asked. Arafat explained that he was on his way to Arabia. Abu Sitta offered to write a letter of recommendation to an acquaintance in Kuwait. It did not take long before Yasser Arafat joined the thousands of Palestinian refugees who were making their fortunes in the Gulf.

If Arafat felt bitterness about Nasser's policies, he gained enormously from the leader's philosophy and style. "I think the major influence on Arafat during the Cairo years and indeed...until the present was the influence of the Egyptian revolution as embodied in Gamal Abdel Nasser," observed Columbia University professor Edward Said. "A kind of maximum leader—a person who embodied principles of a political philosophy and a way of life: a certain kind of selflessness, a certain kind of tremendous commitment which he was able to communicate to their people. Above all, a personal style which made it impossible to get to the revolution without going through him in some way. I think also, along with that, he learnt from Abdel Nasser the techniques, of, well, to put it kindly, manipulating people."[14]

5

The Birth of Fatah

THE HIGH IRON GATES are tightly locked outside the entrance to the residence of Hakim Belawi, the PLO ambassador in Tunis. A battalion of security guards, Palestinians and Tunisians alike, stand with their automatic rifles at the ready. At two o'clock in the morning when a car appears, three gunmen rush to the driver, point their weapons and ask for identification. We fumble in the dark searching for our passports, then quickly hand them over to the men. Telephone calls are made at the gate, but permission is refused for the car to enter the grounds. Commotion ensues. Guns click into place. More guards rush to the car. More questions are asked. We explain that we have been ordered by Yasser Arafat to come for an interview. More phone calls, and finally the gates open, just enough to let the car squeeze through.

In the driveway of the sprawling stone mansion more armed chauffeurs stand beside their parked cars, waiting for the PLO officials meeting inside. Several guards in the doorway nod silently, running their hands over their machine guns as they eye the

Americans. A servant comes to the wide front hall and ushers in the guests.

The opulent villa glitters with crystal chandeliers and reproduction rococo furnishings. Fatah caucuses and PLO conferences take place in the spacious salon, where a newly woven Oriental rug covers the tile floor, and a circle of carved and tufted sofas and matching yellow brocade armchairs offers seating space for a score of people. Another ten can huddle in the adjoining salon, and just a few steps up from there twenty VIPs can dine at the long modern table. Downstairs in the cool basement, Arafat sometimes takes a nap or meets with the Executive Committee. At the moment, a half dozen Palestinians from assorted Middle Eastern countries sprawl about, chain-smoking cigarettes, sipping Scotch, gossiping in Arabic.

Off to one side, the chairman, wearing his usual khaki uniform and kafeeyah, stares intently at a television showing cartoons. Few diversions please Arafat as much as Bugs Bunny, Roadrunner, or Tom and Jerry dashing across the screen, and when the tiny mouse outsmarts the wicked cat, the chairman smirks with pleasure.

Another of his pleasures, he says, comes from children. "I have many children," he insists. "All children are my children." Not just the orphaned Palestinians of the refugee camps, but the children of his brother Fathi, of his late brother Gamal, and of the people in this room. When, a few minutes later, the young son and daughter of Bassam Abu Sharif arrive, exhausted after a long journey from their home in Lebanon, Arafat jumps up to greet them, and just as quickly, his personal photographer jumps up to snap the picture. "They are my children," he says, smiling as he embraces the sleepy youngsters. "This gives me full satisfaction. All the children are my children."

Abu Sharif's two children were with him in Beirut during the eighty-eight days of siege in 1982. The thundering sound of bombs bursting in the air one morning drew his son out to the balcony of their apartment where the little boy could watch the Israeli airplanes whizzing by. But the deafening explosions overwhelmed the child. Terrified, he urinated helplessly on the balcony floor. Seeing his son too scared to control himself, Abu Sharif went to the bedroom, found his Kalashnikov and brought it to the boy. "You can stop the planes yourself," he told him, and showed him how to shoot the automatic rifle. The child's fingers were too little to wrap around the weapon, and he needed his father's help to hold it. As they pointed the gun in the air and pulled the trigger together, the planes turned and disappeared from the sky. "He never peed like that again," says Abu Sharif, who adds that, like the PLO, his son feels he controls events instead of events controlling him.[1]

But at three A.M. *in Tunis, Abu Sharif's son cannot stop himself from nodding off to sleep. As the session continues, the boy and his sister keep dozing off until, finally, they are allowed to leave. More kisses from Abu Amar, more photographs, and the weary children are led away and tucked into bed.*

Later this morning Yasser Arafat might also sleep here. But then again, he might not. His aides complain that they are often told to meet the chairman for breakfast, and then they cannot find him at nine A.M. *"I must search every morning for him," says Akram Hanieh, the thirty-year-old PLO liaison with the occupied territories.*[2] *Arafat may leave this embassy residence at dawn and move on to a different house, perhaps the home of Salah Khalaf, now second in command to Arafat and a rival for his power.*

The chief of PLO security, Salah Khalaf, has the bearing of a general, and everywhere one looks about his hidden villa, security soldiers shouldering Kalashnikovs are on guard. Patrolling near the gatehouse, resting on the grass, standing at the door, sitting in the entry, the sharp-eyed Palestinians are on the lookout. And when the stern-faced Abu Iyad, as Khalaf is called, moves about the city in his armored Mercedes, the guards encircle him like chickens around a mother hen. The strong and stern-faced Abu Iyad resides on an estate formerly used by the ambassador of Libya, a stunning mansion complete with sweeping circular staircase, faux zebra rug in the foyer and a specially constructed iron door to shield his bedroom.

But if Abu Iyad's villa does not feel safe tonight, there are other places the chairman might choose to stay. Wherever he decides to go, he will immediately walk around the house, sniffing about instinctively to make sure he is safe. Until the spring of 1988, Arafat might have slept at the home of Abu Jihad, but the spray of bullet holes on the walls of his late friend's bedroom are too grim a reminder of the dangers that always lurk around him.

Today the Abu Jihad house is more a museum than a home: framed photographs of a smiling Abu Jihad look out from coffee tables; pictures of him are printed on scarves worn by his wife; an unfinished letter, now frozen in bronze, written at the time of his assassination to the leaders of the intifada, hangs as a memorial to his work. His widow, Um Jihad, still drained from the experience, welcomes foreign guests and guides them about the well-furnished villa, describing in detail the bloody murder of her husband, whom she calls "the father of the intifada." Slowly, tearfully, she tells us the sobering story of twenty-four killers coming in the middle of the night.

"When we heard the noise, I was sleeping, and Abu Jihad was at the desk writing a letter. I heard the noise, and I woke up. I saw him running to his pistol. He took his pistol and went outside the bedroom. I asked him what was happening and he didn't reply. It happened very quick.

"When Abu Jihad went outside the bedroom he was in the corner by the door. I was behind him, near him. I saw the four men in the other door, and he quickly shot one bullet. He pushed me to another corner, and the first one came and shot Abu Jihad in his head. I tried to carry him, to touch him. The first one prevented me and put his machine gun on my body. I closed my eyes and prayed.

"I saw everything. The killer was young, not more than twenty-two, brown hair, blue eyes and a sporty body. He had a mask. He didn't say anything. He just shot Abu Jihad and put me against the wall and put his gun behind me and prevented me from moving. I saw another one come and shoot Abu Jihad, who was on the floor." She pauses, her eyes burning with the memories. *"The second one came and shot Abu Jihad again, the third man shot Abu Jihad again. The fourth shot him also. They killed the two bodyguards before, and the gardener, a Tunisian boy. After that, they entered our bedroom and shot in it. I was still outside. I thought they killed the baby. I heard him crying. He was two and a half years old. They still kept shooting. They shot near his bed.*

"When I cry, I cry in a low voice. But when the man came and shot Abu Jihad for the fifth time, I cried in a high voice, 'Stop!' My daughter, Hanan, who was sixteen years old, heard my voice and came quickly. She asked 'What happened?' One of them said to her in Arabic, 'Go to your room!' When they went away, I opened the door of the balcony and I saw many people running. I saw not less than twenty-four persons running and I cried 'Help!' but no one came. The policemen came after half an hour. . . . He had seventy-five bullets in his body. . . . He was dead from the first shot."[3]

Only moments later Um Jihad painfully relates the vivid tale again to a delegation of Yugoslav Communist officials, the repetition immortalizing her husband. A Palestinian activist herself, Um Jihad admits she was always aware of the risks. "Every day I thought about his dying," she says. Then shaking her head, she adds in disbelief: "I never thought I would see him die in my house."

Despite the ghostly atmosphere, as she shows her visitors around, they cannot help but notice the splendor of the villa. The spacious white rooms with white tiled floors; the two airy salons, one furnished with curving white sofas, the other decorated in a splash of floral print; the ample dining room, big enough for a piano that provides a touch of Western culture; and upstairs the elegant bathrooms and large bedrooms all reveal a luxurious life-style that contrasts sharply with Arafat's austerity. It is just this asymmetry that elevates the chairman above his colleagues; yet it is he who approves the funds for the dozens of sumptuous villas and PLO embassies not only here but throughout Africa and Europe, he who approves the money for the cars, the food, the liquor and the lavish lifestyles of all the other PLO officials. Their beautiful homes and bountiful lives contrast sharply with Arafat's asceticism and provide proof of his pure devotion to the cause.

For a few short years, even Yasser Arafat enjoyed some of the material pleasures that money provides. He arrived in Kuwait in 1957, not as a warrior but as a well-employed engineer. To some, the Persian Gulf emirate was a desolate stretch of sand where the local government hired refugee Palestinians to do its work, and corrupt Bedouin sheiks oiled the palms of bureaucrats to smooth the way for contracts. But for the Palestinians, who made up almost 50 percent of the civil servants and 80 percent of the teachers, the British Protectorate was a fertile oasis spilling forth jobs, money and opportunity. Here, they could turn their university educations into lucrative positions. Tens of thousands of Palestinians poured into the oil-rich emirate to seek their fortunes from pearls that clung to the seabeds and petroleum that oozed from the earth. By 1990 there were some twenty Palestinian billionaires living in Kuwait.

If Kuwait offered little for the Palestinians to buy with their salaries, at least it provided them with houses and cars and allowed them the funds to send back home to their families. Those still waiting in the refugee camps in the West Bank, Gaza, Lebanon or Jordan could pretend they were temporary residents of those wretched ghettos, expecting to go back to their former homes, marking off the numbered street blocks with the names of their villages, arranging the marriages of their children to others within their clans, making bank deposits with the money sent from the Gulf so they could plan for *al-Awda*, their return.

That same hope of going back to Palestine filled the hearts of those arriving in Kuwait in the early 1950s. The undeveloped Gulf state was a barren desert wracked with heat where thick, brown mud trickled through the town and well-fed rats roamed the streets. The mud and wooden houses which the government gave to the workers had no running water, much less refrigerators or air-conditioning; the sparse supply of fruits and vegetables cost a prince's fortune in the open market and spoiled quickly in the sun. As for entertainment, the pious Moslems forbade drinking liquor in public; bars and nightclubs were nonexistent, and almost all socializing was done at home. The only relief from the boredom was to swim in the shark-infested, phosphorescent gulf or to go hunting with falcons.

Yasser Arafat arrived in the British Protectorate secure with an engineering job provided by the Public Works Department and a bungalow in Solaybiahat, an area designated for unmarried engineers. By the time he moved to Kuwait, electricity had been installed, and Arafat's brick bachelor quarters, once home to British personnel, offered a comfortable place complete with a private garden. But the strict society not only separated the bachelors from single women, it even kept the engineers' section apart from the area for physicians where his brother Fathi would later live, from the neighborhood assigned to teachers where Abu Jihad would soon be ensconced, and from the sections where married people dwelled.

Most days, Arafat dressed nattily in his favorite shiny white sports coats and black sharkskin trousers and worked on public engineering projects. Besides the salary of about $30,000 per year he received for overseeing the building of roads, highways and bridges, Arafat added to his riches by accepting private assignments, working on homes and villas for local sheiks. It did not take long before the independent-minded Arafat formed a contracting company with several other engineers, making even more money from large construction projects. "I had three companies!" he says.[4] With his lucrative work, he was quickly accumulating enough money to become a wealthy man. "You know, I was approximately a millionaire," he boasts. "Yes, I was very rich."

Yet the only luxury items he could buy were automobiles. Now, years later, he grins as he recalls his extravagant youth and asks, "You know how many cars I used to have?" Counting off the fingers on his hands, he answers: "Between six and seven: one Thunderbird in Lebanon, one Volkswagen in Damascus, one Chevrolet, and three or four other cars were with me in Kuwait. I used to change my cars frequently." He pauses to enjoy the memory. "But my favorite car was my Thunderbird."

If Arafat found pleasure in driving his cars, his passengers often did not. Says Zakaria Neel, an Egyptian who worked with him in Kuwait, "The only fault with Arafat's driving is that all the time he is driving he talks and uses his hands." One afternoon Arafat gave Neel a lift in his wide-finned sports car. On the way to a company restaurant, Arafat started talking about Palestinian politics. The more he talked, the more excited he became, and he soon forgot to steer the wheel. Terrified, as the car swerved across the road, Neel turned to him and screamed, "This is the last time I will ever ride with you!"[5]

But frightened passengers did not stop Arafat. He often drove with friends to neighboring Iraq, to Syria and to Lebanon in his two-toned Thunderbird convertible, where the fashionable boutiques filled with European clothes lured him into shopping sprees. Lebanon, then the Switzerland of the Middle East, offered a rich relief from the arid starkness of Kuwait. Palestinians came in droves to dine in Beirut's fine restaurants, gamble at the casinos, or take off from its international airport for European trips.

"I visited France, Vienna and Greece," Arafat recalls, but his eyes roll upward at his favorite memory, a vacation trip to Italy. "When I became rich, I insisted to go and live for a week as a lord in Venice. You know why?" Eyes twinkling, he relishes his recollection of revenge. He could more than make up for his earlier two-day stay in Venice, that terrible time when, as an impoverished student, he had been forced to sleep outdoors and eat only apples. Now, the prosperous engineer bought a first-class ticket, flew to Italy, and checked into one of Venice's most luxurious hotels. "The one on the big island," he recalls. Without money to worry about, he could enjoy sitting in the colorful gondolas as they floated through the Grand Canal or relaxing at the open air cafes near St. Mark's Square watching the women walk by. As Omar al-Khatib, one of his friends from Cairo, remembers, "He was a typical young man. If he saw a pretty young woman, he would whistle at her."[6] Or he might have indulged in other bachelor fantasies. But pushing away any lascivious thoughts now, Arafat brushes the air with his hand and says, "What I did is something not to be mentioned."

Kuwait, the source of Arafat's material wealth, would soon become the wellspring of his revolutionary movement. If his days were spent earning a living as an engineer, his evenings were an indulgence in politics. Only a few months after Arafat arrived, Abu Jihad followed, eager to organize a small group of freedom fighters, and by the fall of 1957 the friends had their first reunion. There were frequent conversations with other Palestinians, mostly over dinner at Abu Jihad's home, where the air swirled with the heat of political talk.

Like other Palestinians consumed with the notion of their homeland, Arafat and Abu Jihad were driven by the urge for armed struggle. Underground groups like theirs, forming all over the Middle East, in Syria, Saudi Arabia, Qatar, Iraq and Gaza, carefully concealed their existence from local Arab governments, which saw the Palestinians as a dangerous threat. Abu Iyad, who joined them in 1959, explains, "The Arab governments wanted to know everything and wanted it to be under their sponsorship and supervision. We were afraid they would abort any new organization." Even Haj Amin, the mufti, was seen as a threat by Nasser and had been forced to leave Egypt, escaping to Lebanon in 1959.

But unlike the other Palestinian groups—pro-Nasser cliques, pan-Arabists, or Islamic fundamentalists who counted on Arab unity to help their cause—Arafat and Abu Jihad firmly believed they had to maintain their independence from other Arab ideologies. They differed as well in their organizational structure: instead of a group headed by an autocratic leader, theirs would be a collective leadership, each member responsible to the others. With this in mind, on October 10, 1959, they started to create the infrastructure for a military organization.

The group, however, was nameless. After some discussion, they hit

upon the self-aggrandizing Palestinian National Liberation Movement, but its Arabic acronym, HATAF, forebodingly spelled "death."
Cleverly, they turned the letters around, forming the word FATAH.
Boasts Arafat now, "This name was chosen in '58. I named it. I came
up with it personally." Explaining the meaning of Fatah he says: "It
is something from the Koran. Fatah means to open the gates for the
glory. Fatah means opening. You can say that you have obtained
fatah in your studies, in your commerce, in your military actions, in
your marriage. Fatah means something glorious for a person, for a
group, for a country, for a nation, for everything."

Their first project, to publish an underground magazine, would be
subsidized by the cash-rich Arafat, and also by Haj Amin. The
mufti's son-in-law, Muheideen al-Husseini, says, "Haj Amin himself
was wealthy. He was born wealthy. I'm sure that he helped Arafat
financially later, when he started Fatah. When it first started, most of
the finances were coming from Haj Amin."[7] Years later, in 1967 and
1968, says the son-in-law, they would meet at his house in Amman.
"Haj Amin felt that Arafat would be the right leader for the
Palestinian nation."

Fatah's periodical, like the one Arafat had started in Cairo, would
raise the Palestinian consciousness and spread the word of revolution
to Palestinians around the world. But finding a publisher trustworthy enough to share their secret and courageous enough to risk it,
would prove more difficult. Only after months of searching did they
locate a small publishing firm in Tripoli, Lebanon, that was willing
to take on the venture.

Their first edition, a roughly put together diatribe printed in 1959,
aptly named "Our Palestine" (*Filistinuna*), was a quick success. Its
angry call to armed struggle and its resolute cry for a homeland
sparked fire in the hearts of Palestinians eager for a rallying point.
Although it was banned in Syria and Egypt, the group smuggled in
copies that reached the refugee camps. Almost immediately, would-
be activists responded. The periodical's box number brought a
promising number of subscriptions and, even more important, the
names of dozens of potential members.

If the founders of Fatah had had any second thoughts about the
seriousness of their intent, the publication of the magazine wiped
away their doubts. With Arafat in charge of military activities and
Abu Jihad responsible for organizing members, the single, secret

group grew into a network of underground cells, eventually spreading around the Middle East and to Europe. Within a few years they would be joined in Kuwait by Salah Khalaf, their friend from the Moslem Brotherhood, Farouk Kaddoumi, an intense revolutionary who worked at the Ministry of Health, and Khaled al-Hassan, a Palestinian who rose to prominence and wealth in Kuwait as general secretary of the Municipal Planning Board. Salah Khalaf explains the structure of the underground group: "Members were selected in a vertical manner, meaning that the members didn't know about each other. Only the organizer knew of his membership. The number varied from ten to fifteen in each cell, and it was secretive from 1959 until 1965." Each member contributed part of his salary to the organization and weapons were bought "from the black market everywhere." Khaled al-Fahoum recalls that Arafat added generously to the group's coffers. "In '65, when we first met, he had 60,000 dinars, around 200,000 dollars, and he donated it all to Fatah."[8]

In December 1962, the group witnessed the success of their Arab brothers, the Algerians, in their revolution against the French. Spurred on by this victory over colonialism, Fatah became Arafat's primary concern. He disappeared frequently from his engineering job in Kuwait, traveling undercover on forged passports to covert meeting with revolutionaries in Egypt, Syria, Algieria and Jordan.

The PLO ambassador to Egypt, Said Kamal, remembers the first time he was introduced to Arafat in Cairo in 1963. Kamal belonged to the Arab National Movement, an underground pan-Arab organization led by George Habash, a Christian Palestinian who had studied medicine at the American University of Beirut. Although Kamal was loyal to Habash's radical Marxist organization, as an activist, he was aware of a Kuwait-based group "attracting some attention, led by a man named Arafat al-Husseini." The tall, intense Kamal, in turn, was known to Fatah activists, who felt sure that his sympathies lay with Palestine.

Fatah's secret representative then in Cairo, Abdul Hamid, wanted Arafat to meet Said Kamal. He invited Kamal to dinner at his apartment late one night. "Come at midnight," he said. "A man from the central committee, Mr. Ahmed, an Algerian, would like to meet you. He is a specialist for the Palestinian section." Kamal arrived at the flat, started talking with Mr. Ahmed, and quickly realized from his accent and mannerisms that something was wrong. Kamal signaled to his host, took him aside and whispered, "Look, I am not so silly. That guy is not Algerian." The "Algerian" came over to the pair. "I am Abu Amar," he said apologetically. "I am Palestinian, but I came here with an Algerian passport."[9] Their identities properly established, the conversation now turned serious. Arafat asked Kamal to join Fatah and begged him to persuade the others in the Arab National Movement to change loyalties as well.

In February of 1963 Fatah formed its first central committee, led collectively by Arafat, Abu Jihad, Khaled al-Hassan and Abdel Karim (no longer active). Specifically designed to be the core of the organization, the fifteen-member central committee is still the most powerful group within Fatah, although its theory of collective leadership is more rhetoric than reality. In fact, early clashes arose between Khaled al-Hassan, who advocated group leadership, and Yasser Arafat, who believed that the reins of command could only be in the hands of one man.

But for the most part, the group worked well together, and when, that same year, Omar Khatib, a former schoolmate in Cairo who had moved to East Jerusalem, paid a visit to Kuwait, he found the work of the committee highly impressive. "It was the first time the concept of Fatah was offered seriously. They gave me the structural organization, the internal constitution of Fatah. I took it and went back to Jerusalem and started organizing in the name of Fatah." The many secret groups competing for membership in the West Bank towns of Ramallah, Nablus and Hebron attracted only twenty or thirty young activists each. "I started talking to these groups under the name of Fatah," says Khatib, and by 1965, with the help of Arafat and Abu Iyad, he had brought the militant organizations, which now included several hundred people, under the Fatah umbrella.

It was in 1963, as well, that the brother of Khaled al-Hassan was first approached by Fatah. Hani al-Hassan had been working in Germany, where he had attended university and organized Palestinian students. By 1963 he was president of international GUPS, which included thirty-two branches in Europe, and had built his small German group into an impressive organization of 3,000 Palestinian students and 5,000 Palestinian workers.

Aware of Hani al-Hassan's widespread influence over so many potential members for their own group, the Fatah leaders invited him for a meeting in Kuwait. When he arrived he met first with Arafat and was struck by his intensity. "He is consumed by his ideology," says Hassan. "It is his weakness and his strength." The strength, he explains, is that "with this quality he could join all the currents around him." But the weakness meant that "sometimes, you don't have a long-term strategy."[10] The men debated angrily over the role of Jordan. Arafat felt that it should stay a separate entity. Hassan believed that the Hashemite Kingdom should be overthrown and become a base for Palestinian operations. He had been in Jordan in 1955 on his way to the West Bank. "I got a bad feeling," he says. "I saw what they were doing in the West Bank. They were miserable.... The Jordanians, then, were like most of the Arab countries. You weren't allowed to say you are a Palestinian. They were oppressing you mentally, psychologically. They were also not giving the Palestinians their rights."

In a meeting, Abu Jihad urged Hani al-Hassan to combine his group with Fatah, telling him that Fatah had hundreds of cells everywhere. "Through this tactic, he convinced me that they were militarily powerful. He said they had helicopters, rockets, etc." Actually, says Hassan, whose own huge group had no military strength, "Fatah had no more than ten to twenty cells and no more than seventy or eighty men."

But Hassan was seduced and promised to link his organization with the Kuwait-based group. He returned to Germany and ordered his members to work one Sunday a month, contributing the paycheck of twenty dollars each to the revolution. He recalls, "Abu Jihad came every month or two to collect the money."

Later Hassan would become a central player in the midst of an internal Fatah fight. The organization became split in two: Arafat, eager to get started in the armed struggle, led one contingent dubbed the "mad group"; Hani's brother, Khaled al-Hassan, who believed it was better to wait until they had several thousand fighters, led a larger contingent called the "wise group." Explains Hani al-Hassan: "They all wanted the military option, but when to start and how to start was the difference. The 'wise current' said they needed at least 3,000 fighters, and weapons everywhere, and enough money to pay for those who would later be martyrs. The 'mad current' said that a revolution is like a human being. It cannot be created. You have to be born as a baby, then become a young man, then a real man."

The difference in tactics almost destroyed the group. Anxious to stop the "mad current" from acting impetuously, Khaled al-Hassan blocked the flow of funds. But his brother Hani, with access to enormous amounts of money from his European members, soon became the financial backer for Fatah.

If the Fatah leaders were divided in their approach to military actions, they were united in their anger over a new group being formed in Egypt. The Egyptian president, Gamal Abdel Nasser, was worried about unrestrained Palestinian commandos who might wreck his 1957 armistice with Israel and bring him into war. At the same time, he wanted to show support for his Palestinian brothers, who could potentially overthrow him. Nasser decided to create a Palestinian organization which would be under his control. As Hani al-Hassan recalls, the idea really belonged to United States official George Ball: "Shukeiry [the leader of the organization] told me that George Ball had said there should be a voice of the Palestinians to speak for them. He told me that Nasser and the Arabs, in cooperation with George Ball, have helped to create this organization."

In January 1964, Nasser invited thirteen Arab leaders to the First Arab Summit in Cairo. Using the excuse that Israel was diverting water from the Sea of Galilee to the Negev desert and could, therefore, afford a sizable increase in its population, Nasser declared that there should be an official Palestinian group to fight the Israelis. Its political arm was to be called the Palestine Liberation Organization; its military side, which would not be a separate army but battalions under the control of Arab governments, would be named the Palestine Liberation Army. The thirteen Arab leaders agreed to the idea and at Nasser's suggestion, chose Ahmed Shukeiry, a bombastic orator and an official of the Arab League, as the head of the new organization. In May 1964 the PLO held its founding conference in Jordanian-administered East Jerusalem. Under Shukeiry's leadership, the 422 Palestinian delegates, who came from throughout the Middle East and Europe, accepted both the Constitution of the PLO and the Palestine National Charter. The Charter, or Covenant, called for armed struggle against the Zionists and the destruction of the Jewish state. Its vitriolic language declared:

"Armed struggle is the only way to liberate Palestine. Thus it is the overall strategy, not merely a tactical phase. The Palestinian Arab people assert their absolute determination and firm resolution to continue their armed struggle and to work for an armed popular revolution for the liberation of their country and their return to it.

"Commando action constitutes the nucleus of the Palestinian popular liberation war. This requires its escalation, comprehensiveness and mobilization of all the Palestinian popular and educational efforts and their organization and involvement in the armed Palestinian revolution.

"The liberation of Palestine, from an Arab viewpoint, is a national duty and it attempts to repel the Zionist and imperialist aggression against the Arab homeland, and aims at the elimination of Zionism in Palestine.... The partition of Palestine in 1947 and the establishment of the State of Israel are entirely illegal, regardless of the passage of time, because they were contrary to the will of the Palestinian people and to their natural right in their homeland, and inconsistent with the principles embodied in the Charter of the United Nations, particularly the right to self-determination.

"The Balfour Declaration, the Mandate for Palestine and everything that has been based upon them, are deemed null and void. Claims of historical or religious ties of Jews with Palestine are incompatible with the facts of history and the true conception of what constitutes statehood. Judaism, being a religion, is not an independent nationality. Nor do Jews constitute a single nation with an identity of its own. They are citizens of the states to which they belong."

The PLO was welcomed by Palestinian groups around the world. But it was identified more as an arm of the Egyptian government than as a self-reliant entity. If Fatah stood for anything, it was independence from Arab states. It wasn't long before the two organizations would clash, and within only a few years, Fatah would take over the PLO.

The formation of the PLO served as a catalyst for Fatah. Arafat's contempt for the Egyptian-dependent organization stirred his urge to fight and drove him to plan Fatah's first military action against Israel. That operation against an Israeli water installation in 1965 marked the graduation of Fatah from an intellectual exercise into an intimidating force.

Fatah's strength would be its military threat, its ability to wreak havoc not only inside Israel but within the Arab world. Its clenched fist held the secret to its power, the determination, the willfulness, the stubborn belief that the Arab world needed it more than it needed the Arab world. It would stake that claim again and again, in Syria, in Jordan and in Lebanon, harassing and tormenting the Arab authorities until they expelled Fatah's leaders from their lands. Thousands more Palestinian fighters would die in struggles against the Arab states than in battles against Israel. Yet all the while, Yasser Arafat, the masterful consensus builder, cunning politician and shrewd tactician, would coerce the Arab rulers to his side. They might set fire to his actions, but never could they stop his dream arising from the ashes.

II

Israel: In Fear

6

Fatah's First Raids

FOR ISRAELIS, *Yasser Arafat is anathema, the embodiment of hate, the terrorist who inflicts only pain and suffering upon the Jews. Mention Arafat's name and Israelis speak of the horrors of Ma'alot and Kiryat Shmonah, towns where innocent children and adults were killed, brutal acts done by faceless murderers of the PLO. For years, Israelis have watched Arafat's efforts to play both peacemaker and warrior and have been enraged by his pose with both an olive branch and a gun. Arafat is perceived as a man emotionally and constitutionally incapable of deciding in favor of peace; even if he did, Israelis say, he could not deliver it.*

Israeli doubts predate the creation of the state; even during the 1920s and 1930s Arab terrorism made its mark on the Jews. Then in 1947, when the Arabs in Palestine were given an opportunity to live side by side with the Jews, the Arabs rejected coexistence and declared war against the newborn state of Israel. For sixteen years afterwards the Palestinians lived as hapless refugees; virtually non-entities, they huddled in tents in Jordan and throughout the Middle

East, had no national identity, no organization, and no army. Nevertheless, they staged raids from Gaza, threatening Israel on its Egyptian border.

The creation of the PLO in 1964 reflected a growing Palestinian need to organize and a conflicting agenda of the key Arab states such as Egypt. Fatah made its first attack in early 1965, placing a bomb in an Israeli water project. The device, crudely made, did not explode, but was detonated by Israeli soldiers. Later, Israelis laughed at the incident when, in a parody of the Palestinian struggle, the commander of the perpetrators, Ahmed Musa, was killed. He was shot, not by Israelis fighters, but by a Jordanian soldier who opened fire when the fleeing man refused to give up his gun.

It was several years before Israelis began to take seriously the actions of Palestinian guerrillas. Numerous bombs placed in public places created an atmosphere of fear. People in Tel Aviv, Haifa and Jerusalem, shocked by a series of explosions set off in crowded markets and busy bus stations, walked warily and watched uneasily for unguarded packages. Somehow they learned to live with the constant threat of guerrilla attack, always glancing over their shoulders as they moved steadily forward, building a country. But the Israeli view was shaped by PLO terrorism between 1969 and 1974. Two incidents in particular were powerful reminders of this perception.

Early in the morning of April 11, 1974, three Palestinian terrorists snuck into a school in the northern Israeli town of Kiryat Shmonah. Fortunately, the building was empty; the children who ordinarily stayed in the school were away on a trip. But the terrorists, members of George Habash's PFLP, raced to another building, a nearby apartment house. The guerrillas went from apartment to apartment, opening fire on astonished civilians, hurling the hand grenades and shooting the automatic weapons they had planned to use on the youngsters. Within minutes they had murdered sixteen innocent people, including eight children. By the time Israeli soldiers surrounded the house, the terrorists had barricaded themselves in the building. As more shooting occurred, the Palestinians were killed, blown up by their own explosives.

The Israeli public was shocked by the news of Kiryat Shmonah. But one month later, on May 15, 1974, they were distraught. This time three DFLP terrorists arrived at midnight in Ma'alot, a northern town where Jews from Arab countries came to make a new start in Israel. The guerrillas first attacked a truck filled with Arab women on the outskirts of town. Firing Kalashnikovs, they killed one passenger and injured ten others. The terrorists moved on to Ma'alot, where they broke into a private house and murdered the family living there. But their real goal was the school building. This time tragedy struck. Inside the school were one hundred children and four teachers. Weary after a trip from their home in Safed to a visit in the Galilee, the children and their teachers lay fast asleep.

The guerrillas seized the building and took the children hostage. Over loudspeakers they announced that they would free the youngsters in exchange for the release of twenty Palestinian prisoners who had been tried and convicted as terrorists. After debate, the Israeli Cabinet agreed to the guerrillas' demands for an exchange. But the ministers refused to give in to their demands to keep the children hostage until the freed prisoners arrived in Damascus. Israeli paratroops were sent to surround the schoolhouse. At six P.M., the deadline announced by the guerrillas when they would either make the exchange or blow up the building with everyone inside, the Israeli government gave the order for its soldiers to attack. Defense Minister Moshe Dayan had been at the building. He wrote in his memoirs: "The scene was shattering, the floor covered in blood and dozens of wounded children huddled against the walls. Our soldiers had killed the three terrorists but before they were shot the assassins had managed to murder 16 of the school children and wound 68."[1]

The entire nation grieved. Gripped by this double horror of Kiryat Shmonah and Ma'alot, they could regard the Palestinians only as terrorists bent on murder. For most Israelis, it was difficult to think of the Palestinian issue as having a political dimension; at best it was a security problem that had to be dealt with accordingly.

Although later there were opportunities for movement in the peace process, particularly through Camp David and Jordan. Israelis felt they themselves had yielded, only to be spurned by irredentist Palestinians who wanted all of their land or nothing. Any peaceful, if still ambiguous, sounds that emerged from moderate Palestinians were quickly muffled by Palestinian extremists who talked only with guns and terror.

When rock-throwing incidents boiled over into an uprising in December 1987, many Israelis pointed to the attacks as proof of the inherent danger that lay in any peace with Palestinians. Nevertheless, the sympathies of many other Israelis were roused. The intifada managed to portray the suffering of the Palestinians at the same time that it showed Palestinians willing for the first time to take responsibility for themselves. The uprising also demonstrated that there were costs to the Israeli occupation, costs that could be managed only through a political solution. Many more Israelis spoke of territory for peace, and some even supported talks with PLO leaders. When, in December 1988, the Palestinian leadership softened its stance and accepted Israel, some Israelis welcomed this new willingness of the PLO to deal on a political level and believed it to be serious. Others could not forget the forty years of Palestinian irredentism, the claims to recover all of Palestine, the terrorist methods for achieving that goal. Even Israelis who dared to consider Arafat a legitimate political leader had to question his ability to control his organization. New terrorist attacks since December 1988, even if not approved by Arafat, were evidence to Israelis that the PLO chairman is untrustworthy. A Palestinian entity on their border, they say, would be fertile ground for growing extremism. Iraq's invasion of Kuwait served as an additional reminder to Israelis of the depths of Arab hate: the Palestinian problem could be solved tomorrow, yet many Arabs would still try to destroy the Jewish state.

Now tattered scraps of green and black cloth, the remnants of torn-down PLO flags, hang from telephone wires in remote West Bank villages like Artas; charred remnants of burned tires block the road to the university town of Bir Zeit; high walls topped by chicken wire and entrances cut off by huge oil cans enclose the inhabitants of Dahashia refugee camp; metal shutters are slammed down on the shops of Arab merchants in Ramallah; piles of stones collected by Palestinian children sit waiting to be thrown at Israeli cars on the Bethlehem road; the bodies of two Arab "collaborators" are found massacred outside their homes in Beit Furik: scenes from the intifada. But the uprising has been overshadowed by the aggressive acts of Saddam Hussein. the Iraqi leader has roused the loyalty of bitter Palestinians, who rally to his threats of war against the Jewish state. The air is laced with the scent of fear. To the Israelis, the sullied hand of Arafat is everywhere.

For those who had lived in Israel since 1948, war was a way of life. The early struggle in Palestine, the battles in the War of Independence, and then again during Suez, had all taken their toll. No Israeli had gone unscathed; everyone claimed close relatives and friends killed by the Arabs. Yet since Suez in 1956, Israeli life had been fairly calm. The Egyptian army had retreated in disarray, and the armistice signed in 1957 allowed the Jewish state to catch its breath and continue to build once again.

During the late 1950s and through much of the 1960s the economy thrived and the society grew. Israel's agricultural advances and technological know-how, its public health policies and regional planning concepts not only flourished at home, but proved of great use in establishing links with the Third World. Isolated by the Arabs in the Middle East, Israel sought friends in the continent to her south. Despite Moslem pressure in Africa, the Jewish state succeeded in building a relationship with a number of African countries, forming an alliance, it hoped, with this important new voting bloc in the United Nations. As agricultural minister, Moshe Dayan traveled extensively. Foreign Minister Golda Meir kicked up her orthopedic heels in Ghana learning African dances and trying to teach the natives how to do the hora. In Liberia, Meir was spirited away to undergo secret initiation rites as a tribal chief; in Cameroon, this woman who paid little attention to her own appearance helped select a beauty queen; and in the Ivory Coast she was greeted by an African band playing a rare rendition of "Die Yiddishe Mama."[2]

While Israeli officials established ties in Africa, later broken by those countries after the 1967 war, their experiences in Asia were far more frustrating. The Japanese government's attitude was circumspect at best. With China, the Israelis suffered the influence of Yasser Arafat, Khalil Wazir and other Palestinian revolutionaries. The Chinese slammed the door on the Jews while Maoist ideologues delivered free arms and training to the Arab guerrillas.

At home Israel resolved its most pressing domestic problem by building its largest water project. In a region that suffered from parched lands and scorching heat, irrigation was a major concern. But by pumping water from the fourteen-mile-long Sea of Galilee, the lake fed by the Jordan River, the Israelis could send the water from the north of the country through 200 miles of canals and irrigation pipes to the arid Negev Desert in the south.

The project, originally suggested by the United States, was opposed by the Arabs, who sought to divert the Jordan River at its sources in Syria and Lebanon. Nevertheless, the Israelis could relax. It seemed as if the Arabs had learned their lesson: Israel would not tolerate hostile aggression.

Israeli officials knew the Arab leaders were no longer interested in war, at least not yet. To hide their own reluctance and fight their smaller battles, the Arabs had created the PLO and formed the Palestine Liberation Army (PLA), which would operate under the directive of the Arab governments. The original excuse for creating the organization had been to stop the Israelis from pumping water from the Galilee, an action which, they complained, would not only permit Israel to sustain itself, but would even give it the ability to grow.

Israeli intelligence was aware that small groups scattered around Lebanon, Kuwait, and Syria had been formed by people like Yasser Arafat, George Habash and Ahmed Jabril. These Palestinian guerrillas sneered at the newly formed PLO and the PLA, bluntly suggesting they were not the iron fighters proffered by the Arab states, but merely papier-mâché puppets dancing on the Arabs' strings. This, they declared, was not the way to get their land back.

The Israelis watched and waited, aware that these groups believed that only a full-blown Arab war with Israel would allow them to reconquer their land and establish their own state. As they saw it, the only possibility of enticing the Arab states into that war was to attack the Israelis with small commando raids, provoking the Jewish state into retaliatory strikes. They knew that the Israeli military would make reprisals against any Arab governments that allowed the raids to be staged over their borders. And in the end, enough retaliations would rouse the reluctant Arab countries into war against Israel.

The actions began like splinters, tiny slivers of Arab wood insinuated beneath the Israeli skin, annoyances easily removed, quickly forgotten. The first irritant drifted in with the New Year, a present from Yasser Arafat in Damascus. On the morning of January 3, 1965, Aryeh Zizhik, an Israeli engineer working for Mekorot, the water authority, was making a routine inspection of the Beit Netopha canal in the Galilee, part of the system that sent water from the northern Galilee to the southern Negev. As he looked down into the fairly shallow canal, his eye caught something floating toward the bottom. Zizhik notified the border police, who ordered him to close the canal and drain the area. When the authorities arrived, they found a sack, covered in plastic, tied with leather belts, and filled with ten sticks of gelignite, batteries and an old alarm clock. The bomb, too poorly assembled to work, had been set to explode several hours later.

Israeli border police worked fast to find the saboteurs. Bedouin scouts tracked the guerrillas' footsteps eastward, down to the Jordan Valley, but were forced to call a halt to their search when they found that the tracks stopped just south of the Sea of Galilee. The gang had crossed the river into Jordan. The soldiers were thwarted.

That same day, Israelis listening to Arab radio broadcasts or reading the Beirut newspapers learned of "Military Communique Number One," which claimed that "Asifa forces moved toward the occupied territories in order to open the battle against the enemy." The news was met in Tel Aviv and Jerusalem with little more than a shrug. To the Israelis, the name Asifa meant nothing, probably just another Arab gang trying to gain some publicity for itself. In fact, they would find out, Asifa was a cover name for Fatah. The underground group led by Yasser Arafat and Khalil Wazir planned to use its base at the Ain al-Helwe refugee camp in southern Lebanon as a launching pad for strikes. But if the guerrillas were caught, they would give the name Asifa, protecting the rest of the cells from detection.

The guerrillas continued the raids: during the months of January, February and March 1965, they carried out ten sabotage operations, seven from the Jordanian-administered West Bank or across the river from the East Bank of Jordan, and three from across the Egyptian-held Gaza Strip. Twice the Israelis discovered and dismantled explosives set by the Fatah *fedayeen* from Gaza; but to the dismay of the Israeli public, a third bomb exploded, killing seven Israelis patrolling the area. The Israeli government responded with warnings delivered to the United Nations Armistice Committee, but it had little effect.

By the end of 1965, the Palestinian Arabs had carried out thirty-five guerrilla operations, twenty-eight launched from the West Bank and Jordan, four from Gaza, three from Lebanon. The Israelis considered their targets—setting explosives in water pipes, on rail-road lines, on craggy roads and in border settlements—to be attacks on civilian areas. Israelis scoffed when they heard the efforts announced on Arab radio, bold reports that wildly exaggerated both the actions and their results. Several different groups of Palestinian fighters, grandly named the Heroes of the Return or the Palestine Liberation Front, took credit for these operations, but the most active seemed to be Fatah. In Israel, the word Fatah was spat out with contempt.

The minor casualties, however, did not greatly concern the Israelis. They could continue to shrug and sneer at the outrageous claims made on Arab broadcasts. The attacks on nonmilitary targets and the avoidance of direct confrontation with the army were worthy only of disgust. Such cowardly operations, carried out like thieves in the middle of the night, struck most Israelis as despicable, the work of thugs, gangs and mercenaries. Ahmed Hijazi, the one guerrilla who was caught and brought to trial, turned out to be a common criminal with a history of robbery and theft against Israeli citizens.

Israeli officials were aware that the leaders of three of the Arab countries rimming Israel—Hussein of Jordan, Nasser of Egypt, and the Christian-led government in Lebanon—were doing their best to stop these reckless guerrilla groups; nevertheless, their best was not good enough. The raiders were still crossing their borders, and reprisals had to be made. The Israeli Defense Forces retaliated with military attacks on two West Bank towns, and an attack across the East Bank of the river inside Jordan. In September 1965 a special Israeli infantry unit dynamited eleven irrigation pumps in the West Bank border town of Kalkiya, while Israeli Prime Minister Levi Eshkol told his cabinet that Jordan could have prevented the recent border raids. Front-page headlines in the *Jerusalem Post* on Monday, September 6, declared that the "Kalkiya Attack Is Warning to Jordan, Eshkol Says," while a news story reported that "since May, Fatah raiders operating mainly from Jordanian territory have carried out eight sabotage raids into Israel. Most of these were directed against water installations." The report, datelined Kibbutz Eyal, continued: "The reprisal action, intended to demonstrate to the Jordanian authorities that Israel is no longer willing to brook its half-hearted measures to check El-Fatah raids into Israel, follows the most recent incident on the night of September 1, when the diesel water pump of this kibbutz was blown up." The Fatah incursions had become pernicious.

Israeli authorities also noted with some concern that the Palestinian commando groups were gaining prestige in the Arab world, ironically, thanks in some measure to the Arabic broadcasts of *Kol Israel*. The military radio station harshly denounced the guerrilla attempts, but the stronger the denunciations, the more effective the guerrillas seemed; the angrier the reports, the more heroic the Palestinians appeared to the other Arabs. Israelis observed, however, that at the Arab Summit in Casablanca in December 1965, Egyptian President Nasser actually called for a halt in the guerrilla activities and that Nasser's resolution was adopted, with only Syria abstaining. The Arab governments knew that Israeli retaliatory strikes would be aimed at them, not at the Fatah commandos racing across the border. They had no desire to suffer the consequences of the Palestinians' irresponsible actions.

Nevertheless, while Israelis mocked the methods, the number of raids increased. During the summer of 1966, fifteen guerrilla attacks took place in Israel, most of them emanating from the Jordanian-administered West Bank. By the time the Jewish high holidays arrived in the autumn of 1966, Israelis were no longer laughing. On October 7, 1966, Palestinian commandos snuck across the demarcation line from Jordanian-administered East Jerusalem into Israeli West Jerusalem. The terrorists set sticks of dynamite under three houses in the Romema quarter, near the central bus station of Jerusalem. The explosion wounded an elderly woman and destroyed two homes, while under a third house, police found a bundle of six sticks marked "high explosive, dangerous, Hercules Powder Co." This time the prime minister rushed to the scene and spoke to the crowd of anxious civilians. The bombing had occurred in the period of Rosh Hashanah and Yom Kippur, the celebration of the New Year and the solemn Day of Atonement, a time when the Bible speaks of entries made in the Book of Life, when good deeds and bad deeds are properly noted. Using the biblical reference, Eshkol stiffly warned the Jordanians, "Our notebook is open and we are writing it down."

One month later, a mine exploded in the southern part of the country near the Jordanian border, close to the settlement of Nehosha; three Jewish soldiers were killed, and six more wounded. The government felt it had been pushed too far. The following week, Israel launched its biggest retaliation raid since Suez. Heavily armed Israeli units crossed the mountainous border near Hebron and, in less than a day, shot down a Jordanian air force plane, destroyed several army posts and a police station, and as a message to the guerrillas, blew up at least ten houses in the Arab village of Samua where the fighters were based.

West Bank Arabs took to the streets in anger, protesting that King Hussein had not protected them. Men, women and children marched through the towns, closed down shops and schools, threw rocks and burned tires to block Jordanian vehicles. The demonstrations were so numerous from Hebron to Nablus that the king, declaring a military government in the West Bank, sent tanks into the city of Nablus, set curfews and shut down newspapers.

But neither the Israeli reprisals nor Hussein's repressive actions could stop the guerrillas. In early 1967, commandos traveled ten miles from the border to the Israeli city of Arad, where they planted explosives. What disturbed the Israelis was not just the dynamite but the daring of the terrorists traveling twenty miles inside Israel, ten miles to the city and ten miles back to the border. Obviously, the guerrillas were well equipped and well organized to carry out such an operation. The irritant had become an infection.

During 1967, the attacks continued at almost double the rate of the year before. The Israeli retaliations and the resulting West Bank protests further escalated the already mounting tensions between Israel and the Arab states. Not only were relations worsening on the Jordanian front, but Syrian attempts to divert the water supply from the Jordan River and skirmishes with Syrian shepherds over Israeli cultivation of northern border areas reached the point where armed clashes were almost constant. By the spring of 1967, Israeli kibbutzim were attacked three dozen times, and heavy Syrian artillery was pointed at Israeli border settlements.

On the morning of April 7, 1967, Syrian troops opened fire on an unarmed tractor ploughing fields near a northern Israeli settlement. The Israeli military retaliated swiftly. By early that afternoon the air force was deployed, and while Syrian citizens watched, Israeli Mirages destroyed six Soviet-supplied MIG fighter planes in the air, two of them near Damascus. By five o'clock Syrian airplanes had disappeared from the sky, and five Israeli tractors were back out ploughing the border fields. Prime Minister Eshkol noted that his notebook could be closed and a new one opened with "pages of peace."

One month later, amidst Syrian and Jordanian calls for Egyptian support, Egypt's President Gamal Abdel Nasser began moving 80,000 of his troops towards the Sinai peninsula, demanding that the United Nations remove its Emergency Forces from Sinai and Gaza. U.N. Secretary-General U Thant shocked the Israelis when he immediately agreed to the withdrawal of the peacekeeping forces. As the general in charge of the U.N. forces said "shalom" to the Israeli chief of staff, the troops belonging to Ahmed Shukeiry's PLA replaced the withdrawing international forces. Ironically, the PLA's first chief of staff, Wajih al-Mandani, had fought side by side with Moshe Dayan when they both served in the British army against the Vichy government in Syria. But in 1967 the PLA and its men were on the warpath against Israel. As they deployed in the Sinai, Nasser imposed a blockade on the Gulf of Aqaba, effectively closing the Israeli port of Eilat and ending Israeli shipping through the Straits of Tiran. The Israelis interpreted this as an act of war. The move was followed on May 30 with a visit to Cairo by King Hussein, who signed a mutual-defense pact with Nasser. The king returned home, the PLA's Ahmed Shukeiry at his side, the Jordanian army now under the command of the Egyptians. One day later, Iraq signed up with Egypt. The Israelis felt surrounded, and they prepared for war.

On Monday morning, June 5, the Israeli air force struck first at the Egyptian air bases from Suez to Cairo. Within hours, they had destroyed the Egyptian air force. Egypt's allies, Syria and Iraq, responded quickly by dropping several bombs on Israel. They did little damage. Despite Israeli messages to Hussein promising not to attack if the king stayed out of the war, Jordan joined its Arab allies. The Israelis returned the fire in the air, and within hours they had wiped out the Jordanian air force and nearly half of that of Syria. Ground fighting lasted only slightly longer: the struggle with Jordan moved from artillery fire on the heights of Mount Scopus to gun shots in the narrow streets of the Old City in Jerusalem. By June 7 Israel had "liberated" Jerusalem; on June 8, the Egyptians, who had fought a bloody battle in Suez and Gaza, surrendered unconditionally; on June 10, the Syrians waved a white flag in the Golan Heights.

Yasser Arafat, who had driven to the Syrian front in his Volkswagen car, never even got to fight.

Within six days the Israelis had virtually destroyed their enemy. They had tripled the size of their territory with the conquest of the West Bank and Gaza, the entire Sinai and the Golan Heights; they had increased the number of Arabs under their control by 1,100,000, and, they thought, had wiped out the infectious guerrillas. Wrote Golda Meir, "We most profoundly hoped that we would achieve a victory so complete that we would never have to fight again.... The defeat *was* total, and the Arab losses *were* devastating...."[3] But the Palestinians had only begun their plague of terror.

7

The Constant Threat

YITZHAK SHAMIR, *the seventy-five-year-old head of the right-wing Likud government, welcomes visitors to his modern office in a building near the Knesset. Contemporary furnishings decorate the large, square room that seems too big, at first glance, for the short, stocky prime minister. Dressed in a navy-blue suit, the gray-haired, mustached politician sits in a low-slung leather chair, his feet barely touching the floor, surrounded by a team of advisers who take careful note of the conversation. Shamir came to power bearing the title "the little terrorist," a name given him by Israeli journalists. As chief of operations of Lehi, also known as the Stern Gang, Shamir was one of three leaders of the underground movement which murdered British soldiers and officials during the Zionist national struggle. Lehi's most infamous operation was its April 9, 1948, attack on the Arab village of Deir Yassin. In retaliation for the murder of the Jewish residents of the Gush Etzion settlement, 120 Jewish guerrillas, members of the Stern Gang and Irgun, entered the tiny village near Jerusalem and opened fire on the Arabs. Some 250*

127

people were massacred, their bodies left in the streets as a message to Arabs in neighboring villages. Although the operation was immediately denounced by the Haganah and other Jewish groups, for many Israelis the bloodbath of Deir Yassin remains a stain on their history.

The tough-minded Shamir projects an image of crablike stubbornness. Although constantly underrated by his opponents, he is a consistently adept politician who maneuvers well and knows his own constituency. His views about the PLO and the intifada reflect the thoughts of many Israelis who continue to despise the PLO and the thoughts of a sizable minority who maintain an ideological commitment to a Greater Israel.

When he speaks, he surprises his listeners with his slow, thoughtful style. "Intifada," he says, "is a very dangerous weapon, first of all for the Palestinians themselves. They have sustained many casualties and sufferings, without bringing peace nearer to this part of the world. It has to be stopped....It's in the interests of the Palestinians to stop...because it doesn't serve anybody's interest, including their own. One way or another, it will come to an end."[1]

For hard-liners like Shamir, Israel can make peace with Arab states and coexist with the Palestinians, but not at the price of relinquishing an inch of the biblical Jewish homeland of Judea and Samaria. For them, the PLO charter which vows to destroy Israel, remains as valid today as it was in 1964. For them, the PLO's willingness to compromise represents a new tactic in the same old war. For them, Yasser Arafat is a mortal enemy.

In the fiercely democratic country of Israel, where the smallest cafes resonate with political debate, opinions pour out as easily as coffee and sometimes stick in the listener's throat like stale cake. A large constituency, represented by politicians including Shamir and other disciples of former Prime Minister Menachem Begin, likes to quote Begin's words, "Yasser Arafat is a head of a militarist, Nazi organization."[2]

On the other hand, a group composed of intellectuals and even security and military officials like Yehoshefat Harkabi, the former director of Israeli Defense Forces Intelligence, views the PLO as a reality. Although there are risks in dealing with Palestinian nationalism, they believe there are other risks far worse: war, the loss of the democratic character of Israel, and the moral corruption of the state.

*Harkabi, the man who translated the PLO covenant into English,
says, "I thought it was important to point out the harshness of the
PLO position." But after studying the changes in the PLO's attitude,
Harkabi wrote a book entitled Fateful Decision. This man who calls
himself a "Machiavellian dove" points out that "Jordan and the PLO
accepted the principle of territory for peace. I thought we have to
accept that." Adds Harkabi, "Reality is important."*[3]

*Major General Matti Peled, a former member of Israel's General
Army Staff who helped lead Israel to victory in the Six-Day War, also
believes that the PLO has changed dramatically. Says Peled, "The
PLO themselves, in 1974 and 1977, reformulated their political goal
from that of annihilating Israel to that of establishing their own state
alongside Israel. All the Arab leaders, including Yasser Arafat, the
leader of the PLO, signed a declaration stating that peace with Israel
is the common goal of Arab nations, provided the Palestinians are
allowed the right of self-determination."*[4]

*Somewhere in the center is former Defense Minister Yitzhak
Rabin, the Israeli leader most closely involved with combating the
intifada. As chief of the military, Rabin decided how Israel should
respond to rocks and Molotov cocktails; whether the army uses
plastic, rubber or real bullets, and whether it employs tear gas or
curfews to quell the rioters. Yet Rabin is also the Labor Party official
who fathered the May 14, 1989, peace plan envisaging elections and
Palestinian self-rule in the territories. "I believe we should offer two
alternatives," he says. "A Palestinian one, and a Jordanian one."
Rabin is equally opposed to an independent Palestinian state, but he
concedes: "I don't deny them the right to bring it up. I believe there
should be a Palestinian entity, and full autonomy, by itself, is the
beginning of the creation of the Palestinian entity."*[5]

*More than three dozen daily newspapers express the dizzying range
of views of Israel's four and a half million citizens, and political
parties seem to form whenever more than two people get together;
for the moment, fifteen parties exist in the Knesset. Demonstrators
march continually: right-wing supporters shout for the arrest of
Faisal Husseini, the head of the pro-PLO Arab Studies Society;
liberal Peace Now protesters parade with placards and call for
meetings with the PLO; and the Council for Peace and Security, a
group of retired senior army officials, declares that occupying the
territories reduces the prospects for peace. Some hard-liners insist*

that the Hashemite Kingdom, with its Palestinian majority, should become the Palestinian state, while Labor leaders like Rabin and Shimon Peres argue that the king is a moderating influence in the neighborhood and could be an important ally for Israel. Arafat negates both Labor and Likud: "Shamir is saying it bluntly and clearly that he doesn't want the Palestinians. Peres is saying, 'I just want the Jordanians to do the dirty work. I don't want the Palestinians either.'" Indeed, Peres believes that the PLO is a greater threat to King Hussein than it is to Israel. "If the king and Arafat and I were in the same room," says Peres, "and the only person who had a pistol in his hand was Arafat, and if he only had a single bullet in this pistol, I would not be worried. First of all, he would try to shoot the king."

Public opinion polls taken in Israel before Iraq's invasion of Kuwait showed that 50 percent of Israeli voters would support talks with the PLO if the Palestinian leaders make a compelling, convincing argument that they mean what they say. But Shamir is firmly against such dialogue. In fact, he demoted Ezer Weizman, a Cabinet minister who engaged in talks with PLO leaders, and he pushed the arrest of Abie Nathan, an Israeli activist who met with Yasser Arafat.

Shamir insists that the PLO has no legitimacy, because, he maintains, it is still a terrorist organization. In fact, elements of the PLO have served his purpose by continuing attacks against Israel. As for the PLO chairman, Shamir says, "Arafat does not represent any country. What we have to do is negotiate peace with Arab countries—not organizations."[6]

Shamir reminds his guests that Jews and Arabs have coexisted for centuries and, he predicts, there will be coexistence in the future, but "Arafat is not a partner for peace." The PLO Chairman "is the obstacle. We don't trust him because we know what he's really doing while he sweet-talks the rest of the world. And while he talks peace one moment, he gives orders for terrorist acts as soon as you've turned your back."

Although their opinions differ widely, both the Likud leaders and the Labor leaders have reached their positions because of Yasser Arafat. Indeed, almost everyone in Israel has been affected in some way by the PLO's guerrilla tactics, whether it has meant being in a place where a bomb exploded or knowing someone who died from a terrorist attack. To the left wing, the deaths of innocent civilians *underscores the need to recognize that the Palestinians, like the Jews, are a people with their own legitimate national claims. To the right wing, terrorism is precisely the reason why Israel cannot make peace with the PLO.*

The swift and resounding Israeli victory in the Six-Day War startled the West Bank and Gaza Arabs. Years of listening to radio broadcasts from Amman and Cairo had convinced them that their brothers would destroy the Jewish state and liberate their land. So surprising was the conquest that some danced in the streets, welcoming the Arab soldiers they thought had come to free them. Only when they learned that the blue and white flag they had never seen before was not the banner of some far-off Moslem nation, but the standard of their neighbor next door, did they realize that the men they greeted so heartily were Israelis.

The Israelis called the Six-Day War a miracle. "Everybody thought that within those tiny borders we were going to be overwhelmed," says Israel Harel, chairman of the Council of Jewish Settlements in Judea, Samaria and Gaza. "It was a miracle that we survived. It was a miracle that we defeated the Arabs in six days."[7]

Of all the Israelis, perhaps no group took the meaning of victory more symbolically than the Orthodox students of Rev Tzvi Yehuda Kook. The son of Rev Avraham Kook, the first man appointed by the British as chief Ashkenazi rabbi of Palestine, Rev Tzvi Yehuda Kook had spoken prophetically only three weeks before the June 1967 war. At a celebration of Israel's Independence Day, the charismatic teacher had cried out to his ardent followers, "Where is our Hebron—have we forgotten her? Where is our Shechem [Nablus], our Jericho? Shall we forsake them? And all of Transjordan—it is ours." And then came the miracle of the war, and the land was theirs.[8]

The students of Rev Kook—a small group of rabbis, their families and their followers—believed fervently that their job was to nurture the land of Eretz Yisrael. Aspiring for redemption, Rev Kook's disciples had been taught it would take three major steps to reach their goal: first, that the Jews in the Diaspora must return to Israel, pushed to some degree by the physical danger of being in the Diaspora; second, that the Jewish people must be reunited with the biblical land of Eretz Yisrael in a complete resettlement of the land; lastly, that the Jews turn to God and be observant of His commandments.

The first of these requirements was already under way. Jews throughout the world were steadily returning to Israel, arriving daily from countries as disparate as England and Ethiopia, South Africa and the Soviet Union. Miriam Levinger, the wife of Moshe Levinger, one of the rabbis in the movement, believes that those in the Diaspora are fated to be at the mercy of others. The proof, she points out, was the massacres and the pogroms of eastern Europe, the Holocaust of the Nazis, or attacks by anti-Semites in the United States. Says the Orthodox woman born in New York City: "I think no matter where you are outside of Israel, the Jews are guests in host countries. I see Jews coming to Eretz Yisrael because I don't think they have a true place outside of Eretz Yisrael. Here in Eretz Yisrael I have my government, I have my soldiers, and I don't have to exist on the goodwill of others."[9]

In the months that followed the 1967 war, this militant band of Orthodox extremists planned their strategy to settle the newly acquired territory. While they did, thousands of ordinary Israelis flocked to the West Bank, to the ancient areas of Judea in the south and Samaria in the north, to see and smell and touch the very birthplace of the Jewish nation. In Hebron, they visited the Cave of Machpelah, which Jews had not been allowed to enter since the beginning of the Ottoman Empire 451 years before. Here, at the burial site of the patriarchs, Israelis were spiritually rejoined with Abraham, the father of Judaism, his son Isaac and grandson Jacob, and with the matriarchs, Sarah, Rebecca and Leah. How meaningful that Hebron was the city where David ruled for seven years before he moved to Jerusalem and unified the kingdom. Elsewhere in Judea, they stopped in Bethlehem, birthplace of David and the cradle of Christianity; traveled to Masada, the sweeping fortress where a small band of Jewish zealots took their own lives rather than submit to their Roman conquerors; and drove to Jericho, the world's oldest city, where Joshua fought the Canaanites and blasted his trumpet until the walls tumbled down. In Samaria they visited the tomb of

Samuel; saw the ancient Jewish sect of Samaritans in Nablus; and traveled north to visit the site of Gamla, a city from the time of the Second Temple. Their ancient land of Eretz Yisrael was now truly intact.

But of all the biblical places, none was more meaningful or more sacred than the Western Wall. Within minutes of winning the Old City on the morning of June 7, the chief Israeli Defense Force chaplain, Rabbi Shlomo Goren, rushed to the wall, torah in hand, to say the ancient shehecheyanu blessing and then, joyfully, gave a resounding blast of the shofar. The rabbi, who stayed at the wall for several hours, was joined moments later by Defense Minister Moshe Dayan, Chief of Staff Yitzhak Rabin and the Prime Minister Levi Eshkol. Uniformed soldiers streamed by the holy site, some praying, some weeping, some staring in awe, some slipping their written wishes between the ancient stones. Within hours of the cease-fire, thousands of Israelis, both religious and secular, many still in uniform, swarmed to the Old City to pray at the ruins of the ancient temple. The psalm that had been repeated despairingly so many times by Jews everywhere, "Jerusalem, holy city, may you be rebuilt and reestablished speedily in our day," suddenly became a song of cheer.

On June 10, Dayan announced that East Jerusalem would be annexed, and the city would be reunified. Teddy Kollek, formerly the mayor of West Jerusalem and now mayor of all Jerusalem, drove around to inspect the newly won territory. When an Israeli soldier saw the mayor, he stopped him and said proudly, "We've made your city bigger." Replied Kollek prophetically, "A bigger headache, you mean."[10] On a visit to the Old City, Kollek proudly steered his old friend David Ben-Gurion along the Moslem quarter. As they walked through the poverty-ridden Maghrebi section, down the rancid, narrow alley that led to the Western Wall, the former prime minister was distraught. The overwhelming filth in the streets, the stinking public toilets next to the wall, the meager path that could never afford enough space to the tens of thousands of people who would want to visit the wall, all seemed to Ben-Gurion to be not only an outrage to this sacred site of Judaism but a source of future tensions between Arabs and Jews. That night, it was announced that the Maghrebi section would be torn down.[11]

Still shocked by the overwhelming Israeli victory, the Arabs were distraught by the news that one of the first acts would be the destruction of a neighborhood. Ruhi Khatib, the mayor of East Jerusalem from 1950 to 1967, was at home when the announcement was made. In the early hours of the morning on June 11 Khatib was awakened by a group of people knocking on his door. They had rushed to his house to tell him how upset the North Africans were who lived in the Maghrebi quarter. "I went there to see why," recalls Khatib. "I was not allowed to enter, but people were fleeing. They said they were attacked at 3 A.M. and warned to leave their houses in two or three hours. Then bulldozers came and bulldozed 136 houses."[12] Several months later, in 1968, the houses of the Abu Saud compound, where Yasser Arafat had spent much of his childhood, were also destroyed. Remembers Khatib, the first Arab to be deported by the Israelis, "The wife of Sheik Hassan was kicked out without any chance of collecting her household effects and clothing. She had to find shelter outside the city walls for some time until she died."

As they razed the houses around the Western Wall, the Israelis cleared a broad plaza in front of the holy site, laid out, they discovered, at the end of the first century B.C. Only three days after the bulldozers ravaged the area, 200,000 Israelis descended on the plaza to celebrate the holiday of Shavuot. While Arabs hid fearfully in their homes or peeked curiously through their windows, masses of secular Jews, Orthodox Jews, kibbutzniks and soldiers walked to the wall under the banner of the Star of David. In the weeks and months that followed, archaeologists dug furiously, finding layer upon layer of early fragments of Jewish life. Inscribed coins, pots, utensils, tomb chambers from the ancient Temple, and even an entire Jewish building 1,900 years old, were uncovered. One artifact, the handle of a seventh-century pot, left lying in the ground since the end of the First Temple era, was marked with the Hebrew words La-Melech, meaning "For the King." A fragment from another pot was decorated with two birds and inscribed in Hebrew with the word korban, meaning "sacrifice."[13] For the Israelis these fragments were confirmation that this was the home of the Jewish nation; they would serve as proof to the Arabs that this was the land where the Jews belonged.

Immediately following the Six-Day War, Dayan announced that the integrity of the Arab territory would be kept intact: There would be free movement for the Arabs of the West Bank and Gaza back and forth across the river, allowing them into Jordan and giving them access to the rest of the Arab world; the Arabs would also be permitted to travel without limitations throughout Israel; the territories would be administered by a military governor who would maintain authority according to both Jordanian civil law and Israeli military orders; the West Bank and Gaza would not be annexed.

Some Palestinians, resigned to life under another occupier after the Jordanians and a long list before them, returned to their daily work as farmers, merchants, physicians, lawyers and bureaucrats, making sporadic forays into Israel to visit the villages and towns they had not seen since 1948. Some rang the doorbells on their old houses in Haifa and Jaffa and were welcomed in for coffee by the Jews now living there. Others were rebuffed and sent away. Thousands poured into Jewish Jerusalem to stroll past the shops along Jaffa Road or catch the latest movie at the modern theaters near Zion Square.

A handful of local leaders encouraged modest opposition amongst their citizens. Even before the war, Abdul Jawad Saleh, who had been mayor of El-Bireh, recalls, "I started a voluntary work movement in order to get rid of all negativeness in the Arab mind and behavior."[14] Under his sponsorship, one typical women's group organized projects for sewing and needlework. Headed by local activist Samiha Khalil, it developed into a major center for PLO activism. Other groups, particularly in cities such as Nablus with established intellectual circles and entrenched political activity, quickly formed strong pockets of resistance.

But the most virulent threat to the Israelis came from the leaders of Fatah, who decided, at a meeting in Damascus immediately after the war, to move their military headquarters into the occupied territories. While the Israelis celebrated their victory, Yasser Arafat slipped across the narrow Jordan River into the West Bank. "Directly after the Six-Day War, I went inside the Arab territories where I spent more than four months," Arafat says now. "Four times I went there. Three times through the river, and once over the Abdullah Bridge." Most of the time he wore his *kafeeyah*, but sometimes, he says, he disguised himself as a doctor and "dressed in a suit and tie." It wouldn't be long before his presence would be felt.

"Right after the occupation," says his relative, Sheik Musa Abu Saud, "he came in disguise to my mother, and she was astonished. 'How did you get here?' she cried." She took him to the home of his Uncle Salim, and said, "Here, you were born here," recalls the Sheik.

Arafat took her for a ride in his car. "Since he was not married, and in our religion you are not supposed to have women in the cars, he said the only woman who was invited into his car was my mother." And then, says the cousin, "he just vanished. Just disappeared."[15]

Omar al-Khatib, a Fatah representative in Amman, recalls that in July 1967 he was living on the outskirts of Jerusalem. "A person came to my house in Beit Hanina and told me Arafat was in Jerusalem." Khatib, who had met with Arafat and Abu Jihad several years earlier in Kuwait, was responsible for organizing secret Fatah cells in the West Bank, but was surprised to see Arafat actually in Jerusalem. "He wore a white *kafeeyah* and regular pants and a shirt. He was without the beard," recalls Khatib who sheltered Arafat for a few days. "We talked, and he came to the decision there should be military work."[16]

From Jerusalem, Khatib escorted Arafat to nearby El-Bireh where he received his necessary documents. "Abu Amar got two identity cards from me when I was mayor of El-Bireh," says Abdul Jawad Saleh. "After the occupation, we had a problem of identification. You could move through military blockades from one town to another only with identity cards. We were the first municipality to issue identity cards. He stayed in El Bireh and I gave him two cards as a resident." The mayor's political students escorted Arafat.

Moving around by car or by motorbike, he met secretly with local Arabs in cafes and private homes. Some knew him as the Doctor, or Dr. Fawzi Arafat; others, like Omar al-Khatib, called him "Abu Mohammed." In Nablus, "he stayed with the al-Masri family for a few days," says Khatib. "Then he stayed a couple of days with another family. Then he went to the villages up in the north." But wherever he went, recalls Khatib, the stubborn "Abu Mohammed" "refused to remove his *kafeeyah* at the Israeli checkpoints."

For several months Arafat skulked around the West Bank, sometimes dressed as a shepherd, other times as a physician, working his way from Jerusalem to Ramallah, from El-Bireh to Nablus, and, because Arabs were allowed to travel freely, to cities inside Israel. "I went to Tel Aviv and spent one day there," Arafat says now. "I went to Haifa, to Jaffa, to Acre." Did he cry, he is asked, when he saw what had become of the Arab cities? "Why cry?" he snaps. "I can control my emotions."

Arafat's job, says Omar al-Khatib, was "organizing the infrastructure of Fatah. He organized the military missions. We deliberately did not allow him to get involved in military operations." But, says the PLO official, "he did the basic planning. He was moving around from one house to another, meeting up with people and telling them what to do."

Those who joined the revolutionary movement had to be taught guerrilla warfare. Some were trained by Ŏmar Khatib in the West Bank, but that proved difficult. "You couldn't do practical training with the occupation. You could teach a person how to use the weapon but to actually fire it, you'd be discovered." Other volunteers, he says, "were sent under Arafat's order to el-Hama training camp in Syria. They spent fifteen days in intensive training and then came back."

It was while he was recruiting activists in Ramallah that Arafat encountered Faisal Husseini. The son of Arafat's military mentor, Abdul Kader al-Husseini, Faisal was working in the political office of the PLO and asked Arafat to consider a political strategy against the Israeli occupation. Arafat became suspicious that the son of the legendary Palestinian fighter was too cowardly to fight. Cautiously he cross-examined Husseini until, finally, Husseini passed the test. It was agreed that he would train commandos for Fatah. Arafat brought Husseini to the Ramallah house where he was hiding. "He gave me two machine guns, a Russian Kalashnikov and a Czechoslovak Samosar," recalls Husseini.[17]

In Jerusalem one of the Fatah commanders was Kamal Nammeri, a young man who came from Jordan and Kuwait. Nammeri made his first trip to the West Bank just before the Six-Day War, visiting his uncle, the general manager of a large Jerusalem construction company. Nammeri's cousins welcomed him and one, a young woman, took him touring. While driving along the highway from Tel Aviv to Jerusalem, Nammeri scouted the area for sabotage operations, and seeing equipment used for paving the road, he slipped some sticks of dynamite under the bulldozers. Nammeri's efforts did not go unnoticed; a guard standing nearby tried to stop him, but was killed in the effort.

Not long after Nammeri was caught, his story became well known. What stunned Israeli citizens was not so much the act itself, but that Nammeri's mother was a Jew: Yetta Kleiner was her name. She had come to Jerusalem from Germany and married an Arab man. After the War of Independence, the couple moved to Jordan and Kuwait where they raised their family. It was there that her son, Kamal Nammeri, first heard of Yasser Arafat and Fatah, and it was Arafat himself who recruited Nammeri to become commander of Fatah activities in the West Bank. The uncle Nammeri had visited was a Jewish man, and the cousin who had innocently accompanied him was a Jewish girl. The Israeli public was in shock.

Many of the Fatah fighters who came to the West Bank in 1967 were brought in with the help of Arafat's colleague, Hani al-Hassan. Almost 500 Palestinian students, trained first in Algiers, were snuck across the shallow river into the occupied territories. "It was my job personally to meet the groups that infiltrated across the Jordan River," says Omar al-Khatib. By the end of August, Arafat had set up commanders and bands of fighters in major centers and had smuggled in enough weapons to start carrying out operations.

"After the defeat of '67, nobody expected the Palestinians to start doing anything," recalls Khatib. "Until around September, there was absolutely no control whatsoever. So it was very easy to get weapons across the Jordan River. We brought weapons from the Golan Heights, the weapons the Syrians left behind. They prepared it for shipping down and then across the river. We also used the places where the Jordanian army stored some of their weapons; some of it was left over. The Iraqis were present in Jordan and they helped us transport the weaponry in their cars to the Dead Sea area." The weapons that were used were mostly gelignite, says Khatib. "It's like jelly. It looks like dynamite. You put five or six together and you put a timing device in the middle, and it goes off." Khatib says he crossed the river "about ten times" to smuggle the weapons. "Arafat went across once or twice."

In mid-September a series of guerrilla activities caught the Israeli public by surprise. First, an irrigation pipe was blown up at Kibbutz Yad Hannah; next, rubber tires were set on fire and a general strike called in Nablus. Arab storekeepers rolled down the metal shutters on their shops while truckers refused to drive produce to the markets. Tension developed between workers on strike and those who were not: demonstrations erupted in different cities and some Arabs traveling to work in Israel were fired on by others on strike.

At one point fighting broke out in a northern town between Israeli soldiers and Palestinian protesters, but the Israelis quickly quashed the outburst. Arafat, who was in Ramallah at the time, remembers,

"After a military confrontation in the main square of Jenin between a small group of ours and the Israeli army, six of the Palestinians had been killed." As Arafat recalls it, when a French journalist asked Moshe Dayan, "What about this confrontation with the resistance?" the Israeli defense minister replied: "Resistance? What resistance? You call this resistance? The resistance is like an egg in my hand. I can smash it any time."

During this period, on September 19, a bomb exploded in reunited Jerusalem. Planted in the shabby Fast Hotel near the Jaffa Gate of the Old City, the dynamite wounded seven people. The Israelis suffered nine other terrorist actions that occurred in September. Khatib explains that each operation was watched and analyzed afterwards. "Every group that went to perform a certain operation had one or two people following them who just observed. They came back and reported. These observers reported if the bombs went off at the right time, the numbers of casualties, and if they were arrested." Khatib credits Arafat with the strategy. "It was Abu Amar's idea. He was the military coordinator. He was the one."

Less than three weeks later, on October 8, 1967, Fatma Benawi, an Arab woman, and two men entered the popular Zion movie theater in downtown Jerusalem. The threesome took their seats to watch the film, and after a few minutes got up and walked out. When someone in the audience noticed a package left under their seat, the ushers became suspicious and called the police. The parcel was taken to a vacant lot next to the Jerusalem Central Police Station; when the authorities threw it on the ground, the package exploded. Once again, the Israeli public was stunned. Every Arab became suspect; some were attacked by angry Israelis and their property damaged.

Two days later, thousands of Israelis gathered for a peaceful demonstration in front of the Zion theater, and Israeli artists volunteered to organize a special exhibition to emphasize the fact that the Israelis would not give in to terrorism. Fatma Benawi and her two partners were quickly caught. Says Omar al-Khatib, who helped organize the operation, "She was the first woman prisoner. She came out in the prisoner exchange in 1985 and is now married and living in Tunis." After Fatma Benawi was arrested, Khatib says, "I changed my name and carried a different identity card. My cousin was Ruhi al-Khatib, the [Arab] mayor of [East] Jerusalem [until 1967]. I got a paper from him saying my name was Nazia Mohammed."

The guerrillas carried out ten terrorist attacks in October, eighteen

in November and twenty in December. The Israelis developed a
strategy to protect themselves. National guards or volunteers kept
watch over every public place. People coming into all supermarkets
and banks were asked to open their bags while guards checked them
for bombs. The post office examined every package sent through the
mail. Israelis paid strict attention to bags or suitcases that seemed
abandoned and notified the police. Children were instructed not to
go near packages left in the street and to report them at once to the
authorities. Whenever unattended parcels were discovered, the
streets were closed and special bomb squads were rushed to the
scene. In their heightened efforts, the Israeli police were arresting
guerrillas almost continuously. Arafat was on the run.

"I transported him after one operation to Ramallah and to Nablus
in an UNRWA car!" exclaims Omar al-Khatib. "I had a friend who
worked with UNRWA and their cars were never searched. That was a
good way to do it." On a different occasion when Arafat was in
Ramallah, Omar al-Khatib went to see him. "I found the house he
was staying in was surrounded by the Israeli police. So I went to a
friend's house and asked, 'Was Abu Mohammed arrested?' The
friend told me he had left five minutes before the Israeli military
came." Arafat had hidden in his Volkswagen while the police
searched his house. At another point, Khatib took him to Nablus,
and from there Arafat went to a small village up north. "The Israeli
military surrounded al-Maharia when Arafat was there in September. Some young men took him into the caves in the mountains and
they stayed there a few days. Then he changed his location again."
As Arafat remembers, "The closest call was near Nablus."

Like Arafat, most of the Palestinian terrorists had come from
Kuwait, Jordan or the refugee camps in Lebanon and were considered outsiders by the local population. The West Bank Arabs, many
now working in Israel and enjoying their wages, offered little help to
the guerrillas and then only with reluctance. They were well aware of
the Israeli policy of collective punishment, retaliating against the
villagers as they did against the Arab states. Local villages that
harbored guerrillas were raided, houses demolished, the inhabitants
placed under curfew. As a result, many West Bankers would neither
shelter the guerrillas in their homes nor allow them to use their
villages as bases.

By the end of 1967, the Israelis had successfully arrested 1,000
activists, discovering to their surprise that many of the guerrillas

were not thugs and criminals as they had suspected but educated students. Loyal to their Palestinian leadership, they were intent on pursuing a policy of terrorism in order to call attention to their plight. Some spoke of their allegiance to the Arab National Movement, led by George Habash, some swore a commitment to Syrian-backed groups or the Communists, but more than any other group, they claimed their faithfulness to Fatah. By now, Fatah was infamous, its existence notorious throughout Israel. Although Arafat's name was still not familiar to the Israeli public, his actions had been noted. By December 1967 life had become too dangerous for the guerrillas. Arafat and 300 Fatah fighters were forced to flee from the West Bank.

The frontline Arab states showed no desire to shield the guerrillas. In contrast to the Palestinians, the border countries had agreed to pursue a political course to resolve the Arab-Israeli conflict. On November 22, 1967, the United Nations Security Council had passed Resolution 242 which called for: Israel's withdrawal from territories occupied in the recent conflict; the territorial integrity and political independence of every state in the area and their right to live in peace within secure and recognized boundaries; freedom of navigation through international waterways; achieving a just settlement of the refugee problem; the establishment of demilitarized zones.

The Arab states had suffered enough losses of men and materiel. Neither Syria nor Egypt would allow the guerrillas to operate from their turf; the Lebanese had no army to protect either the Palestinians or themselves. Only Jordan, with a high population of Palestinians in its military and in its midst, could not refuse them refuge. Nevertheless, it was a wary King Hussein who permitted Arafat and his men to move back to the Jordan Valley. Only with a warning to the Palestinians that he would not tolerate commando raids from his country did he allow them to settle in the refugee camp at Karameh.

Despite the king's warnings, the Israelis suffered a barrage of terrorist attacks early in the spring of 1968. All along the border the kibbutzim were continuously shelled, and although no one was hurt, an attack on the children's dormitory at Kfar Ruppin, empty at the time, sent chills down the spine of the Israeli public. The government's response was to send reinforcements along the border: aircraft and artillery were ordered to defend the vulnerable citizens. But on March 18, 1968, no one was protecting a busload of children on a school outing from Herzliya. As the youngsters drove from the seaside resort near Tel Aviv to a desert area near Eilat, the bus hit a mine in the road and exploded. Two children were killed and twenty-seven were injured. The Israeli answer was to mass an attack on Jordan.

IDF tanks and foot soldiers gathered near the bridges to cross the river into Jordan. Defense Secretary Dayan's plan was for the army to destroy the Fatah base at Karameh and return home. But on March 21, 1968, the day of the attack, Dayan was in the hospital, and the fighting proved far more severe than expected. The Palestinians, who had watched the Israeli army deploying on the border, were prepared with shoulder-fired rocket-propelled grenades. The battle was bloody, and as the Israeli army continued moving east beyond the Fatah base and into the mountainous region of the Jordan Valley, they were met by Jordanian aircraft. When Israeli planes and tanks tried to bombard the guerrillas, the Jordanian army protected the Palestinians' flanks, covering their moves with artillery fire. The ten-hour battle was over by dusk, but for the first time in its history, the Israeli army turned back in retreat, leaving four tanks and four armored vehicles in its wake. The Israelis suffered 29 soldiers dead and 90 wounded; 97 Palestinians were killed and 128 Jordanian men were dead.

For the Israelis, Karameh was an embarrassing loss; for Fatah, it was an extraordinary victory. Their spokesman, Yasser Arafat, equated Fatah's small conquest with the Six-Day War. He made certain it was blasted on every radio and headlined in every newspaper in the Middle East. Arafat's picture was emblazoned across the cover of *Time* magazine, where he was heralded as the world's latest freedom fighter. As Arafat explained the struggle, the Palestinians had won the first Arab victory over Israel. They had restored morale and conquered might. The Arab world had regained its pride, and thousands of Palestinian fighters flocked to the Fatah camp. The Israelis had tried to wipe out the guerrilla infection; instead they helped inflame the terrorist disease.

8

Terrorism Escalates

DARK-EYED *Smadar grew up on Kibbutz Rarnot Ninashe, the daughter of a German refugee and a Polish survivor of the Holocaust. Time and again her mother had told her of the horrors she had suffered in Poland; she talked of the shame and fear of being a Jew and of how more than once she had hidden in a hole in the ground, terrified as she heard the footsteps of Nazi soldiers marching in search of Jews.*

In Israel there were thousands of such terrible stories but there was also the joy of Jews at home at last in their own country. No longer did they have to rely on the whims of host governments; no longer did they feel like second class citizens in someone else's state. For the first time Jews could be free to be Jews, proud of their democratic society, their blossoming land, their freedom to do and be whatever they wanted.

At the age of twenty-one Smadar married Danny Haran, the son of immigrants from Shanghai, Jews whose own parents had fled from Russia during the revolution. The couple took an apartment in

143

Nahariya, once a haven for honeymooners during the Roman empire, now a resort town on the Mediterranean. Danny managed a textile factory and Smadar, an artist, painted during the day and taught drawing in the evening. Two years later, in 1975, Smadar gave birth to their first child, Einat. Their second daughter, Yael, was born in 1977. Two years later Israelis celebrated when the government signed a peace treaty with Egypt in March 1979. For Smadar and Danny it seemed that the end of an era was in sight. But the trauma of the Holocaust cast a dark shadow. Despite her happiness, Smadar always sensed enormous danger lurking.

In early April, only days after the Camp David treaty was signed in Washington, the Israeli government reported that six Fatah terrorists armed with rocket launchers, Kalashnikov automatic rifles, submachine guns and pistols had been sent on a mission to Israel. Under orders from Abu Jihad, they had taken a cargo ship owned by Fatah and set sail from Cyprus to the Israeli coast. The Israeli navy had spotted the boat and intercepted it.

Smadar and Danny could rest comfortable with the knowledge that their military was always on the alert. Just three weeks later, as they picnicked with friends on a Saturday afternoon, they relaxed near the sea, gossiping and enjoying the peaceful Sabbath day. In the past the area had been vulnerable to terrorists who had crossed the nearby border with Lebanon. Smadar paid special attention to her five-year-old daughter. The night before, Einat had awakened from a nightmare. Crying and shaking, she said she had dreamed that terrorists had attacked the town and were trying to kill her.

That night, as the family went to bed in their apartment in Nahariya, Smadar hoped that her daughter would sleep peacefully. But around three A.M. the family was awakened by a burst of gunfire. Four terrorists, dressed in khaki uniforms and carrying backpacks jammed with guns and explosives, had set off in a rubber boat from Tyre, eighteen miles away, and landed on the beach at Nahariya. Their outboard motorboat had been spotted on the radar screen by an Israeli soldier on duty, but the sea had been stormy and she shrugged off the blip on her screen as nothing important.

The terrorists made their way to a nearby house and tried to enter, but the building was well fortified. Awakened by the noise in his house, Amnon Sela went to get his gun while his wife called the police. The terrorists, all members of the PLF wing of the PLO, raced down the street to the four-story apartment house at 61 Jabotinsky

Street where Smadar, Danny, Einat and Yael were fast asleep on the second floor. The terrorists ran to different apartments, throwing grenades and blowing open apartment doors. Roused by the blasts, Danny tried to help his family flee, but they had only seconds to escape. The terrorists burst into the apartment, seized Danny and his daughter Einat and searched for Danny's wife. As Danny pleaded with the guerrillas not to take his daughter, his wife hid in terror in an attic crawl space, holding two-year-old Yael as close as she could. While Smadar crouched in fear, she heard her screaming husband and daughter taken away by the terrorists. Panicked that Yael might cry out, Smadar held a cloth tight over her young child's mouth. Danny and Einat were taken out to the beach. As Israeli soldiers surrounded the guerrillas and opened fire, the terrorists murdered Danny and Einat. Only much later, after Smadar came out of hiding, did she realize she had smothered her baby to death.

Smadar Haran never broke down, never let the terrorists feel that they had won a psychological victory over her. Not long after the killings of her husband and two daughters she wrote a poem in her diary:

> *Sometimes, actually, I don't exist any more*
> *Because a mother exists for living children*
> *And I am a mother to dead ones.*
> *So, my daughters, forgive me if I call myself a mother here on*
>   *paper*
> *Because being a mother may have ceased*
> *But not a mother's love that could be this strong.*
> *Not mine.*[1]

W hile the Israeli army suffered defeat at Karameh, thirty-two Israeli families celebrated a victory in Hebron. At the entrance to the Arab city stood the small Park Hotel, and in its dining room the long seder table looked much like Passover tables everywhere in Israel in

April 1968. Glowing with lighted candles, gleaming with china and silver and cups of red wine, the table was laden with food and traditional symbols. On the traditional seder plate were three matzos, a reminder of the unleavened bread which the Jews baked in the desert after they fled from Egypt; the bitter herbs, a symbol of the bitterness of slavery; a lamb shank, a symbol of the sacrificial Paschal lamb in the Temple; a roasted egg, a reminder of the voluntary offerings Jews made in the Temple; charoses, the mixture of apples, nuts, cinammon and red wine that symbolized the mortar used by the Hebrew slaves in Egypt; a dish of salt water, a reminder of the tears shed by the slaves. In the center of the table stood an empty cup, saved for the prophet Elijah, a symbol of hope for the coming of God's kingdom on Earth.

If their table was typical, the celebrants certainly were not. The Jews who rejoiced at the seder in the Park Hotel had made their way to Hebron to help God's kingdom come. The sixty people, including Rabbi Moshe Levinger and his wife Miriam, Rabbi Haim Druckman, Rabbi Eliezer Waldman and a journalist, Israel Harel, had ventured to the Arab city, the site of the cave of Machpelah, so that they could carry out the second step in Rev Tzvi Yehuda Kook's plan to resettle the land of the Jews. God had shown His work, they believed, in the miracle of the Six-Day War. Now it was their turn to help Him. In direct opposition to the Israeli Labor government and its policy of noninterference with the Arabs, these Orthodox Jews announced they would celebrate Passover in the midst of Hebron, a city crammed with 70,000 extremely religious Arabs, a city already blackened by the massacre of its small Jewish community during the Arab riots in 1929.

But ignoring the pleas of Israeli officials to stay away, Levinger and one of his followers arrived at the local hotel, approached the Arab manager and rented the entire place, paying four Israeli pounds for each bed. It was agreed that the Jews could stay for at least ten days, and maybe more. In fact, they had brought along their furniture and belongings; the truck that pulled up to the hotel unloaded the bookcases, refrigerators and washing machines; one way or another, Hebron would become their home.[2]

The Orthodox activists proved a constant nuisance to the government. Even before they sat down to their Passover seder, they demanded weapons from the military governor of Hebron. Their forays into the center of the Arab city armed with the two Uzis and four rifles they received, their attempt to set up shop in the middle of Moslem holy sites, their constant friction with the local mayor, and their requests for government housing and military protection brought about heated debate in the Knesset. Nevertheless, the settlers, it seemed were carrying out part of the plan being drawn up by the Labor leaders. Deputy Prime Minister Yigal Allon, who even stopped by the Park Hotel to wish the settlers well,[3] proposed that the heavily populated Arab areas of the West Bank, like Nablus and Ramallah, be returned to King Hussein, and that corridors be constructed through Jericho and other points to join these cities to Jordan. The Israelis, in turn, would secure themselves by establishing agricultural and military settlements on the strategic sites along the Jordan River. The followers of Rev Kook would fit in with the Allon Plan if they settled in the hills of Upper Hebron, while the Arab city of Hebron would be left intact. Indeed, by 1970 the government approved the settlers' request, and agreed that a community, called Kiryat Arba, would be built in the hills above Hebron. But while the followers of Rev Kook and Rabbi Levinger fought to establish their presence on the land of the patriarchs, the followers of Fatah fought to get it back.

The victory at Karameh and the publicity it attracted in the Arab world brought swarms of volunteers to Fatah. Its ranks swelled: from a group of several hundred students it burst within months into an army of several thousand men. Its presence in Jordan could no longer be sloughed off by the king; in fact, it became a threat to his very existence on the throne. As Fatah grew in numbers, it also increased its activities across the border.

Early in the spring of 1968, Fatah commandos placed bombs at the rear entrance to a kibbutz factory near Natanya, not far from Tel Aviv. The explosion went off in the middle of the night and enraged the Israeli public. More bombs found in other manufacturing facilities, including dynamite in the Dodge automobile factory in Nazareth, did little to increase the Israelis' fondness for Fatah.

But the series of explosions in 1968 that really shook the Israeli public took place in the early evening on the main thoroughfares in downtown Jerusalem. As crowds of people walked along Ha Navim Street, "the street of the Prophets," rushing home from work or on their way to restaurants and movie theaters, a hand grenade, placed in a trash can, exploded. Police cars and ambulances arrived immediately at the scene and helped the wounded. Only a few minutes later, and only 150 meters away on King George Street, another trash can, booby-trapped with a hand grenade, blew up. As police and emergency vehicles rushed from the first scene to the second, a third hand grenade exploded 300 meters away. Twice more, grenades exploded in trash cans. Jerusalem was in a panic. Police and volunteers searched every street and every trash can. In a city with thousands of people on the streets and hundred of trash cans placed about, no one knew where to turn. Ordinary citizens stopped innocent Arabs walking by, cursed, spat, and even beat them while the real criminals got away.

Before the Israelis had a chance to recover, they were hit again. This time the guerrillas attacked the central bus station in Tel Aviv, the most crowded location in Israel. As tens of thousands of people rushed to the buses during noontime, hand grenades, timed to go off together, exploded all around the station. Pandemonium broke out as travelers scattered everywhere, but the police were able to catch three Arab teenagers as they hailed a taxi to Jerusalem. The young criminals, all from Hebron, confessed that they had placed the bombs in Tel Aviv and Jerusalem. Their leader, they told the police, was Abdel Rahim Jaber, a former sergeant in the Jordanian army who had signed up with George Habash's PFLP. Jaber, who had himself set a bomb in a water reservoir in the Negev, had recruited the teenagers, trained them with explosives, given them the hand grenades and sent them off with instructions. The search was on for Jaber, but several weeks passed before he was found. Israeli police discovered the guerrilla, wounded in a minefield, as he tried to escape across the desert near the Dead Sea. Jaber was arrested and imprisoned for life.

PFLP groups carried out a series of attacks on the Israelis. The Ramallah cell, led by a young lawyer, Bashir al-Hairi, recruited local students, including both men and women. In one operation, two young students entered the busy, American-style supermarket just across from the United States Consulate General's office, on Agron Street in Jerusalem. The young man and woman walked down the aisle containing coffee and placed a few bogus cans among the regular stock. After the students left the store, the cans exploded, killing at least one customer and injuring others.

Two other students from the same Ramallah PFLP cell strolled into the cafeteria of Hebrew University and sat down at a table, leaving their book bag on the floor. After the Arab students left the dining hall, the bag blew up, killing several young people and seriously wounding many more.

But if the PFLP was busy, so was Fatah. Among its sophisticated operations was one in which two porters left a discarded refrigerator on the sidewalk outside a building on a main street of downtown Jerusalem. When the refrigerator exploded, thirteen people were killed, including some Arabs. Fatah guerrillas also planted a bomb in a pile of watermelons in Haifa; hid dynamite on a bicycle left at the entrance to a coffee shop on bustling Ben-Yehuda Street in Jerusalem; placed bombs in bus stations and on buses throughout the country; put dynamite in movie theaters in Tel Aviv; and buried explosives in the sand at beach resorts.

Perhaps the most infamous attack was the early Hanukkah gift that Fatah gave the Israelis. On Friday morning, November 22, 1968, the busiest time of the week as Jews prepared for the Sabbath, Ahmad Hassan Zomorrod drove an old car toward Mahane Yehuda, the popular open market in Jerusalem. Throngs of shoppers jammed the stalls of produce, poultry, spices, falafel and other Middle Eastern foods as Zomorrod tried to thread his car through the narrow streets. Zomorrod's blue license plates, signifying that he lived in the West Bank, attracted the attention of an Israeli police-man, who stopped the car and told him he could not drive through the market; however, he could leave the vehicle at the entrance. The Arab followed orders, parked the car, and walked away. Minutes later, the automobile exploded: fifteen people were killed and dozens were injured. The incident enraged the Israelis and set off gangs of Jews who entered Arab neighborhoods crying "Revenge! Revenge!" Graffiti scrawled on the building around the city expressed the Israelis' fury: "Death to the Arabs" and "Death to the Terrorists."

In the course of catching most of the perpetrators of these crimes, the Israeli police discovered the Fatah commander of Jerusalem, Kamal Nammeri, the young man whose Jewish mother had married an Arab. Like him, all the terrorists were given life sentences and assigned to cells where they were separated by organization. The Israeli prisons proved to be a teaching facility for the Palestinians, a place where the fighters enlarged their nationalist conscience while they improved their education. Each cell chose its own commander, set up its own programs, provided school lessons, and even supervised the taking of high school and college examinations.

But if the prisoners organized themselves by fighter groups, and identified themselves as PFLP or Fatah or any other label, the Israeli public cared little. Through radio broadcasts and news reports, they had become familiar with one name, Abu Amar. The man who took credit for Karameh became the symbol of evil in Israeli eyes. The guerrillas' attempt to win back Palestine by frightening the Israelis only made the Jewish public more determined to keep it. They might be willing to discuss the Sinai with Egypt, the Golan with Syria, the West Bank with Jordan, but never would they give their land to these people who wanted all of Israel.

The guerrilla activity slowed down inside the country as Israeli police imprisoned more and more activists in the West Bank. But as the fighters slipped back across the river to Jordan, Fatah's commando raids grew in size and number, always bringing with them the Israeli retaliatory strikes. Israel's pleas to Hussein to put a halt to the incursions were of no effect: the high percentage of Palestinian Arabs within the ranks of the Jordanian army prevented the king from acting. Besides, the Jordanian citizenry was sympathetic to these Arabs who had defeated the Israelis at Karameh.

In February 1969, at a meeting of the Palestine National Council the parliament-in-exile of the PLO, the audacious Abu Amar, now known more formally as Yasser Arafat, and his popular Fatah, which had become the largest of the guerrilla groups, won control of the entire organization, replacing Ahmed Shukeiry and his short-term successor, Yiyuha Hamuda. With Arafat at the helm, the PLO renewed its fervor and strengthened its charter, completely negating the existence of Israel and denying Israel any future right to exist. That year, intent on wiping out the Jewish nation, Arafat's PLO carried out 2,432 attacks on Israel, three times the number of incidents in 1968, and more than twenty times the number carried out in 1967.

The Palestinian revolutionaries, in particular the Popular Front for the Liberation of Palestine (PFLP), led by George Habash, the Democratic Front for the Liberation of Palestine (DFLP) led by Nayaf Hawatmeh, and the PFLP-General Command led by Abu Nidal, all members of Arafat's umbrella organization, were determined to strike at Israelis everywhere. From their base in Jordan, which Golda Meir called "Fatahland," they began a series of infamous terrorist operations that culminated in a massive hijacking.

Not only Israelis, but the entire world watched in horror as the bombings became more barbarous and the hijackings more brazen. On September 6, 1970, PFLP terrorists seized four airplanes as they were flying over European skies. One attempt was foiled when passengers and crew of an El Al flight overcame the terrorists. But the other attempts were all successful. A Pan Am jumbo jet was hijacked just after it took off from Amsterdam on its way to New York. The plane was forced to land in Beirut; the 152 passengers were released, but the airliner was later blown up. A Swissair plane was seized just after takeoff from Zurich; a TWA jet was taken just after takeoff from Frankfurt, the last part of an around-the-world flight. The PFLP terrorists directed these planes to Jordan and forced them to land at Dawson's Field. Three days later, PFLP terrorists hijacked another wide-bodied jet, this one from BOAC and ordered it to land with the others in Jordan. More than 600 passengers were kept on the planes as hostages. Even after most of them were released the next day, sixteen Jewish passengers were held for one month.

The September seizures of the international airplanes were the last test of King Hussein's ability to rule. Palestinian guerrillas had taken such advantage of their popularity in Jordan that they had created their own gangster state within a state, complete with murders, extortion, corruption and assassination attempts. Hussein ordered the Jordanian army to wipe out the terrorists. As a result Syria threatened to invade Jordan and come to the aid of the Palestinians; Israeli aircraft raced in the direction of Damascus as a warning that if the Syrians helped the guerrillas, the Israelis would attack them. The bloody battles that followed between Hussein's forces and the Palestinians would end several months later with the deaths of some 3,000 fighters and the expulsion of the remaining Palestinian commandos from Jordan.

While Israel suffered continuous shellings on its Jordanian border until 1971, it endured on its Egyptian border what President Gamal Abdel Nasser called a "war of attrition." The exhausting, unrelenting struggle started after the Six-Day War when Israel destroyed the infrastructure and industry all along the Canal. Hitting hardest at the heavily populated Egyptian cities of Ismailia and Suez, the Israeli attacks caused the Egyptians to shut down the Suez Canal. Besides the destruction of his aircraft and the demoralization of his people, Nasser suffered hundreds of millions of dollars lost in tariffs from the closed canal. Almost immediately, Egypt began receiving expertise, arms and money from the Soviet government. The nearly 3.5 billion dollars in aid was enough to rebuild the Egyptian military within a year and a half. It took only a few months, however, before the Egyptians started firing once again; in October 1967 they shot missiles that sank an Israeli ship, the *Eilat*, killing forty-seven people. The Israelis retaliated, destroying two Egyptian oil refineries and oil storage tanks. Calm prevailed for several months until the Egyptians regrouped; by April 1968 they began commando raids and started shelling Israeli targets again. At times the low-level fighting heated up to the boiling point, particularly when Soviet-manned Egyptian aircraft fought Israeli airplanes in the skies. Other times it involved sporadic shelling, but the cost of the war was high, in both manpower and materiel.

The war of attrition continued until August 1970, when both Israel and Egypt agreed to a cease-fire. One month later Nasser died and a little-known officer, Anwar Sadat, took his place. But the cease-fire remained in existence. The catalyst was a peace plan offered by American Secretary of State William Rogers based on U.N. Resolution 242, which would have had Israel withdraw to its Egyptian and Jordanian borders, and allowed the return of Arab refugees. Israeli Prime Minister Golda Meir called Rogers "a very nice man" in her memoirs, but, she wrote, "he never really understood the background to the Arab wars against Israel."[4]

The essence of those wars was not the argument over borders between Israel and the Arab states, which Rogers hoped to resolve, but the very land that the Jewish state called its own and which the Palestinians wanted for themselves. No separate peace between Egypt and Israel, or Jordan and Israel, or Syria and Israel, or Lebanon and Israel would give back the land to the Arabs who had lived in Palestine before 1948. Arafat had to bring that to the attention of the world. The only method that seemed to make Americans and Europeans take notice was one that personally affected them. The only answer for some members of the PLO, like George Habash or Nayaf Hawatmeh, was to terrorize the world into action. To the Israelis, it made no difference if Habash's PFLP or Hawatmeh's DFLP carried out the attacks; they were all part of

Arafat's umbrella organization. Whether or not Arafat could control his extremists was irrelevant; the fact remained that he was supposed to be the leader and, as such, was responsible for their actions.

In 1971 Arafat's group began operations on an even broader international scale. In March of that year five Fatah members blew up fuel tanks in Rotterdam, causing one million dollars in damage. In February 1972 they blew up two gas installations in Holland and an electronics plant and an oil pipeline in Hamburg; the following summer they blew up oil installations in Trieste, Italy. During the summer of 1971 Fatah struck at Israelis abroad, exploding bombs in the Jewish National Fund's office in Rio de Janiero and attempting to blow up an El Al plane on its way from London to Tel Aviv by giving a booby-trapped suitcase to an unsuspecting Peruvian woman. But it was the following year that Fatah's own Black September fighters appalled the world. On September 5, 1972, the guerrillas, their faces wrapped behind *kafeeyahs*, seized the dormitories of the Israeli athletes participating in the Munich Olympics. In the bloody aftermath of the vicious hostage-taking, eleven Israeli athletes were killed.

Israeli leaders could hardly accept the notion of turning over their land to despotic terrorists like these, but they could try to negotiate their border with legitimate states like Egypt. With the help of Secretary Rogers, the Israelis and the Egyptians tried to come to some agreement. The discussions went on for three years, but no progress was made.

Anwar Sadat's frustration over the blockaded Suez Canal kept increasing until the summer of 1973 when he felt little choice but to prepare for war. By the fall his forces were ready. On October 6, 1973, while Israelis were in synagogue for Yom Kippur, the solemn Day of Atonement and the holiest day in the Jewish year, Egyptian and Syrian forces attacked Israel. The bombardment caught the Israeli government by surprise. Although the military quickly recovered, the Egyptian forces that had crossed into the Sinai and the Syrian forces that invaded the Golan proved to be strong combatants. The Israeli army pushed them back, but by the time a cease-fire was imposed on October 25, 1973, the Arabs had regained their stature. No longer did they feel impotent in the face of the Israeli military; and no longer did they feel compelled to reject negotiations with Israel; no longer did they feel weak in the world's eyes. The Yom Kippur War, which shook the Israeli government and shocked the

Israeli people, reshaped the thinking of the Arab states. The Arab world had also become empowered by its oil supplies. With the severe shortage of oil in the 1970s the Arab rulers hiked the price of petrol and announced they would not sell their scarce liquid to any pro-Israeli countries. The Arabs could now flex their muscles economically and militarily.

9

Peace with Egypt and War in Lebanon

AT A MEETING in Tunis, we ask Yasser Arafat if he would follow in the footsteps of his former friend, Anwar Sadat. Would he go to Jerusalem to meet with Israeli leaders? The PLO chairman turns livid.

"With Shamir?" he sneers. "Very difficult. Don't forget what happened with Sharon. What happened with the Likud party. Sabra and Shatila," he shouts. "They are my enemies!" Then, almost automatically, he adds, "And I am going to make peace with my enemies."

If a different Israeli leader, perhaps Yitzhak Rabin, invited Arafat to Jerusalem, would he go? "This is my capital," he persists. "Don't forget this is my homeland. I am not in need of his invitation. I would refuse the invitation to Jerusalem. Jerusalem is my capital. This is the point." And then, boasting of his endeavors in 1967, Arafat adds, "I don't need an invitation. I can go alone. I have done it four times by my own means."

Arafat need not worry; Yitzhak Shamir is hardly ready to extend an invitation. In fact, the Israeli insists that if the PLO leader showed up in Jerusalem, he would have Arafat arrested.

The seemingly intransigent positions of Arafat and Shamir almost mirror each other. The PLO leader creeps slowly toward the peace process, his head, as always, turned over his shoulder to watch the hard-line forces behind him. The prime minister crawls as well, looking back at his own right wing as he takes each step forward. Shamir and Arafat each fear their own extremists, but they both also bargain well. And their bazaar, after all, is in the Middle East.

Israeli architect David Cassuto likens Shamir's approach to buying a rug in the souk. "If you enter the shop and then walk right out," *says Cassuto, "the merchant comes running after you. 'Didn't you find anything?' he asks.*

"And you say, 'No, no, no. I don't want anything.'

"So the rug dealer says, 'Okay. But why don't you sit a moment and drink a cup of coffee?' And he immediately puts out ten carpets.

"And then you get up and walk out, and he says, 'No, no, no. Stay. You have to drink another cup of coffee.'

"And then after four cups of coffee and an hour of talking about everything except carpets, he says to you: 'You insult me. You don't find even one that is good for you.'

"Then you leave, and you come back another time. You point out a carpet that you do not want. And then, slowly, slowly, you come to the carpet you do want, and you pay the man a tenth of the price he asked. He is very happy, and you are very happy." But, Cassuto advises, "if you had the idea of saying in the beginning, 'I want this carpet,' he would have told you, 'No. Sorry. This is my mother's carpet. I don't want to give it to you.'"

Says the Italian-born Cassuto, "This is the mentality. We are in Israel and not in the West. We have to think like they think. Because we have to live here. So we have to buy pieces of things. If we say, 'We want this peace very much,' we never will get it. We have to say that we don't want anything; we want to live by ourselves. And then they start slowly, for a little while, to sell the idea of peace. And we have to buy it."[1]

The PLO presented its ideas for peace in Algiers in November 1988, stating that the organization renounced the use of terrorism "in any form." One month later in Geneva, Arafat offered another piece of peace when he accepted United Nations Resolutions 242 and

338, which call for all states in the region to have "secure and recognized" borders, and he recognized Israel's right to exist. Then, in May 1989, in a meeting with French Prime Minister François Mitterand, Arafat went further, declaring that the PLO convenant, the death warrant to Israel, had been superseded by recent events.

But Shamir refuses to accept Arafat's merchandise. "It isn't serious," he tells us. "His December statements don't exist. They aren't serious because I know them, and what they are saying among themselves, and what Arafat and Abu Iyad say. Abu Iyad says now that he never pledged to renounce armed struggle. What is armed struggle, and what is terrorism?" asks Shamir. "Is there a difference between the two? They have never attacked military targets. For them, a passenger of a bus is a military target."[2]

Much to the disappointment of the Israeli right wing, the United States, upon hearing the Palestinian organization's recognition of Israel and its acceptance of the U.N. resolutions, immediately began an official dialogue with the PLO in Tunis. But Shamir insists that the dialogue is detrimental to the peace process. He maintains that the talks weaken the position of the Palestinians living in the occupied territories.

Shamir says the dialogue indicates that for the Americans, the PLO people are the real representatives. So why should someone here risk his life and reputation?"

The risks for the Israelis to enter any kind of peace process, Shamir believes, are far greater than the risks for the Palestinians in the occupied territories. "We are taking risks," he says. "They are not taking any risks, because they will improve their situation. They will have self-government. They don't have it now. They will negotiate with us. They are not negotiating now. They will improve their fate. We will risk ours. They have a chance to improve their situation. We don't. We are struggling for peace."

Both Egypt and Israel paid dearly for peace after the war in October 1973. Israelis measured the cost in terms of humiliation and shame. The streets of Tel Aviv, Jerusalem and Haifa, marked by monuments to the Six-Day War, lack any memorials to those who fought in the Yom Kippur War, save for a cemetery filled with the dead. In the aftermath of the October surprise attacks, the Israeli government was discredited: shaken by its defeat, both Prime Minister Golda Meir and Defense Minister Moshe Dayan resigned in disgrace. The Israeli public was traumatized, overcome with despondence. "After the war I was so depressed, I couldn't go back to work," says Israeli journalist Danny Rubinstein. "There were demonstrations all over Israel, and I went to every one of them. The whole country was in anguish."[3]

While Israelis walked with their heads down, Egyptians strode proudly, their chins held high. President Sadat was quick to rename buildings and boulevards after the Sixth of October, and throughout Egypt tributes to the war still abound. The largest country in the Arab world could finally claim victory over Israel; Egypt had restored pride to the Moslem Middle East and given even the poorest Arabs reason to hope. But the cost of men and materiel was excessive: more than 10,000 Egyptian soldiers were dead and 8,000 taken prisoner; more than 650 tanks, 180 airplanes and 6 missile boats were destroyed.[4] Sadat had won his battle, but at great expense to his people. No longer was he willing to sacrifice his country for the sake of the Palestinians. Egypt was tired of fighting: from now on, the PLO could take care of itself.

After a cease-fire was called, both sides were invited to Washington; talks would start over troop withdrawals. Egyptian forces had crossed to the east bank of the Suez Canal, where 20,000 soldiers of the Third Army were now encircled by the Israelis, while Israeli troops, confronted by the Egyptians, were in control of territory from Ismalia to the city of Suez. Egyptian Foreign Minister Ismail Fahmy flew to Washington in November 1973 for meetings with Secretary of State Henry Kissinger. Within two days Israeli Prime Minister Golda Meir also arrived in the capital.

Tensions were high as the Americans mediated a settlement. The Egyptians refused to talk directly to the Israelis but demanded that the Jewish soldiers withdraw to the cease-fire lines set on October 22. The Israelis demanded direct talks with the Egyptians and a return of their prisoners before their troops moved back. In a private session with the Israeli leader, President Nixon tried to warm the icy atmosphere. He joked with Mrs. Meir that they had something in common; both Israel and the U.S. had a Jewish secretary of state: he had Kissinger, she had Abba Eban. "Yes," said Mrs. Meir dryly, "but mine speaks English without an accent."[5]

Egyptians and Israeli officials welcomed Kissinger's efforts; the secretary began an exhausting series of shuttles between the two states. In early 1974, as a result of Kissinger's persistence, the disengagement process began: the Israelis withdrew from half of the Sinai and later pulled their northern forces out of the Syrian city of Kuneitra.

While Israel took steps towards peace with her neighbors, Yasser Arafat and the PLO continued to make their own kind of war. Now based in the refugee camps of Lebanon, the PLO leaders planned a new strategy for commando raids across the Israeli border. On April 11, 1974, a suicide squad recruited by George Habash's PFLP raided the Israeli village of Kiryat Shmonah and attacked a high school, planning to take the teen-age students hostage. But the terrorists found an empty building, and in their frustration threw hand grenades at a nearby apartment house and opened fire on the Israeli residents, killing eight children and eight adults.

One month later, the PLO struck again, this time in the new immigrants' town of Ma'alot. Equipped with Kalashnikovs and five bags of explosives, three DFLP terrorists took 100 Israeli children hostage and announced they would kill the youngsters unless Israeli officials released twenty Palestinian prisoners. After agonizing over the blackmail, the Israeli government agreed to the exchange, but would not succumb to the guerrillas' demands that the Palestinian prisoners be sent to Damascus before the children were freed. In an effort to save the students, Israeli forces stormed the building. In the bloody struggle that followed, sixteen children were massacred by the Palestinian guerrillas and sixty-eight more were wounded.

As Israelis grieved over the deaths at Kiryat Shmonah and Ma'alot, the government continued its peace plans. The next move, it seemed, would be an agreement with King Hussein in which Israel would be guaranteed her security and Jordan would regain a hold in the West Bank. But Yasser Arafat was quick to short-circuit any such steps.

At a meeting of the Palestine National Congress in the summer of 1974, Arafat preempted Hussein's possible gains in the West Bank by dramatically shifting his position: no longer would the PLO aim to take over all of Israel, at least not at once; now, Arafat announced, his people would accept any "liberated" part of Palestine, meaning, of course, the West Bank as well as Gaza. Arafat's turnaround was seen by Syrian-backed Palestinian hard-liners like George Habash and Ahmed Jabril as a traitorous act. Their response was to withdraw from the PLO and to form a Rejection Front.

Only a few months later, at an Arab Summit in Rabat, Morocco, in October 1974, the Arab rulers, depleted from the wars they had fought against the Israelis, convinced King Hussein that the reins of Palestinian leadership should be handed over to Yasser Arafat. The man who had been crushed by the king in Black September had come out on top. It was announced that the PLO, with Arafat as its chairman, would become "the sole and legitimate representative" of the Palestinian people.

The PLO's newly won status gave it legitimacy in the international arena. Arafat's willingness to accept part of Palestine, and by implication a two-state solution, was seen by many as a step towards moderation. But the Israelis wanted more assurances: they asked that Arafat explicitly recognize Israeli's right to exist and acknowledge that its security must be guaranteed. Israel's requests fell on deaf ears.

To the dismay of Israelis, within days of the Rabat Summit, Arafat was invited to address a special session of the United Nations in New York. Israeli television viewers, their eyes still filled with the tears of Ma'alot, watched in horror as the picture of Arafat loomed across their screens. They thought him ludicrously dressed in his pseudo-military uniform, almost comic with his *kafeeyah,* the guerrilla leader brazenly boasting a holster on one hip and an olive branch on the other. To the Israelis, his demands for a "stolen Palestine" were outrageous; his assertions that his Palestinian state would be secular and democratic were ridiculous; his acceptance only days before in Rabat of "liberated" areas of Palestine was hypocrisy. This man who was held responsible for so much torment in Israel could hardly claim to be a legitimate partner for peace.

Arafat had no credibility with Israel, but there were other potential partners for peace. The Jewish state strove to realign its borders in an effort to coexist with its legitimate Arab neighbors. Yet the closer it came to an exchange of land for peace, the further the Israeli hard-liners pushed their own demands that Israel not give up an inch of soil. The increasing numbers of West Bank settlers who supported Menachem Begin and the Likud coalition considered the Labor Party's proposals of territory for peace to be perfidious.

Indeed, the very rumor that territory might be given back served as a catalyst to Gush Emunim. The extreme right-wing activists of Gush Emunim organized new communities wherever they suspected Israeli sovereignty might be lost. Settlements such as Maleh Admumin were built along the corridor from Jericho to Ramallah, confirming the territory as Israeli. Explains Rabbi David Shisgal of Hebron: "Our presence makes it Jewish. The more Jewish presence there is, the more Jewish it will be."[6]

Israel Harel and his wife were typical of those who put down roots on Arab soil. The journalist and the teacher gave up their jobs in the city and moved with their four children from a comfortable apartment near Tel Aviv to a cramped trailer in the West Bank settlement of Ofra. "Our entire life changed," says Harel, who rarely travels in Israel without wearing his knitted *kippa* upon his head or carrying his machine gun on his shoulder. "I must confess, maybe the standard is lower, but the spirit is much higher ... we felt that wecontinue that path of the first pioneers, the founding fathers.... We are the pioneers of today."[7]

Now a leader of the 70,000 Israelis who joined the settlers movement, Harel believes the move was essential. "For strategic, religious and national reasons, we felt that something has to be done to retain the area of Judea and Samaria." Harel's village of Ofra, he says, was built on a former Jordanian army camp. The neat rows of white and brown houses sit on a hilltop between the Jordan River and the Mediterranean Sea, an important site near Hebron that acts as a backup for the Israeli army. Like all border settlements, the defense units serve as a delaying tactic against possible Arab attack, and its reserve soldiers are well-trained combatants. "This is the main strategic buffer which defends the entire coastal area, the Tel Aviv area. It's not more than thirty miles," says Harel. "But that's all the weight of Israel." While the settlers protected the West Bank, they could point to the continuing PLO commando raids across the Lebanese border as proof that a Palestinian entity would be Israel's death knell.

By the spring of 1977 the right wing had won enough votes to elect Menachem Begin as prime minister. The man whom David Ben-Gurion had called "a fanatic, fascist and dangerous demagogue" would now lead the country. To underscore Likud's ideology of no territorial concession, the coalition soon granted money, housing and military protection for the settlers. Over the course of the next seven years the government would allot one billion dollars to the settlers in the West Bank and Gaza.

To the settlers, the Arabs in the area were merely inhabitants, individual farmers and workers who could stay in their villages as long as they accepted Israeli sovereignty. What the Palestinian Arabs were not, the settlers made clear, was a separate nation like the Jews. "They are part of the greater Arab nation," maintains Harel. "They speak the same language, belong to the same race and the same culture, practice the same religion. There is no difference whatsoever between the Arab who lives next to me here in Ramallah, and the Arab who lives in Cairo, and the one who lives in Baghdad, or Damascus, or Beirut." As Golda Meir had said, there was no such thing as Palestinians: there were only Palestinian Arabs just as there were Palestinian Jews.

The Arabs, increasingly under the thumb of the settlers, continued to lose more land and more water to the Jews; nevertheless, they earned substantial wages as laborers, ironically, helping to construct the houses, schools and stores in the new Jewish communities. In the beginning, says Harel, "we had many contacts, but then the PLO moved in. They threatened those who talked to us and visited us. The Arabs were frightened. They had to disconnect their relations." Harel recalls that some Arabs, and one young boy in particular, would make secret friendly visits to Ofra at night. "He used to come over here, but we couldn't come to them because we endangered them." Two Arabs in a nearby village, he says, were murdered when the PLO suspected them of selling some uncultivated land to the Jews.

While more moderate Israelis shuddered at Menachem Begin's hard-line approach, Egypt's President Sadat surprised them. In a move that astounded the world, the man whose country had been at war with Israel for almost thirty years offered to journey to Jerusalem to meet with Israeli leaders. In November 1977 Anwar Sadat stood before the members of the Knesset, his dark skin and high cheekbones gleaming in the cameras' lights, his well-tailored suit cutting an elegant figure before the nation of pioneers. He made gracious reference to his former enemies Golda Meir and Moshe Dayan and spoke eloquently to the entire Israeli public; here was an Arab leader clearly willing to coexist.

Israelis were ebullient, exhilarated by the possibility of peace with the most powerful country in the Arab world. To them, the Camp David Accords which followed Sadat's initiative established Israel and Egypt as equal partners. The fate of the Palestinians would be decided by Israel and Egypt along with King Hussein of Jordan; Hussein, the Israelis felt, was the only legitimate leader of the Palestinian movement.

Since border disputes could be resolved, it became apparent that the hostility between Israel and its Arab neighbors could be mitigated. Israel and Egypt had signed a peace treaty. The battle was primarily ended between the Jewish state and the Arab states. The only real enemy was Arafat and the PLO. The focus of the conflict had shifted from international borders to the struggle between two communities living on the same land. As Meron Benvenisti, an Israeli expert on Arab affairs explained, instead of being a war between Jerusalem and Cairo, or Jerusalem and Damascus, it had become a war between Jerusalem and Jerusalem.

The Israeli government was willing to give the Arab inhabitants of the occupied territories limited autonomy, and to accept certain rights of the Arabs living on the land, but they refused to accept the notion that these individuals composed a Palestinian nation. Arafat and his people demanded the impossible, a state of their own on the very land that was Eretz Yisrael.

If most Israelis rejoiced over Camp David, two groups of people did not. In a protest of the peace efforts, a small band of fanatic settlers, followers of Rabbi Moshe Levinger, plotted to seize and destroy the Moslems' holiest site in Jerusalem, the Dome of the Rock. At the same time, Arab West Bank activists organized a National Guidance Committee, also with the purpose to undermine the Camp David Accords. The protests and demonstrations led by the Guidance Committee turned violent when its followers murdered six Jewish students in Hebron. Members of the Gush Emunim responded by bombing the cars of three Arab leaders. The explosions mutilated Bassam Shaka'a, the mayor of Nablus, who lost both his legs, and crippled Karim Khalaf, the mayor of Ramallah; a third mayor escaped unharmed. But if the Gush activists seemed brutal to many Israelis, others, like Agricultural Minister Ariel Sharon, saw them as champions of Israel. Under his aegis, settlements seemed to sprout overnight; by 1984, 113 settlements had been built throughout the West Bank.

While small groups of Israelis and Arabs fought each other in the

West Bank, bands of Palestinian guerrillas continued commando operations across the Lebanese border. The unrelenting PLO attacks pounding on small Israeli villages and kibbutzim only served as proof to the Likud government that Arafat was intolerable. A cease-fire arranged by American envoy Philip Habib lasted less than a year.

By the summer of 1982, Ariel Sharon, then the Israeli defense minister, pursued his plan to eliminate the PLO from Lebanon and, he hoped, from the world. On June 6, 1982, Israel began a large-scale, three-front invasion of Lebanon: along the Mediterranean coast, through the central mountains, and near the Lebanese border with Syria. Operation "Peace for Galilee" proved far more difficult than expected when Syrian aircraft and ground forces went into full action against the Israelis. The fighting increased as Israeli troops inched their way towards Beirut. For almost two months Sharon's forces bombarded the city, until the middle of August, when, under pressure from the United States, Israel, Syria and Lebanon, Arafat agreed to withdraw his men from Beirut. In the plan that followed, 14,000 PLO fighters, each carrying a weapon, left Lebanon. But more than 10,000 Palestinian guerrillas, in Syrian-held territory, were allowed to stay. It was only a few months before Arafat returned to Lebanon to fight his Palestinian opponents in Tripoli. But Fatah could not match the Syrian-backed guerrillas. Once again, Arafat left Lebanon in defeat.

The battle that the Israelis had fought on Lebanese turf and in Lebanese skies brought reprobation from the rest of the world. The massacres that followed, by Christian Lebanese forces against the Palestinians in the refugee camps of Sabra and Shatila, brought cries of outrage both overseas and at home. The Israelis had waged a bloody battle against the Palestinians on someone else's soil, but the struggle itself was the same: a fight over the land of Israel. Sharon's pursuit of Arafat and the PLO was in itself a recognition of their existence, and by extension, an implicit understanding that they had to be Israel's partner for peace.

Nevertheless, the Likud leaders refused to deal with the Palestinian issue or with the question of sovereignty over the occupied territories. Arafat's attempts in 1985 to assert himself as part of a negotiating team with Jordan led to a dead end when Israeli officials insisted that they determine which Palestinians would be allowed to sit down at the table. The Israeli leaders could smile smugly with righteousness when King Hussein, furious over Arafat's intransigence, shut the offices of the PLO and expelled the PLO leaders from Amman in early 1986. Likud leaders, however, also refused to deal with Hussein: at a meeting in London in April 1986, Israeli Prime Minister Shimon Peres reached an agreement with the king, but the proposal was rejected by the Cabinet shortly before Yitzhak Shamir took over the rotating government two months later.

The deadlocked talks and Arafat's inability to galvanize any movement towards a two-state solution led the Arabs in the West Bank and Gaza to take action. Frustrated Palestinians living in the refugee camps of Balata and Jabalya threw rocks at Israeli soldiers and burned tires in the road to block their military vehicles. By 1987 the activity had taken on a fervor; on December 9, 1987, following the murder of an Israeli plastics salesman in Gaza and the killing of several Arabs in revenge, the Palestinian uprising began. If the *intifada* was meant to capture the world's attention, it succeeded: night after night for almost a year, television viewers from Atlanta to Zurich watched newly videotaped scenes of the struggle between David and Goliath.

No longer could Israel fight its enemy by traditional means; it could retaliate only with its hands tied. No swift military actions could be taken to stop the uprising. The women and children who stood in the streets to burn tires and throw rocks at soldiers, or who hid behind barricades while stoning the cars of settlers, could not be answered with rockets or missiles or even hand grenades; even rubber bullets were not allowed. If the *intifada* was aimed at catching the attention of Israeli leaders, it certainly succeeded.

10

Skirting the PLO: West Bank Dialogue

ON MAY 14, 1989, *in Jerusalem, the Israelis presented their peace initiative calling for "the continuation of the peace process; the termination of the state of war with the Arab states; a solution for the Arabs of Judea, Samaria and the Gaza district; peace with Jordan; and a resolution of the problem of the residents of the refugee camps in Judea, Samaria and the Gaza district." The document, "based on the Camp David Accords," states that "Israel proposes free and democratic elections among the Palestinian Arab inhabitants" of the occupied territories.*

"Inhabitants?" scoffs Yasser Arafat in Tunis. "We are inhabitants?" he asks angrily, pointing out some prominent Palestinians living in the West Bank. "Faisal Husseini is an inhabitant? Radwan Abu Ayash is an inhabitant? They are Palestinians! Shamir is saying he wants to make peace with Jordan. What he is saying is that he wants to make peace with whom? With the Palestinians? He said

166

with the inhabitants of Judea and Samaria. He didn't mention the Palestinians. I am not an idiot."

From his office in Jerusalem, Shamir responds to us: *"We are not going to solve all the problems of the so-called 'Palestinian people.' The purpose of negotiations is to solve the conflict about these territories."*[1]

Arafat's eyes are ablaze, his lips curled into a snarl, his back straightened to a ramrod: *"Why have negotiations? For what? Elections? For what?"* he demands. Then, his voice calmer, he tells us that he will accept elections, but only *"as a step in the peace process that will lead to the end of occupation. If a commitment and guarantee is given for that, all things will be negotiable."*

"We will never accept it," answers Shamir when we repeat his enemy's words. *"Because for us it is not occupation. We are ready to negotiate about the way we can exist and live together."*

Arafat responds angrily: *"To negotiate what? Give me a full A to Z proposal. And the election is I, or P, or B, or S, or C, or E."*

We ask if he will only participate if a state is guaranteed, and Arafat is quick to counter: *"No. Not a state. From A to Zed."* *"But what is Zed?"* we ask. *"Withdrawal,"* he answers. *"Israeli withdrawal. End of occupation. As President Bush said, end of Israeli occupation. According to 242."*

"I have a different interpretation," Shamir says with a shrug. *"In 242 it was said that Israel would have to withdraw from territories, not from 'the'territories. I say that by our withdrawal from Sinai, we have completed it."*

Says Arafat, *"In Camp David there was withdrawal from Sinai. I am speaking about withdrawal as has been accepted by the whole international community."*

In Camp David, Shamir insists, *"it was never mentioned about any withdrawal except from Sinai. But not from Judea, Samaria and Gaza. It was never said. What does it mean, an 'Israeli withdrawal'? The meaning of it will be a Palestinian state, an Arab state."* In Camp David, he maintains, *"It was said that the Palestinian Arabs living in the territories would participate in determination of their future. What does it mean 'participate'? It means together with us. It means a permanent solution will be accepted by us and them. There are many differences among us, but we have to negotiate until we find a common ground."*

Says Arafat, "I would like to ask Shamir, on what basis is he going to hold the elections?"

"What you are asking is a detail," answers Shamir. "I am not closing any door. What we want now is to talk about the principles of our plan. We have our proposals. We have launched a plan. Let us discuss the plan."

But Arafat insists there must be withdrawal. And then, he adds, the solution will come "according to what the negotiations will decide— a kingdom, a republic, a confederation with Jordan. Can they accept confederation with Israel? I would like it. One state. One government."

Says Arafat defiantly, "We will have peace despite the stupidity of some Israeli leaders."

I n late 1973, two months after Egypt had stunned Israel in the October Yom Kippur war, Prime Minister Golda Meir ordered a top-secret study made of Israel's options in the West Bank and Gaza. The Jewish state had been reminded by the United Nations, meeting that December in Geneva, that the "land-for-peace" principle of Security Council Resolution 242 remained the bedrock for a comprehensive settlement of the Arab-Israeli conflict. The indefatigable Golda, exhausted from the internal strains over the October war and sensing that she was nearing the end of her career, knew it would not be long before Henry Kissinger concluded his peripatetic shuttle efforts to secure a list of Israeli POWs in Syria and would turn his attention to the West Bank and Gaza, the 2,200-square-mile territories that Israel had occupied since the Six-Day War in 1967.

Then, as now, Israel needed a strategy to avoid the mounting pressure for an international conference, fearing such a U.N. conclave would give the Soviet Union and its Arab allies a prominent role in imposing a settlement. The December elections in Israel brought home another reality: even though the Ma'arach, the

Yasser Arafat (center) at age 13 in Cairo. (Courtesy Munib al-Masri)

Arafat in front of his mother's family home in Jerusalem, circa 1941. After the death of his mother, the four-year-old Arafat was sent to live with her family, the Abu Sauds, and stayed in Jerusalem until 1942 when he was called back to Cairo by his father. (Courtesy Munib al-Masri)

For two years, beginning at the age of 16, as he is pictured here, Arafat worked for Haj Amin al-Husseini and his covert organization, helping to buy weapons to fight the Jews in Palestine. (Courtesy Munib al-Masri)

Sheik Hassan Abu Saud, Arafat's mother's cousin, helped raise Arafat and introduced him to his mentor, Haj Amin al-Husseini, who was the spiritual father of the Palestinian nationalist movement. (Courtesy Ruhab Khatib)

Arafat in 1949, when he was an engineering student at the University of Cairo. Arafat spent much of the time during his student days in underground movements against the British and the Jews. (Courtesy Munib al-Masri)

After the Six-Day War in June 1967, the Israelis razed the Arab buildings in front of Jerusalem's Western Wall—the Abu Saud family compound, pictured here, was bulldozed in 1968. (Courtesy Ruhab Khatib)

As the leader of the General Union of Palestinian Students (GUPS) in Egypt, Arafat was invited to attend a Socialist International meeting of students in Prague in 1955. To travel there, Arafat (far left) and his companions stowed away on a cargo ship to Greece. (Courtesy Munib al-Masri)

Arafat and his colleagues invited Hani al-Hassan (on far left) to merge his large European wing of GUPS with Fatah, which he did in 1963, giving Fatah the manpower it never had before. (Courtesy Munib al-Masri)

Meeting with Egyptian President Gamal Abdel Nasser in November 1969. Nasser was an important role model for Arafat. (UPI/Bettmann Newsphotos)

A gathering of colleagues in the early 1970s. Farouk Kaddoumi (second from left) has consistently been a Fatah hard-liner who was used as a frequent envoy to the Soviet Union. (Mimmo Frassineti—A.G.F./Il Venerdì di Repubblica)

Arafat addressed the United Nations General Assembly on November 13, 1974, carrying an olive branch but also wearing a holster (without a gun) to remind the world that he considered armed struggle a legitimate form of resistance. In his speech, Arafat urged the creation of a single state to replace Israel in which Moslems, Jews and Christians could live together in peace. (UPI./Bettmann Newsphotos)

Arafat with Soviet Foreign Minister Andrei Gromyko after Arafat appeared before the U.N. General Assembly in New York. Only a few weeks earlier the Arab states had declared the PLO the sole legitimate representative of the Palestinian people. (Courtesy Bassam Abu Sharif)

Two revolutionary leaders: Yasser Arafat meets with Cuba's Fidel Castro. (Mimmo Frassineti—A.G.F./Il Venerdì di Repubblica)

Arafat on a diplomatic visit in Africa. (Mimmo Frassineti—A.G.F./Il Venerdì di Repubblica)

His head shaved and wearing the ihram, Arafat makes the pilgrimage to Mecca. "I am a good Moslem," he has said in interviews. (Mimmo Frassineti—A.G.F./Il Venerdì di Repubblica)

coalition headed by the Labor Party, emerged as the leading bloc, the opposition had suddenly become powerful because the entire right wing had combined into a bloc of its own.

Although a new Labor-led coalition under Yitzhak Rabin was formed in the spring of 1974, Golda wanted to leave office in June confident that a consensus existed among all of Israel's major parties over policy towards the Palestinian-inhabited lands west of the Jordan River. Israel was committed under Resolution 242 to returning the bulk of the territories to Jordan in exchange for a peace treaty, but Israelis were divided about the shape of a settlement and the road map for achieving it. She did not complete the task, but Rabin agreed on the urgent need for such guidelines. A committee was formed of the top Israeli military, civilian and intelligence officials. It stretched across the political spectrum. In addition to Labor Party leader Yitzhak Rabin, the members included the late Moshe Dayan, Yigal Allon and Herut leader Menachem Begin. There were also representatives from the Mossad, the Israeli CIA; the Shin Bet, the Israeli FBI; a special research and intelligence unit in the Ministry of Foreign Affairs; and senior military commanders. Each was asked to prescribe minimum security requirements in the event of, one, total annexation by Israel; two, return of the territories, or most of them, to Jordan; and three, the establishment of a separate Palestinian state in the West Bank and Gaza.

Although much has changed since 1974, particularly in the wake of Iraq's invasion of Kuwait, the Israeli government's perception of its security needs has remained essentially the same. Despite their deep ideological difference, there is general agreement between Labor and Likud over the nation's basic requirements for maintaining its national security. A senior Israeli government official who participated in the secret study says: "The most fascinating element that came out of these recommendations, which is even more true today than it was then, is that no matter what model of settlement you adopt, it is clear to all agencies that we have to have access to the territories: our security people have to be able to go in, independent of whatever authority exists there, to apprehend and to question anyone suspected of mounting terrorist activities against Israel, and also to bring them out and hold them in a place which is not under the control of whatever authority will exist in these territories." This, he says, "is what they considered the absolute minimum to enable us to maintain our security in case there will be a situation where, in spite of peace between us and that entity, whatever it may be, there are dangers that the population itself, or under incitement and support from outside, will mount activities that are detrimental to our security. The Palestinians will have to understand that they cannot expect any government in Israel to permit the return of something akin to what we had prior to 1967; that they will establish themselves again, that we will be behind the borders, and then, if any kind of enmity develops, they will be able to indulge in the kind of activities they had in the past."[2]

The official lists a second prerequisite for any settlement. "It is agreed by all the major parties that there will not be a return to the barriers, to the borders that separated us physically from the Palestinian Arabs and that, in the context of peace, we will need much more than the kind of 'cold peace' we have with Egypt." There must be open borders, he says, between Israel and the Palestinian entity and also between that entity and Jordan, noting that close to 150,000 Palestinians earn their livelihoods in Israel, and that all three—Jordan, Israel and whatever Palestinian entity emerges—would be natural trading partners. Finally, the official lists a third principle that he says unites all Israelis: that the Jewish state, for reasons of both security and coexistence, "retain a potential for a continued Israeli presence" in settlements in the West Bank.

Provided these three conditions are satisfied, Israeli leaders, still appear willing to consider a plan for a three-way confederation linking Israel and Jordan with a new Palestinian entity that would have limited self-goverment. The roots of Israeli thinking go back more than a decade to still-undisclosed private talks held between former Prime Minister Begin and Egyptian President Anwar Sadat. "They were near the signing of the peace treaty and were faced with a dilemma: What to do about the Palestinian problem, what to do about the claims for national sovereignty on this land?" recalls Yitzhak Shamir.

Because the issue was irreconcilable, Begin and Sadat agreed to postpone the controversy over the competing claims. Camp David proposed a plan for five years of Palestinian autonomy during which Israel would maintain its control in the occupied territories. By the end of the third year, talks were to start with a delegation of Jordanian officials and elected Palestinians to determine the "final status" of the 2,200 square miles of territory.

What was kept secret was that the private talks between Begin and Sadat had actually gone further. The two leaders had lengthy discussions, "without putting them on paper," about the possible shape of a final settlement, says Shamir.

The search for a new formula has led Israeli policymakers to examine the past in an effort to come up with something that stretches the limits of Camp David without creating the embryo of a new, separate state. "We have to design it in such a way that it gives maximum self-expression, but at the same time doesn't enable them to declare they are independent or do something which may harm our interests," says Shamir's close aide Yossi Ben-Aharon. He adds, "there has to be a whole system of checks and balances."

The plan would take effect only once the uprising is calmed. Then Israel's defense forces would be withdrawn from Arab towns and villages and redeployed within secure perimeters. Elections would be held to choose indigenous Palestinian leaders. Israel also appears willing to begin negotiations about the "final status" of the territories as soon as Palestinian self-rule is introduced. The Palestinians would not be precluded from demanding sovereignty or their own state, nor would Israel be precluded from demanding the right to annex Judea and Samaria. Lastly, the transition period before a final settlement is negotiated could be reduced from five years to three or even less, Ben-Aharon suggests.

In this triple-tiered confederal design, Palestinians would elect their own mayors and other officials to seven municipal councils and six smaller local bodies whose powers would include the right to expropriate public lands and issue deeds.

On a second level, Palestinians would elect representatives from the territories to the legislature in Amman, creating a federation between the Palestinian entity and Jordan. The Israelis concede that the bulk of the taxes raised in the territories would have to go to Amman to the new federal structure.

Most important, Palestinians also would choose leaders to represent them at a third level, in a new confederation body with Israel and Jordan. "They would represent the entire territory," explains the official. The seat of the new administration—like that of the Israeli government—might be in Jerusalem, where together with the elected Palestinians on the council there would be appointed representatives of Israel and Jordan.

The three-way confederation, if that were the product of a final compromise, would derive its constitutional authority not from Israel or Jordan or the Palestinians, but from the agreement among all three, making that newly formed body the sovereign entity in the territories. "That's the higher umbrella," says the official, and "the trickiest and most sensitive" part: Israel would be required to cede some sovereignty to create the confederation. Each of the three parties also would have veto power over major decisions, including the allocation of valuable water resources and the establishment of new Israeli settlements in the West Bank.

The confederation would benefit all sides economically. Its currency would be tied to both the Israeli and the Jordanian monetary systems, and its trade arrangements would be similar to those of the European Common Market or the Benelux. The Israelis would be given access to the huge markets of the Arab world while the Arabs would be allowed free use of the Israeli ports on the Mediterranean Sea.

The critical aspect of national identity could be solved by giving citizenship to those who live in the confederation. Although the Israelis refuse to accept a broad right of return, they might accept the notion that every Palestinian could hold a national passport. While Jews living in the confederation could still be citizens of Israel, Arabs living inside Israel could be citizens of Palestine and both would be considered to be living on their homeland.

At the heart of this plan is the conviction that King Hussein must ultimately be brought back to play a central role. For an interim period, Jordan would be primarily responsible for the defense and foreign affairs of the new entity. "I cannot expect Hussein to sign away Arab territory," says the official. "Therefore, I have to design something which we can live with and which will enable him to say to his brother Arabs, 'I did not betray the trust that you gave me.'"

Shimon Peres, the Labor leader who has probably met with Hussein more than any other Israeli, is convinced there also must be some form of Palestinian-Jordanian linkage. "In order to solve the Palestinian problem, we must ask ourselves, 'Where are the Palestinians?' Half of them are in Jordan. Half of them are around Israel. I would like to see one solution for one problem because if we shall have two solutions, two stages—one Jordanian, the other Palestinian—then we shall have competition. You shall have two states; you will have two armies. You have two armies, you shall again have another war. We want one solution, a serious one, a permanent one.

We as Israelis, and shall I say we as Jews, do not want to become a dominating nation. It is against our moral foundations, and I am still convinced that we can talk with Hussein and the Palestinians in the West Bank and find a solution."[3]

Before the plan can become a reality, Israeli leaders recognize they must have a negotiating partner among the Palestinians in the West Bank and Gaza. Therefore, they are deliberately calling on local Palestinian activists to play a more prominent political role. "The test for starting a political process lies in finding a partner among the residents of the territories," says Yitzhak Rabin.[4] Even the hard-line Shamir has met more than fifty times with influential West Bank leaders including several rendezvous in the privacy of his home. It is well understood by Israeli officials that the Palestinians send reports of these conversations to Arafat.

"I have met some of these people among the Palestinian leadership here," admits Shamir. "I think they are more intelligent than the people in Tunis. They understand better the situation here, and they feel better the situation here than the people in Tunis. They feel better the extent of the demands they can put, if they want to be realistic, because they are here under the pressure of the events."

The Palestinians insist otherwise. "Without Arafat, we are nothing," says Radwan Abu Ayash, the head of the Arab Journalists Association.[5] One of the leading activists in the West Bank and Gaza, he adds, "Arafat is viewed in the occupied territories as the Palestinian revolution, the leader of the Palestinian revolution. We can abbreviate the Palestinian revolution with his personality. I don't mean that the sacrifices, the heroes, the patriots are nothing. No. I mean that Arafat as such represents all that." The young West Bank activists, says Abu Ayash, would not have had their long uprising if Arafat and the PLO had not planned it.

While Likud leaders maintain that Arafat cannot be included, and the West Bankers state that he cannot be excluded, both sides are proceeding with the dialogue to create a new reality. The Israelis are ignoring the obvious PLO ties of West Bank leaders, and the leaders themselves are boosting their own credibility. Labor leaders are going one step further, meeting with PLO envoys in Paris, Rome, Vienna and other European capitals. At those meetings both sides have exchanged detailed plans for the possible shape of a final settlement. Arafat contends that even Shamir was regularly briefed by Rabin about the secret talks. "Although he's trying to hide his head like an ostrich, Shamir is having a dialogue with us." Labor party emissaries have even proposed a two-stage process that would lead towards Palestinian self-determination. "I will reveal one thing," says Arafat proudly. "The Israelis are talking about two stages: the first stage is the 'self-administration' or autonomy; and after that, semi-independence." Asked for his reaction, Arafat answers, "Well, independence is good, so semi-independence is half-way."

For Likud ideologues, the PLO can never play a role in resolving the Palestinian dilemma. Shamir's contempt for the PLO leaders in Tunis only strengthens his conviction that the Arabs in the West Bank and Gaza should be responsible for determining their own fate. The PLO leaders, he claims, have no sensitivity to the difficulty of life under occupation. "If you come to them and tell them that today ten Palestinians have been killed, it doesn't move them." He compares the PLO leaders with Syrian President Hafez al-Assad. "Assad could permit himself to kill 20,000 people of Hama. It is not important for him. It is nothing for them. For them, human life, and Arab life included, doesn't mean anything."

The discussion evokes a memory for the former guerrilla fighter. "I know it from personal experience. When I was in the British prison in Palestine, the majority of the policemen were Arabs. I sometimes shared my cell with Arab prisoners, and I saw it. They respected me more than their brothers. For an Arab policeman to beat an Arab prisoner was a pleasure, a sadistic pleasure! They never dared to do it to me, despite the fact that I was a prisoner and he was the policeman. It is just like that. You cannot change a character of a people."

The Israelis, he argues, are very different. His portrayal of the Jews underscores the enormous gulf of understanding that still needs to be bridged. For many Israelis, the Jews have an exclusive claim on suffering which blinds them to the pain of the Palestinians. "When we speak in Jerusalem about what our people feel in Hebron, or other parts of the country, or even about any Jewish people in the most distant point in the world, we feel it like they feel it," says Shamir. "For us, it is a great experience. We are moved by it. We cannot continue our daily life. Normally, for us it makes a great difference. It is not so with the Arabs. They do not feel themselves these difficulties. They are quite indifferent. They don't share the suffering, the hunger, and the sorrow of these people here. They don't take care of it. For the PLO, the life of the Palestinians here is not important."

Radwan Abu Ayash resists Israeli efforts to drive a wedge between Palestinians in the territories who are sacrificing their lives and the PLO leadership in Tunis. He sees the *intifada* as "a continuation of the resistance. There wouldn't have been an *intifada* if the possibilities hadn't been laid out." It was Abu Jihad, he says, who "designed, devoted his work to the occupied territories." He admits that the PLO was taken by surprise when the uprising began. "When the *intifada* came out, it was internal for the first three or four days. But unless the PLO had mobilized the people, in terms of reality on the ground, it would have been a phenomenon for a few days, and then it would have been finished." The massive, spontaneous resistance, he adds, had to have "a buildup in the past and a godfather for the future." And says Abu Ayash, "Arafat is the spiritual godfather of the Palestinian revolution."

Israelis and others may find Arafat too physically unattractive to be either a godfather or a leader. "He's not beautiful," says Abu Ayash, laughing. "Maybe he's not viewed by Europeans and Americans as a Hollywood movie star, but for the Palestinians, he's a symbol. Ask a group of national women, 'Would you like to marry Arafat?' And they would say, 'Yes.' It's also in our culture, that the beauty of men is not such a major factor."

Arafat's visage, so unappealing to many Israelis and Americans, is splashed across posters, pasted across university halls or hung in private homes throughout occupied territories. Considered by the Israeli government to be illegal literature, the posters, along with PLO flags, are grounds for arrest. Nevertheless, few houses in the West Bank and Gaza are without at least a pillow representing the green, white, black and red Palestinian flag, or a photograph of Arafat.

One current joke in the West Bank, however, may tell something of popular attitudes: George Habash has died and gone to Hell. As soon as Habash arrives, he is met by three angels who tell him they will escort him to three different rooms where he can watch the punishment; then he can choose which one he wants. The angels lead Habash down the hall to the first room, where he sees Mikhail Gorbachev; the Soviet leader is boiling in scalding water. Habash shakes his head, and the angels take him to a second room where he sees Ronald Reagan burning in flames. Habash shakes his head again, and asks, "Where is Yasser Arafat?" The angels lead him to a third room. They open the door, and there Habash sees Arafat making love to Marilyn Monroe. "Aah," says Habash. "That's the punishment I would like. The same kind as Arafat." "No," says one of the angels, shaking his head. "That is not the punishment for Arafat. That is the punishment for Marilyn Monroe."

Palestinians may laugh about Arafat's looks, but they respect his singular, unswerving ambition. "One thing that distinguishes Arafat from other leaders of the world, especially the Arab world, is that he's a man with a target, a goal. He has devoted his life to this target," says Abu Ayash.

For the older generation, Abu Ayash notes, "Arafat gets into the folklore, the literature, the songs." Palestinian wedding songs, once poems of romantic love, have become chants of nationalism: Arafat is our leader, the lyrics say; Arafat is the one who we are behind; Arafat, you plan and we sacrifice. "The women sing these songs in the wedding parties, and on social occasions," says Abu Ayash.

As hard as the Israelis try to eradicate his influence, banning any evidence of the PLO and its chairman, Arafat's role is inescapable. "For a child he is the head of state," says Abu Ayash. "The first two things that the kids learn are, 'What's the name of your country?' and 'Who's your leader?' They learn this from each other, from their parents, from the radio, the TV, communications. They learn from him how to put on the *kafeeyah*. He is a school for them, a school of education for the Palestinians."

For many of the activists in the *intifada,* Arafat is the symbol of their movement. But among them are a number of critics who rebuke him, complaining that Arafat has not moved quickly enough to the negotiating table. The *intifada* which he has spawned and nurtured has now created the proper mood for peace. Like Sadat, these Palestinians in the West Bank and Gaza feel victorious in battle and strong enough to settle for peace. But, they complain, Arafat is so afraid of the hard-liners and so concerned with his own power within the PLO that he is frozen in his tracks. And maybe once again, they fear, he will have lost the chance. They acknowledge that the Palestinians should have joined Sadat at the negotiating table. They also recall earlier chances. Although they do not mention his name, they refer to Arafat's mentor, Haj Amin al-Husseini, the first and most important leader in the nascent struggle for Palestinian nationalism, and remember that he turned his back on partition. Had he urged its acceptance, the Palestinians would have had their state in 1947, larger and richer than any they might be offered now.

There are other critics, of course, who argue that Arafat has moved too fast, that he has been so afraid to miss the chance for a deal that he has given away the store. The Moslem fundamentalists insist that Arafat has no right to offer to coexist with Israel; they demand that all of Palestine be taken back and turned into an Islamic religious state. But even more moderate Palestinians, Moslem and Christian alike, complain that Arafat has bargained away too much too soon.

Despite the criticism of Arafat's politics, he is the role model for the Palestinian movement. While many Israelis argue that the Arabs in the territories would rather speak for themselves, Abu Ayash insists that they not only want to identify with Arafat, they want to be part of his personal organization. "He is the symbol of the Palestinian struggle and he is the head of Fatah," says the journalist. "So, many teenagers say, 'I'm with Abu Amar; Abu Amar means Fatah, so I'm with Fatah.'"

Although Israeli authorities have routinely closed down institutions with links to the PLO, Abu Ayash insists that Israeli policies have failed. "Fatah has the government. It has all the institutions. It has the budget, it has the power, it has all the possibilities of reinforcing the goals of the PLO. It has the welfare societies, the health societies, the social societies. All walks of life of the Palestinian society are controlled by Fatah."

Asked if he would have acknowledged Fatah's role before the *intifada* had begun, Abu Ayash smiles and shakes his head no. "Today the peace strategy of Fatah and the PLO allows me to say so."

Even Shamir admits that the PLO strategy has created a new reality, one in which Israel must recognize the legitimacy of some of the Palestinian claims: "We are ready to negotiate about the way we can exist and live together. There are differences among us, but we have to negotiate until we find a common ground. That is all."

III

Syria: Fueling the Rejectionists

11

Intrigue and Death in Damascus

DAMASCUS SEEMS a relic layered with the dust of ancien régimes: a city of Omayyads, Ayubbids, Mamluks, Seljuk and Ottoman Turks and French. The Great Omayyad Mosque, built in the eighth century, stands like a proud lady in the downtown section. Nearby, crowds of Arabs jam the sweltering Hamidiyeh souk, bargaining furiously at the gold counters, lingering over the spices and the cloth. Hidden in a corner of the narrow bazaar, a cool courtyard leads the way to the residence of the Turkish pasha. The rich Moorish architecture of the building sets off the splendid balcony lined with bedrooms for the concubines, and down below the pasha's carriage still waits to take him through the city.

Away from the souk, on the other side of the city, where palm trees still grace the streets and flower stalls abound, elegant stone homes built by the French offer shelter to foreign diplomats, and balconied apartment houses are reminiscent of Mediterranean ports of Marseilles or Antibes.

In the residential area of Rawdah is the presidential palace of

Syrian leader Hafez al-Assad. The windows of the unassuming villa are kept closed, the shutters down, and the security is heavy. Those who are allowed to enter are asked politely to leave their cameras and their bags on the landing. Walking up the two flights of stairs, the visitor enters a large, rectangular room wallpapered in fabric; the heavy velvet curtains are drawn, and the large chandelier is only dimly lit. At the far end are Assad's private offices, behind sliding doors.

The reception room is rimmed with comfortably upholstered chairs, two of them placed perpendicular to each other. Between them is a small table where coffee, tea and lemonade are offered to the guests. Assad's preferred seating, a small brown couch, is positioned facing the only object on the walls, a painting called "The Horns of Hittin."

The huge seven-foot-long canvas shows rearing horses and gleaming sabers, scenes from the twelfth-century battle when the Kurdish General Saladin led his armies in a rout of the Crusaders. The battle ended almost a century of Christian rule in Jerusalem and inaugurated the Moslem Ayubid empire. Saladin's dynasty (A.D. 1171-1250) was followed by the Moslem Mamluk rulers. Together they reigned for more than three hundred years in an empire that stretched across much of the Near East.

Hafez al-Assad grew up in Kardaha, a small village in the Alawite Mountains of northern Syria, a region dotted with the ruins of Crusader castles that were destroyed by Saladin's armies. His childhood hero has left his imprint on Assad. The modern leader has declared a public holiday on the anniversary of Saladin's death, decreed that a profile of the twelfth-century ruler adorn Syrian banknotes and changed the name of a fortress near his birthplace from Zion's Castle to the Castle of Saladin.

Many who have met him believe that Assad sees himself leading a similar battle against the hated vestiges of Europe's latest designs on the Middle East: the Balfour Declaration and the Sykes-Picot pact. The first paved the way for millions of Jews to settle in Palestine; the second carved up areas of the Ottoman Empire into British and French protectorates. The Hittin painting is a reminder to Assad's guests that Israel will eventually suffer the same fate as the Crusaders.

Assad likes to tell his visitors that beginning with the Moslem Omayyads in the seventh century, and continuing with the Moslem

Mamluks, who ruled from 1260 to 1516, and even during the subsequent 400 years of Turkish Ottoman rule, a broad part of the Near East was known as bilad al-Sham, the "Lands of Damascus." This region, which Assad says was called "natural" or Greater Syria, extended from the Taurus Mountains in Turkey east to Iraq, west to Alexandria and south to the deserts of Arabia.

While only briefly a political-territorial entity, its inhabitants shared a common culture, enjoyed economic and other links and often called themselves Syrians. During the Ottoman Empire, the vast area was divided into states or "silayet" with a regional governor, or "wali," in each province. There were walis in Baghdad and Tripoli but the most important of these semiautonomous states were Damascus, Beirut and Aleppo. The region of the Galilee was ruled by the wali of Beirut and the rest of what would become Palestine—notably Tiberius, Nablus and Jerusalem—were ruled by the wali in Damascus.

Not until the British defeated the Turks in 1918 was there a governmental unit of Palestine. As recently as 1978, Syria's official media still called the region southern Syria, deemphasizing the Palestinian right to a separate state. Listening to Assad deliver his lecture, it is clear that for him the seventy-two years since the end of World War I are just a moment in the long span of Middle Eastern history. In 1991, he reminds a visitor, he will be the country's longest reigning ruler, his twenty-one years eclipsing the term of even the Omayyad's first leader.

For Assad, the Omayyad legacy and the later centuries of loose union, when families as far away as Jerusalem looked to Damascus as the heart of the region, remain his blueprint for the future. In textbooks for Syrian students, Assad has staked his historic claim to the area of bilad al-Sham. He sees Syria, Palestine, Lebanon and Jordan as belonging to natural Syria and as a bridge to the Baathist concept of a single, pan-Arab nation. Assad has never recognized the modern state of Lebanon that was formed when the French in the early 1920s robbed Syria of Tripoli, Beirut, Sidon and Tyre and attached them to Christian Mount Lebanon. Syria has not yet exchanged ambassadors, nor does the name Lebanon, or Israel, appear as a separate entity on Syrian maps. As recently as March 8, 1989, Assad stressed that Lebanon and Syria "are one people, in body, blood and bones. We will not leave Lebanon because we are a one people nation."[1]

Assad's view of Arafat also is conditioned by his belief that Syria is the preeminent force in Arab nationalism; that Syria therefore sets the agenda for peace or war in the region, particularly with Israel. As an Arab nationalist, Assad must portray himself as the champion of a legitimate Palestinian movement. Syria's national interests demand it dominate the Palestinian national movement. His clash with Arafat is a fight for control: Assad believes that Syria, which has virtually achieved strategic deterrence with Israel, is the only frontline Arab nation with the territory, military resources and ideological commitment to bargain on behalf of the Palestinians from a position of strength.

The claims of Yasser Arafat to a separate Palestinian identity have irritated Assad and often driven him into direct clashes with Arafat for the allegiance of the Palestinian diaspora. In a meeting with the PLO leader, Assad once exclaimed: "You do not represent Palestine more than we do. There is neither a Palestinian people nor a Palestinian entity. There is only Syria and you are an inseparable part of the Syrian people and Palestine is an inseparable part of Syria."[2]

Today Assad appears to be softening his rhetoric. He looks thinner and grayer, as if his heart problems and undefined blood disease have taken a certain toll on the sixty-year-old leader. He recently told a congressional delegation headed by Senators Robert Dole (R.-Kansas), Alan Simpson (R.-Wyoming) and Howard Metzenbaum (D.-Ohio) that "I am willing to negotiate [with Israel]. But there must be a comprehensive and just settlement and it must be based on the principle of land for peace." The election of a more sympathetic Maronite Christian president in Lebanon and the Taif accords, which provide for constitutional reforms that would redress the political imbalance, have reduced the threat of a political vacuum in Lebanon which Syria's enemies could exploit.

Consequently Assad has become more flexible. As the ruler of a minority regime in Damascus, he is not championing a strong Christian-led Lebanon. But U.S. Ambassador to Syria Edward Djerejian thinks Assad has "crossed the ideological bridge on Lebanon" and no longer believes it is in Syria's interest to have Christian Lebanon defeated.[3] Djerejian recently asked Assad, "Is it true that while you consider Syria and Lebanon to be one nation and one people, you accept that Lebanon and Syria are two separate and independent states?" Assad replied: "Yes, that is so" and acknowledged that he was the first Syrian leader to recognize that.

He is also mellowing towards Arafat. When he talks about his longtime rival, his lips still curl, but a wry, bemused smile crosses his face. He still questions the consistency of Arafat's positions and the overall purpose of his policy, but Assad no longer seems to betray the personal hatred of earlier years. Assad's inability to bring Arafat under his control has led him to work out a modus vivendi with the leader of the PLO.

O n May 5, 1966, in a private home on Mazraah Street in the Asakar district of Damascus, the bodies of two pro-Syrian Palestinians were discovered, shot to death at close range with Soviet-made Kalashnikov rifles. The Syrian secret service ordered an immediate investigation. Within days, they arrested twelve Palestinians, among them personalities who would later become well-known: Yasser Arafat, Khalil Wazir (Abu Jihad) and Ahmed Jabril. One of the Palestinians arrested, Abdul Majib Zahmud, remains in Mezzeh prison today. His mother comes faithfully to plead for his pardon, visiting the prison near the Damascus airport every three months for the past twenty-five years. Throughout his stay in jail, and despite repeated efforts to coerce a confession, Zahmud has consistently denied responsibility for the murders. A fourth man, who went only by the name of Adnan, escaped and has never been captured. "The case is still open," says Defense Minister Moustafa Tlass, who was chief of Syria's highest military tribunal at the time.[4]

In those days, the killings didn't attract much attention either in the Syrian or Palestinian communities. The Palestinians involved, those murdered and those accused of complicity, were unknown young activists and no one rallied to their cause. There were no public protests on their behalf, no demonstrations to arouse public opinion for them. In retrospect, however, this incident was an early sign that storm clouds were gathering. The unresolved murder stands as a living reminder of tensions that began on that spring day and have ever since poisoned the atmosphere between Syria's Baathist regime and Yasser Arafat.

Behind the murders of Captain Yousef Arabi and Mohammed Hikmet, the two Syrian soldiers born in Palestine, was a web of growing strife between competing groups, all espousing a new method of confrontation against Israel. Eighteen years had elapsed since the catastrophe of 1948 in which three quarters of a million Palestinians lost their homeland and became refugees. In 1966, their number had grown to more than a million, scattered throughout the Arab world, most of them in refugee camps and slums surrounding the major Arab cities of Beirut, Damascus, Amman, Nablus and Gaza. For these uprooted Palestinians, never absorbed by their fellow Arab communities, almost nothing was being accomplished by the international community to help them regain their rights.

All the young Palestinians, the alleged murderers and the victims, believed they had found the ideological and practical answer to the Palestinian problem. Inspired by the revolutionary climate in the Third World in the mid-1960s, and by the rhetoric of Ernesto "Che" Guevara and Mao Zedong, they chose to become active themselves. In Vietnam, the pro-Communist forces of Ho Chi Minh fought a war of national liberation against the more powerful armies of the imperialist Americans. In Cuba, Fidel Castro was consolidating his victory over the puppet regime of Fulgencio Batista. In South Yemen, after four years of civil war, guerrillas of the Marxist National Liberation Front were on the verge of ousting the Royalist forces of the British colony of Aden. But Algeria, where the people's war had triumphed and forced General Charles de Gaulle to give independence to the former French colony, represented the most attractive model for the new generation of Palestinian youth.

There was no similar revolutionary struggle for the Palestinian cause in the Arab world. On the contrary, the fight for Palestinian rights was being waged along traditional diplomatic and political lines. In Egypt, the largest and most powerful nation in the Arab world, Gamal Abdel Nasser dreamed of unifying the Arabs under his banner of pan-Arab socialism. With Nehru of India, Sukarno of Indonesia and Tito of Yugoslavia, Nasser created a new Third World movement of nonaligned nations. Supported by the Soviet Union, they would combat the Western-backed Jewish state of Israel.

Nasser convened with great fanfare in January 1964 the "First Arab Summit," inviting thirteen Arab leaders to Cairo to coordinate strategy. At the top of the agenda was Israel's plan to build a major pipeline to channel the abundant waters of the Jordan River to the southern Negev Desert. The Arab leaders vowed to deny Israel its new freshwater source, encouraging Syria to draw off the headwaters of the Jordan at the point it met the Yarmuk River south of the Lake of Tiberius. The Arab states also created a new defense pact, with a unified Arab command to control the troop movements among all thirteen nations and established an office to share military intelligence.

Finally, they agreed upon the creation of a new organization to placate the bothersome demands of the impatient Palestinians. They called it the Palestine Liberation Organization and announced it would allow them to "play their role in the liberation of their country and [in achieving] their self-determination." But their real hope was that the PLO would help the restless refugees advance their claims in an orderly, controlled manner that would prevent them from becoming a threat to the established Arab regimes.

Nasser's candidate to further these aims was Ahmed Shukeiry, a Palestinian lawyer originally from Acre, the son of an aristocratic Arab religious figure. His career moved from brief membership on the Arab Higher Committee to posts with the Arab League and through many years of diplomatic service representing both Syria and Saudi Arabia at the United Nations. His speeches were filled with vitriolic attacks on Israel but his bombastic threats to exterminate the Jewish state achieved little for the Palestinian people. "The problem with Shukeiry," according to Mohammed Heikal, a close confidant of Nasser, "was that he belonged to the generation of Arab lawyers who were leading what was called the 'National Struggle.' He was an intelligent man, not a buffoon, but for them it was oratory and written memorandums."[5]

For many refugees, however, Shukeiry remained the supplicant who maneuvered behind closed doors and cowered before Arab rulers hoping to win their blessing and their money to pursue the Palestinian cause. After more than fifteen years, leaders like Shukeiry had accomplished virtually nothing. Khaled al-Fahoum, a member of the original PLO Executive Committee who worked closely with Shukeiry, recalled the appeal he made to the Saudi King Faisal in the fall of 1964. The Saudi king was furious with Shukeiry, his former United Nations envoy, for ignoring orders to convene an emergency session of the U.N. Security Council. Faisal wanted to protest

Nasser's dispatch of a 40,000-man expeditionary force to South Yemen, where the Nasserist-leaning Marxist guerrillas were fighting the Saudi-backed forces of the South Arabian League.

When Shukeiry and the thirteen other members of the original PLO Executive Committee approached Faisal in his spacious suite at Alexandria's Palestine Hotel, the king was in no mood for dispensing charity. "Your Majesty." Shukeiry began, "you have been known to support the Palestinians. Your father King Abdul Aziz supported the Palestinians. Your brother King Saud supported the Palestinians. We hope you will too." Aware of the tension between them, Fahoum told Faisal, "Your Majesty, the PLO is not Shukeiry's organization. It is for all Palestinians. We humbly ask you to be generous and support us."[6]

Without any hesitation, Faisal unleashed a tirade of invective against Shukeiry. Almost two hours later, when Faisal finished, Shukeiry said meekly, "Thank you, your Majesty." Then he added, "Please don't give me your answer here. Give it to me in Riyadh." The polite, if less than dignified reply, was a masterstroke. Fahoum said that when Shukeiry returned from his audience with King Faisal several weeks later, he had two checks with him drawn on the Saudi National Bank: one was for the PLO in the amount of three million dollars and the other was for the Palestine Liberation Army in the amount of one million dollars. "We established the PLO and opened our first office with the Saudi money," says Fahoum.[7]

But the begging for Arab support, which was repeated in other capitals, was humiliating to the second generation of refugees, who rebelled against the Palestinian establishment. "People were fed up with long speeches and U.N. decisions," says Hussan al-Khateeb, a professor at the University of Damascus. There was a romantic belief in the energy of the Arab masses but no plan for mobilizing them. "We wanted deeds and actions," says Khateeb.[8] Dozens of cells, legal and illegal, were formed all over the Arab world, in Syria, Lebanon, Iraq, Jordan and Egypt. Some supported a variety of pan-Arab formulas for unity. Some of them espoused Marxism or Communism. Others were made up of Moslem Fundamentalists who believed the struggle against Israel was divine and should be a holy war.

"Everything was intermingled then," says Abu Laila, a Palestinian radical. "The different Arab states had so many fingers inside the Palestinian movements that it was difficult to differentiate the different groups.'''[9] In Lebanon alone, there were more than a dozen factions vying for the loyalty of the three-and-a-half million refugees. They included Communists, Nasserites, pan-Arab socialists, Islamic believers, independent Marxists and Christian ideologues.

Among those factions were at least two rival groups that advocated much more militant steps than they believed the PLA was prepared to take. The PLA, made up of Palestinian units inside the regular Arab armies, received their orders from Arab commanders and were totally integrated with existing Arab regimes. The more militant Palestinian groups wanted to pattern their liberation movement along the lines of the Algerian independence struggle, launching guerrilla raids and sabotage operations inside the borders of Israel in order to ignite a people's war. One of the militant groups, the Palestine Liberation Front (PLF) led by Ahmed Jabril and Yousef Arabi, was backed by the Baathist government in Syria. Jabril, a Palestinian refugee who graduated from Syria's military academy with an engineering degree, had become an officer in the Syrian army. Arabi, also a Palestinian, was a commando fighter who rose through the ranks to become a captain in the Syrian army. Both men believed that the socialist revolution preached by the Baathist Syrian regime would resurrect Arab glory, unify the Arab world and then liberate Palestine.

The other group of militants, based in Kuwait, was Fatah. Led by Yasser Arafat, Khalil Wazir, Farouk Kaddoumi and Salah Khalaf, this group of university graduates and young professionals believed the opposite: that by liberating Palestine they would unify the Arab world. In the mid-1960s, they created a military unit called Asifa, "The Storm." But Fatah was handicapped by several things: they had organized four years after Jabril started attracting recruits for the PLF; they were unable to compete with the steady income offered to young fighters by the PLA; they were based in the Gul,f far from the borders of Palestine.

Syria's common border with Israel beckoned Arafat and his cohorts. But even more enticing to the ardent revolutionaries was the Syrian government's sympathy for a guerrilla offensive. Unlike the other frontline states of Jordan, Egypt and Lebanon, Syria had already sponsored several small groups. When Arafat arrived in Damascus in 1965, he cooperated with the Syrian-backed PLF, which was under Jabril's command, but clashes between the two groups became inevitable. "Fatah had absorbed the political people, the organizers and the intelligence operatives but they had almost no one with military experience," says Omar Sha'abi, a PLF guerrilla leader. "The PLF was the opposite. We had the military experience, and we were stronger than Fatah in Syria."[10]

The PLF was also intensely jealous of the freewheeling Fatah leaders, who owed their allegiance to no one. Arafat, says Sha'abi, arrived with 60,000 dinars (about $200,000), money he had accumulated in Kuwait, and used it to bribe Syrian-backed cadres. Trying to entice the PLF guerrillas to join Fatah, Sha'abi remembers that Arafat offered them salaries of 500 Syrian pounds (about $1,500) a month and a bonus of 5,000 Syrian pounds (about $15,000). Says Sha'abi, "With 5,000 pounds, you could buy a house."

But Arafat also offered them something the refugees coveted more than money. "The fondest dream for Palestinians in Syria was to have an Algerian passport," Sha'abi recalls. "Arafat was able to get Algerian passports very quickly." In fact, Arafat arrived in Damascus already armed with Algerian support. Senior Palestinian commandos were sent to Algeria to attend courses in guerrilla warfare. Algerian work permits were provided to resident Palestinians in exchange for their contributing a percentage of their salaries to Fatah. Algerian President Ahmed Ben Bella even allowed Fatah to open its own offices in Algiers on Victor Hugo Street.

Furthermore, when the Algerian government wanted to provide Chinese weapons to Fatah, after Arafat visited Beijing in 1964, Syria didn't stand in the way. The official who helped organize the airlift from Algiers and secretly stockpiled the arms for Fatah in Syrian military warehouses was Syria's air force chief Hafez al-Assad, a lanky, straight-necked commander. There was nothing altruistic about Assad's motives. A member of the minority Alawite sect in a country where the Sunni Moslem majority often viewed them as heretics, the ambitious Assad hoped to win the support of the more than 100,000 Sunni Palestinians living in the refugee camps around Damascus.

There was still bitterness between Egypt and Syria over Nasser's attempts to dominate the United Arab Republic, which the two nations formed in 1958 but which only lasted three years. In Syria, unlike most other Arab countries, the Palestinians could attend universities, join labor unions, serve in government posts and be drafted into the army. They could also organize their guerrilla war against Israel. In return for these privileges, the Syrians expected

Palestinian support in their effort to replace Egypt as the champion of Arab unity. However, Assad and Ahmed Sweidani, the chief of Syrian military intelligence, put limitations on the guerrilla groups: their activities had to be kept secret and they had to be supervised by the Syrian army.

Fatah and the PLF both found these conditions hard to accept. To circumvent the restrictions, the groups secretly moved their units across Syrian territory into Jordan, Lebanon and Gaza. From there they would cross the border into Israel, a convenient way of sparing Syria direct responsibility and protecting it from the threat of Israeli reprisals.

The competition between the two groups to launch guerrilla raids was so strong that even today, after thirty-five years, they still argue over who started the first operation against Israel. The former PLF leader Ahmed Jabril contends that in October 1964 his fighters were the first to operate from Jordanian soil against Israeli targets. Arafat and his fighters claim that they carried out the first operation from Jordanian territory on January 1, 1965, planting explosives at the site where Israeli engineers were channeling water from the Sea of Galilee to the Negev. Captain Yousef Arabi, the murdered Syrian officer, helped Fatah plan the operation.

Despite the fact that no one knows which group organized the first raid, and neither claims to have inflicted any damage on the Israelis, Fatah turned the raid into a propaganda success. The date is still celebrated by the Palestinians as a national holiday. Unlike the impotent PLA of Shukeiry, explains Abu Iyad, "Fatah developed into a mass movement by actually practicing armed struggle."[11]

The Arab world reacted at once, and with indignation. No one had ever heard of a guerrilla group by the name of Asifa. There was a widespread suspicion of a plot to push the frontline Arab states into a military confrontation with Israel at a time when none were prepared for it. The Arab world felt some unknown group was conspiring to dictate the timetable for war. In Egypt, the government-controlled media accused Asifa of being an arm of the fanatical Moslem Brotherhood that had tried to overthrow Nasser. *Al-Anwar*, a pro-Nasser newspaper in Beirut, charged Asifa with carrying out the raid for the CIA. Saudi Arabia derided them as agents of international communism.

Jordan accused them of being pan-Arab revolutionaries who wanted to topple the Hashemite Kingdom. Jordan and Lebanon, afraid that enthusiastic reports would spark riots among their large Palestinian populations, prohibited any mention of Asifa in the media. Even the Palestinian establishment embodied by Shukeiry denounced Asifa as an enemy of the Palestinian liberation movement. At Shukeiry's instruction, official notes were sent to all Arab governments by Ali Amir, the Egyptian general in charge of the Unified Arab Command. The notes ordered that Asifa be crushed so as "not to give Israel an excuse to attack the Arab countries."

Syria was the only country that continued to sanction the guerrilla activities. In fact, Fatah supporter Mohammed Nashashibi, the first Palestinian to graduate from Hebrew University, says Syria gave them ammunition and facilities. Remembers Nashashibi: "All the Golan was a Syrian military zone and no one was allowed through it. But Asifa was allowed to pass through and launch their raids [against Israel] from Jordan."[12] Discussing those crucial years from 1965 to 1966, Defense Minister Moustafa Tlass confirms that Syria helped the guerrillas but also imposed firm conditions on them. "We told them, when you want to undertake an operation, it must be with our knowledge. If we are apprised of it beforehand, we can escort you to the site of the operation and be prepared for the [Israeli] response."

Emphasizing his claim of Syrian generosity, Tlass says his nation even permitted the Palestinians to operate from Syrian territory. Tlass proudly recalls the first raid from the Syrian border in January 1966, that was under the personal command of Syrian officer Yousef Arabi. Cooperating with three Asifa *fedayeen*, Arabi crossed the Golan borders into Israel's Hula Valley and laid mines near an Israeli military checkpoint. When an Israeli armored personnel carrier struck the mines, the Palestinians opened fire. The vehicle was destroyed and three Israeli soldiers were killed.

Tlass says Arafat immediately took all the credit. "We do not celebrate this occasion because it was nothing out of the ordinary. But Arafat tried to make something great out of this. He says Fatah carried out the first operation. This is the first bullet and we will go on. But Arabi undertook the first operation. It was his own military section which carried it out. He personally carried out the operation," says Tlass.

The tension between the Syrian-backed officers and Arafat's guerrilla fighters increased as Arafat became more and more emboldened to continue the raids against Israel. Both sides hurled accusations at one another. Arafat began infiltrating commando units into the Golan without prior Syrian approval. Says Tlass, "In fact, we [the Syrians] provided him with light weapons, explosives, mines, dynamite and bombs and they would sometimes get a shepherd to plant a mine and give him 57 pounds [about $150]." That made Syria even angrier, says Tlass, because "the mine could blow up a civilian vehicle or kill a child. It's not our job to kill civilians. That's why we insisted on coordination with them. They always refused."

In February 1966, a month after the first Syrian-backed raid, Hafez al-Assad became defense minister. One of his first missions was to bring the competing guerrilla factions back under control. Assad was suspicious of Arafat's intentions. Looking back at the intelligence files, he discovered that two years earlier, the man who at the time called himself Abu Raouf was arrested for trying to smuggle dynamite from Lebanon into Syria in the trunk of his Volkswagen. The files revealed Arafat was formally charged with bringing explosives into Syria "for subversive purposes" and was officially declared an "enemy of the state." A few months later, Syrian intelligence was informed that Arafat plotted to sabotage the major oil pipeline, the Tapline, from Syria to Lebanon.[13] To Assad and the Syrians, Arafat's background was full of elements that seemed to make him an ideological foe of the Baath secular, socialist, revolutionary regime.

"From the beginning, it was known that Arafat's origins were in Gaza and with the Moslem Brothers and later on with the Egyptian authorities," says Hussan al-Khateeb, a historian at the University of Damascus.[14] Syria had received intelligence reports from Kuwait about Arafat's earlier imprisonment in Egypt, and there were even rumors that he still belonged to a secret cell of Islamic fundamentalists inside the Egyptian army.

These suspicions surfaced following Arabi's murder on May 5, 1966, in circumstances still shrouded in mystery. Hussan al-Khateeb says that he knew Arabi and that the young soldier "was a problem to everyone because of his enthusiasm. He was not an easy person to handle for those people who are in charge and have their own priorities. He saw nothing but Palestine. He wanted it passionately and right away."

Various Syrian accounts say Arafat had promised to make Arabi the general commander of Asifa but had no real intention of doing so. "He [Arafat] used to make all sorts of promises to us and to the Baath personalities who were governing," says Sha'abi. He didn't take the promises seriously, he said, but Arabi did. The Palestinian captain felt he was entitled to the promotion because of the key role he had played in the first two guerrilla operations.

Some Syrians believe that Arafat, worried that he would be forced to keep his promise, sent two armed men, Hishmet and Zahmud, to assassinate Arabi. Other Syrians say Arabi was wounded in a guerrilla operation against Israel and taken to a Syrian hospital in Kuneitra on the Golan Heights. Omar al-Khatib, the deputy commander of PLO forces, confirms Arabi was wounded in battle. At the time, he says, Arabi headed a group of four who called themselves "The Local Leadership of the West Bank." In the battle at the village of Nugueib (near Irbid), "the Israeli military surrounded the village and Arabi was inside," says Khatib. "Some stayed inside to fight the Israelis while another group went up into the caves to hide out. While they were leaving, they went through an Israeli army encampment. There was a battle and several were wounded on both sides." Other Syrians say that before he died, Arabi told General Abdel Ghani Ibrahim, the Syrian commander at the front, that it was Arafat who betrayed him and ordered he be shot.

Arafat, however, is certain that it was he who was the intended victim. Arafat believes Arabi was planted by the Syrians in the ranks of Fatah to take over the leadership. The plan would have made Ahmed Jabril the commanding officer of Asifa and Yousef Arabi his deputy. If Arafat refused, Arabi's orders were to assassinate him. Arabi organized a dinner at which he would carry out the plot. Syrian intelligence officials cooperated by providing Arabi with a report charging Arafat with illegally smuggling arms into Syria. The security dossier was to be the blackmail weapon. There is proof Syria was behind the plot, according to Khaled al-Hassan. He says Jabril didn't wait for Arafat's death to be announced. Jabril distributed hundreds of copies of a statement condemning Fatah as a Saudi puppet and declaring he would soon succeed Arafat as the commander of all the guerrilla forces.

Another version of the incident suggests Arabi may have tried to reconcile Jabril and Arafat. "Jabril thought by the time Fatah arrived here, he had already made huge strides towards organizing the Palestinians. Those [PLF] people thought they were the avant-garde to liberate Palestine," says Hussan al-Khateeb. This version suggests that neither Arafat nor Jabril accepted Arabi's invitation because neither trusted the other. Instead, they sent their seconds: Hishmet for Arafat and Adnan for Jibril. When Hishmet allegedly provoked an argument with Arabi, he shot him and then Adnan shot Hishmet.

Finally, there is the Israeli version of what happened. Israeli intelligence sources say there was a showdown between Arafat and Assad after a squad of Asifa commandos booby-trapped an Israeli truck. The civilian occupants were killed. Assad, furious that Asifa had ignored his orders to coordinate with the Syrian General Staff, ordered an end to Asifa's activities and had Arafat imprisoned. Arabi is said to have informed the Fatah cells that Arafat had been ousted and that he, Arabi, was succeeding him. Even before Arafat was released from prison, his Asifa cohorts found Arabi in the Yarmouk refugee camp and assassinated him.[15]

Whatever the truth, Syrian leaders today still blame Arafat for Arabi's murder. Hafez al-Assad released Arafat fifty-five days later but only after the Arab League intervened on his behalf. According to Moustafa Tlass, the release was arranged on condition that Arafat be expelled from Fatah and exiled from Syria.

The Arabi affair poisoned relations between Fatah and the Baath regime. The mutual antagonism between Arafat and Assad intensified after Arafat was elected chairman of the PLO in 1969 and Assad became president of Syria in 1970. Even though in later years the two men occasionally surmounted the personal hatred between them to cooperate, their ideological differences proved to be too profound to overcome. Their goals and aspirations are basically contradictory. The Palestinian movement headed by Arafat dreams of a return to its homeland in Palestine. The Baath party of Hafez al-Assad dreams of the rebirth of one Arab nation, the nation of Greater Syria, in which Palestine would only be a small part of southern Syria.

Beyond their revolutionary zeal, in the 1960s, the Baathists had little in common with the Palestinians. The rulers of Syria were self-styled Marxists who preached godless socialism and Arab nationalism. In the ideology of Fatah, there was no room for Communism or class struggle and little mention of the oppression of the masses, social equality or pan-Arabism. On the contrary, Arafat received the bulk of his support from oil-rich, anti-Communist sheikdoms of the Persian Gulf. Instead of pan-Arab socialism, he stressed Palestine, Palestine, Palestine. According to Jamil Hilel, a PLO spokesman who lived in Damascus, the Syrians "wanted to minimize the number of Arab states—not add to them. In their pan-Arab ideology, there was no need for a Palestinian state. They thought the area of Palestine should be free of Israeli occupation and be returned to Syria or Jordan."[16]

Arafat, however, wanted to recover his homeland. Assad thought he had the key: a Greater Syria that would form the geostrategic heart of a unified Arab nation and be the military focus for a coordinated assault against Israel. By the end of 1966, the visions of Arafat and Assad were about to collide. Arafat believed time was short: the growing numbers of Jews immigrating to Israel and the Israeli development of nuclear weapons would quash forever the dream of a return to Palestine. For Fatah, the sleeping Arab giant had to be awakened and pushed into a new war with Israel. But Assad did not want war until he felt strong enough to win it. He championed the Palestinian armed struggle but saw it as a substitute for conventional war with Israel, not a prelude to it.

In early July, temporarily stripped of his membership in Fatah and no longer permitted to carry a weapon, Arafat left Mezzeh prison and made arrangements to board a Saudi flight to Riyadh. Before he reached the airport, however, Arafat received a phone call from Ahmed Sweidani, the chief of military intelligence. Sweidani was the Syrian who had persuaded Assad to free Arafat. Surprisingly, he asked Arafat to stay in Damascus and promised he would help him rebuild Fatah. Sweidani said he would provide him with 200 Kalashnikov rifles and 100,000 pounds ($300,000). Sweidani had his own agenda, but it was nonetheless an offer Arafat couldn't refuse.

"Sweidani hated the PLF," says Sha'abi. "After Sweidani connected with Arafat, it was clear he would have opportunities that we wouldn't have. We were convinced that unity was no longer possible—that Fatah's mentality was one of hegemony and manipulation towards the other factions."

While Arafat was imprisoned, Sweidani kept the hopes of other Fatah leaders alive. The military commander who had taken the place of the Fatah prisoners was Um Jihad, who credits Sweidani with saving their lives. She says Sweidani provided the weapons that helped ensure the continuation of the Asifa raids. After Arafat and her husband Abu Jihad were imprisoned, she says, she thought she would never see either of them again. A Syrian official had told her: "They are determined to find Arafat guilty, and they are making it a criminal offense so they can hang him."[17] Her husband was among the first to be freed. Several weeks later, in early July 1966, when Arafat appeared at her front door, Um Jihad couldn't believe her eyes. "I can still remember the moment. He was very happy and I cried. He took my hand and kissed it."[18]

The Fatah raids continued. Between 1965 and March 1967, there were 200 operations by the *fedayeen*. On April 7, 1967, Israel finally decided to retaliate. The Jewish state sent its warplanes over Syria to avenge the shelling of a kibbutz on the shores of the Sea of Galilee. Six Soviet-built Syrian MIG-21s were shot down. Israeli bombers buzzed Damascus. The message was clear: No longer could Syria harbor the Palestinian guerrillas and escape massive Israeli reprisals. Defense Minister Moustafa Tlass goes so far as to outrageously suggest there may even have been a secret alliance between Israel and Fatah to lure the Arabs into the June war. Tlass says, "Maybe there was an Israeli plan which involved Fatah. Israel was going to attack anyway. But Fatah provided the pretext."

12

Nasser, Habash and Hawatmeh

GEORGE HABASH MOVES SLOWLY *into the hotel room, his right side still showing signs of paralysis caused by a careless East German surgeon several years ago. His once-handsome face is still strong, though, the thick dark eyebrows and mustache contrasting with his closely cropped gray hair. The sixty-five-year-old former physician hardly looks like a terrorist. The pocket of his light-blue shirt is embossed with a designer insignia; his trousers are neatly pressed. Married, and the father of two daughters, he wears a gold wedding band and on his good wrist he sports a stainless steel watch. The man who masterminded the most spectacular international hijackings bends his body carefully to take a seat on the couch. He shakes hands with us, offering his right hand, although he barely can move it, and dismisses his bodyguards from the room. Across from Habash, sitting atop a chest of drawers, is a detailed floor plan of an Israeli prison, a sign that the crippled revolutionary may still be plotting new operations inside Israel.*

George Habash was born in Palestine in 1925 in the city of Lydda, now called Lod by the Israelis. The son of a Greek Orthodox wheat

198

merchant, he grew up in Jerusalem, a Christian surrounded by sparring Moslems and Jews. The bitterness he witnessed, and the war that would follow, were the fault of the British, he believes, the imperialists who imprisoned him and gave away his country. It was Palestine that he cared about, and Palestine that would become his cause.

As a student, he believed in Marxist ideology, but before he became a practicing revolutionary, he studied medicine at the American University of Beirut. Later, as a physician, he would offer free services to the poor Palestinians in the refugee camps. He began his work in politics while still in medical school, organizing a group called the Association of Young Arab Men, who protested against British imperialism in the Middle East. In one demonstration, against the Baghdad Pact which sought to preserve British bases and thwart Soviet influence, thirty students were injured.

The young men, expelled from the American University, were welcomed to Cairo University by the socialist Egyptian leader, Gamal Abdel Nasser. Nasser had set the precedent for the student rebellion, leading a revolution and forcing the British out of Egypt in 1952. A year after they arrived in Cairo, the Association of Young Arab Men held their first congress and changed their name to the Arab National Movement, keeping George Habash as their leader. As they searched the Egyptian campuses for recruits, the leaders of the ANM constantly crossed the path of another student group, the General Organization of Palestinian Students, led by Yasser Arafat. The competition between the two men began in the halls of Cairo University and continues today.

On this August day, Habash has come from his headquarters in Damascus to the Tunis Hilton, accompanied by a fleet of bodyguards. Although a competitor of Arafat, and an adversary of Assad as well, Habash has come to rely on Syria for protection and a place to train his forces. His Damascus base, however, is something of an embarrassment; the interests of the PFLP, which is regarded by some Palestinians as a legitimate alternative to Fatah, are not well served by being lumped together with Ahmed Jabril's PFLP-GC, Saiqa, the Popular Struggle Front (PSF) and other fringe groups entirely dependent on and controlled by Syria. Lately, Habash has aligned himself with Iraqi leader Saddam Hussein.

Hundreds of Fatah supporters have begun to pour into the city, *several weeks before Fatah holds its first congress in almost two decades to choose a new leadership. Habash is there to persuade them to topple Arafat, whose 1988 peace initiative, he believes, has yielded nothing tangible for the Palestinians. In the hotel room now, the aging Marxist speaks to us about Arafat, criticizing his bourgeois ways. Despite his infirmities, Habash has not abandoned any of his revolutionary zeal. The model for Palestinian liberation should be the struggle waged by the Vietnamese, he says. The problem with "brother Arafat," he remarks condescendingly, is that Arafat is "more pragmatic than necessary."*[1]

Beginning in 1973, Habash explains, when Arafat started cooperating with Egypt's Anwar Sadat, the Fatah leader constantly modified his political position in an effort to win a state for the Palestinians. "You cannot mobilize the masses with a political stance that constantly changes," says Habash. Instead of telling the Palestinian diaspora that his strategy would get them a state in two or three years, Arafat should have told them "if you want a state, you will have to fight and fight and continue fighting." Habash asserts that Arafat's approach is doomed to failure: without confronting Israel militarily, he believes, the Jewish nation will have no reason ever to recognize the rights of Palestinians to form their own state. Arafat, he says, engages in "wishful thinking."

Habash says he doubts the current PLO strategy will be more successful than previous diplomatic solutions; thus he still withholds public support for Arafat. He did not walk out of the 1988 Algiers PNC meeting which formally pledged the PLO to a two-state solution, but he is personally a long way from accepting Israel's right to exist. "When Israel shows at least some signs that she is ready to sit down with the PLO, you can ask me this question," he says bitterly. "We are not ready to talk about this unless Israel recognizes the PLO and our rights. For the time being Sharon, and even Shamir, are talking about 'all' Palestine. Don't blame me if my response is that all of Palestine is my country. I have been living this way for forty years."

And even today Habash does not completely renounce the PFLP tactics he fathered almost a quarter of a century ago. "We are not terrorists," he says. "We are freedom fighters." For the moment, he notes, "we are concentrating all our efforts on the intifada and the fight inside Palestine. The intifada is the jewel." Nevertheless, when we ask if he would resort to the same kind of hijackings that made his

name a household word in the 1970s, George Habash answers: "If
the Israelis pressure us more than necessary, that becomes the only
means to say to the world that we are still here and will not stop
struggling for our rights." He pauses for a moment, thinking of how
his words might be misconstrued, and then adds: "We will pursue
anything that will be a credit to our aims."

———————————————

————————

Y asser Arafat was a sideshow before June 1967. After the Six-Day
War, he became the main attraction.

Arafat and Abu Iyad were in Damascus on June 9, 1967, when they
heard Gamal Abdel Nasser's unexpected announcement on the
radio: the Egyptian president had decided to resign in the wake of
the Arab debacle during the Six-Day War. "It was as if we had
suffered a double defeat, military and political—political because for
us, despite everything, the fall of Nasser meant the end of all hope,"
says Abu Iyad.[2] For Mohammed Heikal, a close confidant of Nasser,
it was a nightmare never forgotten. Egypt was defenseless: humiliated in the war with Israel, stripped of its heroic leader, its armies
defeated so totally they could no longer secure the Suez Canal. "No
one had the luxury anymore of dreaming great dreams," says
Heikal.[3] Throughout the Arab world, there was widespread despair.
A few days later, Nasser withdrew his resignation after waves of
popular protests urged him to stay.

On June 11, 1967, Arafat and George Habash met for the first
time. They lunched at the Abu Kamal restaurant in Damascus, where
"we talked about forging a wide front to start a new era of struggle
which would be more successful than the Nasser era," Habash
recalls. The Marxist revolutionary told Arafat, "Maybe the Arab
armies are defeated but the Palestinian and Arab people certainly are
not." Habash told him that before there could be a successful war
against Israel, Jordan would have to become theirs. "The reactionary
Arab regimes can't accept the Palestinian revolution because it is
against their interests," he explained. "When Israel and the United
States pressure them to get rid of the Palestinian guerrillas, those

Arab regimes will fight us," he predicted. "That's why you can't simply declare war against Israel and ignore Jordan." Arafat protested, but Habash kept arguing. "All right, you say you have nothing to do with Jordan. But Jordan has something to do with you." Arafat believed Jordan could be neutralized and the Palestinian battle could be waged from its soil. No, said Habash, Hussein and his Hashemite Kingdom would have to be overthrown.

As Habash saw it, they could use Jordan as a base to attack not only Israel but its bankroller, the United States. Israel, he argued, was merely the device which the capitalist warmongers used to secure America's geostrategic position in the Middle East. "We knew we were fighting Israel, but we were not ready to say our fight was only against Israel," says Habash now. He believed the United States had inherited the role of British imperialism. "They wanted Israel to be the tool against the Arabs, and they wanted to fight their battles through the Jews." Before long, Habash would see to it that Americans, too, became the victims of a special branch of guerrilla warfare.

The day after their lunch, Arafat and Abu Iyad hastily organized a conference to chart a blueprint for their new war of national liberation: orders were given to collect the weapons the Arabs had abandoned on the battlefield or had left in weapons depots: a list was made of international arms dealers; Khaled al-Hassan and Abu Mazzen were ordered to raise money in Saudi Arabia and other Gulf states. There was much to be done. New commando bases would have to be set up along the Jordan River and in southern Lebanon. Militants, including Arafat, were ordered to slip into the newly occupied West Bank and Gaza to rebuild the underground network of guerrilla cells. Delegations were sent to Egypt, Syria, Iraq and Algeria seeking guns and guidance on renewing the armed struggle. Only Algeria and Egypt encouraged the envoys. Iraqi President Abdel Rahman Aref was noncommittal. Syrian President Nureddin al-Atassi emphatically warned against launching new raids inside the occupied territories: "You will lose and drag us all along with you in the catastrophe," he told Abu Iyad. "Give us time to catch our breath."

Arafat ignored the advice of the Arab rulers and attempted to launch a popular uprising in the West Bank and Gaza. But within a few months, it was clear it would not materialize. The Israeli security agencies had uncovered hundreds of cells, imprisoned more than

1,000 Palestinians and destroyed the homes of countless collaborators. Arafat received little help: neither Jordan nor Syria were eager
to repeat the lesson of a few months back. The rules governing
fedayeen activities in Amman and Damascus were stricter than ever.
Arafat turned to Egypt but also found little enthusiasm there.

When Khaled al-Hassan arrived in Cairo in the fall of 1967 to seek
an appointment with Nasser, neither the Egyptian leader nor his
aides were particularly interested. Egyptian intelligence agencies
informed Nasser that Fatah had links to the Moslem Brotherhood, which had tried earlier to assassinate the Egyptian leader.
Fatah's headquarters, they warned him, were in Damascus. "The
Syrian regime at the time was composed of some left-wingers who
had crazy ideas about popular struggle and the people's war," says
Heikal, who at the time headed the Egyptian Information Office.

He recalls that Habash, during a meeting with Nasser two years
earlier, had warned the Egyptian leader about Arafat. Nasser was
told there were "some young elements based mainly in Kuwait who
wanted to take the Palestinian struggle into the occupied territory
[Israel]," Heikal says. Nasser advised them to wait, scribbling a note
on the margins of a piece of paper Habash had brought with him. He
wanted to make sure Arafat got the message. The note said: "This is
not the time to escalate inside Israel because that may have serious
repercussions." Nasser went on to explain that as soon as Egypt
withdrew its 40,000-man expeditionary force from Aden [South
Yemen], "we will be ready to shoulder the responsibilities of
escalation." The Egyptian defeat in June 1967 changed the climate.
"We looked to Arafat as the savior," admits Heikal, adding, "maybe
that desperation induced Nasser to see him." After several more
efforts to arrange an appointment, Heikal finally agreed to meet
with Khaled al-Hassan in October 1967. After the meeting, Hassan
went back to Damascus and returned a few weeks later, this time
with Farouk Kaddoumi and Abu Iyad.

They had come to persuade Heikal to support their armed
struggle. But he was suspicious of Abu Iyad, the former Moslem
Brother, and had hardly heard of Yasser Arafat. Heikal was the
opposite of the Palestinian guerrilla: he was elegantly attired in
hand-tailored suits, with a fat cigar in his mouth and a condescend-
ing attitude. "This man," Abu Iyad said to himself, "is incapable of
feeling the slightest sympathy for the Palestinian cause." Frustrated
by Heikal's studied nonchalance, they insisted on seeing a more

responsible official, complaining they were being prematurely condemned as Moslem Brothers and as tools of the Syrian regime. While
the Arab armies were silent, they said, their guerrillas were active.
Fatah had ordered that not a single day go by without a shot being
fired against the Israelis in the West Bank and Gaza. "All right, get
this man, get Arafat. We'll see," Heikal finally relented.

Arafat arrived from the West Bank in early November wearing his
doctor's disguise, a shirt with an open collar and a white sports coat.
Heikal told the three Palestinians—Arafat, Farouk Kaddoumi and
Abu Iyad—that he had arranged for them to meet someone in
authority, but he parried their efforts to find out who it was. Nasser
was suspicious of their presence in Cairo and called Heikal. "I have a
report in front of me on your friends," Nasser said, "and it says they
are planning to assassinate me."[4] Heikal told Nasser to disregard the
report. "Our intelligence agencies [Mokhabarat] sometimes get their
information from the guy sitting in front of the corner drugstore,"
he quipped.

The next day the foursome left together in Heikal's car. The
Palestinians thought they were going to meet Ali Sabri, secretary-
general of the Arab Socialist Union, Egypt's only political party. "Are
you armed?" Heikal asked them, looking at Arafat now outfitted in
his khaki uniform. The men answered no but Heikal had noticed
something bulging beneath Arafat's flak jacket. He repeated the
question. Again they said no. The car turned in the direction of
Heliopolis and headed for Manchiyat al-Bakri, the presidential
compound. "They thought they were going to see the chief of staff,"
Heikal recalls. "Then we made a right turn and entered the driveway
of Nasser's home." As they walked in, one of Nasser's security
guards noticed Arafat's gunbelt protruding from his jacket. The
guard motioned to Heikal, who asked Arafat to unbuckle his holster.
Arafat removed his revolver and gently laid it on the table in the
hallway.

The guerrillas walked into the living room to greet Nasser. The
Eygptian president immediately asked them about Fatah's ties to
Syria and its earlier links to the Egyptian underground. "Was it true
that many Fatah members were Moslem Brothers?" Nasser asked.
Arafat replied that he was brought up and educated in Cairo, had
fought to oust the British from Port Said, and felt he was practically
an Egyptian citizen. He told Nasser he had left for Kuwait in 1956,

had made a great deal of money there but felt he had a responsibility to Palestine. From Kuwait, Arafat told him, he had gone to Syria, where he and his colleagues were hassled by the authorities. Arafat boasted that now they controlled an underground network of cells in the West Bank and Gaza. The Fatah leader spoke, too, about the weapons they had acquired and bragged of the merits of the rocket-propelled grenades the group was using.

The meeting lasted two hours, and by the end Nasser was impressed. "I trust the assurances you gave me about your intentions." he told them, saying he was satisfied they were not employed by any Arab regime and only devoted to the cause of Palestine. "I am ready to help," Nasser said, "provided the sound of gunfire is heard every day in the occupied territories so the flame of Palestinian resistance will not go out." Heikal was instructed to coordinate political matters. Nasser suggested they meet with General Sadek, the chief of Egyptian intelligence, and recommended they give him a shopping list of their military needs. Before they got up to leave, Nasser admonished them not to direct their venom against neighboring Arab regimes. The Egyptian president advised the three guerrilla leaders to confine their liberation struggle—"all of it"—to the West Bank and Gaza Strip. Almost while Nasser spoke, George Habash was working to create a Marxist guerrilla organization with much more ambitious aims. His PFLP would target not only Israelis in the West Bank but Israelis and Americans everywhere.

In the months ahead, Arafat tried to follow Nasser's advice to limit the struggle to the liberation of Palestine. Increasingly, however, that put him at odds with Habash's PFLP, which was formed in December 1967 when his two pan-Arab guerrilla factions, "The Heroes of Return" and "Youth of Revenge," merged with Ahmed Jabril's Palestine Liberation Front. The PFLP initially tried to include Fatah. Abu Iyad attended the first organizing session but boycotted the ceremony at which the unity decree between Habash and Jabril was signed.

Meanwhile, Arafat's popularity was rising. The dramatic March 1968 battle at Karameh had demonstrated that Palestinians were willing to fight and die for their cause; as a result, thousands of young Palestinians volunteered to become Fatah's new *fedayeen*. The rift with the PFLP, however, was widening. Fatah and the PFLP each accused the other of desertion: Arafat contended Habash's forces were nowhere to be found during the battle at Karameh, while Habash countered that Fatah had stolen the "victory" from the Jordanian army.

The ideological split between them also deepened. Habash believed Palestine would only be liberated after the masses had revolted against the frontline Arab regimes and replaced them with Marxist dictatorships. For Habash, the revolution had to begin by provoking a confrontation to topple King Hussein. It was not the pirated Fatah victory at Karameh, he contended, but the PFLP which had struck the first blow to liberate Palestine. Habash's fighters, based at the al-Wahdat refugee camp in Amman, fought with Jordanian troops who tried to disarm the PFLP, inflicting heavy casualties. "Fatah didn't fight, but we fought, and because the Jordanian army was so weak, we won the battle," recalls Habash now. Arafat agreed the guerrilla war had to be escalated but he didn't want to overthrow existing Arab regimes; instead he sought their backing, understanding that to obtain his goals, he might also have to deal, through them, with Habash's archenemies: the United States and Israel.

Not only was there conflict between Fatah and the PFLP, but tensions were growing with Saiqa, a third group established by the Syrian Baath party, whose *fedayeen* were fighting alongside Asifa guerrillas. Saiqa leader Sami Kandil, a former leader of GUPS (General Union of Palestinian Students), says that Arafat thrived on the disunity and deliberately fomented it. "His slogan was 'divide and rule,'" Kandil recalls. "He used all the means at his disposal to turn the student leaders against each other. He tried to expel factions that opposed him and when that didn't work, he provoked fights among them. Arafat has survived by exploiting the contradictions among the Arab regimes."[5]

The bickering worried the Syrian chief of staff, Moustafa Tlass, who feared that the reckless competition between the three groups would draw Syria into another war with Israel. The number of guerrilla attacks from Jordanian soil had quadrupled to fifty-two a month. Syria, which was paying for the training of the 6,000 Palestinian fighters headquartered in Damascus, wanted to unify all of them under its command. "It cost the Baath party $300,000 a month just to pay the salaries of the officers and soldiers. We used to give them weapons free of charge," says Tlass.[6] The chief of staff worked day and night to smooth their differences.

In the spring of 1968, "for four continuous months, I tried to reunite the Palestinian factions," says Tlass. The meetings began after sundown and continued until well past midnight. "All the leaders were assembled in my office. I had the core of the resistance: Yasser Arafat, George Habash and Ahmed Jabril," recalls Tlass. "Let them unite—even against us—but let them unite," Tlass says he felt at the time. The Syrian commander charges, however, that Arafat never intended to cooperate with anyone. "He wouldn't listen to the advice of Assad, Gamal Abdel Nasser, Houari Boumédienne or King Faisal. He works independently."

Despite Tlass's accusation, Arafat's cooperation with Arab regimes was beginning to yield results. In the summer of 1968, Nasser took Arafat along on an official state visit to the Soviet Union. Arafat was provided with an Egyptian passport, given an assumed name, and made a member of the official delegation. Heikal recalls that the flight from Cairo to Moscow was unusually bumpy. He laughed with Nasser when the fearless Palestinian warrior become airsick. Heikal joked about the incident with Arafat, but Arafat was furious. "Isn't it true?" Heikal asked him in front of other passengers. "Yes," Arafat replied. Always concerned about his image, he added, "But it shows me in a bad light."

They arrived in Moscow and Nasser had meetings with the top Soviet leadership: General Secretary of the Communist Party Leonid Brezhnev, Foreign Minister Andrei Gromyko and Prime Minister Alexei Kosygin. But no senior Soviet official agreed to receive the Palestinian. Despite the fact that Moscow broke diplomatic relations with Israel after the Six-Day War, Gromyko never stopped reminding visitors that he had lobbied at the United Nations in 1947 for the creation of the Jewish state. In November 1967, the Kremlin had supported U.N. Security Council Resolution 242, which implicitly called on the Arab states to recognize Israel once the territories seized in the June war were returned to Egypt, Syria and Jordan. Such recognition was anathema to Fatah. So it should have come as no surprise to Arafat that the most senior Kremlin official who saw him was a low-ranking Central Committee staffer who was in charge of Moscow's relations with Third World liberation movements.[7]

Arafat, however, had accomplished his mission. A few weeks later, the Soviet ambassador to Egypt provided the Cairo regime with a list of weaponry for Fatah. "They gave them equipment valued at half a million rubles [about $500,000]," says Heikal, including hand grenades and antiaircraft weapons, all of which were transshipped through Cairo. "They wouldn't deal with the PLO directly. They didn't want to rush into a venture with someone they hardly knew." It was just the beginning of a long relationship. Arafat would make many trips to Moscow, persuading the Soviets to provide training camps and other facilities for the PLO. On one such visit, he was accompanied by Khaled al-Fahoum, the former PNC speaker, who recalls that the Soviet leaders were puzzled by Arafat's behavior. They could not understand why after working all day long Arafat boycotted the official banquets. "He was fasting," recalls Fahoum.[8] It was Ramadan, the ninth month of the Moslem year. "In the summer in Moscow, daytime goes on until ten o'clock at night. Arafat didn't eat anything from daybreak until ten P.M."

While Fatah was building its arsenal, the strife-ridden PFLP broke into factions, with Ahmed Jabril and Nayaf Hawatmeh each leading dissident groups. Jabril did not like Habash's brand of radical Arab politics. "We didn't believe in his Marxism-Leninism," says Omar Sha'abi, a PFLP-GC commander.[9] Jabril also could not support Habash's desire to topple existing Arab regimes. "When we were jointly in command of the PFLP, they used to make hostile statements about Syria and Iraq. We needed to have good relations with Syria and Iraq," says Sha'abi. But most of all, Jabril didn't believe that Arab unity was a necessary precondition to liberating Palestine. "The PFLP tried to be a party of all Arabs everywhere," says Sha'abi. "We were a patriotic Palestinian faction." In October 1968, Jabril formed the PFLP-General Command (PFLP-GC).

The split with Hawatmeh was more profound. He left the PFLP in the autumn. "We represented a wing inside the PFLP at the beginning," recalls Yasser Abed Rabbo, a DFLP leader.[10] "We considered Nasser and the so-called progressive Arab regimes responsible for the 1967 defeat. But we felt the answer was a new organization, based on Marxist principles, which would act as an alternative to Nasserism on one hand and to the traditional, orthodox Arab leftist parties on the other," he explains.

Hawatmeh says there were serious political and ideological differences with Habash. In the heyday of the Egyptian revolution, all the mass movements supported Nasser's brand of anti-imperialist, pan-Arab socialism. The Arab National Movement (ANM) founded by Habash was a suitable umbrella for most Palestinians. But after the breakup of the union between Egypt and Syria in 1961, it became increasingly clear that Nasser's brand of pan-Arabism was at odds with the Palestinian nationalist aspirations to liberate their homeland. "In August 1968, we held a congress of our Palestinian branch inside the movement, and at that congress the split took place," says Hawatmeh.[11] Since his followers, who espoused Palestinian patriotism and more traditional Marxism, had a majority inside the ANM, "we ended the Arab Nationalist Movement and gave each of the branches in the Arab countries the freedom to develop their own independent stand," he says.

On February 22, 1969, Hawatmeh officially announced the formation of the Democratic Popular Front for the Liberation of Palestine (DPFLP), which later abridged its name to the DFLP. Arafat quickly appealed to him for support in Fatah's effort to take over the Palestine Liberation Organization. In return for agreeing to join Shukeiry's PLO, Fatah, the DFLP and other *fedayeen* groups were promised a majority of seats in the Palestine National Council, the PLO's parliament-in-exile. When the fifth PNC met in Cairo that February, 57 of the 105 seats had already been allotted to guerrilla groups. Fatah won 33 of those seats, a majority which enabled it to choose the members of the PLO Executive Committee. They unanimously elected Arafat as chairman and new head of the PLO. Habash's PFLP boycotted the PNC, opposing the move to unify the *fedayeen* groups, and refused to join the new Fatah-controlled PLO.

Arafat and Hawatmeh found a new common cause: opposing Habash, who had emerged as Fatah's chief rival. The PFLP drew its support from among the poorest Palestinians in the refugee camps; thus its message, that the "proletariat should elect the leadership of the national movements," had broad appeal to the young, impoverished ideologues. In March 1968, three months after the formation of the PFLP, Habash was arrested in Syria for illegal possession of firearms and ammunition. Habash says that a fellow physician, Wadi Haddad, who later masterminded the PFLP's airline hijackings, led a daring rescue mission to spring him from jail. Arafat suggests Habash was released because he pledged to coordinate with Syrian authorities to bring Fatah under their control. Habash probably didn't need much persuading. When he emerged from prison in October 1968, the PFLP leader publicly accused Fatah of being chiefly a movement of "the petty bourgeoisie" whose leader, Yasser Arafat, was more interested in courting Nasser, Hussein and the Baathist leaders of Syria than in liberating Palestine. It was at this time that Habash adopted his political motto for the campaign to unseat King Hussein: "The road to Tel Aviv runs through Amman."[12]

Yasser Abed Rabbo says Habash's "infantile, extremist left-wing" sloganeering helped drive the DFLP into the arms of Fatah. "While dealing with the bourgeoisie is evil, there is something worse and that is occupation," says the DFLP leader. "We believed unity was essential, so we made alliances with Fatah and Syria." Habash could not cooperate with Fatah without abandoning his main target: Jordan. Hussein was the real culprit. His acceptance of Resolution 242 implied Jordanian recognition of Israel within its pre-1967 borders. Hussein was offering the unthinkable: a peace treaty with Israel merely for the return of a 2,200-square-mile slice of territory on the West Bank and Gaza.

Even Hawatmeh concedes that by late 1968, after the al-Wahdat battle in November, Hussein was "preparing to use his army to liquidate the Palestinian resistance movement." It was also clear to both Habash and Hawatmeh that the new American president, Richard Nixon, and his national security adviser, Henry Kissinger, intended to pressure Jordan to strike at the Palestinians. For Habash, there was only one answer that would deal with all his adversaries— the Americans, Jordan and Israel—only one formula that could force the Arafat-led PLO to abandon its conciliatory diplomacy and wage a real war to liberate Palestine.

On July 23, 1968, a new era of airline hijackings began when the PFLP seized control of El Al Flight 426 from Rome to Tel Aviv. The Boeing 707 was forced to land in Algiers, where it sat on the ground for forty days while the Palestinians negotiated for the release of sixteen guerrillas imprisoned by the Israelis. The non-Israeli passengers were released immediately. Later the Israeli women and children were freed, but the remaining male passengers were held as ransom. Israel eventually agreed to the Palestinian terms. Says Habash: "Nobody was harmed. We gave strict instructions not to hurt anyone."

But that was not the case on December 26, 1968, when another El Al airliner was stormed by PFLP commandos while still on the ground in Athens. One passenger was killed and two stewardesses were injured when the Palestinians, armed with hand grenades and machine guns and screaming "We want to kill the Jews," took over the plane. The PFLP hijackings continued, climaxing in September 1970 when the group devised its most daring operation: the diversion of four airliners, three of them to Dawson's Field in Jordan, where Habash hoped to spark a revolution to bring down Hussein. After several terrifying days, the passengers were freed, and for the benefit of the worldwide television audience, the planes were spectacularly blown up.

Habash still defends the terror tactics. "At the time, the Palestinian cause was not well known in the world. There probably were fewer than half the American people who were even aware of it," he says. "We wanted to do something that would force people to ask, 'Why are they doing this?' We felt we had the right to attack any targets that would harm Israel and Zionism because they are linked together outside Israel." Boasts Habash: "We achieved our goal: the Palestinian problem instantly became known all over the world."

Hawatmeh maintains that, despite the DFLP's own terror operations, "We opposed hijackings" or any "military operation outside the occupied territories," including terrorist acts against Israeli targets abroad. Hawatmeh claims: "This is one of the differences between the DFLP and the PFLP and between the DFLP and Black September, which was headed by Abu Iyad." It was the Black September group that would later commit terrorist massacres at Khartoum and Munich. Hawatmeh says he has fought to persuade the PNC to condemn terrorism outside Israel's borders at every council meeting since 1974.

But the main issue over which the DFLP and the PFLP clashed in the late 1960s was over Hawatmeh's attitude towards Israel. A devoted Marxist, Hawatmeh could hardly ignore the fact that the Soviet Union had historically supported the creation of a Jewish state in Palestine. His ideology dictated he come to terms with Zionism and its consequences: the emigration of hundreds of thousands of Jews to Israel since the proclamation of the Balfour Declaration in 1917. "We were talking about something heretical: the coexistence of two nationalisms inside Palestine," says Abed Rabbo. He explains: "Politically, we were talking about a state with two national movements—Jewish and Palestinian." The DFLP did not, and today still does not, accept Zionism. As a practical reality however, the DFLP was willing to accept the results of Zionism: the dramatic Jewish influx into Palestine.

That set Hawatmeh on a collision course with Habash. The PFLP position on Zionism was a maximalist one: it supported an armed struggle to regain the entire state of Palestine and force the expulsion of all Jews who had come to Israel since 1917. The 1964 PLO Charter also was unequivocal on this issue. It said only the small number of Jews (about 60,000) who were in Palestine before 1917 could remain. In 1968, the DFLP formulated this idea of a single, democratic, secular state with equality for the Jews and Arabs living under its nonsectarian Arab rule. This meant, of course, the elimination of the state of Israel and the destruction of the nation built on the Zionist doctrine.

But from Hawatmeh's point of view, he had made an important concession: the DFLP was ready to accept Jews in Israel as inhabitants of Palestine with equal citizenship rights. He believed this was a conciliatory move; the Palestinian diaspora, which had no state of its own, was ready to recognize that there were Jews in Palestine who had come because of Zionism, and these Jews were going to remain. While still far from accepting Israel or the right of the Jews to a state of their own, the DFLP nonetheless was opposing more radical calls for the deportation of the three million Jews to the countries from which they fled. Henceforth, the DFLP said, it was only necessary to change the regime and unite the whole country under one government that would not be religiously based: neither Jewish nor Christian nor Moslem.

Hawatmeh says Arafat congratulated him for devising the concept of a single democratic, secular state. "He told me it was a stroke of genius," says the DFLP leader. The fourth PNC meeting, in February 1969, formally ratified this position, and it became PLO policy. The PNC reaffirmed its commitment to armed struggle to liberate all of Palestine. Nevertheless, for the first time the mainstream Palestinians believed they were no longer simply waging a guerrilla struggle but also were offering a political formula that could lead to future negotiations. By the end of the 1960s, Arafat and Hawatmeh were moving closer ideologically. The outcast was George Habash, who proved to be so strong that neither Fatah nor the DFLP could contain the approaching showdown with Jordan—the consequences of which would be disastrous for the Palestinians.

13

Lebanon: The New PLO Battleground

THERE ARE *Syrians who say with contempt that Yasser Arafat inevitably will create the kind of corruption and chaos in Tunis that he caused in Jordan and Beirut. For the moment life remains quiet in Tunis. But Beirut still burns from the years that Arafat spent there.*

His Lebanese sojourn was the PLO's longest, from 1971 to 1982. He arrived in Lebanon almost two decades ago, expelled from Jordan and escorted out by the other front-line states. Only Lebanon did not have the wherewithal to stop him: too weak because of a growing division within its own population, the Lebanese Moslems actually invited him in to help them. In the beginning it seemed that Arafat could keep the peace by maintaining the balance between the feuding Moslems and the Christian communities. But by May 1973 the Lebanese army, the official troops of the Christian-led government, began attacking PLO camps just outside Beirut. It was during this period that Arafat himself appealed for help. Just after the first clashes, Arafat made an appointment with the chief of staff of the Lebanese army. They met at the Makassat hospital in Beirut and tried to reach a cease-fire.

But Arafat did not rely on this meeting alone. Earlier he had asked his friend Nada Yashruti if she would speak to the Christian President, Suleiman Franjieh, and try to arrange a truce. "She was working with us," says Arafat now, acknowledging "she had already accepted" his proposal of marriage. The night that the Chairman met with the Lebanese army chief of staff, Yashruti went to the presidential palace in Beirut. She appealed to the president to do what he could. After the meeting Yashruti left the official residence and headed back to her apartment near the Aroushi district of Beirut where she was assassinated.

Neither the meeting with the chief of staff nor Yashruti's efforts led to a truce with the Christians. Instead the fighting intensified, and the Lebanese army worked its way towards the PLO headquarters in Beirut. Located in the Fakhani district and code named Number 17 (from its phone number 317-052), the headquarters were in an area bounded on one side by the Gamal Abdel Nasser Mosque, on another by the Sabra refugee camp, on a third side by the Arab University, and on the fourth side by the sports stadium below which the PLO stashed its weapons. The ten square meters where the Palestinians' headquarters were scattered, it was joked, was Arafat's miniature republic.

But even the head of this miniature republic was vulnerable to attack. The Lebanese army soldiers were in formation on the Khalde road, the airport route lined with apartment houses and residential buildings that led to the city. The troops, inside their armored personnel carriers, encircled the PLO offices from above and fired a barrage of shells two miles downhill into the Fakhani area. Majoub Omar, a physician and close friend of Arafat's, was with the PLO leader at the time. "He took his Kalashnikov and RPG and went to the street to fight," he recalls. Although Omar tried to stop him, protesting that fighting was a job for younger men, Arafat refused to stay in hiding. "Fighting is something in his blood," says the friend.[2]

By 1975 the battle had spread throughout Beirut, far beyond the refugee camps and slums, reaching middle-class sections and the Jewish neighborhood of Wadi Abu Jamil. Nestled between the elegant shopping street of Hamra and the luxurious hotels on the seaside, the small streets of the Old Jewish Quarter were crammed with almost two thousand people and a large synagogue. Although they were neither committed Zionists nor combatants, the Jewish Lebanese citizens, many of them businessman and bankers, were particularly vulnerable to PLO radicals. "If any extremist Palestinian group had gotten to them, they could have been massacred easily," says Roger Edde, a Christian Lebanese leader.[3] "But Fatah wanted to make the point to the West that it protects non-Moslem minorities." Confirms Arafat proudly, "We protected the Jewish community in Beirut. My special guards were responsible for them."[4]

Fatah spokesman Ahmed Abdul Rahman remembers that occasionally during meetings with the chairman, Jewish representatives would come to the PLO offices asking help to obtain gasoline, food, heating oil and electricity. "The chairman gave them all they wanted," says Abdul Rahman.[5] Nevertheless, despite Arafat's efforts to quarantine the area, the neighborhood became a frontline in the fighting, and Edde remembers, "the PLO gave them a secure escort for evacuation."

The intensity of the shellings required more protection for the Palestinian refugees as well, but unlike the Jews, the Palestinians had nowhere to flee. The solution was to build underground shelters in the camps. Arafat put Abdul Jawad Saleh, an engineer and a member of the PLO Executive Committee, in charge of the project. But Arafat also told a friend of his brother Fathi to hire the contractor for the bunkers and gave him a budget of twenty million Lebanese pounds.

The bunkers were constructed, but the job was so shoddy that "the first time it rained," recalls Abdul Jawad Saleh, "the shelter at the Ain al-Helwe camp, which was supposed to protect five hundred people, was flooded with so much water that the shelter was useless."[6] Saleh went to Arafat and complained, mentioning that the contractor had pocketed much of the money himself. Arafat shrugged. "He said he would be pleased if I also stole maybe five million," says Saleh. Instead, Saleh fired the contractor. "I didn't fire him because he was technically ignorant, but because he was stealing the money for himself. When you do that, you force the contractor to use inferior materials." For months Arafat would not speak to Saleh about the incident. When the subject finally came up, the chairman was bewildered by Saleh's anger. "He just couldn't understand why I was mad," says the engineer. Not long after, Saleh was expelled from

Fatah. But the shelters, rebuilt under Saleh's direction, protected many of the refugees not only from the attacks of the Lebanese army but during the bombardment by the Israelis in 1982.

Lebanon somehow seemed destined to become a Middle East battleground even before the arrival of thousands of Palestinians. It was the French who sowed the seeds for the nation's nightmare by making the Christian Maronites the masters of a Greater Lebanon at the end of World War I. The Maronites regard themselves as direct descendants of the ancient Phoenicians, inventors of the alphabet and allies of the tribes of Israel. Dividing up the spoils of the Turkish Empire with Britain in 1920, France took two main areas for itself, Mount Lebanon and the region of Syria. Traditional Moslem populations were abutted to the Maronite, Greek Orthodox and Greek Catholic areas that stretched across the vast mountain range extending from Becharre in the north to Jezzine in the south. The Moslem areas were inhabited by Sunnis and Shiites who had considered themselves separate entities throughout 400 years of Ottoman rule.

In the north, the fertile Akkar plains and seaport at Tripoli were annexed; in the south the area around the coastal city of Sidon; in the east the Bekaa Valley with its capital of Baalbek. Also incorporated into Lebanon were the Moslem cities of Beirut and Tyre. The resulting population of the new state of Lebanon was 53 percent Christian and 47 percent Moslem. But all of this territory was to be consolidated under Christian leadership.

The remaining areas of this French mandate were confederated into the new nation of Syria. In 1920, the French joined the Ottoman provinces of Damascus and Aleppo and two years later added the Alawi and Druse states to this confederation. The new Syrian nation, however, had lost the vital ports of Tyre, Sidon, Beirut and Tripoli and the Bekaa Valley and had found its borders sharply curtailed and its outlets to the Mediterranean vastly reduced. What further angered Syria was that the League of Nations, the United States and Britain all recognized the independence of Lebanon in 1926.

The fighting began almost at once when Moslems in the regions that had been annexed to Lebanon rejected the legitimacy of the new state and called to be united in "historic" Syria, with Damascus as its capital, under a single Arab ruler: the Hashemite King Faisal, son of Sharif Hussein, leader of the Arab revolt against the Turks.

Although the new state of Lebanon was considered an Arab country and the Lebanese spoke Arabic, to the Moslems it was as alien as a Jewish state in Palestine. They knew the words of the Koran: a Moslem cannot be judged or led by a non-Moslem. Says Maronite leader Roger Edde, "The whole issue is whether a Christian-led state in what the Moslems have considered an Islamic area for fourteen hundred years can remain led by a non-Moslem."

The nature of Lebanon's population compounded the problem. Christians felt themselves a minority even before they were one. Before the areas were combined, the Christians made up 78 percent of the population of the semi-independent, autonomous entity of Lebanon; after the area was expanded, they represented only 53 percent. The massacres of Armenians in Turkey in 1915 and the widespread persecution of Christians in Egypt following the assassination of a Christian Coptic prime minister in 1910 were a reminder of what could happen to them if they loosened their grip on power. In the mid-nineteenth century in Mount Lebanon, eleven thousand Christians had been slaughtered by the Druse, together with Sunni and Shiite peasants; the Moslems in Damascus were inspired by the act and massacred thousands more Christians living there.

Under the French mandate after World War I, the Christians were given the power to rule the country, and the president and the prime minister were chosen from among the Christian community. In 1933, however, in an effort to appease Moslem desires to rejoin Syria, the Maronite president, Emile Edde, chose a Sunni Moslem as his prime minister. This effort to assuage the injustice felt by the Moslems led to an unwritten national compact. The compact was based on a 1932 census—the last the Christians would allow—which showed them to be a bare majority and the Maronites to be the largest single religious group among the Christians. The Moslems agreed to give up their claim to be part of Syria; the Christians agreed to give up the protection of the French. Under the terms of the compact, Lebanon (which means "The White," a reference to the snow covering the summit of Mount Lebanon) became fully independent on November 16, 1943.

The compact provided that the president and his executive branch would be Maronite; the prime minister would be a Sunni Moslem and the speaker of the parliament a Shiite. The Maronites also insisted on having the right to appoint the commander-in-chief of the armed forces, the head of internal security, the chief justice and the governor of the central bank. The division of power in parliament also protected the Christian dominance: for every five Moslems, six Christians had to be seated; the same ratio applied to jobs in the civil service.

France proudly announced to the world that Lebanon was not, like its neighbors, an Arab nation but a new hybrid in the Middle East: *Zou Wajeh Arabi,* "a nation with an Arab face." The problem, of course, was that despite the deft French effort to create a modern nation-state, the communal realities couldn't be changed. Lebanon simply wasn't composed of people who considered themselves a "nation," but of competing religious groups, almost equal in population, who didn't really want to be united under a single ruler.

Tensions between Christians and Moslems continued throughout the next two decades. In 1958, there were two attempts by leftist Moslems to overthrow the presidency of Camille Chamoun; United States Marines had to be dispatched by President Dwight Eisenhower to save the weak Lebanese regime. Unrest continued, and by the late 1960s, Lebanon was beginning to crack under the signs of stress.

Unlike the other front-line states, which disciplined the Palestinian *fedayeen,* Lebanon was too weak and divided to stop them. Here they could establish their base camps, bring arms with impunity into the open seaports, and enjoy the high style and easy money of Beirut. They brought with them not merely their talents for building political and paramilitary organizations but an attractive ideology and an eagerness to help the Moslem communities redress the political imbalances in Lebanon.

The pitfalls of the Palestinian presence were made abundantly clear when Israeli commandos delivered a massive blow in retaliation for the July 22, 1968, PFLP hijacking of an El Al airliner. The El Al plane was en route from Rome to Tel Aviv when it was seized in Athens and diverted to Algiers. Under the cover of darkness, Israel sought to punish the Lebanese government both for harboring the PFLP in Beirut and for allowing the escalation of border attacks against Israel. Although there were only about 150 Palestinian *fedayeen* in Lebanon in 1968, they were about to make their presence felt. As hundreds of travelers watched in astonishment from the airport terminal in Beirut, Israeli jets flew overhead. Within minutes the Israelis started bombing the Boeing 707 jets belonging to Lebanon's Middle East Airlines; all fourteen planes on the ground were demolished.

The retaliatory raid marked the first time Lebanon had suffered as a result of the Arab-Israeli conflict since the war of 1948. It marked the beginning of a new stage in the Palestinian struggle, one that would tear the fragile fabric of Lebanon's Christian-Moslem compact and plunge the country into two decades of continuous bloodshed from brutal religious and sectarian killing.

The Israeli raid galvanized the Lebanese Moslems. "The Sunnis headed by Rashid Karame started to say we must back the PLO because this is the greatest Arab cause and they should be allowed to operate from Lebanon. The Christians said no and this led to the resignation of Rashid Karame's cabinet," says Edde. In 1969, when Charles Helou, the Maronite leader of Lebanon, tried to persuade another Moslem to become his prime minister, no one would take the job because, says Edde, "he would have been assassinated or boycotted by the Moslem community." Without a Moslem prime minister, Helou could not put together a government. The price of the Sunni leadership for sharing power was a demand that the Palestinians be given new rights to govern themselves within Lebanon.

In November 1969, the Christian, Moslem and Palestinian leaders finally agreed to a meeting in Cairo to reconcile their differences. Helou appointed General Emile Boustani, the army commander who was eager to be elected president himself in 1970, as leader of the Christian delegation. Under the watchful eyes of Egyptian President Nasser, Boustani signed a pact with Yasser Arafat. Boustani thought the pact would help him win Moslem support in the coming elections; signing the pact, however, guaranteed that Christians would not support his candidacy.

Boustani also thought the pact would limit the PLO threat by confining the Palestinians to their camps. In fact, the 1969 Cairo Agreement mortgaged Lebanon's future: it was a declaration of

Palestinian independence from the government. It gave the Palestinians unparalleled freedom of movement in a front-line state, one that assured that Lebanon would become the main battleground of the Arab-Israeli conflict for the next decade. The Palestinians had gained something no Arab nation had been willing to cede to them: the right to organize their guerrilla struggle from front-line territory.

At the time, however, everyone thought they had gained something. The Christians were able to form their government with Suleiman Franjieh as president. The Moslems got their candidate, Rashid Karame, named as prime minister. But the Palestinians were the big winners. Their refugee camps would finally be freed of the hated "deuxième bureau," the Lebanese secret police who supervised the camps and often tortured the Palestinians. Henceforth, they would organize and police themselves, be allowed to carry arms, and be able to launch guerrilla attacks against Israel from Lebanese soil—all without the Lebanese armed forces having the right to restrict them.

Syria, which had never given up its claims on Lebanon, also gained. Franjieh, the new president, owed his victory to the Syrians. It was not the first time they had come to his aid. In the 1950s, Franjieh was given political asylum in Damascus after he was involved in a massacre in a Maronite church. As Lebanon's minister of agriculture, he had signed accords to give farm aid to the Soviet Union, Syria's main bankroller. Now Syria lobbied Lebanese parliamentarians to help Franjieh. They gave him a narrow one-vote victory over Lebanese army candidate Elias Sarkis. When he assumed power in 1970, Franjieh pledged to establish closer ties with Syria while promising to scrap the Cairo Agreement. But even with Syrian support, he could not control the Palestinians.

In fact, had Arafat known what would happen to the Palestinians in Jordan less than a year later, he could hardly have maneuvered more cagily to protect them. Ten months before the Jordanian crackdown of Black September, the Palestinians already had secured a place to which they could retreat. "How could you run against the tide of this Palestinian national movement and its members, thrown out of Jordan? How could you prevent them from coming and staying in the camps in Beirut?" asks Edde. In September 1970, left with nowhere else to go, the guerrillas made Lebanon the main staging area for their war against Israel.

That suited the Arab world, which was tired of sacrificing its blood for the Palestinian cause. Saudi Arabia and the Gulf states readily agreed to finance the Palestinian withdrawal from Jordan. It was an inexpensive insurance policy, a guarantee that the Palestinian revolution would not spread outside Lebanon and that future Arab-Israeli fighting would be confined to its border with Israel.

But the PLO did not limit its attacks to the Israeli border. It established its new headquarters in Beirut, the intellectual, political and business capital of the Arab world. The sparkling jewel on the Mediterranean seacoast was a sophisticated hybrid of Western and Arab civilization: more newspapers were published in Beirut than in the rest of the Arab world as a whole. Beirut's universities were a magnet for scholars throughout the Middle East—not only the renowned American University of Beirut but Saint Joseph's University, a Jesuit school where students could pursue postgraduate work in engineering, law, medicine and economics. Many current Middle East leaders hold diplomas from AUB. The financial community of Beirut also was among the wealthiest in the world. The Lebanese pound was a stable, seemingly inflation-proof currency, comparable to the Swiss franc. Lebanon also had the biggest gold reserve in the Arab world.

The PLO, with its newly found status etched into a formal pact, could not resist exploiting its opportunities. Refugee camps, including two large ones at Tel Zatar and Qaratina located in Christian areas, were turned into fortified military bases. Checkpoints were set up at the international airport inside the Moslem sector of Beirut. The Western-style democracy provided opportunities for the PLO that were nonexistent in other Arab societies. Marxist-Leninist theoreticians, espousing their fashionable ideologies at schools and universities, attacked the free enterprise system that had made Beirut the most important commercial center of the Middle East. These Marxist idealists sought to develop a class consciousness among impoverished Shiites, which only exacerbated the existing hatreds between Christians and Moslems.

The roots of the coming civil war were being sown. Not only were Lebanese Moslems increasing their numbers and becoming a majority, but waves of Palestinians were coming in to reinforce them. After the 1948 war, fewer than 150,000 Palestinians sought refuge in Lebanon. By 1972, the Palestinian presence had swelled to almost

400,000, augmented by the 3,000 *fedayeen* and their families who had fled Jordan. Fatah's army was no longer a ragtag force of a few hundred fighters but a potent army of 10,000 commandos who spearheaded an even larger coalition of Moslem militias. They included 5,000 Palestinians of the Syrian-supported Saiqa and troops of the Palestine Liberation Army.

Also allied with the PLO were smaller Moslem militias, including Ibrahim Quleilat's pro-Nasser al-Mourabitoun ("The Ambushers"), which became the main Sunni fighting force in Beirut, and Moustafa Saad's People's Liberation Army, a Sunni militia in Sidon. The Baathists, the Communists and the Syrian Socialist Nationalist Party (SSNP) also had small squads of fighters. In Tripoli, a mostly Sunni city, a Moslem fundamentalist militia, known as al-Tawhid al-Islami ("Islamic Unity"), was forged under the leadership of Sheikh Saed Shaban and was funded by both the PLO and Iran.

Together they formed a powerful alliance of factions loosely linking the cause of Islam with the ideological fervor of Marxism-Leninism. Their supporters were Sunnis, Shiites and Druse, members of organizations that spanned the political spectrum from the Communists and SSNP to pro-Iraqi and pro-Syrian Baathists and the followers of Nasser's pan-Arab socialist movement.

Their aims were not always the same, but that mattered less than the power they wielded. In 1973 Kamal Jumblatt, a feudal Druse chieftain, founded the National Movement to unite the pan-Arabist factions under the leadership of his Marxist Progressive Socialist Party. With support from PLO leftists, it sought to ignite a revolution not only in Lebanon but throughout the Arab world.

Meanwhile, Rashid Karame, scion of a family of notables from Tripoli, and Saeb Salam also vied for the PLO's favors. These more traditional Sunni politicians wanted to preserve the power of conservative Arab regimes. They supported the Palestinian cause but not the revolt against the established order. They wanted to use the PLO to consolidate their own power in Lebanon, to force a shift away from the Maronites to the Sunnis, but they did not want to bring everything down around them.

The third part of this new alliance was led by a dynamic Iranian-born Lebanese cleric, the Imam Musa al-Sadr. He formed the Movement of the Disinherited and its military wing, Amal, to give hope to the real underclass of Lebanese society, its one million

Shiites. They felt their alliance with the PLO would serve their ulterior motives: the creation of an Islamic republic in Lebanon. These Shiites were rapidly becoming a political force in their own right. Driven from their villages in the south by Israeli reprisal raids against the PLO, more than 100,000 Shiites fled to the southern suburbs of Beirut. There were no jobs for them in the already overcrowded capital except as well-paid mercenaries for the PLO.

"The PLO took over the capital to such an extent that we felt like foreigners in our own country," says the Christian Edde. "The Palestinians had the money and the military logistics to back all these groups and to start arming, training and financing the Shiites," he adds. Edde remembers his student days at AUB when he debated Moslem intellectuals and French leftists on whether Lebanon itself should exist. "We were arguing that we understand and support the rights of the PLO. But we told them their fight should be inside the occupied territories. They could not liberate Palestinian lands and get statehood by trying to bring down the Lebanese state," says Edde.

Yet by early 1973 that seemed to be the PLO's aim. "They convinced the Sunnis they were the army of liberation from the Maronites," he says. "They were the army of the Moslems." Meanwhile, the PLO was continuing its raids against Israel. The Jewish state tried to contain the new threat by unleashing a torrent of attacks against guerrilla bases in the south. Forty major assaults were carried out against Palestinian targets, sending an unmistakable message: Israel would not hesitate to use the full brunt of its military force in Lebanon if the Christian-led government there failed to eliminate the new PLO threat.

In tandem with Israeli desires, on a December 1973 visit to Lebanon, U.S. Secretary of State Henry Kissinger warned Franjieh he had an unpleasant choice: either use his army to put a halt to the PLO takeover or surrender Christian Lebanon to them. Seeking to arrest the anarchy, Franjieh ordered the PLO to stick to the terms of the Cairo Agreement and confine its fighters to the camps. By May, the Lebanese Air Force began its own bombardments of the Palestinians with Hawker Hunter propeller planes. The first "War of the Camps" was now underway.

A unanimous outcry arose from the Arab world, and the Syrians threatened to intervene. The Lebanese army was forced to discontinue its assault. As Kissinger writes in his memoirs, "The result was that the Lebanese government, one of the most moderate in the Middle East, was the most passionate advocate of a Palestinian homeland: It was a way to get the Palestinians out of Lebanon!"[7] Left without a viable military option, Franjieh sought to appease the PLO. When Arafat addressed the United Nations in November 1974, following the PLO's anointment as the only legitimate representative of the Palestinian people, it was Franjieh who introduced him to the world body. That simple act, of course, added new legitimacy to the PLO presence in Lebanon.

By the beginning of 1975, the Lebanese armed forces no longer were very effective. Moslem officers started to bolt from the highly trained, professional corps of soldiers; left without many troops, the Franjieh government was now forced to support private militia groups. The remaining Christian contingents of the Lebanese army began to train, arm and fund the Phalangists and other paramilitary groups.

The most important of these militias were the Kata'ib, the Phalangist battalions, founded by Maronite pharmacist Pierre Gemayel after he returned from the 1936 Olympics in Nazi Germany. Other Christian militia included Dany Chamoun's "Tigers" of the National Liberal Party, formed in 1959 by his father, the former president, after he left office; Tony Franjieh's "al-Marrada," based in the northern city of Zugharta, and Etienne Saqer's "Guardians of the Cedars," an extremist group which wanted to rid Lebanon of all Moslems and reconstitute the ancient Phoenician state.

After a series of bloody confrontations, all these groups were forced to unite under the leadership of the Phalangists, led by Bashir Gemayel. They called themselves the Lebanese Forces. Meanwhile, the Lebanese army split into two competing groups. Ahmed Khatib, an Arab officer, led a defection of Moslem soldiers which began operating with Syrian help against the Christian militias. Major Saad Haddad forged an informal alliance with Israel, receiving training and even uniforms from the Jewish army, and waged his own war against PLO positions in the south.

Beirut itself was a battleground. Christians were being systematically kidnapped, tortured and often assassinated when they crossed from one sector of the city to the other. The chaotic conditions were strengthening the Jumblatt-Arafat alliance. The Syrian leadership watched, increasingly fearful that the PLO would rage out of control and bring down the established Lebanese government. President Assad initially tried to contain the situation by inviting Arafat, in March 1975, to join in a common front with Syria. But the PLO leader again refused to submit to Syrian domination, and by the spring of 1975, the war was paralyzing Beirut.

The bus filled with Palestinians from Tel Zatar, the largest refugee camp in Beirut, made its way slowly through a crowded downtown street in the Christian part of the city. The area, Ain Rummaneh, was policed by a group of Maronites who had formed their own militia to defend their Christian neighborhood against an alliance of Palestinian and Moslem factions threatening the Lebanese capital. The Palestinians on the bus were returning home from a rally in Shatila, a camp in the Moslem sector of Beirut. Hanging from the windows of the bus and covering the license plates were posters promoting Ahmed Jabril's PFLP-GC. Unknown to the passengers, on that April day in 1975, about an hour earlier a car with Palestinians had opened fire on a group of Christians emerging from a wedding at a nearby church. Among those in the wedding party was Pierre Gemayel, the founder of the right-wing Christian Phalange party. Four people, including Gemayel's personal bodyguard, were shot and killed by the Palestinians.

On this day, the Christian Phalangists sent a return message to the Moslems by instantly avenging the shooting that had followed the Maronite church service. The Christian militia stopped the bus and boarded it. The Palestinian passengers found themselves trapped. Everywhere they looked there were armed Christian militia. There was little they could do to protect themselves; within minutes twenty-seven passengers were killed.

The episode is generally considered the spark that ignited the civil war between the PLO and its Lebanese Moslem allies on one side and an alliance of the official Lebanese army and private Christian militia forces on the other side. But it was not an isolated incident: events like the murder of the Palestinians on the bus were becoming more frequent. In December, Bashir Gemayel, a Phalangist militia leader, decided the only way to stop the random killings in Beirut was to clean out the Palestinian camps in the Christian-controlled areas. Instead of limiting the actions of the Palestinians by containing them within the camps, the Palestinians had turned the camps into bases from which they could control traffic in and out of the Christian towns. The most important of these camps was at Qaratina, strategically situated on the main Mediterranean coastal road which linked Beirut with Tripoli. The Palestinians set up roadblocks at the Qaratina bridge to prevent Christians from reaching their homes in the north.

On December 6, 1975, Phalangist militiamen entered the refugee camp and gunned down almost 200 Palestinians. The Phalangists also cleaned out Beirut's port area, burned and looted the Shiite slums, and ransacked the nearby refugee camp of Debaya. This camp, set high on the hill above the Nahar al-Kalb River in the heart of the Christian area near Juneih, controlled access from East Beirut to Mount Lebanon.

Less than a month later, in January 1976, PLO forces retaliated by overrunning Damour, a Christian suburb that connected Moslem West Beirut with the south. Damour was the major Christian enclave between Beirut and Sidon, the coastal capital of the Druse-inhabited mountains of the Shouf. Barely a single house was left standing. Every one of Damour's 2,000 inhabitants either fled or was slaughtered.

Within the city of Beirut, any symbol of Lebanon's occidental, capitalist heritage was fair game. Banks, swank seaside hotels, elegant boutiques and French casinos all were robbed. "The Phalangists and the PLO and the Syrian-backed militias and the National Movement fighters were sharing the spoils. They were covering for each other," says Edde. Fatah spokesman Ahmed Abdul Rahman recalls the chaos, but claims the PLO played the key role in protecting the Central Bank of Lebanon where all of its gold was stored. "There was no order in the city, but Arafat is a responsible person, so he took many decisions. Some street groups had stolen from many banks in Beirut, so Arafat sent about sixty-five fighters to surround the Central Bank."

Nevertheless, on January 20, 1976, members of Fatah's Force 17, the private security arm of Yasser Arafat, broke into the headquarters of the British Bank of the Middle East. The team, under the command of Ali Hassan Salameh, the former Black September leader, was aided by fighters of the Syrian-backed Saiqa. Together they dug a tunnel from the basement of the Catholic Capuccin Church to the adjoining basement of the bank. The Syrian defense minister, Moustafa Tlass, recalls the incident and says that Arafat brought in mafioso from Corsica to help break open the main vault.[8] The deposits of gold bars, stock certificates, jewelry and foreign currencies were so huge, he says, that the PLO had to hire a fleet of trucks to haul away the loot.

In February 1976, as the summer presidential elections approached, the Arafat-Jumblatt alliance began an offensive against Mount Lebanon, trying to force Franjieh to step down six months before the official end of his term. This irritated Assad, who had nurtured his ties with Franjieh and the Maronite leadership. Assad's own minority Alawite heritage made him a natural ally of the minority Christians. They had a common enemy: the Sunni majority which had dominated Syria for hundreds of years. In Syria, too, the Christians were a minority, only about 10 percent of the population, but they were more numerous than the governing Alawites, and were an ally for Assad. The Syrian leader was waiting for the Lebanese Christians to turn to him to save the unity of Lebanon. When the time came, the Christians were so desperate they practically pleaded for Assad's help.

By March, the Lebanese army could no longer stop the hemorrhaging. The presidential palace at Baabda was surrounded, and Franjieh fled for his life to Junieh, the Christian port. The Moslem militias were threatening to take over the Maronite stronghold of Mount Lebanon when Assad decided Syria must intervene. The war was no longer being fought for a more just distribution of political power. Assad had persuaded Franjieh to accept a constitutional reform plan that reduced the authority of the Maronite president and gave Moslems equal representation in parliament. But the Moslems, now a majority, could no longer be appeased.

Assad had to face some unpleasant realities. A Lebanon controlled by a Sunni Moslem regime could become a direct threat to his minority Alawite government. Assad was already being threatened by Sunni fundamentalists in Hama. Jamil Hilel, the PLO spokesman in Damascus, says, "The Syrians wanted to prevent the Phalangists from being pushed out altogether because an alliance between the National Forces of Jumblatt and a strong PLO would make Lebanon hard to crack for the Syrians."

On May 31, after a series of reconnaissance forays by Syrian squads earlier that month, Syrian armored columns, led by 2,000 troops and sixty tanks, crossed the border into Lebanon. They arrived with Franjieh's acquiescence and the tacit approval of both Israel and the United States. Kissinger sent a secret envoy to warn Assad that if Syrian forces didn't move to counter the PLO threat, Israeli troops would. Assad had little choice. If he did nothing, one of two nightmares would become reality: either Lebanon would become dominated by the Sunnis, or the Phalangists would create a Christian ministate backed by Israel.

Kissinger negotiated a secret understanding between Israel and Syria that paved the way for a de facto Syrian presence in Lebanon. Under the terms of these "red line" agreements, Syria could not (1) introduce Soviet-built surface-to-air missiles (SAMs) that would threaten Israeli reconnaissance flights or air strikes against PLO strongholds; (2) deploy any units larger than a brigade south of the Damascus-to-Beirut highway; (3) deploy any units beyond a line running along the Litani River in southern Lebanon and (4) use the Syrian air force over Lebanese territory. Syria also agreed not to threaten Junieh, fifteen miles north of Beirut.

But the fighting intensified. By mid-June, the Syrian forces, 10,000-strong, had become the largest of the twelve armies in Lebanon. They met little opposition from PLO forces, who were encouraged to surrender, and captured Beirut, the Bekaa Valley and Tripoli, and were advancing south to the port city of Sidon. Says Tlass, "We were able to gain control of 80 percent of the country." The battle at Sidon was an indication of how the PLO really felt about the Syrians. A small group of Fatah guerrillas, led by Colonel Abu Musa (Said Musa Muragha), commander of PLO forces in southern Lebanon, ambushed a Syrian armored column. The *fedayeen* destroyed four tanks and a small number of armored personnel carriers. Several Syrian soldiers, including two officers, were killed. The next day, reports reached Assad that the delirious Palestinians had amputated the heads of two of the Syrians and were kicking them around like footballs.

On June 21, 1976, the Lebanese army, commanded by a young brigade commander, Michel Aoun, used the cover of Dany Chamoun's Tiger militias to lay siege to the strongest camp ever built by the PLO, at Tel Zatar. The camp was situated on the road which linked the Christian eastern suburbs of Beirut with the presidential palace at Baabda in an industrial area where thousands of Palestinians were employed. The tacit Israeli-Syrian alliance forged by

Kissinger now assumed a more practical shape: Israeli observers were on the ground advising Chamoun's militia while Syrian officers, under the command of Rifat al-Assad, the president's brother, helped advise Aoun. The Christian army commander did not permit his forces totally to surround the camp, thus allowing many of its residents to flee to Moslem areas. But when the siege was finally lifted fifty-two days later, the death toll was alarming: more than a thousand Palestinians and Shiites had been murdered in the assault.

The Christians continued to battle the Palestinians in areas under their control while the PLO tried to clear Christians out of the area between Beirut and Sidon, trying to take over the southern part of the country and push the Christians back into their northern homeland. For the Christians, this was not a civil war at all: it was a war between those who identified with the traditional, Christian Lebanon, or "Green Lebanon," and all the values of Western civilization, and those determined to destroy them. They saw themselves as the guardians of Lebanon's independence, its territorial integrity and sovereignty. Partition was tantamount to surrender.

By August, the Syrians and their Christian allies had reversed the offensive of the Jumblatt-Arafat forces. In October, newly elected President Sarkis invited the Syrians to form a peace-keeping force to police the succession of fragile cease-fires. Assad traveled to Riyadh for a minisummit with Egyptian, Saudi and Kuwaiti leaders who agreed to fund a Syrian-led Arab deterrent force, "al-Radda." Later that month, the force received the formal backing of the Arab League at a full Arab summit in Cairo. Saudi Arabia, Sudan, the Persian Gulf states and Libya provided token troop contingents but withdrew them several months later, leaving 30,000 Syrian forces behind.

In mid-November, the Syrians took control of Moslem West Beirut and ordered the disbanding of the PLO militias. Assad declared that the nineteen-month-old civil war was now officially over. But the war between Assad and Arafat was just beginning. Says Edde, "Arafat condemned the Syrian invasion in 1976 and he hasn't stopped for a second in condemning it since then." Adds Damascus University Professor Hussan al-Khateeb, "If you want to date the real deterioration in Palestinian-Syrian relations, you would have to say it began in 1976 when the Syrian army entered Lebanon and Arafat's propaganda machine started suggesting the Syrians came to dethrone the king and his kingdom."[9]

14

Exile from Beirut: Revolt Against Fatah

THE SYRIAN DEFENSE MINISTRY *in Damascus sits stolidly on a hill, a gray stone structure projecting indomitable strength. Inside the building, gray corridors lead to the offices of army, air force, and naval commanders, and up a flight of stairs is the office of Moustafa Tlass, the minister of defense. Behind the heavy mahogany doors, the enormous room first strikes the visitor for its riot of colors. On the floor lies a wall-to-wall carpet, a patchwork of Oriental patterns in pinks and oranges and greens. French-style armchairs upholstered in a drab olive fabric line the perimeter, and modern paintings splashed with vibrant hues hang on the walls. At the far end sits the defense minister's elaborate wood desk. On it is displayed a silver model of a Soviet antiaircraft missile mounted on a green metal tank, a gift, the minister says, given when the Syrians purchased a number of these weapons from Moscow. Over the desk, like an altar, hangs a photograph of Syrian President Hafez al-Assad, but this is no ordinary image; the frame is a kinetic assemblage of red, white and green blinking lights that flash continually around Assad's face.*

The minister himself is a handsome man in his sixties, his gray hair, blue eyes, and trim physique a familiar sight to many of Damascus's flirtatious women. He is well known for his romantic phrases, his poetic flair and the body of literature he has penned, most notably *The Rose of Damascus*, a series of verses and floral photographs published in a luxurious, leather-bound volume.

If some smile at Tlass's literary efforts, none laugh at his influence with Assad. Even though the defense minister is a Sunni Moslem— the leading Sunni in a cabinet of Alawites, a minority Islamic sect whose co-religionists, like Assad, come mainly from the mountain village of Kardaha—he and the Syrian leader have been close military colleagues for more than thirty years. Tlass and Assad helped bring the socialist, secular pan-Arab Baathist party to power and together helped overthrow the regime of Jadid Salah. In the 1960s, Tlass first met Yasser Arafat, and though they too started out as friends, their relationship later soured after the Syrians entered Lebanon to stop the civil war. Few in the Arab world speak openly with such venom about Arafat, and few have permitted the PLO leader so little room.

But it was not always this way. Tlass was once one of the PLO's most fiery supporters. At one time, he wanted to mold the map of Palestine in a miniature, three-dimensional relief and require every soldier in the Syrian army to wear it as a pendant around his neck. Tlass asked Arafat for 800,000 pounds to manufacture the ornaments. "We argued and brought the price down to 500,000 pounds," says Arafat's aide, Omar al-Khatib.[1] "We made an enormous number of the plastic medallions. But it didn't cost Tlass more than 200,000 pounds," the PLO official says with a wry smile.

In the early stages of the Lebanese civil war, when the PLO was aided by Syrian-backed Saiqa forces, Arafat and Tlass worked together: the PLO's weapons and logistical support were allowed to be transported through Syria. The two military chiefs also tried to attract more recruits from among the Lebanese Sunni and Shiite communities. Both the PLO and Syria's ruling Baath party were secular entities and therefore regarded with some suspicion by Moslem fundamentalists. Tlass thought of a way to convince the recruits to join them and approached Omar al-Khatib, Fatah's deputy military commander in Beirut. "He came and told me he was interested in printing thousands of copies of the Koran in a fancy cover," says Khatib. "So I told Abu Amar." Arafat agreed. "I gave Tlass a half million Lebanese pounds. That's almost two hundred thousand dollars," says Khatib.

The relationship between Tlass and Arafat became strained a year later when Syrian forces marched into Lebanon to protect the Christians from the advance of the PLO. About 3,000 Palestinian fighters were arrested and interrogated. Arafat, it seems, had convinced them that the secular rulers of Syria's Baath party were allies of the right-wing Christians. "When I heard that, I visited them and issued an order," says Tlass, who wanted to prove he was a practicing Moslem. At the same time Tlass hit on an idea to sell the Korans. "Whoever had memorized the Koran could get out of prison," he announced.

Khatib says that earlier Arafat had agreed to help Tlass "get certain favors, to have Tlass provide certain kickbacks, not monetary but political kickbacks, to guarantee certain things for the PLO in Syria. We used to buy weapons from China and Eastern Europe and bring them in through Latakia. The arms were put in Syrian storage depots. To make it easier to bring these weapons in, we had to be nice to Tlass." The Syrian defense chief says Assad had done many other favors for Arafat. "We gave them weapons free of charge," rocket launchers, Kalashnikov rifles, mines and other explosives. But, says Tlass, in the showdown between Syrian and PLO forces, "they used them against our tanks and armored vehicles." Omar al-Khatib responds irately, "We took absolutely no weapons from the Syrian army. All we had came from what we bought or was donated but not from the Syrian army. We even built a factory for RPGs in Syria, and when we started production, the Syrian army took it over!"

During the bloody June 1982 siege of Beirut, Syrian defense chief Tlass recalls that the PLO received ten new Mercedes ambulances as a gift from Kuwait. Each of the ambulances was worth about $60,000. But Tlass says Arafat never used them to transport the wounded. "He had no need for them. He doesn't like to fight; therefore there will be no wounded," says Tlass. "We bought them from Arafat for about half price and he put the money in his pocket."

The Syrian defense minister contends "there are more than a hundred stories like this." On one occasion, he says, a group of Kuwaiti businessmen gave Arafat a check for $800,000. The check was made out to the Palestine Liberation Organization. "Arafat *insisted it be crossed out and rewritten in his name." Adds Tlass, "Every time an Arab head of state wants to give him a check, he insists on having his name on it. So no one can do anything because Arafat has all the money. He has a strange obsession with money," notes Tlass. "He suffers from the same complex as King Hussein, only he wanted to be richer than King Hussein. I think they are almost equal now."*

Tlass alleges Arafat even tried to bribe him. The PLO leader proudly presented the Syrian defense chief with a gift of a BMW, he says. "When I sent it to Beirut for repairs, I found out it was stolen from the American Ambassador in Amman," says Tlass. A former U.S. embassy official in Jordan confirms the theft of the vehicle. Tlass gave the luxury automobile back but not to the U.S. government. "I returned it," says the Syrian with a sly grin, "to our military intelligence." Omar Khatib responds: "If I tell you what belongs to us that's in the depots of the Syrian army, you will be absolutely shocked. During the Israeli surrounding of Beirut, we got large numbers of weapons and foodstuffs and medical stuff, and the Syrians took it all. We got ambulances on the ships and the Syrians even took those."

Tlass makes no effort to hide the friction with Arafat. He says half-jokingly, "Arafat wants to sing solo, even though he sings off-key." But Tlass genuinely believes Arafat has done a disservice to the Palestinian cause by not cooperating with any Arab governments. "Of course there should be a state that directly supports the Palestinians, but that state should be adjacent to Palestine—either Syria, Jordan or Lebanon," says Tlass. Arafat, however, "wronged Jordan and King Hussein expelled him. He wronged Syria and Hafez al-Assad kicked him out. He was expelled by everybody, so he surrendered to Israel. And in Tunis, the Tunisians will expel him as well," predicts the Syrian. "He causes destruction wherever he goes."

After 1976, it became clearer each day that Syria had no intention of withdrawing its 40,000 troops from Lebanon. Not only the PLO leadership but ordinary Palestinians living in Lebanon began to regard Syria as their enemy. Meanwhile, a new threat to the PLO was emerging to the south.

By May 1977 Israel had a new government led by Menachem Begin, the Herut party leader who headed the ruling Likud coalition. Begin did not have much respect for the Kissinger "red line" agreements that had been tacitly concluded with the Syrians by his Labor party predecessor, Yitzhak Rabin. Rabin had not wanted Israel involved in internal Lebanese feuding. From Rabin's perspective, a weakened Lebanon, with Christians fighting Moslems, reduced the threat of war against Israel. Syria's presence in Lebanon didn't worry Rabin; if they policed the PLO, so much the better for Israel. This new balance of power did not satisfy the new Likud leadership. Begin wanted the Christian militias to unite in a single, paramilitary force so they could join Israel in the fight to wipe out the PLO in Lebanon. Taking his cue from Begin, Lebanese Phalangist leader Bashir Gemayel began a new war to unify the Christian militias under his umbrella. His Phalangist forces first assaulted Franjieh's al-Marrada fighters in the north.

Concerned that a strong Christian alliance with Israel could threaten Syria's presence in Lebanon, Assad threw his support behind Tony Franjieh. After the first clash between the two Christian militias, the Phalangists launched a major attack and struck the village of Zugharta, Franjieh's main stronghold. The Phalangist brigade was led by Samir Geagea. Thirty-two Marrada partisans were killed, among them their leader Tony Franjieh, the thirty-six-year-old son of the former president, his thirty-two-year-old wife Vera and their three-year-old daughter Jehane. Suleiman Franjieh immediately invited the Syrians to remain and, in 1978, the Syrian army ousted the Christian Phalangists from Byblos near Beirut and cleared a path all the way north to the Cedars of Lebanon.

Israel, however, was now openly supporting Gemayel's militiamen, and after several months of pounding by the Phalangists, the Syrians withdrew from East Beirut, Junieh and Byblos, and redeployed their forces in the Bekaa Valley. Today those three areas constitute the region the Christians have labeled "Free Lebanon." Meanwhile, Begin had emerged from the historic Camp David talks with an Egyptian-Israeli treaty of peace, the first signed between an Arab nation and the Jewish state. He now dreamed of liberating Lebanon and declaring from its capital the words both he and Anwar Sadat had pronounced on the lawn of the White House: "No more war."

The Israeli policy shift was felt at once. The new peace treaty forged another alliance: Assad and Arafat were able to shelve their differences and unite behind a common strategy aimed at countering the increasingly heavy Israeli bombardments in southern Lebanon. Syrian Defense Minister Tlass reveals that "we even asked for the formation of one state combining Syria and the PLO." He says he spent an entire month trying to persuade Arafat to accept it, but, says Tlass, "all my efforts were in vain."[2]

Arafat wanted to operate alone.

Meanwhile Gemayel was continuing his Israeli-supported strategy in the north. On July 7, 1980, the Christian Phalangists launched a surprise attack against the second of the Christian militia strongholds, Dany Chamoun's headquarters at the resort towns of Al-Safra, Metin and Jebiel. In the battle of Christians against Christians, hundreds were slaughtered, many while still in their swimming pools. Chamoun fled into exile in Paris, and the renamed Lebanese forces of the Phalangists absorbed Chamoun's Tigers' military and command structure.

By the spring of 1982, Syria had been promised by the United States that Israeli forces, which were now bombarding PLO targets in the south, would not advance beyond the Awali River, about thirty miles into Lebanon. But in April, Assad and Arafat anticipated a major Israeli offensive, and Syria signed an accord promising to help the PLO repel the expected Israeli invasion. To this day, Arafat feels double-crossed by Syria's abandoning the Palestinians in the south, leaving them at the mercy of the Israelis. He contends it was only when the Israelis advanced and threatened the Syrians in the Bekaa that Assad ordered his troops into battle. "In one day, they [the Syrians] lost 110 airplanes, their entire surface-to-air missile system in Lebanon and 100 T-72 tanks," says Mohammed Nashashibi, who heads the PLO office in Damascus. "The Syrians brought their tanks into battle without air cover during daylight hours and they were knocked out, methodically, one by one. It was a massacre."[3]

By June 13, after barely a week of fighting, West Beirut was besieged and Arafat was trapped like an animal, scurrying into hastily-dug-out bunkers to escape the unrelenting Israeli bombardments. PLO commandos had to retreat into the Syrian-controlled Bekaa while the *fedayeen* leadership was forced to transfer its headquarters from Beirut to Damascus. Once again, it seemed to the PLO, Israel was doing Syria's dirty work for it, and Syria was reaping the reward. Under the terms Philip Habib, President Reagan's special Middle East envoy, worked out for the PLO's withdrawal from Beirut, their 14,000 fighters could leave by sea or go to Damascus via the Beirut-to-Damascus highway. "We received all of them in Tartous, north of Tripoli," says Nashashibi. Among the humiliated arrivals were George Habash and Nayaf Hawatmeh, the PFLP and DFLP leaders. "Like the rest, they were disarmed and sent to a special camp. Then they were released," says Nashashibi, "but they were never given back their arms." Arafat, the last one to leave, refused to go to Damascus. He sailed to Athens to show his contempt for Syria and to underscore his abandonment by the rest of the Arab world.

It was only a matter of weeks before Arafat began emerging from his latest exile, 1,500 miles away in Tunis. He knew there was only one place where he might be welcomed back, provided, of course, he accepted the jurisdiction of the monarch there. With most of the world having written him off, that seemed a small price to pay for a reconciliation that would advance the Palestinian cause. Arafat recognized he needed to be rehabilitated, and only King Hussein of Jordan could do that for him. Besides, nothing would anger Assad more. So he began, towards the end of 1982, to lobby Palestinians planning to attend the sixteenth PNC session in Algiers early the following year. Arafat asked them to refrain from an outright rejection of President Reagan's peace plan, which had been made public on September 1, 1982, while Arafat was still on the high seas heading for Athens. He wanted to have the leeway to explore a modus vivendi with Hussein that emanated from an opening in the new American approach. The Reagan plan had incorporated some positive elements: a call for Israeli withdrawal from territory occupied since 1967 and a recognition that the Palestinians in the West Bank and Gaza Strip had to govern themselves. Most important, the plan left open the possibility that a Palestinian state confederated with Jordan could emerge from the negotiating process, even though the United States might be opposed to such an outcome. Prime Minister Begin had immediately, and categorically, rejected the Reagan plan, which, of course, assured that it would be considered more carefully by the PLO.

After intense debate at the February 1983 PNC meeting, Arafat thought he had enough support to broach Hussein with a new offer of cooperation. In early April, for three straight days, Arafat tried to resolve his differences with Hussein and his advisers and forge a common approach to new peace talks. Indeed, on April 4, a joint Jordanian-PLO commission drafted a statement which was approved by the two leaders. It called for Hussein to lead a negotiating team that would include Palestinians who would not be PLO members but would be chosen by the PLO. However, the next day, the PLO Executive Committee flatly rejected the agreement and, on April 8, Arafat cabled Hussein that for the time being he could not give him a mandate to negotiate with the Reagan administration on the PLO's behalf.

As far as many in the Palestinian leadership were concerned, the damage had already been done. Shamed by the specter of their televised withdrawal from Beirut, and angered by the Israeli-inspired Phalangist massacres two weeks later at Sabra and Shatila, the sight of a humbled Arafat now courting the monarch who had forced them into exile was too much to bear. The straw that broke the camel's back, as far as Syria was concerned, was the discovery that Arafat had given sanctuary, in Tripoli, to fifty Moslem fundamentalists who had led a bloody religious uprising in Aleppo in northern Syria.[4] Eighty young Syrian officers, members of Assad's own Alawite sect, were murdered in the revolt. Assad himself now decided Arafat had to be deposed as the leader of the Palestine Liberation Organization.

Assad did not have to look very far to find disgruntled Palestinians. A reform movement had been forged of Fatah forces critical of the promotions Arafat had made in his officer corps. They wanted to democratize the way PLO leaders were chosen. This faction was led by an experienced warrior who had been injured six times while commanding Palestinian forces in southern Lebanon, once by Syrian agents in Nabatiyah. Colonel Abu Musa (Saed Musa Muragha), was a respected soldier and had a sizable following among Palestinians. His new group, "Fatah Uprising," declared war on Arafat, attacking the autocratic system which he used to exercise power. They wanted proportional representation in the PLO's labor unions, its welfare and women's groups, in all PLO bodies, from the ruling central council to mass organizations, and within the PNC. Nevertheless, argues PLO spokesman Jamil Hilel, "The call for democratization should be differentiated from the motives of the people who wanted to split the PLO and overthrow Arafat."

Abdul Hadi al-Mashash, a leader of the new faction, says the revolt to topple Arafat began when the PLO leader named loyalists "who never fought against the Israelis" to replace officers who refused Arafat's command to abandon Lebanon. These officers suspected Arafat had concluded a secret pact with Habib that would compel them to quit Lebanon just as thousands of their compatriots had been forced into their latest exile from Beirut. "There were about sixty officers Arafat ordered to shift," says Mashash.[5] "But we refused." Of the total of 15,000 Fatah/Asifa troops in Lebanon, "about 3,000 left with the other cadres for Tunis, Iraq, Yemen, Sudan and Jordan. The rest [about 12,000] remained with us," says the rebel leader. They weren't about to quit Lebanon just because Arafat ordered them to. Explains Mashash, "We consider the Lebanese arena a basic one. Lebanon is not just a geographical place but a political one."

Assad also liked Abu Musa's uncompromising ideology. "Arafat turned his back on the PLO Charter when he agreed to recognize Israel. We stick to the original principles of Fatah," says Mashash. "We are committed to continuing the armed struggle because we believe that entity in Palestine [Israel] can never be a partner for peace. Arafat believes he can achieve a political settlement and that such a solution requires us to abandon a part of Palestine. We believe that *all* of Palestine is the homeland of the Palestinians and we will never abandon it."

For Assad, Abu Musa was a convenient ally, and in May 1983 the Syrians began providing logistical support for the rebels. Emboldened by their new benefactor, Fatah Uprising denounced Arafat in public, charging him with executing a "military and organizational coup d'état in Fatah." Arafat responded at once, stripping the rebels, who numbered about 400, of their supplies of food, fuel and money. In June, Arafat went to Damascus and bitterly castigated them. Sheik Saad al-Din al-Alami, the Moslem Mufti of Jerusalem, issued a *fatwa,* a religious ruling, denouncing Assad's efforts to wipe out Fatah and calling for his assassination.[6] The rival Baathist regime in Iraq cut financial aid to Syria and also called on its people to overthrow the "oppressive tyrant," who the Iraqis charged was allied with Israel to destroy the PLO.

"We suggested arbitration but Arafat refused, threatening to confront us with arms," says Mashash. Venting his frustration at his inability to attract Arafat's attention, a disgruntled Palestinian fighter on the outskirts of Tripoli exclaimed: "What am I supposed to do? Chase Arafat in an airplane!" Learning of the heated exchange between Arafat and the rebels, Assad gave Arafat only two hours to leave Syria. On June 24, 1983, Arafat went to the airport. On the way, says Jamil Hilel, Syrian-backed rebels tried to murder him. "The assassins were waiting in two to three cars but something happened that foiled the attempt." Hilel refused to unravel the mystery. Arafat talked his way onto a commercial flight back to Tunis.

For five years, from that day in the summer of 1983 to the funeral of Abu Jihad in 1988, Arafat did not return to Damascus. "He was despicable," even at the funeral, says Tlass. "He did not attend the funeral procession." After the ceremony, when Assad agreed to meet him, Arafat politely asked for his advice, recalls Tlass. The Syrian leader told Arafat to end his feud and unite with the Damascus-based Palestinian factions. Instead, says Tlass, "He left Assad's office and decided to kill Abu Musa—under the pretext that he could not unite with dead people." Adds Tlass, "He was conducting sabotage operations against Syria. He wanted to overthrow Assad and the entire Syrian regime."

The final showdown, however, was still to come. Assad mobilized Saiqa together with the forces of Ahmed Jabril's PFLP-GC and Abu Musa's Fatah Uprising and drove the Fatah fighters out of the Bekaa and north into Tripoli. There Assad hoped to teach Arafat and his men a lesson they would not soon forget. In late September Arafat called Assad's bluff and traveled incognito by boat from Algiers to Tripoli to confront the rebel forces. "He went because he wanted to be with the besieged Palestinians and to show the Syrians that he was prepared to make a stand," says Hilel. Tlass is more cynical about Arafat's motives. "He went because he thought we were not going to attack him," charges Tlass bitterly.

For Assad, Arafat's unexpected appearance in Tripoli was more than a mere annoyance. His presence in the Moslem capital of northern Lebanon, with its strong links to the Moslem Brotherhood, was a direct challenge to his minority Alawite rule. In February 1982, Assad had ordered his troops to quash a rebellion of Sunni fundamentalists in Hama. A city northwest of Damascus known for the piety of its 180,000 Moslem inhabitants, Hama was also known for its long tradition of resisting rule by the secular central government in Damascus. In the resulting massacre, 20,000 Syrians, many of them civilians, were murdered.

Assad believed he now faced a similar threat. He was not going to sit idly by while fundamentalists in Tripoli linked their cause with fundamentalists in Hama or Aleppo and turned the majority of Sunnis against him. In Assad's mind, Arafat had chosen to fight in Tripoli because it was near the mountain home of the Alawis on the Syrian border. What was close to their mountains had to be under their control if the Alawites wanted to survive.

One by one, charges Tlass, Arafat intended to liquidate each of the groups which operated with Syrian support in areas controlled by Syrian forces: the Baath Party, Jumblatt's Progressive Socialist Party, the Communist Party, the SSNP, Franjieh's Marrada units and the Amal and Hezbollah militias of the Shiites. "He started by killing the members of the SSNP. Then he started killing the Communists," says Tlass.

The Syrian defense minister telephoned Marshal Nikolai Ogarkov, chief of the Soviet general staff, to alert him to what Tlass believed was a CIA plot to eliminate the Communists. "He told me the Soviets had discussed the matter with the CIA. They told him they had not issued an order to liquidate the Communists," says Tlass. But the Syrian official didn't believe them. He reminded Ogarkov that when Sadat expelled two thousand Soviet advisers from Egypt, he wasn't acting explicitly on CIA instructions either. "He told me he understood, and for five years Arafat was not welcome in Moscow. They knew he sided with the United States," says Tlass.

Assad issued a death warrant for the PLO leader, he confirms. Backed by the Syrian army, the rebels used heavy mortars to shell Fatah positions. Israeli vessels also pounded Arafat's men from the sea. Says Tlass, "I warned them I would be attacking with tanks. I fired six rounds near his position. I told him the next round would land on his head. He had to know we would kill." Tlass says he used a commencement address to the graduating officers at the Aleppo Air Force Academy to make sure Arafat got the message. The speech was carried on Syrian radio. In the event Arafat didn't hear it, Tlass made sure it was conveyed through other channels. Military attachés of seventeen nations attended the ceremonies in Aleppo. "One of them was certain to relay the message," says Tlass.

By December 1983, after ten days of particularly intense fighting, Assad's forces surrounded the Fatah guerrillas and again had Arafat trapped like a caged animal. "We suffered," says Mashash, "because we realized that dozens of Palestinians were being killed and even though they were fighting on Arafat's side, they were a loss for the Palestinian revolution." Few in the international media thought the bearded revolutionary would live to tell his tale again. With the deft talent of a statesman, Arafat appealed to France, to Egypt and to the United States. The French arranged passage aboard a Greek ship sailing from Tripoli and provided an armada to protect him. The United States restrained the Israelis. In Arafat's wake, a flotilla of 4,000 Fatah fighters also left Lebanon.

Instead of returning to Tunis, Arafat sailed to Ismailia on the Suez Canal, and from there he was helicoptered to Cairo. The ensuing reconciliation with Hosni Mubarak, Egypt's president, was a turning point for Arafat. "It wasn't simply that Egypt had good relations with Syria's main enemies, Jordan and Iraq, and bad relations with Libya, Syria's principal ally. It was that these three countries encircled Syria and were a fairly powerful grouping," says Hilel. "He was siding with one Arab regional power against the Syrian axis."

The decision to travel to Cairo was an intensely personal one, says Hilel, who recalls Arafat's saying that "since the Syrians forced me to leave, I will go to their enemy." But it also liberated Arafat from the constraints of having to achieve unity by appeasing the splinter PLO factions. He now was free to pursue the political option with the only Arab nation that had already made peace with Israel. "It was time," announced Arafat after a two-hour meeting with Mubarak, "to begin thinking about the creation of a Palestinian government-in-exile." The Egyptian leader was pleased. After almost two decades of revolutionary struggle, Yasser Arafat now appeared to be changing course, embracing the need to compromise, to become responsible for achieving something politically for the Palestinian people.

At least that was the verdict of Arafat's Palestinian adversaries. He was denounced as the "Sadat of Palestine" by PFLP-controlled newspapers. Assad called him a traitor and tried to persuade Farouk Kaddoumi and Salah Khalaf to dump him, offering each of them Syrian support if they agreed to take over the PLO. Even sympathetic organizations, such as France's Radio Monte Carlo, charged Arafat was following in the footsteps of the traitorous Camp David accords.

To defeat Assad at his own game, Arafat now had to prove he still could command the support of a majority of Palestinians. He tried but failed to convince the Algerian government to host the next PNC.

Algiers offered to host it, but only if Arafat first achieved a consensus among the warring PLO factions. So, once again, he turned to his old sparring partner King Hussein. The timing was right. In 1984, Hussein was just as eager to regain his tarnished Palestinian credentials and quickly welcomed Arafat's initiative: the seventeenth PNC congress would be held in Amman, Jordan, in November 1984. The hot war with Assad now became an icy cold war of wits.

Assad's strategy was simple: to deprive Arafat of a needed quorum of 255 delegates, two-thirds of the 383 active PNC members. Assad funded a new Palestinian National Coalition of four resistance groups: Abu Musa's Fatah Uprising, Jabril's PFLP-GC, Saiqa and Samir Ghosha's Palestine Popular Struggle Front (PPSF). Assad also had the tacit support of George Habash's PFLP, Nayaf Hawatmeh's DFLP and Talat Yaqub's faction of the Palestine Liberation Front (PLF). As soon as the coalition announced itself and publicly criticized the PLO's reconciliation with Egypt, Arafat cut off funding to all three groups. They later formed the nucleus of the National Salvation Front which was determined to boycott the PNC in Amman.

Spearheading the battle to make sure Arafat fell short of the required quorum was Khaled al-Fahoum, the PNC speaker, who claimed to represent a hundred PNC members, mostly PFLP, DFLP and independents, living in Damascus. On November 10, 1984, Fahoum sent Arafat a cable asking him to postpone the planned parliament-in-exile. Two days later Arafat formally requested that King Hussein convene the PNC in Amman.

"Therefore," says Fahoum, "it was my duty as chairman of the National Council to warn the members and ask them not to go because it will deepen the split in the PLO." Did Assad, as widely rumored, threaten those who planned to go to Amman? "Not a single passport was confiscated," says Fahoum. But he admits "it was suggested by some senior Syrian officials around Assad that anyone who goes to the Amman conference will not be allowed to come back to Syria." Says Fahoum, "Not a single one went from Syria."

The forty to sixty PNC members who lived in Lebanon also had a difficult time getting to Amman. That left Arafat with only his hardcore of Fatah supporters, somewhat less than 200, and the 60 PNC members, mostly independents, who lived in Amman. He needed every one of them to achieve the required quorum of 255. "He did his best," charges Fahoum, booking every available hotel room and sending first-class tickets for any delegate who promised to make the flight from Europe or the United States. Fahoum says that when he knew he would not make it, Arafat promised them money and cars. "The present PNC chairman even got a house in Amman," says Fahoum.

This was hardball: the coalition of Syrian-backed groups publicly threatened to blow up the home of anyone who participated. Did Arafat muster the necessary support to convene the PNC? He says he did: 261 members, six more than required, attended the session. According to Fahoum, he fell short. "They had 246 or 247. I am sure. I have their names," the rival PNC speaker declares. Fahoum even convened a rival Palestinian congress in Damascus.

The PNC met for a week, beginning on November 22, and unanimously reelected Arafat as chairman. It voted support for his efforts to coordinate with Jordan on a new diplomatic tack to "regain Palestinian and Arab lands" and expelled the PFLP-GC's Ahmed Jabril, one of Arafat's bitterest enemies. In the wake of the PFLP and DFLP boycott, nine of the seats on the Executive Committee were filled with Fatah supporters and independents. Six were left vacant for the return of other candidates.

The battle with Assad and his PLO allies was far from over. A month later, on December 23, 1984, Fahoum appeared on Syrian television, vehemently denouncing Fahd Kawasmeh, one of the new members of Executive Committee. Kawasmeh was the former mayor of Hebron. He had been deported by Israel and had thrown his support to Arafat. The day after Fahoum attacked him, Kawasmeh was assassinated in front of his home in Amman.

For the next three years, Arafat tried to pursue a common strategy with Hussein. Only after it failed and Hussein publicly accused Arafat of being responsible for its failure, did Habash and Hawatmeh agree to return to the PLO fold. Their reconciliation with Arafat took place in March 1987, when the next PNC meeting was held. Almost the entire active membership of 384 delegates (minus the 181 reserved for Palestinians living under Israeli occupation in the West Bank and Gaza) attended the eighteenth parliamentary session in Algiers.

The proposal for a Palestinian-Jordanian confederation was officially rejected; instead, the PNC unanimously endorsed creation of an independent Palestinian state. The return of the PFLP and DFLP leaders marked the collapse of the National Salvation Front and ended an eleven-year effort by Assad to control the Palestinian movement. It was Soviet leader Mikhail Gorbachev who played the decisive role with Assad. During a visit to Moscow in late spring, on the eve of the 1987 PNC meeting, Assad was pressed by Gorbachev to abandon his decade-long campaign to unseat Arafat.

At the end of their meeting, the Soviet and Syrian leaders issued a joint communique. It acknowledged that the PLO was the only legitimate representative of the Palestinian people and gave official backing to its efforts to participate in preparatory talks for an international peace conference. Knowing he had won one of the most important battles of his career, Arafat emerged from the PNC session in Algiers and called the reconciliation "a victory for our people." Then, with a broad smile beaming from his bearded face, he declared: "We will get together and return to al-Quds," the Arabic name for Jerusalem.

IV

Jordan: Brothers and Foes

15

Hussein and the Hashemite Kingdom

THE WHITE SUN *scorches the roof of the old Chevrolet as it speeds towards the Jordanian capital of Amman. The road stretches across a flat plain, then twists and turns through mountain passes, and here and there, past the brown dust that seeps through cracks in the windows, we glimpse a farmer working his fields, or a Bedouin walking his camel, or a sleepy family at rest outside their hut. Out of nowhere a sign appears, only a few words and arrows, but they announce, with startling certainty, that this is the heart of the Moslem world. One arrow points to Damascus, another to Mecca and Medina, a third bends towards Baghdad, and a fourth aims towards Amman. The Hashemite Kingdom is a crossroads of the Middle East; but the sign gives no hint of Jordan's traditional isolation in the Arab world.*

In the fairy-tale city of Amman, seven gentle hills give rise to modern, whitewashed villas; the roads are lined with cypress trees and aromatic eucalyptus is fragrant in the mountain air. A visitor notices first how gleamingly clean the streets are, how pretty the houses built with Jerusalem stone, how well-dressed the people, and how so many of its citizens bear familiar names: Nashashibi and Nabulsi, Masri and Rifai, Dajani and Abu Saud, family names as common, it seems, in Amman as they are in Jerusalem, Ramallah or Nablus. The sparkling streets give little evidence of the blood that has been shed here, of the bitter struggle between Palestinians who call themselves Jordanians and swear their loyalty to the king, and Palestinians who are often frustrated with the Hashemite monarch and his claims to rule them.

Oddly, for an Arab capital in a desert country, the only one in Bedouin dress in this residential part of town appears to be the doorman at the Intercontinental Hotel, a tall, smiling fellow wearing a costume of colorful robes, scuffling about in his sandaled feet, his head wrapped in a kafeeyah that would keep him cool if he were riding a camel. But here in the city one is more likely to see him in a convertible with the top down, or to find his cousin in the Royal Guard driving a silver Mercedes from the king's fleet. Ask either one how he feels about King Hussein, and he will flash a broad smile, put his hand on his chest and say, "My heart belongs to His Majesty."

Every fable must have a king, of course, and Jordan has its own, a dashingly handsome man with sad eyes who seems to bear on his shoulders the course and curse of Middle Eastern history. He is the aristocratic version of an image often seen in the homes of Palestinians: a picture of a heavy old woman carrying the globe on her back. King Hussein has carried that sphere of weight, thanks in great part to those same Palestinians who contest his rule over their lives. Yet they have been a part of that kingdom since Hussein's grandfather, Abdullah, arrived in 1921 to found the country. Tradesmen, people of commerce and government administrators, they traveled back and forth from Nablus and Jerusalem, crossing the spit of water that is the Jordan River as easily as they crossed the cobblestones of the Old City.

Palestinians and Hashemites both are plentiful in the service of the king, their ministerial offices located in his palace. Like the castles and fortresses in storybooks, this one is set high on a hill, protected by stone walls that separate it from the thicket of people who crowd the downtown streets. Beyond the black iron gates and guardhouse, miles of manicured park surround the pale stone buildings of the king's estate. Along the road to his private office building, fire engines, ambulances and extra cars are at the ready, and royal soldiers guard the checkpoints. Inside the entrance to the Palladian-style building and in the marble corridors of power, the king's guards keep a careful eye on guests. Too much has happened to this man, too many would-be assassins have come too close; everyone must be scrutinized.

At the end of a long hall cushioned with green and gold carpet, past a portrait of Abdullah, the king stands in a doorway. Smiling graciously, he shakes our hands and ushers us into his private chambers. The office, like the man, is surprisingly small and almost humble; surely any CEO would demand a more imposing space. The monarch moves towards one side of the room and suggests that we take a seat, although he says, gesturing to the elegant French furniture, that he never knows for sure how the chairs are arranged because "they are always changing things around."[1] Whether these changes are born out of the need for security or a penchant for decorating remains unsaid.

His Majesty, as Hussein is called by everyone around him, speaks almost in a whisper, as if his voice might cause a disturbance. With a well-bred British accent he addresses male guests, almost humbly, as "sir," a manner learned, perhaps, in his days at Harrow and Sandhurst. As he listens, he takes a cigarette and lights it with a shell-shaped silver lighter, and in the habit of almost all Middle Easterners, as soon as he finishes one cigarette, he starts another. Behind him, on his desk, is the most telling work of art in the room, a bronze bust of John Fitzgerald Kennedy. The sculpture of the assassinated president cannot help but serve as a reminder of how dangerous leadership can be. Indeed, Hussein has said that if being a head of state is like being in prison, then being a king is like having a life sentence.[2] Perhaps his first glimpse of the awesome dangers came at the age of sixteen when he walked at his grandfather's side.

The old, jowled Arab king with the twinkling eyes and the schoolboy dressed in the captain's uniform of the Arab Legion stood together in the courtyard of al-Aqsa Mosque, proud members of the Hashim clan who had come to the holy site to say their Friday prayers. Abdullah and Hussein had arrived from Amman the evening before, spent the night with a friend named Nashashibi in the neighborhood of Sheikh Jarrah, and drove the next afternoon through the streets of Jerusalem. They had stopped at the tomb of the old man's father and proceeded towards the Abu Saud compound, where Haj Amin al-Husseini had controlled the Arabs of Palestine and Yasser Arafat had sat at his feet, in the Haram al-Sharif. As their automobile approached the courtyard of al-Aqsa, the boy and his grandfather, a bodyguard protecting them, stepped from the car and walked up the steps of the gold-domed building. Two thousand other Moslems had already gathered inside, but the mosque's distinguished, white-bearded sheik made it a point to come to the door, bow down and kiss the hand of the king. The sixty-nine-year-old Abdullah planned to give a eulogy for Riad al-Sulh, the former Lebanese prime minister, who had been killed in Amman only five days earlier. Before and after the murder of the Lebanese leader, warnings and rumors of plots against King Abdullah had filled the air, and even he felt this might be his last visit to the mosque. But determined to show himself a free man in a city in his own kingdom, he had insisted they come, and they did. Within seconds the violent hand of the Middle East would swoop down and snatch him from life.

King Hussein has had his own confrontations with would-be assassins. Probably his narrowest escapes came during Black September, that period in 1970-1971 when the PLO set out to destroy him and ravaged his country in their wake. His view of Arafat will always be tarnished by that time. Yet their relationship has been ambivalent; both pragmatists, they are cooperative as well as competitive. The king must contend with the reality that his country has a split identity: Jordan is the home of the largest number of Palestinians living outside the occupied territories; moreover, the majority of people living in Jordan are Palestinian. For Hussein, the Palestinian issue does not merely involve the fate of those who are on the West Bank; what happens to them may decide the future of his kingdom on the East Bank. To keep both groups of Palestinians content, Hussein needs Arafat.

The PLO leader needs King Hussein. To keep his claim of leadership of the Palestinians, Arafat must maintain access and amity with the king. In addition, Jordan's geography makes it a vital ally for Arafat; for him it is the back door to Palestine. While Hussein may not be as popular as Arafat with the Palestinians, he has given *them a home in Jordan, and they are aware that by and large it is a better one than they would have in Syria, Lebanon or any other Arab state.*

———————————

————————

The first shot that rang out on June 5, 1916, signifying the start of the Arab Revolt against the Ottoman Empire, was fired by King Hussein's great-grandfather, Sharif Hussein of Mecca. The Sharif, head of the Hashemites, could easily claim leadership in the uprising that marked the beginning of the Arab thirst for nationalism. The Hashim clan were direct descendants of the prophet Mohammed, offspring of Mohammed's daughter, Fatima, and her husband Ali, the only line of males who could be called Sharif of Mecca and who were guardians of the Holy Places.

Even before the prophet Mohammed was born, King Hussein's ancestral Bedouin family was prominent. The Hashim clan, from the tribe of Quraysh, had established itself centuries earlier in Mecca, where Ishmael is said to have come with his mother, the servant Hagar, after Abraham expelled them and sent them into the desert. It was here that the angel Gabriel led them to their first drop of water at the Well of ZamZam. Here, too, it is believed, Abraham, the father of both Ishmael and Isaac, came to build a house of worship, and pagans later came to pray to more than 300 gods. Idols made of gold or wood or stone, the gods for fertility, beauty and other desired attributes, were placed in a stone cubicle, the Kabah, set at the site of Abraham's temple.

Mohammed was born in Mecca in A.D. 570, a member of the same Quraysh tribe as the Hashims, and it was to Mecca that he returned victorious 58 years later to preach his new religion of Islam. Upon his arrival in Mecca, Mohammed visited the Kabah, demolished the idols of the pagans and placed the legendary Black Stone, believed to be a remnant of Abraham's temple, inside the cubicle. Wherever they may be in the world, Moslems still turn towards the Kabah five times daily when they kneel on the ground to pray.

Before Mohammed left the city, he stood on the plain of Arafat and spelled out the duties of a Moslem, including at least one pilgrimage to Mecca to partake in the special rituals of that visit, called the Haj. Before entering the sacred city, male visitors must humble themselves before God and wrap their naked bodies in the *ihram,* throwing a special cloth over the chest and shoulders, wrapping another cloth around their bottom half, and slipping their feet into sandals. The pilgrims must walk at a fast pace around the Kabah, touch the Black Stone, drink from the Well of ZamZam, and either shave their heads or cut their hair. A photograph of Yasser Arafat, on the wall of his office in Tunis, shows him in Mecca, his head shaved and his body wrapped in the *ihram.*

Mecca served not only as a center of religion, the holiest place in the Moslem world, but also as a respite for commercial travelers from the time of the Romans until the end of the Ottoman Empire. Traders carrying silks, spices and jewelry from India as well as frankincense, myrrh, gold and copper from southern Arabia stopped to rest before bringing their goods to the Roman regions further north. From this city along the coastal strip called the Hejaz, on the western plain of the great Arabian desert, they traveled by camel to Damascus and from Damascus to Constantinople, Europe and the rest of the civilized world. Later the Ottoman Turks would build a railroad along this very route.

But it was Islam that won Mecca its fame and it was the Moslem religion that endowed the Hashemites with their right to claim the leadership of the Arabs. In 1916 Sharif Hussein of Mecca had ambitions to reestablish the Arab kingdom once called Greater Syria. At the urging of his second son, Abdullah, the Sharif contacted the British to seek their support for an Arab revolt against the Turks. The father had tried earlier to negotiate Arab independence with the Turks but had found instead that the Ottomans wanted to obliterate the Arabic language. In exchange for siding with the British during World War I, the Sharif wanted British guarantees that, following the war, they would help establish a self-ruling Arab kingdom with Sharif Hussein at the helm.

It seemed only fair, then, that at the end of World War I, when the secret Sykes-Picot agreement became known and the Balfour Declaration was reaffirmed, the British would come through with their promise. But instead of giving the Sharif his one large kingdom, they divided the region into fiefdoms: Sharif Hussein and his oldest son

Ali were given the small kingdom of the Hejaz; his son Faisal, who had fought so well alongside T. E. Lawrence and successfully sabotaged the Turkish railways, claimed the throne in Damascus; his son Abdullah would be given the oil-rich area of Iraq. When Faisal became ruler of Syria, the Arabs in Palestine, led by Haj Amin al-Husseini, proclaimed themselves part of his kingdom and celebrated his inauguration by demonstrating in the streets of Jerusalem. The Ottoman Province of Syria, in fact, had included the territory from the Taurus Mountains in the north to the Sinai Desert in the south, and from the Mediterranean Sea in the west to the Iraqi steppes in the east, so the Hashemites believed that all of this region would be theirs. But Faisal was allowed to stay on the throne for only a matter of months before he was ousted by the French. Subsequently, the British made Faisal the King of Iraq, the land to the east of Damascus.

Abdullah had first met T. E. Lawrence during the Arab rebellion in Jedda, mounted on a white mare, and surrounded "by a bevy of richly armed slaves," as Lawrence wrote in his memoirs, *Seven Pillars of Wisdom*. Lawrence considered Abdullah too clever, and gave him a critical look. "His eyes had a confirmed twinkle; and though only thirty-five, he was putting on flesh. It might be due to too much laughter. Life seemed very merry for Abdullah. He was short, strong, fair-skinned, with a carefully trimmed brown beard, masking his round smooth face and short lips. In manner he was open, or affected openness, and was charming on acquaintance."[3]

Abdullah had been raised and educated in Constantinople, where he was active in Turkish politics, a member of the Ottoman parliament. He was ambitious for his clan and the cause of Arab nationalism. It was he who had first thought of the idea of an Arab revolt and had helped his father work out an agreement with the British. After the war, when his brother Faisal was ousted from the Syrian throne by the French, Abdullah left his father in Hejaz, took a bevy of soldiers and rode off towards Damascus to try and regain Syria for the family. On the way, in March 1921, he stopped in the small backwater town of Amman, met with British officials, and was summoned to Jerusalem for a conference with the colonial secretary, Winston Churchill. Churchill tried to resolve the discrepancy between what had been promised to the family and what, in reality, could be achieved. The colonial secretary listened while Abdullah argued politely that Faisal should be reinstated as the ruler of Syria, and that he wanted to be king of Palestine and the eastern region of the mandate known as Transjordan. With that as his family base, Abdullah envisioned a kingdom of Greater Syria for the Hashemite clan. "He believed in an Arab revival, and the Arabs' right to regain a position they once had amongst nations," says his grandson, King Hussein. "He suffered many setbacks, as did the revolt itself, and the Arab world was divided and occupied in parts."

The British were not interested in an Arab war against the French in Syria, and they had already announced the Balfour Declaration, promising part of Palestine to the Jews. Take Transjordan, Churchill told him, the area to the east of the Jordan River, and from there Abdullah would most likely win control of Damascus and forge the Greater Syria of which he dreamed. The British, who wanted to maintain a presence in both Palestine and Iraq, would pay him 5,000 pounds a month to run a police force and would help him administer the area by sending a British resident who would report to the high commissioner in Jerusalem. Abdullah, always a pragmatist, grabbed the opportunity, and only a few weeks later, on April 21, 1921, he officially took over Transjordan, which from the time of the Roman conquest in A.D. 106 had been part of the province of Arabia.

Although Syria had been signed off to the French, the British had managed to keep the southern section, the region of arid mountains that flanked the eastern bank of the Jordan River. This desert that once contained the biblical lands of Edom, Moab, Ammon and Bashan was linked to the British mandate of Palestine by its people and its administration. Its inhabitants included farmers, shepherds and goatherds, but mostly they were Bedouins: dark-eyed, dark-skinned Arabs who raised camels and roamed the desert for grazing lands. Famed for their flashing swords and fighting spirit, these tempestuous nomads traveled without thought across borders and other people's property. They slept in tents, dressed in flowing burnooses, wrapped their heads in *kafeeyahs*, and lived off dates and camel's milk. Devoted Moslems, with few exceptions, they considered the Hashemites to be their rightful leaders.

But when Abdullah was given the territory, the 2,000 people who welcomed him in Amman were not the desert Bedouins, but Circassians, non-Arab Moslems who left the Caucusus Mountains after the Russians took over their land in the late 1800s. The fair-haired, blue-eyed Circassians had fled from Russian massacres and worked their way further south, first to Bulgaria and Turkey and then deeper into the Ottoman Empire in Syria, Palestine and Jordan. Wherever they settled, they were considered good fighters and loyal to their host government. Those who came to Amman, the city known to the Romans as Philadelphia, found not much more than a stopping place along the route from Mecca to Damascus. At the time when the Hejaz railway was built by the Turks in 1900, as many as 200,000 Moslems traveled to Mecca each year to make the Haj. But there was little else in the town to give it importance; bare, hilly and provincial, it had been an insignificant part of the Ottoman Empire, and seemed destined to remain that way under the British.

Although Abdullah's administration was placed in Amman, the Hashemite saw himself as the leader of all the Arabs in Palestine and the area which he dubbed eastern Palestine, better known as Transjordan. Under the Ottomans, the administrative areas had been organized along horizontal lines, with the districts stretching east to west from the desert to the sea. Although they had used the natural border of the Jordan River and established the district of Palestine and the district of Jordan, people traveled easily back and forth and families were often divided between nearby cities. Those who resided in Jenin often had close relatives in Irbid, and those who lived in Nablus frequently had family in Salt. Indeed, the Peel Commission partition sponsored by the British in 1937 would call for the Arab areas of Palestine to be merged with Transjordan.

Abdullah's own background was similar to that of the Arabs who lived in Nablus, Safad, Hebron and Jerusalem, city people who were educated and traveled, and he called on them to help him form his government. The officials whom he chose as his prime ministers included Tawfik abul Huda from Acre, Samir Rifai from Safad, and Ibrahim Hashim from Nablus; without their political acumen and their training in the Ottoman and British civil service, he would have had almost no one capable of organizing an administration. These Arabs from Palestine, in turn, considered themselves loyal subjects of Abdullah and true citizens of Transjordan. Throughout his rule he sought help in running his government from the Arabs in Palestine and encouraged them to come to the East Bank. But a large faction of Palestinian Arabs, under the strong leadership of Haj Amin al-Husseini, the mentor of Arafat, had no interest in following Abdullah. Their aim was to expel the British and establish their own sovereign Arab state on all of Palestine. The friction between the followers of Haj Amin and the followers of Abdullah would lead tragically to the king's murder and place a pall over his grandson's life.

Abdullah owed much to the British, who not only paid his expenses, but also helped organize his police force of Bedouin fighters. Under the command of the British Captain F. G. Peake, the members of the Arab Legion saved Abdullah from attack in 1924 by the fanatical forces of Abdul Aziz ibn-Saud. A rival Bedouin from Central Arabia, ibn-Saud had already deposed Sharif Hussein from his throne in Hejaz and aimed next for Amman. The Arab Legion returned the favor and served the British in good stead. During World War II, under the command of General Glubb, it fought successfully against the Iraqis and the Vichy government in Syria, pro-Nazi forces supported by Haj Amin and his adherents.

By 1946 Abdullah had proved himself capable of running the country; ensconced in his palace on a hill in Amman with his two wives and one black concubine, he was crowned king of the Hashemite Kingdom of Jordan. The coronation and celebration were the stuff of legends: thousands of people were invited from all over, including Jews from Palestine, who feasted on such extraordinary fare as shish kebabs of whole camels roasting on open spits. Seven camels, a Bedouin delicacy, were stuffed with seven lambs, the lambs stuffed with seven chickens which, in turn, were stuffed with other savories.

But Abdullah saw himself as more than just a hedonistic king: he was the leader of the Moslems and in the forefront of the struggle for Arab nationalism. From his throne in Jordan, Abdullah still had hopes of uniting the Fertile Crescent, the countries of Jordan, Palestine, Iraq, Syria and Lebanon, into the Kingdom of Greater Syria. In Iraq, he could count on his brother Faisal, who was still on the throne; in Lebanon, Abdullah found strong allies in the Maronite Christian community; in Syria, he gathered support from Arab nationalists angry at the French; and in Palestine, Abdullah could gain the Arab areas if he backed the Jews in their struggle for a state. Allied with him in Palestine were the influential Nashashibis, who, like Abdullah, were willing to accept the idea of partition rather than lose everything; his bitter enemies, the Husseinis, led by Haj Amin, had supported the Nazis and were opposed, at any cost, to a Jewish state. The rest of the Arab world had little patience with Abdullah: suspicious of the British influence on him, disgusted by his tolerance of the Jews, and fearful of his hunger for Palestine and more, they turned their backs on the Hashemite ruler and expressed their support for Haj Amin as the rightful head of Palestine.

A pragmatist and a statesman, Abdullah often met with members of the Jewish community in Palestine. "It doesn't surprise me," says King Hussein now, "that he was in touch with leaders on the west side to try to find out what could be done and to explore possibilities. He was honest and courageous to voice his views." In November 1947, a few weeks before the United Nations partition plan was announced, Abdullah was introduced to Golda Meir. They met for the first time in Naharayim, a town on the Jordan River where the Jerusalem Electric Corporation had a hydroelectric plant and where Abdullah had gone on several occasions to meet with Jews. Golda Meir, the acting head of the Political Department of the Jewish Agency, arrived with two Jewish experts on the Arabs, Eliahu Sasson and Ezra Danin. Over cups of thick coffee the Arab king and the Jewish woman discussed the fate of their peoples. "Abdullah was a small, very poised man with great charm," Golda Meir wrote in her memoirs. "He soon made the matter clear: He would not join in any Arab attack on us. He would always remain our friend, he said, and like us, he wanted peace more than anything else. After all, we had a common foe, the Mufti of Jerusalem."[4] From then until the spring of 1948 there were numerous contacts between the Jews and the Jordanians.

"He was a realist," says King Hussein. "He wanted to contain the problem as much as possible, and to see if there was any way of resolving it. He understood what the creation of the state of Israel meant, and what backing it had, and the threat if there wasn't a solution. He sought a solution both of the Palestinian-Israeli problem and of the Arab-Israeli problem."

Despite Abdullah's attempts to work out a peaceful solution, he was alone in both his personal ambition and his support for the Jews. The pressure from the other Arab states was unbearable; no one else was willing to accept either the Jews' right to a state nor Abdullah's claim to the Arab territory of Palestine. By the beginning of May 1948 Abdullah had been lobbied so heavily by Egypt, Syria, Lebanon and Iraq that he had little choice but to join forces with the Arab League against the coming Jewish state. In a final meeting with Golda Meir near the royal palace in Amman, he tried to persuade her to accept an autonomous Jewish home within his kingdom and promised that Jews would be represented by half the seats in his parliament, would hold ministerial positions in his cabinet and would be under his protection.

The Zionists refused his offer, while simultaneously the Arabs, under the leadership of Haj Amin, refused to accept a partitioned Palestine. On May 14, 1948, the Jews declared their state of Israel, and the Arabs declared war. Abdullah let it be known to the British that he was intent only on taking the part of the mandate that the Arabs in Palestine had refused; if the Jews accepted his wish, he would keep his troops away from their areas.

Late that night Abdullah stood at the Allenby Bridge, his advisers next to him, his soldiers just behind. Minutes past midnight the Hashemite king raised his pistol, as his father had done at the start of the Arab Revolt, and fired a shot. His troops charged across the bridge. Their goal was Jerusalem and the territory along the West Bank of the Jordan River; the areas that the Jews had settled in would remain untouched. Abdullah's Arab Legion advanced through Jericho and into Ramallah; the Iraqi troops were close behind; the Egyptians scrambled from the south; the Syrians and the Lebanese rushed in from the north; as for the Palestinian Arabs, they were disorganized and, as Arafat still vividly recalls, soon stripped of their weapons by the Arab League. But the five Arab armies were outmanned, outtrained, and outweaponed by the Jewish forces, the Haganah.

The results were an embarrassment for the Arabs. Only Abdullah's troops, composed of less than 5,000 Bedouin fighters, and the Iraqis succeeded in gaining territory. By June 11, the Jordanians held the Old City, including the Jewish Quarter; together with the Iraqis they also had won the Arab lands along the West Bank of the Jordan River. A truce was declared on June 11, 1948, but fighting broke out again until a second truce was declared on July 18. The murder of the United Nations mediator, Count Folke Bernadotte, by Yitzhak Shamir's Stern Gang delayed the peace. The following spring, under the auspices of Dr. Ralph Bunche of the United Nations, the Jordanians, without any other Arab delegates, met with the Israelis on the island of Rhodes and signed an armistice. One of the delegates on the Israeli side was Yehoshefat Harkabi, who would later translate the PLO covenant into English. It would be Harkabi, too, who would be among the first to call for Israeli talks with the PLO.

In 1950, with the approval of the West Bank Palestinians, Abdullah officially united the West Bank with the Hashemite Kingdom. That act dramatically altered the nature of Jordanian demographics; the population nearly tripled from 450,000 to 1.2 million and now included 400,000 Palestinians living in the West Bank, plus 200,000 refugees who had fled their homes from the Jewish areas to the West Bank, and 100,000 refugees who had fled to the East Bank.

Abdullah, considered to be the temporary caretaker of the West Bank, was keenly aware of the need to keep a balance between Jordanian East Bankers and West Bankers: unlike Palestinian refugees such as Arafat who had fled to other countries, all who came to Jordan were given full citizenship and voting rights; within two months there were West Bank ministers serving in the government, and West Bankers occupied half the seats in the Jordanian parliament. Many of those invited into the government had been supporters of Haj Amin al-Husseini, but some, like Anwar Nusseibeh and Kamal Arikat, had switched their loyalty to Abdullah. Others, however, like Abdullah Nawas of Jerusalem and Abdullah Rimawi of Ramallah were still strongly opposed to the king. The multitude of refugees, who were neither as well educated or well off, welcomed Abdullah's offers of shelter and citizenship but despised his closeness to the British and continued to dream of regaining Palestine for themselves.

Over the years, Abdullah had shown a particular affection for his grandson Hussein and had helped directly with his education. "He was almost a father," says Hussein. Sitting in his palace office, the king still wears a pained expression when he speaks, ever so quietly, of his last days with his grandfather. "I was with him during the last six months of his life. He supervised my tuition in theology and Arabic. At the same time, I accompanied him throughout his day, every day." The king pauses. "I loved him so much," he says. The man who trained the young student allowed him to peek behind the curtains of the kingdom and watch the inner workings of statesmanship. "Standing or sitting in the background, I could hear and see and observe. I got to understand much more than I would have."

But the young Hussein would also be witness to the brutality of his enemies and, in particular, of Haj Amin al-Husseini, who had never forgiven Abdullah for taking part of Palestine. Rumors of plots abounded after the annexation and the king, told of threats against his life, had received a brutal warning when in July 1951, after a meeting about Greater Syria with the former Lebanese Prime Minister Riad al-Sulh, the Lebanese was assassinated in Amman. Despite numerous pleas from his advisers, including his Palestinian prime minister, Samir Rifai, and his Palestinian personal secretary, Nasir Nashashibi, to stay away from Jerusalem, Abdullah insisted on Friday visits to al-Aqsa Mosque whenever he could. The King had a deep love for the city where his father, Sharif Hussein, was buried and where the most important mosque was located in the Haram al-Sharif. Unbeknownst to anyone in Amman, Abdullah had also made plans to meet with two Jewish leaders in Jerusalem, and an appointment had been scheduled with Reuven Shiloah and Moshe Sasson for Saturday, July 21, at the home of a mutual Arab friend.[5] But his invitation to his personal secretary and his favorite grandson, sixteen-year-old Hussein, was to join him for Friday prayers in Jerusalem, and after spending the morning with friends in Ramallah, on Friday, July 21, 1951, Abdullah insisted they go to the mosque. "It was one of the worst days of my life," says King Hussein.

Together the two Hashemites, protected by royal bodyguards, were driven through Jerusalem. They stopped at the tomb of Hussein's great-grandfather, Sharif Hussein, and then proceeded to the courtyard area around the al-Aqsa Mosque where 2,000 Moslems had gathered for noontime prayers. As they stepped from their car, both Hussein and Abdullah noticed a profusion of troops surrounding them. The young boy asked if it were a funeral procession; Abdullah told one of his aides not to imprison him with so many guards.[6] Grandfather and grandson went forward and walked up the steps of the mosque.

An old sheik came out to welcome them. As their bodyguard slipped off his shoes and stepped into the requisite slippers, Abdullah, his grandson and the sheik walked inside the building. Seconds later, an unknown man came from behind the heavy door of the mosque, and pistol in hand, took aim at Abdullah and fired. The single bullet went straight to Abdullah's head; the king fell dead, his turban rolling across the ground. More shots were fired, and one bullet hit Hussein in the chest. But fortunately for the young boy, his grandfather had insisted he wear his military uniform; the large medal covering his heart deflected the bullet and saved his life.

The young Hussein was bewildered and grief-stricken. "It was the loss of a man I loved and cared for, and I was attached to, and who I respected and admired. At the same time," he says, "a man who asked me to promise him a promise just a few days before—which I didn't really comprehend the significance of at the time—that I should do everything I could. He felt that he was coming to the end of his days, and he wanted me to promise that I would follow in his footsteps, and make sure that his work was not lost. I did make that promise and didn't realize what it meant. But I came up with the reality just a few days later."

Abdullah's assassin was a twenty-one-year-old Palestinian belonging to a violent Moslem group that had worked for Haj Amin al-Husseini; the plot had been hatched by relatives and friends of Haj Amin, including Abdullah al-Tal, the chief instigator, and Musa al-Husseini. Haj Amin denied any involvement in the scheme. Four of the plotters were hanged, but Hussein could never forget that Palestinians murdered his grandfather Abdullah.

Hussein bin-Talal succeeded to the throne of Jordan officially on May 2, 1953, exactly the same day as his young cousin and classmate, Faisal, succeeded to the throne of Iraq; it was only a few months after Gamal Abdel Nasser had won control of Egypt by a coup d'état against the British. At eighteen, the role of king was almost overwhelming for a young man who had already been a firsthand witness to the brutal side of Arab rule. Just out of Harrow and Sandhurst, he favored fast cars and pretty young women to a more serious life. In the early days of his rule, the young Hussein would devilishly disguise himself as a taxi driver, and after picking up passengers, ask them what they thought of the new king, Hussein.

Yet he was the fated inheritor of his grandfather's strong will and independent thinking. Hussein was to be king not only of the Bedouins and Circassians of Jordan, but of the 300,000 Palestinians who had fled to the West Bank and East Bank after the 1948 war with Israel. Many of them had hoped that Abdullah's assassination would mark the end of Jordan's claim to Palestine and the end of Jordan's ties with the British.

Hussein was a Moslem, a direct descendant of the prophet Mohammed and destined to rule the followers of Islam, and he was heir to the Hashim clan that led the Arab Revolt, determined to lead the way to Arab nationalism and Arab unity. But he had at least two major obstacles in his path: the Palestinians, who wanted their own state, including the West Bank, Gaza and Israel, and Nasser, who believed himself to be the real leader of the Arab world. From the beginning of their reigns, Hussein and Nasser would be enemies: while the king always saw himself as an ally of the West, Nasser leaned toward the Soviets; while the Hashemite viewed himself as the head of the Moslems, the Egyptian viewed himself as a guiding light for socialism; while Hussein perceived himself as the rightful leader of the Palestinians, Nasser perceived himself as their liberator.

Few Bedouins or Circassians challenged Hussein's authority, and cosmopolitan West Bankers joined the government as ministers, members of Parliament and active players in politics. In efforts to unify his country, Hussein insisted over the years that all citizens of the country call themselves Jordanians. References to Palestinians were frowned upon and even the name was dropped from books. But among the Palestinians who were moving from the West Bank to East Bank were many who had contempt for the king and his ties to the British as well as for the primitive ways of most East Bankers. West Bankers, although not allowed to call themselves Palestinians, always made reference to where they had come from and identified themselves as from Nablus or Jerusalem or Ramallah. While the King suffered their vocal criticism, the more militant Palestinians ran raids across the river into Israel trying to antagonize the Jewish farmers whose fields lined the border. Jordan became the victim of massive Israeli retaliation; although the Palestinian *fedayeen* attacked individual Israeli farms, the Israeli army went after entire Jordanian villages, destroying Kibya and others. Hussein, badly in need of arms to protect his country, sought help from the Turkish and the British. They suggested that Jordan join an anti-Soviet defense pact that already had been signed by Iraq and Turkey in February 1955, and in return, Jordan would receive British help.

Hussein was agreeable, but the Palestinians in his country, particularly those who favored the pro-Soviet Egyptian leader Nasser, were vehemently opposed. To them, Britain represented weak Arabs under colonial repression while Nasser was the symbol of Arab strength. The Egyptian president, they believed, would lead the way to a Palestinian homeland by uniting the Arab world, and his military prowess came from the Soviets. When four West Bank ministers resigned in protest in December 1955, Hussein understood there would be an uprising if he joined the Baghdad Pact. As the mood of the country turned more and more anti-British, Hussein felt compelled to keep the Palestinians calm and untangle himself from the web of relationships he and his grandfather had built with the British.

In March 1956 Hussein demanded the resignation of the British commander of the Arab Legion, General Glubb, and set out to Arabize his troops. To protect himself further, he organized a handpicked group of Bedouins to be his royal bodyguards; their leader would be Hussein's uncle, Sharif Nasser.

But the anti-Hussein feeling was mounting within the Palestinian community. The king, who claimed to be their protector, was accused of defaulting on his duties when the Israelis attacked the West Bank. The Palestinians in the West Bank wanted things both ways: they insisted that they had the right to rule themselves in what they considered to be part of Palestine, and yet, living in Jordan as full citizens, they wanted the king to defend them. They challenged Hussein's authority at the same time that they demanded his protection.

In October 1956, with his citizens in an uproar over another major Israeli reprisal against the West Bank village of Kalkiya, Hussein tried a different tack. This time he held the first real elections in his constitutional monarchy. Unfortunately for the king, the winners in the voting were left-wing West Bankers led by a Palestinian lawyer, Suleiman Nabulsi. Nabulsi's pro-Soviet positions were in direct conflict with Hussein's intensely pro-Western and Islamic beliefs. The Palestinian prime minister was more inclined to take his directions from Nasser or Haj Amin in Cairo than from Hussein.

The Israeli raids had brought the country to a feverish pitch; demands for war against the Jewish state were encouraged by similar cries from Egypt and Syria. To maintain calm, Hussein signed a pact with Syria and Egypt, justifying it as a move towards pan-Arab unity. The pact was short-lived. When the British, the French and the Israelis attacked the Suez Canal on October 29, 1956, Hussein offered to send in troops to help Nasser. But the Egyptian leader refused the offer, expressing his preference for a political solution over a military battle he knew he could not win. Nevertheless, Hussein, after expelling the British from Jordan, invited Syrian, Iraqi and Saudi troops into his country. The prime minister objected, seeing this as a test of his own power. The clash was bitter, and made even more so when, a few days later, Nabulsi opened diplomatic relations with the Soviet Union and the People's Republic of China.

At the same time, the United States government, under President Eisenhower, issued a doctrine declaring that they would send their troops anywhere in the Middle East to stop Communist aggression.

Hussein and his advisers were distraught. Not only were the Palestinian leftists a threat to Jordan, but as Hussein became aware, they were a danger to his throne. They plotted with Egyptian and Syrian leaders, had direct meetings with Soviet military officials, infiltrated the intelligence agency, which was primarily Hashemite, bribed army officers, and lured the head of the army, General Ali Abu Nowar, a longtime friend of the king's, to their side.

During those years, "I cautioned Nasser," says the king. "I built this country up to the best of my ability, after Arabizing the command of the Arab forces and ending the Anglo-Jordanian treaty, and beginning a phase of relations with Great Britain based on mutual respect and cooperation. I had worked in the Arab world to try to stem the tide of communism at that stage out of the suspicion and fear that we were getting out of one kind of foreign domination and ending up under another."

But Hussein's pleas went unheeded, and by April 1957 the feud between the king and Nabulsi exploded in an open fight. Mass riots in support of Nabulsi in the Palestinian refugee camps combined with a mutiny in the army, now under the control of the king's former confidant, Ali Abu Nowar, led to a bitter showdown. Tense days followed for the king, who was inches away from being toppled by his traitorous friend. Nevertheless, in a last-minute move, Hussein, who had been isolated in his palace, appeared before his soldiers at the main army base in Zerqa. His personal visit rallied the support of his Bedouin troops, who hailed his arrival and embraced him as their leader. Hussein was saved, and a new government was formed. Ali Abu Nowar, who could have been executed for betrayal, was ordered by the king to be exiled, and years later was allowed to return to Jordan.

Hussein's ouster of the Nabulsi government was seen by the United States as a friendly move in support of the Eisenhower Doctrine. The U.S. returned the favor by sending the Sixth Fleet to the Eastern Mediterranean for protection, and it began giving economic and military aid to Jordan. Hussein used the aid to strengthen Jordan's infrastructure, improving the roads, electricity and communication system in the East Bank. At the same time, his unhappiness over West Bank politics was made clear when he neglected to make badly needed improvements on that side of the river. The stronger he made the East Bank, the greater would be the loyalty from those living there, while if he strengthened the West Bank, he believed that would only aid his rivals.

The American position in the Middle East further alienated Egypt and Syria, who united their socialist countries in February 1958 to form the United Arab Republic. Hussein, always fearful of pro-Soviet governments, countered by joining his economically poor country in a federation with the far richer state of Iraq, led by his cousin King Faisal. But this Arab union was soon dissolved after Faisal was assassinated in July 1958 in a revolution led by the Iraqi Free Officers.

Faisal's murder left Hussein even more isolated in the Arab world. The enmity with Egypt and Syria had grown so strong that the king could not even fly his airplanes over their territory. In November 1958 when he tried to fly his Royal Jordanian Air Force plane over Syria on the way to Switzerland for a vacation, two Syrian MIG-17 fighter planes tried to force it down. The MIGs pursued the king's plane until it was inside Jordanian territory. Hussein called it "the narrowest escape from death I had ever had," and "an attack on a head of state as yet unparalleled in history."[7] The incident only reinforced Hussein's alienation in the Arab world and his fear of left-wing Palestinian supporters of Syria and Egypt.

More assassination attempts occurred over the next two years, the worst of which happened in April 1960 when explosives were planted in the offices and inside the desk of the prime minister, Hazza Majali. Majali had been in conference with Zeid Rifai, the son of the former prime minister, when the bombs went off. Majali's office was totally destroyed, the walls crumbled and the debris fell on the office below, where more government officials were killed. Although the king was on vacation in the countryside at the time, the assassination message seemed hand-delivered to him. Joyful radio announcements from Cairo only reinforced Hussein's belief that the Syrian and Egyptian leaders were out to kill him.

Not long after, another attempt was made on Hussein's life. This time the plot was discovered when a bottle containing nose drops from the king's medicine chest spilled onto the sink, sizzling with acid that had been put inside. At the same time, a number of palace cats were found dead on the ground, poisoned by food prepared by the king's assistant cook.

Hussein's relations with the Arabs went from bad to worse when, in the autumn of 1962, the Egyptians supported a socialist revolution against the emir of Yemen and the Jordanians backed the ruling monarchy. Although the coup attempt failed, to the Palestinians living in the West Bank, as well as those in Egypt, the uprising reinforced their hopes of a coup against King Hussein.

That same year the Arabs were infuriated when Israel announced it would accept the recommendations of an American plan to divert water from the Jordan River. Although Hussein was not opposed to the idea and, in fact, quietly agreed to its principles, his Arab brothers refused to consider the scheme, which would have included signing an agreement with Israel, implicitly accepting the existence of the Jewish state.

A few months later, a coup against the Iraqi leader brought in a Baathist government which quickly allied itself with the Baathist government in Syria. They, in turn, signed an agreement with Egypt for a triple union. Although once again Jordan had a Palestinian prime minister, the West Bank Palestinians, and particularly those who lived in Jerusalem, were in an uproar, furious that Jordan was not part of this new Arab unity, which, they believed, would lead to the return of Palestine.

It was the Israelis who unintentionally brought about the king's reunion with the other Arab states. When the Israelis officially put their water diversion project into operation in 1964, Egyptian President Nasser called for an Arab summit. With all Arab rulers invited to attend the meeting in Cairo, Hussein could not afford to stay at home in isolation. But the agenda of the meeting was decidedly against him. Not only was it agreed to try to prevent Israel from proceeding with the water project and to organize a consolidated army, the Unified Arab Command, led by an Egyptian officer, but far worse for Hussein, the decision was taken to form a Palestinian Liberation Organization with an army of its own dedicated to the establishment of a Palestinian state. This newly created PLO would prove to be far more threatening to Hussein than even the obvious plots against him by the Egyptians and the Syrians. This new organization would challenge him on the basic questions of who was a Palestinian, who was a Jordanian, and who had the right to represent the people in both the West Bank and the East Bank of the Hashemite Kingdom of Jordan.

16

Black September/White September

<hr>

IN THE DRAWING ROOMS *of Amman, polite conversation rarely touches on one's origins. Although approximately 60 percent of the three million people who live in Jordan have Palestinian roots, loyal subjects of the king refer to themselves as Jordanians. Ask East Bankers whose parents were born in Nablus or Ramallah if they are Palestinian, and they will often ignore the question; sometimes they will answer yes; sometimes, they will call themselves Jordanians of Palestinian origin.*

"In Jordan you can't speak about Palestinians," says the king's adviser Zeid Rifai, whose own father came from Safad. "Who is a Palestinian?" he asks. "It is difficult to differentiate the Palestinians from Jordanians....After World War I and the partitions, people woke up one day and members of families found themselves in two different countries. That doesn't change them into Palestinians and Jordanians, because the whole area was one country. So, in Jordan, you don't know who is who."[1]

Across the Jordan River on the West Bank, the historian Abdul

Latif Barghouti agrees that the people living on both sides of the river are part of the same historic larger family. "Most Palestinians believe there was an Arab continuity in this area. The Canaanites populated Greater Syria: Syria, Lebanon, Jordan and Palestine." Barghouti, a professor at Bir Zeit University, points out that one of the most important traits that unite the people of the area is language. "We can understand one another very easily when we are using our colloquial languages, whether in Palestine, Syria, Lebanon or Jordan," he says. "But with other countries, we communicate in the colloquial with difficulty."[2]

West Bank physician, Yasser Obeid, concurs with the strong link. "If I had to choose between an independent Palestine or a Palestine connected to Jordan, I would rather have it connected to Jordan." Nevertheless, he adds, "There is nobody here who is pro-Jordanian and anti-Palestinian."[3]

But West Bankers who call themselves Jordanians are rare indeed. "Who are the Jordanians?" asks Radwan Abu Ayash, a West Bank activist. "They are our brothers, sisters, aunts and uncles." And yet in 1970, during Black September, he says, "I couldn't believe that such an Arab regime should extend hell to the Palestinians." Abu Ayash's wife lived in the Hussein refugee camp in Amman during the siege. "She was a child then. I've heard some terrible stories from her," he says. "Till now she is terrified of cats. She can't see a cat. Why? Because I'm very sorry to say that she saw cats eating human bodies, and they became wild. She saw many images of people killed." Now, says Abu Ayash, "I fear being sent to Jordan."[4]

The PLO ambassador to London, Faisal Oweida, goes further. Jordan, he says, owes its very existence to the Palestinians. "I believe Jordan was created in the first place to absorb the Palestinians coming out of Israeli-occupied areas. The Jordanians were created for that reason, because there was no Jordan. There was no monarchy called the Hashemites. Nothing. Abdullah was created for that purpose."[5]

Abdullah, of course, would have disagreed, as did his grandson, King Hussein. "He came to Jordan upon the invitation of the people of Jordan," says the king. "He created it."[6]

Like Abu Ayash, Oweida's bitterness stems from Black September and the fighting that took place a few months later when the PLO fedayeen were forced out of the kingdom. After the Jordanians expelled the guerrillas, he "couldn't tolerate to work with the

Jordanians anymore," says Oweida, *who was employed by the Jordanian government as head of the English section of its broadcasting system. "We couldn't even talk as Palestinians."* But, he adds, *"it wasn't only then. Ever since they took over the West Bank, we were to be Jordanized. There were pictures of Hussein. You couldn't say, 'I am a Palestinian.' You had to be Jordanian. Everything was Jordanian. Nothing Palestinian. Even in their books, the name Palestinian was dropped."* The heavy stress on *"Jordanization"* brought about a backlash from the West Bank residents. *"That's why,"* says Oweida, *"one thing that always stuck in our minds was, we always mentioned our cities. Instead of saying Jordanian, you would say, 'I am from Nablus, from Jerusalem.' That was our rebellion."*

Tahir al-Masri, whose family comes from Nablus, has served in numerous high posts in the Jordanian government. He observes that "half of the people here are Palestinians." Yet he notes that the idea of a Palestinian state makes the Jordanians uncomfortable. "The Jordanians believe that a state of Palestine would be totally Palestinian with no Jordanians, while Jordan is half Palestinian."[7]

Masri's cousin, Munib al-Masri, is quick to tell new acquaintances that he is from Nablus and points out other Nabulsis with great pride. The moderate-thinking, Amman-based businessman is now a close friend and adviser to Arafat, and was asked to serve the king as a liaison to the PLO resistance movement after Black September. "I was close to the movement," he explains, then quickly adds, *"I am proud to be Jordanian and Palestinian at the same time."*[8]

Like a foster mother with her arms outstretched, Jordan welcomed the homeless fleeing Israel. From the onset of the Arab-Israeli conflict, Jordan had become the sanctuary for the Palestinians; more refugees took up residence in the Hashemite Kingdom than in any other Arab country and Jordan was the only Arab state that had extended citizenship en masse. In Hussein's eyes, there was no question of who represented the Palestinians; he did. And yet, the thirteen Arab rulers who met at the first Arab Summit in Cairo created a Palestinian organization which would inevitably undermine the king. Theoretically, the newly formed Palestine Liberation Organization was an overt bow to the Palestinians with the covert understanding between the sovereign states that now the freewheeling *fedayeen* would be under Arab control. At the urging of Gamal Abdel Nasser the Arab leaders agreed to sponsor the PLO headed, at Nasser's suggestion, by a master of hyperbole, Ahmed Shukeiry. The Palestinian lawyer Shukeiry had made his reputation at the United Nations where, as the representative first of Syria and then of Saudi Arabia, he ranted and raved about driving the Jews into the sea and destroying the Jewish state.

King Hussein arrived at the meeting an isolated figure in the Arab world, skeptical of his colleagues and suspicious that the new group would start organizing *fedayeen* activities, bringing the Arab countries into another war. Hussein knew that Nasser would not tolerate guerrilla operations from Egyptian territory. The danger would be solely to Jordan. But the king needed to participate in gestures of Arab unity. He yielded support for the group, but as a concession to the king it was agreed that the organization was to cooperate with Jordan. In addition, it was decided that the Arab states would form a United Arab Command which would combine their military forces in defense against the Zionists.

Immediately following the summit, Shukeiry traveled around the Arab world recruiting representatives for the new organization. In May 1964 the 422 newly selected members of the Palestine National Council converged in Jerusalem for their first meeting and quickly named Shukeiry the chairman of the PLO. Under his guiding hand, the congress set the stage for the future, approving a charter, the National Convenant, which declared that "Palestine is an Arab homeland" and announcing its aim to liberate Palestine. The basic structure of the PLO was organized with three major components: a leadership body consisting of a fifteen-member executive committee; a military branch to function under the control of the Arab states as the Palestine Liberation Army; a financial offshoot, the Palestine National Fund.

Although it had been agreed at the PNC meeting that the headquarters of the PLO would be in Jerusalem, Shukeiry quickly set up shop in Amman where, in his typically rabid rhetoric, he promised the world that the Palestinians would "wash our knives with the blood of the Jews." But in spite of the lawyer's bluster, few people listened. Even the Israelis shrugged off his outrageous oratory. "Between 1964 and 1968 the PLO under Shukeiry was an instrument of the Arab states. No one took them seriously," recalls Shimon Shamir, an Israeli authority on Egypt. "It was designed to prevent the emergence of genuine Palestinian expression." Instead of drumming up support for the Palestinians, Shukeiry's bombastic diatribes unwittingly created sympathy for the Jewish state. "He did a lot of service for Israelis," says Shimon Shamir.[9]

King Hussein may have overestimated the dangers from Shukeiry, but his instincts were right: trouble was brewing. The formation of the PLO attracted not only millions of dollars but thousands of volunteers, thereby weakening other Palestinian groups such as Fatah and the Syrian-backed Saiqa. To gain a psychological advantage and attract more militant Palestinians, Arafat and the others immediately began aggressive operations from Syria into Israel.

Within two years the Fatah activities, organized in Syria but often launched from Jordanian soil, would reach such a fevered pitch that the kingdom would suffer badly from Israel's harsh retaliatory blows. Angered by these constant operations and using them as a pretext, Hussein ordered the closing of the PLO offices in Amman in July 1966 and shipped Shukeiry off to Gaza. Nevertheless, the Fatah raids continued and so did the Israeli reprisals, more often attacking Jordan, which was within easy reach, rather than Syria, where the guerrilla bases were too deeply sheltered from Israeli strikes.

In November 1966, a Fatah mine killed three Israeli soldiers who were driving along a patrol route. The Israelis struck back at the *fedayeens'* base in Samua, killing twenty-one Jordanian soldiers, wounding thirty-seven more, and wiping out all of the houses in the West Bank village. Riots and demonstrations broke out throughout the West Bank as well as in the refugee camps in the East Bank as Palestinians flailed against Hussein for not protecting them. Only a week earlier, Egypt and Syria had signed a defense pact. Why wasn't Jordan part of the pact? they demanded. Why hadn't Jordan struck back at Israel? Had the army of the PLO been allowed to stay, they claimed, their villages would have been saved. To make matters worse, Shukeiry called for the establishment of a Palestinian state in Jordan. The United Arab Command, formed just to fight such Israeli actions, was impotent, and Hussein complained bitterly to Nasser for the lack of support, accusing Egypt of hiding behind the United Nations Emergency Forces in the Sinai.

Despite Hussein's concerns that the raids and reprisals were quickly bringing the Arab world towards the brink of war, the *fedayeen* could not be stopped. In fact, their aim was to encourage Israeli retaliation in the hope that these strikes would incite the Arab leaders into war against the Jewish state. The Fatah raids increased, often from the Syrian border where the guerrillas attacked Jewish settlements. By April 1967 the Israelis were so irate at the constant provocations that they ordered their planes to fly over Syria; they destroyed six Syrian MIGs in mid-air combat. In Egypt, Nasser responded to the attack on his Syrian ally by sending two army divisions into Sinai and calling for the withdrawal of the United Nations forces. King Hussein followed the movements with growing fear as U.N. Secretary General U Thant complied with Nasser's requests, paving the way for the Egyptian leader to send more troops into Sharm el-Sheik.

Recalling the events, the king says now, "We were watching when the Egyptians decided to move their forces into Sinai. At that point I realized that war was inevitable: we had fallen into a trap. I knew the facts, that we didn't have the means to win, at least even to defend what we had in our hands." With a heavy sigh, he adds, "I was extremely worried."

On May 22, 1967, Nasser ordered the closing of the Straits of Tiran, an important sea outlet for the Israelis, and announced the deployment of the Egyptian army. "Here we were," says Hussein. "War was inevitable." From the king's point of view Nasser had several choices: "He could have called an Arab summit to discuss the matter; he could have referred the situation of a possible Israeli threat to the Arab world; or, he could have chosen what he chose. His choice, in my view, was the worst. I remember hearing the news and being horrified."

In Amman the king was receiving messages from the Israelis assuring him that if he stayed out of the war, Jordan would not be attacked. But he firmly believed that the Israelis badly wanted the West Bank, and throughout the kingdom there was a deafening clamor to join with the Egyptians. Hussein was caught in a corner, boxed in on one side by a cacophony of cries to join a war he knew he could not win, and on the other side by the painful understanding that if he did not join Egypt, he would lose his throne in a civil war.

Lighting a cigarette and drawing deeply, the king recalls the mounting tension at the time. "I looked at the internal scene in

Jordan," he says quietly. "Jordan had been attacked by Israel time and time again for actions that might have originated elsewhere. So in the eyes of Israel, we were one, we and Egypt. As far as the West Bank was concerned, I knew it was a target for Israel: its close proximity to the sea; the claims. One way or the other it was in jeopardy. In fact, when we had these attacks, we called upon help from the others, which never came. Nonetheless, there was the joint defense agreement. We had to help them as we expected help from them if we were in trouble." On May 30, Hussein flew to Cairo. Within hours he signed a defense pact with Nasser, placed his troops under the command of the Egyptian forces, and most unhappily returned home with Ahmed Shukeiry at his side.

For Hussein, entry into a war with Israel was little short of suicide. "It was clear that the Arabs were nowhere ready or equipped to deal with the problem. Israel was the superior power in the area in terms of its forces and abilities," he affirms. Then again, Hussein felt he had no choice. "If we had not partaken in it, Jordan would crumble from within because already, we were paying for not being able to resist the attacks that were leveled against the villages in isolated areas along the Israeli line. Israel would have stepped in. So at that point I went to Egypt and talked with Nasser and he sent Shukeiry back with me here. I was trying to get people together somehow, in the hope that maybe we can salvage something. Maybe a show of solidarity would help avert the disaster. But if it came, that was the best way to face up to it."

Hussein was correct: disaster came swiftly. The war broke out at 8:45 A.M. on June 5, 1967, when the Israelis made a surprise strike at the Egyptian air bases. By noon the Egyptian air force was destroyed. Nevertheless, at the same time that Egypt's defenses were crumbling, Nasser telephoned the king to tell him that his forces were winning the war and were about to take the Negev. Perhaps with a sense of encouragement that he too could gain territory, Hussein snubbed the Israeli request to stay out of the war and sent Jordanian warplanes into the air. By 2:30 that afternoon the entire Jordanian air force was wiped out. The next day Jordan had lost the West Bank, and on the morning of June 7, Jordanian ground forces could no longer hold the Old City; Jerusalem, which held so much emotion for him and had been such an important symbol to both his grandfather and his great grandfather, was lost to the Jewish state. By June 9, the Israelis had decimated the Syrian forces as well and had taken the Golan Heights.

Within six days the war was over: an extraordinary victory for the Israelis; a brutal humiliation for the Arab states. For Hussein, the loss meant utter shame: the king had lost the Arab land that his grandfather Abdullah had worked so diligently to save in 1948. In addition, Jerusalem, holy city for the Moslems and hallowed symbol of the Sharif of Mecca and the Hashemite dynasty, was gone. The windows of the royal guest house in Amman that once reflected the lights of Jerusalem would now reflect the tears of the king. For Jordanians the war had brought anger and disgrace: the country had forfeited half its territory, and with 200,000 new refugees pouring in from the West Bank, had increased its Palestinian population from 650,000 to 850,000. There were now more Palestinians in the Hashemite Kingdom than in all other Arab countries combined. As the citizens of Jordan listened to their radios just after the cease-fire, they heard the solemn voice of the king declare, "Our calamity is greater than anyone could have imagined."[10]

The enormity of the 1967 defeat forced Hussein to focus on internal matters. The institutions of the state had been destroyed and the king had to concentrate on rebuilding his army, his air force and his country's economy. Hussein turned to the Saudis and after convincing Faisal that Jordan was Saudi Arabia's "window on the West," received generous sums of money to purchase new weaponry from the United States and Britain. Eventually, he hoped, he could work out a political agreement with Israel to win back Jerusalem and the West Bank. While the king concentrated on repairing damage at home, Yasser Arafat was already plotting new provocations, this time from inside Palestine.

Immediately following the Six-Day War, a Fatah convocation in Damascus decided to send Arafat into the Israeli-occupied West Bank to organize military operations. He was to cross back and forth between Jordan and the West Bank. "For me it was not a problem," says Arafat now, "because I am well trained. I was one of the experts in the Egyptian army as a commando, special forces." Those who live in the area laugh at the suggestion that this was a dangerous feat. Remarks Adnan Abu Odeh, a close aide to the king, "In summertime the Jordan River is a creek. When Arafat went to the West Bank in '67 it was very easy to wade across."[11] In addition, the Israelis were too busy enjoying the spoils of victory to pay attention to border crossings.

Between stays in the West Bank, Arafat moved about the Jordan Valley, sometimes sleeping in the mud houses of the refugee camps, other times in mountain caves. Nizar Amar, a Fatah official, recalls the first time he received instructions from Abu Iyad to leave Lebanon and meet Arafat. "He asked me to go to Jordan and look for a man named Abu Amar, and the address was very strange. The address was on one of the mountains close to the River Jordan in the valley of al-Awar. We had a Palestinian guide, and we walked for about an hour in the mountains, and then we walked into a cave." A young man, small and soft spoken, greeted them. "I was surprised by his appearance and that he called me by name. I didn't know that Abu Amar was a leader. I thought that he was a man in charge of dealing with the media." What was most impressive, says the official, was that Arafat told them, "I just came from Jerusalem to meet you. Then, I have to cross the river and go back to Jerusalem." Says Nizar Amar, "That was the greatness, having someone from the leadership inside the territories."[12]

Arafat's activities, however, were less than a huge success. Many Palestinians living in the West Bank had begun working inside Israel, and their new salaries were far more important to them than the disruptive activities of the *fedayeen*. Giving shelter to the guerrillas meant risking their homes and their jobs if the Israelis found out, and they usually did. Those who volunteered to join the movement were untrained and amateurish, and arrests often came right on the heels of an operation.

Although the Fatah venture in the West Bank lasted only six months, the troublesome stage was set for the king. By November 1967 Hussein had helped to write United Nations Resolution 242 calling for: "a just and lasting peace in which every state in the area can live in security"; "withdrawal of Israeli forces from territories occupied in the recent conflict"; the "acknowledgement of the sovereignty, territorial integrity and political independence of every state in the area and their right to live in peace within secure and recognized boundaries free from threats or acts of forces"; "achieving a just settlement of the refugee problem"; and "guaranteeing the territorial inviolability and political independence of every state in the area." As Arafat and the other guerrilla leaders read the resolution, there was no mention of a Palestinian state. They were convinced that even if Jordan regained the territories, the king would not hand them over to the Palestinians.

By December 1967 the Israelis had captured 1,000 *fedayeen* based inside the West Bank. Arafat was forced to flee across the border into Jordan, a fighter embittered by the U.N. resolution but emboldened by the knowledge that at an Arab summit in Khartoum three months earlier the Arab leaders had agreed on "the rights of the Palestinian people in their own country."

Hussein laid out no welcome mat for Arafat, nor, he let it be known, would be tolerate the kind of activities that had led to the disastrous Six-Day War. But the doors of the country were open. Explains the king, "We had Iraqi troops within Jordan, we had Palestinian elements, and others began to come from different states. Suddenly the world seemed changed. Jordan became a place for all the contradictions." The Palestinian fighters called on their Iraqi friends; dressed in Iraqi uniforms and driving Iraqi vehicles they arrived in Jordan without permission from the king and entered the world of mounting chaos.

While the king tried to maintain order, the guerrillas took up positions in the refugee camps of the Jordan Valley, particularly in the village of Karameh just four miles from the river border where the local Palestinian residents rushed to receive them. Still shattered by the June defeat, citizens and soldiers alike gave full support to these enthusiastic fighters. Many in the army, which had a large percentage of Palestinian soldiers and officers, saw the *fedayeen* as a means for the Arabs to save face, and even better, to regain their territory. "There was the feeling," recalls the king, "that the West Bank and all of Palestine were under occupation. Therefore, people should resist occupation. As far as I am concerned, that was the legitimate right of any people under such conditions." Although Hussein says that his "way of thinking was that resistance should be organized, and this would take place in the occupied territories," he acknowledges that the Jordanian army had disintegrated. "There were popular moves to resist" and few ways to stop the tide of emotion, he says. The *fedayeen* represented the only hope of the Jordanians, who gladly gave them money, food and shelter. "People wanted them, the Arabs wanted them, everybody wanted them," explains Adnan Abu Odeh, an advisor to the king. "You couldn't stand against them. It was snowballing."

Arafat went to work planning a barrage of attacks that included planting bombs and shelling the buildings of the Jewish kibbutzim in the West Bank, bringing about heavy Israeli bombardments in return. All too frequently, the victims of the Israeli retaliations were the Jordanians who farmed land in the fertile valley. Marwan Kassem, the Jordanian foreign minister, recalls that at the time he had a farm in the area. "I don't remember getting a penny from my farm from '67 to '71 because that was a continuous active front. Those who paid for it were the Jordanians who helped the Palestinians," he says. "The planes, the Phantoms, it was a training ground all the way from the north of Jordan to the Dead Sea." Kassem's house was in the northern part of the valley. "The first time it was blown up was in the spring of '65. I was then at the U.N. It was the first time the Israelis got their commandos airborne by helicopters in that area. In '67 it was destroyed. And in '68 it was demolished." After the third strike, he says disgustedly, "we built in another place."[13] The few who were determined to make their farms survive were forced to go down at night to water the trees. Says Adnan Abu Odeh, "There was no agriculture. It was a battlefield."

Hussein called for a meeting at the palace with the guerrillas. "I tried to show that they were getting out of hand," recalls the king. "I did indeed have a meeting here in this very building with them for the first time. While talking with them, I was trying to determine who Arafat was. I was very surprised that this was the leader," he says with a smile.

Fatah spokesman Ahmed Abdul Rahman recalls meeting Arafat in the village of Karameh at the beginning of March 1968. "I remember he had an office there. He said, 'Where is the flag?' and they brought the flag. It was in a regular house, and then he asked for a table and chair, and he began to work. He asked about the location of various groups of fighters and wanted to know what happened to them and what was happening in politics, what was happening with Nasser. I thought he was a madman, because you cannot control his attention. He controls all the attention of others, but no one can control his attention." Abdul Rahman smiles and shakes his head. "I was an intellectual, a leftist. I believed in Marxism-Leninism. For Arafat, all these mean nothing. He believes in activity."[14]

On March 18, 1968, the Fatah *fedayeen* set a mine on the road from Tel Aviv to the Negev. When an Israeli schoolbus drove over it, the vehicle exploded: two children were killed and twenty-seven were wounded. This time the Israelis screamed for revenge, and the Jewish army went into action deploying men, weapons and ammunition just across the narrow river.

"They had the intention to move in," recalls the king, "and you could see it developing and happening. We heard very often about it. The troops came down and were lined up. We realized then that that was coming. We almost predicted the time and day exactly." Remembers Arafat, "They were massing in an arrogant way."

While they watched the Israelis flex their muscles, the *fedayeen* leaders prepared to flee. George Habash, Ahmed Jabril and others insisted that their fighters withdraw to the mountains. But Yasser Arafat was just as insistent that the Palestinians should stay and face the Israelis, not so much for the military battle, which they could never win, but for the political victory they could score. "We cannot defeat them but we can teach them a lesson," he told his guerrillas.[15] On March 19 he sent Ahmed Abdul Rahman to Damascus with a message for the leadership based there. "At that time, Arafat had the first historic decision in his life, a decision to face the Israelis," he observes. "I saw the Israeli tanks, and I thought he was mad." The spokesman breaks out in a grin. "I still think he's mad." Nevertheless, three hundred fighters agreed to stay. "Arafat read well the psychology of the masses and the Arab leaders," notes Abdul Rahman. "They didn't believe what happened in June; they needed martyrs in order to have morale."

Against the suggestion of Iraqi military advisors to hide in the mountains, Arafat ordered his men to build trenches at Karameh. Some *fedayeen* would stay in the camp; others would fight in the hills. The Jordanians put their army on alert, deploying whatever elements of their army they could at the approaches to the Jordan Valley and in the city of Salt. "There was armor, infantry and artillery," says the king.

Before dawn on the cloudy morning of March 21, 1968, the Israelis began their attack, a three-pronged approach that covered fifty miles from north to south across the narrow river and into the Jordan Valley. Says King Hussein: "I was apprised of it at six in the morning. So I moved on to army headquarters and we watched the casualties. There were teams from the army formed to go in behind and cooperate against their armor. Fortunately, the Israeli air force was not able to create as much damage as it could have, because the weather was favoring us with low clouds. Some of their units did reach Karameh."

Karameh became a bloodbath as the Israelis bombarded the *fedayeen* hiding in the trenches and wiped out the entire village, leaving little evidence, except for a mosque, that it had ever existed. But as the Israelis moved forward into the valley, they encountered more *fedayeen* under the cover of the regular Jordanian army. The guerrillas fought hard, destroying Israeli tanks with their heavy shelling; the Jordanian troops also blasted the enemy tanks, and the Israelis were stopped in their tracks. "It was a very hard battle," says the king. "We fought to the best of our abilities." He notes that the Israelis were reluctant to leave any casualties behind: "It caused them more losses because they had to fight over every casualty. If there was a piece of equipment lost, they tried to retrieve it." By 10 P.M. the Israelis withdrew, leaving behind four tanks and four armored vehicles. The Israelis claimed 28 of their soldiers dead, and some 100 wounded; the king's army said that 207 Jordanian soldiers were killed and 97 Palestinian *fedayeen* were dead.

As young men were fighting to their deaths all around him, Yasser Arafat led the battle. At least that is what Omar al-Khatib, the Fatah representative in Amman, recalls: "Arafat was leading the battle. He was with the group that was supposed to go towards the mountains. Instead, he headed towards the river near al-Menara. He continued to fight there all day. We dug trenches at Karameh, and he was fighting from within the trenches. He fought until they withdrew."[16] But stories persist in Jordan that Arafat had disappeared. "Arafat ran away to Salt," says Zeid Rifai, a former prime minister and close friend of the king. Another official, Adnan Abu Odeh, agrees. "Arafat wasn't at Karameh," he says flatly. "He was having breakfast in Salt."

Whether Arafat was fighting or eating during the battle, there is no doubt he made a feast of the Israeli retreat. Hours after the struggle, the help from the Jordanian army was forgotten: Arafat was on the radio and briefing reporters, broadcasting Fatah's victory to the world. Says the king, "We were not aware of the importance of putting all the facts out at the time. There was a battle," he shrugs. "There were many battles." Adds Zeid Rifai, "In a shameful way, they stole that battle in the media." Today, Abu Iyad acknowledges, "The Jordanian army helped us a great deal in this particular battle." But the result of the radio propaganda would be more than words. Says Adnan Abu Odeh, "They planted the seeds of hatred against the army."

Arafat's face, with a mustache but not yet a beard, dark sunglasses and his soon-to-become-familiar *kafeeyah,* appeared on the cover of

Time magazine and on television in the fist interview in the West. The story captured the imagination of the Arab media who called it "the light in the darkness of the June defeat." The name Karameh, which means dignity or pride, became a symbol, and the battle became a legend in the Arab world; shamed and degraded by the searing defeat of the Six-Day War, the Arabs were given back their self-esteem through the magic of Yasser Arafat. Ironically, the Palestinians, pariahs before Karameh, suddenly became the champions of the Arab world.

With shrewd understanding of the Arab psyche, Arafat arranged a public funeral in Amman for the dead *fedayeen*. But instead of bringing dozens of bodies to the capital, he carried only seventeen, each a trophy of Fatah martyrdom. As tens of thousands of Arabs lined the streets and massed around the Palestinian leaders, their shouting voices chanted, "Fatah! Fatah! Fatah!" The frenzy was on. "We are all *fedayeen*," exclaimed King Hussein.[17] And they were: thousands of Palestinians and other Arabs flocked to Karameh; within three days 5,000 volunteers had signed up with Fatah. But within the fruits of victory lay the seeds of destruction. "It was very good, and it was sort of suicide for us," says Khaled al-Hassan, who rues the day that Fatah accepted the masses. "With all the ideas they had, you could not control them all."[18]

The success at Karameh raised Arafat's stature in the eyes of his old mentor Haj Amin al-Husseini, who willingly handed over the crown of leadership to the younger man. Muheideen al-Husseini, son-in-law of the mufti, recalls the meetings in his house in Amman: "Haj Amin felt that Arafat would be the right leader for the Palestinian nation after him. He thought he could carry the responsibility."[19] But the mufti was concerned about the recklessness of the fighters. "They were giving arms to everybody. All you had to tell them was, 'I am with you,' and they would give you a Kalashnikov. Arafat decided to go big at any cost!" Haj Amin warned Arafat not to repeat the old mistakes. "Something like this happened in 1936," the old leader said. "Know our mistakes and avoid them. Otherwise, you're not doing your duty. This is not a war," he cautioned. "You are supposed to work as an underground movement. Take only those people you are sure about." The work should be so secret, said Haj

Amin, "that you should not make even the air feel that you are there and you are moving."

But instead, revolutionary fervor spun the air like a whirlwind. Not only did Fatah attract the fighters, it magnetized Marxists, Maoists, socialists, Communists, Baathists, and members of other radical parties that had been banned in Jordan. But more than anything, it galvanized those who wanted to overthrow King Hussein. "Instead of talking about fighting Israel," recalls the king's advisor Adnan Abu Odeh, "they started to talk about fighting the regime. They raised the banner, 'The road to Jerusalem is through Amman,' and everybody took it for granted that they had to fight the regime." Abu Laila, spokesman for the DFLP admits, "We were calling for a strategy of overthrowing the king. We were thinking of a coup or a putsch."[20]

For George Habash, the leader of the PFLP, the issue was clearly political: "We believed from '67 that the reactionary Arab regimes cannot accept the presence of the Palestinian revolution; it is against their interests. When Israel will press them, and America also, to get rid of the Palestinian guerrillas, they will fight against the Palestinian guerrillas. That is why we said to our comrades in Fatah that you cannot say we are fighting against Israel only and have nothing to do with Jordan. All right. You have nothing to do with Jordan, but Jordan has something to do with you, and you have to take this point into consideration."[21]

Yet while Habash and his PFLP and Hawatmeh and his DFLP plotted against Hussein, Arafat stood fast in his belief that the king's presence was crucial to their cause. The Israelis and much of the West felt that Jordan was the logical place for the Palestinians: If the Palestinians took control of Jordan, Arafat believed, they would lose their claim to their real homeland. Omar al-Khatib, the Fatah representative in Jordan, insists that "Fatah had no aims in Jordan. We believed and still do that the presence of King Hussein in Jordan is a security valve for the Palestinian people. We fought any attempt to depose him." Concedes Adnan Abu Odeh, "Fatah continued to talk about Palestine, more about Palestine and less about the regime."

Nevertheless, the gun-toting guerrilla groups led by Habash, Hawatmeh and Arafat completely ignored Jordanian law and organized themselves into separate fiefdoms, governed by their own codes of behavior. "Each one had its own office here, its own training camp, prisons, courts, everything," recalls Zeid Rifai. In a further show of independence, the PFLP developed a new style of airline terror.

Arafat still concentrated on border raids, beefing up Fatah's weaponry with Soviet Katusha rockets and new supplies from Syria and Iraq; the Israelis responded with heavier reprisals. Wary of the chaos in his own country and worried that the competing efforts of the terrorists would weaken the Arab struggle against Israel, the king called for another meeting at the palace. "Certainly this kind of approach was leaving the Israelis the chance to hit back at the army, at the civilian population, at the economy," he explains. "In many cases we found the Israelis were hitting targets that we didn't know existed. Obviously we were in a state of chaos and lack of control. Then," says the king, "The Israelis struck on the valley itself and prevented such crossings from taking place. The result was that the organizations moved into the cities." With the army still on the front line, close to 70,000 *fedayeen* took control of the capital. "In Amman they were running the show," recalls Zeid Rifai.

While the Jordanian army paid the price for the border raids, the guerrillas, drunk with power, swaggered around Amman using their newly acquired arms to intimidate both citizens and soldiers. The refugee camps, already transformed into bases in the Jordan Valley, became training camps and weapons warehouses in town. "The city was like a fortress for them," says Zeid Rifai. "They ran it." The *fedayeen* set up roadblocks and checkpoints, confiscated cars and demanded money. The donations once given gladly to the guerrillas became extortion payments made at gunpoint. Motorists, merchants, businessmen and bureaucrats were all prey to the terror tactics. "There were areas where even a soldier going for a weekend holiday could be killed if they didn't like his looks," says Zeid Rifai who recalls that his daily commute to work became a dangerous obstacle course. "I had to pass through Jabal Hussein which is a part of the city close to a refugee camp," he remembers. "It was the only road to the palace, and there was a PFLP roadblock there. They would stop every car, search it, kidnap people, take the cars." Rifai and his escort cars refused to stop. "When we got to a hundred yards away from the checkpoint and they realized we weren't going to stop, they opened fire on us, and the soldiers fired back. Nobody got killed, but we'd shoot our way through. In the evening we'd shoot our way back. It became a ritual." Meanwhile, Hussein watched in torment from his palace, begged by some of his advisors to crack down on the terrorists, but warned by others that the *fedayeen* were still more popular with the Jordanian citizens than the king himself.

By early November 1968 the Jordanian army, though greatly sympathetic to the resistance movement, had been pushed too far; sense of a crackdown by the military was in the air. The guerrilla leaders called a meeting, and it was pointed out by Habash and Hawatmeh that there might be an attack. On November 4, the assault came against two camps near Amman, Jabal Ashrafiyeh and Jabal Hussein. The attack by the army was proof to the radical Palestinians that the real enemy was Jordan, not Israel. "The first battle after Karameh was on November 4, 1968," states George Habash, who claimed victory over the military. "King Hussein was beaten. He couldn't get rid of the guerrillas."

Although that particular struggle had been fought between the PFLP and the army, it was Arafat who was seen as the major player in the resistance effort. It was he who took on the role of moderating influence, often conferring with the king or government officials to work out a modus vivendi. It was Arafat too, who maintained popularity with the large number of Palestinians serving in the Jordanian army. Acting as a mediator, on one occasion after clashes between regular soldiers and *fedayeen* he reached an agreement with the military. Afterwards, he and a Jordanian official went together for an inspection of the camps where a curfew had been ordered. When they arrived at the village the streets were deserted. "You could see nobody," recalls Fathi Arafat who was there with his brother. "Everyone was in their houses. But inside they were chanting 'Abu Amar, Abu Amar.'"[22] His position had become so strong that Arafat had enough votes for Fatah to take control of the resistance movement: in February 1969 Arafat was named Chairman of the PLO. The organization changed from a dull instrument of the Arab states to a lethal weapon of the guerrillas.

"Abu Amar became a ruler," says Khaled al-Fahoum, a member of the Executive Committee. "There were a lot of prisons in Jordan. He sentenced people to death, pardoned people, married people, divorced people. He was a leader. It was a state within a state. He considered himself to be stronger than the king."[23] Arafat's strength increased even more after the PLO received financial support from the Saudis. With the earlier help of Haj Amin, Arafat had met King Faisal; now, in March 1969, the PLO leader sent his colleague, Khaled al-Hassan, to plea for Saudi help. The result was a tax imposed on all Palestinian workers in the Gulf which would go directly to Fatah, a 12 million dollar annual grant to the PLO, and twenty-eight truckloads of weapons that arrived almost immediately in Amman. The PLO was becoming stronger while the Hashemite government was growing weaker. The constant clashes with the Israelis were not helping Hussein either, since he was feeling pressure from both the army and ordinary citizens to strike back.

As the fighting continued on two fronts, one against the Jordanians, the other against the Israelis, Arafat moved continuously around the country, staying briefly in one military camp or another. "Our main food in the training camps was tuna and sardines," recalls Omar al-Khatib. "When he wanted to eat something good, he would come to my house in Amman. He liked stuffed grape leaves and stuffed squash."

Most of the time the commando leader catnapped at the bases, but "If he needed to rest," says Khatib, "he would come to my house and sleep in my bed." Khatib recalls that Arafat would always bring candy for the children, and always was shy with the family. "Anything he did in the house he did real quietly. He would scout out my son to make sure there was no one on the way to the bathroom." Clad in pajamas, the PLO leader was afraid to encounter Khatib's wife who might be in her nightgown.

Although Arafat maintained his leadership over the *fedayeen,* the number of freewheeling guerrilla groups multiplied into dozens, decreasing the chairman's ability to control the radicals. Support was weakening among Jordanian citizens as well, although popular sympathy still ran in favor of the fighters. After all, they were still the ones sustaining the struggle against Israel, the only ones, it seemed, who could possibly win back the West Bank and Jerusalem. Muheideen al-Husseini, a member of the Jordanian parliament at the time, says that like most people, "I had feelings towards the Palestinians," but he adds, "I was for law and order. It was terrible to live here: everybody had arms and thought that he was the son of God. They were terrorizing anybody, all over Jordan." Not only the Jordanians were suffering. On August 29, 1969, the PFLP extended its operations beyond the Middle East and hijacked a TWA plane en route from Rome to Israel, forcing it to land in Damascus.

As life became more lawless, the king made an attempt to restore order, and in February 1970 he appointed a hard-line minister of the interior, Rasoul Kilani. The new official immediately announced that no weapons could be carried within city limits, and no vehicles could be driven without proper registration. The reaction was a violent outburst and more clashes with the army. Recalls George Habash, "They issued an order on February 10, 1970, saying, 'We only want to organize your guerrilla fight against Israel, and we want to know the places of the arms, the TNT.' But we knew what they wanted. That is why we took volunteers to do battle at that time. Later, our brothers in Fatah followed us. We won that battle."

The *fedayeen* showed their muscle by attacking a Jordanian police station. The fighting lasted several days but the king was so concerned about armed conflict with the guerrillas that he eventually ordered the army confined to their barracks. In reality, the country had disintegrated into two states, one in support of the *fedayeen,* the other in support of the king. A meeting was called for the two leaders to discuss a truce. The king was convinced that Arafat wanted to restore calm, but even within the ranks of Fatah there was dissension from the commander of the Palestinian forces, Abu Daoud, who believed that the king should be overthrown. Arafat cleverly managed to bow to both sides. "Arafat is a survivor," says Adnan Abu Odeh. "When he was with the king, he was respectful. When he was with the others, he opposed the king. That is Arafat." Adds a PLO supporter, Munib al-Masri, "Arafat could have controlled the PFLP and the DFLP, but he wanted them as allies."

By the beginning of June 1970 the clashes between the well-armed *fedayeen* and the splintered Jordanian army had reached a high point. The guerrillas were able to take complete control of several sections of Amman and even the hotels became terrorist bases. At the luxurious Intercontinental Hotel, Palestinian fighters swung their weapons through the lobby as they forced payments from the guests. Across the street at the American embassy a diplomat who had gone to visit a refugee camp was taken hostage and held almost twenty-four hours.

The day of June 9, 1970, the king recalls, "was one of those days that started with severe fighting in Amman, with shooting everywhere. I was living outside the city, and I decided to go in and see what was happening and if it had quieted down. My role during the last six months was to try to calm people down, and to try to get help with the Arab leaders, with anyone's help, to get some sense into the situation." But it was too late.

On this particular day, the king had been informed by Zeid Rifai that the guerrillas were attacking the building of the Jordanian intelligence agency. Hussein insisted that he go with Rifai to army headquarters, and they set off with a motorcade of two cars in the front, two open jeeps and two cars in the back. "We got to an intersection in a town called Sweileh," recalls Rifai, "and there was a checkpoint for the Jordanian military police." But the government troops had deserted the post, leaving the king and his convoy vulnerable. "The bar across the road was down. We stopped the motorcade and one of the soldiers went to lift the barrier. At that moment, heavy machine gun fire started from the hill on the side of the road. They killed the soldier, and then a .50-caliber machine gun started moving towards us. It started attacking the escort cars who returned the fire." Zeid Rifai, who had been sitting in the back seat, got out of the car. The king was in the front, next to the driver. "I saw the bullets getting closer," Rifai remembers. "I opened the door and asked His Majesty to get out of the car. He didn't say anything." Recalls Hussein, "I was really dazed and angry at them." The king muttered "*Ighss,*" how dare they.

"He finally got out of the car," says Zeid Rifai, "and there was a ditch on the side of the road, and he went into it. I was standing on one side of the ditch, and the commander of the royal guards was standing on the other side. We saw the bullets getting closer and we probably had the same idea at the same time: we both wanted to jump to cover His Majesty." They jumped and the two aides collided in mid-air. The men landed with a thud on the king. The driver quickly turned the car around and they all got in. Suddenly the king opened the door and got out again. "I jumped out after him and asked what he was doing," says Rifai. "He said, 'I left my beret in the ditch.' He got his beret and came back." Adds Hussein, "Thinking back, it might have been a silly thing to do, but I just couldn't leave it there." Later when they returned to the palace, the king took to his bed and stayed there for three days with a bad back. The king joked, "You did more damage than the commandos; so next time, leave me alone."

One week later, Hussein signaled a change in strategy. Announcing that he would be in control of the military, he switched his army commander to the major general who had helped the *fedayeen* earlier at Karameh. The move met with approval from the guerrillas, and Arafat agreed to a truce. In addition, Hussein called on a more moderate man to become prime minister, invited nine Palestinians to join his cabinet of seventeen ministers, and announced that Jordanians would no longer be drafted and could join the guerrillas. Hoping to sustain the calm, Hussein invited all Arab rulers to Amman, assuring them separate meetings with the PLO and his government. After their arrival on June 27, the king agreed to recognize the Palestinian Resistance Movement and accepted their legal right to be in Jordan. In Hussein's favor, the guerrillas were required to keep their bases out of the towns and cities and were not permitted to carry their weapons within the city limits. In spite of protests from Habash and Hawatmeh, a peace pact was officially signed on July 10, 1970. But the radicals did not miss the opportunity to make their feelings clear. On July 22, 1970, six terrorists from the Popular Struggle Front hijacked an Olympic Airways plane flying from Beirut and forced it to land in Athens.

Despite Hussein's attempts, peace was not meant to be. Only a few days later the United States unveiled a well-intended proposal spelled out by Secretary of State William Rogers. The plan called for reaffirmation of U.N. Resolution 242; Israeli withdrawal to the pre-June 1967 borders with Jordan; a united Jerusalem whose political fate would be determined in the future; settlement of the refugee problem; an end to the war of attrition; and a cease-fire between Egypt and Israel. The Egyptian and Jordanian responses to the plan were positive; the PLO's answer was rage. Political peace between the Arab states and Israel was unacceptable to the PLO; calling Nasser a traitor, they announced they were determined to keep up the struggle no matter what. The rift became clear at the end of July when Arafat paid a visit to Egypt. Not only did Nasser refuse to see him, but he sent a message that the PLO needed to be taught a lesson. Hussein believed Nasser wanted a crackdown on the guerrillas.

Pressure was also mounting from the United States and Israel. The Americans held back their secret subsidies to the king for government salaries, suggesting that Hussein become tougher or see his throne topple.[24] The Israelis, tired of the endless border attacks, were threatening to wipe out the guerrillas once and for all. The following month the Jordanian government took more drastic measures and moved the army, fortified with tanks and artillery, closer to Amman.

The action brought a warning to Hussein by a representative of Nasser. "We had a special office, code named 'the hulk,' within the office of the Egyptian military attache in Amman who was in contact with Fatah," recalls Mohammed Heikal, a close advisor to Nasser. "We gave an ultimatum to the king that he should stop right away."[25]

Informed of impending doom, the guerrilla factions called a general meeting of their military leaders to assess the situation. Says Hussein Rahtib, who attended the conference, "Everyone exaggerated. They thought they had 138,000 fighters and that they would destroy Hussein. They thought all the Jordanians would rise up against the king."[26] To Habash the struggle against Hussein, an ally of the West, was as vital as the struggle against the Jewish state. "We knew that we were fighting Israel," says the PFLP leader, "but we had to see at the same time that our fight was linked with our fight against imperialism. We were not ready to say that our enemy is only Israel, because historically, you know what British imperialism did." While Habash and Hawatmeh urged the others to fight, says the Syrian professor Hussan Rahtib, "Arafat was accused of appeasing the regime." In truth, he adds, "Arafat and Fatah were in-between. They foresaw there would be a clash with the king. They weren't in any hurry. They felt they were in control of Jordan." The king, in turn, believed that Arafat was not decisive with his factions. "Unfortunately," says Hussein, "he wasn't as firm or as strong as he could be." At the end of August 1970 fighting erupted in a residential neighborhood of Amman.

Two days later the king's car was ambushed again, this time on a trip to the airport to pick up his daughter who had just arrived from school overseas. As the king and his escorts drove along, he recalls that suddenly "The hair on the back of my neck stood up....I opened the window a trifle, and somehow I had the feeling that just around the next corner, we would be under fire." As the cars turned, the waiting guerrillas opened a burst of gunfire on the palace cars, but the king was able to escape.

Hussein was humiliated even more a few days later when, hoping to quiet the clashes, he backed down and tried to prevent his own troops from entering Amman. As the king went to speak to the army officers, he was taken aback by what he saw. There, flying from a radio aerial was a brassiere. He could hardly miss the contemptuous message that the army considered him too cowardly to fight.

While the clashes continued inside the city for several days, the PFLP stunned the world with a series of sensational hijackings. On September 6, under the direction of Wadi Haddad, the number two man to Habash, PFLP member Leila Khaled and another guerrilla attempted to hijack an El Al plane. Less than ten minutes after take-off, the two terrorists, a man and a woman, dashed into the aisle of the Boeing 707, waving hand grenades and pistols. When the guerrilla fired his gun, an airline steward tackled him; in the ensuing struggle, the terrorist was killed. Passengers jumped up to help and used their neckties and string to subdue the woman. The plane was able to proceed on its normal course to New York. But that same day other PFLP gunmen hijacked a TWA Boeing just after take-off from Frankfurt on its way to New York and forced it to land at Dawson's Field, an airstrip near the Zerqa army base in Jordan. More PFLP terrorists hijacked a Swissair flight carrying some Israeli passengers and brought it to the same landing field. Meanwhile, a fourth PFLP group commandeered a Pan Am 747 and forced it to land in Cairo. The following day the guerrillas blew up the Pan Am plane. Three days later the PFLP hijacked a British jumbo jet and brought it to Dawson's Field also. There were now three hijacked airplanes and almost 600 terrified passengers held hostage in Jordan.

Furious with the terrorist operation, Arafat ordered a convoy of food and medical supplies sent to the hijacked passengers. But tensions were so strong between Fatah and the PFLP that Habash's men stopped the convoy. The following day Arafat threatened to resign unless the innocent people were released. George Habash recalled: "At that time, regarding this particular action, I remember that he was against it."[27]

The hijackings had won the Palestinians the world's attention. Dozens of international journalists were drawn to the story and rushed to Jordan to cover it. While the terrified passengers sat at gun point on the planes, PFLP leaders summoned two of their press officials from Beirut, Bassam Abu Sharif and Ghassan Kanafani. "We were called to Amman to talk to press and passengers," recalls Bassam Abu Sharif. "I talked to two hundred to three hundred passengers. We talked about Palestine. I did my best under the circumstances to make them relax and laugh. When I went there, they were relaxed, but," he says, "I didn't like to. When I was talking, I was always thinking about what if...?"[28]

As the Palestinian tried to calm the passengers, one elderly woman asked him where they were. "Are we in Kenya?" she said. Abu Sharif said no.

"Young man," said the woman, "If I want to buy a ticket to go to Kenya, is it close?"

"It is close," he answered.

"So," he recalls, she took out a wad of 20,000 dollars and "gave me money to buy a ticket to Kenya. I told her to keep her money, and 'I will buy you a ticket.'" Abu Sharif told her not to show the money to anyone else "because they might think you are trying to bribe them. If people think you are trying to bribe them, it wouldn't take much effort to shoot you." And then, he says with a shrug, "They were released the next day and were taken to the Intercontinental Hotel. There, I gave her a ticket to Kenya with my compliments."

After Abu Sharif finished talking to the passengers, he says he went to the decision makers to persuade them to release the majority of people. "If you want to make a political point," Abu Sharif told them, "let all the women and children leave." Although hundreds were released, fifty-six people were kept on the plane. "They were important for political reasons," he says, "especially those with two passports, Israeli and American." With the Jewish passengers still held hostage, the PFLP pressed their demands that a hundred Palestinian prisoners be released from Israeli jails.

The following day the exhausted passengers were told to go to Ashrifiya Hospital where their papers would be put in order. Says Abu Sharif, "I remember that I stamped the old lady's passport and signed it for seven years." He laughs and says, "After they were released, they all wanted a stamp as a souvenir." Except for sixteen people whom the PFLP continued to hold, the passengers had been freed by an agreement worked out with Nasser. The Egyptian leader sent private planes for the people to leave the country; in return, says Abu Sharif, "all the prisoners we wanted were released to Nasser." None of the hostages were hurt, he says, "except for one girl. Six months later she said she was harmed: She said because of the hijacking, she lost her sex drive." He adds with a smirk, "The case was dropped because we sent her a young man."

While the PFLP controlled the hijackings, the king could do little to affect the situation. His pleas to Arafat were of little use since the chairman also carried little weight with Habash. Nevertheless, Arafat did use his influence to help with the release of the passengers, and on September 14, an agreement was reached between the government and Arafat allowing guerrilla bases to exist outside the cities and towns. Two days later, in the hope of restoring law and order, the king announced a military government. That same day the world watched in horror as the PFLP blew up the three airplanes they were holding. "That operation wasn't a terrorist one," claims Bassam Abu Sharif. "It was more than that. Terror is easy. This operation was brain-breaking. It was a real violent entry into the minds of people. They succeeded. They got headlines all over the world."

As the charred remains of the airplanes blackened the ground, the new government planned its strategy. On September 17, 1970, it was decided the army would enter Amman. The city became racked with tension as citizens took to their homes and the guerrillas readied themselves in trenches. Arafat called for a general strike and announced he would give the king forty-eight hours to pack and leave. The next morning the sounds of gunfire shattered the air. Black September had begun. "We call it White September," says Zeid Rifai, recalling that the fifty-two different guerrilla groups operating in the country had committed 44,000 violations against Jordanian law.

Once the fighting started, shelling was heavy, even reaching the palace; telephone and electrical lines were torn down almost immediately; food and water quickly became difficult to obtain. For two days the battle continued, worsened by the intervention of Iraqi and Syrian troops near the northern city of Irbid. After Israel scrambled its air force and threatened to attack, however, the Syrians pulled back. Today the man who was the Syrian military commander, Moustafa Tlass, accuses the Palestinians of scrounging for cover. "Arafat and his clan ran away to Syria," he says, "so we withdrew the two batallions."[29] The Jordanian army fought hard, but some 5,000 soldiers and officers defected, far more than Hussein had hoped, far fewer than the *fedayeen* expected. Amman was a battlefield, and so were the areas to the north.

The new United States ambassador, Dean Brown, arrived, taken by armored car to see Hussein. On September 20, after pleas of help from the king, the United States sent the Sixth Fleet near Jordan and ordered 20,000 troops on alert. But the Arab rulers offered hardly any aid: the Iraqis and the Syrians fought against the king; the Saudis watched and waited, offering no funds or weapons to Hussein; the Libyans and the Kuwaitis cut off diplomatic relations with Jordan. The Egyptians monitored events from afar, silently supporting the PLO, urging Hussein to stop. "We thought it would be a bloody battle," says Mohammed Heikal, who was Egyptian minister of information at the time. "The Palestinians are no match for that inside Amman, and they could have been liquidated. We were racing against time to stop, and were asking for a cease-fire right away, a summit conference in Egypt right away." The Egyptians organized a delegation to Amman, led by the president of Sudan, General Numeiry, and including among others the Egyptian vice president, Hussein Shafi'i, the foreign minister of Kuwait, Sheik Sabbah, and his private secretary. Numeiry worked doggedly to arrange a cease-fire. By the time a truce was called on September 24 and accepted by Arafat the next day, the last of the hostages were released. Some 2,000 people were dead.

With the cease-fire in place, Numeiry called for a summit in Cairo and met with Arafat at the office of the military attache in Amman. Outside the Egyptians' office, Jordanian soldiers patrolled the area. While the delegates talked to Arafat, one man slipped off his robes. "The Jordanian guards were counting heads," says Heikal. "They gave Arafat the robes of the secretary, took him to the plane right away, and he came to Cairo."

The battle that had been carried out with bullets in Amman became a war of words in Egypt. The Arab leaders who participated in the summit conference all stayed at the Nile Hilton Hotel. Mohammed Heikal recalls that before Hussein arrived, "Arafat would be the first to rush to your room and say, 'I have a telegram that says one million people died.'" Responded Heikal, "Yasser, there is nothing to substantiate that. Just wait and give us time so that we can note the balance of military power between you and the king is in his favor." Added the Egyptian, "We have to put the king under pressure, and to put pressure on him, you cannot give him an ultimatum. You are dealing with a sovereign state."

Pressure from Nasser and Numeiry, as well as the presence of Arafat as an equal balance to Hussein, one at either end of the U-shaped table, brought about an agreement that did not please the king. The results were a promise of "full support for the Palestinian revolution." The conference ended on September 28 and Nasser escorted the leaders to the airport. On his way to see off the Sheik of Kuwait the Egyptian president suffered a fatal heart attack. The Arab world grieved over the death of Nasser and was surprised by the succession of Anwar Sadat.

When Hussein returned home, he changed his government again, signaling a hard-line cabinet led by Wasfi Tel, the king's longtime adviser and close friend. "He was a tough guy who wanted to see law and order. He hated confusion. He was a man of his word and a man of vision," recalls Munib al-Masri. With Wasfi Tel serving as both prime minister and defense minister, the Jordanians hoped they would turn the guerrillas out of Amman once and for all. A six-month plan was outlined to clear the *fedayeen* out of the cities.

The prime minister wanted to make sure he had the cooperation of the PLO. He invited the fair-minded Masri, a loyal Jordanian and a supporter of Arafat, to join the government. "Amman was a shambles," says Masri. "I had never seen it like this. I accepted the post to be minister of public works. The movement knew I had accepted and was coming to clean up the country. And we did, in six to eight months." Masri arranged the first meeting between the prime minister and Arafat, and for nine months, from October 1970 to May 1971, daily meetings continued. "From two in the afternoon until two in the morning for five or six days a week, we met at the ministry solving petty things between the government and the PLO. Many times the government and the movement side ate lunch and dinner and sometimes slept at my house. Mostly we talked about attacking units, the damage they had done, the location of arms. Many times they would agree, or Arafat would agree, and certain factions didn't want the agreements to be consummated."

In May, Arafat sent a message to Masri that he wanted to meet with him. With Wasfi Tel's approval, Munib al-Masri, Abdul Majeed Shoman, the head of the Arab Bank, and the Saudi ambassador drove off to the Jerash forest to find Arafat in the mountains, hoping they could bring him back to Amman to talk peace with the government. "The ambassador was very nervous and scared," recalls Masri. "We went to see Arafat in his underground cave. The cave was dark and smelly, and I didn't like it. He had been living there for two months." Masri suggested they hold their meeting outside in the ambassador's Buick. Arafat agreed. When the minister suggested that Arafat talk with other government officials, the PLO leader said okay. Says Masri, "Then he talked to us about the atrocities of the Jordanians and made us all cry, even the Jordanian army officer who was with us."

Arafat squeezed into the back of the car between the ambassador and Abdul Majeed Shoman for the ride back to Amman. "When we came to checkpoints," says Masri, "they wanted to shoot the guy with the Kalashnikov. The soldier would say, 'You killed my brother.' Arafat would answer, 'Listen, soldier, you are talking to the head of the revolution. You should be respectful.'" After this happened at six or seven checkpoints, says Masri, "The Saudi was very nervous and he would recite something. Shoman was braver than I, but I thought we were gone."

When the car reached a junction where one road leads to Amman, the other to the Syrian border, Arafat looked at Masri and said, "Let me do two or three things at the border. Then I will come with you." Masri agreed. Arafat suggested they wait. "I will come back after six or seven hours," he lied. The others went on to Amman, but Masri decided to stay in the Jordanian border town. "I waited seventeen hours, and he didn't show up." Finally, Arafat called Masri to the town on the Syrian side. "I don't want to go to Amman," he told Masri, "because I don't want to go as a fugitive. I want to be received as a head of state. Please go on, and I will see you." Several months later, Arafat moved on from Syria to Lebanon.

On June 1, 1971, the guerrillas killed a farmer in Jerash, and the prime minister ordered the army into action. Well-equipped and now eager to rid the country of the *fedayeen,* the Jordanian soldiers, led by a Palestinian officer, fought hard for six weeks in the forests of Jerash. Brash threats by Abu Iyad against the lives of both Wasfi Tel and King Hussein may have spurred on the government forces who pushed hard until the guerrillas were wiped out in mid-July. At least fifty of the Palestinians were so afraid of what the army might do to them that they fled across the Jordan River and turned themselves over to the Israelis. But the bloody battle would come back to haunt the prime minister.

For several months the PLO attempted to return to Jordan. At the urging of Arafat and his adviser, Khaled al-Hassan, Saudi King Faisal took an active role in trying to work out an agreement. By November, Wasfi Tel had agreed to a document that would recognize the PLO as the sole representative of the Palestinian people but with the condition that it would only operate in Jordan as a political body. At a meeting of the Arab League in Cairo in November 1971, in which the agreement was to be officially signed, four men stood near the Sheraton Hotel. The group, members of Fatah's new radical Black September wing led by Abu Iyad, were waiting for Wasfi Tel. As the Jordanian prime minister approached the entrance to the hotel, the group moved in and assassinated him. "They thought that he was responsible for the Jerash massacre," says Munib al-Masri sadly. "He was sincere to the cause, but he was misunderstood."

The personal loss to the king was great, but Jordan had gained enormously by routing the PLO. Hussein's alliance with the United States afforded him the money and technology to develop the country and expand his relations with the US. In addition, after a state visit in 1971, the American government agreed to reorganize and reequip the Jordanian military. As the PLO moved on to Lebanon to create the same kind of chaotic state within a state that they had in Jordan, the king could only look on with relief and despair. Even Arafat, who had tried to bring some kind of order to the anarchy of the movement, would have to take some responsibility for the new Black September faction that rose within Fatah.

With Abu Iyad as the head of Black September, and European operations directed by Ali Hassan Salameh, the group went on to hijack a Sabena airplane in May 1972. Four Fatah terrorists brandishing explosives seized the Boeing 707 which carried one hundred people and forced it to land at Lod Airport in Israel. When Israeli soldiers stormed the plane, they overcame the terrorists. Six people died in the ensuing struggle; the rest were able to escape.

The infamous reputation of Black September reached its nadir in the kidnapping and death of eleven Israeli athletes at the Munich Olympics in September, 1972. Heavily armed terrorists captured the athletes in their dormitory at the Olympic Village. They blindfolded them, tied their hands and held them hostage in a room, demanding that 200 Palestinian prisoners be released from Israeli jails. The Fatah gunmen killed two of the Israelis in the room; nine more of the athletes died in a shoot-out at the Munich airport where they were taken the following day.

A year later Black September struck again. Under the command of Abu Iyad, Fatah guerrillas took an American Ambassador, Cleo Noel Jr., his deputy, George Curtis Moore, and a Belgian diplomat, Guy

Eid, as hostages during a reception at the Saudi embassy in Khartoum. The terrorists demanded the release of Abu Daoud who had been the head of Palestinian forces during Black September and was captured by Hussein's troops. The Fatah guerrillas also demanded freedom for Palestinian prisoners in Israel, West Germany and the United States. Among those they wanted released was Sirhan Sirhan, the Palestinian who assassinated Robert F. Kennedy. When their demands were not met, the terrorists murdered the ambassador and the two other diplomats. Abu Iyad admitted that "Arafat did have knowledge of Black September but was not aware of the logistics or operational details." He claims that the PLO tried to help resolve the crisis and denies that Arafat had any direct contact with the terrorists: "He does not know who they are. He never talked to them. We have documents that show this." Abu Iyad insists the Fatah leaders were surprised by the attack, but admits, "We did contact those in charge and...they released all of those detained and were only left with the American ambassador and his assistant. We asked them to release them and then, 'come up with your demands in a communique.'" Adds the head of intelligence for the PLO, "We did all that we could."[30]

But a BBC documentary, completed in early 1990, suggests that the order to murder the diplomats came from Arafat's headquarters: "Intelligence intercepts showed that the terrorists used a radio telephone to maintain constant contact with the PLO, and according to this censored State Department cable, the code word giving the order to murder the diplomats came from Arafat's PLO headquarters in Beirut."[31] A high-ranking State Department official says: "They were involved up to their eyeballs. The reality was that Abu Iyad was running it. In those days, if Fatah was involved at a minimum, Arafat was involved."

Despite Arafat's earlier efforts to concentrate the struggle inside Israel, the brutality of the Black September operations convinced many that the PLO was an international terrorist organization. Within a few years, the United States officially refused to deal with either Arafat or the PLO, thereby placing King Hussein in a difficult new role. The head of the Hashemite dynasty was torn between working to save the West Bank for his kingdom and conceding it to the Palestinians who tried so hard to destroy him.

17

Reaching for Peace: Territorial Compromise

INSIDE AL-NADWA, *King Hussein's pale stone palace, the spacious rooms are elegantly designed with richly patterned silk rugs, and fine French antique furnishings. The whitewashed main salon zings with splashes of ruby red; the sitting room shimmers in peacock blue, enhanced with a pair of mother-of-pearl throne chairs; and in the hallway, a display of gold and silver daggers dazzles the eye. All seems comfortable in this family-sized house that is home to the king and his American-born fourth wife, Queen Noor, and to the seven youngest of his twelve children. Here the ruling couple can relax over tacos and television, take in old movies or American football games; here the children can run around the sprawling garden or feed the animals in the vest-pocket zoo that accommodates two gazelles, two cranes and a clan of rabbits.*

But hints of fear emerge from time to time in conversation with the queen. On a stifling hot afternoon, the royal consort suggests a stroll

*on the lawn; the house is not air conditioned, she remarks, and the
bulletproof windows cannot be opened, a safety feature installed
during the siege in 1970. It is true, she acknowledges, that His
Majesty wears a pistol, and though she denies that he never takes it
off, it is clear that the king feels safer when it is close to his body.*

*"I pray for him daily," says the thirty-eight-year-old queen. "We
live in a turbulent region."[1] The former Lisa Halaby married Hussein
in 1978, long after the horror of Black September. But the personal
history of the Hashemites, bloodstained with the murder of King
Abdullah and an unending series of assassination attempts against
Hussein, makes her wary of letting down her guard. Admiring of her
husband's patience and persistence, she credits him completely for
the country's advances, but shivers just a little when she speaks about
his life. "He's had every imaginable experience, positive and negative," she observes.*

*Of all his experiences, perhaps the shattering years after the Six-
Day War have left the greatest imprint. The king's relationship with
the PLO will always be marked by that time: their defiance of his
throne, their threats on his life and their damage to his country
robbed him of any hope of easy unity between the West Bank and the
East Bank. Today, the symbol of that hostility is Yassar Arafat.*

*Although the monarch may not check the chairman's sleeves for
hidden daggers, the king embraces Arafat with caution. Just as Arafat
deals cautiously with the king. "It's a funny relationship," observes
an American who has negotiated with them both. "It reminds me of
two chess players who hate each other's guts; the grandmasters, you
know. It's almost time for the big tournament, and they look at each
other, and on one hand they hate each other, but on the other hand
there is a sense of real respect."*

B y July 1971, Hussein had expelled the PLO and Arafat found
himself chairman of an organization whose main fighting force was
no longer welcome in Jordan, Egypt or Syria. In Jordan, the
Palestinians who were left were forced to disarm and required to
abide strictly by Jordanian laws. In Egypt, Arafat lost his benefactor

when Nasser died in September 1970 and Anwar Sadat, a relatively obscure colonel in the Egyptian army, succeeded him. In Syria, Assad had led a successful coup and was now president. The Syrians had learned a lesson from Jordan. Says Defense Minister Moustafa Tlass, "We told Arafat that we don't let anyone fight without our knowledge. Either I command or he commands." He adds angrily, "Who is that son-of-a-bitch to vie with me for authority? I am commissioned by the state to be secretary of defense, not Arafat. Arafat has no authority to engage in military planning on my soil. He has to be subject to my directives—or get out!"[2]

The lack of a guerrilla base created a desperation that played into the hands of PLO militants. Hussein was widely suspected of having saved his throne during Black September by collaborating with Israel and the United States and was isolated in the Arab world. Even when he tried in March 1972 to offer West Bank and Gaza Palestinians a measure of independence from Jordanian rule, his plan was immediately denounced by both his Arab neighbors and the Palestinian leadership in the occupied territories. Hussein suggested that two somewhat autonomous entities be formed, one on the East Bank, the other on the West Bank, and that they be connected through a federation headed by the king. The PLO charged his proposal for a United Arab Kingdom was a scheme constructed with Israel to foreclose any possibility of an independent Palestinian state.

Now even Fatah, which had tried to forestall an open split with Hussein during Black September, called for the king's ouster. Its central committee charged that "the source of the dispute is the Hashemite family in Jordan, its history of conspiracy against our people and cause, and its role in serving imperialist ends in the area." Fatah vowed "to oppose this family and overthrow the royal regime in Jordan."

The PFLP and Black September escalated their attacks and by the end of the year, Syria and Lebanon, which were receiving the brunt of Israel's retaliatory strikes, imposed even tighter restrictions on the PLO. Fatah turned once again to Jordan where, it decided, it had to recover its guerrilla base. Fatah drew up a plot, organized by Abu Iyad, to bring down Hussein. Abu Daoud, the commander of Palestinian forces during the 1970–71 Black September period, was put in charge. In January 1973, what was unofficial PLO policy received the formal imprimatur of the eleventh Palestine National

Council meeting in Cairo. The 450 members of the Palestinian parliament-in-exile formally committed the PLO to a policy of overthrowing Hussein and at the same time rejected proposals for a two-state solution.

In February, the Jordanians imprisoned Abu Daoud, triggering the Black September terrorist operation in Khartoum in which the American ambassador to Sudan and two other diplomats were murdered. In April, Israel retaliated with a daring raid against the alleged masterminds of the Munich massacre and other Black September operations. Landing at night on a Beirut beach, the Israelis drove to the apartments of Kamal Udwan and Mohammed Youssef Najjar and murdered them, along with Palestinian poet Kamal Nasir, in their sleep. Abu Iyad says it was only a stroke of luck that he wasn't at the same apartment at the time.

During the summer, Fatah tried to dissociate itself from the leadership of Black September. Abu Iyad instructed Ali Hassan Salameh to order his operatives to sever their links with Libya and Iraq, the two nations largely responsible for funding Fatah's terrorist wing. Defying his orders, two key operatives who had been liaisons to these nations defected to them: Ahmed Abdel Ghaffar (Abu Mahmoud) to Libya and Sabri al-Banna (Abu Nidal) to Iraq. Arafat personally ordered death sentences for both of them although apparently only one was carried out. When Abu Mahmoud visited Beirut in 1974, he was shot and killed, reportedly by the Israeli secret services.

Meanwhile a friendship was developing between Egyptian President Sadat and Syrian President Assad, who had served as a pilot in a Syrian unit in Egypt when the two nations were joined briefly in the United Arab Republic from 1958–61. While Israel was preoccupied with its war against terrorism, Egypt and Syria were quietly rebuilding their armies. On September 9, Sadat invited Arafat, Abu Iyad and Abu Lutuf (Farouk Kaddoumi) to meet with him at Burgh al-Arab, the presidential compound in Alexandria. Sadat suggested he would like to see a contingent of Palestinian troops among the Egyptian forces on the Suez Canal. The Egyptian president was planning a joint attack with the Syrian army against strongholds in the Golan Heights and Sinai peninsula that Israel had captured in the Six-Day War. Sadat envisaged the assault as a limited offensive that would get the stalemated Arab-Israeli peace process back on track. As for asking Hussein to join the action, there was little love on either side.

Sadat disapproved of the actions of Black September. "King Hussein had decided to liquidate those forces and so fought them ruthlessly." It was "a massacre in the full sense of the term," he wrote in his memoirs, *In Search of Identity*.³ At the same time, Sadat lacked confidence in the Jordanian military strength. On his part, Hussein was not interested in another Arab-Israeli war. His country had not yet fully recovered from the last one; the cost, in terms of territory, money and morale, had been too high.

Unknown to the Jordanians, over lunch with Arafat and his colleagues, Sadat hinted to the three PLO officials that Egypt was running out of patience with Israel but said little that tipped them off to the pending surprise. "What we need is a spark, only a spark which will make everyone aware there is a dormant problem," Sadat told them. In mid-afternoon, Mohammad Heikal drove the Palestinians back to Cairo. Curious about what Sadat had in mind, Abu Lutuf started pummeling Heikal with questions about the wisdom of deploying Palestinian troops on the Suez Canal. Abu Iyad said he thought it was a good idea. "At least they will be a reminder to the Egyptians that there is a Palestinian element," he said. "By the way, what is this 'spark' that Sadat was talking about?" asked Abu Iyad. Heikal tried not to give anything away. "I didn't want to betray Sadat," he said.⁴

On October 1, Arafat instructed a group of Palestinian officers and about 120 soldiers to take up positions in the Canal Zone. Five days later, on October 6, 1973, on the most sacred Jewish holiday, Yom Kippur, Egyptian troops succeeded in surprising the Israeli army and crossed to the East Bank of the Suez Canal. Abu Iyad was in Cairo and went to see Sadat. "Didn't I tell you about the spark?" asked Sadat. "This is the spark," the Palestinian replied incredulously. "This isn't a spark. It's a fire!"

In fact, Palestinian units, part of the 5,000-man PLA force attached to the Syrian army, were helicoptered behind Israeli lines and seized four hills in Kuneitra on the Golan Heights. Efforts to infiltrate another 1,000 guerrillas from Jordan into southern Israel, where they planned to attack from Beersheba to Eilat, were unsuccessful. Heikal blamed King Hussein, who allegedly would not answer the phone when Sadat repeatedly tried to call him. Hussein was concerned that the Palestinian forces would bring Israeli retaliation against the kingdom. Towards the end of the war, Hussein ordered some Jordanian divisions to the Golan to help the Syrians.

But by the time they arrived, the Syrians had lost too much ground to the Israelis and were only a few hours away from a cease fire.

When the sixteen-day October War was over, Egypt had won what was widely hailed as a victory, even though it took U.S. intervention to keep the Egyptian Third Army from being routed by the Israeli troops which had encircled it on the East Bank and cut off its supply routes. The Palestinians, having participated in the fighting, now seemed ready to join the peace process reignited by the United Nations in Geneva at the end of October.

However, in November 1973, Kissinger, who had become secretary of state in addition to his post as national security adviser, began his "shuttle diplomacy," negotiating an unprecedented Egyptian-Israeli troop disengagement accord. By December, King Hussein, impressed with the new American willingness to use its clout with Israel, proposed that Kissinger try to persuade Golda Meir to withdraw Israeli forces from the West Bank and Gaza in return for a peace treaty with Jordan.

In early 1974 Kissinger raised the issue with the Israeli leader, trying to convince her to make at least a gesture by giving Jericho, an Arab town on the Jordan River, back to the Hashemite Kingdom as a sweetener that would make it easier for Hussein to begin talks on the territorial division of the West Bank. Faced with the prospect that Jordan might actually achieve through negotiations what their fighters had been unable to win through force, the PLO began to reassess its own strategy.

On February 24, 1974, the fifth anniversary of the Democratic Front for the Liberation of Palestine (DFLP), its secretary-general, Nayaf Hawatmeh, dropped a political bombshell on his fellow Palestinians. "We are fighting for our people's right to establish its national authority on its own land after the occupation has been ended," he declared. The speech was an answer to Kissinger's suggestion that Jordan take over any part of the West Bank that was evacuated by the Israeli army. The euphemism that Hawatmeh used, "national authority," was meant to send an unmistakable signal to Hussein that Palestinians—and not Jordanians—would establish their homeland on the West Bank. It was the first step towards the PLO's embracing a mini-state solution.

In April, Hawatmeh elaborated on his proposal in an interview with the *Washington Post*. In it, he spoke openly about the need for two states to exist in "historical" Palestine. Fatah was deeply divided over the policy, with Abu Lutuf leading the opposition, but Arafat thought it was "a stroke of genius," says Hawatmeh.[5] Arafat also told Hawatmeh he would work to persuade the 450 members of the PNC to endorse the stand at their upcoming congress. Hawatmeh and Arafat were fought tooth and nail by Habash's PFLP. But they were able to work out a fragile compromise when the twelfth PNC met in Cairo in June and July.

The new political program affirmed that "The PLO will struggle by every means, the foremost of which is armed struggle, to liberate Palestinian land and to establish the people's national, independent and fighting sovereignty on every part of Palestinian land to be liberated." The move was intended to serve notice to Hussein that any part of the territory evacuated by Israeli troops—even one inch—should be under Palestinian and not Jordanian control.

Says Hawatmeh, "We saw that the idea of a single democratic, united Palestinian state with Palestinians and Jews was no longer a practical goal. There were facts on the land: an Israeli state and the Palestinians had nothing." He says he told his PLO brethren, "We must think of a more realistic policy that takes the balance of power—regionally and internationally—into consideration. We must develop a Palestinian policy that is realistic and attainable." For Hawatmeh, that was only a Palestinian mini-state on the West Bank and in Gaza. He is candid: "We know that there is not another place we can take."

But even an implied two-state solution was heresy to Habash, who still accuses Arafat of being "more pragmatic than necessary."[6] If the PLO was prepared to establish its control on any part of Palestine, Habash pointed out, it was prepared to recognize Israel. His logic was irrefutable. Once the PLO signaled a willingness to establish Palestinian sovereignty on some part of Palestine—and not on the entire area—it was signaling its willingness to compromise over other parts of Palestine. For Habash, that meant renouncing the claim to Tel Aviv and Haifa and Jaffa and other cities.

All of them understood—as did Arafat and the overwhelming majority of Palestinians—that establishing a "national authority" in any part of Palestine was the first step towards recognition of the Jewish state. After all, one couldn't establish sovereignty without negotiations with Israel, and negotiations eventually would mean recognition.

For the next several years, there were, in effect, three PLOs. The first was the one dominated by Fatah. The second was the Syrian-sponsored Saiqa, formed from the sizable units of PLA forces in the Syrian army. The third was the Habash-led Rejection Front which tried to exploit the tensions between the two other PLOs.

During that period Arafat had a difficult time defending his PLO stance. The Palestinian diaspora, particularly in the refugee camps, was not ready to abandon the dream of going back to the towns and villages where they grew up. For them, the right of return was a sacred principle that the PLO was now asking them to abandon or, at the very least, postpone until a later stage of the guerrilla struggle.

By May 31, 1974, Kissinger had succeeded in getting Israeli troops, which had advanced in the October War within artillery range of the outskirts of Damascus, to withdraw from Syrian territory north of the Golan and from Kuneitra, the only heavily populated area in the Golan Heights captured in the June 1967 war.

The Israeli pullback followed an earlier agreement with Egypt to withdraw Israeli forces from the Suez Canal and allow Egypt to reopen the waterway. By the summer, negotiations had begun with Egypt for a second disengagement under which Israel would withdraw along the length of the Sinai border. The intensified pace of Kissinger's Middle East shuttles created a climate in which Israel appeared ready to make territorial compromises in return for a new Arab willingness to reduce the presence of military units on Israel's borders. In talks with King Hussein, Kissinger suggested applying the same formula with Jordan that he had used so successfully with Syria and Egypt.

By spring, Yitzhak Rabin had succeeded Golda Meir as Israel's prime minister and was promoting a more expansive version of the Allon Plan. That idea, conceived by Deputy Prime Minister Yigal Allon, had called for the territorial division of the West Bank. It proposed that Arab towns and villages in the mountain ranges of the West Bank be returned to Jordanian jurisdiction while Israel would retain forces along the length of the Jordan River, in the valley where the Jewish state had already established dozens of settlements.

The rationale behind the plan was that these forces would occupy the uninhabited floor of the valley as a buffer zone. Israel would be able to protect its eastern front with the natural borders of the river and steep canyons that made moving towards the mountains more difficult. In return, the Jewish state was prepared to give away the heavily populated areas from Hebron in the south to Jenin in the north. A narrow corridor would connect the Palestinian towns and villages with the Jordanian East Bank. The connection would be Jericho, the only town along the river with an Arab population.

Hussein learned from Kissinger that Israel would negotiate a withdrawal, but only from Jericho, and only as a first step towards implementing the Allon Plan. For Hussein, the proposal meant regaining Jericho, which was desirable, but losing the seven-mile-long strip stretching the length of the Jordan Valley. More importantly, Jordan would be making a territorial compromise inside the 1967 borders and signing away land to Israel. Hussein was ready for a withdrawal similar to the one that had been negotiated with Egypt and Syria, and proposed a five-mile withdrawal by both sides along the entire front, as a first step towards regaining the land he lost in 1967. But he could not accept less than Egypt and Syria had received. The king turned down the Israeli plan.

Aware of the possible consequences of Israel's refusal even to consider a unilateral withdrawal from Jericho, Kissinger tried but failed to persuade Israel to come up with a plan that would meet Hussein's needs. Rabin was willing to listen but his hard-line opposition, reflecting the mood of a frustrated Israel public still reeling from the October defeat, loudly proclaimed it was not ready to give up one inch of territory in what it called Judea and Samaria.

Earlier that year, Kissinger told an audience of American Jewish leaders in Philadelphia: "I predict that if the Israelis don't make some sort of arrangement with Hussein on the West Bank in six months, Arafat will become internationally recognized and the world will be in chaos. If I were an adviser to the Israeli Government, I would tell the prime minister: 'For God's sake, do something with Hussein while he is still one of the players.'"[7]

Kissinger made his prediction on February 8, 1974. Eight and a half months later, on October 28, 1974, the leaders of the Arab world, meeting in Rabat for the seventh summit, formally annointed the Palestine Liberation Organization as "the sole legitimate representative of the Palestinian people" and declared that only the PLO had the right to establish "an independent national authority...in any Palestinian territory that is liberated." Hussein was heartsick as he heard the words. He had argued against them to no avail. Now, even if he regained the dynastic land won by his great-grandfather and his grandfather, he would be forced to hand it over to the PLO. To make matters worse, the United Nations supported Arafat's position when it applauded his appearance before the world body two weeks later on November 13, 1974.

The Arab leaders at Rabat had done just what Kissinger predicted. After a decade of armed struggle with Israel, trench warfare with the PLO's Arab brothers and bitter feuds within its own leadership, the guerrilla organization had won the most important victory of all. As far as the Arab world was concerned, the West Bank no longer belonged to Jordan.

For most of the next decade there was little contact between Arafat and Hussein. The PLO leader spent his energies at war in Lebanon, until he was compelled to withdraw his forces in 1982; the king used his efforts to develop his country and cultivate ties with, among others, the Israelis. The example of King Abdullah had not been lost on Hussein: it was far better to maintain a dialogue with the leaders of the Jewish state, not only as a means to peaceful coexistence, but in order to regain the Arab territories that belonged to the Hashemite Kingdom. "He has had hundreds of hours with every single top Israeli official," acknowledges a senior American diplomat who has been sworn to secrecy by the State Department. The thick dossier filed in the American embassy in Amman under the code name "Sandstorm" is replete with meetings between Hussein and Golda Meir, Shimon Peres, Yitzhak Rabin, Moshe Dayan, Abba Eban and even Yitzhak Shamir. Time and again the king piloted his own private helicopter to Tel Aviv, Aqaba or an island in the Red Sea, or jetted to secret meetings in London and Paris. "I have tried everything possible to see what could be done with the situation," says the king now. "I could not compromise on territory. It was my responsibility to work for Palestinian rights but also for territory for peace and implementation of [U.N. Resolution] 242 which I contributed to and, in fact, was involved in formulating myself. I tried. I left no door unopened."[8]

There were endless meetings, as well, with Arab leaders and American officials. Most noteworthy were the repeated trips to Amman in the mid-seventies by Kissinger, who led Hussein to believe that eventually Jordan, like Egypt and Syria, would recover its territory through negotiations with Israel. To this day Hussein feels disappointed that Kissinger never fulfilled his promise.

Shortly after President Jimmy Carter took office in 1977, the American diplomatic drive shifted from Kissinger's step-by-step approach to a broader international effort. The Americans sought to court Soviet support for reconvening the U.N.-sponsored Geneva Conference that had last met at the end of the October War in 1973. That meeting had not only reaffirmed Resolution 242 but had passed Resolution 338, which called for immediate steps towards a comprehensive Arab-Israeli settlement between all the parties concerned.

On October 1, 1977, following a lengthy meeting between U.S. Secretary of State Cyrus Vance and Soviet Foreign Minister Andrei Gromyko, an agreement was hammered out for reconvening the Geneva Conference. "The joint statement represented our conviction that a just solution to the Palestinian problem was morally and politically essential to any lasting Middle East settlement. I believed it was possible to find a formula that would enable PLO members who were not 'well-known' to be among the Palestinians at a peace conference," Vance wrote in his memoirs.[9] Indeed, the Soviets for the first time had explicitly agreed to commit themselves to the aim of normal relations with Israel and its Arab neighbors. They had also agreed that the conference could be reconvened for the purpose of starting direct talks between Israel and each of its Arab foes without explicitly mentioning either the PLO or its demands for an independent state. In return, the Palestinians could attend the conference as part of a single Arab delegation and later could negotiate directly with Israel.

The PLO was pleased with the U.S.-Soviet accord. But Israel categorically refused to attend a Geneva peace conference based on the joint declaration. Israeli Foreign Minister Moshe Dayan particularly objected to the recognition of "the legitimate rights of the Palestinian people" included in the communique. However, on October 11, after a hastily arranged trip by Dayan to Washington, the Israeli cabinet endorsed the principle of a Geneva peace conference, making clear there could be no discussion of a Palestinian homeland nor any participation by even low level PLO members. Hussein was looking forward to attending the international conference. "Carter got in touch," recalls the king. "I visited with him. He was very interested in doing something. I got in touch with the

Egyptians and Syrians. I found the Egyptians reluctant to have the Syrians involved. I went over to Syria from Egypt because Carter said, 'If you don't respond, you aren't getting anywhere.' So we managed to get the Syrians to move a little on their side. We were still talking about a collective Arab effort to resolve the whole problem."

But Sadat, afraid that he would be outmaneuvered by the Syrians, the Soviets and the Palestinians, decided to take matters into his own hands. The Egyptian leader invited the PLO chairman to hear him address the opening of the new session of parliament on November 9, 1978, but the contents of the president's speech had not been divulged. On the day of the speech, Sadat looked anxiously for Arafat, but the PLO leader was still in Libya where he was working on a rapprochement between Qadaffi and Sadat. At Sadat's request, the PLO envoy in Cairo, Said Kamal, telephoned Arafat. The chairman said he could not be at the Parliament before eight P.M. "So Sadat delayed for one and a half hours," says Kamal, who met Arafat at the airport and escorted him to the parliament. When the two leaders met, the Egyptian president told a delighted Arafat that he was willing to go to the end of the world to make peace, therefore, he said, he was going to Damascus for a rapprochement with the Syrians. But a few minutes later, in front of the entire People's Assembly, Sadat announced his willingness to go to the end of the world, *not* excluding Israel, to make peace. The Sadat initiative to Jerusalem was born.

Afterwards, Arafat remembers asking Sadat, "Are you serious?" But, says Arafat, "He didn't answer me. Because it wasn't actually in his written speech. Did you know that? He suddenly changed his text and began to say, 'I am ready to go, to make peace, everywhere, even to Jerusalem.'" The friendship between the two men evaporated immediately. "It was the last time I saw him," says Arafat quietly. "Then I left."

Arafat felt that Sadat had betrayed him. The PLO leader believed he had won a major victory in gaining implicit American recognition of the PLO. "Don't forget," says Arafat now, "we were coordinating together to go to Geneva. In the summer of '77 we had the Egyptian-American communique in which was mentioned, for the first time, recognition by the American administration for the PLO. Officially. Mentioned in this communique between [Egyptian Foreign Minister] Ismail Fahmy and Vance." The Israelis, however, had refused to accept PLO members as representatives to the conference, and Arafat had made a major compromise. "According to my agreement with Sadat himself, I would send with the joint Arab delegation some [non-PLO] Palestinians with American nationality." Adds Arafat defiantly, "I appointed them."

Just two days after Sadat had announced he would visit Jerusalem, Hussein was in touch with the Egyptian president. The king recalls his surprise at not being informed of the decision: "I said, 'Why?' He said, 'I don't want you to assume any responsibility, or anyone else to be involved. So I decided. It was my own initiative.'"

Although Arafat cut himself off from Sadat, Hussein tried to maintain a relationship with the Egyptian leader. Just before Sadat departed for the United States for the Camp David talks in September 1978, Hussein sent him a letter. "I wrote because of Carter," says the king, "and I said, 'Please, if the Israelis are too adamant, and you not getting anywhere, do not settle for a partial solution. The problem is the West Bank and Gaza, and the problem is a problem of the region. A separate attempt to resolve it will not help us.'" The king says he was assured by Sadat that Egypt was seeking "to get the Israelis and the Americans to move, to try to resolve the whole thing." There was even a slim possibility that Hussein might join Sadat at Camp David.

In mid-September, Hussein, who had flown to London in anticipation of an invitation to join Sadat, received a phone call from Camp David. "He said he was about to leave," recalls the king. "He had tried his best and put my reputation and Egypt's on the line. Unfortunately, the Israelis are not coming through." Hussein replied, "If this is the case, then we have gone this far." Expecting the talks to collapse, the king invited Sadat to meet him in Morocco a few days later. The next day, September 17, 1978, Hussein and his new wife, Queen Noor, left for Spain for a brief vacation with the Spanish monarchs, King Juan Carlos and Queen Sophia. "We woke in the morning and heard the news on the radio about the signing of Camp David," says Queen Noor. Hussein was shocked. "It was a very difficult time," she adds. The Jordanians canceled the meeting in Morocco and flew home to Amman. The agreement called for a five-year period of autonomy for the Palestinians in the West Bank and Gaza, and stated that after the third year of continued Israeli rule, the Palestinians could bring their demands to the negotiating table. Although Camp David offered Jordan an equal role in determining the "final status" of the territories, there was no prospect that the occupied territories would ever revert to Jordan. From Hussein's perspective, Jordan was being asked to continue acquiescing to the Israeli administration of the West Bank and Gaza without being offered any real hope of regaining the Arab land. "Jordan was placed in a role that would cause it to be responsible for Israel's security in the occupied territory, without our being involved in anything, without our being consulted," says the king. "So that was that."

No one was more aware that the road to political rehabilitation ran through Amman than Yasser Arafat. When Adnan Abu Odeh, King Hussein's most influential adviser of Palestinian origin, suggested to Khaled al-Hassan they could exploit an opening in the Reagan Plan to win American recognition of the PLO, Arafat was only too willing to cooperate.

The plan had been announced on September 1, 1982, the day after Arafat and the PLO *fedayeen* withdrew from Lebanon. The proposal required Israeli withdrawal in return for peace and placed a freeze on settlements in the occupied territories. Its basic concept was that the West Bank should become neither a Palestinian state nor a permanent part of Israel, but an "association of the West Bank and Gaza with Jordan"; and that there should be negotiations between Israel and a joint Jordanian-Palestinian delegation to determine the final status of the occupied territories. The United States also broadened its interpretation of autonomy, as outlined in the earlier Camp David accords, and pledged to assure the Palestinians free elections leading to "real authority over themselves, the land and its resources."

Within hours of the plan's announcement, Israeli Prime Minister Menachem Begin rejected it. The king was more cautious, noting that the main idea of association with Jordan was one that he had suggested years earlier. Arafat made little comment.

Within a week the Saudis hosted an Arab Summit in Fez. Bolstered by the swift Israeli rejection of the Reagan Plan and attempting to force the PLO onto a political track after its defeat in Beirut, the Arab leaders formulated their own proposal, the Fahd Plan. It was noteworthy in two respects: for the first time, the Arab world recognized de facto Israel's pre-June 1967 borders; without specifically mentioning Israel, the assembled leaders called for the U.N. Security Council to guarantee peace "among all states in the region." At the same time it reaffirmed the Palestinians' right to self-determination and statehood.

Hussein's close aide, Adnan Abu Odeh, noted that President Ronald Reagan had called for the new entity on the West Bank to be associated with Jordan. Therefore, he argued, when the PLO demands an independent state, it is sabotaging its chances of winning recognition. Abu Odeh proposed a clever gambit to further the PLO's goals. "We will say to the Americans, this association is a confederation," he explained. Do not worry about self-determination, he advised.[10] If Jordan formally recognizes the PLO as the exclusive agent for the Palestinian people, the PLO clearly will head up whatever entity emerges. The PLO no longer will need to demand self-determination because, the Jordanian adviser said slyly, "self-determination will have already taken place."

The tactic appealed to Arafat and at a PNC meeting in Algiers in February 1983 the PLO leader received a mandate to cooperate with Hussein. In April, Arafat and Hussein agreed that Jordan could explore opportunities presented by the Reagan plan to advance the peace process. But the PLO Executive Committee, meeting in Kuwait, refused to give Arafat the authority. PLO radicals regarded the overtures to Hussein as further proof of Arafat's weakness and submission to the west.

But King Hussein needed Arafat as much as Arafat needed King Hussein. Arafat could help Hussein blunt American demands that Jordan play a more active role in the peace process. The Hashemite monarch had asked to buy $1.9 billion worth of F-16 fighter bombers and other American armaments. Many in Congress were angry that Hussein had not followed Sadat's example in making peace with Israel—by early 1985 it was clear that some move in that direction was the litmus test for any new arms package. But Arafat also needed Hussein. His base in Tunis was almost a three-hour flight from the Middle East. Arafat wanted to be closer to his constituency in the West Bank and Gaza. Amman was on the roadmap.

Besides, Hussein had paved the way, renewing diplomatic relations with Egypt and allowing Abu Jihad to reopen the PLO's offices in the Jordanian capital. Hussein had also taken a bold step to help Arafat rebuild his stature within the fractured Palestinian community. In November, 1984, Hussein hosted the 17th Palestine National Council in Amman. By permitting Arafat to hold the PNC meeting in Jordan, Hussein was helping Arafat win back the mantle of PLO leadership. But he also was reminding Arafat and West Bank Palestinians of their need to rely on Jordan to advance their cause. The success of the PNC, which barely managed to rally a quorum of Arafat loyalists, also had a message for Syria: Jordan and the PLO henceforth would cooperate to resist efforts by the Damascus-based National Salvation Front to sabotage the peace process. Hussein confirmed his desire to cooperate with the Palestinians and gave the delegates a choice: "a Jordanian-Palestinian formula" for regaining the West Bank and Gaza; or proceeding without Jordan, in which case he said, "Godspeed, you have our support. The decision is yours."

On February 11, 1985, following four months of secret talks between Adnan Abu Odeh and Khaled al-Hassan, the PLO and Jordan formally agreed on a framework for governing their future relations and on common approach to peace with Israel. The principle of "land in exchange for peace" was reaffirmed. Both sides committed themselves to the need for an international conference to be attended by the five permanent members of the U.N. Security Council and the parties to the conflict. The PLO was named as "the sole legitimate representative of the Palestinian people" and thus entitled to be represented at the conference. The mode of that representation would be a joint Jordanian-Palestinian delegation. There was no specific mention of Resolution 242 in the joint accord, although the PLO agreed to endorse all U.N. resolutions, "including the resolutions of the Security Council." The issue of self-determination also was fudged. While affirming the Palestinians had this right, the joint accord pledged they would exercise it only after a West Bank-Palestinian federation had been formed with Jordan. Hussein reasoned that he could persuade the Reagan administration to begin direct talks with the PLO if the organization dropped this demand; in any event, once the West Bank was "liberated," the PLO would be able to assert its authority there so there was no need to make "self-determination" an irrefutable precondition now.

With self-determination seemingly finessed in this manner, the Jordanian-PLO accord provided an important new opening for the United States. Hussein understood—as Arafat did not—that Washington could never force Israel to do something it deemed against its interests, but he also was aware that without U.S. coaxing, Israel would be unlikely to come to the negotiating table. The timing was appealing because in Israel a national unity government assumed power in 1984, headed by Labor Party leader Shimon Peres. Although Peres had to account to his right-wing Likud coalition partner for any foreign policy departures, he thought he could revive Hussein's interest in territorial compromise, a hallmark of Labor Party platforms in the 1970s. While intent on restoring his relationship with Arafat, Hussein also renewed a series of secret liaisons with Peres in the spring of 1985.

For Peres, as for American officials, the Jordanian option presented a viable alternative to the arguments of Ariel Sharon and other Likud leaders. The hard-liners argued that "Jordan is Palestine," and therefore there was no need for any compromise, certainly not one that would return any part of the West Bank to Jordan or would give sovereignty to the local Palestinians. The Likud position, Peres believed, was untenable because it left only two options for Israel: nearly two million Arabs would have to be forcibly incorporated into Israel, a demographic time bomb for the Jewish state; or the Palestinians would need to be "relocated" in other Arab states, which meant mass deportations.

In his secret talks with Hussein in the spring of 1985 and in Paris where they met in October, Peres offered another solution, an interim one. The formula was Camp David with a twist: There could be three years of "power-sharing" with Jordan while the final status of the territories was decided in negotiations between Israel, Jordan and the inhabitants themselves. Israeli and Jordanian forces would jointly administer the West Bank and Gaza. There would be a total freeze on new Jewish settlements and 500,000 acres of land previously owned by the Hashemite Kingdom would be returned to Jordan.

For Hussein, the Israeli plan offered a return of Jordanian control and kept open the possibility that a Palestinian entity could be federated with Jordan. The entity would owe its allegiance to the Hashemites who, in turn, would be responsible for handling the defense of the Palestinians and their foreign affairs. The whole scheme was based on 242. The United Nations resolution called for reuniting the eastern and western banks of the Jordan River, which for Hussein meant that the territories would be reincorporated, in whole or in part, into his Hashemite Kingdom. Furthermore, its attractiveness for Hussein lay in the fact that there was no mention in 242 of the PLO or any rights of a "people" to self-determination, independence or statehood.

Under international law, Arab East Jerusalem was also considered part of the West Bank. The United States had never recognized reunited Jerusalem as the Israeli capital nor had Washington acceded to Israeli annexation of East Jerusalem. (The United States has never recognized anyone's claim to sovereignty over any part of Jerusalem.) There was, thus, a comity of views between the United States and Jordan: both wanted the PLO to publicly accept 242 as the price for getting a seat at the negotiating table. But the U.S. demanded more: explicit PLO recognition of Israel and renunciation of terrorism. Nevertheless, even if the PLO met all the American conditions, Israel still vowed to destroy the group it considered a purely terrorist organization.

Hussein believed he could resolve these contradictions by offering the PLO representation in a joint delegation to an international conference. The king tried to persuade Arafat that the Reagan Plan offered confederation with Jordan, and therefore the PLO could wait to exercise self-determination until after the territories had been freed from Israeli control. The only precondition to the plan's implementation was the PLO's acceptance of 242. But Hussein and Reagan would have a difficult time.

"You Americans are saying I should give up my last card and accept the state of Israel when Israel doesn't accept me and doesn't accept the idea of a Palestinian state," Arafat said indignantly in response to the plan. "I'm supposed to accept Begin and Shamir and the Israeli state, and they say we will never accept a Palestinian state or the PLO or Arafat! What is it you Americans are offering? If I accept your card, then you will talk to me. Big deal. What are we going to talk about? What's the agenda? You're not offering me anything except a dialogue. I said I am going to negotiate with my enemies, with the Israeli government. That is enough." Hussein clearly had his work cut out for him.

18

Double-crossed by the PLO

IN THE SMALL CIRCLE *of influential people surrounding the king, the name Rifai appears again and again, often at the most critical times. Samir Rifai, a Palestinian from Safad, had been chosen by King Abdullah to be one of his closest advisors. It was Samir Rifai who was prime minister in 1952 when Abdullah was assassinated and who had begged him not to visit Jerusalem. Samir's brother, Abdul Moneim Rifai, was chosen by King Hussein to be prime minister during Black September. But it is Samir's son, Zeid Rifai, who has long been a close personal friend as well as chief adviser to King Hussein. The two men were classmates at college, and the king chose Rifai as his private secretary in 1967, and then made him head of the Royal Cabinet two years later. While he was still in his thirties, in May 1973, Rifai was tapped to become prime minister and served in that role from 1973 to 1976, dramatically improving Jordan's relations with Syria. Since 1978 he has been a member of the Senate and was its deputy leader from 1979 to 1980. In 1985 he was again asked to become prime minister and served until 1989.*

In some ways, he is Hussein's alter ego, able to express views publicly that the king never can. He participated in the meetings with Arafat and the other guerrilla leaders after the Six-Day War and for several years after; he served the king throughout the period of Black September and was in the car with Hussein when the king's automobile was attacked by gunfire in 1970. Although there was little contact between Hussein and Arafat in the years immediately following Black September, once a rapprochement began in 1983, it was Zeid Rifai who helped smooth the way for a political process to start.

Now, as he ushers us into his home in Amman and leads us to the atrium, he speaks about Arafat and a grimace crosses his face. The reason for Rifai's bitterness stems in great part from discussions he held with Arafat in 1985 when the Jordanian official believed he had achieved some progress in possible talks between the PLO and the United States. But Arafat, he feels, let him down and, what was worse, embarrassed the king in front of the Americans. Hussein admits it was an awkward time but blames much of the trouble on hard-line radicals. "One of the problems we had during that time," says the king, *"was probably certain Arab quarters telling the PLO that something better could be achieved. I think no one was as close to the Palestinian problem or the American scene,"* he adds, *"but that didn't help."*[1]

"His Majesty is deeply hurt by Arafat," says Rifai. *"He feels betrayed by him. But as His Majesty always puts it, if he wanted to be personal in relationships, then he would be talking to very few leaders in the world."*[2] *Like Arafat, Hussein is called flexible by his friends, flaccid by his enemies. Both men are able to forget the past and look pragmatically towards the future. "It is a matter of priorities,"* explains Rifai. *"He forgets personal injuries in order to achieve what he believes is good for his people, or for the Palestinians. It is not a matter of getting along with the man. Arafat is the leader of the Palestinians and you have to deal with him."*

Despite the disappointments, Rifai believes that Arafat is now so firmly committed to peace that it is too late for him to reverse course. "I don't think he can change back. The alternative before Arafat is not an alternative policy, but an alternative leadership. If he changes his position, then he would lose credibility. In a way, he should be supported because if the concessions he is given don't achieve any results, then the political, peaceful approach to the settlement is buried.

And people will start thinking about extremist measures, such as violence, terrorism, another war, another leader. Then the chance for peace would be lost forever. So personal feelings aside, Arafat should be supported now. If the Israelis continue their intransigence and the U.S. continues its unwillingness to pressure them, then not only Arafat will pay the price, but the whole area will pay."

F ew Jordanians were as acutely aware of Arafat's ploys as Zeid Rifai when he embraced the PLO chief and kissed him on both cheeks. Rifai considered the PLO a necessary evil, necessary for protecting Jordan from Arab claims that Hussein was trying to cut a separate deal. At the same time Rifai may have believed that Jordan could corner, then co-opt, Arafat on its terms. As he greeted Arafat's entourage he led them all to the patio of his well-guarded Amman home. It was an early spring day in 1985. Arafat arrived with three of his key aides, Hani al-Hassan; Mohammed Milhem, the deposed mayor of Halhul; and Abdullah al-Zaki Yahya, the PLO ambassador to Jordan. Accompanying Rifai were Foreign Minister Tahir al-Masri and two of His Majesty's closest advisers from the Royal Court, Marwan Kassem and Adnan Abu Odeh.

The prime minister led them through the spectacular white villa and out to the patio. On one side they could see a sitting area of wicker chairs covered in comfortable ivory-colored cushions. As they walked along the marble mosaic floor, wind chimes rang and palm trees moved gently in the breeze. Their host guided them to a shaded setting on the far side that seemed like a scene from the Tales of the Arabian Nights. Blue and gold paint covered the intricate woodwork of the atrium and gold leaf trimmed the mosaic tiles on the floor. The men took their seats on the chairs arranged in a horseshoe, and Rifai began the discussion.

He outlined the plan that Hussein intended to propose to President Reagan on his upcoming trip to Washington. In reality, the plan was an outgrowth of ideas proposed by Egyptian President Hosni Mubarak, the accord the PLO had reached with Jordan and the secret meetings Hussein had held with Shimon Peres. Secretary of State George Shultz and his principal Middle East advisers, Assistant Secretary of State Richard Murphy, U.S. Ambassador to Israel Thomas Pickering and U.S. Ambassador to Egypt Nicholas Veliotes, played key roles in putting the plan into motion. It consisted of a series of half steps that if taken in sequence would lead to American recognition of the PLO and the scheduling of an international conference at which both Israel and the PLO would be represented.

The idea of half steps was intended to make it easier for the PLO to accept Resolution 242, which remained the operative United Nations document that implicitly recognized Israel's existence. As a first step, Mubarak proposed that Murphy agree to meet with a joint delegation of Jordanians and Palestinians. The Palestinians would be chosen by the PLO, but none of them could have any past or current affiliations with terrorist groups, be members of Fatah's Central Committee or the ruling bodies of other PLO factions. "Non-declared PLO Palestinians," was the way Murphy later described them.

The meeting would be convened to discuss three points: U.S. recognition of the Palestinians' right to self-determination within the context of a confederation with Jordan; PLO acceptance of 242; and PLO recognition of Israel's right to exist. Once both sides had publicly declared their acceptance of these principles, there would be further talks with the United States. A senior PLO delegation, perhaps led by Arafat himself, would be invited to Washington to pave the way for direct peace talks with Israel that would take place at the United Nations-sponsored conference.

Rifai's guests sat around a stone-encrusted round table as servants poured tea and coffee. The mood was an expectant one. Could these eight people—four Palestinians and four Jordanians—seize the opportunity to achieve the breakthrough that had eluded all their predecessors? Rifai reminded Arafat that he should submit a list of seven or eight Palestinians from which four would be chosen as participants in the joint delegation to meet Murphy and the Americans. "Do you understand what is required?" Rifai asked him. "You submit the names. It's all right for them to be PNC members or affiliated with the PLO but they can't be prominent personalities and they can't be people who were involved in any act of terrorism."

He went on: "When the list is accepted, the delegation will meet with Murphy. After that you declare your acceptance of 242, your renunciation of terrorism and your willingness to negotiate with the state of Israel. After that, there is a second meeting in Washington, which perhaps you can go to. Is that clear?" Arafat replied flatly, "Yes. It is very clear." Eager to be certain that he understood all the facets of the plan, Rifai said, "Abu Amar, after the [initial] meeting, you will declare your acceptance of 242?" Again, the PLO leader answered, "Yes. I just told you so." Still doubtful, Rifai said, "Abu Amar, you are absolutely sure that once the meeting is over, you will immediately declare your acceptance of 242?" Now an angry Arafat replied, "What is this? I am not a child when it comes to politics. I know the price I have to pay. I just told you I would." Summing up then, Rifai said, "So, you have absolutely no doubt that after the meeting, you will declare your acceptance of 242." At this point, Arafat got up and exclaimed: "You really are overdoing it. I just told you I will. I said okay. The matter is closed."

After Arafat and his entourage left that afternoon, Abu Odeh took Rifai aside and said, "You were talking to the chairman of the PLO. Why did you repeat the same question three times? I really felt hurt myself. You were so cruel to him. Why?" And Marwan Kassem told Rifai, "You weren't asking him questions. You were cross-examining him." The prime minister replied: "I just don't believe him. The man changes his mind. I had to make sure. He can repeat his answer a hundred times. I still don't believe he's going to do it. I just can't see it happening."

The Reagan administration, however, was excited about the prospect that Jordan and the PLO might be prepared to proceed together into peace talks with Israel. For the first time, the PLO had agreed it would be only indirectly represented and only by Palestinians who, although of its choosing, would not be officials of the PLO. Israel could reject any member of the Palestinian delegation it claimed had such ties, in effect, canceling the PLO out of the process.

American policymakers thought Israel could hardly expect a better deal. They were eager to set the whole process in motion before October 1986, when the rotation agreed upon by the Likud and Labor blocs would put the more hard-line Yitzhak Shamir in place as Israel's prime minister. Shamir already was making felt his opposition to the Peres-Hussein deal. During a trip to Jerusalem, Shultz tried to persuade him to overlook the fact that the PLO would be engaged in the process, citing the veto power Israel would retain. Only Palestinians who had proved their reasonableness would wind up in the talks, Shultz argued. Shamir reportedly shot back, "There is no good or bad PLO."

During their White House talks in May, Hussein officially presented his plan to President Reagan. He conveyed Arafat's new willingness to accept 242 and 338 if other pertinent United Nations resolutions also were endorsed as the basis for an international conference. For the PLO, these were General Assembly resolutions such as 181, which partitioned the British mandate into an Arab and Jewish state; others that affirmed the Palestinian right to self-determination and independent statehood; yet others that equated Zionism with racism and endorsed the Palestinian right to use all means against the occupier, including armed struggle.

On May 29, during a joint press conference in the White House Rose Garden, Hussein was asked why he called his plan the "last chance" for peace in the region. Reagan, trying to protect Hussein from having to respond, abruptly ended the session, saying neither of them would take any more questions. Then Reagan turned to the reporters and said, "I think the conditions have never been more right than they are now to pursue peace. And who knows whether those conditions will ever come as close together as they have now. So that's why I think the term 'last chance' is used. And I think we ought to keep that in mind, that perhaps it is the last chance."

What none of the reporters knew at the time was that Arafat had secretly promised to recognize Israel's existence, accept 242 and renounce terrorism. Reagan and Hussein even discussed a timetable. Invitations to a "ceremonial" opening of the international conference would be sent out in early fall. The conference itself would begin in November. For the first time Israel would be able to confront each of its Arab enemies—Jordan, the Palestinians, Saudi Arabia, Iraq, perhaps even Syria—at the negotiating table instead of on the battlefield. They would be gathered under the watchful eye of the United Nations with the United States and the Soviet Union, as well as Britain, France and China, overseeing the history-making event.

Assistant Secretary of State Murphy began working at once to put together a list of Palestinians who would be acceptable to the PLO as participants in the planned initial round of talks with the United States. Names were exchanged with Khaled al-Hassan, who made several trips to Washington in June and July. Murphy also travelled to the region, carefully keeping the Israeli Government informed of his progress. Finally, on July 17, 1985, the deputy chief of mission at the U.S. Embassy, acting at Shultz's direction, gave Prime Minister Peres the names of seven Palestinians whom Arafat had approved and provided to King Hussein a week earlier. They were:

Khaled al-Hassan, Arafat's political adviser and co-founder of Fatah;

Hatem Husseini, the former chief of the PLO office in Washington;

Henry Cattan, a Paris lawyer who had written extensively about Palestinian issues;

Fayez Abu Rahmeh, a highly-regarded Palestinian lawyer in Gaza who was not a member of the PLO;

Nabil Sha'ath, a non-Fatah "independent," important PNC leader and Cairo businessman who had been an articulate moderate voice among Palestinians;

Hanna Siniora, a West Bank pharmacist-turned-newspaper editor who used *Al-Fajr*, the PLO's proxy voice on the West Bank, to plead for coexistence and a two-state solution;

Fayez Sayigh, a Palestinian economist;

Salah Taamri, a Fatah operative in southern Lebanon, married to King Hussein's first wife, Muna, who had spent a year in the Israeli prison of Ansar before being freed in a 1983 prison exchange.

Since only three members of the group—Cattan, Abu Rahmeh, and Siniora—did not belong to the PLO, it is likely Arafat knew they would be the only ones who would even be considered. And at that juncture there is every reason to believe Arafat was acting in good faith. However, less than twenty-four hours after he got the list, Peres made two of the names public, announcing them in front of the Israeli Knesset. Of the seven Palestinians, only Siniora and Abu Rahmeh were acceptable, he said. The public battle was being waged. "How is it possible," asked Deputy Prime Minister Shamir on July 18, "that this terrorist organization [the PLO] should suddenly be a dialogue partner for the United States, which stands at the forefront of the war against world terrorism?" In Amman, Hussein couldn't believe his ears. "We were furious because we gave the names to the United States, not to Israel," explained Tahir al-Masri.

Nonetheless, in early September, the *Washington Post* reported that Murphy planned to meet soon in Amman with the joint Jordanian-Palestinian delegation. There was feverish activity. In

Cairo, Avraham Tamir, an aide to Peres, met with President Mubarak and his senior adviser Osama al-Baz in an effort to expand the list. Al-Baz was running the names by Arafat, flying to Tunis or meeting the PLO leader elsewhere in the Arab world. Peres indicated he would accept other West Bank Palestinians such as Faisal Husseini whose affiliation with the PLO would not be automatically vetoed by his coalition partner. Final agreement with Israel remained elusive and George Shultz decided it was not the time to confront the divided government there with a fait accompli. He asked Murphy to postpone his meeting.

The American and Israeli rebuffs to Hussein were not all he had to contend with. Hardline members of the PLO Executive Committee were digging in their heels against the Arafat initiative. But it was Soviet opposition that was the most unexpected. Moscow apparently feared that if Hussein succeeded, Soviet and particularly Syrian interests, would suffer from the new U.S.-PLO relationship. In March 1985, less than a month after the Jordanian-Palestinian accord, Arafat couldn't get a visa for himself or any other PLO official to Moscow to brief Soviet officials. Foreign Minister Andrei Gromyko was against the accords. Masri says Arafat finally had to "inject himself into the funeral of [Konstantin] Chernenko" just to get a brief audience with Gromyko. "We tried the same thing," says Masri, "but the Soviets wouldn't see any Jordanian official. They saw the accord as an American plot to deliver the PLO to the United States. They have always suspected Arafat and his moderation. Now, the king, who is a close friend of the United States, was doing the job for them [the Americans]."[3]

During the summer, Arafat wanted to send a PLO delegation to the Moscow Youth Festival. So did Abu Musa, the Syrian-backed claimant to Arafat's Fatah throne, who was in Damascus and "wanted to send his group to represent Palestine," says Abu Odeh. "The Soviets said, 'We might have you both.' To the PLO, that was a sign that the Soviets were not sure what side they were on. Both went."[4] Later, the Soviet Union was the only permanent member of the Security Council that refused to receive a joint Jordanian-Palestinian delegation. It was while that delegation was in London in mid-October, preparing for a meeting with British Prime Minister Margaret Thatcher, that the deepening internal PLO divisions over the initiative, fueled by Moscow, broke into the open and put Arafat's gambit in serious jeopardy.

A succession of terrorist incidents had worsened the climate for peacemaking. On September 25, three Israelis, Reuven and Esther Paltzur of Haifa and Avraham Avneri of Arad, all in their fifties, were murdered while asleep aboard their yacht in the Larnaca marina off Cyprus. Israel said the two men and one woman were tourists who had taken advantage of a long Yom Kippur holiday weekend to sail from Haifa to the nearby Mediterranean island. They were the victims of a hit squad of Fatah's Force 17, the elite commando group that had been formed by Ali Hasan Salameh. Fatah denied this allegation, charging the three Israelis were Mossad agents who were tracking the PLO's efforts to resupply their fighters in southern Lebanon. Abu Iyad charged they were targeted because the PLO had evidence these three were responsible for Salameh's 1978 murder. Meanwhile Israel declared "the murders would not go unpunished."

On October 1, 1985, eight Israeli F-16 jets swooped down on the seven-acre compound the PLO was using as its headquarters in Hamman al-Shat, a suburb of Tunis. The mission, more than 3,000 miles, was the longest ever flown by Israeli fighter-bombers which were refueled in mid-air. About twenty-four members of Arafat's immediate staff, including Mohammed Natour, the commander of Force 17, were killed, as well as fourteen Tunisians. Nearly a hundred others were injured. An Israeli defense expert later confided that information provided by Jonathan Pollard, the American naval intelligence official who was recruited to spy for Israel, was invaluable in helping plot the attack. Pollard gave the Israelis hundreds of documents pinpointing the precise location of Arafat's compound, the extent to which Tunisian and Libyan radar defenses reached into the Mediterranean and—so they wouldn't detect the attack—the exact movement of Soviet, French and American vessels in the region.

Six days later, on October 7, 1985, an Italian cruise ship, the *Achille Lauro*, was hijacked by four Palestinian terrorists who reportedly were acting on the orders of Mohammed Zaidan (Abul) Abbas, the leader of a small, Iraqi-supported pro-Arafat faction within the Palestine Liberation Front. Abul Abbas was a member of Fatah's Executive Committee. A senior PLF guerrilla leader who calls himself "Bilal," says that the real PLF mission—its first outside Israel—was to sail to the Israeli port of Ashdod, where the terrorists were to have commandeered two Israeli patrol boats guiding the *Achille Lauro* into the harbor. The PLF commandos then were to reconnoiter with a waiting guerrilla squad and hijack a bus filled with Israeli civilians. The Israelis were to be murdered in cold blood. "We call it an operation from which there is no return. We have some fighters like this," the young PLF guerrilla says.[5]

He explains that the hijackers panicked when they thought they had been discovered by an undercover Mossad agent, a seductive woman who was posing as an Italian security officer aboard the cruise liner. At first one of the young Palestinians thought she was interested in a shipboard romance. "She asked him to come to her room. He thought she wanted to make love," says Bilal. He was ordered by the commander of the squad "not to make this kind of connection because you will forget your mission." As the cruise continued, they thought she had become suspicious of them when she discovered they were travelling on South American passports. None of the four spoke Spanish. Their fears seemed confirmed when a general announcement was made that all personal passenger luggage would be examined after leaving Alexandria en route to Port Said, the last stop before reaching Ashdod. The general custom, explains Bilal, was to wait until a cruise ship entered Israeli waters.

In their hand luggage, the four were carrying plastic explosives and two bombs. Concerned they would be discovered, the leader of the group suggested, says Bilal, "We have about six hours between Alexandria and Port Said. Why don't we open the bags now so that we can prepare the explosives?" It was noontime and they expected the general announcement of the midday meal. But the public address system was not working, so the ship's stewards went from room to room to inform the passengers who had remained on board. Just as the Palestinians were beginning to assemble the bombs, there was a knock on their door, asking them to come to lunch. When there was no answer, the steward kept knocking. According to Bilal, the Palestinians thought they were going to be arrested, and smashing the door down, they ran out of their room, toting their machine guns and yelling that they were taking over the ship. During the hijacking a sixty-four-year-old, wheelchair-bound American, Leon Klinghoffer, was brutally murdered and tossed overboard.

Israeli officials as well as many Americans pointed to Arafat as the instigator. He denied that he had planned the operation and charged the leader of the PLF's military wing had been bribed by the Syrians. The goal of the terrorist act was not only to avenge the Israeli bombing of the PLO's headquarters in Tunis. It was, claims Arafat, also aimed at sabotaging the pending PLO peace mission to London which had been announced by Mrs. Thatcher and King Hussein. "We are also the victims of this terrorism," Arafat claims. He charges the "Syrians infiltrated Abbas' group. This was an example of Syrian dirty business. They penetrated them [PLF]—the Syrian intelligence services. I know everything about it," he adds, noting that he had already left on an official visit to the Sudan when the hijacking took place and so could not have masterminded it.

Arafat contends that Syrian agents knew the hijacking would strengthen Israeli hard-liners and advance their goal of overthrowing him by identifying him with a terrorist act that from all outward appearances seemed to have been conceived, directed and executed by the Fatah leader himself. Arafat insists it was Abul Abbas who gave the order to the hijackers to give up and return to Alexandria after Hani al-Hassan, who was in Cairo, radioed PLF headquarters in Damascus. Bilal, the PLF leader, says Hassan telephoned "our military leader and asked if they were our fighters." He replied that they were. Arafat says that he subsequently "froze the status" of Abul Abbas and has not permitted him to participate in Executive Committee meetings since 1985.

To this day, Arafat contends his actions saved the lives of the *Achille Lauro* passengers. "I received official thanks from the Italian government. I have a letter from the Prime Minister [Bettino Craxi]. I saved four hundred. The Department of Justice even dropped the request for the arrest and extradition of Abul Abbas."

But the State Department contends that Arafat was complicit in the attack. "He was aware that an operation was being planned even if he didn't know the specific target or how it came out. To say he had no idea that Abul Abbas was planning something is ludicrous," a senior U.S. policymaker says. He points to the fact that Abul Abbas was elected to the PLO Executive Committee in 1984. The PLF claim that the attack against Ashdod was planned in revenge for the Israeli bombing of the PLO's headquarters in Tunis is just as far-fetched, the official says, because it was virtually impossible to have planned the attack with a week's notice. The National Security Agency, he adds, has wiretaps pointing to the probability that the attack was conceived several months before the raid on Hamman al-Shat and perhaps as early as November 1984.

Israeli intelligence officials also contend that after the terrorists used the *Achille Lauro*'s radio telephone to contact the PLF coordinator in Genoa, he used a short-wave frequency to get in touch with PLO headquarters in Tunis. On October 16, 1985, the Israeli Government released transcripts of tape recorded conversations that Abul Abbas conducted with the terrorists on October 8, the second day of the hijacking, from the Egyptian harbor of Port Said. The tape recordings show that Abul Abbas knew the hijackers by their codenames and that he told them "it was not *our* goal to take control of the ship" and therefore they should apologize to the passengers and release them. Finally, the Israelis contend it was Arafat who, at the April 1987 PNC meeting in Algiers, backed the reelection of Abul Abbas to the executive committee after being pressed by Abu Nidal, the notorious leader of the breakaway Fatah Revolutionary Council.

Regardless of whether or not it was the PLF objective, the *Achille Lauro* affair effectively ended any prospect of a Palestinian meeting in London with Sir Geoffrey Howe, the British foreign secretary. A spokesman for the Abu Nidal faction in Libya threatened that if Ilia Khouri, the anglican bishop of Ramallah, and Mohammed Milhem, the deposed mayor of Halhul, went through with their plans to issue a joint statement with Howe accepting 242 and renouncing terrorism, they both would be murdered. King Hussein had worked assiduously throughout the fall to bring off the meeting. In September, he persuaded Mrs. Thatcher, while she was on an official visit to Jordan, to announce that she would welcome two members of the PLO Executive Committee on an official visit to Britain as part of a joint Jordanian-Palestinian delegation. "We know Bishop Khouri and Mr. Milhem to be men of peace," she said in announcing the initiative at a farewell press conference near the Red Sea port of Aqaba. "They personally support a peaceful settlement on the basis of the relevant United Nations resolutions and are opposed to terrorism and violence. I know they will reaffirm their positions during their stay in London." In responding to questions, she added: "I hope this will help the United States to take a similar step."

Working closely with Howe, Hussein and his advisers drafted a statement that pledged the PLO to oppose "all forms of terrorism and violence from whatever sources." It included an explicit acceptance of Israel's existence and endorsement of the relevant United Nations resolutions. The plan was for Khouri, who had approved the text in Amman, and Milhem to issue the declaration "as individuals" and not on behalf of the PLO as a whole. But even that proved too much for the traffic to bear. "It seems that this statement didn't get to any of the Palestinian leadership either here [in Jordan] or abroad [in Tunis]," says Tahir al-Masri, a member of the joint delegation. When Milhem saw the text, he erupted angrily. "What is this? I never heard you say we would accept 242," he said to the Jordanian foreign minister. Masri explained that the British would cancel the meeting "if we don't issue such a statement." Milhem said, "I can't accept 242 and recognize Israel just like that—neither in my personal or any other capacity—because I don't have the authority."

After a flurry of telephone conversations between Milhem, Khaled al-Hassan and Arafat, and long, fruitless efforts to reword the statement, the meeting was canceled. Howe announced that he had initially agreed to the meeting because he had received "unambiguous assurances" that the two PLO representatives would both renounce terrorism and recognize Israel, but was now convinced that the PLO had no intention of following through. Hussein was furious. He had personally given the assurances to Howe and travelled to London to be on hand for the momentous announcement. A seething king publicly blamed the PLO for the breakdown. A relieved Israeli leadership announced that the PLO never had any intention of taking either step because it was, as the Jewish nation had always contended, purely a terrorist organization.

Seeking to undo some of the damage Fatah had suffered, Arafat travelled to Cairo and on November 10 issued what became known as the "Cairo Declaration." It was his first attempt, in the wake of the Larnaca killings and the *Achille Lauro* hijacking, to grapple personally with the need to say something publicly about terrorism. Arafat's announcement stopped short of what the United States and the rest of the world wanted to hear. He condemned "all forms of terrorism" abroad and vowed that the perpetrators would be punished. But he made clear that continuation of the "armed struggle" inside the occupied territories, was a legitimate act of resistance and would continue.

Tensions were running high between Arafat and Hussein, but the Jordanian leader still felt he had one last chance to persuade the PLO to join the peace process. Arafat was to visit Amman in January. Hussein asked President Reagan for a new carrot: a written commitment from him that the PLO would be invited separately by the U.N. Secretary-General to the international conference if it accepted the American preconditions. Such an invitation, Hussein believed, would convey the official recognition not simply of the United States but also of most of the 159 countries that comprised the entire membership of the United Nations. The opportunity to sit across the negotiating table from the Government of Israel would give the PLO what it had always said it wanted: Israeli recognition of the PLO as the "sole and legitimate" representative of the world's five million Palestinians.

"I didn't think he [Hussein] was going to get this, at least not in writing," said Zeid Rifai. "He got it one day before Arafat arrived in Amman." The United States agreed that "when it is clearly on the public record" that the PLO had accepted U.N. Resolutions 242 and 338, had renounced terrorism and signalled its readiness "to negotiate with Israel," a separate invitation would be issued to the guerrilla organization. "We separated the issue of invitation and participation," says American Ambassador-at-Large, Wat Cluverius. "We accepted that the U.N. Secretary-General would issue an invitation, but participation had to be such that it wouldn't drive the Israelis from the table."

As Zeid Rifai recalls, "King Hussein wanted to break the news to Arafat himself so he invited him to lunch at the palace with his advisers Milhem and Yahya." Arafat was shown the letter from President Reagan. "Your Majesty," he said, "this is a miracle. If someone had told me this was going to happen, I wouldn't have believed him." Then Hussein said, "All right, now all you have to do is give me your acceptance of 242. We will not make it public. We will inform the White House but we'll keep it between us and when invitations are extended to the international conference, you will make your public declaration."

Arafat answered: "How can I accept 242 without self-determination for the Palestinian people?" Says Rifai, "That was the first time that he mentioned the words 'self-determination' in more than a year of joint negotiations." Rifai reminded him of the conversation that the eight of them had at his home months earlier. The puzzled Jordanian minister said, "You were willing to accept 242 just to get a meeting with Murphy. Now we've obtained an invitation for you to an international conference." Quietly but firmly, Arafat denied ever having said anything of the kind. But, said Rifai, looking right at Milhem and Yahya, "I wasn't the only one there. Perhaps you should ask them if they remember whether you said, not once but four times, you would accept 242." Arafat didn't respond. Both Yahya and Milhem averted Rifai's stare, lowering their heads and gazing at the food on their plates. Hussein said nothing. "We didn't want to embarrass him so we just let it go," says Rifai.

Arafat agreed he would make a new effort to draft language that would be acceptable to the Americans. Wat Cluverius, who held the rank of a roving ambassador to camouflage his official behind-the-scenes role, flew into Amman and used Jordanians, West Bank Palestinians and private American intermediaries, including Judith Kipper, a liberal academic with extensive knowledge and broad experience in the Middle East, in an effort to come up with a workable formula. The PLO circulated three different drafts: one written by Hanna Siniora and other moderate West Bankers; one written by Palestinian diaspora businessmen, including Abdul Majeed Shoman; and one written for PLO hard-liners by a former Egyptian prime minister. "Each of the groups who were working on drafts thought that theirs had a chance," says Cluverius.[6] Some progress was made when in the second of three proposed statements, the PLO pledged its readiness to attend an international conference and negotiate a peaceful settlement of the Palestinian problem with the Israeli Government on the basis of "the pertinent United Nations resolutions, including Security Council Resolutions 242 and 338." While the statement denounced terrorism, it fell short of the unambiguous declaration that had been sought because it reaffirmed, in addition to 242 and 338, all the other U.N. resolutions which included demands for Israel's destruction.

Arafat took all three proposals to Hussein. "He went to see the king alone because he couldn't have witnesses from these groups," says Cluverius. "He presented all three drafts. He was obviously running moderate drafts with his moderates and hard-line drafts with his hard-liners like Abu Iyad. Each draft had footnotes which none of us, the Jordanians or Americans, had seen before." The key footnote read: "All of the above is contingent upon recognition by the United States of the right to self-determination." The following day the U.S. delegation was shown the PLO proposals. One of the American officials recalls the king telling him, "Look at what that fool gave me. I rejected it out of hand."

The American told Jordanian official Tahir al-Masri: "This is nonsense. If this word [self-determination] is mentioned, I cannot accept any statement. No way. Who the friggin' hell does the PLO think it is—a superpower?" So, Masri says, "we delivered the American position to Arafat."

On January 26, 1986, the talks broke down, and less than three weeks later, in a remarkable, three-hour speech laced with allusions to Arafat's duplicity, King Hussein washed his hands of the entire effort. Although stopping short of abrogating the accord, he suspended all coordination with the PLO, subsequently closing Fatah offices and institutions and expelling its officials from Jordan. In his speech, Hussein implied that the Palestinians in the West Bank and Gaza deserved a better leader than the unreliable Abu Amar.

Adnan Abu Odeh is more generous to Arafat. The PLO, he says, is still the Palestine *Liberation* Organization. "They had to replace the slogan of liberation [of all of Palestine] with something that is just as attractive: an independent state. They could not tell the Palestinians that they had given up the liberation of Jaffa and Haifa for a confederation [with Jordan]. We understood the confederation was the baby that would be born out of any negotiations. They wanted to believe that the baby was an independent state, and only then a confederation."

Arafat also insists he cannot be blamed for the collapse of the peace effort. "If there is a Canadian problem, would you ask Queen Elizabeth to solve it?" he asks. In his mind, Jordan and the United States were conspiring against him. "I will tell you a secret," Arafat says. "In October 1985, I received a very important message from the occupied territories. Our people sent someone to warn me against the approaching catastrophe. They told me of the secret [Peres-Hussein] accord that had been reached between the Israelis and the Jordanians. Zeid Rifai was responsible for it. Under the terms of this agreement, the PLO was eliminated from the process. Nothing would be done with the PLO."

The year-long peace effort broke down, says Arafat, "because there was a secret [U.S.-Jordanian agreement] to annihilate me. They were trying to offer John the Baptist's head on a silver platter to Salome." The United States, he charged, never seriously considered his second formula because King Hussein refused to consider it. It was "dead on arrival," says Arafat, "because it contained the word self-determination."

Arafat's view of Hussein is virtually a mirror image of Hussein's view of Arafat. Says Rifai, "Arafat wanted the United States to accept his own interpretation of self-determination as an American and Israeli guarantee against Jordan. He was afraid it [the exercise of self-determination] would be at his expense. He always considered Jordan his competitor, not his partner. He wanted assurances that could be used against this competitor and to safeguard and guarantee his own role."

That preoccupation, the need to maintain his leadership of a democratically structured but deeply divided organization, always is Arafat's highest priority, Rifai believes, and severely limits his options. "Everything else is secondary. He's constantly fighting on so many fronts, trying to appease so many factions—that is why he has missed so many opportunities for peace. If his priority had been just to end Israel's occupation [of the West Bank and Gaza], and to liberate the people under occupation at any cost, it would have been much easier. But that is a non-starter to him," says Rifai, "because his own leadership is not guaranteed."

There were outside pressures on Arafat. The PLO Executive Committee had met secretly in Kuwait and voted unanimously to censor Arafat's efforts. PLO hard-liners also were undermining Arafat. "I was told," an American official says, "that Abu Iyad had gone to the king and said, 'Don't be fooled. He has no authority to make a deal. In the Executive Committee meeting, he wasn't given the authority.'" Israel also helped PLO hard-liners by publicly attacking the Jordanian effort. The Soviet Union made its displeasure felt in a variety of ways. And the United States, yielding to pressure from Jerusalem and the American Jewish community, reneged on the initial promises that were made to King Hussein.

From Arafat's perspective, the personal and political risks in opting for peace in 1986 outweighed the possible rewards of playing the one card he still had left: recognition of Israel. "I will play that card at the table. If I play it now, what cards do I have left for the negotiations? I am not Sadat. I don't have one million soldiers. I don't have the Suez Canal. I am only chairman of the Palestinians. I have to be honest with them. I have to keep something for these small Palestinian children, for their future. I don't have any other card."

Yet in December 1988 he played that card when he publicly and unequivocally accepted 242 and 338, renounced terrorism and accepted Israel's existence. The PLO did not win any of the gains it could have by cooperating with Hussein two years earlier. It did not win self-determination for the Palestinian people, formal U.S. recognition, an international conference, a meeting with a high-ranking State Department official or an invitation for Arafat to visit Washington. After almost two decades of playing hardball with the United States, why did this consummate politician and wily folk hero finally yield without having won even the promise of a homeland for the Palestinian people?

The answer, in part, is that in December 1987 the Palestinians themselves began to throw off the yoke of occupation with the outbreak of the *intifada*. The uprising not only captured the attention of the world's media, put Israel on the defensive and bolstered the self-image of the Palestinians, but also had a dramatic impact on Jordan. Towards the end of July, eight months after the *intifada* began, Hussein acted boldly to change the political balance. He cut Jordan's legal and administrative ties to the West Bank and Gaza and renounced his claim to sovereignty over the territories. The Jordanian national assembly, which had been reconstituted in 1984, was dissolved, along with the thirty seats held by deputies representing West Bank constituencies. Thousands of Palestinian teachers, the bulk of the West Bank civil servants on the Jordanian Government payroll, were told the Hashemites would not longer give them stipends in addition to their regular Israeli salaries. Funds were cut to *al-Nahar*, a pro-Jordanian newspaper in East Jerusalem. Jordan also announced it was terminating a $1.3 billion development program. Its state-run television network even ceased to provide the weather for the West Bank and Gaza.

Although the steps were largely symbolic—the billion-dollar development program had barely begun—the message from Hussein was clear: no longer could the Israeli Labor Party contend that the road to resolving the Palestinian problem runs through Amman. The Jordanian option had come to a screeching halt. If Israel wanted peace with the Palestinians in these territories, it had a choice: it could confront the PLO on the stone-littered battleground of the West Bank or sit down with the PLO at the negotiating table.

The United States also no longer had a choice. If Washington sincerely wanted peace, it had to give up the illusion that Jordan could replace the PLO. The message to the PLO was just as clear: the time had come for it to shoulder both the economic and political burdens incumbent with its claim to be the "sole and legitimate" representative of the Palestinian people. If the West Bankers complained of injustices, they could take their complaints to Israel or the PLO, but not to Amman.

A reflective King Hussein admits he had a difficult time deciding to cut off the Palestinians. "Basically, we are unionists," he says. "We responded to the Palestinian desire in the 1970s of having this union established, and it was very close to our hearts. We felt a sense of responsibility for the occupied territories, and we suggested that if they were returned to us, they would be placed under international auspices where the people could decide what their future could be: either union again, or federation, or an independent Palestinian state."

But, adds Hussein, "we finally realized there was an impasse: Israel wouldn't move; the world wouldn't move; and the Palestinians had to be involved in the solution of the Palestinian problem. So we responded to that. Our disengagement was the result of realizing that these people want the responsibility of shaping their future in their own hands. They want to represent themselves." Says a wistful King Hussein, undoubtedly thinking back on the accomplishments of his grandfather Abdullah and his great grandfather, the Sharif of Mecca, "Gone are the days of one nation."

V

The United States: Secret Channels

19

Unlikely Spies

A QUIET CALM *soothed the atmosphere on the Achille Lauro cruise ship that October morning as it sailed in the eastern Mediterranean towards Port Said. Earlier there had been a frenzy of activity on board as most of the passengers disembarked at Alexandria. They would spend the day sightseeing and would meet the luxury liner later that night. Only eighty of the 774 passengers remained on the ship: two Americans, Marilyn and Leon Klinghoffer, had little choice but to stay on board since his heavy wheelchair was too cumbersome to maneuver off the boat and through the crowded Egyptian streets.*

The usual call to lunch failed to come over the loudspeaker; instead, crew members knocked on cabin doors, announcing that the noontime meal was being served. The Klinghoffers decided to dine in the lounge near the restaurant, enjoying another relaxing afternoon on the twelve-day cruise from Genoa, Italy, to Ashdod, Israel. Sitting at the table they chatted with others who had stayed on board, but their conversation was interrupted by loud noise. Suddenly several men appeared; brandishing weapons they shouted at the passengers

337

and demanded their passports. The Klinghoffers did as they were told; like the others they handed over their documents.

The gunmen flipped through the passports. Passengers with Jewish sounding names and those who were British were separated from the rest and ordered to the main lounge. Marilyn Klinghoffer pushed her husband's wheelchair as she was told to do. Terrified, the passengers could hear the men speaking Arabic and mentioning the name "Arafat." Only a few days earlier PLO headquarters in Tunis had been bombed and rumor was rampant that the Israelis had carried out the raid. The innocent passengers had become instant pawns in the Middle East game. But this game was no diversion.

Minutes turned into hours as the guerrillas threatened the passengers' lives, announcing demands that fifty Palestinian prisoners be released from Israeli jails. "Arafat good; Reagan bad," chanted the terrorists, who took their orders from Abul Abbas, the head of the PLF faction of the PLO. The passengers asked to use the bathrooms but were refused permission to leave the lounge. Finally the women were allowed to use the ladies' room. The hijackers threw a blanket on the floor; men were ordered to urinate there. Hours began to seem like days.

The terrorists ordered the passengers up a flight of stairs to the bow of the ship. Marilyn Klinghoffer could not maneuver her husband's wheelchair up the steps and sixty-nine-year-old Leon could not climb himself, even with help. She couldn't leave his side, his wife pleaded; he suffered from high blood pressure and was too weak to be left alone. One of the Arabs whacked her feet with the butt of a pistol. Marilyn Klinghoffer went with the other passengers.

Upstairs, the Mediterranean heat beat down on the ship's bow. The passengers were ordered to stand in the blazing sun and face in the direction of Syria. Around the perimeter of the bow they could see huge cans of petrol, placed there deliberately. If anyone fired on the cruise ship, the oil cans would explode; everyone on board would be dead. Tormenting the hostages, the terrorists played with live grenades and shoved them into their captives' hands, releasing the pins as they did. The horrified women watched in tears. From down below, they heard gun shots. Marilyn Klinghoffer asked about her husband. Where is he? she wanted to know. He is in the infirmary, the gunmen said, suffering from his high blood pressure. But the terrorists had shot her husband in the head, then forced other passengers to throw his body and wheelchair overboard. Over the *ship's radio the guerrillas told a Palestinian contact that he was only the first of many who would be killed.*

For forty-four hours the passengers were held at gunpoint as the PLF guerrillas ordered the ship's captain to sail first to Syria, then to Cyprus. When both countries denied it permission to dock, the ship returned towards Egypt. Heading for Port Said, but still outside Egyptian waters, Egyptian authorities ordered it to stop. The hijackers surrendered and the eighty passengers were released, shaken but grateful for their freedom. Marilyn Klinghoffer could never forget that her innocent husband was killed by Palestinian terrorists.

As Americans watched the tragic story unfold on television, they could not forget, either, that Palestinians were too often involved with terrorism: international airliner hijackings, bombings in Europe, numerous attacks in Israel. Seeing the irate American Ambassador to Egypt, Nicholas Veliotes, shout expletives when he learned that the terrorists had lied and said no one was killed only reinforced the feeling that the PLO leader, Yasser Arafat, was up to his old trickery. Arafat could affect anger over the hijacking of the Achille Lauro, but there was little reason not to hold him responsible for the actions of his own organization. In the eyes of the American public, Arafat's offer to try the terrorists himself seemed paradoxical. Abul Abbas, whose group had carried out the operation, was even a member of the PLO's Executive Committee. Each time it seemed that the PLO had changed and was about to engage in a political process—this time at talks in London—its members carried out another terrorist attack. Regardless of whether he was personally responsible or not, one man stood for all the terrorism, all the horror, all the deaths: that man was Yasser Arafat. Most Americans simply could not condone doing business with him. So deep and widespread was the image of the PLO as an organization involved in terrorism, often against Americans, that for thirteen years and four presidencies, from September 1975 to December 1988, the United States banned any substantive talks with the PLO. That pledge was made in secret to the Israeli government and originally did not specify the renunciation of terrorism (this was added by Congress a decade later). Yasser Arafat still refers to the ban contemptuously as "the Kissinger taboos." The written pledge—that the United States "will not recognize or negotiate" with the PLO until it recognizes Israel's right to exist—was contained in an annex to the fall 1975 accord in which Israel agreed to withdraw its forces from Sinai. The Jewish state demanded the explicit American assurance in return for abandoning the Abu Rodeis oil fields, valuable air bases and the Sinai's strategic Gidi and Mitla passes, sacrifices it regarded as heightening the risks to Israeli security. But Kissinger, who negotiated the agreement, also saw the ban as a way of pressuring the PLO, using the bait of American recognition as a lever to coerce the organization to adapt their policies to Israel's existence as a permanent state in the region.

When Jimmy Carter entered the White House in 1977, Kissinger denied that he ever intended the pledge to become a straitjacket for American presidents. "I'm tired of having my position misrepresented," the former high-ranking Nixon and Ford adviser told a source close to Carter. "I never gave the Israelis veto power over our dialogue with the PLO. All I said was that we wouldn't officially recognize them nor negotiate with them. I didn't say we couldn't have any contact with them."[1]

The Carter administration, seeking to provide the PLO with an incentive to change its policy, reformulated the ban, accentuating the positive: the United States would enter talks with the PLO as soon as the PLO recognized Israel and accepted two key United Nations resolutions. "There is a commitment to talk if the PLO takes that step," explained Harold Saunders, a close adviser to both Kissinger and his successor Cyrus Vance.[2]

But the courting failed, and by 1980 the newly elected Ronald Reagan, a strong supporter of Israel, reverted to the original Kissinger formulation, adding a new condition that required the PLO to explicitly renounce terrorism in order to earn a dialogue with the United States. In 1986, Congress enacted all three prohibitions into law. Henceforth, no president could authorize any member of his administration to hold "substantive" talks with the PLO until it had publicly (1) accepted Israel's right to exist; (2) endorsed U.N. Security Council Resolutions 242 and 338, and (3) renounced terrorism. These were the catechisms and they were enforced with theological rigor. Contacts with the PLO were expressly forbidden: a "contact" was defined as making an appointment to sit down and discuss substance. An unavoidable social encounter, however, was not forbidden. So an American diplomat did not have to leave a dinner party that was also being attended by a member of the PLO. If they encountered one another, they could talk—but not about the substance of the Arab-Israeli dispute.

The law, like any other act of Congress, carried strict penalties. When the media discovered that it was being bent or broken, the administration was forced to publicly reprimand and even fire some of its high-ranking envoys. Even before the law was passed, Andrew Young, the U.S. ambassador to the United Nations was forced to resign for allegedly violating the policy. And yet from the day Jimmy Carter took office to the last days of the Reagan administration more than thirteen years later, a myriad of both official and unofficial contacts with the PLO were approved by the president or his secretary of state. Many of these encounters were with Arafat himself and took place at PLO headquarters in Beirut or Tunis, or in Cairo or Baghdad. Most were kept secret. If they did leak to the press, they were publicly denied or justified on grounds of "security," that is, required to protect or rescue American lives, which several of these contacts succeeded in doing.

But, under the cover of security, far more extensive efforts than have ever been publicly documented were made to persuade the PLO to accept the American terms for a dialogue. Indeed, the Carter and Reagan administrations, despite protestations to the contrary, privately regarded the Kissinger commitments as a hindrance on their own freedom to maneuver. But there was more to it than that. Wiser heads in both administrations realized that unless the PLO could be persuaded to accept Israel's existence, there was little chance for progress towards a lasting Arab-Israeli peace. Without resolving the Palestinian problem, they knew Arab states would not be willing to make peace with Israel. To resolve the Palestinian problem required talking to the PLO. Thus, getting the PLO to the altar, and once there to utter the American vows, was the big prize that came to dominate more than a decade of behind-the-scenes American diplomacy, much of which remains secret today.

They were the most unlikely of spies. Robert C. Ames, the husky, six-foot-four former athlete who sported tinted aviator glasses and wore cowboy boots, even in summer, and Ali Hassan Salameh, the aristocratic, German-educated son of an Arab sheik martyred in the

1948 war against Israel. Salameh was rugged and handsome and married to the beauty queen of Lebanon. Ames, the father of six children and a veteran of LaSalle University's 1954 NCAA championship basketball squad, was an undercover CIA agent who rose to become one of Secretary of State George Shultz's most trusted Middle East advisers. Salameh, a confidant of Yasser Arafat, was the founder of Force 17, Arafat's elite personal security squad implicated in numerous terrorist operations. Salameh himself purportedly planned the 1972 massacre of eleven Israeli athletes at the Munich Olympics.

Ames and Salameh had an uncommon friendship forged by the necessity of protecting American lives at a time when the public was told the United States had no official contact with the "terrorists" of the PLO. Both men paid with their lives. Salameh was the victim of an Israeli-planted car bomb in Beirut and Ames of a truck bomb, planted by radical Shiite Moslems, that blew up the American Embassy in Beirut. Their deaths, in 1979 and 1983, ended an unusual chapter in the cloak-and-dagger relationship between the United States and the Palestine Liberation Organization, a relationship that began when Ames and Salameh met covertly in the Lebanese capital in 1969 and that continued until it emerged into the light of day in Tunis in December 1988.

In those two decades, promises were made. Favors were done. Deals were struck. Seldom were the promises kept, the favors reciprocated or the deals honored. The trail is littered with deceit, treachery, betrayal and the murder of an American ambassador and his deputy in the Sudan. And yet, the untold story is not about PLO terrorism. It is about what was quietly accomplished between the United States and the PLO. It is about the help the PLO secretly provided in securing the release of American hostages and in protecting the lives of American diplomats. It is about undisclosed efforts to court the PLO and how close they repeatedly came to success.

At the root of American policy are two United Nations resolutions: 242, which was adopted at the end of the 1967 Six-Day War, and 338, which was adopted at the end of the 1973 October War. The fifteen nations of the Security Council, including the five permanent members, had unanimously endorsed the resolutions which became the bedrock for all Middle East peace efforts. The resolutions called for Israeli withdrawal "from territories occupied" in the two wars in return for a binding peace. This meant Israel would be asked to give up much of the land it had won from Egypt, Jordan and Syria, whose governments accepted the two resolutions, but only when these nations signed peace treaties with the Jewish state. Although they didn't mention Israel per se, the resolutions affirmed the right of "every state in the area...to live in peace within secure and recognized boundaries free from threats or acts of force."

For the PLO, however, both the Kissinger taboos and the resolutions of the United Nations were seen as a threat to their liberation struggle. In October 1974, the PLO had won the backing of the Arab world for its claim to be the "sole and legitimate" representative of the Palestinian people. In PLO eyes, this meant that five million Palestinians dispersed throughout Jordan, the Israeli-occupied West Bank and Gaza Strip and the rest of the Arab world owed their allegiance to Yasser Arafat and his guerrilla organization. The Kissinger promise to Israel was a slap in the face of the PLO. Coming less than a year after the Rabat decision, it meant the United States would not accept the legitimacy of the Arab decision elevating the PLO over Jordan, which also claimed to represent the Palestinians, unless the PLO accepted the two U.N. resolutions. To do that, Arafat argued, would be tantamount to surrender.

The PLO leader attacked the resolutions for treating the Palestinians as refugees, as displaced persons who had a right to be rehabilitated by some humanitarian gesture but little more. The resolutions, he contended, failed to recognize the Palestinians as a "people"; had they done so, they would have recognized their right to claim self-determination and other "political" rights normally associated with statehood. "We are not beggars. The problem is not that we do not have enough to eat," says Arafat. "This is not a welfare case."[3]

By the mid-1960s, Robert Ames had developed sympathy for the homeless Palestinians. He was serving his first undercover post as the U.S. consular officer in Dahran, Saudi Arabia. His subsequent years in Kuwait, Lebanon and South Yemen convinced him that the Palestinian struggle was a genuine liberation movement. Eventually the United States would have to recognize their nationalist aspirations and deal with the least anti-American of the potpourri of Palestinian factions, split among Marxists, pan-Arab Nasserites, pro-Syrian socialists, Islamic fundamentalists and Christian businessmen. Ames had witnessed a revolution first-hand in Yemen. He had watched helplessly as Soviet-backed revolutionaries had overthrown the British colonial government and installed a Marxist-Leninist regime. The new, radical government had its roots in the Arab Nationalist Movement that was founded by George Habash in the 1950s and which later grew into the Popular Front for the Liberation of Palestine (PFLP). Ames believed Arafat's more moderate Fatah wing was the logical faction to support and, in 1969, from his post in Beirut, he established contact with Arafat's security chief, Ali Hassan Salameh.

Ames told him that the Nixon administration was interested in a dialogue and that his credentials as a relatively junior diplomat in the U.S. Embassy should not deter him from establishing contact. This was a chance for the PLO to be heard in Washington. In seeking to open a channel of communications, he added, he was acting on the authority of the National Security Council and its new director, Henry A. Kissinger. Ames and Salameh agreed to exchange information on security threats. The NSC decision was a wise one. When Ames met Salameh, the PLO was a force to be reckoned with. The 350,000 Palestinians in Lebanon had established their own mini-state within Lebanon's borders. A Lebanese Christian commander, General Emile Boustani, who aspired to become president in 1970, was so eager to gain the support of Lebanon's Sunni Moslems that he cut a deal to give the Palestinians extraordinary extra-legal rights. The pact, known as the Cairo Agreement, was signed on November 3, 1969, under the watchful eye of Egypt's President Gamal Abdel Nasser. It gave the PLO the right to carry arms, launch guerrilla raids against Israel from bases in southern Lebanon and organize and police the refugee camps. Salameh controlled a 6,000-man army which ruled the camps.

The CIA was so impressed with his ability to maintain order and protect American interests, including the American University of Beirut and the U.S. Embassy in Moslem West Beirut, that in 1970 Salameh was offered a "positive inducement"—three million dollars—to work for the agency. The offer was made to him through an intermediary in Rome. Salameh was outraged and for the next several months ignored Ames' phone calls. In early May 1972, the CIA discovered Salameh's clandestine activities. Promoted to direct Black September's operations in Europe, Salameh masterminded the hijacking of a Sabena airliner to Israel's Lod Airport. In the wake of the attack, Israel created its own counterterrorist wing within the *Ha Mossad L'Tafkidim Meyuhadim*, the Institution for Special Tasks, or Mossad.

By the end of May, there was another terrorist attack at Lod Airport, planned by the PFLP but executed by the Japanese Red Army. Arriving on an Air France flight from Rome, three guerrillas opened fire on innocent civilians while ostensibly waiting for their luggage. There were more than 100 Israeli casualties. By late summer, Arafat's close associate Abu Iyad had assumed control of Black September operations. On September 5, the last day of the 1972 Munich Olympics, eight of his Fatah loyalists captured the Israeli complex in the Olympic Village and held nine Israeli athletes. They would all be shot unless Israel agreed to release 200 PLO prisoners. At the nearby Furstenfeldbruck military air base, the nine athletes and two other Israelis, and five of the terrorists, were killed in a bloody melee.

CIA contact was not reestablished with Salameh until the mid-summer of 1973, a few months after Black September turned its wrath on an American diplomat, Cleo Noel, the U.S. Ambassador to the Sudan, and his deputy George Curtis Moore. In March, the two Americans, together with a Belgian diplomat, were machine-gunned to death during a reception at the Saudi Embassy in the Sudanese capital of Khartoum. Within weeks of the brutal murders, Ames was approached by Salameh and told that the latest killings were a result of a feud within Fatah that had erupted when the Lebanese Government began to crack down on *fedayeen* operations from Palestinian camps in southern Lebanon. "We were telling ourselves that unless we could take Jordan, our liberation movement was finished," said Abu Daoud.[4]

Salameh also told Ames that Arafat had opposed Black September's tactics and was willing to undertake a commitment in the future to protect the lives of American diplomats. Ames contacted Richard Helms, the U.S. Ambassador in Iran, who informed Kissinger of this intelligence during the July visit to the United States of the Shah of Iran, His Majesty Reza Pahlavi. There was no immediate response. But on October 10, 1973, the fourth day of the Yom Kippur War, Salameh sent another overture to Washington. This time, he said, Arafat was willing to join peace talks if the United States stopped supplying arms to Israel. Less than a month later, on November 3, 1973, the first officially-approved secret meeting between the United States and the PLO took place in Rabat, Morocco. Kissinger sent General Vernon Walters, the deputy director of the Central Intelligence Agency. Ali Hassan Salameh represented the PLO. The meeting, Kissinger wrote later, had been scheduled "just preceding my trip to Cairo," the first high-level mission since the end of the October War, "thus ensuring PLO quiescence during this delicate phase."[5]

Both Kissinger and Walters said the meeting achieved its goal. "After it," Kissinger wrote, "attacks on Americans, at least by Arafat's faction of the PLO, ceased." Walters boasted that he had been sent "to talk to a most hostile group of terrorists. I saw them alone and unarmed in a part of the world sympathetic to their cause. My position made me a major target. I had studied their past, their hopes, their dreams, even their poetry. I was able to convey to them the message that I had been ordered to deliver. We were able to communicate and there were no further acts of blood between us."[6]

Salameh proved his usefulness almost immediately to the Nixon administration. At the meeting with Walters, he alerted him to an assassination threat against Kissinger; consequently, his arrival in Lebanon was rerouted to a military airfield in the Christian-controlled, eastern part of the country. But no sooner had Salameh restored his credentials with Washington than the alarm bells sounded again. A Libyan was caught trying to bring drugs into Italy. He confessed that he was part of a group that intended to murder President Nixon. The Libyan said he had "operational contact" with Salameh. CIA officials became irate. Salameh was called in and given a stern dressing down by Ames. It turned out, however, that the Libyan was part of a scam to discredit Arafat and the PLO. Salameh redeemed himself by chasing down the real perpetrators and agreed to make himself useful in exchanging intelligence information about similar plots. It marked the resumption of genuine operational cooperation between the CIA and the intelligence wing of Fatah.

By late 1973, however, it was clear American officials weren't the only ones who were interested in Salameh. David Ignatius, foreign editor of the *Washington Post*, wrote that a bizarre incident took place in Vienna which suggested that others were curious about America's new willingness to court the PLO. An unidentified Palestinian called the U.S. embassy and claimed he had been authorized by Arafat to provide intelligence information on threats to American citizens. To prove his links to Arafat, he told the embassy officer to listen for a specific message on Radio Damascus. It would concern the Kuwait chapter of the GUPS. The message was broadcast on the day and at the exact time he predicted. Ames contacted Salameh. Arafat denied any knowledge of the overture, and his intelligence operatives tracked down the Palestinian. Under questioning, he admitted he was a Mossad agent. The man was executed and the PLO later showed his confession to the CIA.[7]

The operation should have come as no surprise to Salameh. Beshir Gemayel, the Lebanese Phalangist leader, had tried to warn him that Israeli Prime Minister Menachim Begin had put Salameh at the top of the Israeli hit list. The Mossad had narrowly missed when it tried, in 1973, to settle scores for the Munich massacre. They had tracked Salameh, or so they thought, to Scandanavia. A squad led by Raphael Sequr and Mike Harari, the elusive Israeli who later served as an aide to Panama's General Manuel Antonio Noriega, burst into a Norwegian restaurant. They fired and killed a dark-skinned Arab. The diners were horrified. After the smoke cleared, the Arab turned out to be a Moroccan waiter.

On March 7, 1974, a second meeting was held in Rabat between Walters and an expanded team of PLO officials. They included Khaled al-Hassan, the co-founder of Fatah and its leading intellectual, and Fatah information chief Majid Abu Sharar, a prominent leftist who was mysteriously assassinated in Rome in 1981. In 1974, Khaled al-Hassan had resigned his seat on the fifteen-member Executive Committee and was publicly supporting a two-state solution and coexistence with Israel. Walters was interested in finding out what he thought about the PLO's recent flirtation with Moscow and whether he supported the 1973 decision of the Palestine National Council to seek Hussein's overthrow. Apparently impressed with Khaled al-Hassan's reasonableness, Walters, at one point, said: "If we had dealt with Vietnam the way you are dealing with the Palestinian question, we would have solved the Vietnam problem a long time ago and without all these casualties." The Palestinian leader admits he liked the burly American and asked him "to convince your government they have to be sensible and talk to people. You cannot solve a problem with somebody without talking to him." Walters agreed and, according to Khaled al-Hassan, suggested the United States would respond positively if the PLO abandoned its efforts to organize terrorist attacks against Americans. The PLO subsequently sought a mandate from Arab leaders to begin a political offensive. "We thought we heard an instruction from the United States in 1973," says Hassan. Even Kissinger, he notes, confirms the U.S. offered a sweetener at the initial Walters meeting. "We proposed to treat the Palestinian problem not as an international but as an inter-Arab concern," writes Kissinger.[8] The message he says Walters was to deliver was that "it was up to the PLO to straighten out its relationships with other Arab states." Then the United States would respond. Khaled al-Hassan insists that "we followed through at Rabat on what the United States said it wanted and we didn't get anything for it." The ensuing disappointment increased PLO suspicions about their role in any potential negotiation.

In October 1974, at the Arab Summit meeting in Rabat, the PLO was named as the only legitimate representative of the Palestinian people. A month later, in November, Arafat seemed to win another endorsement of his claim, this time from the United Nations, which agreed to hear him speak to the General Assembly. The PLO thought it was doing what Kissinger wanted. While in New York, there was a third secret United States-PLO meeting, this one in the exclusive Towers of the Waldorf-Astoria Hotel. On the 36th floor, in the suite of the U.S. ambassador to the world body, Ames introduced his successor in Beirut to Salameh.[9] A year earlier, the PLO chieftain had pledged Fatah would not go after Americans. The PLO had enforced that pledge. Now the promise was being extended. Salameh, eager to win American recognition of the PLO, pledged Fatah would make an effort to police other PLO factions and promised to provide intelligence on their operations.

By the fall of 1975, however, the PLO felt it had been had. Instead of winning American recognition, Kissinger had provided the secret assurances Israel had sought: the United States would not recognize or negotiate with the guerrilla organization until it accepted Israel's right to exist. Kissinger reasoned neither Egypt nor Jordan would make peace with Israel if the PLO gained in legitimacy. But as far as Arafat was concerned, the United States had cast the die for his Arab brethren to betray him. Arafat knew, however, the United States would soon again need the PLO. With the civil war heating up in Lebanon, only the PLO could protect the lives and property of Americans in West Beirut. The Kissinger "taboos" would not halt cooperation with the United States. They would, instead, force it underground.

For Robert Ames and Ali Hassan Salameh, the new era began when Kissinger signed the secret annex, in the form of a side letter, to the 1975 Egyptian-Israeli Sinai accord. Henceforth, official contact with the PLO would only be warranted when there was a threat to American lives. Precisely because the Kissinger pledge was such a litmus test of devotion to Israel, and nobody in the White House wanted to be "seen a thousand miles from the PLO," there had to be a Robert Ames, says Geoffrey Kemp. "It had to be done in the context of security and not policy," explains Kemp, a former Reagan administration policymaker.[10] For the next eight years, until he was murdered in Beirut in April 1983, Robert Ames embodied American policy towards the PLO. He became the CIA's national intelligence officer, its chief Middle East analyst and top undercover operator. He became George Shultz's resident Palestinian expert and a close personal friend. Ames' relationship with Khaled al-Hassan and with Abu Hassan Salameh reaped dividends for the United States.

The most important of them was the protection provided by Salameh's 6,000-man militia for the safe evacuation from Beirut of more than 250 American diplomats, teachers, businessmen and their families. On June 19, 1976, Arafat's Force 17 was sent to guard the U.S. embassy. Two routes were set up, one from an oceanfront swimming club to the ships of the U.S. Sixth Fleet and the other through the Shouf Mountains along the Beirut-to-Damascus highway to the borders of Syria. Kissinger sent his personal thanks and President Ford paid a public tribute to Arafat. "The PLO," Ford told reporters, "and all other parties in the Lebanon area have cooperated completely in making it possible for us to evacuate the Americans and the other nationals without any incident whatsoever."

So grateful was the CIA that when Salameh married Georgina Rizik, "Miss Lebanon," the agency invited the newlyweds on an all-expense-paid honeymoon trip to the United States. They went to Hawaii and Florida's Walt Disney World as well as other sites Salameh had longed to see.[11] The *New York Times* later noted that "this uniquely American gesture compounded Mr. Arafat's bitterness and sense of betrayal when Salameh was slain."[12] Salameh ended his trip in Washington. In suburban Virginia, there were talks with CIA officials; some consideration was even given to scheduling a "walk by," a seemingly spontaneous chat with then CIA Director George Bush. But even such VIP coddling couldn't protect Salameh from the Mossad.

By May 1977, when Menachem Begin became prime minister, Salameh had once again become a target of those seeking to settle the score for the Olympics massacre. On January 22, 1979, Salameh who had earned the sobriquet of "the uncrowned king of Beirut," was killed instantly, the victim of a car bomb on a downtown street in West Beirut. Israeli leaders made no secret of their role in eliminating one of the few remaining Black September leaders. But one PLO official still thinks the Mossad may have had another motive. He believes the assassination was aimed at sabotaging the budding secret dialogue with the United States. "The Israelis opposed anything that might bring us to good terms with the Americans," says Khaled al-Hassan. "Salameh was killed," he adds bitterly, "because he was doing fine with the American channels."[13]

20

The Kissinger Taboos

IN THE BOMBED-OUT BACKROOMS *of Beirut, in the refugee camps of southern Lebanon and in the salons of Tunis, endless meetings have taken place between Yasser Arafat and American emissaries. The envoys, some self-appointed, some officially delegated, have spent hundreds of hours trying to persuade the PLO leader to recognize Israel. Only that recognition, they insisted, would bring him what he wanted: direct talks with the United States. Perhaps the most difficult part of the process was to disabuse Arafat of the notion that the United States controls what Israel does. The Americans, they kept repeating, could not deliver Israel to the PLO. The Palestinians would have to express the message themselves.*

"That's part of the education process a lot of us tried to do with him," says one of the American envoys who saw Arafat more than fifty times. "God, that took so much. Intellectually, he just couldn't deal with that. It wasn't until the Soviets started having increasing trouble controlling Syria," he says, that Arafat began to understand. "He knew what had to be done. He always said he knew exactly what

had to be done. There was no question." The irony, says the American, who was traveling back and forth to Israel for meetings with Abba Eban and Moshe Dayan, is that "he even had some messages to relay to the Labor Party." But he adds, "He said the reason he couldn't do it was that the political situation wasn't right." The American heaves a sigh. "He loves to talk. I used to say that his basic exercise was mental gymnastics. That's how he got his physical exercise."

When Arafat needed a change of scenery, says the envoy, "he and I would drive. We would arrive 'somehow' at a place and, my God, it was amazing! His favorite thing was when he would go into the camps. It was like the Pied Piper. The children just wanted to touch him, and hold his hand, and play with him. I used to try to convey this to some of the people in the policy community in Washington, and they had no idea that he was a heroic father figure....To understand him, you have to understand he really sees himself the way George Washington saw himself. He's the father of his people. He sees himself that way. I used to tell him, 'Don't be arrogant. Not everybody thinks you're the father of all the Palestinian people.' And he'd say, 'But the people see me like this.' He'd measure it by the kind of reaction he'd get from the children. It was better than the flag. As much as the ugly portrait turns people off here, it had the complete opposite effect on people there."

The American would brief officials at the State Department whenever he returned from his visits. And before he set out again, the policymakers would brief him. "I remember one visit I made. The State Department told me that the CIA said Arafat was dying of kidney failure—he was in the Gaza Hospital in Beirut. This was on Tuesday, and I was supposed to see him Saturday. I was going to cancel my trip; I mean, if the guy's dying, what am I going to do? So I sent a message through my contact and they said, 'We'll get back to you tomorrow.' They called an hour later and said, 'He wants to see you.' I thought, 'God, how dramatic. He's dying of kidney failure and he wants to see me.' What do you say to somebody in that kind of situation? I arrived, and all the soldiers who met me at the airport were very stern and somber. They took me to the Gaza camp and to the hospital. The whole atmosphere was very uptight. We finally get to where he was, and it turns out he was passing a kidney stone."

Deep misunderstandings and much misinformation are woven through the fabric of the United States-PLO relationship. "He knows quite a bit about our country," says the envoy. "He knows a lot about the American revolution." Drawing a parallel with his own armed struggle, Arafat would ask, "Was it right for us to hide behind trees and shoot British soldiers? Why was that right, and this armed struggle is not right. What's the difference?" Says the American, "He really does not see a moral dilemma over the people who have died because of what he's done."

T he emissaries were mostly private Americans, often representing peace groups that had a vested interest in courting Arafat, including the Quaker-backed American Friends Service Committee and the Foundation for Middle East Peace, whose president Merle Thorpe and director Gail Pressberg have worked assiduously for greater Israeli-Palestinian understanding. The groups often included well-known academics, religious leaders, and former policymakers and congressmen, such as Illinois' Paul Findley and California's Pete McCloskey.

They included Jewish leaders, such as former Commerce Secretary Philip Klutznik and Howard Squadron, as well as retired policy-makers who Arafat used to relay messages to the State Department or White House. The only official channel was the CIA's Robert C. Ames, who often worked with these unofficial envoys, and who became deeply involved himself, during the 1982 evacuation of the PLO from Beirut, in a secret negotiation to break the Kissinger quarantine.

The story begins when shortly after becoming president, Carter reformulated the Kissinger ban in a way he hoped would encourage the PLO to accept its terms. At first Carter misspoke, inadvertently broadening the ban by saying the United States would not even "talk" to the PLO until it accepted Israel and the two United Nations resolutions. Even Kissinger had not intended that "talks," in lieu of negotiations, be precluded. Realizing his mistake, Carter subsequently amended the understanding with Israel. Instead of stating the terms negatively, Carter publicly promised that the United States *would* open a dialogue with the PLO as soon as it accepted 242 and 338 and publicly declared that Israel had a right to exist. To make it easier for the PLO, Carter was prepared to allow Arafat to include in his acceptance of 242 the PLO's complaint that the resolution failed to recognize the Palestinians' national rights.

At the opening of the March 1977 Palestine National Council meeting at the Arab League headquarters in Cairo, Arafat responded to the new president's overtures by telling an American television interviewer that he "trusted" Carter. Palestinian confidence that an opening to the United States was possible increased when Carter referred to Palestinian aspirations for a "homeland" in a speech in Maine later that year. A flurry of diplomatic activity involving Saudi Arabia and Austrian Chancellor Bruno Kreisky was aimed at achieving a formula that would meet Carter's conditions. The effort failed when Secretary of State Cyrus Vance, during an August visit to the Saudi summer resort of Taif, was told Arafat had rejected the specific language Carter had proposed.

Ames remained the only link authorized to have "substantive" talks with the PLO under the cover of discussing security issues. But other officials, aware of the secret Carter initiative, believed they had his blessing for steps to advance it. In some cases, like that of Milton Wolf, the U.S. ambassador to Austria, they were acting with official authorization. In other cases, like that of U.N. Ambassador Andrew Young, the emissaries went beyond their instructions and later were forced to pay a price when their clandestine activities became public.

In early June of 1979, Ambassador Wolf, a fundraiser for many pro-Israeli causes in the United States, encountered a leading PLO moderate when he boarded the private jet of Karl Kahane, a wealthy Austrian Jewish businessman, for a flight from Paris to Vienna. Wolf had persuaded Bruno Kreisky, the Austrian chancellor, to have eye surgery performed at the Massachusetts Eye & Ear Hospital and had accompanied him to Boston for the operation. After the surgery, Kreisky suggested to Wolf that they take the morning Concorde flight to Paris so they could get back to Vienna on the same day. As soon as they landed at Orly Airport, Kahane's privately chartered

Falcon 20 pulled up alongside the supersonic Air France jet to whisk them back to Austria.

What Kreisky failed to tell Wolf was that the PLO's Issam Sartawi would be joining them for the Paris-to-Vienna portion of the trip. "On that plane was Patricia Kahane, his daughter, and another guy who I thought was her boyfriend. Introductions were made after we took off. It happened to be Sartawi," recalls Wolf. The Palestinian, a surgeon who had practiced at the Cleveland Clinic in Wolf's native city, had been authorized by Arafat to make contact with Israelis and wanted to inform the State Department of the initiative.

"How's Cleveland?" Sartawi asked Wolf as soon as they were airborne. "When he started to talk about the Middle East, I told him I'm proscribed against talking to you until your organization recognizes 242 and 338. If you do that, you don't have to talk to me. I'll take you to the president," Wolf says he told the PLO envoy. Wolf immediately sent a cable to the State Department reporting the contents of his impromptu talks. "It was received with much interest. They sent me back a cable which was very supportive," he says.

Less than a month later, Arafat visited Vienna, and Sartawi and Wolf, now operating with Vance's authorization, continued to meet. Letters, including one in which Kreisky provided language Arafat had given him for recognizing Israel, were exchanged. But in August 1979, after Saudi Arabia failed to be able to give Vance the promised PLO commitment to 242 and 338, the Wolf story became public.

An anonymous State Department official leaked the contents of the classified cable traffic to Wolf Blitzer, the Washington correspondent of the *Jerusalem Post*. When the story appeared and the *New York Times* asked about it the next day, State Department spokesman Thomas Reston told reporters the Austrian envoy had been "reminded on July 2 and again on July 7 of the official policy against substantive discussions with the PLO." But, says Milton Wolf, "I was never reprimanded. Vance never instructed me not to have meetings." In fact, he believes the official who leaked the story of his encounters with Sartawi did so deliberately to deflect attention from another senior administration official who was holding his own meetings with the PLO.

On July 26, 1979, Andrew Young, the Carter administration's U.N. envoy, met secretly with Zehdi Labib Terzi, the head of the PLO's observer mission to the United Nations. The meeting took place in the apartment of the Kuwaiti ambassador who was spearheading an effort to amend U.N. Security Council resolution 242 to include reference to the Palestinians' right to self-determination and a state of their own. The conversations were bugged by Israeli listening devices and after the exercise became public a few weeks later, Young was forced to resign. Asked about his resignation, Vance said Young had lied to him about the reason for the meeting with Terzi and he had been embarrassed to learn of its substance from the Israelis. "The timing of my letter of resignation was coincidental with the news stories that broke" about Young, insists Milton Wolf. "What happened was that somebody who didn't want to see Young get injured by himself threw me into it—[but] mine was authorized."

Apart from these officials and the self-appointed goodwill ambassadors, who were always ferrying messages back from Arafat, there also were four emissaries who operated secretly and with more regular and sustained contact with the PLO.

One of them was an American ambassador. The other three were private citizens. But all four were empowered directly by the president, his national security adviser or the secretary of state to conduct talks with Arafat and his senior political and military advisers, including Abu Jihad (Khalil Wazir), Khaled al-Hassan, Hani al-Hassan and Bassam Abu Sharif. The contacts forged by these envoys—Landrum Bolling, John Gunther Dean, John Edwin Mroz and Rita Hauser—all were kept secret from Israel. At least two of these four believe that when the Israelis discovered their efforts, they sought to disrupt them, and on one occasion may even have unwittingly provided the weapons that were used in an assassination effort.

Taken as a whole, these four Americans spent more than 1,000 hours in private talks with Arafat and his deputies. They had more than 150 meetings with him and his advisers in at least five different Arab countries. On several occasions, visa restrictions were waived and senior PLO officials traveled incognito to Washington, holding talks in the heart of the nation's capital. Almost all of this took place behind the back of the Israeli government. Once, the efforts appeared to be so close to persuading the PLO to recognize Israel that some in the State Department still believe one envoy's year-long efforts may have contributed to the Israeli decision to invade Lebanon.

The first of these Americans used by the Carter administration was Landrum Bolling. He had at least forty authorized meetings with Arafat between the period beginning in the spring of 1975, when Jimmy Carter was campaigning for the Democratic presidential nomination, and the spring of 1981, when he was asked to maintain his links by officials in the incoming Reagan administration. (Later his role was curtailed by Secretary of State Alexander Haig.) In his memoirs, National Security Adviser Zbigniew Brzezinski doesn't identify Bolling. He refers to him merely as "a prominent American, active in educational matters," and concedes that, through him, "a number of informal messages" were exchanged with Arafat in a "quiet effort to establish some sort of understanding with the PLO."[1]

Before the end of the Carter administration, Brzezinski himself became the only senior White House official to meet Arafat while in office. He chatted briefly with the PLO leader during celebrations in Algiers marking the twentieth anniversary of the Algerian revolution. The greeting provoked some criticism at home. "I got a telegram from the White House inspired by domestic advisers to the president," says Brzezinski. He wired back that "in accordance with civilized practice, I shook hands with the Algerian president, the brother of Fidel Castro, the Romanian minister of transport, Arafat, and some other dignitaries."[2]

Bolling was the president of Earlham College, a Quaker institution in Indiana, when he was asked by the American Friends Service Committee, in the wake of the June 1967 Arab-Israeli war, to meet with Arabs and Israelis in the West Bank and Gaza. He soon found himself in the role of a messenger, shuttling between Cairo, Amman, Tel Aviv and Washington. Bolling did not meet Yasser Arafat until 1975 when he was introduced to him by Eric Rouleau, an Egyptian-born Jew who at the time was a correspondent for the prestigious French daily *Le Monde*.

In the spring of 1975, Bolling sought to help Sartawi and Sabri Jiryis, head of the PLO's research institute, set up an information office for the PLO in Washington. Bolling arranged for them to obtain visas to the United States and asked Dean Brown, the former U.S. Ambassador to Jordan, to take the request to open a Palestine Information Office to Secretary of State Kissinger. Brown says Kissinger told him he had no objection so long as the Palestinians registered as foreign agents (required of all foreign lobbying groups) and complied with proper filing procedures. Within days, however, the American-Israeli Public Affairs Committee (AIPAC) discovered what was going on and demanded it to end. Kissinger quickly reversed himself. "He sent INS (Immigration and Naturalization Service) gumshoes to the hotel where Sartawi and Jiryis were staying and told them you have twenty-four hours to get out of the United States," says Bolling. "It was really rotten," recalls Brown, who at the time was president of the Middle East Institute. "I knew Henry had changed his mind. I went over to see them to tell them they should leave the country. But while I was meeting with them, the State Department called my old secretary and said they were trying to find Dean. When she told them where I was, they told the INS and sent them to the hotel."[3] (Sartawi was later assassinated on April 10, 1983, in a hotel lobby in the Portuguese Algarve during a meeting of the Socialist International. He was killed by terrorists linked to the Abu Nidal Organization.)

In the period leading up to the 1976 Democratic convention, Bolling had lengthy talks with Jimmy Carter about the Middle East. He helped write position papers for the party's platform committee and for the Democratic candidate during the campaign. But what made Bolling's subsequent meetings with Arafat so unusual was the fact that he had a direct pipeline to Carter after he was elected. "After he got in, he told me anytime I wanted to get ideas to him to call Rosalynn," said Bolling. On one occasion, he gave the First Lady a one-page handwritten memorandum summarizing his meeting with Arafat. He got a xerox of it back with President Carter's notes in the margin.

On another occasion, in September 1977, Brzezinski gave Bolling a formula for Arafat to use for recognizing Israel and promised the United States would open a dialogue with the PLO if he used it. Brzezinski even told the envoy to tell Arafat, "It doesn't have to be exactly these words." Arafat told Bolling he was willing to say all those things but that he would have to get the formal approval of his executive committee. He asked Bolling if he could stay another twenty-four hours. Bolling agreed, but Arafat kept him in Lebanon for three days. Finally Bolling said he had to leave for Baghdad. Arafat promised to send a courier to Washington with a written response. The messenger, an aide to Sartawi, arrived about ten days later. Bolling took the document to the White House and gave it to

Brzezinski. It was so full of doubletalk that the NSC adviser exclaimed: "This guy's got to be kidding. Who does he think we are? A bunch of dopes?"

On a third occasion, Brzezinski was furious over a statement Arafat had made, in the course of an interview with a Kuwaiti magazine, accusing the White House policymaker of having reneged on a secret promise to the PLO. The comment, he says, threatened to undermine delicate talks with the Israeli government. "I want you to get Arafat to retract that statement," Bolling was told. Arafat arranged, during an interview with another Arab magazine, for the same question to be asked. He told Bolling he thought Brzezinski would be pleased with his response. A few days later, Carter invited Bolling to a black-tie dinner at the White House. Brzezinski approached him. He had read the second interview in which Arafat softened his earlier accusations. "I want you to tell Arafat I'll never forget this," he says Brzezinski told him. The former NSC adviser still refuses to discuss the details. "Arafat did somewhat straighten it out," concedes Brzezinski. He says he learned, "If you're reasonably tough with him, you can usually get what you want."

For Bolling, the five-year period remains a somewhat disappointing one. He ascribes his failure to a very simple thing: Arafat "thought he could get a dialogue started with us without saying the full range of words we wanted him to say." At the same time Bolling believes the Kissinger taboos were an "illogical and unjustifiable policy to begin with." He explains, "We don't talk to the PLO because we approve of the PLO or because we like the PLO or because we love Arafat. It's not a blessing we confer on the PLO. It goes to the heart of why you have diplomatic relations with anybody. We talk to the PLO because we want to see peace in the Middle East."

Similar convictions motivated John Gunther Dean. "Talking to people does not mean I approve or condone whatever the person does. It's just a question of looking after our interests," he says.[4] Over a three-year period, from September 1978 to July 1981, while Dean was the American ambassador to Lebanon, he held more than thirty-five secret meetings with PLO officials, including several with Arafat's top aide, Abu Jihad (Khalil Wazir), who was in charge of the PLO's military operations. Dean is a career diplomat who retired from the State Department in 1989 after serving as the U.S.

ambassador to Cambodia, and also to Denmark, India and Thailand. In meeting PLO officials in Beirut, he was operating on the instructions of Vance and was reporting directly to Harold Saunders, the assistant secretary of state for Near Eastern and South Asian affairs. His first Beirut mission was to recover the body of Francis Meloy, Jr., his predecessor, from the PLO. Fatah sources insist Meloy was assassinated by PFLP guerrillas in order to subvert the secret American dialogue with Arafat's Fatah lieutenants. Dean says he was pleased with the cooperation he received from Fatah in recovering Meloy's remains and in identifying the guerrillas who were responsible for his murder.

But the events that brought Dean into regular contact with the PLO, and led to an assassination attempt against him, involved the November 4, 1979, takeover of the U.S. embassy in Iran when sixty-three American diplomats were taken hostage. Dean confirms that after appealing directly to Abu Jihad shortly after the kidnapping, both the PLO military chief and Arafat made special trips to Teheran to try to persuade Ayatollah Ruhollah Khomeini to release the captives. "The PLO saw this as a way of ingratiating itself with the United States. It showed they have a certain amount of influence in certain places and that they are supported in other areas" where the United States is not, says Dean. Of course, what the PLO was offering was the other hand of terrorism: protection from it. The PLO wanted to show it could work with the United States to stop terrorism and thereby establish itself as a recognized player on the Middle East scene.

As it happened, Iran was one place where the PLO had some influence. It had helped provide security forces to guard Khomeini during his years of exile in Paris. At its guerrilla bases in southern Lebanon, the PLO had helped train some of Khomeini's leading revolutionaries. They included Ali Akbar Mohtashemi, who later became Khomeini's Interior Minister.[5] Also, shortly after Khomeini's forces ousted the regime of the late Shah Reza Pahlavi, Hani al-Hassan, was invited to Teheran to install the satellite communication system for the new Islamic republic. The PLO official "saw everything, every cable, every document, that went in or out," says Gary Sick, President Carter's chief White House analyst on Iran. After the revolution that brought Khomeini to power, the PLO was even permitted to occupy the former Israeli embassy. The hostage crisis

Lebanon, 1982. At the urging of the Lebanese and after an agreement with the Americans, 14,000 Fatah guerrillas were forced to leave the country. Here, Arafat marches with Abu Jihad (Khalil Wazir), deputy Fatah chief and commander of PLO military forces in Lebanon. (Courtesy Bassam Abu Sharif)

Arafat embraces a Palestinian woman as he and his forces withdraw from Lebanon. (Courtesy Bassam Abu Sharif)

Conferring with Egyptian President Anwar Sadat in July 1977. Soon after, Sadat announced he would visit Jerusalem; Arafat reacted by refusing to meet with him ever again. (UPI/Bettmann)

Arafat, Abu Iyad (center), the PLO's second-in-command, and George Habash (right), leader of the Popular Front for the Liberation of Palestine, at a meeting of the Palestine National Council in Algiers in 1987. (Reuters/ Bettmann)

Jordan's King Hussein welcomes Arafat. The two leaders have been wary allies for more than two decades. (Courtesy Bassam Abu Sharif)

Arafat meets with Egyptian President Hosni Mubarak in 1983. (UPI/Bettmann)

Arafat with Abul Abbas, leader of the Palestine Liberation Front and member of the PLO Executive Committee. Abbas masterminded the hijacking of the Italian cruise ship *Achille Lauro* and the June 1990 guerrilla attack on a Tel Aviv beach. (UPI/Bettmann)

At work aboard a borrowed jet, Arafat reads through piles of reports and faxes. He makes about ten trips a month and never tells colleagues where they are going until the plane is off the ground.   (Mimmo Frassineti—A.G.F./Il Venerdì di Repubblica)

لتلبية هذه الزيارة ، وهكذا تمت يوم (۱۹۸۸/۱۲/٦) ورافق الاخ ابو عمار كسـل

من يـاسـر عبد ربّـه ومحمـود درويش ، وفي بداية الحوار تمّ وزير الخارجية السـويـدي

اندرسـون ، عرض هذا رسالة وردته من جورج شـولتز ، وهذا نص الرسـالة :

Ink. Utr.min.

1988 -12- 0 4

SECRET

THE SECRETARY OF STATE
WASHINGTON

December 3, 1988

Dear Sten:

I received through Ambassador Wachtmeister your message
concerning the meeting in Stockholm next Tuesday. I greatly
appreciate the constructive approach which you are taking
toward this issue.

The attached papers constitute my reply to the question you
raised in your message. I want to make three points in this
regard:

-- First, we will not engage in any effort to make this
the start of a negotiation over language; in other
words, we will not accept counter-drafts.

-- Second, I am aware that the PLO may wish to add,
following the statement that we have proposed,
certain positions to which they feel committed and
from which they would claim their basic statement is
derived. We would have no objection to their doing
so, provided those positions neither condition nor
contradict their acceptance of our conditions.

-- Third, nothing here may be taken to imply an
acceptance or recognition by the United States of an
independent Palestinian state.

You may share this letter with your visitor if you believe
it would be useful.

Sincerely yours,

George P. Shultz

Attachments:
As stated above.

His Excellency
Sten Andersson,
Minister of Foreign Affairs of Sweden,
Stockholm.

SECRET

Copy of a classified letter from United States Secretary of State George P.
Shultz to Sten Andersson, Sweden's Minister of Foreign Affairs, dated
December 3, 1988. Andersson was the key intermediary between Shultz and
Arafat. The letter set out U.S. conditions for beginning an official dialogue
with the PLO and provided certain still-secret assurances that the Palestinian organization had sought.

Arafat pictured with a poster for the *intifada*, the Palestinian uprising in the West Bank and Gaza that began in December 1987. (Mimmo Frassineti—A.G.F./Il Venerdi di Repubblica)

Saddam Hussein embraces Arafat on Iraqi television, August 6, 1990. Arafat had traveled to Iraq four days after its invasion of Kuwait in an attempt to find an Arab solution to the mounting conflict.

A spontaneous moment between Yasser Arafat and Yitzhak Rabin after the White House signing ceremony of the Oslo II accord. Washington, D.C., September 1995 (Arnie Sachs)

A handshake finally breaks the ice. A smiling Bill Clinton and King Hussein look on as Benjamin Netanyahu gives a warm goodbye to Yasser Arafat before they leave the White House. Washington, D.C., October 1996 (Mark Burris, Consolidated News Photo)

was an unexpected boon for them, explains Sick. He says the PLO "saw this as a clear opportunity to make some real headway with the U.S. government."

In New York, Vance authorized Ames to meet with Khaled al-Hassan, Hani's brother, at the Waldorf Towers, and to make a separate appeal through him for Arafat's help with the hostages. The PLO wanted the crisis to end without any loss of life but the hostage-taking by militant Iranian students also served the PLO's own goals. "Our aim was to stop Camp David," admits Hani al-Hassan. "There was no other way to stop Camp David than to make a big problem in the area." The PLO opposed the 1978 Camp David accords because they had led to a peace treaty between Egypt and Israel. The pact had removed Egypt, the most militarily powerful and largest, Arab nation, from the Arab bloc against Israel, and had offered West Bank and Gaza Palestinians an "autonomy" that the PLO believed would never allow them to gain their independence or statehood.

On November 17, a week before Thanksgiving, Arafat says he helped persuade Khomeini to release thirteen of the American hostages, the women and the blacks. According to Hani al-Hassan, the PLO had to cash a large number of its chips, overcoming opposition from Ahmed Khomeini, son of the new ruler, and other hard-liners. In the end, he says, it was Hashemi Rafsanjani, the speaker of the Iranian parliament (now Iran's president), who personally intervened with the militants to obtain freedom for the thirteen hostages. At a press conference accompanying their release, Hani al-Hassan announced they had been freed for humanitarian reasons, "because we don't believe in dealing with human beings in this manner," but he admitted that the PLO had helped the United States because "it served our cause." Says Hassan, "We dreamed that Arafat would take these hostages to Washington."[6]

Senior Carter administration officials also hoped the PLO would gain credibility from playing a helpful role in the hostage crisis. Harold Saunders, the State Department's top Middle East policy-maker, concedes "we had an interest not just in the PLO's getting the hostages out but in their playing a role in the larger context" of an Arab-Israeli settlement. Saunders says Dean's contacts with the PLO helped the Carter administration win freedom for the first thirteen hostages. "It was through the Dean channel that we learned what would happen, when it would happen, where they [the captive

Americans] would go and who would be included," explains Saunders. He says the fact that the PLO had a direct satellite link between its headquarters in Beirut and the communication system it installed for the Khomeini regime in Teheran also helped the United States in its efforts to free the hostages.

Arafat complains that after he helped get the hostages out the United States stopped using his services and turned to other intermediaries. "I know the Iranians better than you," he says he told a U.S. envoy several weeks later. "They are my friends," Arafat says he reminded the unnamed American. He says he warned him: "You are going to spoil everything by using all these channels." Saunders, however, says that "after a period of time, it became apparent to us that he [Arafat] didn't know what to do either."

In the midst of the Iranian hostage crisis, Dean himself almost became a victim of terrorism. He was angered that Israel had been allowed to carve out a security zone in southern Lebanon. At the time, the Begin Government was making no secret of the help it was giving to Beshir Gemayel, the leader of the Christian Phalangist militia fighting the PLO. Dean says he told his superiors in Washington he would quit if Lebanon was going to be partitioned between Moslem and Christian sectors. "I have never thought that the wandering Jew should be replaced by the wandering Palestinian," he explains.

In the summer of 1980, after publicly criticizing Israeli-Christian attacks on PLO positions in the south, elements of the Phalange militia tried to assassinate Dean in Beirut. He later told a closed-door session of the Senate intelligence committee that "American weapons were provided and were used" in the abortive assassination effort. The weapons could only have come from Israeli stocks. "I have the (weapons) numbers," says Dean. He was not surprised, he adds, because "some elements' intensely disliked the fact that the American ambassador should talk to everybody," including the PLO. On two occasions, he charges a "friendly" foreign government which he will not identify even "asked for my removal."

If Israel felt it had reason to be disturbed about Dean's clandestine contacts with the PLO, at least his efforts were not kept secret from the Jerusalem government. When John Edwin Mroz, the third American envoy, was authorized by the State Department to approach the PLO in August 1981, the Israelis were kept completely in the dark. Nine months later, it may have been a tip Israel received about the Mroz mission that abruptly ended the dialogue just when it looked like it might achieve a breakthrough.

Mroz first approached the State Department in May 1981 after he was given a document by a PLO diplomat at the United Nations. It contained five points, among them explicit mention of Israel and of the right of all states in the region to co-exist in peace and security. At the time, the thirty-two-year-old American believed he might be able to achieve what had eluded Bolling, Dean and the other would-be emissaries. So did Nicholas Veliotes, Saunder's successor as assistant secretary of state for Near Eastern and South Asian Affairs. Mroz was vice president of the International Peace Academy, which helped the United Nations train forces from 130 different countries for peace-keeping responsibilities throughout the world. In the course of his normal activities, Mroz travelled regularly to the Middle East, so no one would question his need to visit Beirut and other Arab capitals.

The document Mroz brought Veliotes piqued his interest because the PLO had mentioned Israel. The latest Arab peace plan, a Saudi by-product of an August 1981 summit in Fez, contained eight points but no mention of Israel. They included acceptance of the right of all states in the region to exist, but only after a Palestinian state was born. In August, Mroz visited Beirut and had a meeting with Arafat. By then the PLO had expanded the five points to seven, including mention of Israel.

Before Mroz left Washington, he spoke with Veliotes but he still did not have official authorization from anyone in the U.S. government to negotiate with Arafat. When he returned a few days later, however, he was carrying something that enticed the new Reagan administration. It was a handwritten message from Arafat, dated August 4, 1981, in which the PLO leader said he wanted to establish contact with the new administration and hoped this could be done "without having to use filters that are unreliable."[7]

Arafat, says Veliotes, no longer trusted Arab intermediaries because each of them had his own agenda. Mroz seemed suitable, says Veliotes, precisely "because he was an American and a non-Arab." In his first secret message to the Reagan administration, Arafat suggested the seven points of the PLO paper could become a possible framework for a U.S.–PLO agreement.

Sensing an opportunity, Veliotes wrote a two-and-a-half-page memorandum to Secretary of State Alexander Haig, laying out the reasons why he believed it might be worthwhile to ask Mroz to pursue the opening. If Mroz succeeded in getting Arafat to accept Israel, that would be a big bonus for the peace process. The memo to Haig suggested the approach was worth pursuing "on its merits." Making any inroads with the PLO, it went on, would be at Moscow's expense. And even if Mroz failed, the exercise could be worthwhile. It might help keep the Israeli-Lebanese border quiet because the PLO may feel it had a stake in maintaining the secret dialogue with Washington. The fragile cease-fire along Lebanon's border with Syria also might be preserved. That was important because otherwise Israel would refuse to implement its peace treaty with Egypt. New hostilities in Lebanon also would frighten Israel and the Jewish state might not complete its scheduled withdrawal from Sinai on April 23, 1982.

When President Reagan arrived for his summer vacation at his home near Los Angeles, Haig brought Veliotes' request to Reagan for his approval. To carry out the delicate mission, Veliotes says he asked Wat Cluverius, a veteran Middle East diplomat, to be "my action man." Cluverius, a deputy assistant secretary and former ambassador to Bahrain, would be Mroz's "handler," his conscience and his official link to the State Department. Meanwhile, Saudi Arabia was asked to backstop the process, with Crown Prince Fahd confirming the authenticity of each side's proposals.

On August 29, 1981, Mroz returned to Beirut for the second time that month and gave Arafat a curious document: an unsigned, typewritten letter which said the Reagan administration welcomed the opportunity to discuss the seven points. The fact that the letter was unsigned reflected the hesitancy of the administration in engaging its prestige in something that could not only fail but was politically explosive. Arafat even had personally asked Mroz to help get visas for two senior PLO officials to tour the United States. Haig granted the visas, hoping it would help build confidence.[8]

Mroz kept travelling throughout the fall and winter of 1981. He shuttled, sometimes for five or six weeks at a stretch, between Beirut and other Arab capitals. He had already met more than twenty-five times with Arafat, their talks consuming some 200 hours, and had decided with his wife, to adopt a Palestinian child, an orphan of the guerrilla struggle with Israel. By the time Mroz completed his mission nine months later, he had spent more than 500 hours with Arafat and met privately with him on more than fifty occasions.

By spring 1982, his mission started to show promise. A succession of Arab leaders visited Washington and told Haig that Arafat was serious about the effort. Says Veliotes, "Maybe they didn't know all the details (of the Mroz mission) but it was clear they were carrying water for Arafat at his request." Haig reminded them to make sure Arafat understood the PLO had to renounce terrorism as well as accept 242, 338 and Israel's right to exist. There was another matter Mroz was instructed to bring up with Arafat. Reagan was preoccupied with the crisis in Central America, where his administration was covertly supporting the Nicaraguan contras, the counterrevolutionaries trying to overthrow the Sandinista government. U.S. intelligence confirmed there was heavy PLO involvement in training and arming the Sandinista regime. Mroz was told that Arafat could prove his sincerity by curtailing these activities.

At their next meeting, Arafat said there was nothing he could do about Nicaragua but he offered to renounce terrorism as part of a formal pact with the United States. While the mission now seemed to be making headway, the chief obstacle continued to be Arafat's demand that the United States accept the principle of self-determination for the Palestinian people. The PLO could not recognize Israel without such guarantees because, Arafat exclaimed to Mroz "This is the last card we have to play and we need it for the negotiations with Israel." Mroz, according to Veliotes, was instructed to respond, "Mr. Chairman, it is the indispensable card you have to play to get into the game."

Veliotes says he periodically reported to Haig. He did so in private, deliberately putting nothing in writing in order to maintain the secrecy of the operation. He says he told Haig, "The beauty of this is that I'll run it for you, and if anything goes wrong, I can take the blame." Meanwhile, Ames was brought in to help brief Mroz. By late spring, Veliotes and Cluverius had devised a formula they thought would overcome the self-determination hurdle. It finessed the issue of Palestinian statehood by declaring that the United States, since the days of the Founding Fathers, had traditionally supported the principle of self-determination. That did not mean the United States would endorse an independent Palestinian state but neither would the U.S. oppose the creation of a state if it was the outcome of direct talks between the PLO and the Israeli government. In fact, Arafat was told if he said the magic words about recognizing Israel, he could say whatever else he wanted about independence and statehood in the following paragraph.

Arafat liked the formulation and indicated he would sign a document pledging his readiness to recognize Israel. "I gave him [Mroz] my approval for the existence of Israel as a fact in the region," Arafat told us. Mroz also insists "we got down to the point where it was three or four words. That was all. We had a special phrase [to resolve the dispute over self-determination]. In fact, it took three or four trips to Beirut just to get agreement on that phrase. But we got it."

But in April 1982, when Mroz returned from a meeting in Beirut, he found the White House and State Department had cooled to his mission. When a top Reagan administration policymaker was told the Veliotes-Cluverius-Mroz formula might achieve a breakthrough, the official reportedly blurted out: "You mean, We're actually going to do it! We didn't mean to do it. Please, don't do this to us!"

By that time, Arafat had referred the draft text to the executive committee for formal approval. Although he will not reveal the wording, Mroz says the language, was "very, very close, within a few words" of what Arafat accepted in December 1988 to get a dialogue started with the United States.

On May 5, Mroz and Arafat met for the last time, although neither of them knew it: they planned a final meeting a month later to sign the document they had been negotiating for almost a year. Meanwhile, Veliotes was getting nervous. "I told them [Mroz and Cluverius] that piece of paper has no status as far as the U.S. Government is concerned and I may have to disavow it," he says. "If it came back that Arafat would accept this as a formula, then we'd have to go and see. I'm not going to make a big deal about it. Let's see what happens."

But the June 5 meeting never took place. In May 1982, Israel was seeking U.S. support for its plan to clean out the "nests of PLO terrorists" in southern Lebanon. While Mroz was in Beirut in May, Israeli Defense Minister Ariel Sharon came to Washington to brief Haig on the plans for the operation to rid Israel's northern border of the guerrilla threat. Sharon showed Haig maps for the planned invasion but Haig says he made clear both he and President Reagan were very much opposed to it. Haig cautioned Sharon against undertaking such an operation in the absence of an "internationally recognized provocation." That caveat probably was the origin of the belief that Haig gave Sharon a yellow light for the invasion.

Arafat, who is always ready to embrace any conspiratorial excuse, believes there was such sabotage. "During that period, while he was sending Mroz to offer me a deal, Haig was making plans with Sharon to invade Beirut," Arafat charges. Veliotes does not dismiss Arafat's suspicions out of hand. As early as February of 1982, in his presence, Veliotes says that Brandon Grove, the U.S. consul-general in Jerusalem, briefed Haig over breakfast at the King David Hotel. Veliotes says Grove told Haig that "the signs are all pointing towards Sharon engineering an early invasion of Lebanon to 'solve' the Palestinian problem. My cynicism comes from the fact that Haig obviously believed that you could solve the Palestinian problem." To this day, Arafat maintains he had accepted the document he "was negotiating" with Mroz, and adds, "I was waiting for the continuity of these talks."

The invasion began on June 6, three days after Israel's ambassador to Great Britain Shlomo Argov was gunned down outside London's Dorchester Hotel by elements of the Abu Nidal faction. Despite the fact that Abu Nidal and his Libyan-supported group were outside of and opponents of the PLO, the maiming of Argov provided the "internationally recognized provocation" for Israel to attack PLO camps in Lebanon. Today, Mroz is not eager to discuss the possibility that his efforts may have contributed to Israel's motivations for invading Lebanon. "That's a pretty nasty thing for me to think about," he says, "that a secret negotiation with Arafat may have been one of the reasons for the timing of the Lebanese invasion."

21

The Reagan Plan: A Political Bonus?

AMONG THE MANY IMAGES of Arafat that have appeared before the world, few are as vivid as the television pictures of the PLO chairman leaving Lebanon in the summer of 1982. Defeated and outwitted at last by the Israelis, it appeared that the guerrilla leader would go off to oblivion, never to be heard from again. But listening to Arafat now, in the lavish salon of the PLO ambassador's residence in Tunis, it is hard to believe it is he who left defeated. Drawing from a well of righteous indignation, Arafat talks smugly about the Israeli attack on the PLO in Lebanon. Despite the fact that the fedayeen were forced to leave, somehow it is Arafat who appears the victor. He sneers at the Israeli commander, Ariel Sharon, and snickers at how the Israeli Defense Forces tried to outsmart the Palestinian fighters in Beirut. "Arrogance of power!" scoffs Arafat as he tells of Sharon's attempts to surround the fedayeen in the city. "With all his power he failed to invade Beirut. With all his huge forces, he failed to invade

368

me!" Arafat laughs at the advances Sharon had claimed to make. "They said their tanks had advanced ten meters. Ten meters. Scandal!" says Arafat, pointing out that the length of an entire tank is 17.6 meters. "He knew he couldn't defeat me!" boasts Arafat.[1]

With great relish, the PLO leader recalls a story told to him by Egyptian officials. A few weeks before Menachem Begin gave the order to invade Lebanon, it seems, Ariel Sharon was invited on an official visit to Egypt. Prior to the trip, Egyptian Prime Minister Kamal Hassan Ali had been approached by Arafat, who was convinced that Israeli troops were massing at Israel's northern border, preparing to make an attack. Arafat asked the Egyptian to raise the issue with the Israeli defense chief.

According to Arafat, the two men were enjoying afternoon tea when the Egyptian cautioned Sharon he might be underestimating the strength of Palestinian forces. It would be a fatal mistake to invade Lebanon, said the Egyptian. It could drag Israel into a lengthy land war and cost many casualties. It could also put Sharon's own career in jeopardy, Hassan Ali suggested. You are the second most powerful figure in the Likud, he told Sharon. Why risk your future on such an enormous gamble?

A white-gloved servant had just finished pouring the tea. Steam was still rising from the cup when, suddenly, Sharon got up and announced, "I won't drink it. I will come back to finish my tea. You'll see. After I finish the operation in Lebanon, I'll be back and the tea will still be warm." Arafat grins when he tells the story. "Sharon never returned," the PLO leader adds with a wry grin.

The three-month period from early June, when Israeli forces rolled into Lebanon and 72 hours later reached the outskirts of Beirut, to the end of August, when Arafat boarded a ship for Athens, taking 14,000 fighters with him, encapsulated all the conflicting tugs in which the PLO has always been pulled. There was Arafat, being hunted, constantly changing his headquarters from the basement bunker of one building to another, trying to escape assassination and fight a guerrilla war against impossible odds. There was the guerrilla chieftain, surrounded by his top lieutenants, an unwelcome guest in an Arab capital, with his Moslem allies trying to persuade him to surrender. And there was the larger-than-life Palestinian leader, forced to find yet another exile, trying to salvage some shred of recognition for a cause that seemed all but lost.

It was precisely the kind of scenario Arafat relished. From his bunker, he could prey on the conscience of the world. He could later boast, "I gave Sharon a lesson. Show me one man who says the Israelis won the battle in Beirut." For Arafat, merely to survive was a victory, particularly since the world had witnessed how none of his Arab brethren had rushed to his rescue.

Beirut was, in some ways, similar to the battle that catapulted Fatah to fame at Karameh. Despite heavy losses, the Palestinians had shown they could fight for themselves against a powerful adversary. In Lebanon, they had battled Israeli forces longer than the armies of five Arab nations in all five wars against the Jewish state. The Palestinians had fought without tanks, without missiles and without aircraft, using mostly light, hand-held weapons against an enemy that sent in the full brunt of its air force, helicopters and armored divisions. When the dust settled, the PLO had killed several hundred Israelis. Even the Syrian effort to fuel an insurrection within Fatah to overthrow Arafat ultimately failed.

But it was the American role that was the most decisive in saving Arafat and in persuading him to begin a political offensive from his new home in Tunis. Even in his bunker in Beirut, he continued receiving American envoys, including Representative Paul Mc-Closkey (R.-California) and a team of five other congressmen who thought they saw an opportunity, at the height of the Israeli siege, to coax Arafat to accept Israel. Without that acceptance, McCloskey says he told Arafat when they met on July 28, 1982, "there's nothing we can do in Congress to change American opinion."[2] He says Arafat replied, "I have recognized Israel. I have recognized the United Nations resolutions. I recognize all of the U.N. resolutions relating to the Palestinian question." McCloskey asked if he meant to include 242 and 338? "Yes," he says Arafat replied. The PLO leader wrote out his acceptance on a small scrap of paper and gave it to the congressional group. At a press conference later that day, the seeming breakthrough was announced by the delegation. The next day, however, it was denied by every PLO spokesman from New Delhi to New York. "Innocents Abroad" and "Congressmen Duped" were some of the headlines that appeared in American newspapers.

Arafat, however, never denied McCloskey's account. Interestingly, there are other signs that he may have been considering a political compromise during the siege of Beirut. About two weeks before McCloskey's meeting with Arafat, another senior PLO operative, Khaled al-Hassan, was quietly granted a visa to visit Washington so that he could keep Arafat informed on the progress of an Arab League delegation invited for talks on July 19–20 with President Reagan and Secretary of State Shultz. The Arab team was headed by Saudi Foreign Minister Prince Saud al-Faisal and Syrian Foreign Minister Abdel Hadim Khaddam. The Kissinger ban meant that Khaled al-Hassan had to be invisible. Arafat hoped the Arab League mission would get the best possible deal for the PLO: a political quid pro quo for quitting Beirut. In his mind, it was a device for evading the need to deal with the U.S. man on the ground, who was demanding an unconditional pullout.

In July, the PLO did not like the terms being offered them by Philip Habib, President Reagan's envoy in Beirut, and was encouraging a Franco-Egyptian effort at the United Nations to introduce a new Security Council resolution to supplant 242. The draft text called for mutual Israeli-PLO recognition and for direct PLO involvement in any Lebanese peace talks. Intense U.S. lobbying, however, prevented the resolution from being seriously considered, and the daily Israeli aerial and coastal bombardments finally forced the PLO to negotiate through Habib. From his headquarters near the presidential palace in Christian East Beirut, Habib dealt with the PLO through Moslem intermediaries, including Shafik al-Wazzan, Lebanon's prime minister, and his predecessor Saeb Salam. They regularly travelled across the heavily-shelled "green line" to the western Moslem sector of the city, where they relayed the demands Israeli leaders were dictating to Habib.

Since PLO forces were completely surrounded in a 14-mile enclave in West Beirut, and had little food and no electricity or water, it was easy for Israeli forces to impose their will. Says Habib, "The terms were very simple. You get out, you take no heavy arms, only personal weapons." At one point, a dispute arose about whether rocket propelled grenades were hand-held as opposed to crew-served weapons. "The Israelis refused to let them take the RPGs," Habib says. The other conditions were that all 14,000 fighters had to withdraw. They could leave by sea or overland to Damascus. In return, Habib explains, Israel agreed the PLO fighters would not be harassed. "They would leave with dignity and the Palestinians left behind [non-combatants, women and children] would not be disturbed."[3] The subsequent massacre, after the PLO withdrawal, of more than 1,000 Palestinian civilians by Phalangist militia forces stands in Arafat's memory as the blackest symbol of American deception.

But when Khaled al-Hassan arrived in early July at The Madison, a stately hotel in Washington, D.C., where world leaders often stay, he thought there still was a chance for the PLO, in its darkest hour, to win American recognition. He knew the odds were against them: President Reagan had publicly defended the Israeli invasion and Secretary of State Haig had called it "an historic opportunity to rid Lebanon of the PLO." But a new secretary of state succeeded Haig in the first week of July 1982. He was a former economics professor and California businessman whose job as the chief executive officer of Bechtel, the international construction and engineering corporation, had brought him into regular contact with the Arab world and with Palestinians. One of George Shultz's friends was Hassib Sabbagh, the chairman of the largest Arab construction company who was a member of the Palestine National Council. Moshe Arens, the Israeli ambassador to the U.S., was particularly worried about Shultz's sympathies. Arens told Lawrence Silberman, a former Ambassador to Yugoslavia and friend of Shultz, that the new secretary had been a major fund raiser for Paul McCloskey in his June 1982 primary campaign to win the Republican Senate nomination.[4]

Khaled al-Hassan knew, however, that an old friend, the CIA's Robert Ames, was close to Shultz. Ames had already been brought into a small circle of informal advisers asked to meet with the new cabinet officer at his Palo Alto, California, home. They included Irving Shapiro, the board chairman of DuPont, and Silberman, who at the time was vice president of the Crocker Bank in San Francisco. "Ames was introduced to me as the most informed CIA fellow on the Middle East," says Silberman. Neither Silberman nor Shapiro knew that Ames also was the architect of ongoing talks with Yasser Arafat, Abu Jihad and other senior PLO officials. Shortly after he took over, Shultz gave Ames another assignment: to help the State Department draft the outlines for a new American approach to the Arab-Israeli conflict. On September 1, 1982, that approach surfaced publicly as the Reagan Peace Plan.

While it was being formulated in July and August, Hassan says he and Ames met regularly in Washington. Ames even was able to put an advance copy of the plan into Arafat's hands through an Arab intermediary who traveled to Beirut.[5] The new administration's approach was distilled from talks with Egypt and Israel that had followed the Camp David accords and from fourteen months of discussions with other Arab heads of state.

The autonomy provisions of the Camp David accords called on local West Bank and Gaza Palestinians to negotiate—with Israel and Jordan—the procedures for holding elections and creating an interim self-governing regime in the occupied territories. The autonomy talks, though, were virtually stillborn, as no Palestinians would participate without public PLO backing. Israel ruled out any PLO role. Meanwhile, Arab leaders complained that the United States was taking no position of its own about the desired outcome. What did the Reagan administration believe should happen to the West bank and Gaza? they asked. Was the United States still committed to the land-for-peace formula embodied in 242? Did America believe Israel had a right to biblical Judea and Samaria? Did the Palestinians have a right to a state?

The Reagan administration realized it had to answer these questions—if it wanted to avoid a public drubbing—before the scheduled Arab summit in early September. That was also the target date for getting Arafat out of Beirut and the combination provided an opportunity. Khaled al-Hassan felt if he could persuade Arafat to recognize Israel and accept Resolutions 242 and 338 before Reagan delivered his speech, the United States might accept self-determination for the Palestinian people.

He based his belief, he says, on secret commitments given to him by Ames. "He was not talking to me as a CIA man," says Hassan. Ames had been transferred as an ex-officio adviser to the White House and the State Department. "He was a kind of liaison. Therefore he couldn't lie to me. A CIA man can lie. He couldn't," he says. During a mid-July luncheon at Georgetown's Four Seasons Hotel, Khaled al-Hassan says Ames promised that if Arafat accepts 242, the Reagan plan "will include provisions that will be very satisfactory to the Palestinian people."

Ames added tantalizingly, "There is a promise to meet with Arafat at a high level in either Riyadh or Cairo." Hassan could not believe his ears. "Bob, are you sure? I am going to send this to Arafat." The official replied, according to Khaled al-Hassan, "Look, if you are willing to leave Beirut and accept 242, a decision has been made that Arafat will be met by a very high-ranking policymaker in Riyadh or Cairo."

Nicholas Veliotes, the assistant secretary of state in charge of the Middle East, confirms that Ames was not free-lancing. The secret offer for a high-level meeting was, says Veliotes, American policy. He had communicated it to a number of important Arab leaders. "If Arafat would accept our formulation, I told him [Ames] I would be ready to meet with Arafat immediately or with anyone he would designate wherever he wanted," says Veliotes.

On July 19, 1982, Khaled al-Hassan cabled Arafat from Washington: "Now we are at a point where we have to make policy and not diplomacy."[6] Time was short. The PLO official suggested Arafat make his pronouncement before the meeting that the Saudi and Syrian foreign ministers had scheduled with President Reagan 24 hours later. He even provided this suggestion: make a personal declaration that the PLO has "no objection to 242," provided it is clear it calls for "the full withdrawal of the Israelis from all the territories occupied in the 1967 war." Make it clear that recognition of Israel is acceptable "if the right to self-determination is connected with it." Finally, Khaled al-Hassan suggested, propose the immediate opening of face-to-face talks with Habib in Beirut. His cable concluded: "The usual Arab approach of wait-and-see should be avoided:" it would be a "fatal mistake" to miss this opportunity.

The PLO leadership met in Beirut to consider Khaled al-Hassan's appeal. At 3:30 A.M. on July 20, only hours before the two Arab envoys were to meet Shultz, Arafat cabled his reply. It was negative. The PLO would gain nothing by the U.S. recognition of self-determination because there were no guarantees such recognition would lead to an independent Palestinian state. Without such commitments by the United States, self-determination would flounder like "a fish in the water," the cable said.[7] Khaled al-Hassan tried once more. Don't worry about being hooked, he cabled Abu Jihad. Just condition your acceptance on American fulfillment of its promise.

Khaled al-Hassan remains convinced that "those who had suggested the proposal" were in a position to deliver, although he still is not sure who authorized Ames and Veliotes. By the time Arafat replied, 24 hours later, it was too late. The meetings with Shultz and Reagan were over, and Arafat was annoyed that he had not heard directly from Khaled al-Hassan about their results. Arafat cabled him: "Until now we have not received anything regarding the discussion except what you said on the phone to Abu Jihad. I want something documented and official so as to move in light of it. We cannot move in light of a telephone conversation."[8]

Other carrots may later have been offered to Arafat. Towards the middle of August, Hani al-Hassan, who was in Beirut, revealed that an unsigned, typewritten letter, pledging the United States "will take into consideration the PLO desire for a political bonus," was received through the Lebanese mediators Shafik al-Wazzan and Saeb Salam. Arafat told us that "Habib handed me a paper with the words 'political bonus to be deferred.' It came through Saeb Salam." What that "bonus" was is unclear. It could have been the Reagan Peace Plan. Or it could have been a promise that self-determination would be written into the plan. In any event, Habib denies ever making an offer of any "bonus" for PLO withdrawal.

Arafat believes he was, again, the victim of a conspiracy engineered by the architect of the ban on official talks with the PLO. "In the final hours before the [Reagan] plan was made public, Kissinger interfered. I have proof from the Egyptians and the Saudis. The Reagan administration wiped 'self-determination' out and instead wrote that the Palestinians have a right to participate in their future through 'association' with Jordan," charges Arafat. He adds bitterly: "Self-determination is not 'with' anybody."

Kissinger was part of an ad hoc group Shultz consulted to advise him in his early weeks in office. During one informal meeting, Kissinger reportedly exclaimed: "Why in hell do we want to give the PLO anything after we have gotten rid of it? We should never let the PLO get back in a central role." But there is no evidence that Kissinger sabotaged any consideration of including self-determination in the Reagan Plan, or that there was ever any serious consideration of including it. There is, however, some indication that self-determination for the Palestinians was discussed by Shultz and his senior advisers and that Arafat's claims may therefore not be far-fetched. After the departure of the Arab League mission in late July, Saudi Ambassador Faisal Alhegelan and Egyptian Ambassador Ashraf Ghorbal were delegated to represent the Arab League in Washington and met regularly with American officials over the terms for the PLO withdrawal. Nabil Shaath, another senior PLO figure, also visited Washington in August and recalls Alhegelan's coming to see him at the Palestine Information Office.

Shaath says the Saudi diplomat quoted Veliotes telling him that if Arafat is realistic and accepts Resolution 242 and Israel's existence, the Reagan Plan "can be your political boat to a Palestinian state." Veliotes confirms Shaath's account. In one of the last meetings he held with Shultz on the Reagan plan, Veliotes says he saw "a problem that was going to make it difficult for the Arabs to accept the plan." The problem, he says he told Shultz, was that "there is no provision for self-determination or an independent state." Heated debate ensued and a few days later, a garbled version of the internal dispute was leaked to the New York Times. It cast Veliotes in the role of arguing for the inclusion of self-determination and being overruled, which was not far from the truth. As a result, says Veliotes, as soon as Arafat left Beirut, "I started getting this: Where's the bonus? What's the bonus? I was furious. Someone must have said it. But I don't think it was us. We thought stopping the destruction of Beirut and its inhabitants, including the PLO, was in itself a form of bonus." The most likely explanation is that Saeb Salam encouraged Arafat to believe it was being seriously considered.

Another possible explanation for Arafat's belief he would get some form of "bonus" was the fact that approval had been given for Habib to meet with Arafat. Shultz okayed the idea, according to Habib, because he thought it would help speed the PLO withdrawal. "I was under instructions to abide by the commitment given by Kissinger to the Israelis," says Habib, so he informed Prime Minister Begin of his intent to deal directly with Arafat.[9] To help ease Israeli concerns, Habib arranged solely for "proximity" talks: Arafat would be on one floor of a building and Habib on another. "We could get done in ten minutes what would take five days to do," says Habib, because instead of sending emissaries through the shelling between war torn Beirut, the two could "just run up and down the stairs." Begin, however, said no. Not in the same building. That would be recognition, the Israeli leader implored. "You mean I have to be in one building and he has to be in another?" Habib asked. "That's right.

Not in the same building," replied Begin. The proximity talks never took place.

And self-determination never appeared in the Reagan Plan.

Nonetheless, the Reagan initiative was a bold effort to narrow the Israeli-Palestinian playing field. In a nationally televised address on September 1, 1982, Reagan said peace can neither be achieved through the formation of an independent Palestinian state nor by Israel remaining in permanent control of the disputed territories. For the first time, the United States served notice it would oppose the annexation of Judea and Samaria. Declared Reagan, "It is the firm view of the United States that self-government by the Palestinians of the West Bank and Gaza in association with Jordan offers the best chance for a durable, just and lasting peace."

In an accompanying explanation of the plan—"talking points"—that was sent separately to Middle East leaders, the administration also made clear its "preference" for the West Bank and Gaza to be federated with Jordan. Ames tried to explain to his PLO contacts that the new U.S. stand did not preclude the PLO from demanding its state and had intentionally left open the possibility that such a state, confederated with Jordan, could result from the negotiations between the parties involved. "Begin did a wonderful favor for us," says Veliotes. "He leaked the talking points. The Arabs knew the *New York Times* got them from the Israelis. That was the best thing that could have happened, because for the first time the Arabs could trust they got the same thing as the Israelis."

The PLO, however, was not persuaded it had won anything at all. It waited for Israel to denounce the plan and then followed suit. Arafat told us angrily: "What Reagan announced was not what I had been promised." Jordan's King Hussein was initially interested in the plan but, after failing to win PLO acquiescence or Saudi support, Hussein also pronounced it "dead on arrival." Six months later, on April 18, 1983, Robert Ames was murdered in Beirut when a young Shiite guerrilla whose brother had been murdered in the Sabra and Shatila massacres, drove a truck bomb into the American embassy. Ames had been visiting his old post to brief the intelligence chiefs who succeeded him in the region. When Ames was killed, a victim of the terrorism he had spent his life trying to understand and eliminate, the PLO probably lost the most sympathetic advocate it ever had in the high reaches of the American government.

If Arafat felt betrayed by the United States—and even Habib

concedes Arafat was justified in feeling that way after the massacres at Sabra and Shatilla—the PLO leader must have felt even more isolated by the Arab states which had failed to come to his rescue in Beirut. He later learned that the Saudi and Syrian envoys who met with Reagan in July hardly mentioned the plight of the Palestinians. Adding insult to injury, when they emerged from their White House meeting, Reagan said he supported the Israeli goal of driving the PLO out of Lebanon. In the presence of the two Arab envoys, Reagan added, "we will do everything in our power to make that happen."[10]

On August 10, Arafat finally made up his mind to quit the Lebanese capital on the terms Habib originally had offered.

Eleven days later, the evacuation began. It was completed on September 1, 1982, two days ahead of schedule. "It was very orderly," says Habib. "They would drive in trucks to the line between West Beirut and the actual port area. French troops were there to facilitate the crossing. We had a group of Greek officers get on the boats with escorts and there were Italian, American and French troops there." The Palestinians "celebrated, they shot their guns in the air and made their farewells; shells were flying all over the damn place." Habib recalls the scene even had some farcical aspects to it. "The Israelis insisted on a list of names coming out. We had a guy standing there. He would yell out a name. That gave us a count. It was how we knew there were 14,000 who came out. There is a list of 14,000 names. Everyone laughed. None of them are real. It was part of the harassment."

Arafat was on the high seas when Reagan began his nationally-televised address. In his own mind, Arafat quit Beirut because his Moslem allies, he says, begged, "Please, Yasser, this is enough: 52,000 killed and wounded, almost half of them Lebanese! You have to look out for our children." (There were approximately 19,000 killed and 33,000 wounded—84 percent of Arab casualties in Beirut were civilians. More than 600 Israelis were killed in the period after the invasion and before Israeli forces completed their final withdrawal in 1986.)

Today, Arafat admits, "They had a right to say that. I left because I began to feel the responsibility of killing their children." And he adds with a wry smile, "Where am I after all these years? I have my forces back in Lebanon."

22

Shultz's Secret Diplomacy

THEY HAD JUST FINISHED *lunch in the James Madison Dining Room, the comfortable eighth-floor nook used by the secretary of state for entertaining visiting dignitaries. George Shultz suggested to Swedish foreign minister Sten Andersson that they step outside onto the balcony to view some of the sights of Washington. The two men walked past the room's eighteenth-century sideboard from the U.S.S. Constitution and portraits of Martha and George Washington. Outdoors, Andersson glimpsed the monuments to America's struggle for liberty and self-determination. Shultz pointed out the Lincoln Memorial and the Robert E. Lee Mansion that sits above Arlington Cemetery. The memorial to Thomas Jefferson, the drafter of the Declaration of Independence, stood majestically beside the Potomac River.*

Shultz and Andersson had met two years earlier, on March 15, 1986, during the funeral in Stockholm of Olaf Palme, the assassinated Swedish prime minister. Andersson had introduced Shultz to Palme's successor, Ingvar Carlsson. They briefly discussed the Middle East, where Palme had worked single-handedly to try to bring

Arabs and Israelis to the negotiating table. Amid the diplomatic niceties, Shultz put in a good word for an old friend, Wilhelm Wachtmeister, the Swedish count who had served so long as Sweden's ambassador to the United States that he had become dean of the diplomatic corps. The tennis court at the ambassador's Nebraska Avenue residence was one of the best in town; Shultz himself played there, sometimes in doubles matches with Wachtmeister and Swedish tennis star Bjorn Borg.

Shultz was aware that the new Swedish government wanted to reassign its ambassador and was preparing to call him home. He also knew the sociable Wachtmeisters were not eager to leave. "Now that he's dean, you'll have to keep him, Shultz told Andersson. The sixty-four-year-old foreign minister snapped, "You can't decide on what ambassador we'll have in Washington." But then, according to Andersson, Shultz reminded him the vice president, George Bush, was playing matches against Wachtmeister. And "he's beating him," said Shultz. "All right," replied Andersson, "he stays." They laughed. The chemistry seemed right: Shultz and Andersson sensed they could trust each other.

So on April 10, 1988, in the early afternoon, Andersson took advantage of the seclusion offered by the balcony to describe a plan for bringing Palestinians and Israelis together. Shultz listened. The Swedish official told him he had visited the Middle East in March and come away with some strong impressions. He had sent his son at age thirteen to work in an Israeli kibbutz, he told Shultz. On his trip, he had visited Makassed Hospital in East Jerusalem and looked in the eyes of paralyzed Palestinian children. He had visited the desert detention camp at Kziot in the Negev south of Beersheba, nicknamed Ansar (Victory) by the thousands of Palestinians interned there. He had met leaders of the liberal Peace Now movement as well as religious Israelis in their armed settlements on the West Bank and in Gaza.

Andersson told Shultz that in twenty-five years of dealing with the region, the hatreds had never seemed more intense. But he said he also sensed a strong, new desire for peace. In Amman, he had long talks with members of the PLO Executive Committee and in Damascus he had met some of the leaders of the Rejection Front. He told Shultz he left the region convinced the Palestinians themselves were aware that "nobody, neither people, could have one hundred percent of the land over which they had been fighting for such a long time." The Palestinians no longer wanted the destruction of Israel, he said, but a separate state that could coexist, peacefully, with the Jewish state.[1]

Alone now on the State Department balcony, Andersson broached the subject of Palestinian statehood. He praised Shultz's efforts. "I don't look upon your approach so much as a plan but as a process," he told him tactfully. "You are quite right," Shultz replied. Then Andersson raised the issue of self-determination. He quietly expressed his own view that there would never be peace unless the PLO was involved in the process and explained that PLO leaders were reluctant to recognize Israel and renounce terrorism simply to start a dialogue with the United States. Shultz was skeptical. He had heard the PLO refrain before: they would be stripped of all their cards and have nothing left for the bargaining table. Andersson told Shultz he had tried to persuade Arafat that his real constituency was the Jews, particularly Jewish Americans who constituted a powerful lobby. Why not meet with a group of them and tell them of your willingness to accept Israel and forswear terrorism? That, the Swede went on, detailing his earlier conversation, would "change the attitudes in this country and open the way for a dialogue."

He told Shultz that Arafat had urged him to pursue that course with the Americans. To break the logjam between the United States and the PLO, he intended to arrange a meeting between Arafat and a group of American Jews. "I knew Shultz couldn't say yes because that [official U.S.-PLO contact] was against the law in the United States. But he could say no," the Swede recalled. Instead Shultz did not respond at all. "I looked upon that as a 'silent' yes. He didn't say it but I felt we were of the same mind."

Two months later, on June 5, 1988, Shultz told Israeli leaders that "the continued occupation of the West Bank and Gaza· and the frustration of Palestinian rights is a dead-end street and the belief that this can continue is an illusion." But Shultz, an ex-Marine, did not trust the freewheeling Palestinian leadership either. The brutal murder of the crippled sixty-nine-year-old Leon Klinghoffer, a passenger aboard the Achille Lauro, still stuck in Shultz's gut. He had a visceral dislike for Arafat and believed that a PLO-led state could threaten the survival of both Israel and Jordan. In his mind, another negotiating partner had to be found for Israel or there would never be any prospect of direct Israeli-Palestinian talks. Shultz tried to reach out to that potential partner when he visited the American Colony

Hotel in East Jerusalem. There he had hoped to meet with local non-PLO Palestinians. Under orders from Arafat, however, none of the West Bank and Gaza politicos showed up; Shultz stood alone at the podium in the hotel's open courtyard reading to hundreds of reporters, some perched on the roof, the statement he had wanted to share in private with the Palestinians. The PLO had upstaged the American secretary of state. But Shultz felt he had gained the moral high ground; he, at least, had shown up prepared to talk to them.

A ndersson wasted little time in pursuing the strategy he had outlined for Shultz. The Swedish minister was being privately encouraged by Arafat's senior political advisor, Bassam Abu Sharif. In March 1988, Abu Sharif had begun drafting a new political position for the PLO, one he hoped would force other PLO officials to adjust to the reality that Israel was there to stay and had genuine security fears born out of the horrible experience of the Holocaust.

The draft statement, which Abu Sharif originally intended to submit as an op-ed article to the *Washington Post,* called for an independent Palestinian state and reaffirmed the PLO's leadership of the Palestinian movement. If Israel wanted to test those assumptions, he wrote, the PLO would agree to internationally supervised elections in the West Bank and Gaza and abide by the results—even if non-PLO candidates were victorious. The document acknowledged Israel had legitimate security needs and promised the PLO would accept a transition period in which the territories could be administered by an international peace-keeping force. Most important, wrote Abu Sharif, the PLO would agree to recognize Israel's right to exist within secure borders and accept U.N. Resolutions 242 and 338 as the benchmark for starting direct talks at an international conference. Abu Sharif put the finishing touches on the document and began circulating it to some American friends.[2]

Andersson was not the first Swedish diplomat to try to resolve the conflict. On September 16, 1948, Count Folke Bernadotte had recommended, in a report to the United Nations, that the right of Arab refugees to return to their homes in Israel be recognized "at the earliest possible date." On the following day, Bernadotte was murdered by members of the Stern Gang. Gunnar Jarring, another distinguished Swedish U.N. envoy, also had tried unsuccessfully to mediate the Arab-Israel conflict in the early 1970s.

For fifteen years, Andersson was secretary-general of Sweden's Social Democrats, Palme's party. His bold plan for an Arafat meeting with American Jewish leaders, at which the PLO leader would publicly declare his acceptance of Israel, had a potential flaw: no members of mainstream Jewish-American organizations could be solicited because word undoubtedly would filter back to Israel. He was convinced Shamir would then act to discredit the Jewish group. If a delegation of prominent Jews could be found, the effort had to be kept absolutely secret. Pierre Schori, the deputy foreign minister, told Andersson he had a friend in Los Angeles, Stanley Sheinbaum, an old-line antiwar Democrat. Schori had met Sheinbaum, a wealthy publisher, while serving on a disarmament commission that was part of the Six Nations Peace Initiative headed by six heads of state including Greek Prime Minister Andreas Papandreou, Swedish Prime Minister Olaf Palme, and India's Indira Gandhi.

At the invitation of Ulf Hjertonsson, a diplomat in the Swedish Embassy, Sheinbaum came to Washington in early 1988 to discuss the possibility of assembling a delegation of prominent Jewish leaders. He suggested the team include Drora Kass, the New York director of the International Center for Peace in the Middle East (ICPME), a group founded in 1982 by former Israeli Foreign Minister Abba Eban and of which Sheinbaum was a board member. He also suggested including Rita Hauser, a gutsy Manhattan lawyer who had served in the Nixon administration and helped promote dialogue between Israelis and Palestinians. Hauser had good connections to the Reagan administration that Sheinbaum felt would be useful down the road. All three—Hauser, Sheinbaum, and Kass— were associated with the ICPME (Hauser was chair of the U.S. chapter), but Hjertonsson insisted the rest of the organization not be informed of the operation. The reason for the unusual secrecy was clear: The Swedes believed they could organize a meeting with Arafat during the course of the year. There would probably be a preliminary session and then a final meeting. The Swedish official said he expected there to be "some developments." He asked Hauser, "Will you help?" Of course, she replied, "that's what we're in business for."[3]

The Swedes' penchant for secrecy became even clearer a few

months later, when Hjertonsson, the deputy chief of mission in the Swedish embassy in Washington, said he was ready to send the names of the PLO officials who would meet them in Stockholm. "Put it in the fax," Hauser told him. "No, no, no," Hjertonsson shot back, and he flew up to New York for a fifteen-minute meeting just to give her the names. Sweden was worried, she says, about the "vaunted Israeli intelligence"; at one point a Washington-based diplomat told Hauser "they have their people in every embassy here and are tapping the lines." On the air shuttle between Washington and New York, the Swedish diplomat even used a fictitious name.

As the Swedish-American effort got underway in the spring of 1988, the PLO tried to refocus attention on the Palestinian uprising so the issue might command attention at the upcoming Reagan-Gorbachev summit. Arab leaders, meeting in Algiers in early June 1988, reaffirmed their commitment to self-determination for the Palestinians and an independent state. But less noticed was Abu Sharif's circulation of his new position paper to journalists covering the summit. He had informed Arafat of what he intended to do but had not shown him the actual document, he says.[4] He took Arafat's silence as a go-ahead to distribute the paper. It called for the acceptance of U.N. Resolutions 242 and 338. The statement, which was published throughout the world the next day, also demonstrated a concern for Israeli fears about security in the Middle East. The Arab summit took another step to help Arafat. In a final communiqué it made clear that at any international conference the PLO could not be subsumed in a joint delegation with any other party to the conflict. It would have to be represented "on an equal footing and with the same rights as the other parties." That was a message to Jordan. The *intifada,* although it began spontaneously, had helped Arafat win an important victory, one that King Hussein could no longer ignore. Hussein read the handwriting on the wall, and only weeks later, in mid-July, he disengaged Jordan from the West Bank.

The impact of Hussein's decision was felt immediately in Tunis. Now, for the first time in its thirty-year liberation struggle, the PLO could determine its political future without Arab interference. Little time was wasted. In early August, only days after Hussein announced his decision, members of the PLO Executive Committee approached a particular Palestinian American on the prospects for a dialogue with the United States. He was Mohammad Rabie, an educator and former classmate of several of the PLO leaders at Cairo University.

Rabie called his friend William Quandt at the Brookings Institution in Washington. As a key aide to President Carter, Quandt helped draft the 1978 Camp David accords. He was highly regarded by professionals in the State Department. When Rabie met with Quandt at his office in mid-August, the Palestinian suggested that the time might be propitious to launch a U.S.-PLO dialogue. "I told him that the PLO would still be required to make an unambiguous statement on 242," says Quandt.[5]

Then he told his longtime Palestinian friend, "Why don't you write your version of what the PLO would be prepared to say and what they would need from the United States? I'll do the same." Quandt wrote the familiar paragraph out in longhand. "Do you think this would be enough for the State Department?" asked Rabie. Quandt suggested they take a few days to work out the language and then meet to compare drafts. Less than a week later, they merged their statements into a single, two-page document. The operating assumption was that neither the United States nor the PLO would act unilaterally: the United States and the PLO would agree beforehand that if the PLO did what was asked of it, the United States would follow through and open a dialogue.

Quandt says he showed the draft to a senior State Department official. "If the PLO could say this, would you be interested?" he asked. William Kirby, a deputy assistant secretary of state, reportedly said he would have to check with others. There was skepticism at the State Department. Says Charles Hill, Shultz's executive assistant, "There were scarcely three days that passed in the course of the 1980s when somebody did not call me or somebody else in the State Department and say we've got a breakthrough: I've just got a message for you from Arafat or this guy or that guy in the PLO. This kind of thing was happening all the time."[6]

Nonetheless, a few hours after Quandt spoke with Kirby, the former Carter aide says, "I got a call back saying the document was very interesting." The State Department official cautioned he couldn't, of course, offer any guarantees of what the American response would be. He wanted to make sure Quandt understood that the United States could not recognize the Palestinian right to self-determination as a quid pro quo for PLO recognition of Israel. Nonetheless, there was enough that was intriguing in what the PLO seemed to be offering. The official told Quandt that he thought there might eventually be some official response.

Rabie returned to Tunis, where he spent several weeks discussing the draft with the PLO Executive Committee. On September 17, Shultz delivered a major speech to the Washington Institute for Near East Policy, a prestigious group of scholars who gathered for their annual retreat at the Wye Plantation on Maryland's Eastern Shore. The speech was an opportunity for Shultz to enumerate to the largely pro-Israeli audience all the reasons for the continuing U.S. refusal to deal with the PLO. Chief among them was the PLO's continuing support for terrorism. But Shultz also was careful not to slam the door on the possibility of future contacts. He even offered the PLO a carrot, declaring "each party is free to bring any position it chooses to the negotiating table. Israelis are free to argue for annexation. Palestinians are free to argue for independence." The statement was consistent with U.S. policy since Camp David.

During the question-and-answer session, Shultz elaborated on his earlier comments. "I suppose under the circumstances it would be surprising if the Palestinians didn't make a run at an independent Palestinian state." He added that the United States would continue to oppose such a state but once the PLO had recognized Israel, it could argue for independence—and, what's more, the United States would support the PLO's right to do so. The message in Shultz's Wye Plantation speech did not go unnoticed at PLO headquarters. Rabie returned to Washington in late September authorized to report that the PLO now was in a position to make the kind of statement Shultz wanted.

But by early fall the Democratic and Republican parties had nominated their presidential candidates; George Bush was engaged in an uphill battle against Massachusetts governor Michael Dukakis, who emerged from the Democratic convention with a sizable lead in the polls. American Jews were upset over Bush's reluctance to fire campaign adviser Fred Malek, a former Nixon administration official, after disclosures Malek had participated in a head count of Jews in the Nixon administration. Malek, who argued that he had simply been following orders from Nixon, eventually resigned from the Bush campaign. But the last thing Bush needed was another scandal, particularly one involving a new, secret effort to woo the PLO. So in late September, Quandt was authorized to convey a message to the leadership in Tunis. The State Department message was a brief one, merely that the Reagan administration hoped to be able to give the PLO "our considered reaction" in about six weeks—after Election Day.[7]

At about the same time in mid-September, Stanley Sheinbaum says, he was called to a meeting in Paris with Swedish diplomat Hjertonsson "to discuss a strategy for what to do after Arafat would assert the three points in Stockholm." But on his flight back home, the American says he realized that rather than worry about what would come later, "our more immediate task should have been how to encourage [Arafat] to take the step....I decided then that it would be essential...to get word to Arafat that the Reagan administration would respond positively. I also decided that such word would have to come from the White House."

When he returned to California, Sheinbaum contacted William A. Wilson, a founder of Ronald Reagan's "kitchen cabinet" and a former ambassador to the Vatican, who had made an allegedly unauthorized visit to Libyan leader Muammar Qadaffi. Wilson agreed to arrange a meeting in mid-October at the Beverly Hilton Hotel in Los Angeles with the White House chief of staff, Kenneth Duberstein, and the president's national security adviser, Lt. Gen. Colin Powell. But at the meeting, Sheinbaum was unable to convince either Duberstein or Powell that President Reagan should get involved: conveying such personal assurances to the world's most notorious guerrilla chieftain was a potentially explosive political bombshell. Redoubling his efforts, Sheinbaum wrote a letter to Colin Powell reiterating his arguments. "Four days later," says Sheinbaum, Powell called Bill Wilson and told him that "my letter had become a 'working document' within the White House, the National Security Council, State, and Defense. More importantly, he told Wilson, I would momentarily be receiving a letter, and that letter indeed arrived."

Written on White House stationery, the one-page letter carried this critical sentence: "There can be no doubt that unequivocal PLO acceptance of Israel's right to exist and United Nations Security Council Resolutions 242 and 338, accompanied by a clear renunciation of violence and terrorism, would be such a step—and there can be no doubt that the United States would respond positively to it." The letter was signed "Colin Powell."

By early October, Andersson was in New York attending the annual fall session of the U.N. General Assembly. He met Hauser there for the first time. In Tunis, the PLO's Executive Committee, its Central Council and the Fatah Central Committee were busy debating the position paper Abu Sharif had already advertised as the new PLO peace plan. Abu Iyad and Farouk Kaddoumi at first fought hard to deprive Arafat of the consensus required to support the document. But flying from Baghdad to Riyadh to Cairo and back a dozen times to Tunis, Arafat won them over. He says the effort consumed more than 600 hours. Meanwhile, with an eye on the November elections in the United States, the Palestine National Council postponed the scheduled meeting of its 450-member parliament-in-exile.

With George Bush the victor in November and now prepared to enter the White House, the PLO began advertising its November 12–15 session in Algiers as the one that would finally act on 242 and 338, recognize Israel and renounce terrorism. The PNC moved in that direction, formally declaring its own independence and the unilateral establishment of a Palestinian state in the West Bank and Gaza with Jerusalem as its capital. But it did not unconditionally accept Resolution 242. The State Department reacted strongly. Spokesman Charles Redman declared that the status of the occupied territories cannot "be determined by unilateral acts of either side but only through a process of negotiations." He added: "A declaration of independent Palestinian statehood is such a unilateral act."

But something less noticeable and significant occurred in Algiers: Arafat's Fatah wing won the grudging support of Habash's PFLP and Hawatmeh's DFLP, the second and third largest among the eight groups that comprised the PLO. The PNC adopted a new political program which accepted 242 as the basis for negotiations at an international conference, provided the talks focused on the need for a full withdrawal to Israel's pre-June 1967 borders and the creation of a Palestinian state. Arafat contended "our political statement contains moderation, flexibility and realism. The ball is now in the American court." Despite Arafat's euphoria, however, American officials were unconvinced. Chiefly, they were disappointed by the failure of the PNC to act unequivocally in two other areas.

Instead of renouncing terrorism against both civilian and military targets, as the United States had demanded, the final PNC communiqué stressed that the U.N. Charter guaranteed the right to "resist foreign occupation, colonialism and racial discrimination, as well as struggle for their independence." Although there was new language asking the U.N. Security Council to guarantee peace and security "among all the countries concerned in the region," Israel was never mentioned by name. White House spokesman Marlin Fitzwater said the document contained "positive elements," but there was no disguising the fact it fell far short of what George Shultz had hoped for.

Still, Andersson sensed that a new page had been turned, that perhaps Arafat now had a genuine consensus to move towards peace with Israel. "Within days after Algiers, we got a phone call from the Swedes that a group led by Khaled Hassan was prepared to meet us in Stockholm," recalls Hauser. She telephoned Sheinbaum and they left Sunday night, November 20, preparing to meet Drora Kass in the Swedish capital. There, waiting to meet them, were al-Hassan and three other PLO officials: Afif Safieh, the PLO's ambassador to the Netherlands; Dr. Eugene Makhlouf, PLO ambassador to Sweden; and Hisham Mustafa, an aide to Abu Mazzen.

Their first meeting on Tuesday morning did not go well. The straight-talking Americans were up against the fudge masters of the Middle East. "Look, I've read two English translations of the [Algiers] political statement and one French translation," she told the PLO team, "and they all read differently. Not only in nuance," she added, "but in wording." Andersson recalls that Hauser had come with a "sign-on-the-dotted-line approach and it was not at all what Khaled al-Hassan was after."

Threatened with an early collapse of his efforts, the foreign minister invited both groups to lunch in his private office. Andersson was tough, particularly with the Palestinians. "Here are some people who are willing to help you make better known to the world what you really did in Algiers," he told them. "You should work together." Sheinbaum recalls that Andersson was so annoyed, "he turned to al-Hassan and in an exasperated tone wondered why the PLO had troubled the Americans to come thousands of miles" if they were not prepared to move forward. "Al-Hassan repeated once more the same concern from earlier in the morning: that they needed firmer assurances that the United States would indeed respond.

"At that point," says Sheinbaum, "I chose to pull out the Colin Powell letter, and all I had to do was to read that one critical sentence. Afif Safieh, one of their delegation, wanted to know what the letterhead was, and I was able to turn it around and show them that it was from the White House. That seemed to impress them as much as the one sentence I quoted above."

Lunch wasn't over until 2:30 P.M. and the Palestinians said they wanted a rest. The next meeting was scheduled for 5:00 P.M. The Americans were sure that during the break their PLO counterparts were on the phone to Tunis, because when they finally returned, Khaled al-Hassan said simply, "Let's get down to work."

As the first order of business, Hauser urged them to resolve the conflicting interpretations of what the PNC had done at Algiers. "There are three different translations. Why don't we try to clarify what was the essence of what you wanted to do in Algiers. That gave me a handle," she says now. In the guise of clarifying, the Americans wrote the Stockholm Declaration with the PLO officials, going well beyond what they did in Algiers. Their most important objective was to persuade the PLO to be unambiguous in accepting Israel and renouncing terrorism. With the help of Anders Bjurner, the Middle East expert in the Swedish Foreign Ministry, the two sides worked late into the night, finally emerging with a document that everyone could support.

In it the PLO accepted the existence of Israel as a state in the region and declared that the "independent state of Palestine" would coexist with the Jewish state in peace. The joint draft also declared the PLO's "rejection and condemnation of terrorism in all its forms." However, it restated a number of previous positions, affirming "the right of the Palestinian people to self-determination" and conditioning PLO acceptance of 242 and 338 on prior agreement to convene an international conference. What was achieved was a step forward over what the PLO had said in Algiers, but it still fell short of satisfying the State Department's demands for unconditional acceptance of Israel and the relevant United Nations resolutions. The document was typed up as "minutes" on Sten Andersson's stationery.

Feeling relieved and proud of their accomplishment, the delegation of American Jews went to dinner with the PLO team. At about 11:00 P.M., Andersson sent a copy of the typed statement to the restaurant. Reading it over, Hauser suggested they all sign it. Khaled al-Hassan refused, contending Arafat first would have to review it and give his okay. "We're not leaving here without signing this," said Hauser. "They went into a panic over whether they could sign." But then Hauser had an idea—why not sign the original that was on Andersson's Foreign Ministry stationery and take unsigned copies home to review. Over dessert, they signed the original and left it with Andersson, taking the other copies with them. It was Wednesday, a day before Thanksgiving; the three exhausted Americans headed home while the PLO team returned to Tunis to brief Arafat.

Meanwhile, Andersson instructed Wachtmeister to request a meeting with Shultz, sending Anders Bjurner to Washington to transmit a personal letter informing Shultz he soon would have "some significant visitors from Tunis" (Arafat and his delegation) in Stockholm. He now needed to know the precise formulation—what Arafat would have to say—that would prompt the start of an official U.S.-PLO dialogue.

Because Shultz was looking forward to a Thanksgiving dinner at home, he did not have time to respond, even in a preliminary manner, until Friday, November 25. On that day, after reading the full text of the still-secret Stockholm Declaration, Shultz told Wachtmeister, according to the Swedish envoy, "Well, this really advances things. It's clear we can do some business here." He promised to provide a reply to Andersson's letter before the arrival of his "significant visitors" the following week.

Within hours of signalling he would comply with Andersson's request, Shultz had to make a more important decision: whether or not to provide a visa for Arafat to come to New York. The PLO leader formally asked for the visa on Friday to address a special U.N. session on the Palestinian issue the following week. So on the same day that Shultz promised he would reply to Andersson's letter, he called a meeting of top White House and State Department officials to advise him what to do about the Arafat request. Assembled around the fireplace in his seventh floor office, he asked each of them to present arguments for and against granting the visa. A majority of fifty-one senators had urged Shultz not to admit Arafat. Israeli Prime Minister Shamir also had gone on record opposing the visa. But unsure of how Shultz himself felt, the officials were guarded in their comments. Only Colin Powell, the president's national security adviser and the highest ranking official there, spoke forcefully for granting Arafat's request.

Michael Armacost, the under secretary for political affairs, and Richard Murphy, the assistant secretary of state for Near Eastern and South Asian affairs, came to Powell's defense. "Murphy said we should give him the visa because otherwise it will tend to change Arafat's behavior," recalled Mary Mochary, a State Department lawyer who attended the meeting. She was the last to speak, just after Murphy. "In my motherly way, I said I didn't think the argument cut that way. I said it would be more appropriate to deny him the visa and give him a goal: if he wanted the privilege to come to the United States he would have to behave appropriately. I suggested we give him an incentive to change his ways rather than reward him in advance." Shultz thanked the group but didn't reveal his thoughts.

That afternoon, against the advice of almost all his advisers, Shultz decided to deny Arafat a visa. The only aides who supported him were L. Paul Bremer, chief of the State Department's counterterrorism office; Charles Hill, Shultz's executive assistant and Mochary. Powell was particularly upset. He had seen the text of the Stockholm Declaration and felt Arafat should be allowed to elaborate on it to the world body in New York. Defense Secretary Frank Carlucci urged that the visa be granted. Vernon Walters, the U.S. ambassador to the United Nations, argued the decision would affront nearly the entire world body.

"All of these people were in a panic that this was the end of our role in the Middle East," said a senior NSC official. Shultz asked his supporters to draft the press guidance and sent it to the vacationing Reagan at his Santa Barbara, California, ranch. Neither George Bush nor incoming Secretary of State James Baker was consulted. When the visa denial was made public on Saturday, November 26, the United Nations immediately announced it was rescheduling the special Palestinian session at its European headquarters in Geneva. Said Murphy, "I saw Geneva as an enormous propaganda circus with no gain for anyone at the end of it.'"[8]

For Shultz, however, the decision was relatively clear-cut, one he felt compelled to make on legal, political, moral and both personal and policy grounds. The Anti-Terrorist Act required that a waiver be refused to anyone who was actively involved in organizing or abetting acts of terrorism. "As far as he was concerned," Murphy explained, "there was ample evidence Arafat had, over the years, accommodated himself to and directed acts of terrorism by units responsible to him. These included Fatah, and later Force 17, which has got to be seen as an Arafat organization."

It was a coldly calculated decision, says another close aide. Shultz felt "we held the cards" and insisted there be "no concessions to Arafat until he met our terms." Few people, even among Shultz's own advisers, were aware that while he took the hard line on the visa issue, exposing himself to a torrent of international criticism, Shultz was privately encouraging Andersson to continue his secret diplomacy. Were the two part of a larger plan to persuade the PLO leader he had no other choice but to comply with the American terms? Was this statecraft at its most cagey or just George Shultz betting his hunch?

As much as anything, Murphy believed the decision was an intensely personal one for Shultz. It was made "deep in his gut,"

Murphy said, at least partly out of loyalty to the murdered Robert Ames and Leon Klinghoffer. For Shultz, "there was something very suspicious and disreputable about Arafat," Murphy added. He simply couldn't stomach the idea of the PLO leader in New York. "It came down to asking that the law be waived for Arafat to be admitted and Shultz said no," Murphy explained.

So, on Saturday morning, November 26, Shultz signed the order rejecting Arafat's request for a visa. The PLO leader was formally cited as "an accessory" to terrorism. In announcing the decision, the State Department said Arafat's presence in New York would pose an unacceptable security risk. Hauser called Sheinbaum as soon as she heard the news. "Well, I guess that's the end of our exercise. I guess I'll never get to the next meeting," she told him.

The move also apparently angered George Bush and James Baker. Bush and Baker feared the underdog image of the PLO leader would be enhanced by Shultz's overreaction. *Time* magazine wrote that "their sense was that he [Shultz] was creating a mess that he could walk away from in a few weeks" but that they would be left having to pick up the pieces of this needless diplomatic debacle.[9] Above all, Bush and Baker feared Shultz's actions would complicate their own intentions to bring peace to the Middle East. The Israeli response was ecstatic. With that single decision, Shultz gained so much goodwill with Yitzhak Shamir and the mainstream American Jewish community that there was almost nothing he could do in his last weeks in office that risked the loss of their support.

"I was very gloomy because I thought our exercise was over," Hauser recalled. But on Friday, December 2, at about noon, Sheinbaum and Hauser got news from the Swedes: the meeting would take place. Anders Bjurner was on the phone. "We believe Arafat will be coming on Tuesday to meet with you. Can you be here on Monday?" Bjurner asked. "By the way, they are bringing a big delegation. You may want to enlarge yours a bit. But be discreet about who you ask."

The Americans got to work. Drora Kass was in Israel. She spent the next few days on the phone to the United States trying to recruit others. Sheinbaum and Hauser did what they could to expand the group. Hauser tried to recruit Martin Lipset, a Harvard professor, but he had a class. Arthur Hertzberg, a respected rabbi and scholar then at Dartmouth University, was jittery that the whole thing would backfire and begged off, Hauser said. They were able to recruit Dr. Abraham Udovitch, a professor of medieval Arab history and chairman of the Department of Near Eastern Studies at Princeton University, and Menachem Rosensaft, national president of the Labor Zionist Alliance and founding chairman of the International Network of Children of Jewish Holocaust Survivors and a member of the Conference of Presidents of Major Jewish Organizations.

On Saturday, December 3, while still the target of derisive attacks from Arab rulers, third world leaders, and even Western European officials, Shultz invited Wachtmeister to his suburban Maryland home. Over coffee, Shultz handed the Swedish envoy a letter. "He asked me to personally fly to Stockholm to deliver it," Wachtmeister recalled. Shultz told him, he said, "I have complete confidence in the security of your communications. But this is too sensitive. Please take it yourself."[10] Attached to the cover letter were two appendices, marked SENSITIVE and SECRET. The first addendum specified the precise language Arafat was to use. The second addendum gave Arafat the precise formulation the United States would use to respond in announcing the start of direct talks with the PLO. All three pages were on State Department stationery. But only the first page, the letter to Andersson, carried Shultz's personal letterhead—THE SECRETARY OF STATE, WASHINGTON—and was signed "Sincerely yours, George."

The cover letter, stamped and underlined SECRET near the top, acknowledged receipt of Andersson's message "concerning the meeting in Stockholm next Tuesday." Shultz wrote that "the attached papers [the appendices] constitute my reply to the question you raised in your message"—namely, what the PLO would have to say and how the United States would respond if the PLO said "the magic words."

Shultz then made three points:

First, that the attached documents were not intended to be "the start of a negotiation over language" and should not be presented in that manner to the PLO.

Second, that the United States "would have no objection" to the PLO's restating "certain positions to which they feel committed," provided such declarations of principle do not contradict their acceptance of the American conditions.

Third, that "nothing here may be taken to imply an acceptance or recognition by the United States of an independent Palestinian state." Shultz concluded with these words, "You may share this letter with your visitor [Arafat] if you believe it would be useful."

At the bottom left-hand corner of the Shultz letter were the words, "Attachments: As stated above." The first page of the official annex provided the words Arafat was to pronounce. On the second page, Shultz committed the United States to respond in this manner: "The PLO today issued a statement in which it accepted U.N. Security Council Resolutions 242 and 338 and recognized Israel's right to exist and renounced the use of force.

"As a result, the United States is prepared to begin substantive discussions with representatives of the PLO. The United States believes that negotiations, in order to reach a sound settlement of the Arab-Israeli conflict, must be based on 242 and 338 and calls on all parties to renew their efforts to search for peace without delay. The United States recognizes that representatives of the Palestinian people have the right to raise in negotiations all subjects of interest to them."

Andersson was delighted. He felt he now had one of the "bookends" in place. Shultz was lined up. In the late afternoon of December 3, Wachtmeister dispatched an aide to hand-carry the Shultz letter to Stockholm. Of course, neither Hauser nor Sheinbaum knew anything about the secret Andersson-Shultz exchange. Nor were the Jewish leaders aware that Shultz knew something else: Arafat would be arriving seventy-two hours later in Stockholm. In the letter, Shultz had deliberately given Andersson the latitude to show his letter to Arafat.

On Monday morning, shortly after they arrived, Andersson invited Hauser and Sheinbaum to his office (Rosensaft and Udovitch only reached Stockholm the next day). For the first time, he informed them, "Arafat is going to arrive tomorrow. He will be accompanied by Yasser Abed Rabbo, Afif Safieh, Mahmoud Darwish, Bassam Abu Sharif and others. I have to announce it to the world today. We have very tight security. We're going to refer to you as 'distinguished American Jewish personalities' but we have to release your names. We have reason to believe that Arafat will sign off on your Stockholm Declaration. It's been discussed within the PLO and it's been approved."

Then Andersson took Hauser aside and told her, "I want to share this with you privately because I know you're very close to Shultz and Murphy. We have this letter from Shultz. It contains the exact text that he needs. We're going to try to get Arafat to issue it at the same time that he endorses the Stockholm Declaration." Hauser immediately told Sheinbaum, "We're into a bigger game than we realized."

No sooner was the announcement made than the Israeli and American-Jewish establishment began their protest. In Jerusalem, the chairman of the World Labor Zionist Movement called for Rosensaft's ouster from all official positions in the Jewish community. The American Jewish Committee "disavowed" the mission, a statement that the AJC later said it felt compelled to make because Hauser was one of its vice presidents. Morris Abram, chairman of the most powerful lobbying group, the Conference of Presidents of Major American Jewish Organizations, attacked the five intellectuals as "willing dupes" for Arafat's latest act of treachery.

Andersson recalls his first meeting with Arafat shortly after he arrived in the Swedish capital: "I took him aside and started reading the last page, what the United States was ready to say. That opened his eyes. Then I told him what he must say. Shultz said you can change the wording but not the content. I told him you can use other words but nothing contrary to what is written here. Then I showed him the letter." At the bottom was the admonition that while "you can let your guest read this letter," under no circumstances should you show it to the delegation of American Jews.

The initial session between the two delegations took place in a small medieval castle in a park in Stockholm, which the Swedish government used as a guest house for Arafat because it could be secured against a terrorist attack. Andersson says he told Arafat on Tuesday that the secret police had seen a car with suspicious plates and wanted him to be aware that the police could not guarantee his security if he went through with his intention to visit the tomb of Olaf Palme. "He just laughed," says Andersson. " 'I'm going to pay my respects,' Arafat insisted. And so he did."

Rosensaft's presence in Stockholm was of particular significance: he alone qualified as a leader of the more conservative American Jewish establishment. At the beginning of the first working meeting, he introduced himself as follows: "I was born in the Displaced Persons camp of Bergen-Belsen. My grandparents were murdered at Auschwitz. I am here as a Jew, as an American, as a Zionist and as the son of two survivors of the Holocaust. I am here out of concern for the State of Israel and the future of the people of Israel." At that point, Arafat interjected: "That makes two of us who are concerned about the people of Israel. Do we also have two who are concerned about the future of the Palestinian people?"

The meeting had its moments of tension. Abed Rabbo, a senior DFLP official, wanted to make the PLO acceptance of Israel contingent on a reciprocal recognition of Palestinian statehood. Rosensaft argued that to have any significance whatsoever, the PLO's recognition of Israel had to stand alone and be unambiguous. In the end, the Palestinians gave in. Shultz also wanted changes. Instead of merely condemning violence, he wanted the PLO to "renounce terrorism in all its forms" both inside and outside Israel. In particular, he wanted the PLO to pledge it would ban "all forms of violence on a mutual basis when negotiations begin." Shultz's intent was to get the PLO to order an end to the *intifada*. In his letter to Andersson, Shultz had forewarned the PLO that "we will not accept counterdrafts." But drafts, and counterdrafts, were being faxed across the Atlantic. He may not have liked it, but he was caught up in the frenzy of haggling in the bazaar called the Middle East.

Important progress was being made, however. The PLO no longer demanded American recognition of its right to self-determination. In October, during a meeting in the Jordanian seaport of Aqaba, King Hussein prevailed on Arafat to drop this demand. "If we're no longer claiming the West Bank and Gaza," Hussein told him, "you don't need to worry about self-determination. It's going to be yours. All you need to worry about is Israeli withdrawal." Hussein's advice to Arafat: "Concentrate on getting the Israelis out."[11]

In return for Arafat's agreeing to abandon his demand for U.S. recognition of the Palestinian right to self-determination, Shultz offered a modest concession of his own. The PLO was informed that if a reporter asked Shultz, he would repeat what he had said at the Wye conference—that the Palestinians had the right to demand whatever they wanted at the negotiating table, including independence. Quandt told Rabie: "That's as close as we can come to recognizing their right of self-determination." The PLO penciled in other changes and gave them to Andersson to transmit to Shultz. Says Abed Rabbo smugly, "We made amendments."

The official PLO minutes of the subsequent top-secret exchanges between Shultz and Andersson reveal that a negotiation took place. "We did discuss the draft [of the annexes] and went back and forth. With the help of the Swedes, we got agreement with the Americans on the following statement that we would make and what they [the Americans] would say." This is what is contained in the annexes marked SENSITIVE and SECRET that are attached to the Shultz letter; in short, what the PLO agreed to say:

"One, in its search for a just and lasting peace in the Middle East, the Executive Council of the PLO, the Executive Committee of the

PLO which will assume the role of the provisional government of the state of Palestine, wishes to make the following additional statement: that it is prepared to negotiate with Israel in order to reach a comprehensive and sound settlement of the Arab-Israeli conflict within the framework of an international conference on the basis of Security Council Resolutions 242 and 38.

"Two, that it is prepared to live in peace with Israel and other neighbors and to respect their right to live in peace within secure and recognized borders [the precise language of 242]. The Democratic Palestinian State, which will be established in Palestinian land occupied in 1967 [the West Bank and Gaza], will act similarly.

"Three, that it condemns individual group and 'state' terrorism in all its forms and will not resort to it."

Andersson said the PLO "was anxious to mention Israeli forms of terrorism." He added, "They didn't use the term 'Israeli' but they had a broader definition of terrorism...that was accepted by Shultz," Andersson said. The PLO insisted its reference to "state terrorism" in the annex applied to Israel.

Apparently convinced that the PLO could not demand an end to the *intifada*, Shultz permitted the PLO to drop his demand for an end to "all forms of violence when negotiations begin." Said Quandt, "Later on, in their notes, they take some pride in saying it was dropped. They bragged to the Soviets that they managed to delete this and didn't have to say it." The PLO achievement was hardly a minor one. Admitted Quandt, "I guess they thought that meant they could keep the 'armed struggle' going."[12]

Abed Rabbo said the PLO also asked the United States to accept an international conference "as the framework for reaching a final settlement." The Reagan administration was hardly enthusiastic about such a conference because it would provide Moscow a prominent role. But that change, too, was incorporated by prior agreement on the third page of the documents. Quandt explained, "It was agreed that Shultz would take questions from newsmen, planted questions." Charles Hill, however, denied Shultz ever agreed to respond to the questions himself. "There was an understanding," Hill admitted, "that there would be Q. and A. that would follow— that we would answer questions. But there was never any under-standing or discussion of who would do it. What happened here is that a lot of the boys who were part of all this were assuming it would be Shultz and they got p---ed off when it wasn't."

The first question that the PLO was told the United States would respond to was: "Does your statement mean that the Palestinians can put on the negotiating table their position on a Palestinian state?"

"Yes," the promised official answer began. It continued: "The Palestinians, as far as we are concerned, have the right to pursue an independent state through negotiations. It is through the process of negotiation and direct exchange between the concerned parties that a lasting result may be achieved."

The second planted question was: "Do you agree that negotiations must be completed within the framework of an international conference?"

The State Department promised it would respond as follows: "The United States has long made its support for direct negotiations clear but we remain prepared to consider any suggestion that may lead to direct negotiations toward a comprehensive peace. The initiative suggested by Secretary Shultz in the beginning of the year called for an international conference to begin direct negotiations. Any conference of this type must be organized well so that it does not become an alternative to direct negotiations."

According to Andersson, Arafat's eyes glistened when he showed him the second and third pages of the Shultz letter: the United States had gone further towards accepting an international conference than it had in years. The United States also had agreed that the PLO could "pursue an independent state through negotiations." For two decades, officially and publicly, the United States had consistently opposed such an outcome. While the Reagan administration continued to deny any policy shift, the PLO now believed it had won something which might prove useful in future negotiations. The green light to "pursue an independent state through negotiations" did not, in fact, go beyond the possibilities provided by the 1978 Camp David accords. "This was not a significant concession. It commits us to nothing," the NSC's Peter Rodman said. "It was a standard ploy: to repackage an old negotiating position and tie a nice ribbon around it." But the PLO contended this was the first time the U.S. pledge was made in writing.

"The Swedes did manage to negotiate an understanding that the other things they [the PLO] would say [about statehood and the PLO governing the state] would not be considered contrary," Quandt said. He added: "What clearly happened was that they [Shultz and the PLO] did negotiate over it. This was the culmination of months of trying to find the language of what the PLO would say and what the Americans would say in response." Richard Murphy agreed that more may have been implied than Shultz intended. "We choked up on the word 'negotiating.' The logic to me is that the original of what becomes a two-page annex is Andersson passing [to us] what they [the PLO] plan to say, and yes, if you react at all, you are 'negotiating' in anybody's sense of the word."

Abed Rabbo said it was Shultz himself who proposed a significant change. "We did not use the word 'democratic.' We say the State of Palestine. He [Shultz] used the term 'democratic' State." A senior administration official conceded the insertion of the word 'democratic' but contends, "Up to now the PLO has been a Marxist organization. Democratic is one of our code words." In fact "democratic" is a code word for both the United States and the PLO. For the PLO, it differentiates their organization from the autocratic rule of existing Arab states. For the United States, "democratic" connotes an ideological commitment to pluralism and freedom of speech.

On Tuesday, December 6, while conducting one set of talks with the five Jewish Americans, the PLO quietly submitted the final changes in the text to Andersson, who said he conveyed them to Shultz. Murphy said the PLO called them "minor changes." Abed Rabbo said Andersson told him late Tuesday afternoon that the changes had been accepted. Shultz was irritated, but wanted to clinch the deal, Murphy explained. "All right, it's your position, go ahead" was Shultz's instruction to the PLO, Murphy recalled. "But just be crystal clear about 242, 338, Israel's right to exist and the renunciation of terrorism. Make your explanations, make them in any detail you choose, that's your business, but if you want to enter a political dialogue with the United States, here's the key; here's the door; it has to be opened."

Although these secret annexes did not constitute recognition of the PLO's right to a state, they could spell trouble for future negotiators because Arafat believed the United States had committed itself to more than the mere opening of a dialogue. Abed Rabbo maintained the United States, at least implicitly, had recognized the PLO right to a "Democratic State of Palestine" with the PLO as its "provisional government." As preposterous as it may sound, Arafat also believed he had won important American concessions. He told us, "I have an agreement—between me and Mr. Shultz. It was according to this [accord] that we opened the talks and the dialogue. If you don't believe me, ask Mr. Baker: Are you committed to what Mr. Shultz accepted in the agreement between Yasser Arafat and George Shultz? Are you committed to the accord that was mediated by Mr. Andersson?" Arafat said, "It is written. It is not verbal. We have official documents from the Scandinavian mediator. I have even sent it to President Bush and I signed it."

Even with the Shultz letter, however, Arafat still was not confident enough to follow through on his promise to Andersson: that he would pronounce the magic words at the same time that the Stockholm Declaration was proclaimed at a joint news conference with the Jewish American leaders. The news conference was scheduled for 2:30 P.M. on Wednesday, December 7. The Stockholm Declaration was made public. But nothing more.

The first signs of PLO retreat were visible during a luncheon that day that had been hosted by the speaker of Sweden's parliament. "The Swedes and the PLO are running around, getting up from the table. It was an agitated lunch," Hauser recalled. Arafat told his hosts that before he could say the magic words, he needed the approval of his inner circle, the kitchen cabinet of Executive Committee members. Therefore he had to return to Tunis. He promised he would say the words, precisely as Shultz had given them to him, from his headquarters there. It was a disappointment for Andersson. But he was not the only one disappointed.

The Reagan administration was so confident Arafat was going to finally recognize Israel and renounce terrorism that it informed the Soviet Union—officially. On Wednesday, December 7, Reagan, Shultz and President-elect George Bush met with Soviet leader Mikhail Gorbachev on New York's Governors Island. The purpose of the meeting was to permit Bush, Secretary of State-designate James Baker and Brent Scowcroft, the newly appointed national security adviser, to have an informal, get-acquainted session with the Soviet leadership team. "Scowcroft told me subsequently they told the Russians the PLO was going to issue the 'magic words' and that the United States was going to recognize the PLO," Hauser said. Reagan, she said, told Shultz that if Arafat fulfilled his promise, the State Department would get the immediate authority to open "substantive discussions" with the PLO in Tunis.

Before he left Stockholm, Andersson asked for a letter from Arafat, one he could show to Shultz. Unknown to any of the Americans, the PLO leader confirmed for the first time that "based on Shultz's letter to Andersson, he [Arafat] believed the Executive Committee would allow him to say the 'magic words.'" Andersson revealed that the letter apologized "he was unable to do so in Sweden." Despite his disappointment, the Swedish statesman felt he had finally closed the bookends. Taking his cue from Shultz, Arafat wrote that Andersson should feel free to show his letter to the American policymaker. Arafat felt proud. He had achieved one of his lifelong objectives: he was negotiating an agreement with George Shultz, the American secretary of state.

The Executive Committee met all weekend in Tunis and finally decided that instead of a unilateral statement by Arafat, the words Shultz wanted to hear would be written into the speech that Arafat intended to give on Tuesday, December 13, in Geneva. There, envoys of the 159 U.N. nations—many of them foreign ministers—would gather for the special U.N. General Assembly session on the Palestinian question. With everything now seemingly in place, Thomas Pickering, the U.S. Ambassador to Israel, told Israeli Foreign Minister Shimon Peres that Reagan had decided to authorize a U.S.-PLO dialogue. The leaders of Britain, France, West Germany, Egypt and, of course, Sweden also were told of the U.S. decision. On Monday night, with barely a month remaining of their eight-year term in office, the Reagan administration, and its chief foreign policy architects, prepared for a stunning Middle East breakthrough.

Tension filled the air of the Palais des Nations as delegates watched the small Palestinian figure come down the aisle, smiling proudly, his checkered *kafeeyah* and neatly pressed khaki uniform brightly lit in the glare of television lights. Fourteen years had passed since the November day when the PLO leader, clutching an olive branch and wearing an empty holster, had last addressed the United Nations.

Mounting the stage and taking his place behind the podium, Arafat obviously relished the moment too. "Mr. Chairman and Members: it never occurred to me that my second meeting since 1974 with this esteemed assembly would take place in the hospitable city of Geneva." The rest of his speech, although triumphant in its tone and lasting for over an hour, was not what others had expected.

"We sat there listening for the words," says Andersson. "Arafat had been allowed to use Arabic and he spread the agreement [on the magic words] into three paragraphs that were scattered throughout his speech. We sat there listening. We couldn't find the three paragraphs. We couldn't find the words. It was a magnificent speech but without the right content. I was very disappointed."

A similar scene was unfolding in a small, private room adjoining the secretary of state's spacious office in Washington. There, gathered in front of a television set in the early evening, were several of Shultz's senior advisers, including Murphy, Armacost, Hill, and Max Kampelman, the department's counselor. When Shultz walked in near the end of the speech, they had already drafted a one-page memo for him. The group agreed. The magic words had not been uttered. Not in Arabic. Not in English.

Instead of declaring that Israel had a right to exist, Arafat had said the PLO would seek a "comprehensive peaceful settlement among the parties concerned in the Arab-Israeli conflict, including the State of Palestine, Israel and other neighboring states. Instead of renouncing terrorism, Arafat had merely condemned it—"in all its forms"— and then saluted all "those sitting before me in this hall" who have led "national liberation movements." Even the acceptance of 242 and 338 was still couched amid the usual demands for an international conference and Palestinian self-determination.

Andersson wasted little time in confronting Arafat in his suite at Geneva's Intercontinental Hotel. Hussein and Mubarak had already called to congratulate him. "Yes, it was a magnificent speech," the Swedish official told him. But he added: "I was very disappointed." Arafat's face dropped and the two started to argue. "If I make an agreement between Sweden and the United States," Andersson told him, "I can't change a comma of it afterwards. You changed all the words." Arafat replied that Andersson had no respect for Arab honor and that surely no one could expect the United States to dictate to the PLO. When their tempers cooled, Arafat asked, "Well, what do you think I should do now?" Andersson suggested he should hold a news conference to clarify what he meant to say. Angrily, Arafat told him, "I've already said it. Read the text in Arabic!"

Unknown to Andersson and Shultz, Arafat had come under extraordinary pressure during the Executive Committee meetings in Tunis. Among others, DFLP leader Nayaf Hawatmeh told Arafat, "You can't simply read from an American script. If you do, I am going to denounce you as an American stooge."

No one was more upset with Arafat's latest evasion than Rita Hauser. She was a guest Tuesday night, with Israeli Ambassador

Moshe Arad, on PBS's "McNeil/Lehrer News Hour." She wiped her brow to show how relieved the Israeli envoy had seemed on the program. "The PLO will never do it," she recalled Arad saying off-the-air. Later that night, Hauser was on ABC's "Nightline." Anchorman Ted Koppel likes to isolate his guests, separating them from him and one another. Even though it was 5:00 A.M. in Geneva, "Nightline" had managed to line up Bassam Abu Sharif, who argued that all the points Shultz wanted were in the speech Arafat had delivered.

Hauser became incensed. "I really lost my patience and forgot I was on the air," she said. Shouting at the enlarged image of Abu Sharif that was being beamed live from Tunis, Hauser shrieked, "Bassam, you have the words. You know what they are. You have them written down. For God's sake, why don't you say them?" That night, Hauser's phone rang off the hook. What words? the media wanted to know. To help her fend off press calls, Phyllis Oakley, the deputy State Department spokesperson and a longtime friend, spent the night at Hauser's home.

By the time Arafat got into his limousine Tuesday in Geneva to attend a dinner the Egyptian ambassador was hosting for the fourteen Arab foreign ministers, the State Department had already reacted publicly to Arafat's speech. Spokesman Charles Redman dismissed it as "ambiguous." That word stuck in Arafat's throat. "He was very, very upset. He felt betrayed," says Egyptian Foreign Minister Esmat Abdel-Meguid.[13]

As he kissed the Egyptian in the entry hall of the ambassador's private residence, overlooking Lake Geneva, Arafat told him he had already scheduled a news conference for 10:00 A.M. Wednesday, but only to vent his anger at the Americans. One by one, each of the Arab envoys—only Syria and Libya were absent—congratulated Arafat and told him he had made an excellent speech. "But I sensed a crisis was looming," Abdel-Meguid said, "and thought if he holds the news conference, an historic opportunity will be lost."

A few minutes before dinner, he asked Arafat to join him for a short tête-à-tête in a small, adjoining parlor. Abdel-Meguid phoned Hosni Mubarak, the Egyptian president, and put him on the line with Arafat. "Mr. President," Arafat said, "I've done what was asked of me. You can't demand more, particularly after the brave stand we took in Algiers a month ago. I spoke of both 242 and 181 [the partition resolution]. That is only fair. I can't do more. I've already been stripped naked."[14]

Mubarak promised he would call Reagan and Shultz and try to persuade them to take another look at the speech. But he also asked Arafat to postpone his press conference until Wednesday evening, noting that if he held it at 10:00 A.M., it would be 4:00 P.M. in Washington, thus precluding the possibility that he could talk to Reagan and Shultz beforehand. Arafat agreed. "Everybody in the world was calling in," said Shultz's aide Hill. "We screened out all the ones we possibly could, but some were people we just could not refuse to take a phone call from." One of those leaders was Mubarak. On Wednesday morning, the Egyptian leader made his pitch, pleading with Shultz. Mubarak told Shultz that Arafat had already removed his shirt. "Does the United States also want him to take off his pants?" he asked. Shultz was unconvinced. "I think the Egyptians knew damn well the words were inadequate," said a key Shultz adviser who asked to remain anonymous.

There was another problem: Arafat was not going to admit he was wrong; he needed to save face. Abdel-Meguid called Shultz: "Suppose Sten Andersson, in his speech today, confirms that this is what Arafat meant to say, that Arafat had explained to him that the Arabic was not translated accurately into English, and that the thoughts spread throughout the speech should have been condensed into a single part of it, would that be agreeable to you, Mr. Secretary?"

Under the plan, Arafat would use his news conference to confirm that what Andersson had said in his speech to the world body was acceptable to him, "and the circle," explains Abdel-Medguid, "would be closed." Shultz appreciated the Egyptian's call but underscored the need for Arafat himself to pronounce the crucial words at the news conference. Abdel-Meguid told Andersson of his conversation and the Swedish diplomat returned to Arafat's hotel suite. He gave the PLO leader an advance text of his own speech and said, "When you hold your press conference, don't say 'We recognize,' and then ten lines later say 'Israel.'" That afternoon, in his speech, Andersson—not Arafat—quoted the "magic words" that Andersson had long since committed to memory.

Meanwhile, on Tuesday night and into the morning hours, Arafat was receiving phone calls from many world leaders encouraging him to read the Shultz script. French President Francois Mitterrand called, as did British Prime Minister Margaret Thatcher. Jordan's King Hussein and Iraq's Saddam Hussein phoned. Mubarak called again. In his suite, where he had been up virtually the whole night,

Arafat also was coaxed by a group of wealthy Palestinian business-men, led by Hasib Sabbagh, Munib al-Masri and Abdul Majeed Shoman, all urging him to say the words. A few minutes before the news conference was scheduled to begin, Hauser received a phone call from Abu Sharif. Arafat was in the next room and he wanted to know if she still believed Shultz would honor his commitment. "You must be joking," Hauser replied. "He's written it in the letter, he's told the Russians, the President was in the room. C'mon!"

Finally, at 7:00 P.M. on Wednesday, December 14, a weary but confident Arafat arrived at the Palais des Nations and went directly to the conference room that had been set aside for the press conference. He smiled at the throng of more than 800 reporters, photographers and cameramen, many of whom he knew, and walked briskly to the podium. Taking his glasses out of his breast pocket, he read a statement. It was in English. He stumbled over the pronuncia-tion of some words. "I announce terrorism," he said. Realizing his mistake, he said, "I renounce tourism." Finally he declared clearly and for all the world to hear: "We totally and categorically reject all forms of terrorism, including individual, group and state terrorism."

He noted that in his speech twenty-four hours earlier, "I referred to our acceptance of Resolutions 242 and 338 as a basis for negotia-tions with Israel within the framework of the international con-ference." He then confirmed "the right of all parties concerned with the Middle East conflict to exist in peace and security, including the State of Palestine, Israel and other neighbors in accordance with Resolutions 242 and 338." Youssef Ibrahim, the respected Paris-based Middle East correspondent of the *New York Times,* asked whether his acceptance of 242 was unconditional, as Andersson had declared in this address. "Of course," Arafat replied. Then he added, "Enough is enough. What do you want? Do you want me to do a striptease?"

In Washington, Shultz convened his inner circle for another informal caucus. They listened to an audio cassette of the news conference that had been forwarded by a U.S. Embassy officer in Geneva. They all agreed Arafat had met the test. It was time for the fourteen-year-old boycott to end. The Kissinger taboos, having been satisfied, would be dropped. Arafat finally had opened the door to a dialogue with the United States.

Shultz, however, remained frustrated. Although he refused to admit it publicly, he resented the brazen effort to squeeze more and more out of the United States. If Arafat could try to change the terms of the accord, so could the United States. Instead of taking questions on the desirability of an international conference and the acknowledged right of the PLO to demand a state, as had been previously agreed, Shultz instructed Vernon Walters to make the first announcement in Geneva. Observed William Quandt, "It was Shultz's way of showing he was pissed off with the [PLO's] playing around with the language."

Arafat did not wait to hear Walter's speech. Leaving immediately after his own news conference, the PLO leader went to the airport, walked up the short ramp of his borrowed plane and instructed the pilot of the executive jet to return to Tunis. While Arafat was airborne, Shultz instructed his spokesman to issue the statement announcing the PLO had complied with the U.S. strictures and, therefore, a U.S.-PLO dialogue would get underway in Tunis. Hill denies that Shultz intentionally underplayed the final scene in this drawn-out drama in order to spite Arafat and the PLO. "Everyone assumes that this was such a big deal that he'd go down and make a big press conference out of it," the former Shultz aide said.

It was not that way at all, Hill said. "In the last hours of this, it was extremely fast paced and Shultz was not involved in it. Strangely, for a big chunk of time, he was running around and I was telling him things. We knew we had to get something out on it within a very short matter of time, minutes or half an hour. He said, 'Here's how we'll do it.' He just did it [authorized the statement] and walked away," Hill said. Before long, however, the television networks caught up with Shultz. He told them "as a result" of the Arafat comments in Geneva, "the United States is prepared for a substantive dialogue with PLO representatives." Asked if the United States had caved in, Shultz said, "I didn't change my mind. They made their statement clear."

When he was asked why, after so many false starts, he had finally pronounced the magic words, Arafat was evasive. He contended that the PLO decision to recognize Israel was made in principle in 1974, when he persuaded the PNC to implicitly embrace a two-state formula. "You will remember that we also said we accepted 242 in the [February 1985] Jordanian accord," he claimed. "We did everything we could to give replies to all the superficial excuses given by the Israelis for not making peace."[15]

Why, then, was it so difficult to say the magic words at Geneva? "It was not difficult. I had repeated those words many times," Arafat insisted. "But the Israelis were not willing to hear me." After more questions, he finally admitted that he had been left with little choice. "As I told you, we were discussing this at different levels within the Palestinian leadership, with our Arab brothers and with our friends all over the world. They said that we had to say it."

A senior White House policymaker insisted that Shultz's denial of a visa played a key role in Arafat's conversion. "It dramatized that the United States had the blocking position." The policymaker said, "Arafat can go to bed with Queen Elizabeth and Mrs. Mitterrand but that's totally worthless to the PLO. They are nothing without a dialogue with the United States and they met our terms for it. It [the visa denial] hammered into their heads that they had no choice but to pay our price. They looked for the least painful way to pay it; they wanted it on the cheap. Shultz figured that out early on and hung tough."

Hauser was more skeptical of Shultz's diplomatic skills. "When I think back on it, Shultz was holding them to the standards of exactitude you would expect of an established state with a foreign ministry and a governing apparatus. It finally dawned on me how unsophisticated these guys are. They're a handful of guys and they meet in these endless debates with Arafat trying to hold the whole thing together." For fourteen years, the PLO had been frozen in time, she said. "They encapsulated themselves in the Kissinger language."

It was Sten Andersson more than anyone who, Hauser believed, had found the formula that freed them. Although Andersson, Shultz, Quandt and the American-Jewish team played important roles, there was a much more important reason why, after fourteen years, Arafat finally took the plunge: the *intifada*. The Palestinian uprising gave him the psychological confidence and created the political imperative to move forward. Palestinians demonstrated their willingness to fight and die for the creation of their homeland. Never before had they given the world such persuasive proof of their claims to be a "people" deserving of basic political rights. In the West Bank and Gaza, they established their own state-in-waiting: running their own schools and hospitals, setting up an underground network of social services and a renegade system of law and order that enforced compliance and brutally punished collaborators.

It was up to Arafat to convert twelve months of suffering, and death, into some tangible gain for the Palestinians—or he risked losing control of the revolution. In the past, retaining his own leadership position in the PLO always precluded taking risks for peace. Now, perhaps for the first time, he had to move towards peace to retain his leadership of the Palestinian movement. That meant he had to take risks. The uprising was both an opportunity and a major challenge for Arafat. It created the chance to move the Palestinian issue back to center stage but also sent an unmistakable message: Palestinians in the West Bank and Gaza were fed up with the sloganeering and terrorism. Neither had helped them end the Israeli occupation. They looked to the PLO for practical steps. Their message to Arafat was "If you are our leader, find a way to act like our leader. Deliver us from Israeli occupation."

Arafat heard the call. Even an avowedly pro-Israeli White House official admitted the PLO had changed. "They have swallowed hard," he said. "They have adopted a political strategy: they have repudiated terrorism as much as you could expect them to and they have accepted two states and a negotiation without preconditions."

Arafat concurred: "I am a pragmatist," he insisted. "I know without American involvement, nothing will be achieved. We know America has a very important role to play. Have no doubt. We are not resisting for the sake of resistance. There must be a political process. This is what I am searching for."

The political process received a setback on May 30, 1990, when Palestinian forces loyal to Abul Abbas, who masterminded the 1985 hijacking of the *Achille Lauro,* launched an amphibious attack on a Tel Aviv beach. Israel foiled the raid, killing four guerrillas and capturing twelve others. One of the Palestinian commandos later told investigators he was under orders to kill as many Israeli civilians as possible. Another guerrilla admitted the real aim was to storm the U.S. Embassy across from the beach.

Aware that the raid by the Palestine Liberation Front faction might also have been aimed at undermining Arafat and the political process he sought, Secretary of State James Baker initially sought to give Arafat every opportunity to preserve the dialogue with the United States. Baker called on the PLO leader to denounce the raid and to declare his intention to begin action to discipline Abul Abbas, who held one of fifteen seats on the PLO Executive Committee. Arafat responded that only the Palestine National Council, which elected Abul Abbas to the post, could remove him.

In early June, the Executive Committee met in Baghdad and issued a statement opposing "any military action that targets civilians." It also appointed a committee of inquiry to look into allegations that the PLF raid was targeted against civilians and to recommend what action, if any, should be taken to punish Abul Abbas. But the PLO stopped short of specifically denouncing the May attack and said nothing about Abul Abbas.

With forty-seven American senators threatening to garner majority support for a resolution to force the administration to terminate its talks with the PLO, President Bush decided on June 20 to suspend the eighteen-month-old dialogue. Bush implied that the talks could resume "pending a satisfactory response from the PLO of steps it is taking to resolve problems associated with recent acts of terrorism." Referring to the PLO, Bush said: "I hope they will see in my statement a rather temperate view that, though we are specific in calling for the condemnation of this particular terrorist act, once that is done we can resume talks.... The peace process must go forward and it must go forward along the original lines."

The May 30 incident underscored that armed struggle would undoubtedly remain a cardinal tenet of PLO policy. Israelis pointed to the May 30 attack as a devastating reminder that Israel would have to remain vigilant in its defense against terrorism. Arafat's support for Iraq, following its invasion of Kuwait, also appeared to have put the U.S.-PLO dialogue into a deep freeze. Yet Arafat did not retreat from his acceptance of Israel and, in endorsing U.N. Resolutions 242 and 338, had recognized the need for the Jewish state to have secure and defensible borders. In the eyes of the Palestinians, this was a "historic compromise."

Perhaps even more significant was the fact that Arafat appeared to have accepted a principle that the United States had made a prerequisite for peace since the 1978 Camp David accords: a willingness to negotiate over the Palestinian demand for statehood. Israeli Prime Minister Menachem Begin implicitly accepted this when he agreed in 1978 to negotiate the "final status" of the occupied territories. The Palestinians rejected the autonomy or self-rule promised by Camp David because there were no guarantees it would lead to statehood. Without such guarantees, no Palestinians were willing to gamble on the outcome of the negotiations.

Arafat appeared to have implicitly accepted much of what the PLO rejected in 1978. Former President Jimmy Carter told us, "Arafat authorized me to say that he now endorses Camp David."[16] Arafat even spoke approvingly of what Egypt achieved from the treaty with Israel. "In Camp David there was Israeli withdrawal from the Sinai," Arafat said. "There must be something. I am not demanding a state. I am asking for what the President of the United States already has declared is his goal. I am only asking for what already has been accepted by the whole international community. By President Bush. By the European Economic Community. By the Soviet Union. By the Chinese. I am asking for withdrawal: Israeli withdrawal and the end of occupation."

In fact, Arafat had accepted key provisions of the Camp David accords:

—Direct peace talks with Israel. "With whom else are you going to make peace? With my friends?" he asked. "With my enemies, of course! I have accepted the same thing our forefathers refused. We have accepted the premise that we must live together." Arafat said he was ready to negotiate with Israel or appoint others to do so. In early 1990, he also signaled his willingness to permit a delegation of non-PLO residents of the West Bank and Gaza, approved in advance by Israel, to begin talks about organizing democratic elections in the territories.

—Acceptance of the United Nations resolutions that were the foundation for the Camp David accords. "I am accepting what the Israelis, for many years, asked us to accept: 242 and 338. What is the meaning of 242?" Arafat asked. Answering his own question, he said: "Withdrawal. But 242 is not a one-way street. There is two-way traffic. Peace for territory. Not only peace for one side and hell for the other side!"

—A transition period during which talks would begin to determine the "final status" of the West Bank and Gaza. Arafat no longer ruled out such a period of autonomy, provided the PLO received assurances from the United States that it would lead to some form of self-determination. In late 1989, a senior PLO official wrote the following draft proposal which was communicated to the administration: "If the United States is serious about peace, the timetable [for such a transition] could be six months. To build a bridge of trust, three years would not be totally unacceptable. As an outside time frame, the Palestinians would be ready to consider a five-year proposal."

—The right of return to their homes in Palestine. In February 1990, Arafat tried to reassure Israeli leaders that a Palestinian homeland would not be flooded with millions of returnees, although he insisted that all Palestinians, in principle, be afforded that right. "We regard the right of return as enshrined in international law and in U.N. Resolution 194. However, we are ready to discuss the conditions of its application on the basis of Resolution 194," Arafat wrote in a letter to a global conference of Jewish leaders in Jerusalem.

—Confederation with Jordan and acceptance of negotiations without a predetermined outcome. While maintaining his demands for a Palestinian state, Arafat no longer insisted on such guarantees as a prerequisite for talks with Israel. He said: "Let's leave that to the negotiations." With a mischievous glint in his eye, he asked: "Would Israel accept a kingdom? Or a republic? Or a confederation with Jordan?" Turning serious, he said such a confederation could be "immediate and simultaneous" with the birth of a Palestinian state. In practice, that would mean Jordan would manage the foreign and defense policies of the new entity. The confederation could even open borders between Jordan, the West Bank and Israel, Arafat suggested. "Could the Israelis accept confederation with Israel? I would support it," he said.

—Elections in the West Bank and Gaza. Despite the fact that the PLO still smarted from 1976 elections in which pro-PLO mayors were democratically elected but the results were negated by Israel, Arafat said he supported an electoral process. He insisted, however, that such elections had to be linked to a plan for the withdrawal of Israeli troops. "If a commitment is given for that, all things will be negotiable. We will find a formula and we will start," he said. "Give me a full A-to-Z proposal and tell me if the elections are A, B, C, P or S. I accept Z now as what the president of the United States has declared is his goal: Israeli withdrawal. Elections for withdrawal, as a step in the peace process that will lead to the end of occupation." Arafat added, "I am an old man. Don't force me to self-destruct. I am pragmatic. I am not negotiating just for the sake of negotiations. I am willing to negotiate for the sake of my people."

23

The Gulf War

THE PLO HAD BEEN IDLING *for more than half a year as the peace process wilted and then disappeared in the summer heat. Arafat was wilting too: the PLO dialogue with the United States had been cut off after the May 1990 attack on the Tel Aviv beaches by PLF guerrillas loyal to Baghdad-based Abul Abbas. Arafat knew he had little time to show any fruits of his November 1988 decisions to opt for peace with Israel. His agreement with George Habash had a two-year deadline: by the end of 1990 the PFLP leader would remind the PNC members that Arafat had failed to produce any concessions from Israel and therefore a more militant approach was required. Ironically, Iraqi president Saddam Hussein was one of the prominent Arab leaders who had encouraged Arafat, in December 1988, to accept the U.S. terms for beginning a dialogue.*

But all that had faded in the wake of the August 2, 1990, Iraqi invasion of Kuwait. Only three days later, Arafat rushed to his jet and flew immediately to Baghdad. Once again the guerrilla was on the go, seeking the role of peacemaker, racing to keep himself in place. Arafat was continuing his perpetual-motion machinations. Here was a chance to bring the Palestinian issue and Yasser Arafat back into world view. Yet the chairman faced a major problem: For almost two years the PLO had looked to Iraq to help pay the costs of the intifada, to balance the increasing influence of Egypt on the Palestinian organization, and to gain the benefits of power from the emerging strength of Saddam Hussein. Now Arafat was caught on one side by the PLO's pro-Iraqi policy and on the other by its relations with the moderate Arab states which had long provided funding and with the

413

West, which had recently given it recognition. Typically, Arafat resorted to his old method of being all things to all people. Within hours of the invasion, the PLO leader had devised a peace plan; within days he had scurried to Egypt, Algeria, Saudi Arabia, Sudan, Libya and Iraq, trying to act as a middleman.

The pages of this book were being printed as news of Iraq's invasion of Kuwait hit the airwaves. Arafat appeared in Baghdad, embracing his friend the president, Saddam Hussein. Then, at the hastily arranged Arab Summit in Cairo, it seemed that Arafat had bolted from his friendship with Hosni Mubarak, that he had turned his back on the West and was siding with Saddam Hussein.

We rushed to the telephone and called our publisher. "Stop the presses," we begged. "We've got to add an epilogue." "We'll give you three days," they told us. "But not a minute longer." We phoned our contacts in Tunis, pleading for one last meeting with the PLO leader before the book was bound. Over and over we heard, "We'll see what we can do, but you know he isn't talking to anyone." At last, Bassam Abu Sharif promised he would arrange an interview in Tunis. "But you need seven or eight days," he warned. "He comes and goes. No one gets to see him unless they are willing to spend a week here." We tried our best to explain that our deadline was hours, not days. This was Saturday, and we had only until Tuesday or Wednesday. A Palestinian friend in London who has direct access to Arafat assured us he would help. "Come over," he said, "and I'll do my best to help you see him."

We booked a flight to Tunis and stopped overnight in London, hoping our friend there would solidify the commitment. We arrived at one A.M. and he promptly picked up the phone to Tunis. We could hear Arafat's voice on the other end. "Abu Amar will lunch with you on Wednesday," our friend said. "It is definite. The lunch will be hosted by Hakim Belawi," the PLO ambassador to Tunisia. We went to sleep confident that the interview would take place.

The Swissair flight to Tunis, with a change of planes in Geneva, arrived on schedule, and at three P.M. Tuesday we went directly to the Tunis Hilton. When we called Bassam Abu Sharif, however, we were told he was not in Tunis, but in Morocco with "the president." When was he coming back? "We never know," a polite female voice said. The following morning the phone rang; Arafat's adviser Sami Musallam was on the other end. "Meet me at my office at eleven

A.M." *We did, only to be told that the luncheon had been rescheduled for two-thirty. "Don't worry. Everything is fine," he said. But two-thirty came and went and still no Arafat. It was not until ten-thirty Tuesday night that Bassam Abu Sharif showed up. He had just dropped him off at the airport in Tunis; the chairman was going on to Amman.*

We panicked. Our deadline was disappearing and still no interview. "Come with me to Amman on Thursday," Bassam advised. Could he swear to a meeting? No, but at least there we would have a better chance to see Arafat. We nodded okay and he quickly called his travel agent. Sorry, she said. There's no space on the plane. Nor was there space on any other flight to Jordan. We resigned ourselves to staying in Tunis. Maybe the chairman would return soon. We called our publisher and begged for more time. "Two more days," they growled.

When we went to see Sami Musallam on Thursday evening, he showed us a fax in Arabic. On the bottom was a handwritten note from Arafat. "Tell Wallach to come to Baghdad. I'll see them there." Our hearts sank as the safety of Amman disappeared. Baghdad was not exactly where we wanted to be. But now we had invested too much in this chase to give it up and walk away. We booked the only flight available: seven A.M. to Cairo and from there to Amman. Once we got to Jordan we would figure out how to get to Iraq. We stayed up all night worrying about transportation to Baghdad.

Early Friday we raced to the airport in Tunis and noticed an announcement that a charter flight was leaving directly for Amman. The clerk at the counter advised us there was still some space available. We went scurrying for a ticket.

Happy to be on the plane, we squeezed our way among a hundred teenagers who were planning to spend a year in the Gulf. The plane left late, and we arrived in Amman in the afternoon. Abu Yassin, a PLO official who prefers the name "Mr. Sami," was there to meet us. Mr. Sami had the run of the airport: Jordanian customs officers saluted him and rushed us through with full diplomatic treatment. We were out of the terminal so quickly, our baggage was left behind. "We've got to get to the Palace Hotel immediately," he told us as the Mercedes sped along the streets of Amman. Bassam Abu Sharif was waiting in a handsome suite. He greeted us with only a few words: "Our flight on Iraqi Airways leaves at four o'clock." He handed us the tickets. Ordinarily, an open return is nothing to fret about. In this case, however, we noticed that although we were booked to Baghdad with Bassam, there was no mention of a flight out. Visions of becoming guests of the Iraqi government crossed our minds. "Don't worry. You're our guests," said Bassam. "Everything will be taken care of." We rushed to the car with him and headed back to the airport.

With Bassam leading the way, we were escorted to the diplomatic waiting area, where a group of Arab diplomats, notably the Iraqi ambassador to Jordan and a leading Islamic fundamentalist in the Jordanian parliament, were waiting to greet an arriving Iraqi politician. There was to be a convention of Arab parties in Amman, we learned, and it planned to denounce the American "intervention" in the region. They talked excitedly about the big news of the afternoon: George Habash, the PFLP leader, had arrived a few hours earlier. It was the first time he had been welcomed back to Jordan since he led the effort to overthrow King Hussein in 1970.

Iraqi Airways was using whatever planes it had to evacuate hundreds of women and children from Kuwait to Baghdad and to London. They had dragged out a beat-up Boeing 707, jammed with Iraqis going home, for the Amman-to-Baghdad run. On board we sensed the gallows humor when someone alluded to the shortage of foodstuffs in Iraq. Word had spread there was no longer evaporated milk, bread, rice or sugar. "Did you bring any baby milk?" he asked. "No," we retorted. "What about bread?" His answer came quickly: "You just ate it." Everyone laughed a little too loud, relieved to break the nervous tension, if only momentarily. As the wheels touched down, the steward announced, "Ladies and gentleman, welcome to Saddam International Airport."

Several people from the PLO embassy in Baghdad were there to greet us. But their welcome was worthless, as we discovered that no letter had been sent from the foreign ministry which would allow us to leave the country later. It was Friday, and foreign ministry officials had gone to pray. It took almost three hours of phone calls from the airport before the papers arrived.

Weary from the travel, the tension and the lack of two nights sleep, we climbed into the waiting Mercedes and told Bassam we looked forward to getting in bed. "Please don't wake us in the middle of the night for an interview," we pleaded. Bassam listened in silence. The car sped through Baghdad and entered a walled-in compound. In the *dark we could make out at least an acre of grounds with a swimming pool and a sprawling white villa.*

The car doors were opened. Bassam jumped out and we followed. Inside the house we rushed past several people and found ourselves face to face with Arafat. Exhausted, we pulled out our tape recorder to do an interview. "Please, let's have dinner first," said our host. We walked into the dining room of his modern headquarters in Baghdad, far larger and more lavish than his offices in Tunis. The table was set for almost a dozen people; we could see that dinner would take at least a couple of hours. We brought our tape recorder to the table and turned it on.

----

*S*eated at the dining table, Yasser Arafat says, "I am running very fast. I am running very fast. Believe me; believe me. During the siege of Beirut I was not as worried as I am worried now."

Such flashes of self-doubt surface only briefly with Arafat. But his twitching, a nervous habit, has increased noticeably. The pistol in his holster and the six live bullets perched above it now seem less symbolic and more menacing. For the first time, the reality of being in Baghdad comes home to us. "Imagine," says Arafat, "that suddenly we'll face a cruise missile here, the three of us? Who knows?" Throughout the marble mansion in the Iraqi capital are color photographs of Saddam Hussein and Yasser Arafat, so close their frames touch one another. In one salon a dozen aides vie to flick a remote control, switching from American videos to Iraqi television reports of British hostages nervously sending messages and pleas for negotiations to their loved ones. A young man from Belfast tells the Iraqi newsman that he knows the horror of war.

On the dining table set for the PLO chairman and his extended family of advisers, including Abu Iyad and Abu Khaled, the Palestinian chosen by Saddam Hussein as his personal emissary to Iranian President Hashemi Rafsanjani, are Arab delicacies as well as breaded veal cutlets and a shish kebab of steak. Arafat eats sparingly, using his favorite Kuwaiti honey on some sliced apples carefully stripped of their skin. For Yasser Arafat, there is a bittersweet irony to this Gulf crisis. Throughout his life he has worked to free the Palestinians from the illusion that some other Arabs would be able to win Palestine for them. Now he finds himself tossed back to an earlier era, the guest of yet another Arab ruler who has momentarily clad himself in the mantle of Palestinian nationalism.

There are other ironies, too. As he tries to justify his own support for Saddam, the PLO chairman recalls having made his personal fortune in Kuwait. There, he says, he worked as an engineer for the Kuwaiti government helping to construct the very road that runs through the center of the disputed oil fields. "I know every inch of those seven kilometers by heart. I was the supervisor. I supervised the construction for about six months, replacing one of my workers."

In 1961, when Kuwait called for British, Saudi and Egyptian troops to turn back an earlier Iraqi invasion, Arafat claims he tried to mediate the conflict. "This is a very old confrontation, an old story," he says. When clashes broke out again in 1972, he says, "I took the Iraqi foreign minister in my airplane to Kuwait, where they started talking all the points and eventually compromised." On that occasion, Arafat, with typical theatrics, ordered his bodyguard to carry a white flag as the PLO leader maneuvered through the opposing lines. This time, he says, "I worked to end this conflict from the beginning," and adds that war fever was at such a high pitch that he told the Kuwaiti leadership on the eve of the attack that an invasion was inevitable.

He recounts a tale of frenzied hours spent trying to ward off an Iraqi-Kuwaiti confrontation: "I was in Iraq on Saturday, and on Sunday I was there [in Kuwait]. I advised the Kuwaitis forty-eight hours before the invasion." During long discussions with Saddam Hussein, the Iraqi president was adamant. "We want our rights," he told Arafat. "Let the Kuwaitis give us our rights and that's it!" And he added this unmistakable warning: "If they refuse to give us our rights, don't make the Kuwaitis feel secure about our intentions." The meetings in Baghdad were over at two A.M., and the PLO leader left immediately for Kuwait. Eight hours later he delivered Saddam Hussein's message to the emir, Sheikh Jaber al-Ahmed al-Sabah. He says he warned him that the situation was explosive. "I regret to say that the emir refused to discuss it with me." So Arafat was forced to speak to his old friend Sheik Saad Abdullah, the crown prince who had saved the PLO leader's life two decades earlier when he helped him escape from Amman disguised as a Kuwaiti sheik.

"I told him the climate is very tense." Arafat mentioned three points of contention: Kuwaiti drilling from the Rumailah oil fields; possession of the Bubiyan and Warba Islands in the Shatt-al-Arab mouth of the Persian Gulf, which would give Iraq a deepwater outlet to the sea for exporting its oil; and debts from the Iran-Iraq war. But the emir did not want to hear about it. Says Arafat, "Jaber interrupted and said 'Okay, Arafat, get up.'" Then the Kuwaiti lectured: "What are you doing about Jewish emigration from the Soviet Union?" Arafat says he replied, "I am telling you what is coming, what is going to happen." He warned them that the Iraqis already had 100,000 troops on the border. To keep the troops at bay, he advised the Kuwaitis to "keep the process going, because if we keep talking and negotiating, we will definitely reach a solution. Don't say no. Say 'Yes, but....' If you say no to them, you're closing everything and," he added in an explicit warning that the Iraqis meant business, "you shouldn't feel secure."

When a meeting took place in Jedda the following day, the Iraqis made their demands, and the Kuwaitis answered with a decisive no. The PLO leader was taken aback. Saddam Hussein responded immediately to the no by ordering an invasion. Arafat was trapped: no longer in control of the situation, he was now at the mercy of events. An ally of Saddam Hussein, who had trained and paid for the more than 5,000 PLO fighters in Iraq, but indebted to the Saudis and other moderate Arab rulers who had sustained the PLO and nourished its leadership, Arafat was boxed into a corner.

"To say that Arafat was pressed between two evils is an understatement," says his aide Hassan Khadar. "He is really caught in this crisis. If Arafat stands against Saddam Hussein, if he takes the Egyptian position, it means he is creating new enemies in Iraq." If he supports U.S. efforts to isolate and punish Iraq, says Khadar, he would be playing into the hands of PLO radicals who were already critical of Arafat's alleged soft line towards the Americans. "He had not yet received anything to justify that the dialogue with the U.S. could be productive. There was no way he could now support the American position in the Middle East."

The aide continues: "As for the other devil, if he took the Iraqi position 100 percent, it meant losing the independence of the Palestinian movement, making it subordinate to the Iraqi position and completely destroying his traditionally good relations with the Saudis and Gulf states."

Although it seemed to many that his abstention in the Arab League vote to send troops to the Gulf and his warm physical embrace of Saddam Hussein were clear evidence of a tilt towards Iraq, some of his colleagues, including his senior political adviser, Hani al-Hassan, could be heard condemning the invasion of Kuwait. Says Bassam Abu Sharif, "In fact, the PLO did not at all support the invasion. On the contrary, we have expressed in principle our position: we are against the usurpation by force of any country."

On the one hand, Arafat faced tens of thousands of Palestinians marching in the streets with placards, screaming their support for Saddam Hussein. The majority of the nearly 700,000 Palestinians living in Saudi Arabia and the Gulf, the 1.3 million living in Jordan, as well as the 1.5 million Palestinians in the West Bank and Gaza had long felt bitter towards the pro-American, oil-rich sheiks who had used the talents of the Palestinians to turn the backward, primitive area of Kuwait into a gushing oasis of modern society. Despite the handsome salaries they paid the refugees, the Kuwaiti rulers refused to recognize their need for political rights and citizenship, and they would not allow the Palestinians to be integrated into their societies. Palestinians were treated as second class.

If the Palestinians felt humiliated by these circumstances, they felt despair over the disappearance of the peace process, which began to fade out at the beginning of 1990 when the Israeli coalition government weakened and then was replaced by a hard-line Likud regime. Falling back on old habits, many Palestinians saw Saddam Hussein as the assertive Arab ruler who could save them and win back Palestine: his pan-Arab ideology and rhetorical zeal were reminiscent of Nasser, who had been similarly shunned by the rulers in the Gulf; Saddam's vows to destroy Israel, his threats to use chemical weapons if attacked by the Jewish state and his brazen stance towards the United States glorified his heroic image.

On the other hand, the Palestinians quickly felt the impact of the invasion as thousands of them in Kuwait lost their jobs and their homes. "Don't forget the contributions to their families in the occupied territories—$140 million per month was being transferred from Kuwait," moaned Arafat. Once again they were refugees, victims of the Arab ruler who had promised them paradise. They could look for monetary help neither to Saddam, whom they had supported, nor to the Saudis, whom they had snubbed.

Yasser Arafat knew well that the power of the PLO lay as much in its financial strength as in its popular support. Without control of the money, Arafat is fond of saying, there is no control of power. Although PLO officials claim that Iraq was paying $4 million a month to help fuel the *intifada,* much of the organization's money has come from Saudi Arabia, which together with the Gulf states financed most of the PLO operating budget of some $350 million a year. No wonder that while Arafat was hugging Saddam Hussein, the chairman of the Palestine National Fund, Jaweed al-Ghussein, was condemning the aggression of the Iraqi leader. Once again Arafat tried to speak with multiple tongues, addressing opposing audiences. But this time the world saw his embrace of Saddam Hussein as putting him squarely in the Iraqi camp.

Now Arafat takes quiet pride in what Saddam has accomplished, particularly his deliberate linking of the Gulf crisis to the Israeli occupation of the West Bank and Gaza. Although the linkage is rejected by the Bush administration, Arafat calls it important for the Palestinians: "For the first time [an Arab leader] has connected oil with our cause. This is a unique chance for the Palestinians."

In Arafat's eyes, Saddam Hussein seems to have achieved in a few weeks what the *intifada* failed to do in three years. By creating a crisis that has brought the world to the brink of war, the Iraqi leader has forced the Middle East, and the Palestinian issue at its heart, to the top of the agenda of the two superpowers. Now, Arafat says, there is general agreement that an international conference, sponsored by the United Nations, ultimately will be needed to deal with all unresolved tensions. "Don't forget," he wags his finger, "in December 1988 Saddam Hussein supported me. He accepted the Palestinian peace initiative, the Palestinian-Jordanian accord [1985–86] and he supported Shultz publicly.

"I have declared from the beginning in my peace initiative that I accept a two-state solution according to U.N. Resolutions 242 and 338. I am still committed to what I declared, and not only me but the whole Arab world has adopted the Palestinian peace initiative," he says.

But Arafat has hardened his stance. He says he is still willing to approve a Palestinian delegation for peace talks with Israel and for scheduling elections in the West Bank and Gaza, but the PLO must be represented and the talks must take place under the aegis of the international conference. "Why go lower than that? Why do I have to retreat?" he demands. The bitterness surfaces again. "I can't forget that since I declared my initiative two years ago, there has been no satisfactory response. While I am offering a peaceful solution, nothing from the Americans, and from the Israeli government complete rejection."

Pressed to explain why he is playing with fire by supporting Saddam Hussein, Arafat answers, "Don't forget that he is giving us hope for making something concrete for our cause, especially after the American dialogue was suspended and the Israeli rejection. Why didn't Bush become more even-handed with the Israelis and their raids against my people? Are they blue bloods?" he asks bitterly.

"I will tell you a story," says Arafat. "When this armada arrived in the Gulf, I went to see Saddam. He said, 'Remind me of what you mentioned to me during the siege of Beirut.' I said I mentioned many things. He said, 'No, you said you smelled the breath of paradise. I am like you,' Saddam said, 'I am smelling the breath of paradise.'" Adds the PLO chairman, "This is the martyrdom spirit brought on by this siege."

Asked whether this crisis is an even bigger threat to his survival than Black September in 1970–71 and the Israeli bombardment of Beirut in 1982, Arafat admits the stakes are much higher. "How can you speak of any peace initiative while the drums of war are beating in the whole area? There will be no winner in this next war.... The whole area from Israel to Saudi Arabia to Jordan to Lebanon to Iraq and maybe the whole Gulf will be aflame.... Don't forget that I am a man of history."

There is little hint, however, that Arafat's leadership or his era in history is coming to an end, except for the fact that he is running so hard to stay in place. For the moment Arafat's priorities will be just that: to survive in his own deeply splintered organization. But the strains show as he adds suddenly, "I don't care whether I continue as chairman of the PLO or not. Tell Mubarak I would like to see them appoint another man instead of me! I am ready to give my life for the sake of my people to be free in their free land."

By embracing Saddam Hussein, who he calls "a calculator, no a computer," Arafat is gambling, risking the moral high ground he had begun to claim. Like the Kuwaitis, Arafat's cause was to champion the right of any people to resist occupation. Now, despite his protestations, his mediation seems to many an excuse to avoid taking a stand on principle. "It is not a matter of condemning the invasion," he insists. "It is a matter of how to resolve it." But in assuming an allegedly neutral position, even Arafat can't hide the reality that the gains he has made in the last two years have been seriously jeopardized.

A consensus was growing in the West, and more significantly in Israel itself, that if the Palestinian problem were solved, Israel would find its rightful and permanent place in the Middle East. But Israelis now question if the Palestinian problem were resolved tomorrow, and the Palestinians were given their ministate alongside Israel, whether or not any guarantees could exist to protect them against the aggression of a Saddam Hussein or any other Moslem leader who aspires to become the idol of the Arab masses.

To Israelis, the Iraqi invasion of Kuwait has made Arafat seem more threatening than ever. To those American Jews who believed he was sincere, he seems more hypocritical. In the eyes of two of his strongest Arab supporters, Egypt and Saudi Arabia, he seems less trustworthy and has given them reason to help others reclaim the mantle of Palestinian leadership. In the eyes of the American government, he has undermined chances for an early resumption of the official dialogue. But in his own eyes he has aligned himself with two of the most potent forces in the Arab world, Islamic fundamentalism and Arab nationalism, and has remained true to the Palestinian cause.

Arafat may find some justification in blaming Israeli intransigence for his predicament, and he may be more right than wrong in accusing the United States, when it broke off the dialogue, of playing into the hands of extremists such as Abul Abbas, who wanted to sabotage the peace process. But the bearded revolutionary, the leader who has so successfully preyed on the conscience of the world to publicize the suffering of the Palestinians, now seems, like them, a victim of events that neither he nor they can control. Without the credibility that was beginning to be his, Yasser Arafat is now counting on the success of a much larger figure in the radical Arab world, one whose own survival is in serious jeopardy. Arafat is once again, as in 1948, 1967 and 1973, at the mercy of events far beyond his control, pressured by individuals whose interests are far broader than his, forced to make choices he either cannot or will not make.

There is almost a sixth sense—what Arafat himself in earlier times described as his "dog sense"—that tells him he may be risking his career by this alliance with Saddam Hussein. "I have tied myself to an Arab solution with the future of my nation so that it can continue for new generations," he says, with a tinge of regret in his voice. Nevertheless, whether he survives or not, the Palestinian nationalism which he has fostered, and for which he has been the symbol, will remain a potent force.

When he stands at the end of the interview, the signs of age seem more apparent. There are red patches on his hands, and he seems to have some difficulty moving his joints. "I have burned my hand," he says, blaming it on the "ultraviolet machine, ultraviolet lights. Every time I am using it, I am doing this. The doctor said not more than two minutes but..." Arafat says it comes from lack of sunshine and vitamin E. Explains a friend, "He's been all his life in hiding."

With that, the PLO chairman has decided he has replied to enough questions, even in the eery stillness of the Baghdad night. The phoenix rises brusquely from the table and strides into his office. Never forgetting that he is a master P.R. man, he takes off his *kafeeyah*, asks his guest whether he wants it, and instructs an aide to bring a fountain pen. He signs it, and is about to present it when he recalls that he has not dated it. With his flourishing scrawl he inscribes the date:

Baghdad
September 15
1990

Postscript.

Four days later the phone rings in our hotel room in Baghdad, telling us to be ready in twenty minutes. "The president wants to take you with him on his plane." "Where is he going?" we ask. "They don't tell us," is the answer. A few minutes later we are downstairs in the lobby of the Babylon Hotel.

We are driven to Arafat's house and asked to join him for breakfast. The lavish spread of food would make many in Baghdad tearful. Outside in the real world, bread has virtually disappeared from the stores, even from the city's five-star hotels.

Arafat is unusually upbeat. Asked if there still are chances for avoiding war in the Persian Gulf, he replies, "If there is a will, there is a way. There can still be a political solution." At the signal that the motorcade is ready to roll, Arafat stands and motions everyone to their cars. Outdoors, under an already blazing sun, the PLO aides who will remain behind stand in a semicircle to bid their leader farewell. Arafat shakes each hand and kisses each of the diplomats. He salutes the soldiers of the Palestine Liberation Army and walks toward one of the limousines. The convoy of thirteen vehicles, eight Mercedes, a Chevrolet, several Japanese cars and a Toyota four-wheel Land Cruiser, packed with automatic machine guns, silently rolls through the electronically operated gates. There are no sirens, no motorcycle escorts, almost no noise whatsoever—just the sound of the convoy speeding its way to Saddam International Airport. The motorcade sweeps onto a special VIP ramp and right onto the runway, where a shiny new, green and white Gulfstream II Executive Jet with Dallas, Texas, markings, waits. It is one of four in the personal fleet of the Libyan ruler Muammar Qadaffi.

Inside we are shown to seats in the tiny first-class compartment. Sitting in the seat across from us is the PLO chairman. As he snaps his seatbelt shut, he says that he often uses the Libyan jet as well as those from other Arab countries. He boasts that when he went to Austria to attend the funeral of "my good friend Bruno Kreisky, I used a Saudi plane, a Gulfstream III. I have no trouble with my communications or my transportation."

We ask if he is still in contact with Saudi King Fahd and Egyptian President Hosni Mubarak. "Do you think it is an obstacle for me?" he asks. "You don't understand the realities in this part of the world. I received an official message from King Fahd yesterday," he says, and after the crisis is over, "we'll sit around a cup of tea and solve all the problems. This," explains Arafat, "is the Arab mentality." Arafat says his personal envoy was received by both nations last week. Are you able to phone them? Will they talk to you? he is asked. "I use the phone rarely, because it is an open line. My *sacrephone*," he says of the French cellular mobile phone, talking about it as if he were holding an infant in his arms, "my *sacrephone*. I haven't my *sacrephone*. It is for secret dialogues," he says, revealing once again his love for advanced technological products.

Switching the subject, he asks when President Bush is going to attack Kuwait or Iraq. Before we have a chance to respond, he offers his own prediction: that the attack will either come in the next twelve days or not until November. Why, we wonder, is he so confident? "You know, it's a very important election in your country: the whole Congress and one third of the Senate." When it is pointed out to him that his credibility in the United States, particularly among American Jews, is at an all-time low, Arafat nods. "Butcher Bedfellows," he says. "I read it." Asked if that nickname disturbs him, he winces and replies: "If there is a solution, they will understand. If there is a war, they will understand." Then apparently letting some of the anger out, he adds, "After the third day, they will understand what is the meaning of war. There will be no winners in this next war. Those clapping for the drums of war will be the victims—all of us."

The Gulfstream begins its descent over the hills of Amman. Arafat unfolds his *kafeeyah*, carefully draping himself in it. As he looks out the window at the sparkling city, he is once again the immaculate guerrilla leader, his green fatigues neatly pressed, his black boots polished to a high shine and his pistol in its holster accompanied by gleaming brass bullets. Stepping off the plane and onto a red carpet lined with a Jordanian color guard in red berets, Arafat seems more at home. The color guard snaps to attention. Saluting the troops, he embraces Marwan Kassem, the Jordanian foreign minister, and walks to the VIP reception lounge. With Abu Iyad at his side, Arafat is seated next to Kassem and the Jordanian protocol chief. Smiles and handshakes are exchanged as flashbulbs pop and television cameras record the official welcome. Here, in the one Arab country with more Palestinians than all the others combined, Yasser Arafat, the man without a country, is still received as a head of state.

VI

The Road to Peace

24

Oslo to Hebron:
Handshakes and Heartaches

Yasser Arafat was smiling broadly as he reached out for the Israeli prime minister's arm. Yitzhak Rabin was hunched over a little, his head tilted, his manner spelling reluctance, even resistance, a frown on his face. Agonized as he was, Rabin knew he could not shirk the obligatory handshake. As he haltingly grasped Arafat's arm, we recalled what the PLO leader had told us during our final interview with him in Tunis three years earlier: "I am searching for a new De Gaulle to come and sign the peace of courageous men for the sake of new generations of Israelis and for the sake of our new generations, for their children and for ours." Just as Richard Nixon had been able to go to China and Charles De Gaulle had withdrawn French troops from Algeria, Arafat had repeatedly told us that peace would never become a reality until Israel produced a similarly courageous leader, a hawk who had the domestic credentials to persuade his own public to take risks for peace.

Here, on the South Lawn of the White House on an unusually hot

September day, as a group of children, Israeli, Egyptian and Palestinian, in the Seeds of Peace program joined former American presidents and potentates from 150 nations, we longed for the chance to ask him whether he had finally found his De Gaulle. As Arafat strode past us, he reached behind the roped-off cordons and clasped John's hand, momentarily holding it aloft with his own. "Is Rabin the Israeli De Gaulle?" we asked. "Aaah, you remembered," Arafat replied, as evasive as ever but with a noticeable twinkle in his eye.

Later that day, Arafat seemed relieved as he spoke with us about his emotions. "We have done it. We have done it," he said, "despite all the challenges, all the difficulties, all the pain and all the sacrifices—our casualties, our martyrs, our freedom fighters. It wasn't easy to implement on the ground our dream from the past." For the bearded revolutionary, September 13, 1993, would be forever etched as the day when the president of the United States and the prime minister of Israel witnessed the baptism of a new Palestinian baby. "Here in the Gaza Strip and Jericho will be the area for us to establish our National Authority," said Arafat. "It is a historic moment, not for myself," he said with false modesty, "but for my people and the Israeli people."[1]

In fact, he said, it was the culmination of a policy he had fought hard to persuade the Palestine National Council, the PLO's parliament-in-exile, to adopt in 1974 when it voted to seek a political settlement of the violent Palestinian-Israeli struggle. At Arafat's urging, the PNC had adopted a resolution declaring that the Palestinian "national authority" would be established "on any piece of land" from which Israel withdrew. The Palestinian move signaled the first implicit recognition of Israel.

Arafat confided to us that it was Egypt's Anwar Sadat who had first persuaded him to pursue a political settlement. Shortly after Sadat himself had negotiated Egypt's initial troop disengagement accord with Israel in 1973, he told the PLO leader, "There is this train. It is called a political settlement. If you move, you're okay. But if you stay at the station, the train is not coming back to pick you up. You have to restructure yourself to fit into the approaching negotiations." Arafat returned from his meeting with Sadat to tell his people that both Egypt and Syria were already engaged in indirect talks with Israel through the shuttle diplomacy of Henry Kissinger. "We cannot stay behind. If we are not at the table, we'll be out of the door.

We have to scramble to get to the table. We can be under the table, but we have to be there," Arafat recalled. "So we went back and drafted the ten-point PNC program." He underscored the significance of the 1974 shift. "There was going to be a political settlement. In a political settlement, you don't have liberation. You don't have all of Palestine. You have parts of Palestine. Now, after nineteen years, we have it in the agreement. At last we did it," he sighed.[2]

Despite Rabin's noticeable aversion for Arafat, and Arafat's reluctance to compare him to De Gaulle, Rabin and Arafat have much in common. Born seven years and less than seven miles apart, both men set out to become engineers and aspired to study in the United States. Politics changed their careers. Indeed, both men carried out a lifelong struggle against what the other represented, yet the seeds of their opposition lay buried in the same soil. They fought for the same cause: a secure homeland. They played crucial roles in the same events, the same disappointments, the same victories, but on opposite sides—lives tied by their plight but forever divided by it.

In 1940 Rabin enrolled at the University of California at Berkeley where he had received a scholarship in hydraulic engineering, but he left to join the Palmach, the underground paramilitary force fighting the British to secure Israel's independence. Eventually Rabin became head of the Palmach and was even imprisoned for six months for alleged terrorist activity.

Arafat also wanted to study in the United States, but he, too, joined covert operations against the British. After his graduation as an engineer from Cairo University, he went to work for the Kuwaiti Government. It was in Kuwait that he helped establish Fatah, which also was involved in terrorist activity. But as an engineer, he planned the road through the Rumailah oil fields that thirty-five years later became a major irritant in Kuwait's relation with Iraq and helped ignite the Iraqi invasion and the Gulf War.

Indeed, the road to the historic handshake at the White House began in the aftermath of Iraq's invasion of Kuwait in August 1990. Many of the reasons why the September 13, 1993, agreement occurred when it did can be traced to the Gulf War. It produced profound strategic and geopolitical changes in the region. The defeat of Israel's most powerful enemy by a coalition that included both the United States and the Soviet Union and every major Arab state (with the exception of Jordan, which remained neutral) greatly enhanced

Israel's sense of security. Never before had Egypt, Syria and Saudi Arabia joined forces with the Persian Gulf sheikdoms to combat a former Arab ally.

Israel gained three immediate benefits from the allied victory: the Iraqi threat, including its nuclear potential, was removed; the PLO, which was publicly perceived as siding with Saddam Hussein, was discredited in the West and among its former Arab supporters; and Israel's alliance with the United States was bound tighter than ever. But there was also another by-product of the war for Israel that created a new reality in the region and set the stage for subsequent direct talks in Madrid between the Jewish nation and each of its Arab adversaries. By resisting the temptation to retaliate against the Iraqi Scud missile attacks, the Israeli government tacitly helped the U.S.-led coalition to remain intact and earned IOUs from both its Arab neighbors and the United States.

By striking at Israel's civilian population, Saddam Hussein clearly hoped to involve Israel in the war. Had Israel retaliated against Iraq, it is unlikely that Egypt, Saudi Arabia and Syria—which all have sizable populations of Islamic fundamentalists—would have been able to resist the pressure to abandon the war against Iraq. Indeed, it was Saddam Hussein's goal to transform the conflict from one over Iraq's aggression into a more conventional war to repel an Israeli attack against a neighboring Arab state. Threatened as they would have been by mass protest marches against their regimes, these Arab leaders would eventually have quit the coalition. When Israel refrained (after strenuous arm-twisting by Deputy Secretary of State Lawrence Eagleburger) from providing Iraq with the pretext to turn its invasion of Kuwait into an Israeli-Arab war, the Jewish nation tacitly became an ally of its bitterest foes. Whether they acknowledged it publicly or not, these Arab leaders understood that "the enemy (Israel) of my enemy (the Islamic fundamentalists) is my friend" and that the nature of the struggle in the Middle East was changing.

If Israel felt more secure, the PLO certainly felt weaker and more vulnerable as a result of the Iraqi defeat. Saudi Arabia and Kuwait, which expelled 300,000 Palestinians in the wake of the war, also suspended their payments (estimated at $133 million, or two-thirds of the annual PLO budget) gleaned from the taxes on these expatriate workers who were no longer welcome in their kingdoms. Without work, the Palestinians also no longer sent remittances (estimated at

$400 million annually) to their families in the West Bank and Gaza, depriving the PLO of additional income. As a result, the PLO had to shut down newspapers, health clinics, social welfare centers and hospitals.[3] There was little money to pay the monthly stipends to the widows of martyrs (estimated at 90,000) who had given their lives during the *intifada* and in earlier stages of the Palestinian liberation struggle. Arafat even complained to us that he no longer could pay the salaries of bodyguards for some of his key lieutenants.

Politically as well as financially, the PLO was hemorrhaging. The *intifada*, the Palestinian uprising in the territories, had made heroes of the local Palestinian leadership, who now felt they deserved at least an equal role with Tunis in negotiating on behalf of the two million Palestinians living under Israeli occupation. Some Arab leaders who disliked Arafat's style of leadership became entranced with the prospect that an alternative leadership might emerge to challenge his authority. To make matters worse for Arafat, his chosen heir to the PLO leadership, Salah Khalaf (Abu Iyad), was murdered by an Iraqi-based assassin backed by Abu Nidal, who had infiltrated Abu Iyad's security force.

No one was more aware of the shift in the regional balance of power than Yitzhak Rabin. He told an audience at Tel Aviv University's Jaffe Center for Strategic Studies that "I am convinced our deterrent capability has increased as a result of the crisis in the Gulf." He cited "the fact that this time the United States stood firm and was ready to become involved against an aggression in the Middle East" as the principal reason for Israel's heightened sense of security.[4] Arab leaders also had new appreciation for the U.S. decisiveness. "American credibility is higher now than it has been since the end of World War II because the United States has proven that it stands by its friends," explained Aaron Miller, a senior aide to Secretary of State James Baker. He said that Israel, Saudi Arabia and Kuwait "all know that we made good on our promises and that this was not a precedent for being trigger-happy. The United States tried diplomacy first, but American weapons worked. The ideology of winning," Miller added, "transcends politics: winning means power and power generates respect—not love—but respect."[5] In the wake of its victory in the Gulf War, the United States would soon use its new power to translate the gains made on the battlefield into diplomatic breakthroughs on the ground.

George Bush spoke of a "new world order" that had emerged from

Iraq's defeat and the allied victory in Kuwait. Together with Russia, America would become more active as the behind-the-scenes broker in resolving regional disputes. In the Middle East, it was abundantly clear that the traditional order had received some shocks. For the first time the radicals were in retreat: Libya had been marginalized, the PLO was vulnerable and Syria had lost its principal benefactor, the Soviet Union. Without these threats hanging over them and sensing that something new might emerge from this alignment of Arab states with Israel, Baker felt he could persuade the moderate Arab leaders to sit down with the Israelis at the negotiating table. The result was the Madrid Peace Conference in October 1991. The hard-line government of Yitzhak Shamir agreed to attend only if the PLO was not present. The Palestinians could participate but only as part of a Jordanian delegation made up of Palestinian resident of East Jerusalem and Palestinians from outside the West Bank and Gaza, "diaspora" Palestinians whose credentials would be vetted by the Israeli Government. Unhappy with this slight, Arafat nevertheless agreed to the conditions, knowing that control of Fatah still lay in his hands and that he would be able to pull the reins from Tunis.

Far more significant, however, than the Israeli-PLO wrangling that overshadowed the summit was the fact that the talks themselves were designed as a series of bilaterals between Israel and Syria, between Israel and Lebanon and between Israel and the joint Jordanian-Palestinian delegation. For the first time, Israeli and Syrian as well as Israeli and Lebanese and Israeli and Jordanian negotiators sat across the table from one another.

Unnoticed but perhaps equally significant was the fact that Madrid ratified a new order in which the PLO was no longer able to make its demands for self-determination a precondition for progress on the Israeli-Syrian, the Israeli-Jordanian or the Israeli-Lebanese track. This new approach allowed each Arab nation to put its own self-interest ahead of the liberation struggle of the Palestinian people, and that, in turn, forced the Palestinians to bargain more realistically to achieve their goals. In a sense, Madrid marked the end of the Arab-Israeli conflict as it had existed in the mid-to-late twentieth century. The conflict, of course, continued, but Israel's traditional adversaries now had more immediate concerns, chiefly the threat of Islamic fundamentalism, which was beginning to loom as large as the threat that had united them for more than half a century: the existence of the Jewish state.

Madrid codified this new order and actually enhanced the prestige of the PLO. Haidar Abdul Shafi, a respected Palestinian physician with former ties to the Communist Party in Gaza, used his opening plenary address to pay homage to the absent Fatah leadership. Indeed, if Shamir dreamed of driving a wedge between Fatah and the Palestinian "insiders," he was quickly disabused of this notion. "Practically every night one or more of the Palestinians were flying to Tunis," recalled Ammon Cohen, an Israeli professor at Hebrew University. The Palestinian delegation constantly faxed PLO head-quarters, but the "most sensitive material they had to fly. The flight from Madrid to Tunis was like a domestic flight. They would go, get clearance from Arafat and return."[6] Shamir, of course, knew the fig leaf barely covered their secret—that the PLO was a party to the Madrid conference.

The pattern was now set. As the bilateral talks moved to Washington, and multilateral talks began in Moscow and other European capitals on water rights, arms control, the economy, the environment and the status of refugees, the Israeli Government could no longer maintain the fiction that it was not dealing with the PLO. Ori Nir, a knowledgeable columnist for *Ha'aretz,* the Israeli newspaper, pointed out that while still refusing direct talks with the PLO, Shamir had tacitly accepted the role of the PLO at Madrid in legitimizing Abdul Shafi, Faisal Husseini, Hanan Ashrawi and the rest of their Palestinian negotiators. This perhaps was the most notable achievement of otherwise desultory months of negotiations in Washington. "There has been a gradual shift," Nir explained in the spring of 1992, "from the PLO being the 'sole legitimate representative' of the Palestinian people to its being the sole 'legitimator' for the insiders representing the Palestinian people."[7]

In April 1992 another incident occurred which Arafat himself concedes had a chilling effect on him. His private jet, a Soviet-built turboprop borrowed from Muammar Qadaffi, crashed in a ferocious sandstorm near al-Khufrah in the Libyan desert. As the plane went down, passengers aboard the doomed jet heard Arafat exclaim, "I'm coming! I'm coming!"The pilot and the Libyan stewardess were killed. For fifteen hours Arafat lay in the desert fighting the pain of internal injuries and multiple wounds. He later said that the apparitions of Abu Jihad and Abu Iyad, his murdered colleagues who had founded Fatah with him almost three decades earlier, flashed before his eyes. Arafat told us that seeing their faces as he lay in the sand gave him the fortitude to survive. "I must live," he repeatedly told himself, "to redeem those dead martyrs and pray in the [Al-Aqsa] mosque."[8] In the aftermath of a seemingly miraculous escape from death, many ordinary Palestinians believed that once again the legendary phoenix had risen from its own ashes. But others said another myth had been punctured: the belief in Arafat's invincibility. The sixty-four-year-old guerrilla leader suddenly seemed mortal.

Something else occurred in April 1992 that would set the stage for subsequent secret talks with the PLO. Yossi Beilin, a Knesset member who headed the leftist Mashov faction of the Labor Party, met Terje Rod Larsen, head of the Norwegian Institute for Applied Social Science (FAFO). Larsen had unique credentials as an intermediary: his organization did research on economic conditions in the West Bank and Gaza Strip; he was on good terms with several senior aides to Arafat; and he had direct access to Norwegian foreign minister Johan Jorgen Holst, whose wife, Marianne Heiberg, worked with Larsen at the institute.

At their first meeting, reported David Makovsky in his groundbreaking study *Making Peace With the PLO,* Beilin and Larsen agreed that the only way of breaking the stalemate in the Washington talks was for Israel to begin a direct dialogue with the PLO. But that was illegal under Israeli laws. Beilin did the next best thing. He put the Norwegian in touch with Yair Hirschfeld, a close friend who taught the history of the Middle East at Haifa University. Like Beilin, Hirschfeld believed Israel had to talk to the PLO. Larsen suggested that a "back channel" be established with Faisal Husseini, the most prominent Palestinian in the territories. His links with Arafat and the PLO were well known and at least tacitly accepted by the Shamir government. Beilin and Hirschfeld hardly needed prodding; they had already established a secret link to Husseini. He had been blocked from participating in the Washington talks because he was a resident of East Jerusalem, and his presence, in Shamir's view, would have been tantamount to acknowledging Palestinian rights to a part of the Israeli capital. Over the next fifteen months, Hirschfeld and Husseini met almost weekly, while Beilin met with the Palestinian every few months at his home in East Jerusalem or at the home of an acquaintance in West Jerusalem.

While Beilin was formulating plans for dealing with the PLO, Yitzhak Rabin was putting his energies into helping Labor win the June 1992 election so that he would become prime minister. Rabin did not make the traditional Labor platform—that Israel had no ideological claim to the territories—the central focus of his campaign. Instead, he focused on three issues: settlements, security, and separation. The Bush administration, in a thinly disguised effort to help Labor, had deliberately provoked a crisis in U.S.-Israeli relations by withholding $10 billion in U.S.-backed loan guarantees intended for resettling Russian Jews inside Israel proper. When Shamir insisted on using the loans to resettle new immigrants in Judea and Samaria in the West Bank, President Bush forced a showdown. Shamir banked on winning the ideological vote from Israelis angered over such blatant U.S. interference in Israel's internal affairs. Rabin sensed that Israelis were tired of the five-year-long *intifada* and that the average Israeli did not share the ideological claim to Judea and Samaria. Rabin's campaign promise, that he would change the national priorities to building more schools and better roads and to improving the absorption of immigrants inside the Green Line (that is, pre-1967 Israel), reflected a growing consciousness among Israelis that they wanted to be rid of the Palestinian "problem."[10] Asked in a poll what their solution would be, a majority of Israelis responded that the nearly two million Palestinians in the West Bank and Gaza should be deported to neighboring Arab countries. But when the pollsters pointed out that such a solution might be impractical, virtually the same number replied: "Give them their own state!"[11]

In devising his campaign strategy, Rabin responded to this seeming contradiction among Israeli voters. He promised a settlement freeze that would permit the $10 billion in loan guarantees to be spent on domestic priorities and that he would, within his first nine months in office, secure an agreement with the Palestinians giving them autonomy in the West Bank and Gaza Strip. As a result of the Allied victory in the Gulf War and the deep schisms it had produced in Arab ranks, Rabin argued that the Palestinians no longer constituted a direct threat to Israel's existence. He acknowledged that Palestinian extremists continued to menace the personal safety and security of every Israeli. But he insisted that the threat could be contained. He proposed a combination of military deterrence and the pursuit of policies that would give moderate Palestinians incentives to begin governing themselves.[12] He contended that the real threat to Israel's security—and to the Palestinians who aspired to strike a deal with Israel—came from Hamas and the Hezbollah (Party of God), Iranian-backed militant groups that advocated the violent overthrow of the Jewish nation and its replacement by a fundamentalist Islamic state. Rabin reminded us once again of the Arab proverb "the enemy of my enemy is my friend." He correctly judged that in the "new order" established by the Gulf War, the "enemy" of the PLO and of secular states such as Egypt, Jordan and Syria was these radical Islamic groups. Israel, therefore, could be a "friend."

Separation was the third theme of the Rabin campaign. Just before the election, Rabin used the case of Helena Rapp, a thirteen-year-old girl from the Tel Aviv suburb of Bat-Yam who was murdered by Palestinian terrorists, to bolster his argument that Palestinian territories should not be part of Israel. "Gaza belongs to the Gazans," Rabin told a nationwide audience in the only televised debate with Shamir prior to the election.[13]

Upon his election, in his inaugural speech to the Knesset on July 13, 1992, Rabin set the tone for his first moves to resolve the Israeli-Palestinian conflict and to seek a broader peace with Jordan and Syria. "No longer are we a 'people that dwells alone,' and no longer is it true that 'the whole world is against us.' We must overcome the sense of isolation that has held us in its thrall for almost half a century. We must join the international movement towards peace, reconciliation and cooperation that is spreading all over the entire globe these days—lest we be the last to remain, all alone, in the station." Rabin promised the Israeli people that his peace policies would make them feel more secure. His tactic was a new one for an Israeli leader: by making peace he would defuse the Palestinian and Arab threat. Asked how he would deal with terrorist attacks against Israeli citizens, he replied: "I will pursue peace as if there were no terrorism, and I will fight terrorism as if there were no peace process." Eitan Haber, Rabin's longtime friend and speech writer, said Rabin instinctively knew from his long career as a military commander that "if you want to make drastic concessions on peace, you must show the public you can take drastic measures for security."[14]

In July 1989, we had been invited to Tel Aviv to brief a senior Israeli official in the national unity government on the discussions we were having with Arafat in Tunis. It was an unusual invitation, memorable for us because of the secrecy surrounding it. After a long wait in a small room, we were led down a hall and ushered into the office of the defense minister, Yitzhak Rabin. He had sat behind his desk and listened intently while we talked. "I believe there should be a Palestinian entity," he finally volunteered, "and full autonomy by itself is the beginning of the creation of the Palestinian entity."

Shortly after the Labor Party won the 1992 elections, on his first visit to Washington as prime minister, Rabin spoke at length with us. When we reminded him of that conversation, he reminded us that in April 1989 he had fathered the first Israeli proposal that would have allowed the Palestinians to elect their own representatives for peace talks with Israel. "I'm ready. I proposed it in 1989. I believe there is a chance. I believe if we succeed in starting this way, many new ideas can be brought up, once we find ways of more limited peaceful coexistence and then realize we are really ready to consider more lasting solutions."[15]

As early as the summer of 1992, Rabin understood that the Palestinians would have to be offered more than mere self-rule or autonomy. He did not foreclose the possibility that during the first three years of interim self-government, Palestinians could take steps towards self-determination, including democratic elections to choose their own administrative council. "I believe," Rabin told us, "that there should be a transitional period in the real sense, with the purpose [being] to realize that they [the Palestinians] are a different entity than us: religiously, politically, you can even say *nationally*."[16] While he clearly did not suggest direct talks with the PLO, the logic of his approach would predetermine his course. No previous Israeli leader had offered the Palestinians the prospect of achieving both their *political* and their *national* aspirations. This was, after all, dictated by the doctrine of separation. A month later, in September 1992, Rabin told his nation that Israel must give up "the illusions of the Greater Land of Israel religion" fostered by his predecessors, who viewed every inch of *Eretz Yisrael* as Israel's biblical birthright. "Remember," Rabin intoned, "there is a people of Israel, a society, a culture, and an economy, and that the strength of a nation is not measured by land, the lands under its control, but rather by its beliefs and its ability to foster social, economic, and security systems."[17]

It is unclear whether the defeat on November 3, 1992, of Republican president George Bush and the election of Bill Clinton, a Democrat, had any direct impact on Rabin's strategy. The Democratic Party traditionally won the support of a large majority of American Jews and thus had a legacy of being less critical of Israeli governments. Rabin must have welcomed the fact that for several months at least, during the so-called honeymoon with the new American administration, he would have greater freedom of action. But my mid-November 1992, the first signs appeared that Rabin himself was moderating his own stance towards the PLO. In Washington earlier that year, we had reminded him that Arafat was no longer demanding a Palestinian state as a precondition for recognizing Israel and for beginning direct negotiations with the Jewish state. We recalled what we had told him at our previously undisclosed meeting in Tel Aviv in 1989, when we quoted Arafat as saying: "Give me a full A-to-Z proposal and tell me if the [Palestinian] elections are A, B, C, P or S. I accept Z now as what the president of the United States has declared is his goal: Israeli *withdrawal*. Elections for withdrawal, as a step in the peace process that will lead to the end of occupation." That had marked a sea change in Arafat's position. Israeli troop withdrawal from the West Bank and Gaza now was the price for peace—a state was not a precondition—and no one was more aware of the opportunity this offered than Yitzhak Rabin. "I know, I know," he muttered when we made this observation.[18]

In November he went a step further. At a luncheon for Israeli newspaper editors he remarked that the PLO was gradually evolving from a terrorist organization into something akin to the former World Zionist Organization, alluding to the pre-state Jewish body which became largely symbolic when the government of Israel was formed.[19] In another speech later that month, Rabin for the first time broached the possibility of direct talks with the PLO. "I believe that among the leadership of the territories [West Bank and Gaza] and outside of the territories, *maybe even in [PLO headquarters in] Tunisia,* there are today Palestinian leaders who have wised up, and they understand that they cannot repeat the mistakes of the past.... There are many among them who understand that it is better to establish the nucleus of a Palestinian entity, even if it is administrative."[20] Rabin appeared convinced that the traditional PLO threat of terror had receded and that Israel had an opportunity to strike a deal because the PLO was weak. While he criticized Arafat for failing to give Palestinian "insiders" enough negotiating authority, Rabin never deluded himself about the eventual need, however unpleasant, to address the PLO at its headquarters in Tunis.

On December 1, weeks after these two speeches, Rabin fulfilled his pledge to Yossi Beilin to have the Knesset introduce legislation to repeal the ban on unofficial Israeli contacts with the PLO. To distance himself from right-wing criticism, Rabin did not show up for the vote. Unbeknown to Rabin, on December 4, Yair Hirschfeld held his first meeting with Ahmed Kureah, the senior PLO official, whose nom de guerre is Abu Ala, to discuss creating a secret link to PLO headquarters in Tunis. Hirschfeld proposed that the Norwegians who had been serving as the intermediaries for his talks with Faisal Hussein in Jerusalem host the new direct talks in Oslo. They would begin on January 20, the day of Bill Clinton's inauguration and the day after the bill permitting Israeli contact with the PLO would become law.

On another front, Rabin found himself embroiled in a controversy that sapped his strength at home. Within a period of twelve days eight Israeli policemen were murdered in Gaza. Yielding to what he later characterized as "bad advice" from his defense team, Rabin decided on December 17, 1992, to deport 415 militants, most of them Hamas agitators. He expected Lebanon to accept the deportees, as it had in the past, but Rafik Hariri, a wealthy Maronite Christian businessman with close ties to Syria and Saudi Arabia, and recently appointed prime minister, refused to take responsibility for the deportees. They were left in a mountainous no-man's land. The media flocked to southern Lebanon's snow-capped peaks to interview these newly homeless Palestinians. Cable News Network even set up a satellite dish for talk-show host Larry King to broadcast live from Lebanon. Although Rabin had intended to end the killings in Gaza by deporting the ringleaders, the unprecedented media attention guaranteed that they—and not he—achieved their goal. They were depicted as starving refugees, an image that created sympathy for them and their cause. In the eyes of almost all Gazans, the homeless Hamas militants had become heroes.

Rabin learned his lesson. He needed to find some way to turn the principal security responsibilities for policing Gaza and the West Bank over to his enemy, the PLO. By unintentionally focusing the world's attention on the Islamic fundamentalists, Rabin had weakened the more moderate Fatah loyalists, whom he was going to need when the Palestinian territories were separated from Israel. As the new year began, even as the secret Oslo talks were beginning to make progress without Rabin's knowledge, the Israeli prime minister was forced to take other security measures to close off the territories. His actions reinforced the public perception that Israel might be better off without them. By the early spring of 1993, Rabin was facing a deadline of his own making. He had pledged to come to terms with Palestinians within his first nine months in office.

Meanwhile, Foreign Minister Shimon Peres had learned of the Oslo talks from Beilin shortly after the first round ended. In February he informed Rabin, who dismissed the talks as a low-level exercise. But Peres, convinced that as long as Arafat remained in Tunis, he would try to slow the peace talks, wasted no time in secretly advancing his own peace proposals to the PLO. "I suggested that we propose to Arafat and his staff that they move to Gaza. Once there, they would have the right to vote and to stand for elections; and if elected, they would represent the Palestinians directly in the negotiations with Israel," Peres wrote in his memoir *Battling for Peace.* "My criticisms of the Washington talks were that we were trying to reach a declaration of principles without any reference to specific territorial issues." On November 16, 1992, barely four months after being named foreign minister, Peres used a meeting with senior Egyptian officials to propose a new variation of an old idea—that Palestinians be given control of Gaza. The new wine that Peres poured into an old bottle, a gift the Palestinians had resisted for fear they would feast only in Gaza, was that Israel also would turn over a municipality in the West Bank, either Jericho or Jenin, as a "good faith" offering of its intentions to eventually withdraw from a broader swath of the West Bank.[21] Peres knew the idea (initially proposed in 1968 by then foreign minister Yigal Allon) would have appeal for Rabin, but he wanted some sign of Palestinian interest to make it even more difficult for Rabin to reject.

What intrigued the Palestinians was its emphasis on a *territorial* component in the West Bank as well as in Gaza. "I preferred to offer Jericho as a sign of our intent to continue negotiations, even if 'Gaza First' would be the main policy," Peres wrote in *The New Middle East.*[22] "There were no Jewish settlements in the immediate Jericho area, therefore there would be no need to discuss their fate. We proposed an administrative center to be set up in Jericho to take pressure off Jerusalem, especially since Jericho is not far from Jerusalem," Peres wrote. "Its proximity to the Jordan River opened a preferred solution in my eyes for the future, a confederation between Jordanians and Palestinians."

In March 1993 the PLO, suspicious that the offer was intended to divide the insiders from the Tunis-based headquarters, responded that the proposal, as presented, was unacceptable. Less than a month later, on the eve of a meeting between Rabin and Hosni Mubarak, Arafat sent a message to the Egyptian leader. He signaled that with certain changes, including provisions for Arafat himself to return to Gaza and head the interim government there (tantamount to winning Israeli recognition), as well as provisions giving the PLO control over the bridges linking Gaza to Egypt and the West Bank to Jordan, the proposal might be acceptable.

It would have been amusing to see Rabin's reaction when Osama el-Baz, Mubarak's chief foreign policy adviser, handed Rabin the document with Arafat's assent. It was the first time Rabin had heard of the Peres proposal for a "Gaza-Jericho" deal. Peres subsequently told an interviewer that Rabin "jumped to high heaven" when he read the document.[23] He was particularly agitated over Arafat's demanding control of the bridges into Gaza and the West Bank. That, he exclaimed, posed an unacceptable security risk for Israel because it could no longer control either the weapons or the Palestinians entering the West Bank and Gaza. Rabin was more concerned at the time about potential security risks to Israel than about Arafat's demands to be recognized as the legitimate leader of the Palestinian people on a parcel of land in the occupied territories.

A month earlier, before Rabin even knew of Arafat's conditional acceptance, he had admitted to Ambassador Dennis Ross, the Clinton administration's special coordinator for the Middle East and senior American official in charge of mediating the negotiations, that the five-month-old Washington talks between Israeli officials and Palestinian insiders were going nowhere. Ross's ears had perked up, however, when Rabin, on a fund-raising mission to Washington, noted that only Arafat would be able to deliver the Palestinians because the West Bank and Gaza leaders were too afraid of defying him to negotiate in earnest.[24] Rabin's willingness to acknowledge Arafat and the need to make peace with him "point to the large role that personalities play in peace," said Mohammed Rashid, a key Palestinian negotiator. "Only after Rabin believed in peace did Oslo become possible. We were very worried that these were the ideas of Yossi Beilin or Shimon Peres. One no from Rabin would have destroyed everything," said Rashid.[25] Nevertheless, Rabin emphasized that under no circumstances could he talk directly to Arafat. "Rabin was an incrementalist by nature," Beilin observed. "He did not want a revolution. For him, talking to the PLO was a revolution."

That is why the Oslo process proved so indispensable. It refined the series of Israeli and PLO demands into a "Declaration of Principles" that both sides could accept without betraying their publicly declared positions, so-called red lines. The Oslo accords, painstakingly negotiated over the next six months of secret meetings at the Borregard paper company in Sarpsborg, about a ninety-minute drive from Oslo, consecrated guidelines which both the PLO and Israel felt they could sell to their constituencies. "My authority was to explore, not to negotiate," explained Uri Savir, director-general of the Israeli Foreign Ministry and Israel's chief envoy to the Oslo talks. "I got my instructions from Rabin for my first meeting through Peres. From then on, from the beginning of June, Rabin went through the text of my instructions through his own tête-à-têtes with Peres."[26]

In the end, Rabin could claim victory because the PLO ultimately agreed to postpone any discussion of the settlements, refugees and Jerusalem until the "final status" talks, which were to begin within three years of the implementation of Palestinian autonomy. This was the same time frame contained in the Camp David accords in 1978, and the PLO had spurned it. The concession now angered Hanan Ashrawi, who charged in her own memoir that Arafat had undermined the Palestinians by postponing both issues "without even getting guarantees that Israel would not continue to create facts on the ground that would preempt and prejudge the final outcome."[27]

For Rabin, another PLO concession that emerged from Oslo made recognizing the PLO, and ultimately a meeting with Arafat, more tolerable. While the terms of the DOP stipulated that Gaza and Jericho would be ceded to the Palestinians, nothing in the Oslo accord predetermined that there would be a Palestinian state. The DOP created a timetable for the election of a Palestinian "self-governing council," but the arrangements for Israeli withdrawal were left to future negotiations. "On four of five major issues, they agreed to [things] I had doubted they would agree to," Rabin said in an interview with author David Makovsky. "First, [keeping all of] Jerusalem under the entire interim period. Second, [retaining all Israeli] settlements. Third, overall Israeli responsibility for the security of Israelis and external security. Fourth, keeping all options open for the negotiations on a permanent solution."[28] Rabin could insist, as he did, that on the four major issues of direct concern to Israel's security, he had yielded on none of them: no Jerusalem, no settlements, no refugees and no guarantee of Palestinian statehood.

Of course, Arafat insisted he had achieved just the opposite, and, to a certain extent, he had. Israel's military administration had to be dismantled; thus he could plausibly argue the occupation was finally ending. The Palestinian interim self-governing authority (PISGA), contemplated in the Washington talks, became the Palestinian National Authority (PNA), an embryonic government that had a large measure of control over its Jericho border with Jordan and Gaza border with Egypt. The PNA also would have its symbols of national identity: Palestinian passports, its own police force, the right to levy and collect taxes, a national assembly and, symbolically most important of all, the Palestinian flag flying over "liberated" land, the towns and villages where nearly two million Palestinians had lived for almost thirty years under repressive Israeli rule. What sweetened the deal for Arafat, of course, was the fact that Oslo gave him something that had eluded him throughout thirty years of struggle: Israeli recognition of the Palestinians as a distinct Arab people with him at its head. That achievement, winning recognition as the titular head of state, Arafat deduced, could over time be turned into statehood for the Palestinians regardless of any attempts by future Israeli governments to diminish it.

The final two months of the Oslo negotiations, in July and August, not only involved Rabin and Arafat (culminating in a secret exchange of letters between them) but created the precedents that both governments would use for claiming victory long after the DOP was signed. The Oslo talks were teetering on collapse when the breakthrough occurred. "The talks had broken down. Abu Ala resigned. We were packing. We had sixteen points of disagreement. We couldn't overcome them," Uri Savir recalled. "I went to Abu Ala and said if we can't do the small thing, let's do the big thing. I had handwritten these seven points," including the sweetener the PLO had wanted all along—recognition.[29]

On July 11, Savir presented a one-page paper to Abu Ala listing the preconditions for mutual recognition. He would try to get Rabin's approval if the PLO agreed to these points, he said. (In fact, Rabin had already indicated his willingness to accept the package if the PLO did.) The seven points were: acceptance of the United Nations Security Council Resolutions 242 and 338 ("land-for-peace") as the basis for ending the conflict in the region; PLO recognition of Israel's right to exist in peace and security; formal repeal of the PLO covenant calling for the destruction of Israel; renunciation of the use of terrorism and cooperation with Israel in combating violence from all factions; ending the Palestinian uprising *(intifada)*; committing itself to resolve peacefully all other outstanding issues with Israel; and the PLO was to establish its headquarters in Gaza with Arafat as "chairman of the PLO." "We *needed* him to sign the document as *chairman* of the PLO," Savir said.[30]

Despite the PLO's acceptance of the broad outlines of these seven points, it took a final exchange of letters to break the Oslo stalemate and resolve the two most contentious issues: Jerusalem and the control of security, both internal and external. Neither Rabin nor Arafat communicated directly. They used emissaries: the Israeli was Health Minister Haim Ramon; the Palestinian was Ahmed Tibi, a Gaza physician. During the summer of 1989, when we spent many hours interviewing Arafat, Tibi, an Israeli Arab, was already forwarding to Tunis remarkably detailed plans for a possible settlement that had been authorized by "sources close to Rabin." It certainly was a surprise to us when, in the midst of a lengthy interview with Arafat, an aide presented to him a twenty-page proposal—from Tibi—for devolving authority in the West Bank and Gaza on the Palestinians. Four years later, Tibi was still playing an intermediary role.

On July 19, 1993, Tibi traveled to Tunis carrying a letter from Rabin. He returned home two weeks later with a letter from Arafat. In his letter Rabin attempted to define the security issue as broadly as possible. He insisted on the need for the IDF to be able to retaliate in Gaza and Jericho or anywhere else in the West Bank for any attack. This right would allow the IDF to launch preemptive strikes or to chase alleged terrorists in "hot pursuit" if they sought sanctuary beyond the 1967 borders.

Arafat was just as adamant that the PLO had to be solely responsible for securing their territory against terrorism, suggesting that Israeli responsibilities be limited to "external" security over borders alone. Arafat also demanded that the PLO be able to govern Jericho and Gaza from Jerusalem, the Israeli capital. Rabin countered that the status of Jerusalem could not be negotiated until the conclusion of the three-year interim period. The stage was set for the dramatic showdown in Oslo.

On August 17 Peres flew to Stockholm knowing that for the first time he would have to deal directly with Arafat if the Oslo process was to be saved. An official visit to the Swedish capital had been scheduled for some time, so no one was suspicious. Nor did anyone notice when Norwegian foreign minister Holst, the Oslo mediator, joined Peres, purportedly to discuss an ongoing quarrel between their nations over heavy water fuel for nuclear reactors.

But Holst's real reason for inviting Peres was to save the negotiations. The only path, he believed, was to get Peres and Arafat to talk to each other, despite the fact that neither recognized the other. Holst arrived at the Swedish government residence where Peres was an official guest and gathered Peres's advisers together for a conference call to Tunis, where Arafat was standing by with his advisers. During the long night, Holst worked feverishly with the aides of both men to narrow the differences on security and Jerusalem. (Without an agreement on these, there could be no breakthrough.) Several times, Holst summoned Peres to the phone. But since Peres could not officially speak directly to Arafat, Holst held the receiver for him. "I heard Arafat's voice as it came over the telephone. It was clearly distinguishable as it echoed across the room. I could sense the emotion that gripped the speaker on the other end of the line and the intensity, despite the considerable distance between Tunis and Stockholm," Peres told us. "It was," he noted, "a fateful night when the negotiations could either collapse or end in an accord."

After seven hours, both sides agreed to compromise on the most important issues. Peres conceded that the PLO could control "internal" security, i.e., areas that would be ceded to the Palestinian National Authority; Israel would remain in control of "external" security, the Palestinian-Israeli borders with Jordan and Egypt. Responsibility would be shared for controlling the bridges and border crossings into the West Bank and Gaza.

Arafat had won perhaps his most important victory: control over the territory that would be his.[31]

Arafat, however, yielded on Jerusalem, conceding that the city would be excluded from the Palestinian-administered area in return for Israeli assurances that the Palestinians could maintain Orient House, their quasiofficial presence there. The last-minute horsetrading over Jerusalem was so intense that almost a month passed after the Oslo accords were signed on the White House South Lawn before the compromise became official. Its form, too, was unusual: Shimon Peres wrote a secret letter to Holst conceding the well-being of Palestinians of East Jerusalem was "of great importance and will be preserved" through its existing "economic, social, educational and cultural" institutions. Peres had agreed to write the letter on August 19 but waited until after the September 13 signing ceremony to convey the secret assurances. Under the compromise, Palestinian residents of East Jerusalem were permitted to run for posts in the self-rule council and to vote in Palestinian general elections.

Abu Mazzen (Mahmoud Abbas) replied to Hanan Ashrawi's earlier charge that the PLO had given away too much in the accords by underscoring the "strategic political" nature of the Palestinian gains, "particularly the fact that this agreement is with the PLO and not just a Palestinian delegation" and that they had won recognition "as a people with political rights."[32] Jerusalem and the right of return of Palestinian refugees, he argued, were also issues that should be viewed from a Palestinian perspective: Israel had conceded both were negotiable, even if consideration of them should be delayed until the start of talks on the permanent settlement. "The biggest achievement of Oslo was that the Palestinians agreed to have an interim solution without knowing what the permanent solution would look like," observed Yossi Beilin.[33]

On August 20, in a secret ceremony held in the middle of the night, Uri Savir, Abu Ala and Holst initialed the Declaration of Principles. It was unanimously approved by the Israeli cabinet ten days later. (Two ministers abstained.)

Arafat hesitated and waited until early September to accept the final Israeli conditions. "He was more personally involved in the negotiations than ever before. He spent two weeks closeted with Peres in the end game," Savir recalled.[34] Arafat subsequently agreed that the provisions of the 1964 charter of the Palestinian National Council calling for Israel's destruction would be amended. The PLO would "take part in the steps leading to the normalization of life, rejecting violence and terrorism, contributing to space and stability, and participating actively in shaping reconstruction, economic development, and cooperation."[35] Arafat also acceded to Israel's demand that the PLO recognize its right not merely to exist but to exist "in security." It also promised to prevent acts of terrorism by "all PLO elements and personnel" and discipline violators of the agreement. "Larson told me, after receiving a call from Tunis, 'The seven points are okay.' On September 8 we went to Paris for a marathon session—forty-eight consecutive hours that culminated in an agreement," Savir said.[36]

On September 9 and 10, Rabin and Arafat exchanged a final set of letters. Holst hand-carried Arafat's letter to Jerusalem on September 9. Rabin faxed his reply to Tunis the next morning. President Clinton, who had been fully informed of the accord only on August 27, when Peres flew to Southern California to brief vacationing Secretary of State Warren Christopher, wanted to arrange a public signing ceremony at the White House. On September 9, Clinton telephoned Rabin from Air Force One urging him to attend.

"At the beginning Rabin did not want to come. So Arafat thought, if Rabin is not coming, he's not going to come either," a close Arafat adviser recalled.[37] As late as September 9, Peres and Abu Mazzen were to be the highest-ranking officials. But behind the scenes, Tibi and Ramon continued to try to bring their leaders together. The PLO aide remembers having lunch with Arafat in Tunis when Clinton announced at a press conference that an agreement had been reached. With Arafat also were his wife, Suha, Dr. Tibi, and senior adviser Yasser Abed Rabbo. "We all went down after coffee, about 3:00 P.M., to the small living room downstairs, turned on CNN, and there was Clinton saying that if the two sides decided to come at the highest level, we will receive Arafat and welcome him," the aide recalls. "You see, Abu Amar," exclaimed Suha, staring intently at her husband, "this is an invitation for you to go to the White House."[38]

Arafat forced Rabin's hand by accepting the televised invitation before a formal presidential one was extended. Rabin continued to be reluctant. He was hardly eager to afford Arafat, his enemy for more than three decades, the dignity accorded heads of state. "Rabin really hesitated to go to Washington because he knew there would be a handshake," said Yossi Genosar, a high-level aide to Rabin. "But he also understood that if he and Arafat did not do this handshake, the significance of the DOP would be diminished."[39] Secretary of State Christopher called the prime minister's office to let Rabin know that Arafat was coming. Rabin later admitted that he had "butterflies in his stomach,"[40] but he felt he could not say no to the president, who had been Israel's most stalwart supporter. On the afternoon of September 10, three days before the ceremony was to be held, Rabin personally called President Clinton to let him know that he, too, would be there. Still smarting from his long rivalry with Peres, Rabin neglected to inform his foreign minister that he was indeed going to Washington for the historic occasion. Peres found out only when he heard the news on the radio.

But even the presence of Rabin and Arafat in Washington three days later did not end the wrangling between the Israelis and the Palestinians. "The ceremony was delayed for fifteen minutes. We threatened to pack our bags," recalled Hasan Abu Rahman, a close confidant of Arafat's and the Palestinian Authority's chief represent-ative in the United States.[41] The last last-minute dispute centered on use of the term "Palestinian delegation" in the official DOP docu-ment. Tibi informed Peres that unless it was replaced with "PLO" Arafat and his entourage would head home on the same chartered Moroccan jumbo jet that had brought them to Washington. Perhaps remembering Rabin's slight in failing to inform him that he was going to attend, Peres did not bother to check with Rabin on the proposed change. He signaled his assent, and the ceremony began.

As tense as emotions were between the Israeli and Palestinian leaders who stood together on the White House lawn, relations were hardly better among the Palestinians themselves. Only a handful of people knew just how difficult it had been for Arafat to make the trip to Washington. True, his ideological disagreements with his PLO associates were legendary, and his colleagues' disgruntlement with his conciliatory behavior well documented, but in the last few hours another argument had taken place that, in the context of the PLO, had no historic parallel.

Since 1990 Arafat had been secretly married to Suha Tawil. The marriage was kept hidden for two years, and when it became news, it hit with the force of a bombshell. Not only had the chairman given up his bachelor status, he had married a young, vivacious Palestinian woman who lived in Paris, was a practicing Christian and dressed in designer clothes. The fact that her mother had been active in the peace movement in the West Bank and had been politically close to Arafat for almost twenty years did not assuage the critics. The hard-line freedom fighters in Arafat's circle had no desire to accept their leader's status as a married man, nor did they want him to project that image upon the Palestinian public. In their eyes, Arafat's role as a single man "married to the Palestinian cause" ensured that he would serve as a symbol of the fight to return to Palestine. If he veered from his course, the return to Palestine might also be diverted, his detractors insisting that he was no longer a serious leader.

So upset were some of Arafat's advisers that hours before the flight to Washington, Abu Mazzen, who had actually negotiated the peace between Israel and the PLO, sent a mutual friend to see the chairman. "I hope Suha is not going," the intermediary said diplomatically. "Well, she wants to go," Arafat replied. When Abu Mazzen heard this, he ordered the interlocutor to go back to the chairman. This time the intermediary insisted, "She cannot go. Because if she goes, Abu Mazzen will not go." Arafat turned livid. After all, it was Suha who had pointed out the importance of President Clinton's words on television, and it was she who had encouraged her husband to make the trip to Washington. Naturally, she was eager to accompany him. And Arafat was just as eager to have her at his side. But knowing that Abu Mazzen would keep to his word, Arafat had no choice. He had to yield. Nevertheless, on the long flight from Tunis to Washington, the two men did not speak to each other. While Hassan Abu Rahman and Abu Ala worked on his speech, Arafat sat in his seat and sulked. He was furious, and so was his wife.

When we asked Hassan Abdul Rahman, one of the PLO members who had accompanied Arafat on the plane, why Abu Mazzen was so against Suha's presence, he replied, "His argument was that this is a controversial agreement. The Palestinian people are going to watch what happens on the South Lawn. This is not some sort of social gathering. This is political business. It's not time to celebrate, even for him. This is an agreement that we reached, and it is a tough agreement, and therefore we should not make it a celebration."[42]

The PLO leaders based in Tunis were keenly aware that an enormous gulf existed between them and the people living under occupation in the West Bank and Gaza. The tension and envy were palpable. Those who had lived under Israeli rule for nearly thirty years did not relish being ruled by another outside group, even if they were called Palestinians. They suspected the Tunis faction of being corrupt or worse, of wanting to take over a land that for most of their lives they had not even been allowed to visit. While the insiders had suffered the dangers and humiliation of occupation and even sacrificed their lives and their children's lives in the *intifada*, the outsiders, they believed, indulged themselves in fancy villas and dreamed of glory, plotting how to take over the territories. "We should not convey the wrong message to our people back home," said Hassan Abdul Rahman as he explained Abu Mazzen's attitude. "This is going to be a televised thing. Our people in the West Bank and Gaza are still under occupation. We should not show that we are engaged in any extravaganza. This is a serious business. There is no time to celebrate yet."[43]

But back in their villa in Tunis, Suha was not about to disappear. That was not her style. A spontaneous, strong-willed woman who feels comfortable in the limelight and appreciates the power of the press, she made contact with CNN, and while her husband readied himself for the historic gathering on the South Lawn of the White House, Suha prepared herself for global television. As Chairman Arafat walked to the podium in stride with President Clinton and Prime Minister Rabin, Suha Arafat gave a running commentary on CNN. Looking chic and sounding charming, despite the rebuff, she announced that she had stayed at home to be with the mothers of the martyrs, the wives who were there with her. For most of the world this was the first glimpse of the fair-skinned, glamorous blonde who had married the grizzly guerrilla leader. Half his age and almost six inches taller, attractive, articulate and poised, Suha was proof that Arafat was neither a caricature, as he often appeared to be, nor a clown, as his critics accused him of being, but a human being made of flesh and feelings. As more details of their relationship trickled out, it became clear that their romance was not a public relations ploy by some media savvy PLO advisers, but more nearly a *coup de foudre.*

Suha Tawil had known of, but not actually known, Yasser Arafat since she was four years old. Her father, Daud Tawil, was a wealthy banker from Nablus; her mother, Raymonda Tawil, much younger than Daud, was an intellectual, outspoken and self-reliant woman, herself the daughter of a free-thinking American-born Arab woman and an elite, wealthy Palestinian man. Raymonda was born in Acre, which became part of Israel in 1948, and had engaged in dialogue with Israelis ever since her childhood, when she was sent to a convent school in Haifa. As the only Arab and non-Jew in attendance, she quickly made friends with the Jewish girls, who showed her a life of freedom and independence, quite different from the strict, constrained world of the Arab girls she had known. Several years later, in 1964 after the birth of her five children, Raymonda began hosting literary salons. Jordanian, American and Palestinian thinkers and writers sipped coffee and spoke freely in her Nablus home.

In 1967, following the quick and stunning Israeli victory in the Six-Day War, Palestinian guerrillas began operations in the West Bank, and for three days a battle raged in Nablus. As the Tawils slept on the floor, out of range of gunfire, Israeli tanks rolled up and down the streets, and shooting went on night and day. At home with her children Raymonda spoke admiringly of a man called Arafat, repeating rumors that he was the leader of the *fedayeen* who clashed with the soldiers nearby. On the final day of the fighting, the Israelis went door to door in Nablus searching for Arafat. Raymonda's children were sent to safety in the basement of their house. Huddled with her sisters and brother and their governess, four-year-old Suha could hear gunshots in the streets. Arafat's name was whispered with pride, and although his struggle ended with his ouster from the West Bank, his efforts gave promise to the dream that even in the face of the horrendous defeat, the Arabs could fight back. Less than a year later, when Arafat's picture appeared on the cover of *Time* magazine and in newspaper and television reports around the world, Suha could hardly help but notice.

In the weeks, months and years that followed under the occupation, Raymonda Tawil became more and more politically active, encouraging her children to do the same. But at the same time that she was leading marches and protests, Raymonda was inviting Israeli journalists and left-leaning politicians to join the discussions in her salon. Confrontation and dialogue became her way of life. Along with intellectuals like Herbert Marcuse and well-known figures like Eric Rothschild and Guy Penne, personal assistant to François Mitterand, Raymonda welcomed the French journalist Eric Rouleau, Israeli journalists such as Uri Avneri and Victor Cygielman and political figures such as Ellezer Be'eri, Mapam's expert on Arab affairs.[44] Suha could hear her mother argue persuasively against the occupation and then, just as effectively, argue for coexistence of Palestinians and Israelis. Her mother explained how important it was to describe the Palestinians' plight to anyone, and in particular to any Israeli, who was willing to listen. Only a few months earlier, the world had listened to Yasser Arafat when as leader of the PLO he was invited to address the United Nations General Assembly in New York and spoke about peaceful coexistence. As the unofficial PLO spokesperson in the West Bank, Raymonda was delivering a similar message, and she expected her daughter to do the same.

Suha Tawil grew up in a household that lived and breathed politics. Again and again her mother led demonstrations against Israeli army raids and against Israeli settlers. She marched against deportations and taxes, daringly started the Palestinian Press Service and brazenly served as the spokesperson to the foreign press for the outlawed PLO. But her protests were not only against the Israelis. As

strenuously as Raymonda was fighting the Israelis, she was battling
the Palestinians for the rights of Arab women. Again and again she
challenged her family and friends when they tried to restrain her. By
August 1976 the Israelis had put Raymonda under house arrest. For
Suha, who had just celebrated her thirteenth birthday, this was a
great opportunity. "For me, it was wonderful," she admitted in an
interview with the *New Yorker*. "It was the only time that my mother
was at home—she had always been out demonstrating, striking,
working. But, for poor Mom, she couldn't even go into the garden. I
remember the Israeli military governor of Ramallah telling her, 'You
are not permitted to see the sun.'"[45]

Other parents may have kept their young daughters away from
student protests, but Raymonda urged her children to take part.
Even at the age of ten Suha, a rock in one hand and a picture of
Arafat in the other, demonstrated against the occupation. Marching
or shouting or hurling stones, she dodged the Israeli soldiers' bullets
and suffered the effects of tear gas. It was those experiences that gave
her the same strength and determination as her mother. "If I were not
the daughter of Raymonda Tawil, I don't think I could ever have
married Yasser Arafat. She pushed us all the time—pushed us not to
be passive. When we were very, very young, she made us take foreign
journalists around and show them what was going on. I gave my first
press interview when I was twelve. So, you see, politics and
resistance are in my blood," she told the *New Yorker*.

When it came time to go to college, Suha turned her back on the
West Bank. For years her mother had dreamed of going to Paris to
study, but Daud forbade her to do so. In 1981 Suha carried out
Raymonda's dream and registered at the Sorbonne. In between
classes she discovered worlds not readily available to her before and
indulged in the opera, theater, ballet, film and fashion. Nevertheless,
as a product of her past, she could not leave politics completely
behind. Besides participating in demonstrations against the Chilean
military leader Augusto Pinochet and in support of the African
National Congress, and doing small tasks for the PLO, she took her
master's degree in political science and wrote her thesis, "The Image
of the Arabs in the American Mass Media." It was an ironic topic for
the woman who would marry an Arab leader with a negative image
in the American press.

While she was studying at the Sorbonne in 1985, Suha joined her
family for a summer vacation in Amman. Arafat was visiting Jordan

at the time, and her mother took the opportunity to introduce them to Abu Amar. "I was still a university student, and thought I was terribly worldly and grown-up. But I remember how excited I was just at the thought—the thought of meeting the leader. I had demonstrated for him so often, carried his picture, and been tear-gassed and shot at," Suha told the *New Yorker*. Two years later, in 1987, at the outbreak of the *intifada,* Suha began serving as a liaison between her mother and Arafat. Raymonda had moved to Paris, but with the *intifada* in full swing, accounts were constantly faxed to her from the West Bank and Gaza. While the chairman flew around North Africa and the Middle East, hurrying from Tunis to Algiers to Yemen and Baghdad in search of support, Suha flew after him, hurrying to bring him up-to-date information on the uprising. But Abu Amar indicated he was interested in more than Suha's reports. The vibrant, elegant young woman intrigued him. "If I were younger," he would call and tell her, "I would have married you."[46] Then, in 1989, when the chairman made an official trip to France, staying at the Crillon Hotel, Suha was asked to plan Arafat's schedule. "There was a chemistry between us, it was clear. And in Paris everything came together," she said. "Just like that." A relative notes, "It was a real love story."[47]

They talked, they ate, they talked, and they talked some more. They discovered they shared interests in children, in peacemaking, in astrology. Somewhere, somehow, in their confined courtship, they even danced a tango. She found the chairman "gracious," "gallant," "funny" and "intellectual," far more exciting than the "banal," bourgeois men she had known. Her life with them would be boring. Her life with Abu Amar would be a front-row seat to history. They talked of marriage, and Arafat suggested she join him in Tunis and work on his economic staff. The romance was still a secret, yet a few months later, when we asked one of Arafat's most important advisers if the chairman had any Christian colleagues around him, we were told that there was one Christian he was "very, very close to." When we asked this same man whether Arafat really could love a woman, we were told, "Absolutely, absolutely. I promise you, take my word for it. I promise."

Then, on July 17, 1990, her twenty-seventh birthday, Suha and Arafat were married. Like any newlywed Suha wanted to share their joy with the world. But with the *intifada* still going on, Arafat was nervous about the consequences. "There was mourning at all the houses, there were more tears, there were people being oppressed all over. It was not the right time to announce a marriage," Suha explained to the *New Yorker.* One month later, Saddam Hussein invaded Kuwait. With the world about to go to war, it was certainly no time to celebrate a wedding.

For over a year the Arafats lived a secret life: she, ensconced in a villa, surrounded by dozens of bodyguards wielding kalashnikovs, spending most of her time in a single room devoid of warmth or charm; he, moving from villa to villa, trying to balance Palestinian support of Saddam Hussein against the anger of Egypt, Kuwait and Saudi Arabia, his former Arab allies. By October 1991, when the Madrid Conference took place, word began to trickle out that Arafat and Suha were married. A few months later, in April 1992 when his plane crashed in the desert, their secret crashed, too. The news of their marriage made headlines as large as those of the airplane disaster. The story was broken in *Ha'aretz,* an Israeli newspaper. "I have been looking for a long time," Arafat told *Newsweek,* "and at last I found someone who wanted me."[48] Now the chairman had to balance his love for a frank, effusive and fashionable wife with the fury of his macho, chauvinistic aides. Anticipating their complaints that she was a Christian, Suha converted to Islam, but it made no difference. "I was never welcomed by the PLO leadership," Suha told an interviewer. "I had to have the courage to impose myself on it."[49] She was, however, welcomed by King Hussein. A few months after the plane crash, Arafat was hospitalized in Jordan and underwent major surgery. When Suha arrived to see him, a relative recalls, "King Hussein was really noble. He brought the queen to meet her." The Jordanian king has not been alone in his warm attitude. Morocco's King Hassan has also been fatherly towards Suha. "He takes care of Suha like his own daughter," the relative says.[50]

For Palestinians interested in social causes, Suha's position seemed a blessing. By the time the marriage became public, she was scheduling some of Arafat's interviews, arranging meetings and influencing his agenda. Health care, hospitals and women's rights are high up on her list of priorities. And while the PLO leadership wavered over their leader's support of the peace process, she backed him solidly. "We're a tiny country, and we have no choice," she said in a magazine interview.[51] Sounding words she had first heard as a child, she went on, "We must coexist with the Israelis, and we can learn a lot from them: about agriculture, economic development, women's rights. I grew up in a house where Israelis were coming and going all the time. So, you see, for me making peace with them is not at all strange."

As the ceremony proceeded in Washington, she listened proudly from afar. Watching with the widows and freedom fighters in Tunis, she saw her husband's lifelong enemy reach out to the Palestinian people. Unbeknown to her, Prime Minister Rabin was particularly nervous, not only because of the agreement he was signing, but also because he was fearful that Arafat would behave in his usual manner and try to kiss the Israeli leader on the cheek. Indeed, before the ceremony took place, says Israeli journalist Akiva Eldar, Rabin told one of his aides, "You know, those guys have the habit of kissing you on the cheek. What happens if he will try to kiss me?" Rabin's aides assured him it would be okay. Says Eldar, "They had to promise that this was not going to happen."

Rabin was still uneasy as he rose to speak. But on this day he was eloquent, and in his famous monotone, the Prime Minister declared: "Let me say to you, the Palestinians—we are destined to live together on the same soil in the same land. We, the soldiers who have returned from battles stained with blood; we, who have seen our relatives and friends killed before our eyes; we, who have attended their funerals and cannot look into the eyes of their parents; we, who have come from a land where parents bury their children; we, who have fought against you, the Palestinians, we say to you today in a loud and a clear voice—enough of blood and tears. Enough!

For the first time, Rabin publicly recognized the Palestinians as human beings, equal to the Israelis. "We have no desire for revenge. We harbor no hatred towards you. We, like you, are people; people who want to build a home, to plant a tree, to love, live side by side with you in dignity, in affinity, as human beings, as free men. We are today giving a peace a chance, saying again to you, 'Enough.'"

When it was his turn, Arafat spoke with equal solemnity: "Now as we stand on the threshold of this new historic era, let me address the people of Israel and their leaders, with whom we are meeting today for the first time, and let me assure them that the difficult decision we reached together was one that required great and exceptional courage.

"We will need more courage and determination to continue the course of building coexistence and peace between us. This is possible and it will happen with mutual determination and with the effort that will be made with all parties on all the tracks to establish the foundations of a just and comprehensive peace." The PLO chairman noted that the direction of Palestinian-Israeli relations would now be towards economic, social and cultural cooperation, but that progress would not be easy. Arafat concluded, "Ladies and gentlemen, the battle for peace is the most difficult battle of our lives. It deserves our utmost efforts because the land of peace, the land of peace, yearns for a just and comprehensive peace."

It was President Clinton who spoke about the actual agreement being signed that day. The Declaration of Principles on Interim Palestinian Self Government, he said, "charts a course toward reconciliation between two peoples who have both known the bitterness of exile." Clinton said, "Let us today pay tribute to the leaders who had the courage to lead their people toward peace, away from the scars of battle, the wounds and the losses of the past, toward a brighter tomorrow. The world today thanks Prime Minister Rabin, Foreign Minister Peres and Chairman Arafat. Their tenacity and vision have given us the promise of a new beginning."

Under the terms of the DOP, to which Clinton referred, there was to be a five-year period of transition during which a permanent settlement was to be negotiated; by May 4, 1999, the most difficult and emotional issues—the status of Jerusalem, refugees, settlements and Palestinian statehood—were to be resolved. In the meantime, another agreement had to be negotiated for the implementation of the Oslo accords. The DOP had stipulated that Israeli forces would be withdrawn from Gaza and Jericho as well as other areas of Palestinian self-rule, but it had not determined such basic issues as the size of the Jericho district; whose forces would control the borders; under what circumstances (if any) Israeli troops had the right of "hot pursuit"; and whether clusters of individual settlements would be defined as single blocs, making them easier for Israeli forces to protect.

The implementation talks [Oslo II] began at the small Egyptian resort town of Taba, near Eilat, but quickly were moved to a secret location in Cairo when both sides seemed more interested in posturing for the cameras than in reaching agreement. The December 13 deadline set by the Oslo accord came and went. These were not simply technical talks. Unless and until an agreement could be reached, Arafat could not return to the territories to take up his post as titular leader of his people.

To make matters worse, Arafat was under increasing fire from his family of supporters. Six of the most prominent members of the PLO's Executive Committee, one-third of its body, resigned in protest. They included PFLP representative Abdul Raheem Mallouh, former United Nations envoy Safiq al-Hout, cultural affairs chief Abdullah Hourani and, most painful for Arafat, Mahmoud Darwish. "I will shock you," Darwish declared. Then he announced: "This organization, complete with its hierarchy and structure and figures and perhaps its content, this organization is finished. Forgive me if I say that I am under no obligation to take part in this gamble." The in-fighting between Arafat and Abu Mazzen, his chief Oslo negotiator and most trusted aide, became so bitter that Abu Mazzen withdrew to his home, refusing to talk to the PLO leader, isolating himself in a kind of self-imposed exile. Meanwhile, Haidar Abdul Shafi, who had deliberately boycotted the historic White House ceremony to protest the Oslo accord, led a group of 120 prominent Palestinians in demanding that Arafat democratize the PLO. The reformers called for the institution of a "new mechanism" to check Arafat's power, but after several days of talks, Abdul Shafi returned to Gaza empty-handed. Nor was the dissent limited to senior PLO cadres. In November, violence erupted in Gaza's Bureij refugee camp. Several Fatah commanders were murdered by their more radical rivals; Palestinian police killed twelve protesters and injured almost two hundred more. Gaza itself was on the brink of civil war. "People do not know what Oslo cost us," Arafat sighed as negotiations dragged on into mid-February without an implementation accord.

Then disaster hit. On the morning of February 25, 1994, as the Cairo talks were finally nearing a breakthrough, Dr. Baruch Goldstein, a Jew from the nearby settlement of Qiryat Arba and follower of the extremist Meir Kahane, walked into the Ibrahim Mosque in Hebron's Tomb of the Patriarchs and opened fire on a large crowd of Muslims worshiping on Ramadan. Twenty-nine of them were murdered, and almost a hundred others were wounded, many seriously. Goldstein himself was beaten to death by the enraged crowd, but riots ensued throughout the territories, with thirty more Palestinians being killed.

Hamas boasted that the massacre was what all Palestinians could expect from the "appeasement" of the PLO at Oslo. Rabin telephoned Arafat to express his regrets but resisted ordering the dismantling of the small Jewish settlement in Hebron on grounds that the settlement issue was not negotiable until the start of final status talks. Arafat today believes that Rabin's failure to act against the Hebron settlers in the immediate aftermath of the massacre may have actually emboldened the settlers to act against him. "There are clearly fanatics in the settlements, and the government of Israel needs to take steps against them. They want to destroy the peace process. I told Mr. Rabin this when he called me after the massacre," Arafat recalled.[53] The PLO leader demanded action by the United Nations, not merely a Security Council resolution condemning Israel for the incident but the deployment of an armed international peacekeeping force. Rabin refused to permit the stationing of U.N. troops in Hebron, fearing that would be a precedent for U.N. trusteeship, but agreed to the presence of an unarmed "temporary international presence" in Hebron. The move was barely enough to save Arafat's face, but the force itself proved powerless and was withdrawn less than three months later. "Actually, there were seven lost months after the Washington signing in which not very much occurred," Arafat complained.

On May 4, 1994, an agreement finally was reached in Cairo to implement the DOP. Seven days later, Israeli troops began to pull out of Gaza and Jericho. The Israeli redeployment to specified areas along the Egyptian border and surrounding the settlements was completed on May 18. Unlike the DOP, which required fewer than twenty pages, the new accord contained almost three hundred, with four annexes and six maps. Under the pact, authority was transferred from the Israeli Civil Administration, which had ruled Gaza since 1967, to the Palestinian Authority, and a new Palestinian police force of 9,000 men (7,000 of whom could come from abroad) was formed. Henceforth, in the areas of the West Bank and Gaza under their jurisdiction, the Palestinians would be responsible for their own education, social welfare, housing, tourism, parks, religious affairs, archaeology, commerce and industry, health, transportation, agriculture, employment, electricity, nature reserves, public works, postal services, population registry, telecommunications, pensions, water and sewage, planning and zoning, direct taxation, environmental protection, insurance and the banking system. The Jericho "district" under Palestinian rule was defined as containing approximately 65 square kilometers. Israel remained responsible for ensuring "safe passage" for Palestinians traveling between the Gaza Strip and Jericho during daylight hours, while joint Israeli-Palestinian patrols and mobile units were established to ensure "free, unimpeded and secure" movement on the roads of the West Bank.

In a final compromise, Israeli border officials were able to retain a veto over the entry of persons from Jordan and Egypt into the territories but agreed to remain disguised behind mirrored glass partitions so that Palestinian guards would be the only visible police at the borders. Israel also agreed to release 5,000 Palestinian prisoners, including members of Hamas, on condition they sign a pledge renouncing violence and supporting the peace process. Rabin, however, refused to free anyone charged with killing an Israeli, regardless of whether the victim was an Arab or a Jew. Perhaps the most important breakthrough was not even in the accord: it allowed Yasser Arafat to return to Gaza and Jericho for the first time since he escaped Israeli capture in 1967.

Less than two months later, on July 1, 1994, Arafat made his triumphal return. Thousands of jubilant Palestinians lined the roads to watch Arafat's arrival. Standing shoulder to shoulder in the streets, they pushed and shoved, and some even climbed the trees to get a better look at the PLO hero. Flags of every size waved from buildings, trees and telephone poles and in the hands of the onlookers. Arafat, grinning with pride and waving an olive branch, rode through Gaza on the sunroof of a large Mercedes, flanked by bodyguards. At the main square he stood on the balcony of a large building where a huge Palestinian flag stretched across the entire front. Overwhelmed by the size of the crowd and their exhilaration, he reacted, says Nabil Shaath, "like a child."

"Are these my people?" he asked again and again.

"Is this my sea?" he asked, looking towards the Mediterranean.[54]

While the throngs celebrated in Gaza, the same exuberance spread through Jericho. A few days earlier, when we visited the West Bank town, cars were backed up for miles, their horns blaring, their passengers wildly waving Palestinian flags. Outside the city, at the old Israeli checkpoints where Palestinians once felt intimidated by Jewish soldiers, Palestinian and Israeli guards, now standing side by side, checked the cars and waved them on. In the center of town, smiling Palestinian policemen, proudly wearing their fresh new uniforms, tried desperately to control traffic. Everywhere there was a feeling of triumph and a newly discovered self-esteem.

But as Arafat became ensconced in Gaza and made his first trip to Jericho, King Hussein became increasingly convinced that Jordan could not wait much longer to make its own peace with Israel. At stake were economic, religious and political issues. Hussein had reacted angrily when, after the May 4 accord, Israel sharply reduced Jordanian exports to the West Bank, wanting to retain the Palestinian market for Israelis. Jordan had traditionally been the custodian of the Muslim holy sites in Jerusalem, even paying the salaries of the *waqf* (Islamic Trust) employees who managed them. The Palestinians now established their own *waqf*, even appointing their own *mufti*, or religious leader, as custodian of the Islamic holy sites. The move was a direct threat to the Jordanians. Although in 1988 he had renounced Jordan's claim to the West Bank, the king did not want to lose jurisdiction over the sites that tied him as a direct descendant of the prophet Mohammed to the Al-Aqsa Mosque. Above all, Hussein was eager to sign a treaty with Israel so that Jordan could have a hand in shaping the Palestinian entity that would emerge at the end of the interim period.

Less than two weeks after the Israeli-PLO accord was signed in Cairo, the king and his brother, Crown Prince Hassan, met with Rabin at the home of Lord Victor Mischon, a well-known British politician active in Zionist affairs and a close friend of Shimon Peres. The rendezvous in London was the most recent in a series of more than one hundred clandestine meetings Hussein had held with Rabin, Peres and every Israeli prime minister since the 1950s. Shortly after the London conversation, Crown Prince Hassan met with opposition leader Benjamin Netanyahu, who reportedly assured him that Likud no longer believed that "Jordan is Palestine" (tantamount to advocating Hussein's overthrow). Netanyahu added that he believed Israel and Jordan faced a common threat, the creation of a Palestinian state.[55]

Shortly thereafter Israeli-Jordanian talks resumed in Washington, fortified by President Clinton's decision to forgive Jordan's $700 million debt and a promise to submit to Congress longstanding Jordanian requests for F-16 fighter planes and other weapons, financing for the purchase of Boeing jets and agricultural credits. The negotiations moved so swiftly that by mid-July President Clinton persuaded Rabin and Hussein, who were planning back-to-back summits in Eilat and Aqaba, to move their first-ever public meeting to the South Lawn of the White House. There, on July 24, for the second time in less than a year, two Middle East adversaries agreed to end the state of war between them and pledged to make peace.

What set the Washington Declaration apart from the DOP, the earlier accord with the Palestinians, was the scope of its commitments. Borders were to be opened, new bridges built near the Sea of Galilee in the north and at Eilat in the south directly linking the two nations and skirting the West Bank, daily passenger flights planned, and electrical grids, telephone and police forces joined. Israel also pledged to give "high priority to the Jordanian historic role" in administering the religious shrines in Jerusalem when the "final status" talks began with the Palestinians. But perhaps most far-reaching was the mutual commitment to prohibit any persons or groups from using the territory of the other to mount any threat of "force, weapons or any other means," and to combat any such threats resulting "from all kinds of terrorism." Securing the border with Jordan not only meant greater strategic depth for Israel, but also, in effect, insulated the Palestinian territories and vastly reduced the threat that weapons and terrorists could be smuggled through Jordan into the West Bank and Israel.

After the July 24 accord, Yitzhak Rabin traveled freely to King Hussein's palace in Aqaba, and the two men, bolstered by their earlier clandestine meetings, became close personal friends. Their relationship seemed to set the tone for overcoming the final hurdles to a peace treaty: the return to Jordan of its rightful allocation of water from the confluence of the Yarmuk and Jordan Rivers; the return to Jordan of territory occupied by Israel since the June 1967 war; and provisions to protect Israel against the use of Jordanian territory by a third party. The latter, while outwardly intended to prevent Islamic fundamentalists or radical Palestinians from establishing a beachhead in Jordan, also served notice that Israel had a stake in preserving Jordan's independence and survival against any attempt by the same forces to overthrow the Hashemite regime.

In less than three months, the two nations reached a final accord. Israel agreed to return 50 million cubic meters of water that it had been siphoning from the confluence of the two rivers since the early 1950s. From Rabin's perspective, however, the most important compromise created a precedent he hoped might one day apply to a treaty with Syria. After secretly surveying the region in a helicopter, Rabin agreed to return almost 360 square kilometers of land along its southern border with Jordan which had been incorporated into Israel in 1969. Jordan subsequently allowed Israel to retain almost 30 kilometers of land in return for Israel's ceding of territory in the

Arava border region to which Jordan had never claimed sovereignty. The unique aspect of the compromise, however, was that Jordan agreed to permit Israeli farmers to continue using 1.3 square kilometers of Jordanian land without reimbursement or charge of any kind. In return, Israel allowed Jordan, in the winter, to store 20 million cubic meters of water in Lake Tabors and pump it back during the summer.

Fayez Tarawneh, the Jordanian ambassador to the United States and the chief negotiator for the Hashemite kingdom, noted that the border demarcation was significant "because it is the longest international border Israel has with an Arab country." He noted that the compromise reached on the administration of Islamic shrines in Jerusalem makes clear that "the West Bank is now totally Palestinian land and once Palestinian sovereignty is regained over the Holy City, they will have custodianship over the shrines. But in the absence of any Islamic rule, the Hashemite kingdom, which has administered the shrines since the beginning of the century, will always fill the vacuum."

Tarawneh credited "the unbelievable chemistry and real trust" that existed between his monarch and Rabin for the rapid conclusion of a treaty. "We became brethren and friends," said King Hussein.[56] Tarawneh recalled that when the Israeli and Jordanian negotiators pushed for "maximalist" positions, the leaders themselves "would intervene and get us back in line." Motivating King Hussein and Rabin was the belief that the treaty could be a model for others in the Arab world, he said. "King Hussein considered him his partner. Rabin delivered on everything he promised. He had a very high credibility as far as we were concerned," Tarawneh said.[57] The treaty was signed, in President Clinton's presence, on October 26, 1994, near a desert border crossing just north of Aqaba and Eilat. It was a hot, windy day, but no one seemed to mind. Unlike the strained atmosphere of the Israeli-PLO signing thirteen months earlier, the mood on that day was festive, even celebratory.

The mood, at least for Arafat, quickly soured. On November 18, his newly formed units of Palestinian police confronted several thousand pro-Hamas demonstrators outside the largest mosque in Gaza. In the resulting melee eighteen people were killed and hundreds more wounded. "It looked like we were on the brink of civil war. We really were very lucky that Gaza didn't burn down," Nabil Shaath recalled. Although Arafat was having an increasingly hard time broadening his base of support, Rabin was able to keep the peace talks moving forward through the first half of 1995. The three peacemakers—Rabin, Arafat and Peres—were, after all, recipients of the 1994 Nobel Peace Prize and shared a common stake in making the process work.

Then came the news that Arafat's wife was pregnant. On July 24, 1995, Suha delivered a baby girl, Zahwa, and suddenly the world looked at Arafat through a softer lens. In their Gaza house, a new suite was built upstairs with rooms for the baby and nurse and for the parents. But Arafat, who continues to work late at night, although not as late as he used to, prefers to sleep in his small study downstairs, where Suha joins him.

On September 28, 1995, history again seemed to side with them when Rabin and Arafat, in the presence of President Clinton, King Hussein and Egyptian President Hosni Mubarak, signed an agreement at the White House that formally ended almost three decades of Israeli occupation of the West Bank and Gaza Strip. Over the next thirty-six months, Israel was to withdraw from most of the territory it had captured in the June 1967 war. The accord was accompanied by seven annexes governing future redeployment of Israeli troops and security arrangements; elections; civil affairs; legal matters; economic relations; Israel-Palestinian cooperation programs; and the release of Palestinian prisoners and detainees. In addition, letters were exchanged between the PLO and the Government of Israel, as were twenty-six maps of the new demarcation lines. The whole package, more than four hundred pages, weighed almost eighteen pounds.

Self-rule for the first time appeared to put the Palestinians on the map. The Palestinian Council was to be democratically elected within a few months and could pass laws to govern the territories as well as the people. Israeli troops finally were to be withdrawn from hotbeds like Hebron as well as less controversial towns like Jenin. Henceforth, the two peoples were to fight terrorism together, sharing intelligence as well as manpower and establishing a liaison committee to ensure full implementation of the agreement. The PLO even promised to make good on its earlier pledges of September 9, 1993, and May 4, 1994, that "within two months of the date of the inauguration of the [Palestinian] Council the Palestinian National Council will convene and formally approve the necessary changes in regard to the Palestinian Covenant." [In early May 1996 the PNC met in Gaza and voted, by 406 to 45, to repeal the existing PLO charter and directed a committee to draft a new Palestinian covenant without any provisions vowing to destroy Israel.] Arafat could finally claim, with justification, that a Palestinian state was no longer a dream. The embryo state now existed; only the act of a madman could abort it. Just over a month later, disaster struck again.

On November 4, 1995, Shimon Peres and Yitzhak Rabin appeared at a peace rally in Tel Aviv. Standing with his colleague onstage in front of the crowd of more than 100,000 people, Rabin addressed the gathering, telling them, "I waged war as long as there was no chance for peace. I believe there is now a chance for peace, a great chance for peace." Later in the evening, Rabin joined Peres and the audience and sang the lyrics of "Shir Ha-Shalom," the Song for Peace.

The evening was a great departure for the prime minister. Not one to enjoy large crowds, and certainly not one to sing in front of them, the taciturn Rabin had agreed to the event because he felt so strongly that the peace movement needed his show of support. But the words to the song were not completely familiar, and he read the lyrics from a paper while he tried to keep the tune with Shimon Peres. But the joyous mood of the evening had even touched the usually somber Rabin. "I never saw him so content, so satisfied, so optimistic, as those last three or four hours," said Shimon Peres. "I knew him for fifty years. He had never embraced me in his life; I had never heard him singing." Rabin told the former mayor of Tel Aviv that this had been one of the happiest days of his life. He left the stage, heading for his car. He and his wife were going to a party for Avi Pazner, the new Israeli ambassador to France, at the home of Edo Disentchek, a well-known Israeli journalist.[58]

But only a few steps away from his car, he was approached by a young Israeli. Reaching out to Rabin, he pulled a .22 caliber pistol and shot the prime minister three times, in the spleen, the chest and the spinal cord. Rabin fell to the ground, blood gushing from his chest. His bodyguard fell over him; he had been struck by the last bullet. Rabin was pushed into the car, and the driver raced to the hospital. Two hours later Rabin was dead.

The assassin, an Orthodox twenty-four-year-old law student named Yigal Amir, a member of an extremist militia group called Ayal, had posed as one of the prime minister's drivers. Amir was apprehended immediately and subsequently tried and sentenced to life imprisonment.

To many Israelis the assassination came as a total shock. Never before, they said, had one Israeli killed another. Never before, they said, had a person murdered someone in office. The prime minister's death, it seemed, threw a pall over the entire country. And yet there were some who actually celebrated the news of Rabin's assassination. For months, right-wing Israelis had taunted the prime minister, accusing him of selling out the country, mocking him with ugly placards that depicted him with a *kafeeyah* to look like Yasser Arafat or, even worse, in an SS uniform to look like Adolf Hitler. Although gaining in strength, these extremists were considered only a fringe group. Amir, however, had been trying to kill Rabin for almost a year. Threats against the prime minister had come hours before the peace rally in Tel Aviv. But Rabin had not even bothered to wear a bulletproof vest. His lifestyle, as one of the most revered of Israelis, precluded it. He often left the door to his apartment unlocked, often mingled in crowds. "A flak jacket? Really? What are we, Africa here? This is Israel," Leah Rabin told a journalist who asked if her husband had been wearing any protective gear at the rally.

Arafat must have felt he would suffer a similar fate. Rabin had been more than a partner in the peace process. While there was little personal rapport between the two leaders—indeed Arafat once asked, "Why doesn't he like me?"—he recognized how indispensable the soldier Rabin, the general Rabin, was to the peace process. He was, as Arafat confided to us after Rabin's death, the Israeli De Gaulle. The death of Rabin orphaned Arafat, leaving him more vulnerable than ever. "I've never seen him like this. In his eyes, when Rabin died, I saw such inner sadness and despair," Nabil Shaath recalled. Arafat was advised not to attend the funeral, although he sent senior aides to represent his government. A few days later, Arafat paid a condolence call on Leah Rabin in Tel Aviv. For the first time in anyone's memory, Arafat appeared before photographers without his *kafeeyah*. "He had great respect for Rabin. It showed in the way he took Rabin's death. It was the first time he felt emotional empathy to Israel," Uri Savir said.[59]

However, amid the remorse, and the finger-pointing, the question arose: Could the seventy-two-year-old Shimon Peres, whose diffident, intellectual air made him seem more philosopher than politician, persuade Israelis that he, too, could safeguard their security while pursuing peace?

In the immediate aftermath of the assassination, everything

seemed to get back on track. On November 19, Palestinian self-rule was extended to Jenin in the West Bank. It was the first of several planned Israeli withdrawals. But no sooner had the new year begun than the endless round of revenge that has always plagued the region resumed. On January 5, forces of the Israeli intelligence arm Shin Bet detonated a remote-control device planted in the cellular telephone of Israel's most wanted terrorist, the "Engineer" Yahya Ayyash. Ayyash, the head of the Qassam Brigades, the underground military wing of Hamas, was killed instantly. The assassination undermined Arafat's efforts to persuade Hamas to field candidates in the elections for an eighty-eight-member legislative council in the West Bank and Gaza Strip. Nonetheless, when Palestinians voted for the first time, on January 20, 1996, a surprisingly high 88 percent of the Gaza population cast ballots, spurning the decision by Hamas to boycott the election.

Just over a month later, Hamas took its revenge. On February 25, there were two suicide bus bombings in Jerusalem and Ashkelon, then another a week later, then one more on Monday, March 4, at the crowded Dizengoff shopping center in the heart of Tel Aviv. The Israeli death toll was sixty, many of the victims children costumed to celebrate the Jewish holiday of Purim. Sarah Duker and Mathew Eisenfeld, two American college students who were engaged to be married, were also killed.

The bombings were aimed at the heart of the peace process, and they could not have been more adroitly timed. Peace finally seemed to be taking hold: the Israeli economy was booming; the right wing was finally in remission; Syria was at the negotiating table; and the first democratic Palestinian elections in history had been held without incident. Suddenly the same mobs that had branded Rabin a traitor turned their fury on Peres. An angry and anguished nation demanded retaliation.

Peres acted at once. To prevent new infiltrations, he closed the borders with the West Bank and Gaza, sending the fledgling Palestinian economy into a tailspin. More than 100,000 Palestinian laborers could no longer reach their jobs inside Israel. "Palestinians as well as Israelis paid the price for the suicide bombings," explained Dennis Ross. Per capita Palestinian income plummeted. Goods could no longer move between the West Bank and Gaza. "The hopes of Israelis were supplanted by fears," Ross said.[60]

Arafat tried to assuage Israeli fears, cracking down on Hamas as never before. For the first time, he began publicly calling his Hamas opponents "terrorists." "It's a terrorist organization, and I condemn any organization behind it," he said on February 25. Furious with his own security force, he chided them: "You are not men. You should wear skirts. Find the Hamas leaders."[61] As a result, hundreds of Islamic activists were arrested, and several institutions were raided, including Islamic University in Gaza, which was cordoned off by the Palestinian police. Arafat ordered that the university be closed in its current form and reopened as a branch of Cairo University. He even arrested five of the thirteen men on Israel's most-wanted list and put out an all-points alert for Mohammed Deif, the current head of the Qassam Brigades, and Muhyi al-Din al-Sharif, known as "Engineer No. 2" because he was believed to have succeeded the martyred Ayyash. Although Arafat's earlier strategy had succeeded in dividing Hamas into separate political and military wings—there had been no suicide bombings in Israel for six months before the February attacks—he received little credit from the Israeli public. Arafat himself, however, now understood the threat was aimed as much at him as it was the Israelis.

On March 7, Arafat convened the first Palestinian legislative council in Gaza and proclaimed " the birth of a new democracy in the Middle East." Despite the pomp provided by an Egyptian military band, dozens of diplomats and an honor guard that snapped to attention when he walked by, Arafat did not try to conceal his frustration. Shouting over a winter storm that raged at the palm trees and rained hail on the glass roof over his head, Arafat announced: "The peace of the brave that began with the declaration of principles signed by the PLO and Israel will go on, will go on, will go on!" As he spoke, he was banging his fist on the rostrum. "We will not allow any enemy of the Palestinians, inside or outside, to take it away. We will not allow violence or terrorism to stop this peace process." The day was a proud one for Arafat. Each speaker greeted him as *rais,* a word that connotes ruler, and as he swore in the eighty-eight members of the new parliament, he replied: "We are witnessing the birth of a new democracy in the Middle East. We are witnessing a new Palestinian struggle for an independent state, with Jerusalem as its capital."

What do you fear about Peres? Rabin was asked in the mid-1980s by Michael Kramer, an American journalist. According to Kramer, he replied with reluctance but finally said, between cigarettes,

"Shimon is in love with an idea, land for peace. Sometimes that's fine. Obviously we wouldn't have peace with Egypt if we hadn't given up the Sinai. But I worry that in seeking a larger peace, Peres, to prove that he's tough, might overreact in a way that's harmful."

The words sounded prophetic in mid-March 1996. According to the Shi'a guerrilla forces of Hezbollah in southern Lebanon, Israel violated an unwritten 1993 accord that neither side would attack civilians just north of the so-called security zone that Israel had occupied since 1978. Several Lebanese civilians were killed by Israeli missiles and mines, the Hezbollah charged. Israel denied those attacks were intentional and charged that pro-Iranian guerrillas used them to justify a major new offensive against Israeli civilians in the towns in the northern Galilee.

At first, Peres was reluctant to be drawn into a new war in Lebanon. But after repeated volleys of Katyusha rockets slammed into these Israeli villages, wounding 36 civilians and driving another 250,000 Israelis into bomb shelters, the new prime minister felt he had no other recourse. He ordered Operation Grapes of Wrath. The IDF would strike with all the might they had: artillery, missile boats, helicopter gunships and American F-16 fighter bombers. Although the targets were supposed to be Hezbollah guerrilla bases and mobile rocket launchers, almost from the start the Israelis assaulted Lebanese cities and villages, roads and power stations. Peres announced that his aim was to destroy the infrastructure of the guerrillas wherever it could be located. Unfortunately, the Hezbollah forces often took refuge amidst the squalid Palestinian refugee camps.

For two weeks, the Clinton administration appeared to countenance the raids, perhaps in part because many people thought Peres was ridding himself of the stigma of being soft while simultaneously bolstering his domestic image for the upcoming May 29 presidential elections. In the first two weeks of Operation Grapes of Wrath, there were more than a thousand air raids. More than 15,000 artillery shells were fired. More than 400,000 Lebanese fled north to U.N. refugee camps in Beirut.

And yet the world waited. Then suddenly there was a new round of bombardments, more devastating than the last. On April 12, Israeli artillery struck at the lower Bekaa Valley, killing nine Palestinian civilians, including a two-year-old girl and a one-hundred-year-old man. The next day, Israelis attacked an ambulance south of Tyre, killing eight Palestinians—two men, two women and four children. The Israelis claimed that the men were Hezbollah guerrillas who used the ambulance as cover for their escape. For four days, between April 16 and 20, Israeli missiles pounded the Ein Helw refugee camp, while gunboats bombed the coastal highway near Sidon. And then, on Thursday, April 18, an Israeli F-16 fired at the Nabatiya home of Fawzieh El-Aabed, killing her and seven of her Palestinian children, including a four-day-old daughter. The house was said to be a Hezbollah stronghold.

A few hours later a new tragedy began. Two Katyusha rockets and six mortars were fired by Hezbollah forces from a position less than three hundred yards away from the United Nations compound at Qana. The U.N. post had been there since 1978 and was well known to the Israelis, who also knew, despite their later denials, that the camp harbored civilian refugees. According to a senior Israeli defense official, an Israeli reconnaissance squad had been sent into the vicinity of the camp to determine the source of the Hezbollah rocket attacks. One of the squad members was hit and radioed back to IDF headquarters for help. "It is our custom that when any one of our men comes under direct fire, and is hit, to retaliate without regard to the concept of proportional force," the official conceded.[62]

That was as close as any Israeli official came to admitting that the attack was a deliberate effort to retaliate against the Hezbollah, even if that meant killing innocent civilians. For almost a quarter of an hour, an Israeli 155-mm howitzer shelled the U.N. compound at Qana. The carnage was enormous: more than one hundred refugees—one-sixth of the camp's population—were killed, and another one hundred were wounded. "I couldn't count the bodies. There were babies without heads. There were people without arms and legs," recalled Swedish U.N. Captain Mikael Lindvall.

General Stanislaw Wozniak, the Polish commander of the U.N. force, flatly rejected Peres's claim that the IDF was unaware that there were civilians at the camp. "They knew we were sheltering civilians in this U.N. post. Simply, you don't attack civilians. You don't attack U.N. positions," he declared. U.N. spokesman Timor Goksel added: "We asked Israel several times to stop firing on the Fijian headquarters, telling them that we had civilian victims, but in vain."

Two days before the attack, a Blue Helmet peacekeeper from Fiji, a Pacific island that supplied most of the forces at Qana, had tried to persuade Hezbollah fighters to move their positions farther away from the U.N. outpost. He was shot in the chest during the Israeli attack. "We were breaking our backs to stop Hezbollah from using the United Nations as a shield," said spokeswoman Sylvana Foa.

Prime Minister Peres later apologized for the fact that "citizens of Lebanon were killed," but he put the blame squarely on Hezbollah, warning Syria that unless it withdrew its 30,000 occupation troops, untold new "tragedies would befall Lebanon." Perhaps with Rabin in mind, Peres added: "The right to defend ourselves is not dependent on anyone's permission."

There were less than six weeks until new Israeli elections in May. These were the first in which the prime minister would be directly elected by popular vote instead of being chosen by the party that won a majority of seats in parliament or hammered together a majority of its own and smaller parties. As the Labor Party leader who had inherited Rabin's mantle, Peres seemed to have a comfortable lead over his Likud challenger. But the seventy-two-year-old Peres miscalculated the mood of the Israeli public. Instead of focusing on a presidential campaign, he directed his attention to running the country, gambling that his early double-digit lead in the polls would insulate him from attack by his media-savvy, American-reared opponent, Benjamin Netanyahu. It was simply inconceivable to the intellectual elder statesman that someone as young and brash as Netanyahu, whose marital problems and reported love affairs filled the gossip columns, could pose a serious challenge. Although he lacked combat experience, the Polish-born Peres was not always seen as a dove. Reared at the side of David Ben-Gurion and Golda Meir, he is one of the last of the leaders who experienced the emergence of Israel as a modern state and is widely credited with making its army a powerful force. As the chief weapons procurer for the young nation, he concluded Israel's first major arms agreement with France, transforming the pre-state underground militias into a modern army, the Israel Defense Force (IDF). Peres also helped cement Israel's independence in the post-1948 period by securing the Dimona nuclear reactor. Throughout his long career, he has been slighted by some for his constant feuds with Rabin, but others saw the two competitors for Labor Party power as a perfect match, one outgoing, polished and visionary and the other reclusive, pragmatic and tough. Peres never imagined that after a half century of service to his nation, the Israeli people would choose to sever the bond that tied him to the martyred Rabin and to their long mutual leadership.

But the popular "Bibi," as Netanyahu was known when he served as Israel's envoy to the United Nations, had made the battle against terrorism his trademark ever since his brother became the sole Israeli fatality in the daring raid to rescue an Israeli airliner at Entebbe, Uganda, in 1975. "Shimon didn't take Bibi seriously. He didn't focus enough on security," said a senior State Department official. Nor did Peres prepare adequately for the only nationally televised debate, on the eve of the election, despite the fact that Netanyahu was being coached by American media mogul Roger Ailes.

Netanyahu's Kennedyesque youth and stiletto-like swipes at his opponent produced better sound bites than the soft, wiser tones of the silver-haired politician. When the votes were counted, neither candidate had won a convincing majority. But Netanyahu emerged with just over 50 percent, his margin of victory 30,000 votes, a bare one percent of Israel's 3 million eligible voters. Indeed, had even half of the 80,000 Arab citizens of Israel who submitted blank ballots voted for Peres, the results might have been different. But a sizable number of Israel's eligible Arab voters, who traditionally supported Labor as well as their own small parties in the Knesset, were still fuming from the Palestinian death toll in the April bombing of the Lebanese refugee camp at Qana.

The media wrote that Bibi, who immediately instructed his aides to cease using his nickname as it no longer befitted his high office, had won because he promised the Israeli public what Peres had failed to deliver, "peace with security." Indeed, the results reflected the frustration with a peace process that had not ended terrorist attacks. Many Israelis blamed Arafat for failing to control extremists within his community. Even American officials put the best face on what was clearly a devastating defeat for President Clinton, who had openly backed Peres. Dennis Ross noted that Netanyahu was the beneficiary of several shocks to the Israeli psyche, beginning with Rabin's assassination and culminating in four bombs in nine days. These events, and the Hezbollah provocations that led to Operation Grapes of Wrath and the tragedy at Qana, "shook Israelis to their core," creating a "trauma" in which the "hopes of Israelis were supplanted by fears," said Ross.

For Yasser Arafat, the trauma was more personal. "I didn't sleep all night, not at all," he told an American describing the way he spent the night of the election. "Peres went to sleep and Netanyahu went to sleep, but I didn't sleep at all," he said, on the verge of tears. "How could they lose? No Rabin? Why no Rabin?" Arafat repeated as he tried to fathom Peres's failure to invoke the legacy of his martyred ally. "It was a criminal campaign. Why didn't Peres run his own campaign? Why did he turn it over to fools? The debate was a mistake, a serious mistake. So much at stake, so much chance. They couldn't lose it, but they did." And he repeated, as if talking to himself in a stream of consciousness, "Peres went to sleep thinking he's won, and Netanyahu thinking he's lost, but I didn't sleep all night. I cried, I was so angry and upset. Now we have so much problems."[63]

The questions asked repeatedly were: Who was Netanyahu and what did he stand for? What would happen to the peace process? What would happen to the agreements signed in Oslo? Optimists pointed to the fact that Netanyahu had participated in the 1991 Madrid conference as the spokesman for then prime minister Shamir. With the Israeli electorate deeply divided, they said he would have a golden opportunity to do what former American president Richard Nixon had done in China, cementing his place in history by forging a genuine majority for peace—with security. Indeed, when Netanyahu swore in his cabinet on June 18, he declared he would fulfill the obligations of the Oslo accords.

Others were pessimistic. One high-ranking American official in Israel told friends that there could be no comparison with Nixon going to China or even the hard-line Israeli leader Menachem Begin giving back the Sinai to Egypt. "Here there is an ideological, religious commitment to the West Bank. Bibi still calls them Judea and Samaria," said the senior policymaker. The doubters pointed to Netanyahu's party platform, which declared that "the eastern border of the state of Israel will be the Jordan River [incorporating Judea and Samaria]," which obviously was inconsistent with the creation of a Palestinian state in the West Bank. They pointed to his vow that "settlement in all parts of the Land of Israel is an expression of our right to the land and it represents an inseparable part of our national security." Autonomy, not independence, seemed the most Netanyahu was willing to offer. He would pay lip service to continuing negotiations and to the Oslo accords but, in the view of these skeptics, only as a ruse to buy time to implement his own program. "Hold the Peace; Keep the Process" was the way Serge Schmemann of the *New York Times* described the shift. "Yes to continuing negotiations with the Palestinians and the Syrians. Yes to improving relations with Egypt, Jordan and other Arab states. No to a Palestinian state. No to any division of Jerusalem. No to giving up the Golan Heights. Add to this an intention to use the army bullishly against terrorism, and a readiness to build new Jewish settlements in the West Bank, and there you have it," the *New York Times* correspondent wrote.[64]

Nor did his inner circle make much of an effort to disguise the shift. They said it was the reason why the Israeli public had elected Netanyahu and rejected Peres. "We live in a period in which there is a juxtaposition of high hopes and bitter disappointments," explained Dore Gold, Netanyahu's chief foreign policy adviser. "In the last four years there have been political breakthroughs, but Israelis have seen an upsurge in terrorism in the heart of our cities and a massive increase of fatalities—two hundred since Oslo, the same number as in the last decade. The launching pad for many of these operations," he said pointedly, "was the territory under the control of our negotiating partner."[65]

Thus, few were surprised when a new policy emerged demanding that Israel regain the right of "hot pursuit" of suspected Palestinian assailants into Palestinian-controlled areas throughout the West Bank and Gaza Strip. In the final round of the Oslo talks, Rabin had reluctantly conceded that while Israel would retain control over settlements, settlers and Israelis traveling in these areas, Palestinians would be primarily responsible for securing their newly acquired territories against terrorism. This last-minute concession reflected an important gain for the Palestinians, because it implied that they would gain control over the land. Supervision of the borders was to be shared, as were security responsibilities for about a quarter of the territory of the West Bank, but in the areas under Palestinian jurisdiction, the Palestinian Authority was responsible for "internal" security. Now that basic tenet of the Oslo accord seemed in jeopardy.

Having toughened Israel's positions on these issues so soon after his inauguration, it was hoped that Netanyahu would move quickly to address his Arab peers directly. Jordan's King Hussein, perhaps intrigued by a new Israeli leader who would strongly police the Palestinians, was virtually alone in pleading that the Arab world give Netanyahu time. But while he did make contact with King Hussein and Egypt's Hosni Mubarak, Netanyahu studiously avoided Yasser Arafat. As he had done before, for so many years, Arafat waited for the Israeli leader to pick up the phone. But there was neither a phone call nor a fax. Instead, it was more than a month before Netanyahu sent his aide, Dore Gold, on a mission to Gaza, an occasion as telling for its lack of enthusiasm on the Israelis' part as for its actual occurrence.

The envoy arrived at Arafat's headquarters carrying a single sheet of paper. It contained no salutation and no signature. Scrawled on the page was a brief list of Israeli prerequisites for continued dialogue, six demands intended to chart the new rules of the road. If the Palestinians helped to "prevent terror, extradite terrorists and cease incitement against Israel," the Israeli Government would lift the closure and permit more laborers to work in Israel, the "non-paper" (because it was not an official document) said. After the February suicide bombings, Israelis deliberately decreased the size of the Palestinian work force inside Israel, denying permits to the majority of the 125,000 Palestinian laborers. As punishing was the closure of the road that linked Palestinian enclaves in the West Bank with Gaza. "One box of tomatoes in Gaza costs 3 shekels [to produce]," said Arafat. "In the West Bank, if we could get them there, they would sell for 30 shekels. We are out of olive oil here [in Gaza], but there's a surplus in the West Bank and we can't bring it here. We can't export our flowers, so we are feeding them to the goats," he said. "We have the best-scented goats," he liked to add.[66]

The message Gold now carried offered to reverse that trend—but at a price. Arafat and Gold talked. But when Arafat asked him questions, Gold refused to answer, saying that his instructions did not permit him to elaborate on the terse unofficial document.

"All the things Arafat now seeks—more land, a state, control over water, the right of return for refugees, a freeze on settlement—are red lines for Netanyahu. The only reason Arafat might play along with the process is if he finds some tangible economic benefits in it," Schmemann wrote, adding that "the Palestinian Authority's main problem today is not frustrated national aspirations, but poverty."[67] In describing his initial meeting with Arafat, Gold said he sought to convey that "there has been too much talk of borders and what kind of [Palestinian] entity will exist." The starting point for cooperation must be "a firm and fundamental recommitment to the principle of nonviolence."[68]

Almost three more months elapsed before Netanyahu and Arafat finally came face to face. Their meeting was provoked by Israeli President Ezer Weizman, who announced that he would meet with

Arafat if Netanyahu didn't. The brief strained session between the Israeli prime minister and the Palestinian Authority president took place on September 4 at the Erez checkpoint, a military base on the border of Israel and the Gaza Strip.

Despite his air of contempt, Netanyahu believed that his behavior towards Arafat would be seen by the other Arab leaders as separate and different from the way he behaved towards them. Indeed, he assumed that Israel's economic ties to the Arab states could be strengthened even as the peace process weakened. But in late June, when Arab leaders convened in Cairo for a summit, they showed their support for Arafat and the Oslo accords. Although rejecting calls by Syrian President Hafez el-Assad to harshly denounce the new government, the leaders nonetheless issued an unambiguous warning: any retreat from the peace process by the Israelis would be matched on the Arab side. Egypt pointedly warned that it would cancel the Middle East economic summit set for Cairo in November if Netanyahu was not more forthcoming to the Palestinians. Fueling the anger further, Syria ordered troop deployments near the Israeli border. Israel responded in kind, stirring the spector of war.

While Netanyahu stalled on the next step in the process, the already delayed redeployment from Hebron, and the Arab governments repositioned themselves, Arafat was locked in the middle. His fate was linked to the peace process. Without positive movement, his survival seemed in jeopardy. Indeed, the next step taken by the Israelis appeared to many Palestinians to be a deliberate provocation, an attempt to weaken him further. In September 1996, in the middle of the night, the Israeli Government opened a new exit to an archeological tunnel that winds along the Temple Mount, the site of Jewish and Muslim holy shrines in Jerusalem's old city. The ancient tunnel, built by Jews in the time of Herod, exited near the Via Dolorosa in the Muslim quarter in East Jerusalem. None of Israel's previous prime ministers, not Peres, not Rabin, not even Shamir, had allowed the tunnel to be opened there. They recognized that to do so would be interfering and inciteful. Nevertheless, Netanyahu, perhaps to appease Infrastructure minister Ariel Sharon, the ex-general, and other hawks in his cabinet, turned a deaf ear, and with an attitude that seemed to many to reek of arrogance or ignorance or both, he ordered the tunnel exit to be opened, claiming it was merely a step that would help accommodate the tourist traffic.

The Arabs reacted immediately. Violent clashes took place between Palestinians and Israelis, and even worse, between Palestinian police and Israeli soldiers. The Israeli's nightmare began to play out as Palestinian police shot at Israeli soldiers. During the *intifada*, the Palestinians had thrown stones, rocks or Molotov cocktails, but now a force of some thirty thousand Palestinians, armed and trained by the Israelis, was using those rifles against them. Within a few days, sixty Palestinians and fifteen Israeli soldiers were killed and hundreds more injured. Ironically, among his own constituents, Arafat appeared stronger, first as he urged his people to fight, and then, after pleas from Israeli and American officials, as he urged them to stop. But the volatility and unpredictability brought fear, not just in the region, but in America as well. Bill Clinton, whose presidential campaign had boasted of foreign policy success in the Middle East and who was less than two months away from victory, now felt threatened in the same part of the world that had helped defeat former presidents George Bush and Jimmy Carter.

Clinton acted swiftly. On October 1, he convened a White House summit with Netanyahu, Arafat and King Hussein. For two days the leaders talked, and at one point, by a prearranged plan, President Clinton and King Hussein excused themselves from the room, forcing the Israeli and Palestinian leaders to be alone and communicate. The next day, at the end of the nonstop, forty-eight-hour meeting, Clinton called a press conference. Netanyahu and Arafat sat in silence, their hands folded in their laps, looking stonily at the cameras. But a short while later, as they were leaving the White House, Netanyahu clasped Arafat's right hand in both of his, shaking it vigorously for several seconds, while Clinton beamed. Said Netanyahu, the "children of Israel are safer tonight" because the summit "cemented the principle that the path to peace is through negotiation and not through violence." He told reporters that talks would immediately resume on Hebron and that if lower-level negotiators did not resolve the dispute, "Arafat and I will sit down until we solve it. We agreed to do that." But Nabil Shaath, a senior Arafat aide, countered soberly: "There is no agreement about anything."

Despite the inconclusive White House summit and some strident Arab calls on him to cancel it, Egyptian President Hosni Mubarak defied critics and in early November convened the third annual Middle East Economic Conference in Cairo. Bringing businessmen from the Gulf, even Saudi Arabia, and other Arab nations together with Israeli entrepreneurs was the brainchild of Jordan's Crown

Prince Hassan and Shimon Peres. They had proposed the idea in October 1993 during an Oval Office meeting with President Clinton shortly after the signing of the Israeli-Palestinian Declaration of Principles. "At first, we thought it was a wild idea that could not be implemented before a comprehensive settlement achieved peace on all fronts," said Jordanian Ambassador Fayez Tarawneh.[69] But the profit motive proved as effective as any political motive. More than nine hundred businessmen showed up at the first economic summit in Casablanca in the fall of 1994. A year later, almost two thousand dealmakers came to Amman to exchange business cards, listen to lectures about the prospects, real or imagined, of regional cooperation and to plan possible joint ventures with the captains of Israeli industry. The attraction was an Israeli economy that produced an annual GNP of $80 billion. By any practical yardstick, given Arab attitudes towards the Netanyahu government and the turmoil in Palestinian streets over its settlement policies, the Cairo conference should never have happened. "We debated this issue," and there were strong bureaucratic battles over whether it should be held, said Osama el-Baz, Mubarak's most senior and trusted adviser. But it took place. In fact, a record number of Arab and Israeli businessmen, more than three thousand self-styled entrepreneurs and executives, came to Cairo to market their wares. El-Baz said that Cairo was told in no uncertain terms, particularly by European and Asian multinationals, that "if we postpone the conference, let alone cancel it, we will be hurting the cause of peace. We were told that investors will not invest in an unstable region where everything is subject to political whims." Despite the daily headlines, "we wanted everyone to think that the Middle East is an area that is stable and where the future is bright," he said.[70]

But there was little reason for optimism in the fall of 1996. By March, some eight months earlier, Israel was to have completed its redeployment from Hebron and seven other West Bank cities. But September, October and November had come and gone, and although the troops had been withdrawn from the first six by the Peres government, nothing had happened in Hebron, an Arab city of almost 150,000 people. Both Muslims and Jews claim a biblical right to the heart of the city, where they take turns worshipping at the Tomb of the Patriarchs, the burial site of Abraham and Sarah, called Ibrahimi Mosque by the Muslims. Arafat had already agreed that Israel could redeploy its troops around the nearby settlements.

Netanyahu demanded that, in addition to protecting the settlements, Israel have the right of "hot pursuit" into Palestinian-controlled areas. Otherwise a would-be terrorist could attack a Jew and escape into the sanctuary of the Palestinian-controlled city. Thus, Netanyahu demanded that Israel have the exclusive right to protect the 450 zealously nationalistic Jews living near the very place where Abraham had bought a burial plot for his wife Sarah and where he was later buried with his son Isaac and grandson Jacob. Less than twenty of these ultra-Orthodox believers had come after the seemingly miraculous Israeli victory in the June 1967 war to spend Passover in the burial place of their Patriarch. It was God, they said, who had delivered the Israeli army, which had vanquished four Arab armies in only six days, and it was God who compelled them to establish a settlement there. Now they and their followers were entrenched in Hebron. The handful of zealots had become several hundred, and none of them were moving from the ancient Hebrew capital where King David had ruled for seven years before going to Jerusalem. Dennis Ross, the American envoy, spent almost the entire month of October trying to mediate an agreement. He quit when it became clear that while substantive differences were being narrowed, there was still too much mutual distrust between Arafat and Netanyahu to close the gaps.

By December, in the absence of a Hebron agreement, violence flared again. Breaking a five-month lull in armed assaults, Palestinian gunmen attacked a family of Jewish settlers who were driving on an Israeli-built road that bypassed the Palestinian-ruled town of Ramallah. A twelve-year-old boy and his mother were killed in the drive-by shooting. Israel announced that the gunmen belonged to the Popular Front for the Liberation of Palestine (PFLP), the Damascus-based guerrilla group led by George Habash which opposed the PLO's accords with Israel. Less than twenty-four hours earlier, following the announcement of Israeli plans to build 132 high-rise apartments for Jews inside Ras al-Amud, a depressed Palestinian area in East Jerusalem, the PLO had warned that the plan was a "time bomb" and there would be an "explosion" of violence.

But Netanyahu seemed oblivious to the warnings, seizing on the murders to announce that he would restore financial subsidies for the settlements and to deliver a harsh message to Arafat. "This is a test now for the Palestinian Authority. We expect them to extradite, to help us find these murderers of women and children [who apparently fled to Ramallah] and return them," said the Israeli leader. "Whoever thinks that through acts of terror he can uproot the Jewish people from its country, from the heart of the Jewish homeland, should know that we will uproot him."

Tensions increased when Israeli troops cordoned off Ramallah to conduct a house-to-house manhunt for the gunmen. Arafat and his closest advisers were losing hope that Netanyahu had any intention of honoring the agreements negotiated and signed by his predecessors. "The policies of Netanyahu are destroying the whole peace process," Arafat told a visiting American. "And not just with me," but with "Tunisia, Qatar, Oman, Jordan and Morocco." For the Palestinians, hopes to economic gains were quashed by border closures. "Look at these flowers," Arafat said, gesturing to the small vase on the table in front of him. "We cannot export them. We lose $7 to $9 million every day." Unlike richer nations, noted Arafat, the Palestinians could hardly afford it. "We are not Saudi Arabia," he said, noting that "even Saudi Arabia would feel that loss. It is a tragedy."[71]

Arafat worried that Netanyahu would use a Hebron pact to expand the construction of new Jewish settlements and avoid fulfilling the remaining obligations of the Oslo accords. The pact required Israeli troop withdrawals in three six-month intervals from rural areas of the West Bank. The withdrawals were to have begun in March 1996 after the scheduled Hebron pullout and were to be completed by September 1997. Although the Palestinians insisted these would give them control of 85 percent of the territories, Israeli officials said that Oslo had deliberately left the extent of the withdrawals to future negotiation. But those talks, like the ones on a permanent settlement, had never begun. Netanyahu now suggested that final status talks should begin as soon as the Hebron accord was reached—implying that the final Israeli withdrawals would be scrubbed—and that the negotiations should be aimed at a permanent settlement in which the emerging Palestinian entity would resemble Puerto Rico, an American protectorate, or Andorra, a Spanish colony. The Israeli leader said either would be an appropriate model because in both Puerto Rico and Andorra national groups manage their own affairs without risking the dissolution of the nation in which they live and without threatening the majority.

To Arafat, this seemed like a ploy aimed at sabotaging the Oslo accords. They called, after all, for the three most difficult issues to be dealt with in final status talks: the future of Jerusalem, the fate of Jewish settlements and Palestinian demands for statehood. Arafat had agreed at Oslo to put off consideration of these highly emotional issues until the end of the third year of the interim accord. But now Netanyahu was saying something different. The only subjects, he insisted, which remained for negotiation were the disposition of "open territory" essential for protecting Israel's security and the issue of what "authorities" the Palestinians would receive in a permanent settlement. In any event, he said, those civil powers would "not be consonant with the concept of sovereignty," which seemed to exclude a Palestinian state. "Most of Judea and Samaria is unpopulalted," he said, deliberately dismissing Arab farmland, and is "crucial to Israel's security."

With such hints of what was in store, it was Arafat who now turned a cold shoulder on the talks over Hebron. Without specific assurances that the Hebron pullback would be followed by a precise timetable for the completion of Israeli withdrawals from the West Bank, there would be no Hebron agreement, he warned. The Israelis were prepared to set a deadline for the first withdrawal, but Netanyahu refused to agree to any additional pullbacks.

Meanwhile, as Christmas approached, both sides signaled their willingness for one more try. Once again the State Department's Dennis Ross and his capable deputy Aaron Miller sped to the region. Once again, following several days of intense negotiations that frequently concluded at dawn, Arafat and Netanyahu agreed to meet, on Christmas Eve, at the Erez border. Forty-eight hours before their meeting, a private American intermediary hand-carried a message to Arafat from Dore Gold "on behalf of the prime minister."[72] Unlike earlier missives, this one was remarkably thoughtful and reasoned. It implored Arafat to put himself in Netanyahu's shoes so he could sympathize with the nature of the hard-line opposition he faced from the settlers in Hebron and from the hawks in his own cabinet. The message noted that the two leaders had met, but only at times of crisis. That is not conducive to developing the "intimacy" required to create confidence about the future, it went on. Netanyahu "knows that you're suspicious of him" and, the message bearer conceded, "you have reason to be." The only solution: "You have to become partners." There not only had to be personal rapport but also an "intimate connection" between the Hebron accord and what follows, the message said. That, at least, was a hint that Israel might be softening its stance. In particular, Netanyahu "wants to pay attention to what Bar-Ilan said in the *Jerusalem Post* interview."

In that interview two days earlier, David Bar-Ilan, a senior policy adviser, and leading Likud ideologue, showed flexibility.[73] He told the *Post* that Israel ultimately might be able to accept a Palestinian state with strictly defined, limited sovereignty—provided the state was a demilitarized one. "Partition is a fact. The question now is really what sort of partition," Bar-Ilan explained. He said that in some ways a Palestinian state already existed and conceded that if the Palestinians declared statehood, the "whole world will recognize it"—regardless of the Israeli reaction. Netanyahu genuinely wanted peace, he said. Despite his rhetoric, he no longer espoused the idea of "Eretz (or Greater) Israel," Bar-Ilan explained. "I don't think he feels that there is any chance of the Land of Israel remaining completely under the exclusive rule of Israel," he told the *Post*. Finally, he said, Netanyahu is convinced that existing settlements could be expanded without adding "another square inch" to them, thus placating Palestinian fears that he would preclude the outcome of final status talks.

But the message from Gold also contained a stern warning to Arafat: you will be making a "big mistake" if you continue to stonewall. Netanyahu "is concerned you may be waiting for things to get worse, to choose your moment. If you go to violence, you lose it," the American visitor said. "Now is the time to establish a real working relationship" with Netanyahu, he added. Don't put it off and don't resort to violence. "This is the end of the message."

Arafat was defensive. "Why are you saying that I'm delaying it?" he snapped. For the past week, Saeb Erekat, the chief Palestinian negotiator, and his team had tried to iron out the remaining differences with their Israeli counterparts. But when Erekat went to see Yitzhak Molcho, a private Israeli attorney who was helping to draft the legal language of the accord, "after one half hour, Molcho said he had another appointment. The day after that, he stayed for fifty minutes, and the next day one hour. This is not negotiation," Arafat complained. "What could be more important than that?"[74]

As Christmas approached, it was Dennis Ross and Aaron Miller who forced their hand. "Early this morning, at 2:00 A.M., me and Ross spoke with Netanyahu," Arafat said. That set the stage for a three-and-a-half-hour Christmas Eve meeting at the Erez border. "They have made real progress," Ross said afterwards. "They have made the kind of progress that takes us closer to agreement."

But close is never enough in the Middle East. As Ross returned to Washington to brief President Clinton before speeding back to the region for the expected signing ceremony, violence again wreaked havoc on everyone's hopes. However, it was not Palestinian terrorists who were the spoilers. Instead, it was a twenty-two-year-old Orthodox Jewish settler, a soldier with a history of mental problems, who opened fire at 9:55 A.M. on New Year's Day in the vegetable market in Hebron. Witnesses said he fired one round with his M-16 assault rifle, sat down and fired a second volley, twelve shots in all. Six Palestinians were wounded before Private Noam Friedman, who lived in the West Bank settlement of Maale Adunim, was wrestled to the ground by other Israeli soldiers. Friedman, who was carrying three magazines of M-16 ammunition, later told police officers his aim was to destroy the peace pact. "Hebron now and forever," he said in a Jerusalem courtroom.

Both sides moved at once to try to contain the damage. Less than thirty minutes after the shooting, Netanyahu telephoned Arafat to convey his sorrow over "this criminal act." President Clinton also called Arafat, who moved quickly to discourage retaliation. Tempering his anger, Arafat termed the incident "regrettable" while he cautioned against new rioting. Perhaps most important, in full view of hundreds of Arabs Ami Ayalon, the chief of Israel's security service, met in the central square of Hebron with his Palestinian counterpart, Jibril Rajoub. That act alone seemed a dramatic contrast to the September aftermath of the Israeli opening of the tourist tunnel, when Palestinian anger quickly spilled over into violence, leaving thirty people dead.

As 1997 began, Dennis Ross worked feverishly to try to save the accord. "Those who use violence cannot be permitted to be the arbiters of the future," he said. However, after nine hours of talks the envoy facilitated between Yitzhak Mordechai, the Israeli defense minister, and Mahmoud Abas and Yasser Abed Rabbo, Arafat's chief deputies, no deal was reached. Again, there was speculation that, in the wake of this latest shooting, the third by a Jewish religious fanatic in three years, Arafat was insisting on ironclad guarantees that the already delayed Oslo accords be implemented as promised. "There are more burning issues than signing the agreement," Arafat said after a meeting on the same day with Ross. Netanyahu tried to put the best face on the nearly completed pact by insisting it was far improved over the "sloppy" and vague language negotiated by

Shimon Peres. "We are trying to plug the holes, making it a better agreement, a safer agreement, one that we can live with literally," he, told the Associated Press. Concessions put the settlers out of "rifle range" of Palestinian police and assured that the Israelis would not be hemmed in "to the point where they are blocked from expanding."

Despite his efforts, however, support for the Hebron pact was eroding among the members of Netanyahu's coalition government. Led by Infrastructures Minister Ariel Sharon, seven of the eighteen ministers in the cabinet had already announced they would vote against the agreement. Justice Minister Tzabi Hanegbi became the eighth cabinet member to oppose the pact. A day later, the two cabinet members of the religious Shas Party were reported to be wavering.

Although not legally required to, Netanyahu had pledged to seek cabinet approval. If those ten voted against the accord, it would go down to defeat—unless he took the unlikely course of dissolving the government and forming a new "national unity" government with Peres and the Labor Party.

In the wake of the latest incident, tensions between secular and religiously nationalistic Jews also deteriorated. Israel had already lost a revered prime minister to an ultra-Orthodox fanatic who believed God spoke to him. It had witnessed the massacre of twenty-nine Palestinians praying at the Tomb of the Patriarchs by another fundamentalist Orthodox settler, a follower of Rabbi Kahane. Now the red-bearded army private, wearing his *kippa* and a *tzitzit,* the undergarment of an Orthodox Jew, was repeating the same liturgy to an Israeli judge. "When I heard that the agreement was about to be signed to surrender the holy city bought for 400 shekels of silver by our forefather Abraham, I decided that this can't be passed over in silence," Friedman told her. "No one will return it," he vowed, adding "I protest being tried in a secular court and by a woman." It was later learned that Friedman had been hospitalized and undergone seven psychiatric examinations before being inducted into the army. "If these claims that the settler is psychologically ill, which is something that is repeated every time there is a criminal act against Palestinians, are true, why do they insist on arming these psychological patients?" asked Yasser Abed Rabbo, the Palestinian information minister. Chief Palestinian negotiator Saeb Erekat was more pointed. The problem, he said, is that it is the Palestinians in Hebron who need protection from the Jews and not Israelis who need "more security for killers in Hebron."

As Netanyahu and Arafat again dug in their heels, Egyptian president Hosni Mubarak came to the defense of the Palestinian leader. The Israelis, he told a television interviewer, "want to finish the Hebron issue and then sit tight on everything else. When they do not specify a date for the end of redeployment, they create more fears." Mubarak also complained that if Arafat accepted sole Israeli control at the Tomb of the Patriarchs in lieu of joint Israeli-Palestinian patrols, "his acceptance will be met by denunciation and great criticism from the Arab and Islamic states."

This time, however, Dennis Ross and his team did not return home. Instead, in the wee hours of Sunday, he arranged what was to have been a secret meeting between Arafat and Netanyahu at the Erez border crossing. But the meeting swiftly became public, to Netanyahu's apparent regret. "I had hoped the meeting would remain confidential since it seems to me it is paramount that there also be meetings which help build trust and working relations...and which do not have to withstand the lightning flash of cameras," he told a group of Israeli businessmen that same evening. "The fact that [they] were prepared to meet under the cover of darkness reflected how far the conservative Israeli Prime Minister had come in accepting the Palestinian leader as an unavoidable partner," observed Serge Schmemann.[75]

At Ross's urging, Netanyahu used the meeting that began at 2:00 A.M. and lasted until daybreak to offer two new concessions: a date for the release of female Palestinian prisoners and for opening a "safe passage" road to connect the West Bank and Gaza. The Labor government was to have taken both steps after Oslo II, the implementation agreement, was signed in September 1995—but did not. To sweeten his offer, Netanyahu also proposed a timetable for discussing the opening of a Palestinian seaport and airport in Gaza. He already knew from Ross that the nearly completed airport was the apple of Arafat's eye. "It is 3.8 kilometers [long]. Any jet in the world can land there," a beaming Arafat had told a visiting American only a few days earlier.[76]

But no sweetener could satisfy Arafat's insistence on a timetable to complete the three final stages of Israeli withdrawals. In his view, he made compromises in the Oslo pact—to postpone resolution of the emotional issues of Jerusalem, refugees, settlements and statehood—

only because the Palestinians were gaining self-rule in the bulk of the West Bank territory according to an agreed timetable. The Palestinians had signed the Oslo accord without any guarantees that East Jerusalem would ever become their capital; that Palestinian refugees would ever have the right of return; indeed, that there would ever be a Palestinian state.

"When they agreed to delay these issues, the Palestinians made a historic decision," explained Osama El-Baz. "They were betting on the future, gambling that the peace process would create its own momentum." Yossi Beilin, a key Oslo architect, agreed. By conceding that Israel would withdraw from the West Bank by September 1997, "the Palestinians got a kind of safety net, he said.[77] To give away that card now, Arafat believed, would not only leave the Palestinians without the *territorial* card gained at Oslo but would also jeopardize future negotiations over the all-important final status issues. In Arafat's mind, Israel would regain what it had already given up at Oslo: the ability to use its control over additional territory as a bargaining chip to wrest further compromises from the Palestinians on Jerusalem, refugees, settlements and statehood.

Netanyahu, however, refused to provide any deadlines beyond the first redeployment, which he promised would be completed by March. He argued that events had already overturned the calendar. "Remember that the original dates were thrown asunder because we had an assassination, a horrible happening here, an earthquake," Netanyahu told Charlie Rose, host of a highly regarded PBS television talk show. "Then we had terror attacks," he went on. "Then we had an election. Then we had this awful incident where they fired their rifles against us [after the opening of the tourist tunnel]. Each one of them is a cataclysmic event and obviously throws the calendar askew. So you can't come and say, 'Let's hold to the original dates.' You need a different arrangement."

As Dennis Ross worked with Netanyahu trying to close the remaining gaps, violence once more derailed the talks. On January 9, two pipe bombs exploded in garbage cans in a seedy part of Tel Aviv, wounding thirteen people, three of them seriously. Netanyahu broke off his talks with Ross and warned that the process would be imperiled "if it becomes clear that the terrorists who carried out this attack came from the Palestinian Authority."

With Netanyahu in no mood to continue the talks, Arafat left on Friday for Paris. When he returned to the region the next day, he flew to Cairo to meet with Egyptian president Hosni Mubarak. Meanwhile Dennis Ross, who had himself flown to Cairo earlier that day to encourage Mubarak to cease reinforcing Arafat's stubbornness, served notice that he would return home on Sunday. His threat to leave was at least taken seriously by King Hussein, who flew to Gaza Sunday afternoon to urge Arafat to accept a compromise. It would postpone Israel's final withdrawal from the West Bank for almost a year—until August 1998—but the new timetable would be guaranteed by the United States. So would the phased release of five thousand Palestinian prisoners, including female inmates; the opening of a new seaport and airport; and a "safe-passage" truck route between Gaza and the West Bank. For Arafat, the compromise preserved an essential element of Oslo: although the new borders and extent of Israeli withdrawals still had to be negotiated, the Israeli pullout would be completed at least ten months before the May 1998 deadline for resolving the difficult "final status" issues. With this in hand, Arafat agreed to the pact, only hours before Ross planned to head home from his month-long journey. From Gaza, Hussein flew to Tel Aviv, where he relayed Arafat's acceptance to Netanyahu. As the three—Ross, Netanyahu and the king—emerged from an hour-long meeting, Hussein spoke for them all when he said dryly, "I believe, sir, we are on the verge of the completion of a long road."

Two days after Hussein's rescue mission, Arafat and Netanyahu finally met to seal the agreement. The drama began, as usual, on Arafat's clock, shortly after midnight, when Ross and his team closeted himself with the two leaders and their negotiators at the Erez checkpoint. After four months of meetings, the closing session lasted an hour and a half. But this time Arafat and Netanyahu spent twenty minutes alone in what a State Department official called a "four-eyes" meeting. It was a chance for the two leaders to talk about the future.

After they emerged, at about 2:00 A.M., the two negotiating teams were invited in to witness the initialing of the accord by the two delegation heads, Dan Shomron and Saeb Erekat. Fifteen minutes later an Israeli spokesman announced the pact had been signed, and at 2:45 A.M. Dennis Ross came out, flanked by Netanyahu on his right and Arafat on his left. Ross called the accords "fair and balanced." He said that an accompanying note, a formal statement by the United States of what it expected each side to do, "really lays out a road map for the future." The mood that "pervaded this place tonight was really quite striking," he said. "It was very emotional with all of us crowded into a little room," added Aaron Miller.[78] The two delegations embraced. But neither Arafat nor Netanyahu displayed any warmth toward the other. They shook hands stiffly. Then they parted, no doubt contemplating their next task: selling the pact to their hardliners.

As details emerged of the documents—the Hebron accord, the U.S. "Note for the Record" and confidential letters from U.S. Secretary of State Warren Christopher to both leaders—it became clear that while Netanyahu had won concessions providing greater security for nearby settlements and the Jewish enclaves in the heart of the Hebron, he had failed to win the unimpeded right for Israeli soldiers to enter Palestinian-controlled areas—about 80 percent of the city—in "hot pursuit" of alleged troublemakers. In this sizable Arab area, specified as H1 in the new "protocol" accord, the Palestinian Authority would assume complete control. Netanyahu, however, had won the right to police Abu Sneineh (H2), the neighborhood adjacent to the Tomb of the Patriarchs where the 450 religious Jewish nationalists live. Under the accord, Israeli forces would "retain all powers and responsibilities for internal security and public order" in this area, although Palestinians would have a "symbolic" presence at the same site. Israeli-Palestinian mobile units could be called to calm tensions in this area if instructed to do so by the new jointly staffed District Coordination Office. These armed units would patrol the "commanding heights" above Abu Sneineh and the Hebron roads, including Highway 35, which transects H1 and is often used by settlers to reach Jerusalem. To further protect Abu Sneineh and Qiryat Arba, the pact called for buffer zones adjacent to Hebron's old city and the nearby settlement where Palestinian checkpoints would be set up to disarm anyone who tried to smuggle weapons into the area.

Israel won an additional measure of protection: its mobile units would be equipped with short-barrel M-16 automatic rifles that had a longer range and greater accuracy than the Mini-Ingram submachine guns carried by the Palestinians. Indeed, Palestinian firepower was to be more restricted than in any other West Bank city. The Palestinian police force of four hundred was to be equipped with only twenty vehicles and two hundred pistols. The one hundred rifles allotted to them were to be kept in locked compartments that could be removed only by two special sixteen-man units and only after

Israeli authorities had been notified, Finally, on Shohada Street, which bypasses the ancient Tomb, the United States agreed to finance construction of a traffic island, guardrails, shoulder-height barriers and parking areas to separate Palestinians and Israelis, and their cars, entering and departing the immediate area. "This has been one of the most micro-managed peace processes in history," quipped Palestinian activist Hanan Ashrawi. "There were negotiations over a particular street, over the Arab vegetable market [in Abu Sneineh] and over the parking lot," she said.[79]

But by far the most significant gain for Arafat—apart from the fact that Israeli troops were leaving the bulk of Hebron and turning civilian control over to his government—was the affirmation in the Christopher letter to Netanyahu that Israel was compelled to complete its withdrawal from the West Bank "no later than mid-1998." In gaining that commitment, Arafat won an important round in the gamble that he could deliver a state to his people. Indeed, Netanyahu's decision to accept the pullout marked the end of a long period in which Likud ideologues thought they could integrate Judea and Samaria into a "Greater Israel" and force the two million Palestinian "inhabitants" to accept only limited autonomy under Israeli sovereignty. Now, not only the Labor Party, which had comprised half of the Israeli electorate, but a sizable majority of Israelis accepted the need for separation from the Palestinians. "They are agreeing to territory for peace," said an American negotiator. "They are agreeing to a partnership with the Palestine Liberation Organization, whose sole essence means the creation of a Palestinian state."[80]

For Netanyahu, the Christopher letter also contained an important stipulation: all "outstanding commitments" had to be carried out by both sides "on the basis of reciprocity." In his campaign for office Netanyahu had charged that since Oslo, the Labor Party had pursued a policy of "give and give." Now he could claim he had redeemed his pledge to negotiate a new arrangement of "give and take." Under the terms of the U.S. note, the PNC had to fulfill its pledge to ratify a new charter. The Palestinian Authority also would be required to strip Hamas and the Islamic fundamentalists of their arms, extradite wanted terrorists and "combat systematically and effectively terrorist organizations and infrastructure." If they failed to implement those promises, Netanyahu would have a pretext for evading his responsibilities. In the U.S. note, Arafat received similar assurances: the Israelis would have to release prisoners, open Gaza ports (sea and air), guarantee safe passage between Gaza and the West Bank and facilitate trade and people-to-people exchanges. Both sides also agreed to begin talks on a permanent settlement within two months after the Hebron redeployment.

"I am very happy that Netanyahu is signing on to Hebron," said a vindicated Shimon Peres. "To see Bibi Netanyahu and his rightist government declaring that Oslo is the only hope for the Jewish people is not an easy change for them," he said. However, he added, the pact could have been concluded a long time ago. "He delayed for six months and returned to the point of departure," changing only the "technicalities." In the process, precious goodwill was lost. "You can organize security with long-range rifles or short-range rifles," said Peres. "It is the nature of the relationship rather than the range of the rifles that decides the fate of peace."[81]

There is a long way to go before Arafat and Netanyahu establish real trust, observed a participant in the talks. "It is not a warm and fuzzy relationship." But the official praised Netanyahu, who he noted had become more pragmatic and flexible. "Tactically he is prepared to do just about anything to succeed," explained the policymaker. Arafat, too, had matured. "He's much less volatile, much less emotional and more focused."[82]

Although Benjamin Begin, the son of the Israeli leader who negotiated peace with Egypt and Israeli's pullout from Sinai, re-signed, the rest of the cabinet approved the pact. After a day of stormy closed-door debate the vote was 11 to 7. The Israeli parliament followed suit, with the Labor parliamentarians happily casting their ballots in the lopsided 87 to 17 majority (with 15 abstentions). As crowds of Palestinians formed outside the British-built military headquarters in Hebron to witness Israeli commanders turning over the keys to the city, Netanyahu told the Knesset he was compelled to fulfill the Oslo accords inherited from the previous government. "We cannot ignore reality," he declared.

Indeed, more than four years after the signing ceremony on the White House lawn and after clasping the hand of the reluctant Yitzhak Rabin, Yasser Arafat is an inescapable reality. Part conjurer, part actor and always consummate politician, the sixty-eight-year-old Nobel Laureate continues to be a folk hero and a phoenix. He has survived assassination attempts, imprisonment, exile, plane crashes, pronouncements of his political demise, and even Saddam

Hussein. And through it all he has brought his people back to Palestine and given them reason to restrengthen their dream.

In the months and years to come, Arafat will confront many more tests of his patience and endurance before he can legitimately declare himself, in fact as well as in spirit, the president of a Palestinian state. But there is no longer any doubt that he has redeemed much of his promise to his people and that he has largely fulfilled his 1988 pledge to recognize the right of the Jewish state "to exist in peace and security." After half a century of struggle, Yasser Arafat has helped usher in a new era of coexistence for Israel and Palestine. Today he can point with pride to his own role in bringing about "the peace of courageous men, the peace of the brave."

Documents

The Palestinian National Charter as revised by the Fourth PNC meeting, July 1968 (extracts)

Article 1: Palestine is the homeland of the Arab Palestinian people; it is an indivisible part of the Arab homeland, and the Palestinian people are an integral part of the Arab nation.

Article 2: Palestine, with the boundaries it had during the British mandate, is an indivisible territorial unit....

Article 4: The Palestinian identity is a genuine, essential and inherent characteristic; it is transmitted from parents to children. The Zionist occupation and the dispersal of the Palestinian Arab people, through the disasters which befell them, do not make them lose their Palestinian identity and their membership of the Palestinian community, nor do they negate them.

Article 5: The Palestinians are those Arab nationals who, until 1947, normally resided in Palestine regardless of whether they were evicted from it or have stayed there. Anyone born, after that date, of a Palestinian father—whether inside Palestine or outside it—is also a Palestinian.

Article 6: The Jews who had normally resided in Palestine until the beginning of the Zionist invasion will be considered Palestinians....

Article 8: The phase in their history, through which the Palestinian people are now living, is that of national struggle for the liberation of Palestine. Thus the conflicts among the Palestinian national forces are secondary, and should be ended for the sake of the basic conflict that exists between the forces of Zionism and of imperialism on the one hand, and the Palestinian Arab people on the other....

493

Article 9: Armed struggle is the only way to liberate Palestine. Thus it is the overall strategy, not merely a tactical phase. The Palestine Arab people assert their absolute determination and firm resolution to continue their armed struggle and to work for an armed popular revolution for the liberation of their country and their return to it....

Article 10: Commando action constitutes the nucleus of the Palestinian popular liberation war....

Article 12: The Palestinian people believe in Arab unity. In order to contribute their share towards the attainment of that objective, however, they must, at the present stage of their struggle, safeguard their Palestinian identity and develop their consciousness of that identity, and oppose any plan that may dissolve or impair it....

Article 15: The liberation of Palestine, from an Arab viewpoint, is a national duty and it attempts to repel the Zionist and imperialist aggression against the Arab homeland, and aims at the elimination of Zionism in Palestine. Absolute responsibility for this falls upon the Arab nation—peoples and governments—with the Arab people of Palestine in the vanguard....

Article 19: The partition of Palestine in 1947 and the establishment of the state of Israel are entirely illegal, regardless of the passage of time, because they were contrary to the will of the Palestinian people and to their natural right in their homeland, and inconsistent with the principles embodied in the Charter of the United Nations, particularly the right to self-determination.

Article 20: The Balfour Declaration, the mandate for Palestine and everything that has been based upon them, are deemed null and void. Claims of historical or religious ties of Jews with Palestine are incompatible with the facts of history and the true conception of what constitutes statehood. Judaism, being a religion, is not an independent nationality. Nor do Jews constitute a single nation with an identity of its own; they are citizens of the states to which they belong.

Article 21: The Arab Palestinian people, expressing themselves by the armed Palestinian revolution, reject all solutions which are substitutes for the total liberation of Palestine....

Article 22: Zionism is a political movement organically associated with international imperialism and antagonistic to all action for liberation and to progressive movements in the world. It is racist and fanatic in its nature, aggressive, expansionist and colonial in its aims, and fascist in its methods....

Article 27: The Palestine Liberation Organization shall cooperate with all Arab states, each according to its potentialities; and will adopt a neutral policy among them in the light of the requirements of the war of liberation; and on this basis it shall not interfere in the internal affairs of any Arab state....

Article 33: This Charter shall not be amended save by (vote of) a majority of two-thirds of the total membership of the National Congress of the Palestine Liberation Organization [i.e. the PNC] at a special session convened for that purpose.

Text of United Nations Security Council Resolution 242 of November 22, 1967

Adopted unanimously at the 1382nd meeting

The Security Council,
Expressing its continuing concern with the grave situation in the Middle East,
Emphasizing the inadmissibility of the acquisition of territory by war and the need to work for a just and lasting peace in which every State in the area can live in security,
Emphasizing further that all Member States in their acceptance of the Charter of the United Nations have undertaken a commitment to act in accordance with Article 2 of the Charter.
1. *Affirms* that the fulfilment of Charter principles requires the establishment of a just and lasting peace in the Middle East which should include the application of both the following principles:
(i) Withdrawal of Israeli armed forces from territories occupied in the recent conflict;
(ii) Termination of all claims or states of belligerency and respect for and acknowledgement of the sovereignty, territorial integrity and political independence of every State in the area and their right to live in peace within secure and recognized boundaries free from threats or acts of force;
2. *Affirms further* the necessity
(a) For guaranteeing freedom of navigation through international waterways in the area;
(b) For achieving a just settlement of the refugee problem;
(c) For guaranteeing the territorial inviolability and political independence of every State in the area, through measures including the establishment of demilitarized zones;
3. *Requests* the Secretary-General to designate a Special Representative to proceed to the Middle East to establish and maintain contacts with the States concerned in order to promote agreement and assist efforts to achieve a peaceful and accepted settlement in accordance with the provisions and principles of this resolution.
4. *Requests* the Secretary-General to report to the Security Council on the progress of the efforts of the Special Representative as soon as possible.

Text of United Nations Security Council Resolution 338

Adopted by the Security Council at its 1747th meeting, on October 21–22, 1973

The Security Council

1. *Calls upon* all parties to the present fighting to cease all firing and terminate all military activity immediately, no later than 12 hours after the moment of the adoption of this decision, in the positions they now occupy;

2. *Calls upon* the parties concerned to start immediately after the cease-fire the implementation of Security Council Resolution 242 (1967) in all of its parts;

3. *Decides* that, immediately and concurrently with the cease-fire, negotiations start between the parties concerned under appropriate auspices aimed at establishing a just and durable peace in the Middle East.

The Jordanian-PLO Accord of February 11, 1985

Proceeding from the spirit of the Fez summit resolutions, as agreed upon by the Arab [world] and the resolutions of the UN relating to the Palestine problem;

In accordance with international legitimacy, and proceeding from the mutual understanding to establish a special relationship between the Jordanian and Palestinian people;

The Government of the Hashemite Kingdom of Jordan and the Palestine Liberation Organization have agreed to march together towards the realization of a just and peaceful settlement of the Middle East problem and to put an end to the Israeli occupation of the Arab occupied territories, including Jerusalem, in accordance with the following principles:

1. Land in exchange for peace, as laid down in the resolutions of the United Nations, including the resolutions of the Security Council;

2. The right of the Palestinian people to self-determination. The Palestinians will exercise their inalienable right to self-determination when the Jordanians and the Palestinians will be able to realize this within the framework of an Arab confederal union, which [they] intend to have established between the two states of Jordan and Palestine (*dawlatay al-Urdunn wa-Filastin*);

3. The solution of the Palestinian refugee problem in accordance with the resolutions of the UN;

4. The solution of the Palestinian problem in all its aspects;

5. On this basis, the peace negotiations will be held within the framework of an international conference that will be attended by the five permanent

members of the UN Security Council and the other parties to the conflict, including the PLO, the sole legitimate representative of the Palestinian people, in a joint delegation (a joint Jordanian-Palestinian delegation).*

*Words in parentheses did not appear in the PLO version of text.

Text of the joint Stockholm PLO-American delegation statement, presented by Swedish Foreign Minister Sten Andersson, December 7, 1988

The Palestinian National Council met in Algiers from November 12 to 15, 1988, and announced the declaration of independence which proclaimed the state of Palestine and issued a political statement.

The following explanation was given by the representatives of the PLO of certain important points in the Palestinian declaration of independence and the political statement adopted by the PNC in Algiers.

Affirming the principle incorporated in those UN resolutions which call for a two-state solution of Israel and Palestine, the PNC:

1. Agreed to enter into peace negotiations at an international conference under the auspices of the UN with the participation of the permanent members of the Security Council and the PLO as the sole legitimate representative of the Palestinian people, on equal footing with the other parties to the conflict; such an international conference is to be held on the basis of the UN Resolutions 242 and 338 and the right of the Palestinian people to self-determination, without external interference, as provided in the UN Charter, including the right to an independent state, which conference should resolve the Palestinian problem in all its aspects;

2. Established the independent state of Palestine and accepted the existence of Israel as a state in the region;

3. Declared its rejection and condemnation of terrorism in all its forms, including state terrorism;

4. Called for a solution to the Palestinian refugee problem in accordance with international law and practices and relevant UN resolutions (including the right of return or compensation).

Text of Arafat's Geneva Press Statement, December 14, 1988

Allow me to explain my viewpoints before you. Our desire for peace is strategic and not a temporary tactic. We work for peace regardless of whatever may happen, whatever may happen.

Our state provides salvation for the Palestinians and peace for both the Palestinians and Israelis. The right to self-determination means the existence of the Palestinians and our existence does not destroy the existence of the Israelis, as their rulers claim.

In my speech yesterday, I referred to UN Resolution No. 181 as a basis for Palestinian independence. I also referred to our acceptance of Resolutions 242 and 338 as a basis for negotiations with Israel within the framework of the international conference.

Our PNC accepted these three resolutions at the Algiers session. Also in my speech yesterday, it was clear that we mean our people's rights to freedom and national independence in accordance with Resolution No. 181 as well as the right of all parties concerned with the Middle East conflict to exist in peace and security, including—as I said—the State of Palestine, Israel, and other neighbors in accordance with Resolutions 242 and 338.

Regarding terrorism, yesterday I announced beyond doubt—and nevertheless I repeat for the sake of recording stands, I repeat for the sake of recording stands—that we totally and categorically reject all forms of terrorism, including individual, group, and state terrorism.

We explained our stand in Geneva and Algiers. Any talk to the effect that the Palestinians must offer more—do you remember this slogan—or that what was offered is insufficient or that the Palestinians are playing propaganda games or public relations maneuvers will be harmful and unfruitful. That is enough.

All outstanding issues should be discussed on the table and at the international conference. Let it be perfectly clear that neither Arafat nor anyone else can stop the uprising.

The uprising will stop only when practical and tangible steps are taken toward the attainment of its national goals and establishment of its Palestinian state.

Within this framework, I expect the EEC states to play a more effective role in consolidating peace in our region. They assume a political and moral responsibility and they can deal with this.

Finally, I announce before you and ask you to convey these words on my behalf: We want peace, we want peace, we are committed to peace, we are committed to peace, and we want to live in our Palestinian state and let others live. Thank you.

Arafat's Letter to Rabin Recognizing Israel's Right to Exist in Peace, September 9, 1993

Mr. Prime Minister,

The signing of the Declaration of Principles marks a new era in the history of the Middle East. In firm conviction thereof, I would like to confirm the following PLO commitments:

The PLO recognizes the right of the State of Israel to exist in peace and security.

The PLO accepts UN Security Council Resolutions 242 and 338.

The PLO commits itself to the Middle East peace process, and to a peaceful resolution of the conflict between the two sides and declares that all outstanding issues relating to permanent status will be resolved through negotiations.

The PLO considers that the signing of the Declaration of Principles constitutes a historic event, inaugurating a new epoch of peaceful coexistence, free from violence and all other acts which endanger peace and stability. Accordingly, the PLO renounces the use of terrorism and other acts of violence and will assume responsibility over all PLO elements and personnel in order to assure their compliance, prevent violations and discipline violators.

In view of the promise of a new era and the signing of the Declaration of Principles and based on Palestinian acceptance of Security Council Resolutions 242 and 338, the PLO affirms that those articles of the Palestinian Covenant which deny Israel's right to exist, and the provisions of the Covenant which are inconsistent with the commitments of this letter are now inoperative and no longer valid. Consequently, the PLO undertakes to submit to the Palestinian National Council for formal approval the necessary changes in regard to the Palestinian Covenant.

Sincerely,

Yasser Arafat
Chairman, The Palestine Liberation Organization

Rabin's Letter to Arafat Recognizing the PLO, September 9, 1993

Yasser Arafat
Chairman
The Palestinian Liberation Organization

Mr. Chairman,

In response to your letter of September 9, 1993, I wish to confirm to you that, in light of the PLO commitments included in your letter, the Government of Israel has decided to recognize the PLO as the representative of the Palestinian people and commence negotiations with the PLO within the Middle East peace process.

Sincerely,

Yitzhak Rabin
Prime Minister of Israel

The Israel-PLO Declaration of Principles, September 13, 1993

The Government of the State of Israel and the P.L.O. team (the "Palestinian Delegation"), representing the Palestinian people, agree that it is time to put an end to decades of confrontation and conflict, recognize their mutual legitimate and political rights, and strive to live in peaceful coexistence and mutual dignity and security and achieve a just, lasting and comprehensive peace settlement and historic reconciliation through the agreed political process. Accordingly, the two sides agree to the following principles:

ARTICLE I—Aim of the Negotiations

The aim of the Israeli-Palestinian negotiations within the current Middle East peace process is, among other things, to establish a Palestinian Interim Self-Government Authority, the elected Council (the "Council"), for the Palestinian people in the West Bank and the Gaza Strip, for a transitional period not exceeding five years, leading to a permanent settlement based on Security Council Resolutions 242 and 338.

It is understood that the interim arrangements are an integral part of the whole peace process and that the negotiations on the permanent status will lead to the implementation of Security Council Resolutions 242 and 338.

ARTICLE II—Framework of the Interim Period

The agreed framework for the interim period is set forth in this Declaration of Principles.

ARTICLE III—Elections

1. In order that the Palestinian people in the West Bank and Gaza Strip may govern themselves according to democratic principles, direct free and general political elections will be held for the Council under agreed supervision and international observation, while the Palestinian police will ensure public order.

2. An agreement will be concluded on the exact mode and conditions of the elections in accordance with the protocol attached as Annex 1, with the goal of holding the elections not later than nine months after the entry into force of this Declaration of Principles.

3. These elections will constitute a significant interim preparatory step toward the realization of the legitimate rights of the Palestinian people and their just requirements.

ARTICLE IV—Jurisdiction

Jurisdiction of the Council will cover West Bank and Gaza Strip territory, except for issues that will be negotiated in the permanent status negotiations. The two sides view the West Bank and the Gaza Strip as a single territorial unit, whose integrity will be preserved during the interim period.

ARTICLE V—Transitional Period and Permanent Status Negotiations

1. The five-year transitional period will begin upon the withdrawal from the Gaza Strip and Jericho area.

2. Permanent status negotiations will commence as soon as possible, but not later than the beginning of the third year of the interim period, between the Government of Israel and the Palestinian people's representatives.

3. It is understood that these negotiations shall cover remaining issues, including: Jerusalem, refugees, settlements, security arrangements, borders, relations and cooperation with other neighbors, and other issues of common interest.

4. The two parties agree that the outcome of the permanent status negotiations should not be prejudiced or preempted by agreements reached for the interim period.

ARTICLE VI—Preparatory Transfer of Powers and Responsibilities

1. Upon the entry into force of this Declaration of Principles and the withdrawal from the Gaza Strip and the Jericho area, a transfer of authority from the Israeli military government and its Civil Administration to the authorized Palestinians for this task, as detailed herein, will commence. This transfer of authority will be of a preparatory nature until the inauguration of the Council.

2. Immediately after the entry into force of this Declaration of Principles and the withdrawal from the Gaza Strip and Jericho area, with the view to promoting economic development in the West Bank and Gaza Strip, authority will be transferred to the Palestinians on the following spheres: education and culture, health, social welfare, direct taxation, and tourism. The Palestinian side will commence in building the Palestinian police force, as agreed upon. Pending the inauguration of the Council, the two parties may negotiate the transfer of additional powers and responsibilities, as agreed upon.

ARTICLE VII—Interim Agreement

1. The Israeli and Palestinian delegations will negotiate an agreement on the interim period (the "Interim Agreement").

2. The Interim Agreement shall specify, among other things, the structure of the Council, the number of its members, and the transfer of powers and responsibilities from the Israeli military government and its Civil Administration to the Council. The Interim Agreement shall also specify the Council's executive authority, legislative authority in accordance with Article IX below, and the independent Palestinian judicial organs.

3. The Interim Agreement shall include arrangements, to be implemented upon the inauguration of the Council, for the assumption by the Council of all of the powers and responsibilities transferred previously in accordance with Article VI above.

4. In order to enable the Council to promote economic growth, upon its inauguration, the Council will establish, among other things, a Palestinian Electricity Authority, a Gaza Sea Port Authority, a Palestinian Development Bank, a Palestinian Export Promotion Board, a Palestinian Environmental

Authority, a Palestinian Land Authority and a Palestinian Water Administration Authority, and any other Authorities agreed upon, in accordance with the Interim Agreement that will specify their powers and responsibilities.

5.   After the inauguration of the Council, the Civil Administration will be dissolved, and the Israeli military government will be withdrawn.

ARTICLE VIII—Public Order and Security

In order to guarantee public order and internal security for the Palestinians of the West Bank and the Gaza Strip, the Council will establish a strong police force, while Israel will continue to carry the responsibility for defending against external threats, as well as the responsibility for overall security of Israelis for the purpose of safeguarding their internal security and public order.

ARTICLE IX—Laws and Military Orders

1.   The Council will be empowered to legislate, in accordance with the Interim Agreement, within all authorities transferred to it.

2. Both parties will review jointly laws and military orders presently in force in remaining spheres.

ARTICLE X—Joint Israeli-Palestinians Liaison Committee

In order to provide for a smooth implementation of this Declaration of Principles and any subsequent agreements pertaining to the interim period, upon the entry into force of this Declaration of Principles, a joint Israeli-Palestinian Liaison Committee will be established in order to deal with issues requiring coordination, other issues of common interest, and disputes.

ARTICLE XI—Israeli-Palestinian Cooperation in Economic Fields

Recognizing the mutual benefit of cooperation in promoting the development of the West Bank, the Gaza Strip and Israel, upon the entry into force of this Declaration of Principles, an Israeli-Palestinian Economic Cooperation Committee will be established in order to develop and implement in a cooperative manner the programs identified in the protocols attached as Annex III and Annex IV.

ARTICLE XII—Liaison and Cooperation with Jordan and Egypt

The two parties will invite the Governments of Jordan and Egypt to participate in establishing further liaison and cooperation arrangements between the Government of Israel and the Palestinian representatives, on the one hand, and the Governments of Jordan and Egypt, on the other hand, to promote cooperation between them. These arrangements will include the constitution of a Continuing Committee that will decide by agreement on the modalities of admission of persons displaced from the West Bank and Gaza Strip in 1967, together with necessary measures to prevent disruption and disorder. Other matters of common concern will be dealt with by this Committee.

ARTICLE XIII—Redeployment of Israeli Forces

1.   After the entry into force of this Declaration of Principles, and not later than the eve of elections for the Council, a redeployment of Israeli military forces in the West Bank and the Gaza Strip will take place, in addition to withdrawal of Israeli forces carried out in accordance with Article XIV.

2.   In redeploying its military forces, Israel will be guided by the principle that its military forces should be redeployed outside populated areas.

3.   Further redeployments to specified locations will be gradually implemented commensurate with the assumption of responsibility for public order and internal security by the Palestinian police force pursuant to Article VIII above.

ARTICLE XIV—Israeli Withdrawal from the Gaza Strip and Jericho Area

Israel will withdraw from the Gaza Strip and Jericho area, as detailed in the protocol attached as Annex II.

ARTICLE XV—Resolution of Disputes

1.   Disputes arising out of the application or interpretation of this Declaration of Principles, or any subsequent agreements pertaining to the interim period, shall be resolved by negotiations through the joint Liaison Committee to be established pursuant to Article X above.

2.   Disputes which cannot be settled by negotiations may be resolved by a mechanism of conciliation to be agreed upon by the parties.

3. The parties may agree to submit to arbitration disputes relating to the interim period, which cannot be settled through conciliation. To this end, upon the agreement of both parties, the parties will establish an Arbitration Committee.

ARTICLE XVI—Israeli-Palestinian Cooperation Concerning Regional Programs

Both parties view the multilateral working groups as an instrument for promoting a "Marshall Plan," the regional programs and other programs, including special programs for the West Bank and Gaza Strip, as indicated in the protocol attached as Annex IV.

ARTICLE XVII—Miscellaneous Provisions

1. This Declaration of Principles will enter into force one month after its signing.

2. All protocols annexed to this Declaration of Principles and Agreed Minutes pertaining thereto shall be regarded as an integral part hereof.

Done at Washington, D.C., this thirteenth day of September, 1993.

| For the Government of Israel: | Shimon Peres |
| For the PLO: | Mahmoud Abbas |

| Witnessed by: | Warren Christopher | Andrei Kozyrev |
| | United States of America | Russian Federation |

Glossary

Major Palestinian Organizations

ANM: Arab Nationalist Movement. Founded in late 1940s as student movement with Palestinian nationalist branch. Ideological predecessor of George Habash's Popular Front for the Liberation of Palestine.

ALF: Arab Liberation Front. Iraqi-backed radical PLO faction headed by Executive Committee member Abdul Rahim Ahmed. Opposes Arafat peace initiative.

Asifa. The military branch of Fatah used as a cover for the first guerrilla operations against Israel in 1965.

Black September. Terrorist group within Fatah. Operated from 1970–74. Organized attacks against Israeli athletes at Munich Olympics, U.S. diplomats in Sudan and Jordanian officials. Led by colleagues of Abu Iyad: Ali Hassan Salameh, Kamal Adwan, Abu Youssef.

DFLP: Democratic Front for the Liberation of Palestine. Founded in 1969 by Nayaf Hawatmeh when he split with PFLP leader George Habash. First to advocate two-state solution in 1974. Supports Arafat's peace initiative.

Fatah: Reverse acronym in Arabic for Palestinian National Liberation Movement. Formed in late 1950s as secret underground cell in Kuwait by Arafat and Khalil Wazir (Abu Jihad). Gained leadership of PLO in 1969. Largest organization within PLO. Represents mainstream of Palestinian thinking.

Fatah Revolutionary Council. Libyan-backed anti-Arafat radical faction led by Abu Nidal responsible for numerous terrorist attacks. Formed in 1973 when Abu Nidal split from Fatah. Headquartered in Tripoli. Expelled from Iraq and Syria.

506

Fatah Uprising (also known as Fatah Provisional Command). Formed in 1983 with Syrian backing. Led by Abu Musa, a noted Palestinian military commander who attempted to overthrow Arafat after PLO ouster from Lebanon. Based in Damuscus.

Force 17. Fatah faction within PLO formed in early 1970s. Provides personal security forces for Arafat and other leaders. Involved in terrorist operations against Israelis in Cyprus.

National Salvation Front. Alliance of anti-Arafat factions sponsored by Syria. Formed in 1983 to oppose U.S.-brokered PLO withdrawal from Beirut. Included Fatah Uprising, PFLP, PFLP-GC, PPSF, PLF-Yakoub faction and Saiqa.

PLF: Palestine Liberation Front. Iraqi-backed radical PLO faction led by Executive Committee member Mohammed Abul Abbas. Split from PFLP in 1977. Originally worked closely with Syrian intelligence. Reunited in 1987 with opposing PLF faction headed by Talat Yaqoub. Responsible for 1985 Achille Lauro hijacking and 1990 attack on Tel Aviv beach.

PFLP: Popular Front for the Liberation of Palestine. Formed by Marxist physician George Habash, a Christian Palestinian, as outgrowth of ANM in 1967. Responsible for terrorist operations, chiefly airplane hijackings in early 1970s. PFLP is Fatah's main rival within PLO but conditionally supports Arafat's peace initiative.

PFLP-GC: Popular Front for the Liberation of Palestine-General Command. Radical Syrian-backed and anti-Arafat faction formed in 1969 by Ahmed Jabril when he broke from PFLP. Responsible for terrorist operations both inside and outside Israel, including hang-glider attacks, and allegedly involved in bombing of Pan Am 103.

PLO: Palestine Liberation Organization. Formed in 1964 by Egyptian President Gamal Abdel Nasser and other Arab states to gain support of Palestinian nationalists. First led by Ahmed Shukeiry. Replaced by Arafat in 1969. Umbrella organization for Palestine liberation movement. Named sole legitimate representative of Palestinian people at 1974 Arab summit in Rabat. Governed by Central Committee and ruling fifteen-member Executive Committee. Comprises eight main organizations.

PNC: Palestine National Congress. Parliament-in-exile of all Palestinians inside and outside occupied territories. PLO gets its authority from PNC which meets annually to elect Executive Committee and approve PLO policies.

PSF: Popular Struggle Front. Radical anti-Arafat faction led by Samir Ghosheh who split from Habash in 1960s. Based in Damascus.

RPCP: Revolutionary Palestinian Communist Party. Moscow-backed PLO faction led by Executive Committee member Suleiman Najab. Early advocate of two-state solution and supporter of Arafat peace initiative.

Saiqa: Acronym in Arabic for Vanguard of the Popular War of Liberation. Created by Syrian Baathist regime in 1967 as Palestinian military unit. Anti-Arafat faction based in Damascus that split from PLO in 1983. Supports struggle to regain all of Palestine.

Major Palestinian Figures

Yasser Abed Rabbo (Abu Bashir). Assistant secretary-general of DFLP. Member of PLO Executive Committee. Leads PLO team negotiating with U.S.

Abu Amar (Yasser Arafat). PLO Chairman and president of PLO-declared state of Palestine. Co-founder and leader of Fatah.

Abu Daoud (Mohammed Daoud Mahmoud Auda). Commander of all Palestinian fighters in Jordan until Black September in 1970–71. Captured by Jordan after assasination plot against King Hussein.

Abu al-Houl (Hail Abdul Hamid). Member of Fatah. Responsible for Fatah Western section, including West Bank and Gaza.

Abu Iyad (Salah Khalaf). Number two in PLO. Responsible for intelligence and security. Alleged links to Black September group.

Abu Jihad (Khalil Wazir). Former number two in PLO and head of operations inside occupied territories. Co-founder of Fatah. Assassinated in 1988 by Israeli commandos in Tunis.

Abu Lutuf (Farouk Kaddoumi). Hard-line PLO foreign minister and head of PLO political department. Close to Syria and Soviet Union.

Abu Mazzen (Mahmoud Abbas). Fatah representative on PLO Executive Committee. Head of PLO Department of Arab and International Affairs. Responsible for Israeli portfolio. On PLO team negotiating with U.S.

Abu Musa (Colonel Said Musa Muragha). Leader of Fatah Provisional Command. Military commander in Lebanon. Organized National Salvation Front in 1983 in effort to overthrow Arafat. Based in Damascus.

Abu Nidal (Sabri al-Banna). Head of Fatah Revolutionary Council. Removed from PLO Executive Committee for launching unauthorized terrorist operations. Headquartered in Libya.

Bassam Abu Sharif (Abu Sharar). Political adviser to Arafat. Former PFLP activist; switched allegiance to Arafat in 1987. Major moderate voice.

Abu Tariq (Abdul Latif Abu Hijiah). Member of PLO team negotiating with U.S. in Tunis.

Abu Tayyib (Colonel Mohammed Natour). Head of Force 17.

Abul Abbas (Mohammed Abbas). PLF. Member of PLO Executive Committee. Implicated in Achille Lauro hijacking and June 1990 attack on Tel Aviv beach.

Abder al-Rahim Ahmed. Secretary-General of ALF. Head of Popular Organization Dept. Member of PLO Executive Committee. Editor of PLO magazine *Philistinel-Thawra*.

Fathi Arafat. Physician brother of Yasser Arafat. Head of Palestine Red Crescent Society.

Inam Arafat. Yasser Arafat's oldest sister. Brought him up when their mother died. Lives in Cairo.

Hakim Belawi. On PLO team negotiating with U.S. in Tunis. PLO Ambassador to Tunisia. Close Arafat adviser.

Mahmoud Darwish. Independent. Member of PLO Executive Committee. Chairman of Supreme Council for Education, Propaganda and Heritage.

Khaled al-Fahoum. Former PNC speaker based in Damascus. Opposed Arafat's efforts to convene PNC in Amman in 1983.

Jaweed al-Ghussein (Abu Tufiq). Independent. Member of PLO Executive Committee. Chairman of Board of Directors of Palestine National Fund.

George Habash. Leader of PFLP. Marxist Christian intellectual graduate of AUB. Supports armed struggle. Arafat rival within PLO. Born in Lydda in 1926.

Akram Hanieh. Member of PLO Higher Committee for Occupied Territories. Influential adviser to Arafat.

Hani al-Hassan. Leader of Palestinian student movement in Germany and Europe in early 1960s. Close political adviser to Arafat. Joined Fatah in 1963.

Khaled al-Hassan. Abu Sa'ed. Member of Fatah since 1963. Chairman of Foreign Affairs Committee in PNC. Diplomatic troubleshooter and early advocate of two-state solution.

Nayaf Hawatmeh. Leader of DFLP. Greek Catholic graduate of AUB. First major PLO figure to advocate two-state solution. Supports Arafat peace initiative. Born in Jordan in 1935.

Jamil Hilel. DFLP. PLO spokesman in Tunis.

Abdullah Hourani. Independent. Member of PLO Executive Committee. Head of Cultural Affairs Department.

Abdul Kadar al-Husseini. Led military wing of Palestine Arab Party founded by his cousin Haj Amin. Educated Yasser Arafat in tactics of resistance struggle. Killed in 1948 battle for Jerusalem.

Haj Amin al-Husseini. Spiritual father of Palestinian nationalist movement. Appointed by British as Grand Mufti of Jerusalem in 1922.

Ahmed Jabril. Leader of PFLP-GC. Headquarted in Damascus. Major opponent of Arafat's peace initiative. Split from PFLP in 1969.

Um Jihad. Intissar al-Wazir. Widow of Abu Jihad. Fatah activist involved with orphans of Palestinians killed in guerrilla struggle. Elected to Fatah leadership position in August 1989.

Said Kamal. PLO representative in Cairo. Important go-between with Egyptian Government. Member of Fatah. Moderate.

Omar al-Khatib. PLO representative in Jordan. Former deputy to to Abu Jihad in Lebanon. Active in West Bank in 1965–67.

Bishop Ilia Khouri (Abu Mahar). Independent. Member of PLO Executive Committee.

Abdul Hadi al-Mashash. Leader of anti-Arafat "Fatah Uprising" faction. Headquartered in Damascus.

Mohammed Milhem (Abu A'Ala). Independent representative on PLO Executive Committee. Deposed West Bank mayor. Close Arafat adviser. Head of Occupied Homeland and Higher Education Department.

Suleiman Najab. PCP. Head of Department of Social Affairs. Member of PLO Executive Commitee.

Sheikh Abdul Hamid al-Sayeh. PNC Speaker. Member of Fatah.

Omar Sha'abi. Head PFLP-GC Foreign Relations Department.

Nabil Sha'ath. Chairman of PNC Political Committee. Senior adviser to Arafat. Member of Fatah. Moderate.

Abdul Majeed Shoman. Director of Arab Bank, Ltd. Former chairman of Palestine National Fund.

Ahmed Shukeiry. First chairman of the PLO. Appointed by Egyptian President Gamal Abdel Nasser in June 1964.

Hamid Abu Sitta. University classmate of Arafat. Coached him in anti-British, anti-Zionist guerrilla activities in early 1950s. Member of PLO Executive Committee in 1960s.

Jamal al-Surani. Independent. Secretary-General of PLO Executive Committee. Head of Organizations Department.

Zehdi Labib Terzi. PLO representative to the United Nations. Independent.

Abdul Razak Yahya (Abu Anas). Independent. Member of PLO Executive Committee. Head of Economic Department. Senior PLO representative in Jordan.

Salim Zaanoun (Abu Adib). Deputy chairman of PNC. Chief PLO representative in Gulf states. Headquartered in Kuwait. Member of Fatah Central Committee.

Mustafa al-Zabari (Abu Ali Mustafa). PFLP. Head of Department of Palestinian Refugees. Member of PLO Executive Committee.

Notes

CHAPTER 1

1. Interview with authors, July 1989. All quotes from Arafat in this book are from interviews with the authors unless otherwise noted.
2. Interview with authors, July 1989.
3. Interview with authors, August 1989.
4. "Faces of Arafat," BBC documentary, February 1990.
5. Interview with authors, July 1989.
6. "Faces of Arafat," BBC documentary, February 1990.
7. Interview with authors, July 1989.
8. T.D. Allman, "On the Road with Arafat," *Vanity Fair*, February 1989, p. 112.
9. Interview with authors, August 1989.
10. Livingstone and Halevy, *Inside the PLO*, pp. 177-178.
11. Interview with authors, August 1989.
12. Interview with authors, August 1989.

CHAPTER 2

1. Interview with authors, July 1989.
2. Trager, *The People's Chronology*, pp. 6, 14.
3. Mattar, *The Mufti of Jerusalem*, p. 12.
4. Johnson, *A History of the Jews*, p. 396.
5. Ibid., p. 399.
6. Ibid., p. 430.
7. Ibid., p. 435.
8. Mattar, p. 29.
9. Kollek and Pearlman, *Jerusalem*, p. 156.
10. Interview with authors, August 1989.
11. Interview with authors, August 1989.
12. Zua'iter, *The Palestine Question*, p. 65.
13. Gilbert, *Exile and Return*, p. 159.
14. Interview with authors, August 1989.
15. Interview with authors, August 1989.
16. Interview with authors, August 1989.

CHAPTER 3

1. Interview with authors, July 1989.
2. Interview with authors, August 1989.
3. Interview with authors, July 1989.
4. Interview with authors, August 1989.
5. Interview with authors, August 1989.
6. Interview with authors, August 1989.
7. Interview with authors, August 1989.
8. Interview with authors, August 1989.
9. Interview with authors, July 1988.
10. Interview with authors, July 1989.
11. Interview with authors, August 1989.
12. Interview with authors, August 1989.
13. Interview with authors, August 1989.
14. Interview with authors, August 1989.
15. Interview with authors, July 1989.
16. Mattar, p. 100.
17. Ibid., p. 102.
18. Ibid., p. 103.
19. Interview with authors, August 1989.
20. Mattar, p. 104.
21. Ibid., p. 105.
22. Hart, *Arafat*, p. 70.
23. "Faces of Arafat," BBC documentary, February 1990.
24. Hart, p. 71.
25. Ibid.
26. Interview with authors, August 1989.
27. Hart, p. 70.
28. Ibid.

CHAPTER 4

1. Interview with authors, August 1989.
2. Interview with authors, August 1989.
3. Interview with authors, August 1989.
4. Interview with authors, August 1989.
5. Hart, p. 87.
6. Ibid.
7. Ibid., p. 86.
8. Interview with authors, August 1989.
9. Interview with authors, August 1989.
10. Interview with authors, June 1989.
11. Interview with authors, August 1989.
12. Interview with authors, August 1989.
13. Interview with authors, July 1989.
14. "Faces of Arafat," BBC documentary, February 1990.

CHAPTER 5

1. Interview with authors, July 1989.
2. Interview with authors, July 1989.
3. Interview with authors, July 1989.

4. "Faces of Arafat," BBC documentary, February 1990.
5. Interview with authors, August 1989.
6. Interview with authors, August 1989.
7. Interview with authors, August 1989.
8. Interview with authors, August 1989.
9. Interview with authors, August 1989.
10. Interview with authors, July 1989.

CHAPTER 6
1. Dayan, *Story of My Life*, p. 596.
2. Meir, *My Life*, p. 329.
3. Ibid., p. 364.

CHAPTER 7
1. Arnaud DeBorchgrave, *Washington Times*, March 1, 1989.
2. Interview with authors, January 1981.
3. Interview with authors, June 1988.
4. Interview with authors, January 1981.
5. Interview with authors, January 1981.
6. Interview with authors, August 1989.
7. Interview with authors, June 1988.
8. Segal, *Dear Brothers*, p. 11.
9. Interview with authors, June 1988.
10. *Jerusalem Post*, June 11, 1967.
11. Halabi, *The West Bank Story*, p. 34.
12. Interview with authors, August 1989.
13. Kollek and Pearlman, p. 274.
14. Interview with authors, August 1989.
15. Interview with authors, August 1989.
16. Interview with authors, August 1989.
17. Interview with authors, July 1988.

CHAPTER 8
1. Life Magazine, July 1984.
2. Segal, *Dear Brothers*, p. 14.
3. Ibid., p. 17.
4. Meir, p. 383.

CHAPTER 9
1. Interview with authors, August 1988.
2. Interview with authors, August 1989.
3. Interview with authors, November 1989.
4. Shimoni, *Political Dictionary of the Arab World*, p. 77.
5. Kalb and Kalb, *Kissinger*, p. 502.
6. Interview with authors, June 1988.
7. Interview with authors, June 1988.

CHAPTER 10
1. Interview with authors, August 1989.
2. Interview with authors, July 1988.
3. Interview with authors, January 1981.
4. Interview with authors, July 1989.
5. Interview with authors, February 1990.

CHAPTER 11

1. Press conference in Damascus with Lebanese President Elias Hrawi, UPI, January 23, 1990.
2. Ma'oz, Asad, *The Sphinx of Damascus*, p. 114.
3. Interview with authors, August 1989.
4. Interview with authors, August 1989.
5. Interview with authors, July 1989.
6. Khalid Fahoum, interview with authors, August 1989.
7. Ibid.
8. Interview with authors, August 1989.
9. Interview with authors, August 1989.
10. Interview with authors, August 1989.
11. Interview with authors, July 1989.
12. Interview with authors, July 1989.
13. Rouleau and Iyad, *My Home, My Land*, p. 46.
14. Interview with authors, August 1989.
15. Kiernan, *Arafat: The Man & The Myth*, p. 254.
16. Interview with authors, July 1989.
17. Hart, *Arafat: A Political Biography*, p. 207-9.
18. Interview with authors, July 1989.

CHAPTER 12

1. Interview with authors, July 1989.
2. Rouleau and Iyad, p. 51.
3. Interview with authors, July 1989.
4. Rouleau and Iyad, p. 62.
5. Interview with authors, August 1989.
6. Interview with authors, August 1989.
7. Hart, pp. 280-81.
8. Interview with authors, August 1989.
9. Interview with authors, August 1989.
10. Interview with authors, July 1989.
11. Interview with authors, August 1989.
12. Zeev Schiff and Raphael Rothstein, *Fedayeen: Guerrillas Against Israel*, pp. 108-9.

CHAPTER 13

1. Interview with authors, July 1989.
2. Interview with authors, July 1989.
3. Interview with authors, March 1990.
4. Interview with authors, July 1989.
5. Interview with authors, July 1989.
6. Interview with authors, August 1989.
7. Kissinger, Henry, *Years of Upheaval*, p. 787.
8. Interview with authors, August 1989.
9. Interview with authors, August 1989.

CHAPTER 14

1. Interview with authors, July 1989.
2. Interview with authors, August 1989.
3. Interview with authors, August 1989.
4. *New York Times*, Judith Miller.

5. Interview with authors, August 1989.
6. Ma'oz, p. 168.

CHAPTER 15

1. Interview with authors, August 1989.
2. Fallaci, *Interview with History*, p. 51.
3. Lawrence, *Seven Pillars of Wisdom*, p. 67.
4. Meir, p. 215.
5. Shalim, *Collusion Across the Jordan*, p. 606.
6. Lunt, *Hussein of Jordan*, p. 5.
7. Ibid., p. 58.

CHAPTER 16

1. Interview with authors, August 1989.
2. Interview with authors, July 1988.
3. Interview with authors, July 1988.
4. Interview with authors, February 1990.
5. Interview with authors, July 1989.
6. Interview with authors, August 1989.
7. Interview with authors, August 1989.
8. Interview with authors, August 1989.
9. Interview with authors, August 1989.
10. Lunt, p. 106.
11. Interview with authors, August 1989.
12. Interview with authors, July 1989.
13. Interview with authors, August 1989.
14. Interview with authors, July 1989.
15. Hart, p. 260.
16. Interview with authors, August 1989.
17. Lunt, p. 108.
18. Interview with authors, July 1989.
19. Interview with authors, August 1989.
20. Interview with authors, August 1989.
21. Interview with authors, July 1989.
22. Interview with authors, August 1989.
23. Interview with authors, August 1989.
24. Hart, p. 313.
25. Interview with authors, August 1989.
26. Interview with authors, August 1989.
27. "Faces of Arafat," BBC documentary, February 1990.
28. Interview with authors, July 1989.
29. Interview with authors, August 1989.
30. Interview with authors, July 1989.
31. "Faces of Arafat," BBC documentary, February 1990.

CHAPTER 17

1. Interview with authors, August 1989.
2. Interview with authors, August 1989.
3. Sadat, *In Search of Identity*, p. 201.
4. Heikal, Interview with authors, August 1989.
5. Interview with authors, August 1989.

6. Interview with authors, July 1989.
7. Posner, *Israel Undercover*, p. 202.
8. Interview with authors, August 1989.
9. Vance, *Hard Choices*, pp. 186, 193.
10. Interview with authors, August 1989.

CHAPTER 18
1. Interview with authors, August 1989.
2. Interview with authors, August 1989.
3. Interview with authors, August 1989.
4. Interview with authors, August 1989.
5. Interview with authors, July 1989.
6. Interview with authors, July 1988.

CHAPTER 19
1. Interview with Landrum Bolling, March 1990.
2. *American Arab Affairs*, Issue 15, Winter 1985-86.
3. Interview with authors, February 1988.
4. Hart, p. 353.
5. Kissinger, pp. 628-29.
6. Walters, Vernon, *Silent Missions*, 1978.
7. David Ignatius, *The Washington Post*, December 4, 1988.
8. Kissinger, p. 629.
9. Interview with Khaled al-Hassan, July 1989.
10. Interview with authors, April 1990.
11. Ignatius, *Wall Street Journal*, February 10, 1983.
12. *New York Times*, July 10, 1983.
13. Interview with authors, July 1989.

CHAPTER 20
1. Brzezinski, Zbigniew, *Power and Principle*, pp. 101-7.
2. Interview with authors, Spring 1990.
3. Interview with authors, March 1990.
4. Interview with authors, Fall 1989.
5. Interview with Gary Sick, March 1990.
6. Interview with authors, July 1989.
7. Interview with authors, July 1989.
8. *New York Times*, February 19, 1984.

CHAPTER 21
1. Interview with authors, July 1989.
2. Interview with authors, Spring 1990.
3. Interview with authors, Fall 1989.
4. Interview with Lawrence Silberman, July, 1990.
5. *The Washington Post*, December 4, 1988.
6. Khalidi, Rashid, *Under Siege: PLO Decisionmaking During the 1982 War*, p. 156.
7. Ibid., p. 157.
8. Ibid., p. 158.
9. Interview with authors, July 1989.
10. Khalidi, p. 161.

CHAPTER 22

1. Interview with authors, Spring 1990.
2. MacLeod, Scott, *New York Review of Books,* June 22, 1989.
3. Interview with authors, Fall 1989.
4. MacLeod, *New York Review of Books.*
5. Interview with authors, Spring 1990.
6. Interview with authors, Spring 1990.
7. Interview with William Quandt, Spring 1990.
8. Interview with authors, Spring 1990.
9. *Time,* December 26, 1988, pp. 23-27.
10. Interview with authors, Spring 1990.
11. Interview with authors, July 1989.
12. Interview with authors, Spring 1990.
13. Interview with authors, August 1989.
14. Interview with authors, July 1989.
15. Interview with authors, July 1989.
16. Letter from Jimmy Carter to authors, July 1990.

CHAPTER 24

1. Interview with authors, September 13, 1993.
2. Ibid.
3. Makovsky, *Making Peace With the PLO,* p. 108.
4. Rabin speech, Tel Aviv University, May 1991.
5. Interview with authors, September 1993.
6. Interview with authors, February 11, 1996.
7. Interview with authors, March 1992.
8. Interview with authors, May 1992.
9. Makovsky, pp. 13–14.
10. Ibid., p. 85.
11. Jaffe Center for Strategic Studies, Tel Aviv, April 1992.
12. Makovsky, p. 85.
13. Ibid., p. 86.
14. Ibid., p. 87.
15. Interview with authors, September 1992.
16. Interview with authors, September 1992.
17. Interview with authors, March 1993.
18. Interview with authors, March 1993.
19. Makovsky, p. 109.
20. Ibid., p. 110.
21. Ibid., p. 35.
22. Shimon Peres, *The New Middle East* (New York: Henry Holt, 1993), p. 23.
23. Makovsky, p. 37.
24. Ibid., p. 41.
25. Speech, Conference of Center for Middle East Peace and Economic Cooperation, Washington, D.C., December 5, 1996.
26. Interview with authors, December 12, 1996.
27. Hanan Ashrawi, *This Side of Peace* (New York: Simon & Schuster, 1995), p. 261.
28. Makovsky, p. 66.
29. Interview with authors, December 12, 1996.
30. Ibid., December 12, 1996.

31. Makovsky, p. 66–67.
32. Ashrawi, p. 261.
33. Speech, Conference of Center for Middle East Peace and Economic Cooperation, Washington, D.C., December 5, 1996.
34. Interview with authors, December 12, 1996.
35. Arafat letter to Holst, September 9, 1993.
36. Interview with authors, December 12, 1996.
37. Interview with authors, April 3, 1996.
38. Ibid.
39. Ibid.
40. Makovsky, p. 81.
41. Interview with authors, April 3, 1996.
42. Ibid.
43. Ibid.
44. Raymonda Tawil, *My Home, My Prison* (New York: Holt Rinehart Winston, 1979), p. 148.
45. *New Yorker,* May 16, 1994.
46. Ibid.
47. Interview with authors, Paris, November 9, 1996.
48. *Newsweek,* May 4, 1992.
49. *New Yorker,* May 16, 1994.
50. Interview with authors, Paris, November 9, 1996.
51. *New Yorker,* May 16, 1994.
52. Makovsky, p. 77.
53. Interview with authors, October 1995.
54. Interview with Hasan Rahman, April 3, 1996.
55. Makovsky, p. 156.
56. Interview with authors, June 26, 1996.
57. Interview with authors, September 1966.
58. Interview with authors, November 10, 1996.
59. Interview with authors, December 12, 1996.
60. Speech, Conference of Center for Middle East Peace and Economic Cooperation, Washington, D.C., December 5, 1996.
61. Interview with authors, Paris, November 9, 1996.
62. Interview with authors, New York, May 23, 1996.
63. Meeting with American delegation, Gaza, June 7, 1996.
64. *New York Times,* June 9, 1996.
65. Speech, Conference of Center for Middle East Peace and Economic Cooperation, Washington, D.C., December 5, 1996.
66. Meeting with American delegation, Gaza, December 22, 1996.
67. *New York Times,*
68. Speech, Conference of Center for Middle East Peace and Economic Cooperation, Washington, D.C., December 5, 1996.
69. Interview with authors, December 1996.
70. Speech, Conference of Center for Middle East Peace and Economic Cooperation, Washington, D.C., December 5, 1996.
71. Meeting with American delegation, Gaza, December 22, 1996.
72. Ibid.
73. *Jerusalem Post,* December 20, 1996.
74. Meeting with American delegation, Gaza, December 22, 1996.
75. New York Times, TK.

76. Meeting with American delegation, Gaza, December 22, 1996.
77. Interview with the authors, December 5, 1996.
78. Interview with the authors, January 16, 1997.
79. Speech to the Women's Foreign Policy Group, Washington, D.C., January 8, 1997.
80. Interview with the authors, January 16, 1997.
81. Interview with the authors, January 15, 1997.
82. Interview with the authors, January 16, 1997.

Bibliography

Abu Iyad (Salah Khalaf). *My Home, My Land: A Narrative of the Palestinian Struggle*. New York: Times Books, 1978.

Allon, Yigal. *My Father's House*. New York: W. W. Norton and Co., 1976.

Arberry, Arthur J. *The Koran Interpreted*. Oxford University Press, 1983.

Bavly, Dan and Eliahu, Salpeter. *Fire in Beirut: Israel's War in Lebanon with the PLO*. New York: Stein and Day, 1984.

Becker, Jillian. *The PLO: The Rise and Fall of the Palestine Liberation Organization*. New York: St. Martin's Press, 1984.

Bellow, Saul. *To Jerusalem and Back: A Personal Account*. New York: Viking Press, 1976.

Benvenisti, Meron (with Danny Rubinstein). *The West Bank Handbook: A Political Lexicon*. Jerusalem: Jerusalem Post, 1986.

Blitzer, Wolf. *Territory of Lies: The Exclusive Story of Jonathan Jay Pollard*. New York: Harper and Row, 1989.

Brzezinski, Zbigniew. *Power and Principle: Memoirs of a National Security Adviser 1977–1981*. New York: Farrar, Straus, and Giroux, 1983.

Cattan, Henry. *Palestine: The Road to Peace*. London: Longman Group, 1971.

Cobban, Helena. *The Palestine Liberation Organization: People, Power, and Politics*. Cambridge: Cambridge University Press, 1984.

Corbin, Jane. *The Norway Channel: The Secret Talks That Led to the Middle East Peace Accord*. New York: Atlantic Monthly Press, 1994.

Dawisha, Adeed. *The Arab Radicals*. New York: Council on Foreign Relations, 1986.

Dayan, Moshe. *Breakthrough: A Personal Account of the Egypt-Israel Peace Negotiations*. New York: Alfred A. Knopf, 1981.

_____. *Story of My Life*. London: Sphere Books, 1976.

Dimbleby, Jonathan. *The Palestinians*. New York: Quartet Books, 1980.

Edwards, David L. *A Key to the Old Testament*. London: William Collins Sons and Co., 1976.

Elon, Amos. *Jerusalem: City of Mirrors*. Boston: Little, Brown, and Co., 1989.

Fallaci, Oriana. *Interview with History*. Boston: Houghton Mifflin Co., 1976.

Frangi, Abdallah. *The PLO and Palestine*. London: Zed Books, 1983.

Friedman, Thomas L. *From Beirut to Jerusalem*. New York: Farrar, Straus, and Giroux, 1989.

Front Page Israel: Major Events as Reflected in the Front Pages of the Jerusalem Post. Jerusalem: Jerusalem Post, 1986.

Gilbert, Martin. *The Arab-Israeli Conflict: Its History in Maps*. London: Weidenfield and Nicholson, 1974.

_____. *Exile and Return: The Struggle for a Jewish Homeland*. New York: J. P. Lippincott and Co., 1978.

Haig, Alexander M. *Caveat: Realism, Reagan, and Foreign Policy.* New York: Macmillan Publishing Co., 1984.

Halabi, Rafik. *The West Bank Story: An Israeli Arab's View of Both Sides of a Tangled Conflict.* New York: Harcourt Brace Jovanovich, 1982.

Halsell, Grace. *Journey to Jerusalem: A Journalist's Account of Christian, Jewish, and Muslim Families in the Strife-torn Holy Land.* New York: Macmillan Publishing Co., 1981.

Hart, Alan. *Arafat: Terrorist or Peacemaker.* London: Sidgwick and Jackson, 1984.

Hillel, Shlomo. *Operation Babylon: The Story of the Rescue of the Jews of Iraq.* New York: Doubleday, 1987.

JCSS Study Group. *The West Bank and Gaza: Israel's Options for Peace.* Jaffee Center for Strategic Studies, Tel Aviv University, 1989.

Johnson, Paul. *A History of the Jews.* New York: Harper and Row, 1987.

Khalidi Rashid. *Under Siege: P.L.O. Decisionmaking During the 1982 War.* New York: Columbia University Press, 1986.

Kiernan, Thomas. *Arafat: The Man and the Myth.* New York: W. W. Norton and Co., 1976.

Kissinger, Henry. *White House Years.* Boston: Little, Brown, and Co., 1979.

———. *Years of Upheaval.* Boston: Little, Brown, and Co., 1982.

Kollek, Teddy, and Pearlman, Moshe. *Jerusalem, Sacred City of Mankind: A History of Forty Centuries.* Jerusalem: Steimatzky's Agency Ltd., 1972.

Laffin, John. *The P.L.O. Connections: How Has the Wealthiest, Most Bloodthirsty Terrorist Organization in the World Become Accepted—Even Respectable.* London: Corgi Books, 1982.

Laqueur, Walter. *Terrorism.* Boston: Little, Brown, and Co., 1977.

Lawrence, T. E. *The Seven Pillars of Wisdom.* New York: Penguin Books, 1962.

Livingstone, Neil, and Halevy, David. *Inside the PLO: Covert Units, Secret Funds, and the War Against Israel and the United States.* New York: William Morrow and Co., 1989.

Lunt, James. *Hussein of Jordan: Searching for a Just and Lasting Peace.* New York: William Morrow and Co., 1989.

Lustick, Ian S. *Jewish Fundamentalism in Israel: For the Land and the Lord.* New York: Council on Foreign Relations, 1988.

Makovsky, David. *Making Peace with the PLO.* New York: Westview Press, HarperCollins, in cooperation with the Washington Institute for Near East Policy, 1996.

Ma'oz, Moshe. *Asad, the Sphinx of Damascus: A Political Biography.* New York: Grove Weidenfeld, 1988.

Mattar, Philip. *The Mufti of Jerusalem: Al-Hajj Amin al-Husayni and the Palestinian National Movement.* New York: Columbia University Press, 1988.

Meir, Golda. *My Life.* New York: G. P. Putnam's Sons, 1975.

Mishal, Shaul. *The PLO Under Arafat: Between Gun and Olive Branch.* New Haven: Yale University Press, 1986.

Muslih, Muhammed. *The Origins of Palestinian Nationalism.* New York: Columbia University Press, 1988.

Mussalam, Sami. *The Palestine Liberation Organization: Its Function and Structure.* Brattleboro, Vermont: Amana Books, 1988.

"The New Terrorism," *Israel Defense Forces Journal,* vol. 3, no. 1 (Fall 1985), pp. 39–42.

Peres, Shimon. *Battling for Peace.* New York: Henry Holt, 1995.

———. *The Middle East.* New York: Henry Holt, 1993.

Peretz, Don. *The West Bank: History, Politics, Society, and Economy,* Boulder:

Westview Press, 1986.

Perlmutter, Amos. *Israel, The Partitioned State: A Political History Since 1900*. New York: Charles Scribner's Sons, 1985.

Pintak, Larry. *Beirut Outtakes: A TV Correspondent's Portrait of America's Encounter with Terror*. Lexington, Mass.: Lexington Books, 1988.

Political Report of the Sixth General Conference of the Popular Front for the Liberation of Palestine—General Command (April 29–May 8, 1986).

Posner, Steve. *Israel Undercover: Secret Warfare and Hidden Diplomacy in the Middle East*. Syracuse, N.Y.: Syracuse University Press, 1987.

Raban, Jonathan. *Arabia: A Journey Through the Labyrinth*. New York: Simon and Schuster, 1979.

Roy, Susan. *The Gaza Strip: A Demographic, Economic, Social, and Legal Survey*. Jerusalem: The West Bank Data Base Project, 1986.

Sadat, Anwar. *In Search of Identity: An Autobiography*. New York: Harper and Row, 1978.

Said, Edward. *The Question of Palestine*. New York: Times Books, 1980.

————, and Hitchens, Christopher, eds. *Blaming the Victims: Spurious Scholarship and the Palestinian Question*. London: Verso, 1988.

Saleh, Abdul Jawad. *Israel's Policy of De-Institutionalization: A Case Study of Palestinian Local Government*. London: Jerusalem Center for Development Studies, 1987.

Schiff, Zeev, and Rothstein, Raphael. *Fedayeen: Guerrillas Against Israel*. New York: David McCay Co., 1972.

Seale, Patrick. *Asad of Syria: The Struggle for the Middle East*. Berkeley, Cal.: University of California Press, 1988.

Segal, Haggai. *Dear Brothers: The West Bank Jewish Underground*. Beit-Shamai Publications, 1988.

Shaheen, Jack. *The TV Arab*. Bowling Green, Ohio: Bowling Green State University Popular Press, Ohio, 1984.

Shamir, Shimon, ed. *The Jews of Egypt: A Mediterranean Society in Modern Times*. Boulder: Westview Press, 1987.

Shimoni, Yaacov. *Political Dictionary of the Arab World*. Jerusalem: Jerusalem Publishing House, 1987.

Shipler, David K. *Arab and Jew: Wounded Spirits in a Promised Land*. New York: Times Books, 1986.

Shlaim, Avi. *Collusion Across the Jordan: King Abdullah, the Zionist Movement, and the Partition of Palestine*. Oxford: Clarendon Press, 1988.

Slater, Robert. *Rabin of Israel: Warrior for Peace*. New York: HarperCollins, 1996.

Tawil, Raymonda Hawa. *My Home, My Prison*. New York: Holt, Rinehart and Winston, 1979.

Trager, James. *The People's Chronology: A Year-by-Year Record of Human Events from Prehistory to the Present*. New York: Holt, Rinehart and Winston, 1979.

Vance, Cyrus. *Hard Choices: Critical Years in America's Foreign Policy*. New York: Simon and Schuster, 1983.

Wallach, John, and Wallach, Janet. *Still Small Voices*. New York: Harcourt Brace Jovanovich, 1989.

Washington Institute's Presidential Study Group. *Building for Peace: An American Strategy for the Middle East*. Washington Institute for Near East Policy, 1988.

Zamir, Meir. *The Formation of Modern Lebanon*. Ithaca, N.Y.: Cornell University Press, 1985.

Zua'iter, Akram. *The Palestine Question*. Damascus: Palestine Arab Refugees Institution, 1958.

Index